UNITED STATES CODE
ANNOTATED

Title 41
Public Contracts

2011
Cumulative Annual Pocket Part

Replacing 2010 pocket part in the back of 2008 bound volume

Includes the Laws of the
111th CONGRESS, Second Session (2010)

For close of Notes of Decisions
See page III

For Later Laws and Cases
Consult
USCA
Interim Pamphlet Service

WEST®
A Thomson Reuters business

Mat #41162679

315

 PRINTED ON 10% POST CONSUMER RECYCLED PAPER

EXPLANATION

The 2011 Cumulative Annual Pocket Parts and Supplementary Pamphlets updating the U.S.C.A. set contain the laws, classified to the United States Code, of a general and permanent nature enacted by Congress through the final law of the Second Session of the 111th Congress. Additional laws of a general and permanent nature, more recent than those listed above, may be included.

The Pocket Parts and Supplementary Pamphlets updating Federal Court Rules volumes include amendments received to February 1, 2011.

The Pocket Parts and Supplementary Pamphlets updating Federal Sentencing Guidelines volumes include amendments received to March 11, 2011.

These Pocket Parts and Supplementary Pamphlets may also include Executive Orders, Proclamations, selected sections of the Code of Federal Regulations, and Reorganization Plans relating to such general and permanent laws.

Under the same classification will be found the annotations from the decisions of the Federal courts. Notes of decisions of Federal courts include cases published through January 1, 2011. For subsequent judicial constructions, pending the publication of the next supplementary service, see later permanent volumes and weekly Advance Sheets of the relevant Reporters.

Later amendments and judicial constructions and interpretations will be cumulated in subsequent pocket parts and pamphlets.

For additional information or research assistance call the West reference attorneys at 1-800-REF-ATTY (1-800-733-2889). Contact West's editorial department directly with your questions and suggestions by e-mail at west.editor@thomson.com. Visit West's home page at west.thomson.com.

*

WestlawNext™

THE NEXT GENERATION OF ONLINE RESEARCH

WestlawNext is the world's most advanced legal research system. By leveraging more than a century of information and legal analysis from Westlaw, this easy-to-use system not only helps you find the information you need quickly, but offers time-saving tools to organize and annotate your research online. As with Westlaw.com, WestlawNext includes the editorial enhancements (e.g., case headnotes, topics, key numbers) that make it a perfect complement to West print resources.

- FIND ANYTHING by entering citations, descriptive terms, or Boolean terms and connectors into the WestSearch™ box at the top of every page.

- USE KEYCITE® to determine whether a case, statute, regulation, or administrative decision is good law.

- BROWSE DATABASES right from the home page.

- SAVE DOCUMENTS to folders and add notes and highlighting online.

SIGN ON: next.westlaw.com
LEARN MORE: West.Thomson.com/WestlawNext
FOR HELP: 1–800–WESTLAW (1–800–937–8529)

*

UNITED STATES CODE ANNOTATED

TITLE 41

PUBLIC CONTRACTS [REPEALED]

CHAPTER 1—GENERAL PROVISIONS

§ 5. Advertisements for proposals for purchases and contracts for supplies or services for Government departments; application to Government sales and contracts to sell and to Government corporations

HISTORICAL AND STATUTORY NOTES

Repeal of Exemptions

Act Aug. 2, 1946, § 9(b), which provided exemptions from this section in other laws in amounts of $100 or less are repealed, was editorially eliminated from the Code as a result of the enactment into positive law of Title 41, Public Contracts, by Pub.L. 111–350, Jan. 4, 2011, 124 Stat. 3677.

Notes of Decisions

IV. CONDITIONS OF CONTRACTS

157. Miscellaneous conditions, conditions of contracts

Government's statement in settlement offer to contractor whose proprietary cost information was disclosed in contract solicitation, that Government hoped contractor's performance of directed subcontract to date certain would be of such quality that prime contractor would desire to continue relationship beyond date certain, was a "recital" and did not create obligation on Government's part to provide contractor with opportunity to develop relationship with prime contractor separate from obligation to provide directed subcontract through the date certain. Blackstone Consulting Inc. v. U.S., Fed.Cl.2005, 65 Fed.Cl. 463, affirmed 170 Fed.Appx. 128, 2006 WL 618805. United States ☞ 74(6)

V. CHANGES, MODIFICATIONS OR ADJUSTMENTS OF CONTRACTS

194. Cardinal changes, changes, modifications or adjustments of contracts

United States Postal Service (USPS) materially breached mail delivery contract when it attempted unilaterally to add fifty-two boxes to contractor's route, and that act represented a cardinal change to the contract serious enough to justify contractor's refusal to perform the work in dispute and its discontinuance of contract performance altogether. Keeter Trading Co., Inc. v. U.S., Fed.Cl.2007, 79 Fed.Cl. 243. United States ☞ 73(17)

VI. BREACH OR TERMINATION OF CONTRACTS

305. Constructive termination, breach or termination of contracts

Doctrine of constructive termination, pursuant to which government may defend against a breach of contract claim on ground there existed a legal excuse for nonperformance unknown to the government at time of alleged breach, was not applicable to suspension of timber sale contracts by the Forest Service, since Forest Service did not breach the contracts by attempting to terminate; moreover, Forest Service was aware it had legal right to terminate contracts under contract clause, and chose not to exercise that right. Scott Timber Co. v. U.S., Fed.Cl. 2005, 64 Fed.Cl. 130, reconsideration denied 65 Fed.Cl. 131, affirmed 224 Fed.Appx. 972, 2007 WL 1426728, rehearing denied. United States ☞ 73(24)

VII. ACTIONS FOR BREACH

373. —— Miscellaneous damages, actions for breach

Timber contractor who prevailed on claim that the Forest Service breached timber sales contracts when it suspended them to protect endangered bird species was not entitled to damages during period of suspension when the Forest Service was consulting with the Fish and Wildlife Service (FWS) concerning the species pursuant to section of the Endangered Species Act (ESA); because contractor was an "applicant" under the ESA during period of consultation, it was barred by the ESA from harvesting timber,

See Revised Title 41, post

1

and thus breach was not a "but for" cause of damages. Scott Timber Co. v. U.S., Fed.Cl. 2005, 64 Fed.Cl. 130, reconsideration denied 65 Fed.Cl. 131, affirmed 224 Fed.Appx. 972, 2007 WL 1426728, rehearing denied. United States ⟜ 74(13)

§ 6a. Advertisements for proposals for purchases and contracts for supplies or services for Government departments; limited to particular agencies under specified circumstances

HISTORICAL AND STATUTORY NOTES

Government–Owned Furniture Removed to Washington D.C.

Act July 30, 1947, c. 359, Title I, § 101, 61 Stat. 594, which provided that removal of Government–owned or leased furniture, equipment, supplies and other property of employees, and costs of restoration of leased office space may be accomplished without regard to former 41 U.S.C.A. § 5, was editorially eliminated from the Code as a result of the enactment into positive law of Title 41, Public Contracts, by Pub.L. 111–350, Jan. 4, 2011, 124 Stat. 3677.

§ 6a–2. Transferred

HISTORICAL AND STATUTORY NOTES

Codifications

Section, Pub.L. 96–558, Dec. 19, 1980, 94 Stat. 3263, which authorized the Architect of the Cap- itol to contract for personal services with any firm, partnership, corporation, association, or other legal entity, was editorially transferred to 2 U.S.C.A. § 1816b.

§ 6b. Miscellaneous exceptions from advertisement requirements

[See main volume for text of (a) and (b)]

(c) Transferred

[See main volume for text of (d)]

HISTORICAL AND STATUTORY NOTES

Similar Provisions

Provisions similar to former subsec. (e) of this section, which was omitted, which related to the employment of experts or consultants in the Canal Zone, and were contained in prior Appropriation Acts, were editorially eliminated from the Code as a result of the enactment into positive law of Title 41, Public Contracts, by Pub.L. 111–350, Jan. 4, 2011, 124 Stat. 3677.

LIBRARY REFERENCES

American Digest System

United States ⟜64.10.
Key Number System Topic No. 393.

Research References

Encyclopedias

70 Am. Jur. Proof of Facts 3d 97, Proof that a Government Agency was Liable for Improperly Granting a Bid Award to a Bid Applicant.

§ 10a. American materials required for public use

HISTORICAL AND STATUTORY NOTES

Effective and Applicability Provisions

1994 Acts. Pub.L. 103–355, § 4301(c), which provided an Oct. 13, 1994, effective date for an amendment to former subsec. (b) of this section, and former 41 U.S.C.A. § 428, was editorially eliminated from the Code as a result of the enactment into positive law of Title 41, Public Contracts, by Pub.L. 111–350, Jan. 4, 2011, 124 Stat. 3677.

1988 Acts. Pub.L. 100–418, § 7004, which provided a cessation date of April 30, 1996, was formerly set out as a note under this section and was editorially transferred to be set out as a note under 19 U.S.C.A. § 2511.

Pub.L. 100–418, § 7005(f), which provided an effective date of Aug. 23, 1988, was formerly set out as a note under this section and was editorially transferred to be set out as a note under 19 U.S.C.A. § 2511.

Text Repealed by Pub.L. 111–350, effective Jan. 4, 2011

Short Title

1988 Acts. Pub.L. 100–418, § 7001, which provided a short title, was formerly set out as a note under this section and was editorially transferred to be set out as a note under 41 U.S.C.A. § 101.

1933 Acts. Act Mar. 3, 1933, c. 212, § 7, formerly § 5, as added Pub.L. 103–355, Title X, § 10005(f)(4), Oct. 13, 1994, 108 Stat. 3409, renumbered § 7 and amended Pub.L. 104–106, Div. D, Title XLIII, § 432(a)(11), Feb. 10, 1996, 110 Stat. 671, which provided a short title, was formerly set out as a note under this section and was editorially transferred to be set out as a note under 41 U.S.C.A. § 101.

Water Resource Projects; Cofferdam

Pub.L. 100–371, Title V, § 508, July 19, 1988, 102 Stat. 875, which provided that a cofferdam or any other temporary structure to be constructed by the Secretary of the Army, shall be treated in the same manner as a permanent dam, was formerly set out as a note under this section and was editorially transferred to be set out as a note under 41 U.S.C.A. § 8301.

§ 10b. Contracts for public works; specification for use of American materials; blacklisting contractors violating requirements

HISTORICAL AND STATUTORY NOTES

Prohibition on Use of Funds for Construction Contracts with Contractors of Foreign Countries which Deny United States Contractors Fair Opportunities in Construction Projects of that Country's Government

Provisions from prior appropriation acts [Pub.L. 101–516, § 340, Pub.L. 101–514, § 511, and Pub.L. 100–202, § 109] which prohibited the use of appropriated funds to be used to enter into any contract for construction, alteration, or repair of any public building or public work in the United States or any territory or possession of the United States with any contractor or subcontractor of a foreign country, during any period in which such foreign country is listed by the United States Trade Representative as a foreign country that denies fair and equitable market opportunities for products and services of the United States in procurement and bidding, were editorially eliminated from the Code as a result of the enactment into positive law of Title 41, Public Contracts, by Pub.L. 111–350, Jan. 4, 2011, 124 Stat. 3677.

§ 10b–2. Waiver of Buy American Act

HISTORICAL AND STATUTORY NOTES

Similar Provisions

Provisions similar to those in this former section and former 41 U.S.C.A. § 10b–3 were formerly set out as a notes under this section and were editorially transferred to be set out as a notes under 41 U.S.C.A. § 8304.

§ 10c. Definition of terms used in sections 10a, 10b, and 10c

HISTORICAL AND STATUTORY NOTES

Effective and Applicability Provisions

1933 Acts. Section 5, formerly section 4, of Act Mar. 3, 1933, renumbered Pub.L. 100–418, Title VII, § 7002(1), Aug. 23, 1988, 102 Stat. 1545, which provided that the title should take effect on Mar. 3, 1933, but should not apply to any contract entered into prior to such effective date, was repealed in the enactment into positive law of Title 41, Public Contracts, by Pub.L. 111–350, § 7(b), Jan. 4, 2011, 124 Stat. 3855.

Separability of Provisions

Act Mar. 3, 1933, § 6, formerly § 5, renumbered Pub.L. 100–418, Title VII, § 7002(1), Aug. 23, 1988, 102 Stat. 1545, which provided for separability of provisions, was editorially eliminated from the Code as a result of the enactment into positive law of Title 41, Public Contracts, by Pub.L. 111–350, Jan. 4, 2011, 124 Stat. 3677.

§ 10d. Clarification of Congressional intent regarding sections 10a and 10b(a)

EXECUTIVE ORDERS

EXECUTIVE ORDER NO. 10582

Ex. Ord. No. 10582, Dec. 17, 1954, 19 F.R. 8723, as amended by Ex. Ord. No. 11051, Sept. 27, 1962, 27 F.R. 9683; Ex.Ord. No. 12148, July 20, 1979, 44 F.R. 43239; Ex.Ord. No. 12608, Sept. 9, 1987, 52 F.R. 34617, which related to uniform procedures for determinations of bids or offered price of materials of foreign origin, was formerly set out under this section and was editorially transferred to be set out under 41 U.S.C.A. § 8303.

See Revised Title 41, post

§ 11. No contracts or purchases unless authorized or under adequate appropriation; report to the Congress

[See main volume for text of section]

(R.S. § 3732; June 12, 1906, c. 3078, 34 Stat. 255; Oct. 15, 1966, Pub.L. 89–687, Title VI, § 612(e), 80 Stat. 993; Oct. 30, 1984, Pub.L. 98–557, § 17(e), 98 Stat. 2868; Feb. 10, 1996, Pub.L. 104–106, Div. D, Title XLIII, § 4322(b)(4), 110 Stat. 677; July 11, 2006, Pub.L. 109–241, Title IX, § 902(c), 120 Stat. 566.)

HISTORICAL AND STATUTORY NOTES

Revision Notes and Legislative Reports

2006 Acts. House Conference Report No. 109–413, see 2006 U.S. Code Cong. and Adm. News, p. 579.

Amendments

2006 Amendments. Subsec. (a). Pub.L. 109–241, § 902(c), struck out "of Transporta-tion" and inserted "of Homeland Security" following "Department".

LAW REVIEW AND JOURNAL COMMENTARIES

Risk analysis of financing federal government equipment leases. Gregg A. Day and Patrick J. Keogh, 18 Pub.Cont.L.J. 544 (1989).

LIBRARY REFERENCES

American Digest System

United States ☞62.
Key Number System Topic No. 393.

Corpus Juris Secundum

CJS United States § 108, Authority of Boards or Officers to Bind Government.

CJS United States § 114, Appropriation or Provision for Payment as Prerequisite to Validity of Contract.

Research References

ALR Library

19 ALR 408, Liability for Work Done or Materials Furnished, Etc., for State or Federal Governments in Excess of Appropriations.

Encyclopedias

14 Am. Jur. Trials 437, Representing the Government Contractor.

Treatises and Practice Aids

Immigration Law Service 2d PSD INA § 294, Undercover Investigation Authority.

West's Federal Administrative Practice § 603, Differences from Private Contracts.

§ 15. Transfers of contracts; assignments; assignee not subject to reduction or setoff

MEMORANDA OF PRESIDENT

MEMORANDUM OF PRESIDENT

Memorandum of the President, Oct. 3, 1995, 60 F.R. 55289, which related to a memorandum for the Heads of Executive Departments and Agencies relating to delegation of authority under the assignment of Claims Act, was formerly set out under this section and was editorially transferred to be set out under 41 U.S.C.A. § 6305.

Notes of Decisions

All amounts payable, transfers or assignments with section 10a
Operation of law, transfers or assignments within section 15a
Summary judgment 40a
Transfers or assignments within section 10–22
 All amounts payable 10a
 Operation of law 15a

2. Construction with other laws

Despite the bar of the Anti–Assignment statute, the government, if it chooses to do so, may recognize an assignment, thereby nullifying the statute's effect. L-3 Communications Integrated Systems, L.P. v. U.S., Fed.Cl.2008, 84 Fed.Cl. 768. United States ☞ 111(10)

Text Repealed by Pub.L. 111–350, effective Jan. 4, 2011

10a. —— All amounts payable, transfers or assignments with section

Government contractor's assignment to investment company of remaining $50,000 due to contractor but retained by Army on contract to upgrade sprinkler system at Army base did not cover all amounts payable on contract, as necessary for assignee to receive contract proceeds pursuant to valid assignment, under Anti–Assignment Acts, requiring that assignment of government contract must be for all amounts payable under contract and not already paid, where amount payable under contract was 5% of original contract price due at completion in addition to $50,000 retention. Ham Investments, LLC v. U.S., Fed.Cl.2009, 89 Fed.Cl. 537, affirmed 388 Fed.Appx. 958, 2010 WL 2788206. United States ⚖ 71

15a. —— Operation of law, transfers or assignments within section

Where a transfer is incident to the sale of an entire business or the sale of an entire portion of a business, the transfer is considered to have occurred "by operation of law," and the assignment is exempted from the anti-assignment statute. L-3 Communications Integrated Systems, L.P. v. U.S., Fed.Cl.2008, 84 Fed.Cl. 768. United States ⚖ 111(7)

Sale by actual disappointed offeror of its business unit that bid on project to another corporation, and its concomitant transfer of any claims to that corporation, occurred by "operation of law," and thus post-award bid protest of successor-in-interest corporation was not precluded by Anti–Assignment Act, since transfer was not deleterious to government's interest. L-3 Communications Integrated Systems, L.P. v. U.S., Fed.Cl.2008, 84 Fed.Cl. 768. United States ⚖ 64.60(2)

23. Financing institutions—Generally

To qualify for an exception from the Anti–Assignment Acts, an assignment of a government contract must be made to a bank, trust company, or other financing institution; otherwise, the assignment is invalid. Ham Investments, LLC v. U.S., Fed.Cl.2009, 89 Fed.Cl. 537, affirmed 388 Fed.Appx. 958, 2010 WL 2788206. United States ⚖ 71

28. —— Notice of assignment, recognition of transfer or assignment

Assignee's failure to provide the disbursing official for a government contract with written notice and a copy of the assignment of the contract negates the assignment, under the Anti–Assignment Acts, in the absence of a government waiver of the Acts' requirements. Ham Investments, LLC v. U.S., Fed.Cl.2009, 89 Fed.Cl. 537, affirmed 388 Fed.Appx. 958, 2010 WL 2788206. United States ⚖ 71

Bank claiming to be assignee of contractor's rights to payment for work performed on government contract did not comply with notice requirements of Assignment of Contracts Act and Assignment of Claims Act, given absence of evidence that bank sent copies of notice of assignment and assignment instrument to disburs-

ing office designated in government contract. Texas Nat. Bank v. U.S., Fed.Cl.2009, 86 Fed.Cl. 403. United States ⚖ 71; United States ⚖ 111(10)

Government's express acceptance of assignments of claims in purchase agreements pursuant to which minority owners of interests in nuclear power plants sold their interests served to vitiate provisions of the Assignment of Claims Act that otherwise would have precluded their assignment of claims against the United States. Delmarva Power & Light Co. v. U.S., Fed.Cl. 2007, 79 Fed.Cl. 205, appeal filed, affirmed 542 F.3d 889, certiorari denied 129 S.Ct. 2050, 173 L.Ed.2d 1149. United States ⚖ 111(10)

29. Consent or waiver

To determine if the government waived the requirements of the Anti–Assignment Acts, Court of Federal Claims looks to the totality of the circumstances, including specific factors as to whether: (1) assignor and/or the assignee sent notice of the purported assignment to the government, (2) contracting officer signed the notice of assignment, (3) contracting officer modified the contract according to the assignment, and (4) government sent payments to the assignee pursuant to the assignment. Ham Investments, LLC v. U.S., Fed.Cl.2009, 89 Fed.Cl. 537, affirmed 388 Fed.Appx. 958, 2010 WL 2788206. United States ⚖ 71

Army's mere knowledge of government contractor's assignment to investment company of remaining proceeds of contract to install sprinkler system at Army base and guidance to company as to perfecting assignment did not constitute Army's clear assent to assignment, as necessary for government's waiver of requirements of Anti–Assignment Acts, limiting assignment of government contracts to third parties, thereby precluding investment company from receiving contract proceeds under assignment that was null and void, where contracting officer neither modified contract nor sent any payments to purported assignee. Ham Investments, LLC v. U.S., Fed.Cl.2009, 89 Fed.Cl. 537, affirmed 388 Fed.Appx. 958, 2010 WL 2788206. United States ⚖ 71

Government may, if it chooses to do so, waive the provisions of Assignment of Contracts Act and Assignment of Claims Act and recognize an assignment. Texas Nat. Bank v. U.S., Fed.Cl. 2009, 86 Fed.Cl. 403. United States ⚖ 111(10)

Government did not expressly or implicitly recognize offeror's assignment of claim for bid and proposal costs incurred in particular procurement, as required for governmental recognition or waiver to avoid application of Anti–Assignment Act, by recognizing that offeror had assigned different claim for costs incurred in wholly separate procurement. L-3 Communications Integrated Systems, L.P. v. U.S., Fed.Cl. 2008, 84 Fed.Cl. 768. United States ⚖ 111(10)

40a. Summary judgment

Bank president's declaration that she sent copies of notice of assignment and assignment instrument to disbursing office designated in

See Revised Title 41, post

contract between federal agency and government contractor-assignor could not create issue of fact, for purposes of summary judgment motion, as to bank's compliance with disbursing officer notice requirements of Assignment of Contracts Act and Assignment of Claims Act

when declaration was inconsistent with president's earlier deposition testimony and there was no evidentiary support for assertion in declaration. Texas Nat. Bank v. U.S., Fed.Cl.2009, 86 Fed.Cl. 403. Federal Courts � 1120

§ 35. Contracts for materials, etc., exceeding $10,000; representations and stipulations

HISTORICAL AND STATUTORY NOTES

Effective and Applicability Provisions

1985 Amendments. Pub.L. 99–145, § 1241(c), which provided a Jan. 14, 1986, effective date, was editorially eliminated from the Code as a result of the enactment into positive law of Title 41, Public Contracts, by Pub.L. 111–350, Jan. 4, 2011, 124 Stat. 3677.

Short Title

1936 Amendments. Act June 30, 1936, c. 881, § 14, formerly § 12, as added Pub.L. 103–355,

Title X, § 10005(f)(5), Oct. 13, 1994, 108 Stat. 3409, and renumbered § 14 by Pub.L. 104–106, Div. D, Title XLIII, § 4321(f)(1)(B), Feb. 10, 1996, 110 Stat. 675, which provided a short title, was formerly set out as a note under this section and was editorially transferred to be set out as a note under 41 U.S.C.A. § 101.

EXECUTIVE ORDERS
EXECUTIVE ORDER NO. 13126

Ex. Ord. No. 13126, June 12, 1999, 64 F.R. 32383, which prohibited acquisition of products produced or manufactured wholly or in part by forced or indentured child labor, was formerly

set out under this section and was editorially transferred to be set out under 41 U.S.C.A. § 6501.

§ 39. Hearings on Walsh–Healey provisions by Secretary of Labor; witness fees; failure to obey order; punishment

Notes of Decisions

5. Judicial review—Generally

"Preponderance of the evidence" language in hearing provisions of Walsh-Healey Act, which are incorporated by reference into Service Contract Act (SCA), mandates application of standard of review which is somewhat more exacting than "substantial evidence" standard that ordinarily applies to judicial review of agency fact finding. Karawia v. U.S. Dept. of Labor, S.D.N.Y.2009, 627 F.Supp.2d 137. Labor And Employment � 2357

§ 46. Committee for Purchase From People Who Are Blind or Severely Disabled

HISTORICAL AND STATUTORY NOTES

Effective and Applicability Provisions

1971 Acts. Pub.L. 92–28, § 2, which provided an effective date, was editorially eliminated from the Code as a result of the enactment into positive law of Title 41, Public Contracts, by Pub.L. 111–350, Jan. 4, 2011, 124 Stat. 3677.

Short Title

1938 Acts. Section 7 of Act June 25, 1938, c. 697, as added Pub.L. 103–355, Title X, § 10005(f)(6), Oct. 13, 1994, 108 Stat. 3409, which provided a Short Title for the Javits–Wagner–O'Day Act, was repealed in the enactment into positive law of Title 41, Public Contracts, by Pub.L. 111–350, § 7(b), Jan. 4, 2011, 124 Stat. 3855.

Contracting with Employers of Persons with Disabilities

Pub.L. 109–364, Div. A, Title VIII, § 856(a), (d), Oct. 17, 2006, 120 Stat. 2347, 2349, which

provided for the inapplicability of the Randolph–Sheppard Act and the Javits–Wagner–O'Day Act to contracts for the operation and support of military dining facilities, was formerly set out as a note under this section and was editorially transferred to be set out as a note under 41 U.S.C.A. § 8501.

Statement of Policy; Report

Pub.L. 109–163, Div. A, Title VIII, § 848(b), (c), Jan. 6, 2006, 119 Stat. 3395, which provided for the issuance of a joint policy statement relating to the implementation of the Randolph–Sheppard Act and the Javits–Wagner–O'Day Act, by the Secretary of Defense, the Secretary of Education, and the Chairman of the Committee for Purchase From People Who Are Blind or Severely Disabled, was formerly set out as a note under this section and was editorially transferred to be set out as a note under 41 U.S.C.A. § 8501.

Text Repealed by Pub.L. 111–350, effective Jan. 4, 2011

§ 47. Duties and powers of the Committee

Notes of Decisions

Award and decision   4
Injunction   5

_____

2. Persons entitled to maintain action

Incumbent contractor providing laundry services for veterans' hospitals, pursuant to contract with Department of Veterans Affairs (DVA), had standing for bid protest action, under Tucker Act, to challenge DVA's alleged violation of procurement regulation and DVA's new guidelines, giving priority to service-disabled veteran-owned (SDVO) and veteran-owned (VO) small businesses qualified under Veterans Benefits Health Care, and Information Technology Act, although contractor was not SDVO or VO, since contractor had direct economic interest due to substantial chance of being awarded longer-term, gap-filling, follow-on contract based on satisfactory performance as incumbent contractor with resources already in place to meet requirements. Angelica Textile Services, Inc. v. U.S., Fed.Cl.2010, 95 Fed.Cl. 208. United States ☞ 64.60(2)

3. Procurement list

Incumbent contractor's bid protest, challenging Department of Veterans Affairs' (DVA) extension of laundry services contract in order to place services on AbilityOne procurement list for bidder employing blind and otherwise severely disabled individuals, pursuant to Javits-Wagner-O'Day Act, as failing to comply with procurement regulation and DVA's new guidelines giving first priority to service-disabled veteran-owned (SDVO) and veteran-owned (VO) small businesses qualified under Veterans Benefits Health Care, and Information Technology Act, was "in connection with a procurement," within meaning of Tucker Act, conferring jurisdiction to consider bid protest without constraint as to any equitable remedy of removing services from AbilityOne list, since Javits-Wagner-O'Day Act's rulemaking provisions subjecting deletions from AbilityOne list to judicial review under

Administrative Procedure Act (APA) did not supersede Tucker Act's protest jurisdiction. Angelica Textile Services, Inc. v. U.S., Fed.Cl. 2010, 95 Fed.Cl. 208. United States ☞ 64.60(1)

4. Award and decision

Contracting officer (CO) lacked rational basis for failing to comply with Department of Veterans Affairs' (DVA) new guidelines reasonably giving first priority to service-disabled veteran-owned (SDVO) and veteran-owned (VO) small businesses qualified under Veterans Benefits Health Care, and Information Technology Act, by CO intentionally awarding DVA contract to provide laundry services to veterans' hospitals on sole-source basis to nonprofit bidder employing blind or otherwise severely disabled individuals, under AbilityOne program pursuant to Javits-Wagner-O'Day Act, since guidelines were effective immediately, did not exempt placements on AbilityOne procurement list that were being considered but not yet completed, and warranted *Skidmore* deference. Angelica Textile Services, Inc. v. U.S., Fed.Cl.2010, 95 Fed. Cl. 208. United States ☞ 64.15

5. Injunction

Incumbent contractor would suffer irreparable harm in absence of permanent injunction setting aside Department of Veterans' Affairs (DVA) award of contract to provide laundry services to veterans' hospitals to nonprofit bidder employing blind or otherwise severely disabled individuals, under AbilityOne program pursuant to Javits-Wagner-O'Day Act, in contravention of DVA's new guidelines giving first priority to service-disabled veteran-owned (SDVO) and veteran-owned (VO) small businesses qualified under Veterans Benefits Health Care, and Information Technology Act, since contractor would lose ability to compete for contract without injunctive relief. Angelica Textile Services, Inc. v. U.S., Fed.Cl.2010, 95 Fed.Cl. 208. Injunction ☞ 86

§ 48. Procurement requirements for the Government; nonapplication to prison-made products

NOTES OF DECISIONS

Balance of hardships, injunctions and stays
  3
Injunctions and stays   1-4
    Generally   1
    Balance of hardships   3
    Irreparable harm   2
    Public interest   4
Irreparable harm, injunctions and stays   2
Public interest, injunctions and stays   4

_____

1. Injunctions and stays—Generally

Unsuccessful bidder on government contract for custodial and grounds maintenance services

to be performed by nonprofit bidder employing blind or otherwise severely disabled individuals, pursuant to AbilityOne program under Javits-Wagner-O'Day Act, seeking temporary restraining order (TRO) prohibiting government from permitting performance of contract, had substantial likelihood of success on merits of claims that selection and recommendation of successful bidder were inconsistent with stated bidding evaluation scheme and integrity of procurement process was compromised by conflicts of interest and favoritism; it was likely government misapplied factors of geography and quality control systems when ranking bidders, and fact that successful bidder's chief executive officer served

See Revised Title 41, post

7

on board of directors for bid selecting committee raised questions as to integrity of award process. Bona Fide Conglomerate, Inc. v. U.S., Fed.Cl.2010, 2010 WL 4925288. Injunction ⟋ 150

2. —— **Irreparable harm, injunctions and stays**

Unsuccessful bidder on government contract for custodial and grounds maintenance services to be performed by nonprofit bidder employing blind or otherwise severely disabled individuals, pursuant to AbilityOne program under Javits-Wagner-O'Day Act, would likely suffer irreparable harm in absence of temporary restraining order (TRO) prohibiting government from permitting performance of contract; contract performance was imminent and without TRO, unsuccessful bidder could be deprived of a fair opportunity to compete for and perform the contract, and if court later ruled in favor of unsuccessful bidder, relief ordered could substantially disrupt the government, the parties, and the employees with severe disabilities. Bona Fide Conglomerate, Inc. v. U.S., Fed.Cl. 2010, 2010 WL 4925288. Injunction ⟋ 150

3. —— **Balance of hardships, injunctions and stays**

Balance of hardships favored temporary restraining order (TRO) prohibiting government from permitting performance of contract for custodial and grounds maintenance services to be performed by successful nonprofit bidder employing blind or otherwise severely disabled individuals, pursuant to AbilityOne program under Javits-Wagner-O'Day Act; employees of successful bidder who had severe disabilities would be harmed by not being able to perform contract immediately, but these employees would also be harmed by any future disruption of the contract. Bona Fide Conglomerate, Inc. v. U.S., Fed.Cl. 2010, 2010 WL 4925288. Injunction ⟋ 150

4. —— **Public interest, injunctions and stays**

Public interest supported grant of temporary restraining order (TRO) prohibiting government from permitting performance of contract for custodial and grounds maintenance services to be performed by successful nonprofit bidder employing blind or otherwise severely disabled individuals, pursuant to AbilityOne program under Javits-Wagner-O'Day Act, since there was an overriding public interest in preserving integrity of procurement process by requiring government to follow its procurement regulations. Bona Fide Conglomerate, Inc. v. U.S., Fed.Cl. 2010, 2010 WL 4925288. Injunction ⟋ 150

§ 51. Short title

HISTORICAL AND STATUTORY NOTES

Effective and Applicability Provisions

1986 Acts. Pub.L. 99–634, § 3, which provided an effective date, was editorially eliminated from the Code as a result of the enactment into positive law of Title 41, Public Contracts, by Pub.L. 111–350, Jan. 4, 2011, 124 Stat. 3677.

Short Title

1986 Amendments. Pub.L. 99–364, § 1, which provided a short title, was formerly set out as a note under this section and was editorially transferred to be set out as a note under 41 U.S.C.A. § 101.

§ 55. Civil actions

Notes of Decisions

Construction with other laws 2a

----

2. Annulment of contract

Contractor who engaged in prohibited kickback activities on four federal contracts was liable to the government for statutory civil penalties under the Anti–Kickback Act of $259,457.04, representing twice the total amount of the kickbacks, or $219,457.04, plus $40,000 for each kickback "occurrence." Morse Diesel Intern., Inc. v. U.S., Fed.Cl.2007, 79 Fed.Cl. 116,

reconsideration denied 81 Fed.Cl. 311. United States ⟋ 75(6)

2a. Construction with other laws

Imposing civil penalties under the Anti–Kickback Act, and separate civil penalties and treble damages under the False Claims Act for the same acts, is neither duplicative nor prohibited. Morse Diesel Intern., Inc. v. U.S., Fed.Cl.2007, 79 Fed.Cl. 116, reconsideration denied 81 Fed. Cl. 311. United States ⟋ 75(6)

CHAPTER 2—TERMINATION OF WAR CONTRACTS

§ 101. Declaration of policy

HISTORICAL AND STATUTORY NOTES

Separability of Provisions

Section 26 of Act July 1, 1944, c. 358, which provided that if any provision of the Act or the

application of such provision to any person or circumstance, is held invalid, the remainder of the Act or the application of such provision to

Text Repealed by Pub.L. 111–350, effective Jan. 4, 2011

persons or circumstances other than those as to which it is held invalid, shall not be affected thereby, was repealed in the enactment into positive law of Title 41, Public Contracts, by Pub.L. 111–350, § 7(b), Jan. 4, 2011, 124 Stat. 3855.

Short Title

1944 Amendments. Section 27 of Act July 1, 1944, c. 358, which provided a Short Title for the

Contract Settlement Act of 1944, was repealed in the enactment into positive law of Title 41, Public Contracts, by Pub.L. 111–350, § 7(b), Jan. 4, 2011, 124 Stat. 3855.

§ 106.   Basis for settlement of termination claims

HISTORICAL AND STATUTORY NOTES

Settlement of Claims for War Contract Losses Incurred Between September 16, 1940, and August 14, 1945

Act Aug. 7, 1946, c. 864, §§ 1 to 6, 60 Stat. 902, as amended June 25, 1948, c. 646, § 37, 62 Stat. 992; Aug. 30, 1954, c. 1076, § 1(2), 68 Stat. 966, which provided that if work, supplies, or services were provided for any department or agency of the Government, under a contract or subcontract, between Sept. 16, 1940, and Aug. 14, 1945, and a loss was incurred by the contrac-

tors or subcontractors without fault or negligence on their part, then those departments or agencies were authorized to adjust and settle these losses on a fair and equitable basis, if claims were filed within six months after Aug. 7, 1946, and granted claimants dissatisfied with the settlement the right of judicial review, was editorially eliminated from the Code as a result of the enactment into positive law of Title 41, Public Contracts, by Pub.L. 111–350, Jan. 4, 2011, 124 Stat. 3677.

§ 113.   Appeals

HISTORICAL AND STATUTORY NOTES

Abolition of Appeals Board; Termination of Appeals; No Further Appeals Accepted; Return of Erroneous Filed Appeals

Act July 14, 1952, c. 739, 66 Stat. 627, which abolished the Appeals Board and set forth pro-

cedures for the termination of appeals and return of erroneously filed appeals, was repealed in the enactment into positive law of Tile 41, Public Contracts, by Pub.L. 111–350, § 7(b), Jan. 4, 2011, 124 Stat. 3855

§ 114.   Court of Federal Claims

HISTORICAL AND STATUTORY NOTES

Commissioners; Termination of Appointing Authority

Section 4(b) of Act July 28, 1953, which provided that the authority contained in subsec. (a) of this section respecting the appointment of commissioners "is hereby terminated", was editorially eliminated from the Code as a result of the enactment into positive law of Title 41, Public Contracts, by Pub.L. 111–350, Jan. 4, 2011, 124 Stat. 3677.

Section Unaffected by Revised Title 28

Act June 25, 1948, c. 646, § 2(d), 62 Stat. 985, which provided that nothing in Title 28, Judiciary and Judicial Procedure, should be construed as repealing any of the provisions of this section, was editorially eliminated from the Code as a result of the enactment into positive law of Title 41, Public Contracts, by Pub.L. 111–350, Jan. 4, 2011, 124 Stat. 3677.

§ 117.   Defective, informal, and quasi contracts

HISTORICAL AND STATUTORY NOTES

Nonaccrual of Liability

Section 2 of Act June 28, 1954, which provided that no liability shall accrue by reason of the enactment of section 1 of such Act (amending

subsec. (d) of this section) which would not otherwise have accrued, was editorially eliminated from the Code as a result of the enactment into positive law of Title 41, Public Contracts, by Pub.L. 111–350, Jan. 4, 2011, 124 Stat. 3677.

CHAPTER 4—PROCUREMENT PROCEDURES

See Revised Title 41, post

Sec.
254d.   Examination of records of contractor.
266a.   Transferred.

SUBCHAPTER IV—PROCUREMENT PROVISIONS

§ 251.   Declaration of purpose of this subchapter

HISTORICAL AND STATUTORY NOTES

Effective and Applicability Provisions

1996 Acts. Pub.L. 104–106, § 4401, which provided an effective date and applicability provisions was formerly set out as a note under this section and was editorially transferred to be set out as a note under 10 U.S.C.A. § 2302.

1994 Acts. Pub.L. 103–355, Title X, § 10001, Oct. 13, 1994, 108 Stat. 3243, which provided an effective date and applicability provisions was formerly set out as a note under this section and was editorially transferred to be set out as a note under 10 U.S.C.A. § 2302.

1984 Acts. Pub.L. 98–369, Title VII, § 2751, July 18, 1984, 98 Stat. 1203, which provided an effective date and applicability provisions was formerly set out as a note under this section and was editorially transferred to be set out as a note under 10 U.S.C.A. § 2302.

Severability of Provisions

Act June 30, 1949, c. 288, § 604, formerly § 504, 63 Stat. 403, renumbered by Act Sept. 5, 1950, c. 849, § 6(a), (b), 64 Stat. 583, which provided for severability provisions, was formerly set out as a note under this section and was editorially transferred to be set out as a note preceding 41 U.S.C.A. § 3901.

Short Title

2008 Amendments. Pub.L. 110–417, Div. A, Title VIII, § 861, Oct. 14, 2008, 122 Stat. 4546, which provided a short title, was formerly set out as a note under this section and was editorially transferred to be set out as a note under 41 U.S.C.A. § 101.

1996 Amendments. Pub.L. 104–106, Div. D, § 4001, Feb. 10, 1996, 110 Stat. 642, as amended Pub.L. 104–208, Div. A, Title I, § 101(f) [Title VIII, § 808(a)], Sept. 30, 1996, 110 Stat. 3009–393, which provided a short title, was formerly set out as a note under this section and was editorially transferred to be set out as a note under 41 U.S.C.A. § 101.

1994 Amendments. Pub.L. 103–355, § 1, Oct. 13, 1994, 108 Stat. 3243, which provided a short title, was formerly set out as a note under this section and was editorially transferred to be set out as a note under 41 U.S.C.A. § 101.

1984 Amendments. Pub.L. 98–577, § 1, Oct. 30, 1984, 98 Stat. 3066, which provided a short title, was formerly set out as a note under this section and was editorially transferred to be set out as a note under 41 U.S.C.A. § 101.

Pub.L. 98–369, Title VII, § 2701, July 18, 1984, 98 Stat. 1175, which provided a short title, was formerly set out as a note under this section and was editorially transferred to be set out as a note under 41 U.S.C.A. § 101.

1949 Amendments. Act June 30, 1949, c. 288, § 1(a), 63 Stat. 377, amended Oct. 13, 1994, Pub.L. 103–355, Title X, § 10005(a)(2), 108 Stat. 3406, which provided a short title, was formerly set out as a note under this section and was editorially transferred to be set out as a note under 41 U.S.C.A. § 101.

Linking of Award and Incentive Fees to Acquisition Outcomes

Pub.L. 110–417, Div. A, Title VIII, § 867, Oct. 14, 2008, 122 Stat. 4551, which provided executive agencies other than the Department of Defense with instructions, including definitions, on the appropriate use of award and incentive fees in Federal acquisition programs, was repealed in the enactment into positive law of Title 41, Public Contracts, by Pub.L. 111–350, § 7(b), Jan. 4, 2011, 124 Stat. 3855.

Close the Contractor Fraud Loophole Act

Pub.L. 110–252, Title VI, §§ 6101 to 6103, June 30, 2008, 122 Stat. 2386, relating to the Close the Contractor Loophole Act, was repealed in part and transferred in part in the enactment into positive law of Title 41, Public Contracts, by Pub.L. 111–350, Jan. 4, 2011, 124 Stat. 3677. Section 6101, which provided a Short Title for the Act, was transferred to be set out as a note under 41 U.S.C.A. § 101. Sections 6102 and 6103 were repealed by Pub.L. 111–350, § 7(b), Jan. 4, 2011, 124 Stat. 3855.

Implementing Regulations for Pub.L. 104–106

Pub.L. 104–106, § 4402, which provided for proposed revisions to the Federal Acquisition Regulations and such other regulations as may be necessary to implement the National Defense Authorization Act for Fiscal Year 1996, and the publication of final regulations, was editorially eliminated from the Code as a result of the enactment into positive law of Title 41, Public Contracts, by Pub.L. 111–350, Jan. 4, 2011, 124 Stat. 3677.

Implementing Regulations for Pub.L. 103–355

Pub.L. 103–355, Title X, § 10002, Oct. 13, 1994, 108 Stat. 3404, which provided for proposed revisions to the Federal Acquisition Regulations and such other regulations as may be necessary to implement the Federal Acquisition Streamlining Act of 1994, and the publication of final regulations, was editorially eliminated from the Code as a result of the enactment into

Text Repealed by Pub.L. 111–350, effective Jan. 4, 2011

positive law of Title 41, Public Contracts, by Pub.L. 111–350, Jan. 4, 2011, 124 Stat. 3677.

Evaluation by the Comptroller General

Pub.L. 103–355, Title X, § 10003, Oct. 13, 1994, 108 Stat. 3405, which directed the Comptroller General to submit a report to designated committees regarding the effectiveness of the regulations implementing the Federal Acquisition Streamlining Act of 1994, was editorially eliminated from the Code as a result of the enactment into positive law of Title 41, Public Contracts, by Pub.L. 111–350, Jan. 4, 2011, 124 Stat. 3677.

Congressional Statement of Purpose

Pub.L. 98–577, Title I, § 101, Oct. 30, 1984, 98 Stat. 3066, which provided purposes for the Small Business and Federal Procurement Competition Enhancement Act of 1984 , was formerly set out as a note under this section and was

editorially transferred to be set out as a note under 41 U.S.C.A. § 3701.

Commission on Government Procurement

Pub.L. 91–129, Nov. 26, 1969, 83 Stat. 269, as amended Pub.L. 92–47, July 9, 1971, 85 Stat. 102, which established the Commission on Government Procurement, which was to study and investigate statutes, rules, regulations, procedures, and practices affecting Government procurement and to submit a final report to Congress on or before Dec. 31, 1972, on the results of this study, including recommendations for changes designed to promote economy, efficiency, and effectiveness in the procurement of goods, services, and facilities by and for the executive branch of the Government and which terminated such Commission 120 days after submission of the final report, was editorially eliminated from the Code as a result of the enactment into positive law of Title 41, Public Contracts, by Pub.L. 111–350, Jan. 4, 2011, 124 Stat. 3677.

EXECUTIVE ORDERS
EXECUTIVE ORDER NO. 13005

Ex. Ord. No. 13005, May 21, 1996, 74 F.R. 26069, which directed the Secretary of the Department of Commerce to develop policies and procedures to ensure that agencies grant qualified large businesses and qualified small businesses appropriate incentives to encourage

business activity in areas of general economic distress, when assessing offers for government contracts in unrestricted competitions, was formerly set out under this section and was editorially transferred to be set out under 41 U.S.C.A. § 3101.

EXECUTIVE ORDER NO. 13202

Ex. Ord. No. 13202, Feb. 17, 2001, 66 F.R. 11225, as amended by Ex. Ord. No. 13208, Apr. 6, 2001, 66 F.R. 18717, relating to preservation of open competition and government neutrality towards government contractors' labor relations

on Federal and Federally funded construction projects, was revoked by section 8 of Ex. Ord. No. 13502, Feb. 6, 2009, 74 F.R. 6985, set out under this section.

EXECUTIVE ORDER NO. 13502

Ex. Ord. No. 13502, Feb. 6, 2009, 74 F.R. 6985, which encouraged the use of project labor agreements for large-scale Federal construction

projects, was formerly set out under this section and was editorially transferred to be set out under 41 U.S.C.A. preceding § 3901.

MEMORANDA OF PRESIDENT
PRESIDENTIAL MEMORANDUM

Memorandum of the President, Mar. 4, 2009, 74 F.R. 9755 , which related to the development and issuance by July 1, 2009, of Government-wide guidance to assist agencies in reviewing, and creating processes for ongoing review of, existing contracts in order to identify contracts that are wasteful, inefficient, or not otherwise likely to meet the agency's needs, and to formu-

late appropriate corrective action in a timely manner, and such corrective action may include modification or cancelation of such contracts in a manner and to the extent consistent with applicable laws, regulations, and policy, was formerly set out under this section and was editorially transferred to be set out under 41 U.S.C.A. § 3101.

§ 252. Purchases and contracts for property

HISTORICAL AND STATUTORY NOTES

Emergency Relief for Small Business Concerns with Government Contracts

Pub.L. 94–190, Dec. 31, 1975, 89 Stat. 1095, which enacted the Small Business Emergency

Relief Act, was editorially eliminated from the Code as a result of the enactment into positive law of Title 41, Public Contracts, by Pub.L. 111–350, Jan. 4, 2011, 124 Stat. 3677.

§ 253. Competition requirements

[See main volume for text of (a) to (c)]

See Revised Title 41, post

(d) Property or services deemed available from only one source; nondelegable authority

[See main volume for text of (1) and (2)]

(3)(A) The contract period of a contract described in subparagraph (b) that is entered into by an executive agency pursuant to the authority provided under subsection (c)(2)

    (i) may not exceed the time necessary—

        (I) to meet the unusual and compelling requirements of the work to be performed under the contract; and

        (II) for the executive agency to enter into another contract for the required goods or services through the use of competitive procedures; and

    (ii) may not exceed one year unless the head of the executive agency entering into such contract determines that exceptional circumstances apply.

(B) This paragraph applies to any contract in an amount greater than the simplified acquisition threshold.

[See main volume for text of (e)]

(f) Justification for use of noncompetitive procedures

[See main volume for text of (1) to (3)]

(4) In no case may an executive agency—

    (A) enter into a contract for property or services using procedures other than competitive procedures on the basis of the lack of advance planning or concerns related to the amount of funds available to the agency for procurement functions; or

    (B) procure property or services from another executive agency unless such other executive agency complies fully with the requirements of this subchapter in its procurement of such property or services.

The restriction set out in clause (B) is in addition to, and not in lieu of, any other restriction provided by law.

(5) Redesignated (4)

[See main volume for text of (g) to (i)]

(j)(1)(A) Except as provided in subparagraph (B), in the case of a procurement permitted by subsection (c) of this section, the head of an executive agency shall make publicly available, within 14 days after the award of the contract, the documents containing the justification and approval required by subsection (f)(1) of this section with respect to the procurement.

(B) In the case of a procurement permitted by subsection (c)(2) of this section, subparagraph (A) shall be applied by substituting "30 days" for "14 days".

(2) The documents shall be made available on the website of the agency and through a government-wide website selected by the Administrator for Federal Procurement Policy.

(3) This subsection does not require the public availability of information that is exempt from public disclosure under section 552(b) of Title 5.

(June 30, 1949, c. 288, Title III, § 303, 63 Stat. 395; July 12, 1952, c. 703, § 1(m), 66 Stat. 594; Mar. 16, 1968, Pub.L. 90–268, § 2, 82 Stat. 49; July 18, 1984, Pub.L. 98–369, Div. B, Title VII, § 2711(a)(1), 98 Stat. 1175; Oct. 30, 1984, Pub.L. 98–577, Title V, § 504(a)(1), (2), 98 Stat. 3086; Nov. 8, 1985, Pub.L. 99–145, Title IX, § 961(a)(2), Title XIII, § 1304(c)(2), (3), 99 Stat. 703, 742; Nov. 5, 1990, Pub.L. 101–510, Div. A, Title VIII, § 806(c), 104 Stat. 1592; Oct. 13, 1994, Pub.L. 103–355, Title I, §§ 1051, 1052, 1053, 1055(a), Title IV, § 4402(a), Title VII, § 7203 (b)(1), 108 Stat. 3260, 3261, 3265, 3348, 3380; Feb. 10, 1996, Pub.L. 104–106, Div. D, Title XLI, §§ 4101(b), 4102(b), Title XLII, § 4202(b)(1), Title XLIII, § 4321(e)(2), 110 Stat. 642, 643, 653, 674; Oct. 19, 1996, Pub.L. 104–320, §§ 7(a)(2), 11(c)(2), 110 Stat. 3871, 3873; Nov. 18, 1997, Pub.L. 105–85, Div. A, Title VIII, § 850(f)(3)(B), 111 Stat. 1850; Jan. 28, 2008, Pub.L. 110–181, Div. A, Title VIII, § 844(a), 122 Stat. 239; Oct. 14, 2008, Pub.L. 110–417, Div. A, Title VIII, § 862(a), 122 Stat. 4546.)

Text Repealed by Pub.L. 111–350, effective Jan. 4, 2011

HISTORICAL AND STATUTORY NOTES

Revision Notes and Legislative Reports

2008 Acts. Statement by President, see 2008 U.S. Code Cong. and Adm. News, p. S3.

Senate Report No. 110–335, see 2008 U.S. Code Cong. and Adm. News, p. 1829.

Statement by President, see 2008 U.S. Code Cong. and Adm. News, p. S30.

Amendments

2008 Amendments. Subsec. (d)(3). Pub.L. 110–417, § 862(a), added par. (3).

Subsec. (f)(4). Pub.L. 110–181, § 844(a)(2), struck out former par. (4), and redesignated former par. (5) as par. (4). Former par. (4) read: "The justification required by paragraph (1)(A) and any related information shall be made available for inspection by the public consistent with the provisions of section 552 of Title 5."

Subsec. (f)(5). Pub.L. 110–181, § 844(a)(2)(B), redesignated former par. (5) as par. (4).

Subsec. (j). Pub.L. 110–181, § 844(a)(1), added subsec. (j).

Public Disclosure of Noncompetitive Contracting for the Reconstruction of Infrastructure in Iraq

Pub.L. 108–136, Div. A, Title XIV, § 1442, Nov. 24, 2003, 117 Stat. 1674, which required the head of an executive agency that entered into a contract for the repair, maintenance, or construction of infrastructure in Iraq without full and open competition, to publish in the Federal Register or Commerce Business Daily and otherwise make available to the public such contract provisions, was editorially eliminated from the Code as a result of the enactment into positive law of Title 41, Public Contracts, by Pub.L. 111–350, Jan. 4, 2011, 124 Stat. 3677.

Small Business Act

Pub.L. 98–369, § 2711(c), which provided that amendments made by such section do not supersede or affect the provisions of section 8(a) of the Small Business Act, 15 U.S.C.A. § 637(a), was formerly set out as a note under this section and was editorially transferred to be set out as a note under 41 U.S.C.A. § 3301.

CODE OF FEDERAL REGULATIONS

Competition requirements, see 48 CFR § 2406.202 et seq.

LAW REVIEW AND JOURNAL COMMENTARIES

Enforcing competition through government contract claims. Michael K. Love, 20 U.Rich. L.Rev. 525 (1986).

Federal environmental remediation contractual and insurance-based risk allocation schemes:

Are they getting the job done? Major Amy L. Momber, 58 A.F. L. Rev. 61 (2006).

LIBRARY REFERENCES

American Digest System

United States ⊜64.10.
Key Number System Topic No. 393.

Corpus Juris Secundum

CJS United States § 113, Advertising and Proposals or Bids.

Research References

ALR Library

24 ALR, Fed. 2nd Series 133, Application of Requirement in § 107(A) of Comprehensive Environmental Response, Compensation, and Liability Act (42 U.S.C.A. § 9607) that Public Cost-Recovery Actions Not be Inconsistent With National Contingency...

9 ALR, Fed. 2nd Series 565, "Cardinal Change" Doctrine in Federal Contracts Law.

23 ALR, Fed. 301, Standing of Unsuccessful Bidder for Federal Procurement Contract to Seek Judicial Review of Award.

96 ALR 712, Alternation of Plans or Materials as Necessary or Proper Factor in Proposal for or Acceptance of Bids for Public Works.

64 ALR 1281, Subsequent Developments as Authorizing Increase of Amount of Succession Tax Fixed by Taxing Authorities.

Encyclopedias

14 Am. Jur. Trials 437, Representing the Government Contractor.

Am. Jur. 2d Public Works and Contracts § 34, Federal Contracts.

Forms

Federal Procedural Forms § 34:2, Procedures to Promote Competition.

Federal Procedural Forms § 34:3, Procedures to Promote Competition--Exclusion of Sources.

Federal Procedural Forms § 34:4, Procedures to Promote Competition--Contracting Without Open Competition.

Treatises and Practice Aids

Federal Information Disclosure § 14:84, Government Contractors' Data Exemption Claims.

Federal Procedure, Lawyers Edition § 39:3, Promotion of Competition.

Federal Procedure, Lawyers Edition § 39:4, Promotion of Competition--Exclusion of Sources.

Federal Procedure, Lawyers Edition § 39:5, Promotion of Competition--Noncompetitive Procurements.

West's Federal Administrative Practice § 603, Differences from Private Contracts.

See Revised Title 41, post

West's Federal Administrative Practice § 622, Competition Requirements.

West's Federal Administrative Practice § 635, Types of Contracts.

West's Federal Administrative Practice § 640, Research and Development Contracting.

Notes of Decisions

4. Competitive bids or offers

Where a contract has been awarded, but a bid protest has been sustained and the recommended corrective action is to make a new best value determination, the standard competition rules of the Competition in Contracting Act (CICA) and the Federal Acquisition Regulation (FAR) apply, and under such circumstances, if an agency conducts discussions, it must do so with all offerors in the competitive range. Chapman Law Firm Co. v. U.S., Fed.Cl.2006, 71 Fed.Cl. 124, affirmed in part, reversed in part and remanded 490 F.3d 934. United States ⟨⟩ 64.40(1)

5. Modification

Protester failed to show it would have had substantial chance of winning competitive contract for procurement of mobile medical units, and protester, which was not prequalified as Federal Supply Schedule (FSS) contractor, thus was not prejudiced by, and lacked standing to challenge, agency's FSS procurement award to FSS contractor who offered non-FSS trailers in response to FSS request for quote (RFQ); although protester had previously been in sole-source negotiations with agency and claimed to be the sole source of pre-certified trailers, RFQ did not require certification until after manufacture, and protester thus would have faced substantial competition in open bidding from several contractors who could have obtained certifications after making trailers, moreover, protester was rated as high business risk at time of procurement, had requested advance payment in excess of 15% permitted by regulation, and had quoted a price significantly higher than that submitted by successful bidder and other competitors. Mobile Medical Intern. Corp. v. U.S., Fed.Cl.2010, 95 Fed.Cl. 706. United States ⟨⟩ 64.60(2)

Transfer by the Department of Housing and Urban Development (HUD) of house managing and marketing responsibilities for particular geographic area to incumbent contractors that had sufficient capacity to perform the services

was not a "solicitation" subject to competition requirements of the Competition in Contracting Act (CICA), but rather was an in-scope contract modification of existing contracts permitted under their modification clause, and fact that HUD shopped around for the best incumbent contractors in terms of performance and price did not transform its action into a solicitation. Chapman Law Firm Co. v. U.S., Fed.Cl.2008, 81 Fed.Cl. 323. United States ⟨⟩ 64.10; United States ⟨⟩ 70(35)

8. Injunctive relief granted

Preliminary injunction was warranted to prohibit United States and Department of the Interior from proceeding with or awarding a contract to implement a department-wide email messaging system or any related procurement, solicitation, task order, or activity; protestor established likelihood of success on the merits of its claim that process by which Interior restricted competition exclusively to a competitor for messaging and collaboration solutions violated the Competition in Contracting Act and relevant FAR (Federal Acquisition Regulation) provisions and that such violations would cause it irreparable harm by achieving an "organizational lock-in" for a competitor, and costing protestor the opportunity to compete. Google, Inc. v. U.S., Fed.Cl.2011, 95 Fed.Cl. 661. Injunction ⟨⟩ 138.63

9. Review

Disappointed bidder could not raise claim that it did not qualify as affiliate of suspended business concern as basis for contesting its suspension by Defense Logistics Agency (DLA) in connection with solicitation for bids for United States Air Force contract for base operations and maintenance, where bidder did not, in its response to DLA, present this argument and seek decision by DLA on its "affiliate" status, but instead took action to totally eliminate suspended entity's interest in bidder. FAS Support Services, LLC v. U.S., Fed.Cl.2010, 93 Fed.Cl. 687. United States ⟨⟩ 64.55(2)

§ 253a. Planning and solicitation requirements

HISTORICAL AND STATUTORY NOTES

Authorization of Telecommuting for Federal Contractors

Pub.L. 108–136, Div. A, Title XIV, § 1428, Nov. 24, 2003, 117 Stat. 1670, which authorized telecommuting by employees of Federal Government contractors in the performance of contracts entered into with executive agencies, was repealed in the enactment into positive law of Title 41, Public Contracts, by Pub.L. 111–350, § 7(b), Jan. 4, 2011, 124 Stat. 3855.

Notes of Decisions

Amendment of judgment 25
Factors considered in evaluation 20-22
   Past performance 21a
   Responsibility criteria 21b

Master task orders 24
Past performance, factors considered in evaluation 21a

Text Repealed by Pub.L. 111–350, effective Jan. 4, 2011

---

5. Disclosure by government

Air Force procurement regulations did not authorize it to disclose "unit pricing information" involuntarily submitted by contractors. Canadian Commercial Corp. v. Department of Air Force, D.D.C.2006, 442 F.Supp.2d 15, affirmed 514 F.3d 37, 379 U.S.App.D.C. 354, 85 U.S.P.Q.2d 1693. United States ⊸ 64.5

19. —— Miscellaneous cases

Source selection authority's (SSA) decision indicating that bidder lacked back-up plan "although one was not required by the solicitation," in event one of major subcontractors in bidder's teaming arrangement was unable to perform, did not apply undisclosed evaluation criterion solely to bidder in solicitation for contract with National Aeronautics and Space Administration (NASA) to provide cargo transportation to and from International Space Station (ISS), where solicitation notified bidders that teaming arrangements would be evaluated for performance risk, and only bidder's teaming arrangement carried added risk by relying on subcontractors for key portions of work. PlanetSpace, Inc. v. U.S., Fed.Cl.2010, 92 Fed.Cl. 520, subsequent determination 2010 WL 5183959. United States ⊸ 64.40(1)

21. —— Price and value, factors considered in evaluation

National Aeronautics and Space Administration's (NASA) source selection authority (SSA) conducted sufficient trade-off analysis in awarding contract to provide cargo transportation to and from International Space Station (ISS), and thus his decision to award contract to higher-priced bidder was entitled to deference, where SSA explained highly critical nature of procured services, noted high-risk nature of work required to deliver the procured services, provided that he considered overall procurement to be difficult and risky for all offers and the chance of successful contract performance for all proposals to be low, focused on the technical and management risks associated with the proposals and their potential to deliver critical cargo to the ISS in a timely manner, and selected higher priced, but technically superior, far less risky proposal. PlanetSpace Inc. v. U.S., Fed.Cl.2010, 2010 WL 5183959.

Source selection authority's (SSA) assignment of significant weaknesses to bidder's proposal for contract with National Aeronautics and Space Administration (NASA) to provide cargo transportation to and from International Space Station (ISS) was reasonable, where bidder's proposed subcontracting structure relying on major subcontracts for key portions of work represented significant risk to successful performance, and SSA was factually correct in concluding that bidder would not have positive cumulative cash from operations until nearly end of contract. PlanetSpace, Inc. v. U.S., Fed.Cl. 2010, 92 Fed.Cl. 520, subsequent determination 2010 WL 5183959. United States ⊸ 64.45(1)

As required in procurement for design and construction of military barracks for United States Army Corps of Engineers, source selection authority (SSA) justified selection of two higher-priced offerors over disappointed bidder where SSA determined that offers of higher-priced offerors satisfied solicitation's pricing target and that such offerors, unlike disappointed bidder, had exact experience in building barracks-type housing that agency sought and so had better chance to perform successfully, and solicitation, which indicated that non-price evaluation factors were significantly more important than price, gave SSA discretion to reject disappointed bidder's lower-priced proposal in favor of other offerors' technically higher-rated, and price-satisfactory, proposals. Structural Associates, Inc./Comfort Systems USA (Syracuse) Joint Venture v. U.S., Fed.Cl.2009, 89 Fed.Cl. 735. United States ⊸ 64.45(1)

21a. —— Past performance, factors considered in evaluation

Source selection authority's (SSA) evaluation of past performance of prime contractor in teaming arrangement with major subcontractors as "not relevant for purposes of selection" for contract with National Aeronautics and Space Administration (NASA), to provide cargo transportation to and from International Space Station (ISS), was not irrational or contrary to procurement regulations that did not compel SSA to consider past performance of key personnel and subcontractors, where SSA did not employ unstated evaluation criterion by failing to give credit for past performance of key personnel and subcontractors, given contractor's own lack of past performance as prime contractor for which SSA did not penalize contractor, but rather, correctly assigned equivalent of neutral past performance rating. PlanetSpace, Inc. v. U.S., Fed.Cl.2010, 92 Fed.Cl. 520, subsequent determination 2010 WL 5183959.

21b. —— Responsibility criteria, factors considered in evaluation

In conducting trade-off analysis in process of awarding contract to provide cargo transportation to and from International Space Station (ISS), National Aeronautics and Space Administration's (NASA) source selection authority (SSA) did not make de facto non-responsibility determination, based on concerns regarding unsuccessful bidder's responsibility, but rather rejected proposal based upon a legally sufficient and carefully conducted trade-off analysis, where SSA relied upon arguable responsibility criteria as only part of his comparative evaluation of proposals; although SSA was especially concerned with the risks inherent in unsuccessful bidder's proposed use of two different launch vehicles over contract period, its proposed reliance on subcontractors for performance of majority of work under contract, and inadequacy of its proposed measures for controlling subcon-

See Revised Title 41, post

tractor costs, SSA properly weighed factors in comparison to overall highly critical nature of procured services and high-risk nature of work to be performed. PlanetSpace Inc. v. U.S., Fed. Cl.2010, 2010 WL 5183959. United States ⟷ 64.45(2)

24. Master task orders

Transfer of work done under two travel services contracts to successor contractor by means of sub task orders issued under a master task order, which in turn was issued under a master indefinite delivery indefinite quantity (IDIQ) contract held by the successor contractor, did not violate the Competition in Contracting Act (CICA) on ground that master task order exceeded scope of master contract because task order required provision of classified travel services. Omega World Travel, Inc. v. U.S., Fed. Cl.2008, 82 Fed.Cl. 452. United States ⟷ 64.10

25. Amendment of judgment

Although manifest injustice did not require amendment of judgment directing Coast Guard to recompete audit-supporting federal financial management system services through fair and open competition, clarification was warranted that judgment did not proscribe Coast Guard from utilizing lawful noncompetitive procurement procedures, but that Coast Guard had clearly intended to compete such services so that forgoing solicitation, and instead issuing modifications to task order effectively constituted new standalone procurement made after expiration of ordering period for underlying contract, in violation of CICA, and thus, judgment's directive to recompete services through fair and open competition would be replaced with directive to procure services in accordance with law and in manner preserving integrity of procurement process, exercising discretion in reasonable manner. Global Computer Enterprises, Inc. v. U.S., Fed.Cl.2009, 88 Fed.Cl. 466. United States ⟷ 64.60(5.1)

26. Remand

Remand was required for further agency explanation as to whether source selection authority (SSA) performed legally sufficient trade-off analysis or usurped authority of contracting officer and Small Business Administration (SBA) by making de facto non-responsibility determination rather than proper trade-off analysis, in awarding contract with National Aeronautics and Space Administration (NASA) to provide cargo transportation to and from International Space Station (ISS) to bidder with technically superior but significantly higher-priced proposal, where SSA recognized that unsuccessful bidder had lower overall price than awardee's proposal, but did not discuss magnitude of price difference between competing proposals, and indicated that no "typical" trade-off analysis was conducted. PlanetSpace, Inc. v. U.S., Fed.Cl.2010, 92 Fed. Cl. 520, subsequent determination 2010 WL 5183959.

27. Standing

Agency violated CICA's full and open competition requirements by awarding Federal Supply Schedule (FSS) task order to FSS contractor who offered non-FSS trailers in response to FSS request for quote (RFQ), as required for non-FSS contractor's standing to challenge award of task order for procurement of mobile medical units; although successful bidder's FSS modifications were approved prior to award, modifications were outside the scope of successful bidder's FSS contract, as reasonably interpreted, because modifications transformed original trailers from mere shells to medical units that were comparable to sophisticated emergency rooms, modifications increased production and delivery time of original trailers by nearly 100%, and modifications were made pursuant to modification request, in which successful bidder conceded it was adding "new item" to its FSS schedule, and which included 75 pages of technical specifications. Mobile Medical Intern. Corp. v. U.S., Fed.Cl.2010, 95 Fed.Cl. 706. United States ⟷ 64.60(2)

§ 253b. Evaluation and award

HISTORICAL AND STATUTORY NOTES

Effective and Applicability Provisions

1996 Acts. Pub.L. 104–201, § 1074(b)(7), which provided a Feb. 10, 1996, effective date, was editorially eliminated from the Code as a result of the enactment into positive law of Title 41, Public Contracts, by Pub.L. 111–350, Jan. 4, 2011, 124 Stat. 3677.

1984 Acts. Pub.L. 98–577, § 201(b), which provided effective date and applicability provisions, was editorially eliminated from the Code as a result of the enactment into positive law of Title 41, Public Contracts, by Pub.L. 111–350, Jan. 4, 2011, 124 Stat. 3677.

EXECUTIVE ORDERS

EXECUTIVE ORDER NO. 12979

Ex. Ord. No. 12979, Oct. 25, 1995, 60 F.R. 55171, which directed heads of executive departments and agencies engaged in the procurement of supplies and services to establish administrative procedures for the resolution of protests to the aware of their procurement contracts, was formerly set out under this section and was editorially transferred to be set out under 41 U.S.C.A. § 3701.

Text Repealed by Pub.L. 111–350, effective Jan. 4, 2011

Notes of Decisions

Material changes from solicitation   45
Post-award modification   44

---

5.   —— Arbitrary or capricious actions, authority of agency

Contracting officer did not abuse her discretion in deciding not to reinstate bidder for United States Air Force contract for base operations and maintenance after Defense Logistics Agency (DLA) removed it from excluded parties list system (EPLS), where there was competition up to point at which bidder was suspended and price proposals of competitors were evaluated, bidder did not change its price proposal in its final proposal revision (FPR), whereas other bidder substantially lowered its already lower price proposal in its FPR, and it was unlikely that bidder would have received award after divesting itself of suspended entities. FAS Support Services, LLC v. U.S., Fed.Cl.2010, 93 Fed. Cl. 687.   United States ⊂⊃ 64.20

Military Sealift Command's (MSC) evaluation of proposals and lowest-price, technically acceptable award of charter party for vessel, serving as floating military warehouse for global prepositioning program, to awardee whose proposal did not comply with all technical requirements of solicitation was arbitrary, capricious, and violated procurement standards and CICA, where awardee's proposal failed to detail how vessel's climate and humidity control system would meet temperature and humidity specifications, failed to describe components of security and communications systems, maintenance plans, and cocoons, and failed to explain how any of these components met request for proposal (RFP), and award was based on relaxed standards for awardee that were not extended to bid protester. Red River Holdings, LLC v. U.S., Fed.Cl. 2009, 87 Fed.Cl. 768.   United States ⊂⊃ 64.45(1)

6. Discussions with offerors

Contracting agency was not required to conduct discussions with bidder after it reopened discussions with competing bidder, where bidder had been placed on excluded parties list system (EPLS), and contracting officer reasonable concluded that it lacked reasonable chance of obtaining contract after it divested itself of suspended entities. FAS Support Services, LLC v. U.S., Fed.Cl.2010, 93 Fed.Cl. 687.   United States ⊂⊃ 64.40(1)

12. Solicitation terms

Source Evaluation Board's (SEB) consideration of launch and landing (L&L) staffing at Kennedy Space Flight Center (KSC) was consistent with terms of solicitation, as required under Competition in Contracting Act (CICA) and federal acquisition regulations, in evaluating bids to award protective services contract with National Aeronautics and Space Administration (NASA), even though bids were to exclude L&L staffing at KSC that would be addressed in separate task order, since SEB made substantial effort to ensure that contract awardee had understood

that KSC L&L staffing was not part of solicitation, allowed awardee to remove KSC L&L staffing from bid, did not give awardee credit for overstaffing at KSC or penalize disappointed bidder for excluding KSC L&L staffing, and did not rely on any tradeoff analysis exceeding scope of SEB advisor's authority that could have prejudiced disappointed bidder. Coastal Intern. Sec., Inc. v. U.S., Fed.Cl.2010, 93 Fed.Cl. 502. United States ⊂⊃ 64.45(1)

26. Compliance with law and regulations

Statute which requires contracting agencies to evaluate proposals based only on factors set forth in relevant solicitation was not violated when the Small Business Administration (SBA) disqualified contractor from bidding on contract set aside for Historically Underutilized Business Zone (HUBZone) small business concerns, where SBA's decision did not retroactively create a new eligibility requirement but instead represented the SBA's enforcement of one of the requirements already in place. Aeolus Systems, LLC v. U.S., Fed.Cl.2007, 79 Fed.Cl. 1. United States ⊂⊃ 64.15

31. Judicial review

Disappointed bidder could not raise claim that it did not qualify as affiliate of suspended business concern as basis for contesting its suspension by Defense Logistics Agency (DLA) in connection with solicitation for bids for United States Air Force contract for base operations and maintenance, where bidder did not, in its response to DLA, present this argument and seek decision by DLA on its "affiliate" status, but instead took action to totally eliminate suspended entity's interest in bidder. FAS Support Services, LLC v. U.S., Fed.Cl.2010, 93 Fed. Cl. 687.   United States ⊂⊃ 64.55(2)

Bid protestor's complaint alleging that National Aeronautics and Space Administration (NASA) violated Competition in Contracting Act (CICA), Administrative Procedure Act (APA), and federal acquisition rules, in awarding protective services contract, recited sufficient basis for jurisdiction under Tucker Act, as amended by Administrative Dispute Resolution Act (ADRA), providing jurisdiction over bid protests for government contracts and alleged violation of statute or regulation in connection with procurement. Coastal Intern. Sec., Inc. v. U.S., Fed.Cl.2010, 93 Fed.Cl. 502. United States ⊂⊃ 64.60(1)

33. Persons entitled to maintain action

Bid protestor challenging award of protective services contract by National Aeronautics and Space Administration (NASA) was "interested party," within meaning of Tucker Act, conferring standing for bid protest of federal contract, since protestor submitted timely bid and was initially awarded contract that was set aside, so that protestor's economic interests were directly affected by award to competing bidder after reprocurement, and protestor had substantial chance of being awarded contract as only other bidder in competitive range in competition that

See Revised Title 41, post

17

was very close. Coastal Intern. Sec., Inc. v. U.S., Fed.Cl.2010, 93 Fed.Cl. 502. United States ⬅ 64.60(2)

Contractor that would likely have competed for a government contract for travel management center (TMC) services had standing to challenge award of such services by master task order and sub task orders issued under master indefinite delivery indefinite quantity (IDIQ) contract held by another contractor, on ground that master task order exceeded scope of master IDIQ contract in violation of the Competition in Contracting Act (CICA). Omega World Travel, Inc. v. U.S., Fed.Cl.2008, 82 Fed.Cl. 452. United States ⬅ 64.60(2)

40. Injunction

Balance of harms and the public interest weighed in favor of granting preliminary injunction to restrain the Washington Metropolitan Area Transit Authority (WMATA) from selling certain commercial real estate to third party pending resolution of developer's bid protest; WMATA would still have the opportunity to sell the property and purchase a replacement facility once the lawsuit was resolved, and public had an interest in ensuring that WMATA followed its procurement procedures. Monument Realty LLC v. Washington Metropolitan Area Transit Authority, D.D.C.2008, 540 F.Supp.2d 66. Injunction ⬅ 138.63

44. Post-award modification

Reflagging work done on vessel in Singapore did not constitute a post-award material modification of time charter contract awarded by the Military Sealift Command to vessel owner which required reflagging work be preformed in the United States, in violation of the Competition in Contracting Act (CICA), where majority of reflagging work was done in Guam, and vessel was already a U.S. flagged vessel at time the contracting officer accepted the vessel. Sealift, Inc. v. U.S., Fed.Cl.2008, 82 Fed.Cl. 527. United States ⬅ 64.10

A post-award modification of a government contract that materially departs from the scope of the original procurement violates the Competition in Contracting Act (CICA) by preventing potential bidders from participating or competing for what should be a new procurement. Sealift, Inc. v. U.S., Fed.Cl.2008, 82 Fed.Cl. 527.

United States ⬅ 64.10; United States ⬅ 72(1.1)

45. Material changes from solicitation

Source selection authority's (SSA) evaluation of bids for protective services contract with National Aeronautics and Space Administration (NASA) did not consider factors outside of solicitation, as prohibited by Competition in Contracting Act (CICA) and federal acquisition regulations, by downgrading source evaluation board's (SEB) weakness finding for contract awardee's staffing plan that could reflect legitimate business approach allowing awardee to respond to requirements of both basic contract and future task orders, since solicitation provided for possible future task orders and allowed SSA to evaluate bidders' overall approach to provide balance of skills and resources required for contract and task orders, and SSA exercised independent judgment, not bias, in disagreeing with SEB's weakness finding and did not give awardee extra credit for proposed staffing. Coastal Intern. Sec., Inc. v. U.S., Fed.Cl.2010, 93 Fed.Cl. 502. United States ⬅ 64.45(1)

Post-award change in solicitation requirement that vessel owner awarded tanker time charter contract acquire vetting approvals from four commercial petroleum refineries did not constitute a material change in violation of the Competition in Contracting Act (CICA); solicitation acknowledged that an official vetting certificate was no longer required, and thus it was appropriate for the contracting officer to change the type of documentation required to demonstrate that the tanker would be accepted by oil companies listed in the solicitation. Sealift, Inc. v. U.S., Fed.Cl.2008, 82 Fed.Cl. 527. United States ⬅ 64.10

Assuming that vessel owner who was awarded time charter contract by the Military Sealift Command did not obtain required security clearances for corporate officers and ship's officers, that event alone did not constitute a material change from solicitation in violation of the Competition in Contracting Act (CICA); allowing additional time to obtain required clearances was not outside the scope of the original competed contract, because the only agency that could grant the security clearances delayed the processing of the applications. Sealift, Inc. v. U.S., Fed.Cl.2008, 82 Fed.Cl. 527. United States ⬅ 64.10

§ 253c. Encouragement of new competition

HISTORICAL AND STATUTORY NOTES

Effective and Applicability Provisions

1984 Acts. Section 202(b) of Pub.L. 98–577, which provided that section was applicable to solicitations issued more than 180 days after

Oct. 30, 1984, was editorially eliminated from the Code as a result of the enactment into positive law of Title 41, Public Contracts, by Pub.L. 111–350, Jan. 4, 2011, 124 Stat. 3677.

Text Repealed by Pub.L. 111–350, effective Jan. 4, 2011

§ 253d. Validation of proprietary data restrictions

HISTORICAL AND STATUTORY NOTES

Effective and Applicability Provisions

1984 Acts. Section 203(b) of Pub.L. 98–577, which provided that section was applicable to solicitations issued more than 60 days after Oct.

30, 1984, was editorially eliminated from the Code as a result of the enactment into positive law of Title 41, Public Contracts, by Pub.L. 111–350, Jan. 4, 2011, 124 Stat. 3677.

§ 253f. Economic order quantities

HISTORICAL AND STATUTORY NOTES

Effective and Applicability Provisions

1984 Acts. Section 205(b) of Pub.L. 98–577, which provided that section is effective at the end of the 180 day period beginning on Oct. 30,

1984, was editorially eliminated from the Code as a result of the enactment into positive law of Title 41, Public Contracts, by Pub.L. 111–350, Jan. 4, 2011, 124 Stat. 3677.

§ 253g. Prohibition of contractors limiting subcontractor sales directly to United States

HISTORICAL AND STATUTORY NOTES

Effective and Applicability Provisions

1984 Acts . Section 206(b) of Pub.L. 98–577, which provided that section was applicable to solicitations made more than 60 days after Oct.

30, 1984, was editorially eliminated from the Code as a result of the enactment into positive law of Title 41, Public Contracts, by Pub.L. 111–350, Jan. 4, 2011, 124 Stat. 3677.

§ 253h. Task and delivery order contracts: general authority

[See main volume for text of (a) to (c)]

(d) Single and multiple contract awards

[See main volume for text of (1) and (2)]

(3)(A) No task or delivery order contract in an amount estimated to exceed $100,000,000 (including all options) may be awarded to a single source unless the head of the agency determines in writing that—

(i) the task or delivery orders expected under the contract are so integrally related that only a single source can reasonably perform the work;

(ii) the contract provides only for firm, fixed price task orders or delivery orders for—

(I) products for which unit prices are established in the contract; or

(II) services for which prices are established in the contract for the specific tasks to be performed;

(iii) only one source is qualified and capable of performing the work at a reasonable price to the government; or

(iv) because of exceptional circumstances, it is necessary in the public interest to award the contract to a single source.

(B) The head of the agency shall notify Congress within 30 days after any determination under subparagraph (A)(iv).

(4) The regulations implementing this subsection shall—

(A) establish a preference for awarding, to the maximum extent practicable, multiple task or delivery order contracts for the same or similar services or property under the authority of paragraph (1)(B); and

(B) establish criteria for determining when award of multiple task or delivery order contracts would not be in the best interest of the Federal Government.

[See main volume for text of (e) to (g)]

(June 30, 1949, c. 288, Title III, § 303H, as added Oct. 13, 1994, Pub.L. 103–355, Title I, § 1054(a), 108 Stat. 3261, and amended Jan. 28, 2008, Pub.L. 110–181, Div. A, Title VIII, § 843(b)(1), 122 Stat. 238.)

See Revised Title 41, post

HISTORICAL AND STATUTORY NOTES

Revision Notes and Legislative Reports

2008 Acts. Statement by President, see 2008 U.S. Code Cong. and Adm. News, p. S3.

Amendments

2008 Amendments. Subsec. (d)(3). Pub.L. 110–181, § 843(b)(1), redesignated former par. (3) as par. (4), and added a new par. (3).

Subsec. (d)(4). Pub.L. 110–181, § 843(b)(1)(A), redesignated former par. (3) as par. (4).

Effective and Applicability Provisions

2008 Acts. Pub.L. 110–181, Div. A, Title VIII, § 843(b)(3)(A), Jan. 28, 2008, 122 Stat. 239, which provided that amendments by Pub.L. 110–181, § 843(b)(1), should take effect 120 days after Jan. 28, 2008, and apply with respect to any contract awarded on or after such date, was editorially eliminated from the Code as a result of the enactment into positive law of Title 41, Public Contracts, by Pub.L. 111–350, Jan. 4, 2011, 124 Stat. 3677.

Requirements for Purchase of Property and Services Pursuant to Multiple Award Contracts

Pub.L. 110–417, Div. A, Title VIII, § 863(a) to (e), Oct. 14, 2008, 122 Stat. 4547, which provided amendment of the Federal Acquisition Regulation to require enhanced competition in the purchase of property and services by all executive agencies pursuant to multiple award contracts, was repealed in the enactment into positive law of Title 41, Public Contracts, by Pub.L. 111–350, § 7(b), Jan. 4, 2011, 124 Stat. 3855.

Guidance on Use of Task Order and Delivery Order Contracts

Pub.L. 106–65, Div. A, Title VIII, § 804, Oct. 5, 1999, 113 Stat. 704, which provided guidance to agencies on the appropriate use of task order and delivery order contracts, was repealed in the enactment into positive law of Title 41, Public Contracts, by Pub.L. 111–350, § 7(b), Jan. 4, 2011, 124 Stat. 3855.

Provisions Not Affected by Pub.L. 103–355

Section 1054(b) of Pub.L. 103–355, which provided that the Brooks Automatic Data Processing Act and the Brooks Architect–Engineers Act were not affected by Pub.L. 103–355, was repealed in the enactment into positive law of Title 41, Public Contracts, by Pub.L. 111–350, § 7(b), Jan. 4, 2011, 124 Stat. 3855.

LIBRARY REFERENCES

American Digest System

United States ⬅59.
Key Number System Topic No. 393.

NOTES OF DECISIONS

Contracts within section   1

---

1. Contracts within section

Department of Energy's (DOE) award of task order for environmental consulting services and operational assistance, under General Services Administration (GSA) federal supply schedules (FSS), was not "task order contract," within meaning of National Defense Authorization Act (NDAA), requiring mandatory post-award debriefing of disappointed bidders for large task orders under Federal Acquisition Streamlining Act (FASA), since FASA and GSA FSS contracts were separate contracting vehicles, authorized by distinct statutory provisions, and implemented by different parts of federal acquisition regulations. Navarro Research and Engineering, Inc. v. U.S., Fed.Cl.2010, 94 Fed.Cl. 224.   United States ⬅ 64.55(1)

§ 253i. Task order contracts: advisory and assistance services

HISTORICAL AND STATUTORY NOTES

Waivers to Extend Task Order Contracts for Advisory and Assistance Services

Pub.L. 109–364, Div. A, Title VIII, § 834, Oct. 17, 2006, 120 Stat. 2332, which related to waiver authority, was formerly set out as a note under this section and was editorially transferred to be set out as a note under 10 U.S.C.A. § 2304b; subsecs. (b) and (c) were repealed in the enactment into positive law of Title 41, Public Contracts, by Pub.L. 111–350, § 7(b), Jan. 4, 2011, 124 Stat. 3855.

NOTES OF DECISIONS

Contracts within section   1

---

1. Contracts within section

Department of Energy's (DOE) award of task order for environmental consulting services and operational assistance, under General Services Administration (GSA) federal supply schedules (FSS), was not "task order contract," within meaning of National Defense Authorization Act (NDAA), requiring mandatory post-award debriefing of disappointed bidders for large task orders under Federal Acquisition Streamlining Act (FASA), since FASA and GSA FSS contracts were separate contracting vehicles, authorized by distinct statutory provisions, and

Text Repealed by Pub.L. 111–350, effective Jan. 4, 2011

implemented by different parts of federal acquisition regulations. Navarro Research and Engineering, Inc. v. U.S., Fed.Cl.2010, 94 Fed.Cl.
224. United States ⊕ 64.55(1)

§ 253j. Task and delivery order contracts: orders

[See main volume for text of (a) to (c)]

(d) **Enhanced competition for orders in excess of $5,000,000**—In the case of a task
or delivery order in excess of $5,000,000, the requirement to provide all contractors a
fair opportunity to be considered under subsection (b) is not met unless all such
contractors are provided, at a minimum—

(1) a notice of the task or delivery order that includes a clear statement of the
agency's requirements;

(2) a reasonable period of time to provide a proposal in response to the notice;

(3) disclosure of the significant factors and subfactors, including cost or price,
that the agency expects to consider in evaluating such proposals, and their relative
importance;

(4) in the case of an award that is to be made on a best value basis, a written
statement documenting the basis for the award and the relative importance of
quality and price or cost factors; and

(5) an opportunity for a post-award debriefing consistent with the requirements
of section 2305(b)(5) of this title.

(e) **Protests.**—(1) A protest is not authorized in connection with the issuance or
proposed issuance of a task or delivery order except for—

(A) a protest on the ground that the order increases the scope, period, or
maximum value of the contract under which the order is issued; or

(B) a protest of an order valued in excess of $10,000,000.

(2) Notwithstanding section 3556 of title 31, the Comptroller General of the United
States shall have exclusive jurisdiction of a protest authorized under paragraph (1)(B).

(3) This subsection shall be in effect for three years, beginning on the date that is 120
days after the date of the enactment of the National Defense Authorization Act for
Fiscal Year 2008.

(f) **Task and delivery order ombudsman**

The head of each executive agency who awards multiple task or delivery order
contracts pursuant to section 253h(d)(1)(B) or 253i(e) of this title shall appoint or
designate a task and delivery order ombudsman who shall be responsible for reviewing
complaints from the contractors on such contracts and ensuring that all of the contractors are afforded a fair opportunity to be considered for task or delivery orders when
required under subsection (b) of this section. The task and delivery order ombudsman
shall be a senior agency official who is independent of the contracting officer for the
contracts and may be the executive agency's competition advocate.

(g) **Applicability**

This section applies to task and delivery order contracts entered into under sections
253h and 253i of this title.

(June 30, 1949, c. 288, Title III, § 303J, as added Oct. 13, 1994, Pub.L. 103–355, Title I, § 1054(a), 108
Stat. 3264, and amended Jan. 28, 2008, Pub.L. 110–181, Div. A, Title VIII, § 843(b)(2), 122 Stat. 238.)

HISTORICAL AND STATUTORY NOTES

Revision Notes and Legislative Reports

2008 Acts. Statement by President, see 2008
U.S. Code Cong. and Adm. News, p. S3.

References in Text

The date of the enactment of the National
Defense Authorization Act for Fiscal Year 2008,
referred to in subsec. (e)(3), is Jan. 28, 2008, the
approval date of Pub.L. 110–181, 122 Stat. 3.

Codifications

Amendment   by   Pub.L.   110–181,
§ 843(b)(2)(C), which directed striking subsec.
(e), as redesignated by paragraph (1), and inserting a new subsec. (e), was executed as the
probable intent of Congress, even though the
redesignation occurred pursuant to paragraph
(2)(A).

See Revised Title 41, post

Amendments

2008 Amendments. Subsec. (d). Pub.L. 110–181, § 843(b)(2)(A), (B), redesignated former subsec. (d) as subsec. (e), and added a new subsec. (d).

Subsec. (e). Pub.L. 110–181, § 843(b)(2)(A), (C), redesignated former subsec. (d) as subsec. (e), struck out subsec. (e) as so redesignated, and added a new subsec. (e). See Codifications note set out under this section. Subsec. (e), as redesignated, formerly read:

"(e) Protests

"A protest is not authorized in connection with the issuance or proposed issuance of a task or delivery order except for a protest on the ground that the order increases the scope, period, or maximum value of the contract under which the order is issued."

Subsec. (f). Pub.L. 110–181, § 843(b)(2)(A), redesignated former subsec. (e) as subsec. (f). Former subsec. (f) was redesignated subsec. (g).

Subsec. (g). Pub.L. 110–181, § 843(b)(2)(A), redesignated former subsec. (f) as subsec. (g).

Effective and Applicability Provisions

2008 Acts. Pub.L. 110–181, Div. A, Title VIII, § 843(b)(3)(B), Jan. 28, 2008, 122 Stat. 239, which provided that amendments by Pub.L. 110–181, § 843(b)(2), should take effect 120 days after Jan. 28, 2008, and apply with respect to any task or delivery order awarded on or after such date, was editorially eliminated from the Code as a result of the enactment into positive law of Title 41, Public Contracts, by Pub.L. 111–350, Jan. 4, 2011, 124 Stat. 3677.

LIBRARY REFERENCES

American Digest System

United States ⟜64.40, 64.55.
Key Number System Topic No. 393.

Research References

Treatises and Practice Aids

West's Federal Administrative Practice § 525, Bid Protests.

West's Federal Administrative Practice § 630, Contracting by Negotiation--Federal Supply Schedule.

West's Federal Administrative Practice § 635, Types of Contracts.

West's Federal Administrative Practice § 664, Protests and Appeals.

West's Federal Administrative Practice § 822, Subject Matter Jurisdiction--Contract Claim: Jurisdiction, Limitations, Appeals and Interest.

Notes of Decisions

Contracts within section 2

---

1. Protests

Claim for breach of multiple-award Indefinite Delivery/Indefinite Quantity (ID/IQ) contract brought by provider of computer hardware maintenance at federal facility against the United States was, in essence, a bid protest disguised as a contract dispute, and, thus, was barred by the Federal Acquisition Streamlining Act's (FASA) prohibition on task order protests, although provider's action was not a classic bid protest and remedy sought was not a classic bid protest remedy, where provider sought damages based on alleged breach of specific contractual language on ordering provisions in the ID/IQ contract. Digital Technologies, Inc. v. U.S.,

Fed.Cl.2009, 89 Fed.Cl. 711. United States ⟜ 64.55(1)

2. Contracts within section

Department of Energy's (DOE) award of task order for environmental consulting services and operational assistance, under General Services Administration (GSA) federal supply schedules (FSS), was not "task order contract," within meaning of National Defense Authorization Act (NDAA), requiring mandatory post-award debriefing of disappointed bidders for large task orders under Federal Acquisition Streamlining Act (FASA), since FASA and GSA FSS contracts were separate contracting vehicles, authorized by distinct statutory provisions, and implemented by different parts of federal acquisition regulations. Navarro Research and Engineering, Inc. v. U.S., Fed.Cl.2010, 94 Fed.Cl. 224. United States ⟜ 64.55(1)

§ 253k. Task and delivery order contracts: definitions

NOTES OF DECISIONS

Contracts within section 1

---

1. Contracts within section

Department of Energy's (DOE) award of task order for environmental consulting services and operational assistance, under General Services Administration (GSA) federal supply schedules (FSS), was not "task order contract," within

meaning of National Defense Authorization Act (NDAA), requiring mandatory post-award debriefing of disappointed bidders for large task orders under Federal Acquisition Streamlining Act (FASA), since FASA and GSA FSS contracts were separate contracting vehicles, authorized by distinct statutory provisions, and implemented by different parts of federal acquisition regulations. Navarro Research and Engi-

Text Repealed by Pub.L. 111–350, effective Jan. 4, 2011

neering, Inc. v. U.S., Fed.Cl.2010, 94 Fed.Cl. 224. United States ⬩ 64.55(1)

§ 254. Contract requirements

HISTORICAL AND STATUTORY NOTES

Regulations on the Use of Cost–Reimbursement Contracts

Pub.L. 110–417, Div. A, Title VIII, § 864, Oct. 14, 2008, 122 Stat. 4549, which directed revision of the Federal Acquisition Regulation to address the use of cost–reimbursement contracts, was repealed in part and eliminated in part in the enactment into positive law of Title 41, Public Contracts, by Pub.L. 111–350, Jan. 4, 2011, 124 Stat. 3677. Subsecs. (c) and (f)(1) of the note were eliminated, and the rest of the note was repealed by Pub.L. 111–350, § 7(b), Jan. 4, 2011, 124 Stat. 3855.

EXECUTIVE ORDERS
EXECUTIVE ORDER NO. 13201

Ex. Ord. No. 13201, Feb. 17, 2001, 66 F.R. 11221, relating to notification of employee rights concerning payment of union dues or fees, was revoked by section 13 of Ex. Ord. No. 13496, Jan. 30, 2009, 74 F.R. 6107, set out as a note under this section.

EXECUTIVE ORDER NO. 13496

Executive Order No. 13496, Jan. 30, 2009, 774 F.R. 6101, which related to notification of employee rights under Federal labor laws, was formerly set out under this section and was editorially transferred to be set out preceding 41 U.S.C.A. § 3901.

MEMORANDA OF PRESIDENT
PRESIDENTIAL MEMORANDUM

Presidential Memorandum of Mar. 4, 2009, 74 F.R. 9755, relating to government contracting, is set out as a note under 41 U.S.C.A. § 251.

§ 254b. Cost or pricing data: truth in negotiations

HISTORICAL AND STATUTORY NOTES

Effective and Applicability Provisions

1994 Acts . Section 1251(b) of Pub.L. 103–355, as amended by Pub.L. 104–106, Div. D, Title XLIII, § 4321(a)(3), Feb. 10, 1996, 110 Stat. 671, which provided that subsec. (a) of this section shall apply according to the provisions of section 304A of the Federal Property and Administrative Services Act of 1949 on and after Oct. 13, 1994, notwithstanding section 10001(b), set out as an Effective Date of 1994 Amendments note under 41 U.S.C.A. § 254, was editorially eliminated from the Code as a result of the enactment into positive law of Title 41, Public Contracts, by Pub.L. 111–350, Jan. 4, 2011, 124 Stat. 3677.

Limitations on Tiering of Subcontractors

Pub.L. 110–417, Div. A, Title VIII, § 866, Oct. 14, 2008, 122 Stat. 4551, which provided for amendment of the Federal Acquisition Regulation for executive agencies other than the Department of Defense to minimize the excessive use by contractors of subcontractors, or of tiers of subcontractors, that add no or negligible value, and to ensure that neither a contractor nor a subcontractor receives indirect costs or profit on work performed by a lower-tier subcontractor to which the higher–tier contractor or subcontractor adds no, or negligible, value, was repealed in the enactment into positive law of Title 41, Public Contracts, by Pub.L. 111–350, § 7(b), Jan. 4, 2011, 124 Stat. 3855.

Minimizing Abuse of Commercial Services Item Authority

Pub.L. 110–417, Div. A, Title VIII, § 868, Oct. 14, 2008, 122 Stat. 4552, which provided for amendment of the Federal Acquisition Regulation to ensure that services that are not offered and sold competitively in substantial quantities in the commercial marketplace, but are of a type offered and sold competitively in substantial quantities in the commercial marketplace, may be treated as commercial items, only if the contracting officer determines in writing that the offeror has submitted sufficient information to evaluate, through price analysis, the reasonableness of the price for such services, was repealed in the enactment into positive law of Title 41, Public Contracts, by Pub.L. 111–350, § 7(b), Jan. 4, 2011, 124 Stat. 3855.

Eligibility for Contracts and Subcontracts To Be Conditioned On Compliance

Pub.L. 105–261, Div. A, Title VIII, § 808(c), Oct. 17, 1998, 112 Stat. 2085, which provided that not later than 180 days Oct. 17, 1998, the Federal Acquisition Regulation shall be amended to provide that an offeror's compliance with a requirement to submit data for a contract or subcontract shall be a condition for the offeror to be eligible to enter into the contract or subcontract, subject to such exceptions as the Federal Acquisition Regulatory Council determines appropriate, was editorially eliminated from the

See Revised Title 41, post

Code as a result of the enactment into positive law of Title 41, Public Contracts, by Pub.L. 111–350, Jan. 4, 2011, 124 Stat. 3677.

Criteria for Certain Determinations Regarding Price Information

Pub.L. 105–261, Div. A, Title VIII, § 808(d), Oct. 17, 1998, 112 Stat. 2085, which provided that not later than 180 days after Oct. 17, 1998, the Federal Acquisition Regulation shall be amended to include criteria for contracting officers to apply for determining the specific price information that an offeror should be required to submit under 10 U.S.C.A. § 2306(d) or subsec. (d) of this section, was editorially eliminated from the Code as a result of the enactment into positive law of Title 41, Public Contracts, by Pub.L. 111–350, Jan. 4, 2011, 124 Stat. 3677.

§ 254d.   Examination of records of contractor

[See main volume for text of (a) and (b)]

(c) Comptroller General authority

(1) Except as provided in paragraph (2), each contract awarded after using procedures other than sealed bid procedures shall provide that the Comptroller General and his representatives are authorized to examine any records of the contractor, or any of its subcontractors, that directly pertain to, and involve transactions relating to, the contract or subcontract and to interview any current employee regarding such transactions.

[See main volume for text of (2) and (3); (d) to (i)]

(June 30, 1949, c. 288, Title III, § 304C, as added and amended Oct. 13, 1994, Pub.L. 103–355, Title II, § 2251(a), Title IV, § 4103(d), 108 Stat. 3318, 3341; Feb. 10, 1996, Pub.L. 104–106, Div. D, Title XLIII, § 4321(e)(5), 110 Stat. 675; Sept. 23, 1996, Pub.L. 104–201, Div. A, Title VIII, § 808(b), 110 Stat. 2607; Oct. 14, 2008, Pub.L. 110–417, Div. A, Title VIII, § 871(a), 122 Stat. 4555.)

HISTORICAL AND STATUTORY NOTES

Revision Notes and Legislative Reports

2008 Acts. Senate Report No. 110–335, see 2008 U.S. Code Cong. and Adm. News, p. 1829.

Statement by President, see 2008 U.S. Code Cong. and Adm. News, p. S30.

Amendments

2008 Amendments. Subsec. (c)(1). Pub.L. 110–417, § 871(a), inserted "and to interview any current employee regarding such transactions" following "contract or subcontract".

LIBRARY REFERENCES

American Digest System

United States ⬅75(1).
Key Number System Topic No. 393.

§ 255.   Contract financing

HISTORICAL AND STATUTORY NOTES

Relationship Between 1994 Amendments and Prompt Payment Requirements

Section 2051(f) of Pub.L. 103–355, which provided that amendments to this section are not intended to impair or modify procedures required by the provisions of chapter 39 of title 31, 31 U.S.C.A. § 3901 et seq., United States Code and the regulations issued pursuant to such provisions of law as such procedures are in effect on Oct. 13, 1994, except that the Government may accept payment terms offered by a contractor offering a commercial item, was formerly set out as a note under this section and was editorially transferred to be set out as a note under 41 U.S.C.A. § 4501.

§ 256.   Allowable costs

HISTORICAL AND STATUTORY NOTES

Revision of Cost Principle Relating to Entertainment, Gift, and Recreation Costs for Contractor Employees

Section 2192 of Pub.L. 103–355, which provided for revision of cost principle relating to entertainment, gift, and recreation costs for contractor employees no later than 90 days after Oct. 13, 1994 , was formerly set out as a note under this section and was editorially transferred to be set out as a note under 41 U.S.C.A. § 4304.

Text Repealed by Pub.L. 111–350, effective Jan. 4, 2011

EXECUTIVE ORDERS
EXECUTIVE ORDER NO. 13494
ECONOMY IN GOVERNMENT CONTRACTING

Executive Order No. 13494, Jan. 30, 2009, 74 F.R. 6101, as amended Ex. Ord. No. 13517, Sec. 2, Oct. 30, 2009, 74 F.R. 57239, which related to costs allowable in government contracting , was formerly set out under this section and was editorially transferred to be set out under 41 U.S.C.A. § 4304.

§ 263. Performance based management: acquisition programs

HISTORICAL AND STATUTORY NOTES

Enhanced System of Performance Incentives

Section 5051(c) of Pub.L. 103–355, which provided for review of incentives and personnel actions available to the heads of departments and agencies of the Federal Government for encouraging excellence in the acquisition workforce and provide an enhanced system of incentives for the encouragement of excellence in such workforce, was formerly set out as a note under this section and was editorially transferred to be set out as a note under 41 U.S.C.A. § 1703.

Recommended Legislation

Section 5051(d) of Pub.L. 103–355, which provided for submission to Congress by one year after Oct. 13, 1994 of recommended legislation necessary to carry out the section and facilitate and enhance management of Federal Government acquisition programs and workforce, was editorially eliminated from the Code as a result of the enactment into positive law of Title 41, Public Contracts, by Pub.L. 111–350, Jan. 4, 2011, 124 Stat. 3677.

§ 264. Relationship of commercial item provisions to other provisions of law

HISTORICAL AND STATUTORY NOTES

Provisions Not Affected by Title VIII of Pub.L. 103–355

Pub.L. 103–355, § 8304, which provided that nothing in Title VIII of Pub.L. 103–355 shall be construed as modifying, superseding, or as intended to impair or restrict authorities or responsibilities under 10 U.S.C.A. § 2323, section 7102 of the Federal Acquisition Streamlining Act of 1994, the Brooks Automatic Data Processing Act, the Brooks Architect-Engineers Act, section 8(a) and (d) of the Small Business Act, and the Javits-Wagner-O'Day Act, was formerly set out as a note under this section and was editorially transferred to be set out as a note under 10 U.S.C.A. § 2375.

Regulations on Acquisition of Commercial Items

Section 8002 of Pub.L. 103–355, as amended, Pub.L. 108–136, Div. A, Title XIV, § 1432, Nov. 24, 2003, 117 Stat. 1672, which related to list of contract clauses to be included in contracts for the acquisition of commercial end items, demonstration of market acceptance of items, types of contracts for commercial items, contract quality requirements, and defense contract clauses, was repealed in the enactment into positive law of Title 41, Public Contracts, by Pub.L. 111–350, § 7(b), Jan. 4, 2011, 124 Stat. 3855.

§ 264b. Preference for acquisition of commercial items

HISTORICAL AND STATUTORY NOTES

Comptroller General Review of Federal Government Use of Market Research

Section 8305 of Pub.L. 103–355, which directed the Comptroller General of the United States to submit to Congress a report on the use of market research by the Federal Government in support of the procurement of commercial items and nondevelopmental items not later than 2 years after Oct. 13, 1994, was editorially eliminated from the Code as a result of the enactment into positive law of Title 41, Public Contracts, by Pub.L. 111–350, Jan. 4, 2011, 124 Stat. 3677.

§ 266a. Transferred

HISTORICAL AND STATUTORY NOTES

Codifications

Section June 30, 1949, c. 288, Title III, § 317, as added Dec. 17, 2002, Pub.L. 107–347, Title II, § 210(b), 116 Stat. 2934, establishing share–in–savings contracts for information technology in which the Government awards a contract to improve mission–related or administrative processes or to accelerate the achievement of its mission and share with the contractor in savings achieved through contract performance, was editorially transferred to be set out as a note preceding 41 U.S.C.A. § 3901.

See Revised Title 41, post

CHAPTER 5—JUDICIAL REVIEW OF ADMINISTRATIVE DECISIONS

§ 321. Limitation on pleading contract provisions relating to finality; standards of review

Notes of Decisions

III. JUDICIAL REVIEW GENERALLY

Collateral estoppel   111
Res judicata   110

---

92. Jurisdiction, judicial review generally

Wunderlich Act did not provide jurisdiction over contractor's suit in the Court of Federal Claims, where contractor contracted with an agency within the executive branch, and contract was entered into well after the effective date of the Contract Disputes Act (CDA). Parker v. U.S., Fed.Cl.2007, 77 Fed.Cl. 279, affirmed 280 Fed.Appx. 957, 2008 WL 2329271, rehearing and rehearing en banc denied. United States ⇔ 73(15)

105. Burden of proof, judicial review generally

Issuance of change order did not excuse government contractor's burden to prove that tunnel safety work was extra work under the contract so as to entitle it to an equitable adjustment for the removal of streetcar tracks allegedly in excess of the quantity estimated by the contract. Kiska Const. Corp.-U.S.A. v. Washington Metropolitan Area Transit Authority, D.D.C.2010, 736 F.Supp.2d 171. United States ⇔ 70(26)

110. Res judicata, judicial review generally

Contractor's claims for retainage and equitable adjustment against contracting authority fell under the disputes clause of government contract, which required administrative exhaustion of claims before they could be presented to a federal court, and therefore contractor could not have asserted its claims for retainage and equitable adjustment during prior federal breach of contract action that was outside the scope of the disputes clause; consequently, res judicata did not bar the claims for retainage and equitable adjustment, which were not litigated during the

prior federal action. Kiska Const. Corp.-U.S.A. v. Washington Metropolitan Area Transit Authority, D.D.C.2010, 736 F.Supp.2d 171. United States ⇔ 73(9)

111. Collateral estoppel, judicial review generally

Doctrine of collateral estoppel did not preclude government contractor's claims against contracting authority for the retainage and equitable adjustments because contracting authority failed to show that the issues before it were actually litigated, submitted to the jury, or necessarily decided by the judgment in prior breach of contract action between the parties; fact that contractor might have recovered damages for the retainage and equitable adjustments under its alternative breach of contract theory in prior action did not establish that its claims for retainage and equitable adjustment were actually before the jury, and court provided no instructions to the jury regarding a claim for the wrongful withholding of retainage or authority's failure to pay equitable adjustments. Kiska Const. Corp.-U.S.A. v. Washington Metropolitan Area Transit Authority, D.D.C.2010, 736 F.Supp.2d 171.

VI. SUBSTANTIAL EVIDENCE FOR DECISION

287. Miscellaneous issues, substantial evidence for decision

Substantial evidence supported Armed Services Board of Contract Appeals' (ASBCA) finding that government contractor did not meet its burden of proof with respect to showing completion of all work under the contract, and therefore was not entitled to payment of the retainage under contract's terms, which required completion of "all work". Kiska Const. Corp.-U.S.A. v. Washington Metropolitan Area Transit Authority, D.D.C.2010, 736 F.Supp.2d 171. United States ⇔ 73(15)

CHAPTER 6—SERVICE CONTRACT LABOR STANDARDS

§ 351. Required contract provisions; minimum wages

HISTORICAL AND STATUTORY NOTES

Effective and Applicability Provisions

1965 Acts. Section 9 of Pub.L. 89–286, which provided that chapter should apply to all contracts entered into pursuant to negotiations concluded or invitations for bids issued on or after ninety days from Oct. 22, 1965, was repealed in the enactment into positive law of Title 41, Public Contracts, by Pub.L. 111–350, § 7(b), Jan. 4, 2011, 124 Stat. 3855.

Short Title

1965 Amendments. Section 1 of Pub.L. 89–286, which provided a Short Title for the Service Contract Act of 1965, was repealed in the enactment into positive law of Title 41, Public Contracts, by Pub.L. 111–350, § 7(b), Jan. 4, 2011, 124 Stat. 3855.

Text Repealed by Pub.L. 111–350, effective Jan. 4, 2011

EXECUTIVE ORDERS
EXECUTIVE ORDER NO. 13495
NONDISPLACEMENT OF QUALIFIED WORKERS UNDER SERVICE CONTRACTS

Executive Order No. 13495, Jan. 30, 2009, 74 F.R. 6103, which provided that for nondisplacement of qualified workers under successor service contracts, with certain exceptions and exclusions, was formerly set out under this section and was editorially transferred to be set out under 41 U.S.C.A. § 6703.

Notes of Decisions

2. Construction with other laws

Federal Enclave Doctrine precluded claims brought under New Jersey Wage and Hour Law by employees alleging wage violations in connection with role-playing assistance in military base exercises, pursuant to Supremacy Clause; nothing in Service Contract Act evinced congressional intent to apply state minimum wage laws to federal enclaves, nor was application of state law to federal property mentioned therein. Manning v. Gold Belt Falcon, LLC, D.N.J.2010, 681 F.Supp.2d 574. United States ⟜ 3

§ 352. Violations

Notes of Decisions

6. Persons entitled to maintain action

Bid protestor's contention that United States Park Service violated the Service Contract Act in solicitation for ferry services by not requiring bidders to submit wages computed in accordance with the Act constituted a challenge to term of solicitation, and protestor's failure to contest term before submission of proposals precluded its subsequent protest of term in bid protest before the Court of Federal Claims. Blue & Gold Fleet, LP v. U.S., Fed.Cl.2006, 70 Fed.Cl. 487, affirmed 492 F.3d 1308. United States ⟜ 64.55(2)

§ 353. Law governing authority of Secretary

Notes of Decisions

16. —— Exclusiveness of enforcement procedure, administrative review

Unions alleging interference by National Aeronautics and Space Administration (NASA) with negotiations for collective bargaining agreement failed to establish that denial of judicial review would wholly deprive them of meaningful and adequate means of vindicating statutory rights, as required to show entitlement to nonstatutory review of agency's actions; administrative remedies were available to unions under Service Contract Act (SCA). International Ass'n of Machinists and Aerospace Workers, Dist. Lodge 166, AFL-CIO v. Griffin, D.D.C. 2008, 590 F.Supp.2d 171. Labor And Employment ⟜ 1143

26. Standard of judicial review

In the Second Circuit, modified de novo standard of review applies to judicial review of administrative actions under Service Contract Act (SCA). Karawia v. U.S. Dept. of Labor, S.D.N.Y.2009, 627 F.Supp.2d 137. Labor And Employment ⟜ 2357

"Preponderance of the evidence" language in hearing provisions of Walsh-Healey Act, which are incorporated by reference into Service Contract Act (SCA), mandates application of standard of review which is somewhat more exacting than "substantial evidence" standard that ordinarily applies to judicial review of agency fact finding. Karawia v. U.S. Dept. of Labor, S.D.N.Y.2009, 627 F.Supp.2d 137. Labor And Employment ⟜ 2357

27. Weight and conclusiveness of administrative determinations

California-based security company owned by Egyptian that was seeking relief from debarment under Service Contract Act (SCA) failed to establish by preponderance of the evidence either causal link between reprehensible conduct of General Services Administration's (GSA's) Chief Contracting Technical Representative and GSA contract's cancellation or that federal government otherwise acted in bad faith; contractor argued that negative media attention in New York following September 11th terrorist attacks and government employee's racial animus towards contractor's owner resulted in bad faith cancellation of GSA contract, itself an unusual circumstance. Karawia v. U.S. Dept. of Labor, S.D.N.Y.2009, 627 F.Supp.2d 137. United States ⟜ 64.20

28. Burden of proof

Under Service Contract Act (SCA), it is contractor's burden to prove that unusual circumstances warrant relief from debarment. Karawia v. U.S. Dept. of Labor, S.D.N.Y.2009, 627 F.Supp.2d 137. United States ⟜ 64.20

§ 354. List of violators; prohibition of contract award to firms appearing on list; actions to recover underpayments; payment of sums recovered

Notes of Decisions

Culpable neglect 9a

---

3. —— Unusual circumstances, list of violators

Late payments under General Services Administration (GSA) contract did not impact contractor's ability to pay employees and thus did not constitute "unusual circumstances" that warranted relief from debarment under Service Contract Act (SCA). Karawia v. U.S. Dept. of Labor, S.D.N.Y.2009, 627 F.Supp.2d 137. United States ⟾ 64.20

9a. Culpable neglect

California-based security company's numerous and repeated violations of Service Contract Act (SCA) involving underpayment of its employees, particularly after being put on notice as to statute's requirement, constituted "culpable neglect," an aggravating factor that precluded relief from debarment from federal contracting for three years. Karawia v. U.S. Dept. of Labor, S.D.N.Y.2009, 627 F.Supp.2d 137. United States ⟾ 64.20

§ 357. Definitions

HISTORICAL AND STATUTORY NOTES

Effective and Applicability Provisions

1973 Acts. Section 2 of Pub.L. 93–57, which provided that amendment to subsec. (d) of this section made by Pub.L. 93–57 is effective with respect to all contracts entered into after July 6, 1973, was editorially eliminated from the Code as a result of the enactment into positive law of Title 41, Public Contracts, by Pub.L. 111–350, Jan. 4, 2011, 124 Stat. 3677.

CHAPTER 7—OFFICE OF FEDERAL PROCUREMENT POLICY

§§ 401, 402. Repealed. Pub.L. 104–106, Div. D, Title XLIII, § 4305(a)(2), Feb. 10, 1996, 110 Stat. 665

HISTORICAL AND STATUTORY NOTES

Effective and Applicability Provisions

1979 Acts. Section 12 of Pub.L. 96–83, which provided that, except to the extent otherwise provided, amendments made by Pub.L. 96–83 shall take effect on Oct. 1, 1979, was editorially eliminated from the Code as a result of the enactment into positive law of Title 41, Public Contracts, by Pub.L. 111–350, Jan. 4, 2011, 124 Stat. 3677.

Short Title

2003 Amendments. Pub.L. 108–136, § 1401, which provided a Short Title for the Services Acquisition Reform Act of 2003, was formerly set out as a note under this section and was editorially transferred to be set out as a note under 41 U.S.C.A. § 101.

1988 Amendments. Section 1 of Pub.L. 100–679, which provided a Short Title for the Office of Federal Procurement Policy Act Amendments of 1988, was formerly set out as a note under this section and was editorially transferred to be set out as a note under 41 U.S.C.A. § 101.

1983 Amendments. Section 1 of Pub.L. 98–191, which provided a Short Title for the Office of Federal Procurement Policy Act Amendments of 1983, was formerly set out as a note under this section and was editorially transferred to be set out as a note under 41 U.S.C.A. § 101.

1979 Amendments. Section 1(a) of Pub.L. 96–83, which provided a Short Title for the Office of Federal Procurement Policy Act Amendments of 1979, was formerly set out as a note under this section and was editorially transferred to be set out as a note under 41 U.S.C.A. § 101.

1974 Amendments. Section 1(a) of Pub.L. 93–400, which provided a Short Title for the Office of Federal Procurement Policy Act, was formerly set out as a note under this section and was editorially transferred to be set out as a note under 41 U.S.C.A. § 101.

Stylistic Consistency

Section 10005(b)(1) of Pub.L. 103–355, which amended the chapter so that the section desig-

Text Repealed by Pub.L. 111–350, effective Jan. 4, 2011

nation and heading is in the same form and typeface as this section, was editorially eliminated from the Code as a result of the enactment into positive law of Title 41 by Pub.L. 111–350, Jan. 4, 2011, 124 Stat. 3677.

Requirements for use of Appropriations by Executive Agencies for Services by Contract

Pub.L. 102–394, Title V, § 502, Oct. 6, 1992, 106 Stat. 1825, and prior similar provisions, which provided that appropriations must be awarded and entered into under contracts in compliance with appropriations acts, were formerly set out as a note under this section and were editorially transferred to be set out as a note under 41 U.S.C.A. § 1101.

EXECUTIVE ORDERS
EXECUTIVE ORDER NO. 12073.

Executive Order No. 12073, Aug. 16, 1978, 43 F.R. 36873, which related to Federal procurement in labor surplus areas, was formerly set out under this section and was editorially transferred to be set out under 41 U.S.C.A. § 1701.

EXECUTIVE ORDER NO. 12931.

Executive Order No. 12931, Oct. 13, 1994, 59 F.R. 52387, which provided for review of agency procurement rules, reporting requirements, contractual requirements, certification procedures, and other administrative procedures, and agency programs in order to reform Federal procurement procedures, was formerly set out under this section and was editorially transferred to be set out under 41 U.S.C.A. § 1701.

MEMORANDA OF PRESIDENT

Presidential Memorandum, Oct. 28, 1993, 58 F.R. 58095, for the Heads of Executive Departments and Agencies and the President's Management Council regarding streamlining of procurement procedures through electronic commerce, was formerly set out under this section and was editorially transferred to be set out under 41 U.S.C.A. § 2301.

§ 403. Definitions

HISTORICAL AND STATUTORY NOTES

First Adjustment of Small Purchase Threshold

Section 806(a)(2) of Pub.L. 101–510 provided that the adjustment under par. (11) of this section, as amended by paragraph (1), shall be made on October 1, 1995.

Modification of Federal Acquisition Regulations

Section 2752 of Pub.L. 98–369, which provided that, not later than March 31, 1985, the single Government–wide procurement regulation referred to in par. (4)(A) of this section shall be modified to conform to the requirements of Title VII of Pub.L. 98–369, §§ 2701 to 2753, was editorially eliminated from the Code as a result of the enactment into positive law of Title 41, Public Contracts, by Pub.L. 111–350, Jan. 4, 2011, 124 Stat. 3677.

Notes of Decisions

Stages of process of acquiring property 2

---

1. Construction with other laws

Federal agencies' decision to insource work currently performed by contractor did not constitute "procurement," for purposes of Tucker Act provision giving Court of Federal Claims exclusive jurisdiction over decisions made in connection with procurements, and thus federal district court had jurisdiction under Administrative Procedure Act (APA) over contractor's action challenging agencies' decision, where contractor sought only declaratory and injunctive relief, and only challenged agencies' compliance with their own procedures. K-Mar Industries, Inc. v. U.S. Dept. of Defense, W.D.Okla.2010, 2010 WL 4829965. Federal Courts ☞ 1139

Court of Federal Claims had exclusive jurisdiction, under Administrative Dispute Resolution Act (ADRA) amendments to Tucker Act, over government contractor's challenge to Department of Defense's (DOD's) decision to insource weather-related services which were currently provided by contractor under procurement arrangement; despite contention that insourcing was not procurement-related, it was DOD's decision not to procure something, not the act of insourcing itself, that was at issue, moreover, statutory definition of procurement was broad enough to include decision not to procure, either as a matter of "determining a need" for procurement or deciding whether to continue procurement arrangement, and determination that insourcing dispute was within Court of Federal Claims's exclusive jurisdiction was consistent with policy behind ADRA to create a place of uniform jurisdiction over all manner of procurement-related disputes. Vero Technical Support, Inc. v. U.S. Dept. of Defense, S.D.Fla.2010, 733 F.Supp.2d 1336. Federal Courts ☞ 1141

See Revised Title 41, post

2. Stages of process of acquiring property

Incumbent contractor's bid protest, challenging Department of Veterans Affairs' (DVA) extension of laundry services contract in order to place services on AbilityOne procurement list for bidder employing blind and otherwise severely disabled individuals, pursuant to Javits-Wagner-O'Day Act, as failing to comply with procurement regulation and DVA's new guidelines giving first priority to service-disabled veteran-owned (SDVO) and veteran-owned (VO) small businesses qualified under Veterans Benefits Health Care, and Information Technology Act, was "in connection with a procurement," within meaning of Tucker Act, conferring jurisdiction to consider bid protest without constraint as to any equitable remedy of removing services from AbilityOne list, since Javits-Wagner-O'Day Act's rulemaking provisions subjecting deletions from AbilityOne list to judicial review under Administrative Procedure Act (APA) did not supersede Tucker Act's protest jurisdiction. Angelica Textile Services, Inc. v. U.S., Fed.Cl. 2010, 95 Fed.Cl. 208. United States ⟻ 64.60(1)

United States Agency for International Development's (USAID) planning, setting up, defining process and procedure, and keeping official on selection panel for prime contractor's issuance of awards to subcontractors to fulfill task orders related to prime's own contract with USAID for health-related services were indicia of "stages of the process of acquiring property or services," within meaning of statutory definition of "procurement," as required for Tucker Act jurisdiction to review prime's issuance of procurement awards to subcontractors, even though prime was private third party, not government agency. Alatech Healthcare, L.L.C. v. U.S., Fed.Cl.2009, 89 Fed.Cl. 750. United States ⟻ 64.60(1)

§ 405. Authority and functions of the Administrator

HISTORICAL AND STATUTORY NOTES

Improvements to the Federal Procurement Data System

Pub.L. 110–417, Div. A, Title VIII, § 874(a), Oct. 14, 2008, 122 Stat. 4558, which provided for enhanced transparency on interagency contracting and other transactions, was repealed in the enactment into positive law of Title 41, Public Contracts, by Pub.L. 111–350, § 7(b), Jan. 4, 2011, 124 Stat. 3855.

Pilot Program for Development and Implementation of an Inventory to Track the Cost and Size of Service Contracts

Pub.L. 110–161, Div. D, Title VII, § 748, Dec. 26, 2007, 121 Stat. 2035, which provided that no later than 180 days after Dec. 26, 2007, the Office of Management and Budget should establish a pilot program to develop and implement an inventory to track the cost and size (in contractor manpower equivalents) of service contracts, particularly with respect to contracts that have been performed poorly by a contractor because of excessive costs or inferior quality, as determined by a contracting officer within the last five years, involve inherently governmental functions, or were undertaken without competition, was formerly set out as a note under this section and was editorially transferred to be set out as a note under 41 U.S.C.A. § 1122.

Federal Support for Enhancement of State and Local Anti–Terrorism Response Capabilities

Pub.L. 108–136, Div. A, Title VIII, § 803, Nov. 24, 2003, 117 Stat. 1541, which established a program under which States and local governments may procure anti-terrorism technologies or services, was formerly set out as a note under this section and was editorially transferred to be set out as a note under 41 U.S.C.A. § 1121.

Statutory and Regulatory Review

Pub.L. 108–136, Div. A, Title XIV, § 1423, Nov. 24, 2003, 117 Stat. 1669, as amended Pub.L. 109–163, Div. A, Title VIII, § 843, Jan. 6, 2006, 119 Stat. 3389, which provided for establishment of an advisory panel to review laws and regulations regarding the use of commercial practices, performance–based contracting, the performance of acquisition functions across agency lines of responsibility, and the use of Governmentwide contracts, was editorially eliminated from the Code as a result of the enactment into positive law of Title 41, Public Contracts, by Pub.L. 111–350, Jan. 4, 2011, 124 Stat. 3677.

Center of Excellence in Service Contracting

Pub.L. 108–136, Div. A, Title XIV, § 1431(b), Nov. 24, 2003, 117 Stat. 1671, which provided that the Administrator for Federal Procurement Policy should establish a center of excellence in contracting for services, which should assist the acquisition community by identifying, and serving as a clearinghouse for, best practices in contracting for services in the public and private sectors not later than 180 days Nov. 24, 2003, was repealed in the enactment into positive law of Title 41, Public Contracts, by Pub.L. 111–350, § 7(b), Jan. 4, 2011, 124 Stat. 3855.

Reporting of bundled contract opportunities

Section 414 of Pub.L. 105–135, which provided for collection of data regarding bundling of contract requirements when the contracting officer anticipates that the resulting contract price, including all options, is expected to exceed $5,000,000, was formerly set out as a note under this section and was editorially transferred to be set out as a note under 41 U.S.C.A. § 1122.

Congressional Findings and Policy Regarding Consideration of Contractor Past Performance

Section 1091(b)(1) of Pub.L. 103–355, which made Congressional findings regarding past contract performance of an offeror, was formerly set out as a note under this section and was

Text Repealed by Pub.L. 111–350, effective Jan. 4, 2011

editorially transferred to be set out as a note under 41 U.S.C.A. § 1126.

Results-Oriented Acquisition Process

Section 5052 of Pub.L. 103–355, which provided for results–oriented acquisition process guidelines, which are not applicable to Department of Defense, was formerly set out as a note under this section and was editorially transferred to be set out as a note under 41 U.S.C.A. § 1122.

Development of Definitions Regarding Certain Small Business Concerns

Section 7107 of Pub.L. 103–355, which directed the Administrator for Federal Procurement Policy to conduct a comprehensive review of Federal laws, as in effect on Nov. 1, 1994, to identify and catalogue all provisions in such laws that define (or describe for definitional purposes) small business concerns owned and controlled by socially and economically disadvantaged individuals, minorities, and women, and submit a report to Congress by May 1, 1996, was editorially eliminated from the Code as a result of the enactment into positive law of Title

41, Public Contracts, by Pub.L. 111–350, Jan. 4, 2011, 124 Stat. 3677.

Data Collection Through the Federal Procurement Data System

Section 10004 of Pub.L. 103–355, relating to data collection, was formerly set out as a note under this section and was editorially transferred to be set out as a note under 41 U.S.C.A. § 1122.

Profit Methodology Study

Section 7 of Pub.L. 100–679, which provided that Administrator shall conduct a study to develop a consistent methodology which executive agencies should use for measuring the profits earned by government contractors on procurements, other than procurements where the price is based on adequate price competition or on established catalog or market prices of commercial items sold in substantial quantities to the general public, was formerly set out as a note under this section and was editorially transferred to be set out as a note under 41 U.S.C.A. § 1121.

Notes of Decisions

Past performance   4

---

4. Past performance

Army's evaluation of awardee's past and present performance, in awarding contract to provide community health care services to military personnel and their dependents, was contrary to evaluation criteria in request for proposals (RFP) and underlying statutory and regulatory provisions, since Army gave awardee neutral rating that did not help or hinder awardee based on lack of past performance, rather than finding that awardee had failed to comply with material requirement in RFP by not providing past performance information for subcontractors that were to perform major or critical aspects of work, essentially taking awardee's past performance off table or at least reducing any advantage that unsuccessful bidder could otherwise have enjoyed from past performance rating of "excellent." CRAssociates, Inc. v. U.S., Fed.Cl.2010, 95 Fed.Cl. 357. United States ☞ 64.45(2)

§ 405a.   Uniform Federal procurement regulations and procedures

HISTORICAL AND STATUTORY NOTES

Supersedure of Inconsistent Statutory Provisions

Pub.L. 96–83, § 11, Oct. 10, 1979, 93 Stat. 652, which provided that the provisions of Pub.L. 96–83, as amended, shall supersede the provisions of section 222 of the Act of October 24,

1978, entitled "An Act to amend the Small Business Act and the Small Business Investment Act of 1958", former 41 U.S.C. 405a, to the extent they are inconsistent therewith, was formerly set out as a note under this section and was editorially transferred to be set out as a note under 41 U.S.C.A. § 1121.

§ 405c.   Repealed

HISTORICAL AND STATUTORY NOTES

Codifications

Section 405c, Pub.L. 110–417, Div. A, Title VIII, § 841, Oct. 14, 2008, 122 Stat. 4537, relating to ethics safeguards related to contractor conflicts of interest, was repealed in part and transferred in part in the enactment into positive law of Title 41, Public Contracts, by Pub.L. 111–350, Jan. 4, 2011, 124 Stat. 3677. Subsec. (b) was transferred to be set out as a note under 41 U.S.C.A. § 2303 and the section was repealed by Pub.L. 111–350, § 7(b), Jan. 4, 2011, 124 Stat. 3855.

See Revised Title 41, post

§ 413. Tests of innovative procurement methods and procedures

HISTORICAL AND STATUTORY NOTES

Test Program for Executive Agencies

Pub.L. 103–355, Title V, § 5061, Oct. 13, 1994, 108 Stat. 3352, as amended Pub.L. 104–106, Div. D, Title XLIII, § 4302(a), Feb. 10, 1996, 110 Stat. 658, as amended Pub.L. 105–85, Div. A, Title VIII, § 850(f)(1), Nov. 18, 1997, 111 Stat. 1849, which provided that the Administrator for Federal Procurement Policy may conduct a program of tests of alternative and innovative procurement procedures, was editorially eliminated from the Code as a result of the enactment into positive law of Title 41, Public Contracts, by Pub.L. 111–350, Jan. 4, 2011, 124 Stat. 3677.

§ 416. Procurement notice

HISTORICAL AND STATUTORY NOTES

Effective and Applicability Provisions

1984 Acts. Section 303(b) of Pub. L. 98–577, which provided that amendment by Pub.L. 98–577(a) to this section should take effect with respect to any solicitation issued after March 31, 1985, was editorially eliminated from the Code as a result of the enactment into positive law of Title 41, Public Contracts, by Pub.L. 111–350, Jan. 4, 2011, 124 Stat. 3677.

Applicability to Tennessee Valley Authority

Section 303(c) of Pub. L. 98–577, which provided that amendment by Pub.L. 98–577, § 303(a) to this section should apply to the Tennessee Valley Authority only with respect to procurements to be paid from appropriated funds, was formerly set out as a note under this section and was editorially transferred to be set out as a note under 41 U.S.C.A. § 1708.

§ 417. Record requirements

[See main volume for text of (a) to (c)]

(d) Transmission and data entry of information

The head of each executive agency shall ensure the accuracy of the information included in the record established and maintained by such agency under subsection (a) and shall transmit in a timely manner such information to the General Services Administration for entry into the Federal Procurement Data System referred to in section 405(d)(4) of this title, or any successor system.

(Pub.L. 93–400, § 19, as added Pub.L. 98–369, Title VII, § 2732(a), July 18, 1984, 98 Stat. 1197, and amended Pub.L. 103–355, Title IV, § 4403, Oct. 13, 1994, 108 Stat. 3349; Pub.L. 110–417, Div. A, Title VIII, § 874(b), Oct. 14, 2008, 122 Stat. 4558.)

HISTORICAL AND STATUTORY NOTES

Revision Notes and Legislative Reports

2008 Acts. Senate Report No. 110–335, see 2008 U.S. Code Cong. and Adm. News, p. 1829.

Statement by President, see 2008 U.S. Code Cong. and Adm. News, p. S30.

Amendments

2008 Amendments. Subsec. (d). Pub.L. 110–417, § 874(b), rewrote subsec. (d), which formerly read:

"**(d) Transmission and data system entry of information**

"The information included in the record established and maintained under subsection (a) of this section shall be transmitted to the General Services Administration and shall be entered in the Federal Procurement Data System referred to in section 405(d)(4) of this title."

LIBRARY REFERENCES

American Digest System

United States ⟊41.
Key Number System Topic No. 393.

§ 417b. Database for Federal agency contract and grant officers and suspension and debarment officials

(a) In general

Subject to the authority, direction, and control of the Director of the Office of Management and Budget, the Administrator of General Services shall establish, not later than one year after October 14, 2008, and maintain a database of information regarding the integrity and performance of certain persons awarded Federal agency

Text Repealed by Pub.L. 111–350, effective Jan. 4, 2011

contracts and grants for use by Federal agency officials having authority over contracts and grants.

(b) Persons covered

The database shall cover the following:

(1) Any person awarded a Federal agency contract or grant in excess of $500,000, if any information described in subsection (c) exists with respect to such person.

(2) Any person awarded such other category or categories of Federal agency contract as the Federal Acquisition Regulation may provide, if such information exists with respect to such person.

(c) Information included

With respect to a covered person the database shall include information (in the form of a brief description) for the most recent 5–year period regarding the following:

(1) Each civil or criminal proceeding, or any administrative proceeding, in connection with the award or performance of a contract or grant with the Federal Government with respect to the person during the period to the extent that such proceeding results in the following dispositions:

(A) In a criminal proceeding, a conviction.

(B) In a civil proceeding, a finding of fault and liability that results in the payment of a monetary fine, penalty, reimbursement, restitution, or damages of $5,000 or more.

(C) In an administrative proceeding, a finding of fault and liability that results in—

(i) the payment of a monetary fine or penalty of $5,000 or more; or

(ii) the payment of a reimbursement, restitution, or damages in excess of $100,000.

(D) To the maximum extent practicable and consistent with applicable laws and regulations, in a criminal, civil, or administrative proceeding, a disposition of the matter by consent or compromise with an acknowledgment of fault by the person if the proceeding could have led to any of the outcomes specified in subparagraph (A), (B), or (C).

(2) Each Federal contract and grant awarded to the person that was terminated in such period due to default.

(3) Each Federal suspension and debarment of the person in that period.

(4) Each Federal administrative agreement entered into by the person and the Federal Government in that period to resolve a suspension or debarment proceeding.

(5) Each final finding by a Federal official in that period that the person has been determined not to be a responsible source under subparagraph (C) or (D) of section 403(7) of this title.

(6) Such other information as shall be provided for purposes of this section in the Federal Acquisition Regulation.

(7) To the maximum extent practical, information similar to the information covered by paragraphs (1) through (4) in connection with the award or performance of a contract or grant with a State government.

(d) Requirements relating to information in database

(1) Direct input and update

The Administrator shall design and maintain the database in a manner that allows the appropriate Federal agency officials to directly input and update information in the database relating to actions such officials have taken with regard to contractors or grant recipients.

(2) Timeliness and accuracy

The Administrator shall develop policies to require—

See Revised Title 41, post

(A) the timely and accurate input of information into the database;

(B) the timely notification of any covered person when information relevant to the person is entered into the database; and

(C) opportunities for any covered person to submit comments pertaining to information about such person for inclusion in the database.

(e) Use of database

(1) Availability to Government officials

The Administrator shall ensure that the information in the database is available to appropriate acquisition officials of Federal agencies, to such other government officials as the Administrator determines appropriate, and, upon request, to the Chairman and Ranking Member of the committees of Congress having jurisdiction.

(2) Review and assessment of data

(A) In general

Before awarding a contract or grant in excess of the simplified acquisition threshold under section 403(11) of this title, the Federal agency official responsible for awarding the contract or grant shall review the database and shall consider all information in the database with regard to any offer or proposal, and, in the case of a contract, shall consider other past performance information available with respect to the offeror in making any responsibility determination or past performance evaluation for such offeror.

(B) Documentation in contract file

The contract file for each contract of a Federal agency in excess of the simplified acquisition threshold shall document the manner in which the material in the database was considered in any responsibility determination or past performance evaluation.

(f) Disclosure in applications

Not later than one year after October 14, 2008, the Federal Acquisition Regulation shall be amended to require that persons with Federal agency contracts and grants valued in total greater than $10,000,000 shall—

(1) submit to the Administrator, in a manner determined appropriate by the Administrator, the information subject to inclusion in the database as listed in subsection (c) current as of the date of submittal of such information under this subsection; and

(2) update such information on a semiannual basis.

(g) Rulemaking

The Administrator shall promulgate such regulations as may be necessary to carry out this section.

(Pub.L. 110–417, Div. A, Title VIII, § 872, Oct. 14, 2008, 122 Stat. 4555.)

HISTORICAL AND STATUTORY NOTES

Revision Notes and Legislative Reports

2008 Acts. Senate Report No. 110–335, see 2008 U.S. Code Cong. and Adm. News, p. 1829.

Statement by President, see 2008 U.S. Code Cong. and Adm. News, p. S30.

Codifications

Section was enacted as part of the Duncan Hunter National Defense Authorization Act for Fiscal Year 2009 and not as part of the Office of Federal Procurement Policy Act, which otherwise comprises this chapter.

§ 418a.   Rights in technical data

HISTORICAL AND STATUTORY NOTES

Effective and Applicability Provisions

1984 Acts. Section 301(c) of Pub.L. 98–577, as amended Pub.L. 99–145, Title IX, § 961(d)(3),

Nov. 8, 1985, 99 Stat. 704, which provided that amendment by Pub.L. 98–577, § 301(a), which

Text Repealed by Pub.L. 111–350, effective Jan. 4, 2011

enacted this section, should take effect on Oct. 30, 1984 and required regulations should be issued not later than Oct. 19, 1985, was editorially eliminated from the Code as a result of the enactment into positive law of Title 41, Public Contracts, by Pub.L. 111–350, Jan. 4, 2011, 124 Stat. 3677.

§ 418b. Publication of proposed regulations

HISTORICAL AND STATUTORY NOTES

Effective and Applicability Provisions

1984 Acts . Section 302(b) of Pub.L. 98–577, which provided that procedures required by this section should apply with respect to procurement policies, regulations, procedures, or forms that an agency issues in final form on or after Oct. 30, 1984, was editorially eliminated from the Code as a result of the enactment into positive law of Title 41, Public Contracts, by Pub.L. 111–350, Jan. 4, 2011, 124 Stat. 3677.

§ 419. Contracting functions performed by Federal personnel

HISTORICAL AND STATUTORY NOTES

Requirement for Guidance and Regulations

Section 6002(b) of Pub.L. 103–355, which directed Federal Acquisition Regulatory Council to review part 37 of title 48 of the Code of Federal Regulations as it relates to the use of advisory and assistance services, was formerly set out as a note under this section and was editorially transferred to be set out as a note under 41 U.S.C.A. § 1709.

§ 421. Federal Acquisition Regulatory Council

HISTORICAL AND STATUTORY NOTES

Justification and Approval of Sole-Source Contracts

Pub.L. 111–84, Div. A, Title VIII, § 811, Oct. 28, 2009, 123 Stat. 2405, which provided for justification and approval of sole source contracts, was editorially eliminated from the Code as a result of the enactment into positive law of Title 41, Public Contracts, by Pub.L. 111–350, Jan. 4, 2011, 124 Stat. 3677.

Status of the Director of Defense Procurement

Pub.L. 102–190, Div. A, Title VIII, § 809, Dec. 5, 1991, 105 Stat. 1423, as amended Pub.L. 103–160, Div. A, Title IX, § 904(f), Nov. 30, 1993, 107 Stat. 1729; Pub.L. 106–65, Div. A, Title IX, § 911(a)(1), Oct. 5, 1999, 113 Stat. 717, which provided that Director of Defense Procurement of the Department of Defense shall be considered to be an official at an organizational level of an Assistant Secretary of Defense within the Office of the Under Secretary of Defense for Acquisition, Technology, and Logistics for purposes of amendment made by Pub.L. 101–510, § 807 to subsec. (b)(2) of this section, was formerly set out as a note under this section and was editorially transferred to be set out as a note under 41 U.S.C.A. § 1302.

§ 422. Cost Accounting Standards Board

HISTORICAL AND STATUTORY NOTES

Effective and Applicability Provisions

1999 Acts. Pub.L. 106–65, Div. A, Title VIII, § 802(i), Oct. 5, 1999, 113 Stat. 702, which provided that amendments by Pub.L. 106–65, § 802(a), (B), should take effect 180 days after Oct. 5, 1999, and apply to contracts entered into after effective date and to determinations made on or after such effective date, was formerly set out as a note under this section and was editorially transferred to be set out as a note under 41 U.S.C.A. § 1502.

Inapplicability of Standards to Certain Contracts; Construction Regarding Certain Not-for-Profit Entities

Pub.L. 106–65, Div. A, Title VIII, § 802(g), (h), Oct. 5, 1999, 113 Stat. 702, providing that cost accounting standards issued under former 41 U.S.C.A. § 422(f) not apply during fiscal year 2009 with respect to certain contracts formerly set out as a note under this section, was editorially transferred to be set out as a note under 41 U.S.C.A. § 1502

Regulations; Implementation

Pub.L. 106–65, Div. A, Title VIII, § 802(c) to (e), Oct. 5, 1999, 113 Stat. 701, authorizing the revision of regulations on types of CAS coverage and the manner of their implementation, was editorially transferred to be set out as a note under 41 U.S.C.A. § 1502

Notes of Decisions

Cost reimbursement contracts 9	Recovery of asset surplus 8
Interpretation of provisions 7	Review 4
Jurisdiction of Board of contract appeals 6	Statutory interest rate 5

See Revised Title 41, post

4. Review

When interpreting provisions of the Cost Accounting Standards (CAS), the Court of Appeals' task is to ascertain the CAS Board's intended meaning when promulgating the CAS. Gates v. Raytheon Co., C.A.Fed.2009, 584 F.3d 1062, rehearing and rehearing en banc denied 2011 WL 692062. United States ☜ 70(18)

5. Statutory interest rate

Military contractor's violation of Cost Accounting Standard (CAS) by delayed payment of business segment closing adjustment to government for pension fund surplus, resulting in increased costs to government, warranted assessment of interest compounded daily, rather than simple interest, pursuant to statutory interest rate calculated for CAS violations. Gates v. Raytheon Co., C.A.Fed.2009, 584 F.3d 1062, rehearing and rehearing en banc denied 2011 WL 692062. United States ☜ 70(18)

6. Jurisdiction of Board of contract appeals

The scope of the contracting officer's decision regarding a government contract determines the extent of the jurisdiction of the Armed Services Board of Contract Appeals. Gates v. Raytheon Co., C.A.Fed.2009, 584 F.3d 1062, rehearing and rehearing en banc denied 2011 WL 692062. United States ☜ 73(15)

Armed Services Board of Contract Appeals is authorized to exercise jurisdiction over the proper methodology for computing interest under the Cost Accounting Standard (CAS) clause in government contracts. Gates v. Raytheon Co., C.A.Fed.2009, 584 F.3d 1062, rehearing and rehearing en banc denied 2011 WL 692062. United States ☜ 70(18)

Armed Services Board of Contract Appeals is authorized to exercise jurisdiction over the proper methodology for computing interest under the Cost Accounting Standard (CAS) clause in government contracts. Gates v. Raytheon Co., C.A.Fed.2009, 584 F.3d 1062, rehearing and rehearing en banc denied 2011 WL 692062. United States ☜ 70(18)

7. Interpretation of provisions

The intentions of the Cost Accounting Standard (CAS) Board in promulgating the CAS clause incorporated into government contracts are clearly influenced by the authorizing statute, and thus, Court of Appeals looks to that statute when interpreting the incorporated regulation. Gates v. Raytheon Co., C.A.Fed.2009, 584 F.3d 1062, rehearing and rehearing en banc denied 2011 WL 692062. United States ☜ 70(18)

When interpreting provisions of the Cost Accounting Standards (CAS), the Court of Appeals' task is to ascertain the CAS Board's intended meaning when promulgating the CAS. Gates v. Raytheon Co., C.A.Fed.2009, 584 F.3d 1062, rehearing and rehearing en banc denied 2011 WL 692062. United States ☜ 70(18)

8. Recovery of asset surplus

Under the Cost Accounting Standard (CAS), neither contractors nor the government are entitled to a windfall in connection with the application of the CAS; therefore, the government is not entitled to require that its share of the surplus pension assets following a segment closing be paid by the seller in cash when the government receives an equal or greater cost reduction from government contracts with the buyer attributable to the seller's pension contributions to the transferred segment's pension plan, because in such cases, the benefit the government receives from pension cost reductions attributable to the seller's transferred pension asset contribution makes the government whole. DirecTV Group, Inc. v. U.S.,. Fed.Cl. 2009, 89 Fed.Cl. 302. United States ☜ 70(18)

After the Cost Accounting Standard (CAS) segment closing calculation is performed, under CAS provision governing treatment of pension asset surplus or deficit attributable to government's pension cost payments under cost-reimbursement contracts after segment closing, the pension asset surplus attributable to government contributions is recoverable under the allowable cost and payment clause and the credits clause. DirecTV Group, Inc. v. U.S., Fed.Cl. 2009, 89 Fed.Cl. 302. United States ☜ 70(18)

9. Cost reimbursement contracts

Contractor's segment closing payment obligation to government for $273 million in surplus pension assets, under cost-reimbursement contracts, after selling two segments with overfunded pension plans to successor contractors with underfunded pension plans, was satisfied by benefit that government received in pension cost reductions from billions in excess pension assets transferred to successor, on grounds that government could not recover windfall, under Cost Accounting Standard (CAS) allowing segment seller to meet surplus pension payment obligation either through cash payment or cost reduction, even though contractor rather than successor had been reimbursed pension costs by government, and thus, contractor did not owe government any direct cash payment regardless of government's lack of consent or execution of novation agreement prior to transfer of surplus to successor. DirecTV Group, Inc. v. U.S., Fed.Cl.2009, 89 Fed.Cl. 302. United States ☜ 70(18)

Under the Cost Accounting Standard (CAS) provision, governing treatment of pension asset surplus or deficit attributable to government's pension cost payments under cost-reimbursement contracts after segment closing, the credits clause does not require double payment to the government where the evidence establishes that the seller's segment closing payment was satisfied by the cost reduction the government received under its contracts with the buyer due to the pension asset surplus transferred by the segment seller. DirecTV Group, Inc. v. U.S., Fed.Cl.2009, 89 Fed.Cl. 302. United States ☜ 70(18)

Text Repealed by Pub.L. 111–350, effective Jan. 4, 2011

§ 423. Restrictions on disclosing and obtaining contractor bid or proposal information or source selection information

HISTORICAL AND STATUTORY NOTES

Effective and Applicability Provisions

1988 Acts. Section 6(b) of Pub.L. 100–679, as amended Pub.L. 101–28, May 15, 1989, 103 Stat. 57, which provided that section was effective July 16, 1989, was editorially eliminated from the Code as a result of the enactment into positive law of Title 41, Public Contracts, by Pub.L. 111–350, Jan. 4, 2011, 124 Stat. 3677.

Clarification of Frequency of Certification by Employees and Contractors

Pub.L. 101–510, Div. A, Title VIII, § 815(b), Nov. 5, 1990, 104 Stat. 1597, provided that, not later than 30 days after Nov. 5, 1990, the regulations implementing subsec. (e)(1)(B) of this section shall be revised to ensure that a contractor is required to obtain from each officer, employee, agent, representative, and consultant of the contractor only one certification (as described in clauses (i) and (ii) of that section) during the person's employment or association with the contractor and that such certification shall be made at the earliest possible date after the person begins his or her employment or association with the contractor, was editorially eliminated from the Code as a result of the enactment into positive law of Title 41, Public Contracts, by Pub.L. 111–350, Jan. 4, 2011, 124 Stat. 3677.

Promulgation of Regulations

Section 814(e) of Pub.L. 101–189, which provided that, not later than 90 days after Nov. 29,

1989, regulations implementing amendments made by Pub.L. 101–189, § 814, to this section should be issued in accordance with former sections 405 and 421 of this title, after coordination with the Director of the Office of Government Ethics, was editorially eliminated from the Code as a result of the enactment into positive law of Title 41, Public Contracts, by Pub.L. 111–350, Jan. 4, 2011, 124 Stat. 3677.

Suspension of Effect of Subsec. (f)

Pub.L. 101–510, Div. A, Title VIII, § 815(a)(1), Nov. 5, 1990, 104 Stat. 1597, which provided that subsec. (f) of this section have no force or effect during the period beginning on Dec. 1, 1990, and ending on May 31, 1991, was editorially eliminated from the Code as a result of the enactment into positive law of Title 41, Public Contracts, by Pub.L. 111–350, Jan. 4, 2011, 124 Stat. 3677.

Suspension of Effect of Section

Pub.L. 101–194, Title V, § 507(1), Nov. 30, 1989, 103 Stat. 1759, provided that the provisions of this section shall have force or effect during the period beginning Dec. 1, 1989, and ending one year after such date, was editorially eliminated from the Code as a result of the enactment into positive law of Title 41, Public Contracts, by Pub.L. 111–350, Jan. 4, 2011, 124 Stat. 3677.

Notes of Decisions

Particular cases 4

---

2. Conflict of interest

Incumbent contractor who lost out in competition for successor aircraft maintenance contract failed to establish bias on part of source selection evaluation board (SSEB) based on e-mail of member of board critical of contractor's policy of farming out certain work to subcontractors, where contracting agency, in an abundance of caution, removed member who sent e-mail and member who received e-mail from the SSEB, and destroyed hard copy evaluations to ensure that the opinions of former members and their work product did not find their way to reconstructed SSEB. Avtel Services, Inc. v. U.S., Fed.Cl.2006, 70 Fed.Cl. 173, appeal dismissed 501 F.3d 1259, rehearing en banc denied. United States ⊸ 64.40(2)

3. Disclosure

Protester's integrated equipment list for medical mobile unit was not trade secret under Vermont law, and agency thus did not violate procurement integrity statutes and regulations by reproducing list in Federal Supply Schedule (FSS) request for quote (RFQ); although protester took some measures to maintain secrecy of list, protester forfeited any trade secret protection when it publicly displayed model unit at trade shows, from which educated observers could recreate list, particularly since list was composed of small number of items which were logical for inclusion in standard surgery room. Mobile Medical Intern. Corp. v. U.S., Fed.Cl. 2010, 95 Fed.Cl. 706. United States ⊸ 64.25

Names and e-mail addresses of the prospective bidder's employees, whose resumes were part of a previous procurement process, did not fall within the Procurement Integrity Act (PIA) definition of "contractor bid or proposal information" since names and e-mail addresses were not submitted to a Federal agency as part of or in connection with a bid or proposal to enter into a Federal agency procurement contract; furthermore, even if the resumes that were submitted could be viewed as falling within the PIA definition of "contractor bid or proposal information," record did not contain evidence that procuring agency's adviser had access to the resumes. Assessment and Training Solutions Consulting Corp. v. U.S., Fed.Cl.2010, 92 Fed.Cl. 722. United States ⊸ 64.40(2)

Government could not be held liable for violating the Procurement in Integrity Act (PIA) based on allegation that it disclosed confidential information regarding incumbent contractor's business operations to contract awardee after award of successor contract. Omega World

See Revised Title 41, post

Travel, Inc. v. U.S., Fed.Cl.2008, 82 Fed.Cl. 452. United States ⊱ 64.45(1)

Contracting officer's decision not to disqualify offeror under the Procurement Integrity Act for obtaining information concerning incumbent contractor's working conditions, pay, and other deployment details had a reasonable basis, in that such deployment information was in the public domain and incumbent contractor did not demonstrate competitive harm from release of the information. Avtel Services, Inc. v. U.S., Fed.Cl.2006, 70 Fed.Cl. 173, appeal dismissed 501 F.3d 1259, rehearing en banc denied. United States ⊱ 64.45(2)

4. Particular cases

Even if design layout of protester's mobile medical unit was trade secret, protester was not prejudiced by agency's dissemination of layout, and protester therefore lacked standing to bring bid protest claim alleging that agency violated procurement integrity statutes and regulations by releasing layout in Federal Supply Schedule (FSS) request for quote (RFQ) for procurement of mobile medical unit; successful bidder submitted final design layout that was dissimilar to protester's layout, and thus gained no obvious competitive advantage from seeing protester's layout, and final layout was moreover similar to layout which successful bidder previously submitted to agency prior to alleged disclosure of protester's layout, and although successful bidder modified final layout in ways that were similar to protester's layout, modifications were the result of agency regulations and workflow needs, not because of protester's layout. Mobile Medical Intern. Corp. v. U.S., Fed.Cl.2010, 95 Fed.Cl. 706. United States ⊱ 64.60(2)

Staff members within the contracting office did not commit a Procurement Integrity Act (PIA) violation in setting aside a request for proposals (RFP) for a competitive small business procurement. Assessment and Training Solutions Consulting Corp. v. U.S., Fed.Cl.2010, 92 Fed.Cl. 722. United States ⊱ 64.40(2)

§ 425. Contract clauses and certifications

HISTORICAL AND STATUTORY NOTES

Current Certification Requirements

Section 4301(b)(1) of Pub.L. 104–106, which provided for issuance for public comment of a proposal for removal of certification require-ments for contractors and offerors not specifically imposed by statute, was formerly set out as a note under this section and was editorially transferred to be set out as a note under 41 U.S.C.A. § 1304.

§ 427. Simplified acquisition procedures

HISTORICAL AND STATUTORY NOTES

Effective and Applicability Provisions

1966 Acts. Section 1074(b)(6) of Pub.L. 104–201, which provided in part that Pub.L. 104–106, § 4202(c)(1), is amended, effective Feb. 10, 1996, was editorially eliminated from the Code as a result of the enactment into positive law of Title 41, Public Contracts, by Pub.L. 111–350, Jan. 4, 2011, 124 Stat. 3677.

§ 428. Procedures applicable to purchases below micro-purchase threshold

HISTORICAL AND STATUTORY NOTES

Micro-purchase Guidelines

Pub.L. 111–240, Title I, § 1332, Sept. 27, 2010, 124 Stat. 2541, which provided that the Director of the Office of Management and Budget should issue guidelines regarding the analysis of purchase card expenditures to identify opportunities for achieving and accurately measuring fair participation of small business concerns in purchases in an amount not in excess of the micro-purchase threshold, was formerly set out as a note under this section and was editorially transferred to be set out as a note under 41 U.S.C.A. § 1902.

§ 428a. Special emergency procurement authority

HISTORICAL AND STATUTORY NOTES

Authority to Enter into Certain Transactions for Defense Against or Recovery from Terrorism or Nuclear, Biological, Chemical, or Radiological Attack

Pub.L. 108–136, Div. A, Title XIV, § 1441, Nov. 24, 2003, 117 Stat. 1673, which provided that head of an executive agency who engages in basic research, applied research, advanced research, and development projects necessary to the responsibilities of such official's executive agency in the field of research and development, and have the potential to facilitate defense against or recovery from terrorism or nuclear, biological, chemical, or radiological attack, may carry out prototype projects, terminating on Sept. 30, 2008, was repealed in the enactment into positive law of Title 41, Public Contracts, by Pub.L. 111–350, § 7(b), Jan. 4, 2011, 124 Stat. 3855.

Text Repealed by Pub.L. 111–350, effective Jan. 4, 2011

§ 430. List of laws inapplicable to procurements of commercial items in Federal Acquisition Regulation

HISTORICAL AND STATUTORY NOTES

Effective and Applicability Provisions

1994 Acts. Section 8003(b) of Pub.L. 103–355, which provided that no petition may be filed under subsec. (d) of this section until after the date occurring 6 months after Oct. 13, 1994, was editorially eliminated from the Code as a result of the enactment into positive law of Title 41, Public Contracts, by Pub.L. 111–350, Jan. 4, 2011, 124 Stat. 3677.

§ 431a. Inflation adjustment of acquisition-related dollar thresholds

HISTORICAL AND STATUTORY NOTES

Relationship to Other Inflation Adjustment Authorities

Pub.L. 108–375, Div. A, Title VIII, § 807(c), Oct. 28, 2004. 118 Stat. 2011, which provided that this section superseded the applicability of any other provision of law that provides for the adjustment of a dollar threshold that was adjustable under this section, was repealed in the enactment into positive law of Title 41, Public Contracts, by Pub.L. 111–350, § 7(b), Jan. 4, 2011, 124 Stat. 3855.

§ 433 Acquisition workforce

[See main volume for text of (a) to (g)]

(h) Education and training

[See main volume for text of (1) and (2)]

(3) Acquisition workforce training fund

[See main volume for text of (A) to (G)]

(H) Repealed. Pub.L. 110–181, Div. A, Title VIII, § 854, Jan. 28, 2008, 122 Stat. 251

[See main volume for text of (i)]

(Pub.L. 93–400, § 37, as added Pub.L. 104–106, Div. D, Title XLIII, § 4307(a)(1), Feb. 10, 1996, 110 Stat. 666, and amended Pub.L. 108–136, Div. A, Title XIV, § 1412(b), Nov. 24, 2003, 117 Stat. 1664; Pub.L. 109–163, Div. A, Title VIII, § 821(a), (b)(1), Jan. 6, 2006, 119 Stat. 3386; Pub.L. 109–313, § 4, Oct. 6, 2006, 120 Stat. 1737; Pub.L. 110–181, Div. A, Title VIII, § 854, Jan. 28, 2008, 120 Stat. 251.)

HISTORICAL AND STATUTORY NOTES

Revision Notes and Legislative Reports

2008 Acts. Statement by President, see 2008 U.S. Code Cong. and Adm. News, p. S3.

Amendments

2008 Amendments. Subsec. (h)(3)(H). Pub.L. 110–181, § 854, struck out subpar. (H).

Effective and Applicability Provisions

2006 Acts. Pub.L. 109–163, Div. A, Title VIII, § 821(d), Jan. 6, 2006, 119 Stat. 3386, provided that amendments made by Pub.L. 109–163, § 821, which amended this section and repealed provisions set out as a note under this section, should apply with respect to fees collected under contracts described in subsec. (h)(3)(B) of this section after Jan. 6, 2006, was editorially eliminated from the Code as a result of the enactment into positive law of Title 41, Public Contracts, by Pub.L. 111–350, Jan. 4, 2011, 124 Stat. 3677.

Training for Contracting and Enforcement Personnel

Pub.L. 111–240, Title I, § 1343(a), Sept. 27, 2010, 124 Stat. 2545, which provided that the Federal Acquisition Institute should develop courses for acquisition personnel concerning proper classification of business concerns and small business size and status for purposes of Federal contracts, subcontracts, grants, cooperative agreements, and cooperative research and development agreements not later than one year after Sept. 27, 2010, was formerly set out as a note under this section and was editorially transferred to be set out as a note under 41 U.S.C.A. § 1703.

Defense Acquisition University Funding

Pub.L. 109–163, Div. A, Title VIII, § 821(c), Jan. 6, 2006, 119 Stat. 3386, which provided that amounts transferred under former 41 U.S.C.A. § 433(h)(3)(D) as amended by Pub.L. 109–163, Div. A, Title VIII, § 821(a), for use by the Defense Acquisition University shall be in addition to other amounts authorized for the University, was formerly set out as a note under this section and was editorially transferred to be set out as a note under 41 U.S.C.A. § 1703.

See Revised Title 41, post

Acquisition Workforce Training Fund

Pub.L. 108–136, Div. A, Title XIV, § 1412(a), Nov. 24, 2003, 117 Stat. 1664, which provided that purpose of Pub.L. 108–136, § 1412 was to ensure that Federal acquisition workforce adapts to fundamental changes in nature of Federal Government acquisition and acquires new skills and perspectives to enable it to contribute effectively in the changing environment of the 21st century, was repealed in the enactment into positive law of Title 41, Public Contracts, by Pub.L. 111–350, § 7(b), Jan. 4, 2011, 124 Stat. 3855.

Acquisition Workforce Recruitment Program

Pub.L. 108–136, Div. A, Title XVI, § 1413, Nov. 24, 2003, 117 Stat. 1665, as amended Pub.L. 110–181, Div. A, Title VIII, § 853, Title X, § 1063(g)(2), Jan. 28, 2008, 122 Stat. 250, 323, which provided a program to recruit and appoint highly qualified persons to certain Federal ac-

quisition positions, was repealed in the enactment into positive law of Title 41, Public Contracts, by Pub.L. 111–350, § 7(b), Jan. 4, 2011, 124 Stat. 3855.

Architectural and Engineering Acquisition Workforce

Pub.L. 108–136, Div. A, Title XIV, § 1414, Nov. 24, 2003, 117 Stat. 1666, which provided that the Administrator for Federal Procurement Policy, in consultation with the Secretary of Defense, the Administrator of General Services, and the Director of the Office of Personnel Management, shall develop and implement a plan to ensure that the Federal Government maintains the necessary capability with respect to the acquisition of architectural and engineering services, was repealed in the enactment into positive law of Title 41, Public Contracts, by Pub.L. 111–350, § 7(b), Jan. 4, 2011, 124 Stat. 3855.

LIBRARY REFERENCES

American Digest System
United States ⬥41.
Key Number System Topic No. 393.

§ 433a. Federal acquisition workforce improvements

(a) Associate Administrator for Acquisition Workforce Programs

The Administrator for Federal Procurement Policy shall designate a member of the Senior Executive Service as the Associate Administrator for Acquisition Workforce Programs. The Associate Administrator for Acquisition Workforce Programs shall be located in the Federal Acquisition Institute (or its successor). The Associate Administrator shall be responsible for—

(1) supervising the acquisition workforce training fund established under section 433(h)(3) of this title;

(2) developing, in coordination with Chief Acquisition Officers and Chief Human Capital Officers, a strategic human capital plan for the acquisition workforce of the Federal Government;

(3) reviewing and providing input to individual agency acquisition workforce succession plans;

(4) recommending to the Administrator and other senior government officials appropriate programs, policies, and practices to increase the quantity and quality of the Federal acquisition workforce; and

(5) carrying out such other functions as the Administrator may assign.

(b) Acquisition and contracting training programs within executive agencies

(1) Requirement

The head of each executive agency, after consultation with the Associate Administrator for Acquisition Workforce Programs, shall establish and operate acquisition and contracting training programs. Such programs shall—

(A) have curricula covering a broad range of acquisition and contracting disciplines corresponding to the specific acquisition and contracting needs of the agency involved;

(B) be developed and applied according to rigorous standards; and

(C) be designed to maximize efficiency, through the use of self-paced courses, online courses, on-the-job training, and the use of remote instructors, wherever such features can be applied without reducing the effectiveness of the training or negatively affecting academic standards.

Text Repealed by Pub.L. 111–350, effective Jan. 4, 2011

(2) Chief Acquisition Officer authorities and responsibilities

Subject to the authority, direction, and control of the head of an executive agency, the Chief Acquisition Officer for such agency shall carry out all powers, functions, and duties of the head of the agency with respect to implementation of this subsection. The Chief Acquisition Officer shall ensure that the policies established by the head of the agency in accordance with this subsection are implemented throughout the agency.

(c) Government-wide policies and evaluation

The Administrator for Federal Procurement Policy shall issue policies to promote the development of performance standards for training and uniform implementation of this section by executive agencies, with due regard for differences in program requirements among agencies that may be appropriate and warranted in view of the agency mission. The Administrator shall evaluate the implementation of the provisions of subsection (b) of this section by executive agencies.

(d) Acquisition and contracting training reporting

The Administrator for Federal Procurement Policy shall ensure that the heads of executive agencies collect and maintain standardized information on the acquisition and contracting workforce related to the implementation of subsection (b) of this section.

(e) Acquisition workforce human capital succession plan

(1) In general

Not later than 1 year after January 28, 2008, each Chief Acquisition Officer for an executive agency shall develop, in consultation with the Chief Human Capital Officer for the agency and the Associate Administrator for Acquisition Workforce Programs, a succession plan consistent with the agency's strategic human capital plan for the recruitment, development, and retention of the agency's acquisition workforce, with a particular focus on warranted contracting officers and program managers of the agency.

(2) Content of plan

The acquisition workforce succession plan shall address—

(A) recruitment goals for personnel from procurement intern programs;

(B) the agency's acquisition workforce training needs;

(C) actions to retain high performing acquisition professionals who possess critical relevant skills;

(D) recruitment goals for personnel from the Federal Career Intern Program; and

(E) recruitment goals for personnel from the Presidential Management Fellows Program.

(f) Training in the acquisition of architect and engineering services

The Administrator for Federal Procurement Policy shall ensure that a sufficient number of Federal employees are trained in the acquisition of architect and engineering services.

(g) Utilization of recruitment and retention authorities

The Administrator for Federal Procurement Policy, in coordination with the Director of the Office of Personnel Management, shall encourage executive agencies to utilize existing authorities, including direct hire authority and tuition assistance programs, to recruit and retain acquisition personnel and consider recruiting acquisition personnel who may be retiring from the private sector, consistent with existing laws and regulations.

(h) Definitions

In this section:

See Revised Title 41, post

(1) Executive agency

The term "executive agency" has the meaning provided in section 403(1) of this title.

(2) Chief Acquisition Officer

The term "Chief Acquisition Officer" means a Chief Acquisition Officer for an executive agency appointed pursuant to section 414 of this title.

(Pub.L. 110–181, Div. A, Title VIII, § 855, Jan. 28, 2008, 122 Stat. 251.)

HISTORICAL AND STATUTORY NOTES

Revision Notes and Legislative Reports

2008 Acts. Statement by President, see 2008 U.S. Code Cong. and Adm. News, p. S3.

Codifications

Section was enacted as part of the National Defense Authorization Act for Fiscal Year 2008, and not as part of the Office of Federal Procurement Policy Act, which otherwise comprises this chapter.

Acquisition Workforce Development Strategic Plan

Pub.L. 110–417, Div. A, Title VIII, § 869, Oct. 14, 2008, 122 Stat. 4553, which established the Acquisition Workforce Development Strategic Plan for Federal agencies other than the Department of Defense to develop a specific and actionable 5–year plan to increase the size of the acquisition workforce, and to operate a government-wide acquisition intern program, for such Federal agencies, was repealed in the enactment into positive law of Title 41, Public Contracts, by Pub.L. 111–350, § 7(b), Jan. 4, 2011, 124 Stat. 3855.

§ 435. Levels of compensation of certain contractor personnel not allowable as costs under certain contracts

HISTORICAL AND STATUTORY NOTES

Effective Date of 1997 Amendments

Pub.L. 105–85, §§ 808(e), which provided an effective date and applicability provisions, was formerly set out as a note under this section and was editorially transferred to be set out as a note under 10 U.S.C.A. § 2324.

Definition of Certain Terms for Purposes of Section 808 of Pub.L. 105–85

Section 808(g) of Pub.L. 105–85, as amended Pub.L. 105–261, Div. A, Title VIII, § 804(c)(2), Oct. 17, 1998, 112 Stat. 2083, which defined " covered contract", " compensation", and "senior executives" for purposes of section 808 of Pub.L. 105–85, was formerly set out as a note under this section and was editorially transferred to be set out as a note under 41 U.S.C.A. § 1127.

Exclusive Applicability of Provisions Limiting Allowability of Compensation for Certain Contractor Personnel

Section 808(f) of Pub.L. 105–85, which provided that notwithstanding any other provision of law, no other limitation in law on the allowability of costs of compensation of senior executives under covered contracts shall apply to such costs of compensation incurred after Jan. 1, 1998, was formerly set out as a note under this section and was editorially transferred to be set out as a note under 41 U.S.C.A. § 1127.

Promulgation of Regulations

Section 808(d) of Pub.L. 105–85, which directed that regulations implementing amendments made by Pub.L. 105–85, § 808, should be published in the Federal Register no later than 90 days after Nov. 18, 1997, was editorially eliminated from the Code as a result of the enactment into positive law of Title 41, Public Contracts, by Pub.L. 111–350, Jan. 4, 2011, 124 Stat. 3677.

§ 438. Civilian Board of Contract Appeals

HISTORICAL AND STATUTORY NOTES

Change of Name

Except as otherwise provided, any reference to an agency board of contract appeals shall be treated as a reference to the Civilian Board of Contract Appeals, see Div. A, Pub.L. 109–163, Div. A, Title VIII, § 847(e), Jan. 6, 2006, 119 Stat. 3394, set out as a note under 41 U.S.C.A. § 607.

Transfer of Functions

For provisions transferring personnel employed in connection with, and the assets, liabilities, contracts, property, records, and unexpended balance of appropriations, authorizations, allocations, and other funds employed, held, used, arising from, available to, or to be made available in connection with functions

Text Repealed by Pub.L. 111–350, effective Jan. 4, 2011

vested in the agency boards of contract appeals, to the Civilian Board of Contract Appeals, except as otherwise provided, see

Pub.L. 109–163, Div. A, Title VIII, § 847(b), Jan. 6, 2006, 119 Stat. 3392, set out as a note under 41 U.S.C.A. § 607.

§ 439. Public–private competition required before conversion to contractor performance

(a) Public-private competition

(1) A function of an executive agency performed by 10 or more agency civilian employees may not be converted, in whole or in part, to performance by a contractor unless the conversion is based on the results of a public-private competition that—

(A) formally compares the cost of performance of the function by agency civilian employees with the cost of performance by a contractor;

(B) creates an agency tender, including a most efficient organization plan, in accordance with Office of Management and Budget Circular A–76, as implemented on May 29, 2003, or any successor circular;

(C) includes the issuance of a solicitation;

(D) determines whether the submitted offers meet the needs of the executive agency with respect to factors other than cost, including quality, reliability, and timeliness;

(E) examines the cost of performance of the function by agency civilian employees and the cost of performance of the function by one or more contractors to demonstrate whether converting to performance by a contractor will result in savings to the Government over the life of the contract, including—

(i) the estimated cost to the Government (based on offers received) for performance of the function by a contractor;

(ii) the estimated cost to the Government for performance of the function by agency civilian employees; and

(iii) an estimate of all other costs and expenditures that the Government would incur because of the award of such a contract;

(F) requires continued performance of the function by agency civilian employees unless the difference in the cost of performance of the function by a contractor compared to the cost of performance of the function by agency civilian employees would, over all performance periods required by the solicitation, be equal to or exceed the lesser of—

(i) 10 percent of the personnel-related costs for performance of that function in the agency tender; or

(ii) $10,000,000; and

(G) examines the effect of performance of the function by a contractor on the agency mission associated with the performance of the function.

(2) A function that is performed by the executive agency and is reengineered, reorganized, modernized, upgraded, expanded, or changed to become more efficient, but still essentially provides the same service, shall not be considered a new requirement.

(3) In no case may a function being performed by executive agency personnel be—

(A) modified, reorganized, divided, or in any way changed for the purpose of exempting the conversion of the function from the requirements of this section; or

(B) converted to performance by a contractor to circumvent a civilian personnel ceiling.

(b) Requirement to consult employees

(1) Each civilian employee of an executive agency responsible for determining under Office of Management and Budget Circular A–76 whether to convert to contractor performance any function of the executive agency—

(A) shall, at least monthly during the development and preparation of the performance work statement and the management efficiency study used in making that determination, consult with civilian employees who will be affected by that

See Revised Title 41, post

43

determination and consider the views of such employees on the development and preparation of that statement and that study; and

(B) may consult with such employees on other matters relating to that determination.

(2)(A) In the case of employees represented by a labor organization accorded exclusive recognition under section 7111 of Title 5, consultation with representatives of that labor organization shall satisfy the consultation requirement in paragraph (1).

(B) In the case of employees other than employees referred to in subparagraph (A), consultation with appropriate representatives of those employees shall satisfy the consultation requirement in paragraph (1).

(C) The head of each executive agency shall prescribe regulations to carry out this subsection. The regulations shall include provisions for the selection or designation of appropriate representatives of employees referred to in paragraph (2)(B) for purposes of consultation required by paragraph (1).

(c) Congressional notification

(1) Before commencing a public-private competition under subsection (a) of this section, the head of an executive agency shall submit to Congress a report containing the following:

(A) The function for which such public-private competition is to be conducted.

(B) The location at which the function is performed by agency civilian employees.

(C) The number of agency civilian employee positions potentially affected.

(D) The anticipated length and cost of the public-private competition, and a specific identification of the budgetary line item from which funds will be used to cover the cost of the public-private competition.

(E) A certification that a proposed performance of the function by a contractor is not a result of a decision by an official of an executive agency to impose predetermined constraints or limitations on such employees in terms of man years, end strengths, full-time equivalent positions, or maximum number of employees.

(2) The report required under paragraph (1) shall include an examination of the potential economic effect of performance of the function by a contractor on—

(A) agency civilian employees who would be affected by such a conversion in performance; and

(B) the local community and the Government, if more than 50 agency civilian employees perform the function.

(3)(A) A representative individual or entity at a facility where a public-private competition is conducted may submit to the head of the executive agency an objection to the public-private competition on the grounds that the report required by paragraph (1) has not been submitted or that the certification required by paragraph (1)(E) is not included in the report submitted as a condition for the public-private competition. The objection shall be in writing and shall be submitted within 90 days after the following date:

(i) In the case of a failure to submit the report when required, the date on which the representative individual or an official of the representative entity authorized to pose the objection first knew or should have known of that failure.

(ii) In the case of a failure to include the certification in a submitted report, the date on which the report was submitted to Congress.

(B) If the head of the executive agency determines that the report required by paragraph (1) was not submitted or that the required certification was not included in the submitted report, the function for which the public-private competition was conducted for which the objection was submitted may not be the subject of a solicitation of offers for, or award of, a contract until, respectively, the report is submitted or a report containing the certification in full compliance with the certification requirement is submitted.

Text Repealed by Pub.L. 111–350, effective Jan. 4, 2011

(d) Exemption for the purchase of products and services of the blind and other severely handicapped persons

This section shall not apply to a commercial or industrial type function of an executive agency that—

    (1) is included on the procurement list established pursuant to section 2 of the Javits-Wagner-O'Day Act (41 U.S.C. 47); or

    (2) is planned to be changed to performance by a qualified nonprofit agency for the blind or by a qualified nonprofit agency for other severely handicapped persons in accordance with that Act.

(e) Inapplicability during war or emergency

The provisions of this section shall not apply during war or during a period of national emergency declared by the President or Congress.

(Pub.L. 93–400, § 43, as added Pub.L. 110–181, Div. A, Title III, § 327(a), Jan. 28, 2008, 122 Stat. 63.)

HISTORICAL AND STATUTORY NOTES

Revision Notes and Legislative Reports

  2008 Acts. Statement by President, see 2008 U.S. Code Cong. and Adm. News, p. S3.

References in Text

  The Javits-Wagner-O'Day Act, and that Act, referred to in subsec. (d)(1), (2), respectively, is

Act June 25, 1938, c. 697, 52 Stat. 1196, as amended, which is classified to 41 U.S.C.A. §§ 46 to 48c. Section 2 of the Act is classified to 41 U.S.C.A. § 47. For complete classification, see Short Title note set out under 41 U.S.C.A. § 46 and Tables.

§ 440. Contingency Contracting Corps

(a) Establishment

The Administrator of General Services, pursuant to policies established by the Office of Management and Budget, and in consultation with the Secretary of Defense and the Secretary of Homeland Security, shall establish a Governmentwide Contingency Contracting Corps (in this section referred to as the "Corps"). The members of the Corps shall be available for deployment in responding to an emergency or major disaster, or a contingency operation, both within or outside the continental United States.

(b) Applicability

The authorities provided in this section apply with respect to any procurement of property or services by or for an executive agency that, as determined by the head of such executive agency, are to be used—

    (1) in support of a contingency operation as defined in section 101(a)(13) of Title 10; or

    (2) to respond to an emergency or major disaster as defined in section 5122 of Title 42.

(c) Membership

Membership in the Corps shall be voluntary and open to all Federal employees and members of the Armed Forces who are members of the Federal acquisition workforce.

(d) Education and training

The Administrator may, in consultation with the Director of the Federal Acquisition Institute and the Chief Acquisition Officers Council, establish educational and training requirements for members of the Corps. Education and training carried out pursuant to such requirements shall be paid for from funds available in the acquisition workforce training fund established pursuant to section 433(h)(3) of this title.

(e) Salary

The salary for a member of the Corps shall be paid—

    (1) in the case of a member of the Armed Forces, out of funds available to the Armed Force concerned; and

See Revised Title 41, post

(2) in the case of a Federal employee, out of funds available to the employing agency.

(f) Authority to deploy the Corps

(1) The Director of the Office of Management and Budget shall have the authority, upon request by an executive agency, to determine when members of the Corps shall be deployed, with the concurrence of the head of the agency or agencies employing the members to be deployed.

(2) Nothing in this section shall preclude the Secretary of Defense or the Secretary's designee from deploying members of the Armed Forces or civilian personnel of the Department of Defense in support of a contingency operation as defined in section 101(a)(13) of Title 10.

(g) Annual report

(1) In general

The Administrator of General Services shall provide to the Committee on Homeland Security and Governmental Affairs and the Committee on Armed Services of the Senate and the Committee on Oversight and Government Reform and the Committee on Armed Services of the House of Representatives an annual report on the status of the Contingency Contracting Corps as of September 30 of each fiscal year.

(2) Content

At a minimum, each report under paragraph (1) shall include the number of members of the Contingency Contracting Corps, the total cost of operating the program, the number of deployments of members of the program, and the performance of members of the program in deployment.

(Pub.L. 93–400, § 44, as added Pub.L. 110–417, Div. A, Title VIII, § 870(a), Oct. 14, 2008, 122 Stat. 4554.)

HISTORICAL AND STATUTORY NOTES

Revision Notes and Legislative Reports

2008 **Acts**. Senate Report No. 110–335, see 2008 U.S. Code Cong. and Adm. News, p. 1829.

Statement by President, see 2008 U.S. Code Cong. and Adm. News, p. S30.

CHAPTER 9—CONTRACT DISPUTES

Sec.
607.   Agency boards of contract appeals.

LAW REVIEW AND JOURNAL COMMENTARIES

Representing the federal government contractor. James S. Ganther, 70 Fla.B.J. 58 (April 1996).

§ 601. Definitions

HISTORICAL AND STATUTORY NOTES

Effective and Applicability Provisions

1978 **Acts**. Section 16 of Pub.L. 95–563, which provided that Pub.L. 95–563 should apply to contracts entered into one hundred twenty days after Nov. 1, 1978, with exception for pending claims, was repealed in the enactment into positive law of Title 41, Public Contracts, by Pub.L. 111–350, § 7(b), Jan. 4, 2011, 124 Stat. 3855.

Short Title

1978 **Amendments**. Section 1 of Pub.L. 95–563, which provided a Short Title for the Contract Disputes Act of 1978, was repealed in the enactment into positive law of Title 41, Public Contracts, by Pub.L. 111–350, § 7(b), Jan. 4, 2011, 124 Stat. 3855.

Text Repealed by Pub.L. 111–350, effective Jan. 4, 2011

Notes of Decisions

2. Construction with other laws

Under ordinary government prime contracts, subcontractors do not have standing to sue the government under the Tucker Act to enforce a claim for equitable adjustment under the Contract Disputes Act; yet the law allows a prime contractor to sue the government on behalf of its subcontractor, by means of a pass-through suit, for costs incurred by the subcontractor for which the prime contractor is liable. Haddon Housing Associates, LLC v. U.S., Fed.Cl.2010, 92 Fed.Cl. 8. United States ⇔ 74.2

After the passage of the CDA, the Wunderlich Act, authorizing judicial review of agency's fact-finding, only applies to contracts of non-executive agencies or to contracts entered into prior to the effective date of the CDA. Todd Const., L.P. v. U.S., Fed.Cl.2009, 88 Fed.Cl. 235, subsequent determination 94 Fed.Cl. 100. United States ⇔ 73(9)

Court of Federal Claims lacked jurisdiction over bid protestor's claim, construed as objection to contracting agency's termination or breach of contract before its expiration, as section of Tucker Act affording Court jurisdiction over bid protests provides no jurisdiction over claims of wrongful termination or breach which must be brought pursuant to the Contract Disputes Act (CDA). The Ravens Group, Inc. v. U.S., Fed.Cl.2007, 78 Fed.Cl. 390. United States ⇔ 64.60(1)

7. —— Subcontractor

Subcontractor that was allegedly a third-party beneficiary of a contract between the government and the prime contractor was not a "party to a Government contract" under the Contract Disputes Act (CDA), and therefore, under the CDA, subcontractor was not permitted to appeal contracting officer's decision declining to issue a decision on subcontractor's claim for payment based on the government's alleged violation of

its contract with the prime contractor. Winter v. FloorPro, Inc., C.A.Fed.2009, 570 F.3d 1367. United States ⇔ 73(15)

Under the strict interpretation required of waivers of sovereign immunity, the CDA does not permit appeals by anyone who is not a "party to a Government contract other than the Government"; this includes subcontractors that are third-party beneficiaries of the prime contract. Winter v. FloorPro, Inc., C.A.Fed.2009, 570 F.3d 1367. United States ⇔ 73(15)

8. —— Surety, contractor

Sureties that completed performance of contract upon construction company's bankruptcy in construction of federal project were "contractors" for purposes of Contract Disputes Act (CDA), and thus Court of Federal Claims had jurisdiction over sureties' action against United States to recover for losses allegedly caused by deficient design specifications and project mismanagement, even though extant stated liabilities to which company was liable at date of assignment were not assumed, where bankruptcy court that approved assignment confirmed that government retained all defenses. Fireman's Fund Ins. Co. v. U.S., Fed.Cl.2010, 92 Fed.Cl. 598. United States ⇔ 74.1

9. Third party beneficiaries

Subcontractor, as third-party beneficiary of government contract, was not a "contractor" within meaning of the Contract Disputes Act (CDA), as it was not a party to the contract, and thus could not assert a claim for prejudgment interest under the CDA. JGB Enterprises, Inc. v. U.S., Fed.Cl.2004, 63 Fed.Cl. 319, motion for relief from judgment denied 71 Fed.Cl. 468, appeal dismissed 192 Fed.Appx. 962, 2006 WL 2382737, affirmed 497 F.3d 1259. United States ⇔ 73(9)

§ 602. Applicability of law

Notes of Decisions

2. Implied contracts

Any implied contract arising when informant responded to offer of reward by United States Postal Inspection Service (USPIS) for information about assailant who attacked postal worker was one for "procurement of services," and thus within exclusive jurisdiction of Court of Federal Claims under Contract Disputes Act over implied contracts with executive agencies. Goodin v. U.S. Postal Inspection Service, D.Minn.2005, 393 F.Supp.2d 869, affirmed 444 F.3d 998, certiorari denied 127 S.Ct. 930, 549 U.S. 1111, 166 L.Ed.2d 702, rehearing denied 127 S.Ct. 2932, 551 U.S. 1111, 168 L.Ed.2d 258. Federal Courts ⇔ 1141

5. Procurement contracts generally

Army's purchase orders for prototypes of hydration systems constituted "procurement contracts," and thus Armed Services Board of Contract Appeals had subject matter jurisdiction under Contract Disputes Act (CDA) over manufacturer's claim that United States improperly disclosed proprietary data in purchase orders to non-governmental third parties to extent that orders incorporated confidentiality provisions of Defense Acquisition Regulation (DAR) legend on manufacturer's unsolicited proposals, even though Army had not awarded manufacturer final contract, and manufacturer did not sign purchase orders, where purchase orders specified parties involved, delivery instructions, price, payment terms, and transportation instructions. Wesleyan Co., Inc. v. Harvey, C.A.Fed.2006, 454 F.3d 1375, rehearing denied, on remand 2007 WL 3265019. United States ⇔ 73(15)

See Revised Title 41, post

Plaintiff's submission of suggestion proposal to Social Security Administration (SSA) that Supplemental Security Income (SSI) benefits should be delivered to recipients by debit card transaction, rather than by paper check, did not create procurement contract subject to CDA, thus precluding exercise of jurisdiction over CDA claim that government breached contract. Grayton v. U.S., Fed.Cl.2010, 92 Fed.Cl. 327. United States ☞ 73(9)

Contract Disputes Act (CDA) grants the Court of Federal Claims jurisdiction over contracts for the procurement of services and not the provision of services, and intangible forms of consideration, such as a guarantee of payment, do not constitute procurements of services under the CDA. Laudes Corp. v. U.S., Fed.Cl.2009, 86 Fed.Cl. 152. United States ☞ 73(9)

Agreement between mushroom grower and the National Resource Conservation Service (NRCS) in Department of Agriculture, pursuant to which grower would construct and operate spent mushroom substrate (SMS) transfer facility according to NRCS specifications in return for cost-share payments, was a "cooperative agreement" rather than a "procurement contract," and thus it was not subject to the Contract Disputes Act (CDA). Rick's Mushroom Service, Inc. v. U.S., Fed.Cl.2007, 76 Fed.Cl. 250, affirmed 521 F.3d 1338. United States ☞ 73(9)

6. Real property contracts—Generally

Property owners' barter contract with government, in which owners agreed to relocate easement on their property for government's benefit in apprehending illegal aliens crossing border from Mexico in exchange for government's agreement to pave and improve two access roads on relocated easement, was not contract for "procurement of property," within meaning of CDA, requiring submission of certified claim to contracting officer prior to asserting contract claims against government, since government had not acquired any property or services by entering contract, but merely changed property rights to prior easement procured many years earlier, so contract was more akin to collaborative effort to make best use of property rather than buyer-seller agreement. International Indus. Park, Inc. v. U.S., Fed.Cl.2010, 95 Fed.Cl. 63. United States ☞ 73(9)

6a. —— Easements, real property contracts

Property owners' barter contract with government, in which owners agreed to relocate easement on their property for government's benefit in apprehending illegal aliens crossing border from Mexico, in exchange for government's agreement to pave and improve two access roads on relocated easement, was contract for relocation of "real property in being," within meaning of exemption from CDA, since contract concerned relocation of existing easement, not creation of new easement. International Indus. Park, Inc. v. U.S., Fed.Cl.2010, 95 Fed.Cl. 63. United States ☞ 73(9)

7. —— Leases, real property contracts

Agreement for lease of office space to United States Postal Service (USPS) fell within Contract Dispute Act's (CDA) scope, and thus district court did not have jurisdiction over lessors' eviction and collection of monies action against USPS. Grillasca-Palou v. U.S. Postal Service, D.Puerto Rico 2008, 573 F.Supp.2d 493. Federal Courts ☞ 1141

8. —— Financing and subsidy, real property contracts

Contract Disputes Act (CDA) did not apply to alleged contract whereby Mexican exchange houses which purchased United States Postal Service (USPS) money orders from payees residing in Mexico until a surge in mail order fraud would resume cashing money orders in exchange for government's promise to repay money reclaimed because of the fraud; although the USPS received an indirect benefit from role of exchange houses in the postal money order system, that role directly benefited the payees, and thus alleged contract was not a procurement contract for the "direct benefit or use" of the government. Arbitraje Casa de Cambio, S.A. de CV. v. U.S., Fed.Cl.2007, 79 Fed.Cl. 235. United States ☞ 73(9)

10. Services procured—Generally

Alleged oral contract pursuant to which subcontractor provided feedback to the government regarding prime contractor's effectiveness in performing contract in return for a promise of confidentiality and some incidental goodwill was not a "procurement of services" within purview of the Contract Disputes Act (CDA), as there was no obligation to pay for the "services" provided by subcontractor using appropriated funds. Lublin Corp. v. U.S., Fed.Cl.2008, 84 Fed.Cl. 678. United States ☞ 73(9)

11. —— Government provision of services, services procured

Exception agreement, which allowed Department of Defense (DoD) moving contractors under common ownership to continue qualifying for international business despite DoD regulation precluding commonly owned movers from bidding on contracts in the same geographical area, was not a contract for services under the Contract Disputes Act (CDA), but an exemption from government regulations that otherwise would have prohibited contractors from submitting bids to the government; such a contract arose only when government accepted contractors' bid for services. American Red Ball Intern., Inc. v. U.S., Fed.Cl.2007, 79 Fed.Cl. 474. United States ☞ 73(9)

12. Disposal of personal property

Contract Disputes Act (CDA) divested federal district court of jurisdiction over rescission claim that arose out of sale of government property. In re FEMA Trailer Formaldehyde Products Liability Litigation, E.D.La.2008, 583 F.Supp.2d 758. United States ☞ 73(15)

Text Repealed by Pub.L. 111–350, effective Jan. 4, 2011

15. Confidentiality and disclosure

Conceptual information disclosed by manufacturer of hydration system to Army prior to submission of its first unsolicited proposal was not protected by confidentiality provisions, and thus Armed Services Board of Contract Appeals did not have subject matter jurisdiction over manufacturer's claim against Army for improper disclosure of its proprietary data to non-governmental third parties, where proposal did not contain Defense Acquisition Regulation (DAR) legend discussing government use of unsolicited information, and there was no contract between parties at time of disclosure. Wesleyan Co., Inc. v. Harvey, C.A.Fed.2006, 454 F.3d 1375, rehearing denied, on remand 2007 WL 3265019. United States ☞ 73(15)

21. Miscellaneous claims CDA applicable

Claims against United States relating to breach, termination, and overall contract management must be brought under Contract Disputes Act (CDA). Gonzalez-McCaulley Inv. Group, Inc. v. U.S., Fed.Cl.2010, 93 Fed.Cl. 710. United States ☞ 73(9)

22. Miscellaneous claims CDA not applicable

Contractor's claims challenging her termination against officers of Broadcasting Board of Governors in their individual capacities were founded upon protections of First and Fifth Amendments, rather than terms of contract, and thus Contract Disputes Act (CDA) did not apply to contractor's claims, as required for CDA to constitute comprehensive regulatory regime precluding *Bivens* recovery for contractor's claims. Navab-Safavi v. Broadcasting Bd. of Governors, D.D.C.2009, 650 F.Supp.2d 40, affirmed 2011 WL 691363. United States ☞ 50.10(1); United States ☞ 73(9)

Contract Disputes Act (CDA) was not applicable to lodge owner's claim for compensation pursuant to termination provision of term special use permit issued for operation of resort in the Shoshone National Forest, as permit was not issued for the procurement of services for the federal government, which did not own the improvements of the resort site. The Sweetwater, A Wilderness Lodge LLC v. U.S., Fed.Cl. 2006, 72 Fed.Cl. 208, modified on reconsideration, opinion modified on reconsideration 2006 WL 5629499. United States ☞ 73(9)

§ 604. Fraudulent claims

Notes of Decisions

Baseless claims   4
Construction with other laws   ½
Discovery   9
Factual findings   3
In pari delicto   7
Laches   8
Penalties   5
Unclean hands   7
Waiver   6

½. Construction with other laws

Unlike the antifraud provision of the Contract Disputes Act, under which a contractor may incur liability only for the unsupported part of a claim, statute providing for forfeiture of fraudulent claims requires only part of the claim to be fraudulent. Daewoo Engineering and Const. Co., Ltd. v. U.S., C.A.Fed.2009, 557 F.3d 1332, rehearing and rehearing en banc denied, certiorari denied 130 S.Ct. 490, 175 L.Ed.2d 346. United States ☞ 122

A certified claim may be a source of liability under both the Contract Disputes Act and the False Claims Act. Daewoo Engineering and Const. Co., Ltd. v. U.S., C.A.Fed.2009, 557 F.3d 1332, rehearing and rehearing en banc denied, certiorari denied 130 S.Ct. 490, 175 L.Ed.2d 346. United States ☞ 122

2. Contractors liable

Government proved that certified claim of contractor for $64 million was fraudulent to the extent of $50 million, rendering contractor liable for that amount under fraud provision of the Contract Disputes Act (CDA); evidence revealed that contractor did not believe that the government owed it $64 million as a matter of right, but that it submitted claim as a negotiating ploy. Daewoo Engineering and Const. Co., Ltd. v. U.S., Fed.Cl.2006, 73 Fed.Cl. 547, affirmed 557 F.3d 1332, rehearing and rehearing en banc denied, certiorari denied 130 S.Ct. 490, 175 L.Ed.2d 346. United States ☞ 122

3. Factual findings

Court of Federal Claims did not clearly err in finding that $50.6 million portion of government contractor's $64 million claim under the Contract Disputes Act was fraudulent or in assessing a penalty in that amount; contractor's calculation assumed that the government was responsible for each day of additional performance beyond the original 1080-day contract period, without even considering whether there was any contractor-caused delay or delay for which the government was not responsible, contractor apparently used no outside experts to make its certified claim calculation, and at trial, contractor made no real effort to justify the accuracy of the claim or even to explain how it was prepared. Daewoo Engineering and Const. Co., Ltd. v. U.S., C.A.Fed.2009, 557 F.3d 1332, rehearing and rehearing en banc denied, certiorari denied 130 S.Ct. 490, 175 L.Ed.2d 346. United States ☞ 120.1

Court of Federal Claims' factual finding that government contractor made a claim for $64 million, rather than $13 million, under the Contract Disputes Act was not clearly erroneous; claim document itself was unclear, as some of its language supported government's argument that the claim was for $64 million in incurred and projected costs, and some of the claim's language supported contractor's argument that the

See Revised Title 41, post

claim was for only $13 million in incurred costs, but the extrinsic evidence unquestionably supported the court's finding as contractor's complaint stated a total monetary damages claim of $63,978,648.95, and contractor's project manager, who had certified the claim, testified that the claim was for nearly $64 million. Daewoo Engineering and Const. Co., Ltd. v. U.S., C.A.Fed. 2009, 557 F.3d 1332, rehearing and rehearing en banc denied, certiorari denied 130 S.Ct. 490, 175 L.Ed.2d 346. United States ⟜ 120.1

4. Baseless claims

A baseless certified claim is a fraudulent claim under the Contract Disputes Act. Daewoo Engineering and Const. Co., Ltd. v. U.S., C.A.Fed. 2009, 557 F.3d 1332, rehearing and rehearing en banc denied, certiorari denied 130 S.Ct. 490, 175 L.Ed.2d 346. United States ⟜ 120.1

5. Penalties

Penalty of $50.6 million against government contractor for submitting a fraudulent claim under the Contract Disputes Act was not disproportionate to the potential harm that would have been caused by contractor securing a $50.6 million payment from the government, and therefore penalty did not violate the Eighth Amendment. Daewoo Engineering and Const. Co., Ltd. v. U.S., C.A.Fed.2009, 557 F.3d 1332, rehearing and rehearing en banc denied, certiorari denied 130 S.Ct. 490, 175 L.Ed.2d 346. Sentencing And Punishment ⟜ 1567; United States ⟜ 122

6. Waiver

Affirmative defense of waiver was not available to contractor, where contractor failed to suggest in its answer, affirmative defenses, and opposition to government's motion to strike its answer how Attorney General allegedly waived

government's claims for fraud, violation of the anti-fraud provision of the Contract Disputes Act, and violation of the False Claims Act. Hernandez, Kroone and Associates, Inc. v. U.S., Fed.Cl.2010, 95 Fed.Cl. 395. United States ⟜ 122

7. Unclean hands

Affirmative defense of unclean hands was not available to contractor as to government's claims seeking monetary damages for fraud, violation of the anti-fraud provision of the Contract Disputes Act, and violation of the False Claims Act. Hernandez, Kroone and Associates, Inc. v. U.S., Fed.Cl.2010, 95 Fed.Cl. 395. Equity ⟜ 65(1)

8. Laches

Affirmative defense of laches was not available to contractor as to government's claims for fraud, violation of the anti-fraud provision of the Contract Disputes Act, and violation of the False Claims Act, where government was acting in its sovereign capacity to enforce a public right, and to protect the public interest. Hernandez, Kroone and Associates, Inc. v. U.S., Fed.Cl.2010, 95 Fed.Cl. 395. United States ⟜ 122

9. Discovery

Given broad scope of discovery, government was entitled to limited inquiry regarding identity of subcontractors and suppliers referenced in contractor's claims for subcontractor costs, on government's claims for fraud, violation of the anti-fraud provision of the Contract Disputes Act, and violation of the False Claims Act, mindful of the limits of attorney/client and work product privileges, and whether any results might be relevant or admissible were questions reserved for trial. Hernandez, Kroone and Associates, Inc. v. U.S., Fed.Cl.2010, 95 Fed.Cl. 395. Federal Courts ⟜ 1112

§ 605. Decision by contracting officer

HISTORICAL AND STATUTORY NOTES

Effective and Applicability Provisions

1992 Acts. Section 907(a)(2) of Pub.L. 102–572, which provided that amendment by Pub.L. 102–572, § 907(a)(1)(B), enacting subsec. (c)(6), (7) of this section, was effective with respect to all claims filed before, on, or after Oct. 29, 1992, except for those claims which, before such date, have been the subject of an appeal to an agency board of contract appeals or a suit in the United States Claims Court, was editorially eliminated from the Code as a result of the enactment into positive law of Title 41, Public Contracts, by Pub.L. 111–350, Jan. 4, 2011, 124 Stat. 3677.

Section 907(a)(4) of Pub.L. 102–572, which provided that amendments by Pub.L. 102–572, § 907(a)(1)(A) to subsec. (c)(1) of this section was effective with respect to certifications executed more than 60 days after the effective date

of amendments to the Federal Acquisition Regulations implementing the amendments made by paragraph (1)(A) with respect to the certification of claims, was editorially eliminated from the Code as a result of the enactment into positive law of Title 41, Public Contracts, by Pub.L. 111–350, Jan. 4, 2011, 124 Stat. 3677.

Limitations Period for Submissions of Claims Against Government Less Than 6 Years for Certain Contracts in Existence on October 13, 1994

Section 2351(a)(2) of Pub.L. 103–355, which provided statutes of limitation for certain claims, was editorially eliminated from the Code as a result of the enactment into positive law of Title 41, Public Contracts, by Pub.L. 111–350, Jan. 4, 2011, 124 Stat. 3677.

Notes of Decisions

Certification of claim 17-25

Recertification 21a

Text Repealed by Pub.L. 111–350, effective Jan. 4, 2011

2. Construction with other laws

Contractor's claim against the United States, alleging that the United States breached an implied-in-fact contract to facilitate and obtain payment from Iraqi government for contractor's work on a military base camp project in Iraq, fell within jurisdiction of the Tucker Act and not the Contract Disputes Act (CDA), and, thus, contractor's failure to obtain a final decision from a contracting officer, as required by the CDA, did not deprive the Court of Federal Claims of jurisdiction over the claim. Laudes Corp. v. U.S., Fed.Cl.2009, 86 Fed.Cl. 152. Federal Courts ☞ 1102; United States ☞ 73(9)

To satisfy the administrative claim requirement of the Contract Disputes Act (CDA) a contractor must make a written, non-routine demand to a contracting officer, request a final decision, and seek the payment of money in a sum certain, the adjustment or interpretation of contract terms, or other relief arising from or relating to the contract. Ace Constructors, Inc. v. U.S., Fed.Cl.2006, 70 Fed.Cl. 253, affirmed 499 F.3d 1357. United States ☞ 73(9)

4. Claims within section—Generally

Plaintiff's title or characterization of its claims is not controlling, and plaintiff may not avoid jurisdictional bar of Contract Disputes Act (CDA) merely by alleging constitutional torts and regulatory violations rather than breach of contract. Evers v. Astrue, C.A.7 (Ill.) 2008, 536 F.3d 651. United States ☞ 73(9)

Contract Disputes Act (CDA) did not require United States to file its own administrative claim in order to recover equitable adjustment allowed by contracting officer in contract modification, as overpayment to contractor, after Court of Federal Claims had determined, in action filed by contractor to recover further additional amount for unanticipated expenses after contracting officer had made that equitable adjustment, that contractor was not entitled to further additional amount, or any part of equitable adjustment. U.S. v. Renda Marine, Inc., E.D.Tex. 2010, 2010 WL 3909237. United States ☞ 75(2)

Contractor's claim for revision or rescission of Air Force's allegedly unfair and inaccurate performance evaluation, in contractor performance assessment report (CPAR) that was required to be fair and accurate, under federal acquisition regulation (FAR), was "claim," within meaning of CDA, on grounds that contractor sought relief "arising under or relating to this contract," even though contractor had not alleged contractual theory of breach of contract, mistake, or misrepresentation, since claims for extracontractual relief were cognizable under CDA, and connection between contract and evaluation was more than tangential, as FAR requirements were equivalent to mandatory contract term, and performance evaluation related to contractor's performance in same way that any evaluation related to thing evaluated. BLR Group of America, Inc. v. U.S., Fed.Cl.2010, 94 Fed.Cl. 354, reconsideration denied 96 Fed.Cl. 9.

While a "claim" need not use particular language to satisfy CDA requirements, the contractor must submit in writing to the contracting officer a clear and unequivocal statement that gives the contracting officer adequate notice of the basis and amount of the claim. SITCO General Trading and Contracting Co. v. U.S., Fed.Cl.2009, 87 Fed.Cl. 506. United States ☞ 73(9)

A contractor need not assert a specific contractual provision to meet the "matter of right" requirement for a claim seeking relief under the Contract Disputes Act (CDA), but is only required to assert an entitlement that has some legal basis. BLR Group of America, Inc. v. U.S., Fed.Cl.2008, 84 Fed.Cl. 634. United States ☞ 73(9)

5. —— Counterclaims, claims within section

Court of Federal Claims lacks jurisdiction under the Contracts Dispute Act to entertain a government counterclaim unless and until the contracting officer determines that the government has a claim. 1-10 Industry Associates, LLC v. U.S., C.A.Fed.2008, 528 F.3d 859. Federal Courts ☞ 1076; United States ☞ 73(9)

6. —— Penalties or forfeitures, claims within section

Contractor's claim that federal agencies violated their own procedures when they decided to insource work currently performed by contractor did not fall within scope of Contracts Dispute Act's (CDA) grant of exclusive jurisdiction to Court of Federal Claims over contract disputes with agencies, and thus federal district court had jurisdiction under Administrative Procedure Act (APA) over contractor's action; source of rights alleged in action was not contractual, and contractor sought only declaratory and injunctive relief. K-Mar Industries, Inc. v. U.S. Dept. of Defense, W.D.Okla.2010, 2010 WL 4829965. Federal Courts ☞ 1139

6a. —— Performance disputes, claims within section

Contract performance disputes are addressed under the provisions of the CDA. Mission Critical Solutions v. U.S., Fed.Cl.2010, 91 Fed.Cl. 386. United States ☞ 73(9)

7. —— Subcontractor claims, claims within section

Subcontractors are generally not in privity of contract with the government, so as to be able to avail themselves of the Contract Dispute Act's (CDA) appeal provisions; if the prime contractor is acting as the government's agent when it enters into the subcontractor agreement, however, the subcontractor may be permitted to sue the government directly. Winter v. FloorPro, Inc., C.A.Fed.2009, 570 F.3d 1367. United States 👈 74.2

Generally, under ordinary government prime contracts, subcontractors do not have standing to sue the government under the Tucker Act in the event of an alleged government breach or to enforce a claim for equitable adjustment under the Contract Disputes Act (CDA). Harper/Nielsen-Dillingham, Builders, Inc. v. U.S., Fed.Cl. 2008, 81 Fed.Cl. 667, appeal dismissed 321 Fed. Appx. 951, 2009 WL 981976, reconsideration denied 2009 WL 1227719. United States 👈 73(9); United States 👈 74.2

8. —— Miscellaneous requests considered claims, claims within section

Unsuccessful bidder's letter to Army and Air Force Exchange Service (AAFES) official did not satisfy Contract Disputes Act's (CDA) written demand requirement, and thus Court of Federal Claims lacked jurisdiction over bidder's challenge to award of concessionaire contract, where letter concerned different contract, official was not contracting officer overseeing her concessionaire contract, and letter did not address bidder's concessionaire contract. Terry v. U.S., Fed.Cl.2010, 2010 WL 5097766. United States 👈 73(9)

Contractor's claim for revision or rescission of Air Force's allegedly unfair and inaccurate performance evaluation in contractor performance assessment report (CPAR) asserted entitlement to relief as matter of right, under federal acquisition regulation (FAR), requiring government to provide fair and accurate performance evaluation of contractors, in support of validity of contractor's CDA claim, since FAR was intended to benefit both private contractors and government, as contractors were not merely incidental beneficiaries of FAR. BLR Group of America, Inc. v. U.S., Fed.Cl.2010, 94 Fed.Cl. 354, reconsideration denied 96 Fed.Cl. 9. United States 👈 73(9)

Contractor stated "claim" under the Contract Disputes Act (CDA) when he sent e-mail to contracting agency's program manager requesting determination from contracting officer (CO) that agency's cautionary statement in official correspondence regarding the disclosure of communications related to contract be removed from agency's correspondence with him, as e-mail stated in attachments the factual and legal grounds for contractor's contention that contract could not unilaterally be changed by terms of cautionary notice. Parker v. U.S., Fed.Cl.2007, 77 Fed.Cl. 279, affirmed 280 Fed.Appx. 957, 2008 WL 2329271, rehearing and rehearing en banc denied. United States 👈 73(9)

Contractor's letter to contracting officer submitting contract dispute regarding government's alleged unilateral modification increasing scope of work for border patrol station constituted "claim," within meaning of CDA, requiring contractor to submit valid claim to contracting officer as prerequisite to filing CDA action, on grounds that letter set forth sum certain of $840,522.77, although letter submitted sum as best good faith estimate based on contractor's knowledge and belief as of that date and reserved contractor's rights to make any necessary modifications to price based on changes in availability or price of labor and/or material, since contracting officer recognized letter as claim and issued final decision denying claim, and contractor's reservation of rights merely recognized that same claim could increase or decrease in amount by passage of time either at contracting officer level or on appeal. Hernandez, Kroone and Associates, Inc. v. U.S., Fed.Cl. 2009, 89 Fed.Cl. 153, withdrawn from bound volume, opinion not to be published. United States 👈 73(9)

Allegation that contractor's performance evaluation had been issued without observing proper procedures and was substantively erroneous constituted "claim" within meaning of Contract Disputes Act (CDA), and thus Court of Federal Claims had jurisdiction over action seeking judicial review of that decision, since performance evaluation was issue of contract performance, rather than issue of bid protest, when contractor sought future government contracts. Todd Const. L.P. v. U.S., Fed.Cl.2008, 85 Fed.Cl. 34, subsequent determination 88 Fed.Cl. 235, subsequent determination 94 Fed.Cl. 100. United States 👈 73(15)

Contractor's written response to contractor performance assessment report (CPAR) requesting that assessing official correct ratings and narrative contained in initial CPAR satisfied "matter of right" requirement for a valid claim for relief under the Contract Disputes Act (CDA), as contractor was legally entitled to a fair and accurate CPAR. BLR Group of America, Inc. v. U.S., Fed.Cl.2008, 84 Fed.Cl. 634. United States 👈 73(9)

"Certified Restated, Supplemented, and Amended Claims For Monetary Damages" submitted by contractor to contracting officer (CO) satisfied requirements of the Contract Disputes Act (CDA), where claims were the same claims asserted in suit, they were provided with a written demand to the CO seeking a sum certain under the contract, the claims were "in dispute," submission explicitly requested a "final resolution" by the CO, and claims were certified in accordance with the CDA. NCLN20, Inc. v. U.S., Fed.Cl.2008, 82 Fed.Cl. 103. United States 👈 73(9)

9. —— Miscellaneous requests not considered claims, claims within section

Construction contractor's letter to contracting officer for United States Navy on window and roof replacement project, which reiterated contractor's earlier request for extension of time to complete project, was not valid "claim" within meaning of Contract Disputes Act (CDA), and thus Court of Federal Claims lacked subject matter jurisdiction over contractor's breach of contract claim under the CDA, where contrac-

Text Repealed by Pub.L. 111–350, effective Jan. 4, 2011

tor's letter did not provide contracting officer adequate notice of total number of days actually requested in extension, did not state sum certain that contractor sought, and did not request officer issue final decision on contractor's request. M. Maropakis Carpentry, Inc. v. U.S., C.A.Fed. 2010, 609 F.3d 1323. United States ☞ 73(9)

E-mail sent from contractor's counsel to contracting officer (CO) in response to CO's e-mail to counsel, after contractor submitted written responses to Air Force's allegedly unfair and inaccurate evaluation of contractor's performance under air traffic management support services contract that was terminated for convenience, did not constitute "claim," within meaning of CDA, requiring contractor to submit written statement giving contracting officer (CO) adequate notice of basis and amount of claim as prerequisite to appeal of CO's final decision or deemed denial, since counsel's e-mail attempted to persuade CO to change or withdraw evaluation within procurement regulation's performance evaluation procedures, rather than requesting separate CDA relief, so e-mail did not convey notice to CO that counsel intended to assert CDA claim. BLR Group of America, Inc. v. U.S., Fed.Cl.2010, 96 Fed.Cl. 9. United States ☞ 73(9)

Contractor's letter to agency contact did not constitute a "claim" so as to satisfy the Contract Disputes Act (CDA) jurisdictional prerequisites for asserting a claim for nonmonetary relief; overall purpose of letter was to offer a couple of observations relevant to the overall evaluation contained in the initial CPAR (Contractor Performance Assessment Reporting System) with which contractor disagreed, and predated its submission of formal written comments to the initial CPAR. Kemron Environmental Services, Inc. v. U.S., Fed.Cl.2010, 93 Fed.Cl. 74. United States ☞ 73(9)

Contractor's letter sent to counsel for United States Postal Service (USPS), seeking unspecified amount of reimbursement for costs of delays allegedly caused by USPS on contract to construct carrier annex, for additional work performed, and for associated interest, did not qualify as "claim," within meaning of CDA, precluding jurisdiction over contractor's breach of contract claim based on allegedly unpaid costs of continued work, since letter was neither addressed to nor offered to contracting officer (CO) for final decision, letter did not make specific claim for sum certain or establish any entitlement to relief, CO never issued final decision regarding letter, and claim could not have been deemed denied as CO never received letter. L.A. Ruiz Associates, Inc. v. U.S., Fed.Cl.2010, 94 Fed.Cl. 768. United States ☞ 73(9)

Contractor's statement of protest written on memo line of his check to Forest Service, stating that "[payment] remitted in protest and purchaser objects to contents of letter dated 2-27-07 enclosed herewith, as being true and correct," sent to Forest Service receiving bank for deposit, did not constitute claim to contracting office under Contracts Dispute Act (CDA); although contractor had contested accuracy of officer's findings, he did not indicate basis or amount of any claim at that time. Quillen v. U.S., Fed.Cl.2009, 89 Fed.Cl. 148. United States ☞ 73(9)

A complaint filed in the Court of Federal Claims does not seek a decision from the contracting officer or meet the other CDA requirements of a "claim," as necessary for jurisdiction under CDA. SITCO General Trading and Contracting Co. v. U.S., Fed.Cl.2009, 87 Fed.Cl. 506. United States ☞ 73(9)

Contractor's letters to contracting officer (CO) requesting payment either for outstanding invoices or to correct underpayment from "corrupted spreadsheets" did not satisfy the requirements for a claim under the Contract Disputes Act (CDA), where they failed explicitly or implicitly to request a "final decision" therein, as required by the CDA. NCLN20, Inc. v. U.S., Fed.Cl.2008, 82 Fed.Cl. 103. United States ☞ 73(9)

Letters from Department of Defense (DoD) moving contractors under common ownership seeking clarification of how new program would affect exception agreement, which allowed them to continue qualifying for international business despite DoD regulation precluding commonly owned movers from bidding on contracts in the same geographical area, did not constitute a "claim" for purposes of the Contract Disputes Act (CDA), as letters made no demand but only asked for advice. American Red Ball Intern., Inc. v. U.S., Fed.Cl.2007, 79 Fed.Cl. 474. United States ☞ 73(9)

9a. —— Response to evaluation, claims within section

Contractor's comments in response to Air Force's allegedly unfair and inaccurate evaluation of contractor's performance under air traffic management support services contract that was terminated for convenience did not constitute "claim," within meaning of CDA, requiring contractor to submit written statement giving contracting officer (CO) adequate notice of basis and amount of claim as prerequisite to appeal of CO's final decision or deemed denial, even though comments provided notice to CO of basis of claim and relief sought, since contractor did not intend comments to serve as request for CDA relief separate from relief that contractor sought through procurement regulation's performance evaluation procedures, so CO had no notice that contractor intended comments to be treated as CDA claim. BLR Group of America, Inc. v. U.S., Fed.Cl.2010, 96 Fed.Cl. 9.

9b. Contracts within section

Surety's takeover agreement with another contractor, to fulfill surety's performance bond obligations upon default of original contractor, was not procurement contract, as would require contractor to submit claim to contracting officer prior to filing suit, under Contract Disputes Act. Lumbermens Mut. Cas. v. U.S., Fed.Cl.2009, 90 Fed.Cl. 558. United States ☞ 73(9)

See Revised Title 41, post

10. Relating to a contract

Physician's claim that Social Security Administration's (SSA) termination of his consulting contract was so arbitrary that it violated his substantive due process rights related to his contract with SSA, and thus Contract Disputes Act (CDA) deprived district court of jurisdiction over claim, where contract gave SSA right to terminate physician for disorderly conduct, use of offensive language, or quarreling, SSA and contracting officer determined that physician's confrontation with SSA employee qualified as legitimate grounds for SSA to terminate contract under contract's termination and removal-from-duty clauses, source of physician's rights was contract, and only possible remedy for SSA's actions was contractual. Evers v. Astrue, C.A.7 (Ill.) 2008, 536 F.3d 651. United States ⊜ 73(15)

Physician's claim that termination of his consulting contract with Social Security Administration (SSA) violated his procedural due process rights related to his contract with SSA, and thus Contract Disputes Act (CDA) deprived district court of jurisdiction over claim, where physician's claimed property interest consisted of remaining term of his contract, physician's claimed liberty interest was in renewal of his contract and in harm to his reputation as result of contract's termination, and physician sought contractual remedies from SSA and its officers, rather than notice and hearing. Evers v. Astrue, C.A.7 (Ill.) 2008, 536 F.3d 651. United States ⊜ 73(15)

11. Exhaustion of remedies

Statutory time restrictions on the submission of administrative claims are a part of the requirement that a party must satisfy to properly exhaust administrative remedies; therefore, subject to any applicable tolling of the statutory time period, the timely submission of a claim to a contracting officer is a necessary predicate to the exercise of jurisdiction by a federal court or a board of contract appeals over a contract dispute governed by the CDA. Arctic Slope Native Association, Ltd. v. Sebelius, C.A.Fed. 2009, 583 F.3d 785, rehearing and rehearing en banc denied, certiorari denied 130 S.Ct. 3505, 177 L.Ed.2d 1091, certiorari denied 131 S.Ct. 144, 178 L.Ed.2d 36. United States ⊜ 73(9)

Minority small business contractor failed to satisfy jurisdictional requirements, under CDA, for claim of breach of contract by Army and Air Force Exchange Service (AAFES), as nonappropriated fund instrumentality, for alleged interference with, and frustration of, temporary concession contracts for sales of cellular telephone accessories and clothing, since contractor had not submitted written demand to contracting officer and had neither argued in any filings nor averred in her affidavit that she submitted sum certain demand to contracting officer. Baldwin v. U.S., Fed.Cl.2010, 95 Fed.Cl. 238. United States ⊜ 73(9)

Contractor's claim that Army Corps of Engineers acted in bad faith, by refusing to exercise renewal option in contract related to electronic security systems services, had not been administratively exhausted, as required by Contract Disputes Act (CDA), where contractor failed to file claim with Corps' contracting officer representative (COR) before pursuing judicial relief. Government Technical Services LLC v. U.S., Fed.Cl.2009, 90 Fed.Cl. 522. United States ⊜ 73(9)

A plaintiff must exhaust the administrative remedies available under the CDA by submitting a claim to and seeking a final decision from the contracting officer before filing suit against the United States. SITCO General Trading and Contracting Co. v. U.S., Fed.Cl.2009, 87 Fed.Cl. 506. United States ⊜ 73(9)

Under the Contract Disputes Act (CDA), jurisdiction is lacking in the Court of Federal Claims unless a contractor's claim is first presented to the contracting officer and that officer renders or is deemed to render a final decision on the claim. Lublin Corp. v. U.S., Fed.Cl.2008, 84 Fed.Cl. 678. United States ⊜ 73(9)

Court of Federal Claims lacked jurisdiction under the Contract Disputes Act (CDA) over contractor's claim seeking payment for unpaid services and damages resulting from contracting agency's alleged breach of contract, for no less than $500,000, plus interest, costs, and attorney fees, where record did not evidence that contractor submitted a certified claim to the contracting officer for breach of contract damages. Kenney Orthopedic, LLC v. U.S., Fed.Cl.2008, 83 Fed. Cl. 35. United States ⊜ 73(9)

Contractor lacked standing to assert claim that the government breached travel services contracts by terminating them in bad faith, where contractor did not comply with exhaustion requirements of the Contract Disputes Act (CDA) by filing claim with contracting officer (CO) and requesting or obtaining a final decision from the CO regarding its claim. Omega World Travel, Inc. v. U.S., Fed.Cl.2008, 82 Fed.Cl. 452. United States ⊜ 73(9)

13. Persons entitled to maintain claim

Government did not intend to benefit subcontractor's escrow agent by having contracting officer (CO), at request of prime contractor, change prime contract for aircraft hoses to place agent's name on remittance address, thereby precluding agent's third-party beneficiary status to seek damages from government for paying prime contractor rather than agent, pursuant to CDA and Tucker Act, since CO lacked notice that agent was not merely employee of or affiliated with prime contractor, but was distinct third party, no government employee with contracting authority ratified any third-party beneficiary relationship, and agent could not reasonably rely on mere appearance of his name on contract as creating third-party beneficiary rights. Kawa v. U.S., Fed.Cl.2009, 86 Fed.Cl. 575, motion for relief from judgment denied 2009 WL 1704462, dismissed 368 Fed.Appx. 106, 2009 WL 5948861. United States ⊜ 70(5)

Subcontractor's escrow agent was real party in interest in his suit seeking payment from government, pursuant to CDA and Tucker Act, based on alleged breach of implied contract or as third-party beneficiary or assignee of prime contract for aircraft hoses, where agent's name appeared on government's purchase order for aircraft hoses for benefit of subcontractor. Kawa v. U.S., Fed.Cl.2009, 86 Fed.Cl. 575, motion for relief from judgment denied 2009 WL 1704462, dismissed 368 Fed.Appx. 106, 2009 WL 5948861. United States ☞ 74.2

Under the "*Severin*" doctrine," a prime contractor may sue the government on behalf of its subcontractor, in the nature of a pass-through suit, for costs incurred by the subcontractor if the prime contractor proves its liability to the subcontractor for the damages sustained by the latter, a showing which overcomes the objection to the lack of privity between the government and the subcontractor. Harper/Nielsen-Dillingham, Builders, Inc. v. U.S., Fed.Cl.2008, 81 Fed. Cl. 667, appeal dismissed 321 Fed.Appx. 951, 2009 WL 981976, reconsideration denied 2009 WL 1227719. United States ☞ 74.2

14. Time of presentment of claim to contracting officer

Six year time limit in Contract Disputes Act (CDA) was not jurisdictional in nature, as would permit district court to equitably toll limitations period for purposes of Indian tribe's claim that government breached self-determination contract with Secretary of Health and Human Services (HHS); time limit for initiating claim under CDA was not stated in jurisdictional terms, and historical treatment of type of limitation imposed by CDA did not suggest that six-year filing deadline was jurisdictional. Menominee Indian Tribe of Wisconsin v. U.S., C.A.D.C.2010, 614 F.3d 519, 392 U.S.App.D.C. 202. Limitation Of Actions ☞ 104.5

Limitations period for CDA claims of Indian health care contractors, as putative members of class actions that were not certified, seeking ISDA contract support costs, was not tolled under doctrine of class action tolling, since ISDA contractors' failure to present claims to contracting officer within CDA limitations period rendered them ineligible to be potential members of plaintiff class with respect to CDA claims. Arctic Slope Native Association, Ltd. v. Sebelius, C.A.Fed.2009, 583 F.3d 785, rehearing and rehearing en banc denied, certiorari denied 130 S.Ct. 3505, 177 L.Ed.2d 1091, certiorari denied 131 S.Ct. 144, 178 L.Ed.2d 36. Limitation Of Actions ☞ 126.5; United States ☞ 73(9)

Contract Disputes Act's (CDA) six-year limitations period applied to Indian tribe's action alleging that Secretary of Health and Human Services (HHS) breached self-determination contract that allowed tribe to operate health care system for tribal members by failing to compensate it fully for indirect contract support costs (CSC). Menominee Indian Tribe of Wisconsin v. U.S., D.D.C.2008, 539 F.Supp.2d 152, reconsideration denied, reconsideration denied 2008 WL 3919158, reversed and remanded 614 F.3d 519, 392 U.S.App.D.C. 202. United States ☞ 73(15)

Contractor's breach of contract claim, based on Navy allegedly preventing contractor from performing contract to remove and dispose of industrial waste sludge, was timely filed with contracting officer, under CDA provision, requiring claims to be submitted to contracting officer for final decision within six years of accrual of claim, within six years of contractor and Navy executing bilateral modification terminating contract. Nwogu v. U.S., Fed.Cl.2010, 94 Fed.Cl. 637. United States ☞ 73(9)

The passage of time does not transform a claim brought pursuant to the deemed denial provision of the CDA into one covered by the Tucker Act's general six-year statute of limitations. System Planning Corp. v. U.S., Fed.Cl. 2010, 95 Fed.Cl. 1. United States ☞ 73(13)

17. Certification of claim—Generally

The presentment of claims to a contracting officer, as required by CDA, is a prerequisite to suit in the Court of Federal Claims or review by a board of contract appeals. Arctic Slope Native Association, Ltd. v. Sebelius, C.A.Fed.2009, 583 F.3d 785, rehearing and rehearing en banc denied, certiorari denied 130 S.Ct. 3505, 177 L.Ed.2d 1091, certiorari denied 131 S.Ct. 144, 178 L.Ed.2d 36. United States ☞ 73(9)

Contractor made written demand as matter of right, as required for Court of Federal Claims to have jurisdiction over nonmonetary dispute under Contract Disputes Act (CDA), where detailed procedures had been set forth that were to be followed in assessing contractor performance that would be made part of record upon which its future submissions would be judged, with additional steps to be taken when rating would be unfavorable, and contractor alleged that those procedures were not followed and that evaluations it received were not, in fact, accurate and fair. Todd Const. L.P. v. U.S., Fed.Cl.2008, 85 Fed.Cl. 34, subsequent determination 88 Fed.Cl. 235, subsequent determination 94 Fed.Cl. 100. United States ☞ 73(15)

To satisfy the administrative claim requirement of the Contract Disputes Act (CDA) a contractor must make a written, non-routine demand to a contracting officer, request a final decision, and seek the payment of money in a sum certain, the adjustment or interpretation of contract terms, or other relief arising from or relating to the contract. Ace Constructors, Inc. v. U.S., Fed.Cl.2006, 70 Fed.Cl. 253, affirmed 499 F.3d 1357. United States ☞ 73(9)

18. —— Amount of claim generally, certification of claim

Although government would be allowed continued deposition of certified small business contractor's expert witness, limited to alterations he made to his original expert report, and deposition of contractor's principal, limited to reasoning and particulars for reallocation of damages calculation to which expert opined, contractor was not precluded from any further honing of damages calculation, in CDA suit against United States to recover sums allegedly due for work performed at government's request that was beyond scope of fixed-price construction con-

See Revised Title 41, post

tract, since failure of contractor to support CDA claims could have serious ramifications. Hernandez, Kroone and Associates, Inc. v. U.S., Fed.Cl.2010, 95 Fed.Cl. 392. Federal Courts ⟨⟩ 1112

A contractor seeking more than $100,000 must submit a certified claim to the contracting officer before bringing a cause of action pursuant to the CDA in the Court of Federal Claims. OK's Cascade Co. v. U.S., Fed.Cl.2009, 87 Fed.Cl. 739. United States ⟨⟩ 73(9)

21a. —— Recertification, certification of claim

Contractor's renewed claim for price-adjustment for subcontractor's increased labor costs in performing contract to construct hospital replacement did not require recertification, under CDA, for exercise of jurisdiction over claim, pursuant to Tucker Act, where renewed claim was premised on same set of operative facts as those forming basis of prior certified claim, limited only by reduction in amount of claim attributable to settlement agreement. Dick Pacific/GHEMM, JV ex rel. W.A. Botting Co. v. U.S., Fed.Cl.2009, 87 Fed.Cl. 113. United States ⟨⟩ 73(9)

22. —— Amendment of claim, certification of claim

Government contractor was not entitled to amend complaint to add allegations respecting its claim against the government for the costs of responding to landlord's notice of lease termination, where allegations amounted to new claim for costs of litigating termination notice which was not presented to contracting officer, as required under the Contract Disputes Act (CDA). Bannum, Inc. v. U.S., Fed.Cl.2008, 80 Fed.Cl. 239. United States ⟨⟩ 74(9)

Contractor's motion to amend its claim against government to add claim for unpaid contract earnings did not relate back to differing site conditions claims pleaded in its original complaint for purposes of subject matter jurisdiction; new claim was not presented to a contracting officer, claims were not legally and factually intertwined such that demand for relief under one would necessarily be demand for relief under the other, and entitlement to additional contract earnings did not depend on successful prosecution of claim for additional compensation due to alleged differing site conditions. Renda Marine, Inc. v. U.S., Fed.Cl. 2005, 65 Fed.Cl. 152, reconsideration denied 71 Fed.Cl. 782, appeal dismissed 208 Fed.Appx. 880, 2006 WL 3497269, order recalled and vacated 212 Fed.Appx. 969, 2006 WL 3922781, affirmed 509 F.3d 1372, rehearing and rehearing en banc denied. Federal Courts ⟨⟩ 1106

23. —— Separate or joint claims, certification of claim

Trustee's combination of pre-award bid protest and Contract Disputes Act (CDA) action, alleging breach of trust agreement by Department of Interior, Bureau of Reclamation, for administration of state fish and wildlife conservation trust, pursuant to Canyon Ferry Reser-

voir, Montana, Act, by attempting to terminate trustee through unilateral amendment of agreement and then soliciting bids for trustee's successor, warranted bifurcation of proceedings only as to damages on contract claim but not as to liability on either claim, since claims were sufficiently intertwined so that bid protest claim could not be resolved without addressing merits of contract claim, as resolution of both claims turned on common element of validity of attempted termination of trustee, but that element did not extend to damages for breach of contract. Montana Fish, Wildlife, and Parks Foundation, Inc. v. U.S., Fed.Cl.2010, 91 Fed.Cl. 434. United States ⟨⟩ 73(15)

Court of Federal Claims lacked jurisdiction over contractor's claim that government constructively changed contract in its response to request for information (RFI) by requiring controlled compaction in top 1.5 meters in roadway areas, as claim was never presented to contracting officer (CO); claim arose from different set of operative facts than claim presented to CO which sought reimbursement for increased cost of crushing stone to 3 inches as opposed to 6 inches, and for increased cost of spreading 6-inch material in layers with a thickness of 30 cm as compared to spreading 3-inch material in layers with a thickness of 20 cm. AAB Joint Venture v. U.S., Fed.Cl.2007, 75 Fed.Cl. 414, reconsideration denied 77 Fed.Cl. 702. United States ⟨⟩ 73(9)

Contractor's duty under CDA to submit written claim to contracting officer (CO), demanding payment of money in sum certain for reimbursement for costs of delays allegedly caused by United States Postal Service (USPS) on contract to construct carrier annex, for additional work performed, and for associated interest, was not discharged by same claim principle, as would have allowed retention of jurisdiction over contractor's alleged counterclaim or request for set-off from CO's affirmative contract claim against contractor that resulted in $1,131,166 refund owed to USPS, even though contractor's setoff claim and USPS's affirmative contract claim arose out of performance of same contract, since claims did not arise out of same set of facts. L.A. Ruiz Associates, Inc. v. U.S., Fed.Cl.2010, 94 Fed.Cl. 768. Federal Courts ⟨⟩ 1076

24. —— Waiver, certification of claim

Under the CDA, certification of a contractor's monetary claim of more than $100,000 against the United States may not be waived, as the CDA's certification provision was enacted to hold contractors liable for fraudulent, unwarranted, and inflated claims and to encourage settlements. Kenney Orthopedic, LLC v. U.S., Fed.Cl.2009, 88 Fed.Cl. 688. United States ⟨⟩ 73(9)

The CDA requirement that a contractor certify that a claim exceeds $100,000 cannot be waived. SITCO General Trading and Contracting Co. v. U.S., Fed.Cl.2009, 87 Fed.Cl. 506. United States ⟨⟩ 73(9)

Text Repealed by Pub.L. 111–350, effective Jan. 4, 2011

25. —— **Adequacy of claim certification, certification of claim**

Contractor satisfied CDA requirements for commencing suit against United States, by submitting certified claim to contracting officer (CO) alleging that United States owed additional negotiated fee of $7,039,870 pursuant to amendment on contract to provide new security system to protect United States Air Force (USAF) facilities, even though CO had not issued final decision, since contractor's claim was deemed denied by CO after waiting nearly seven years for final decision that CO failed to issue within reasonable time. System Planning Corp. v. U.S., Fed. Cl.2010, 95 Fed.Cl. 1. United States ⟨=⟩ 73(13)

Government contractor that sought to challenge termination of its timber-harvesting contract with Forest Service satisfied requirements of Contract Disputes Act (CDA) by submitting its claim to contracting officer in letters. Wyoming Sawmills, Inc. v. U.S., Fed.Cl.2009, 90 Fed.Cl. 148, subsequent determination 94 Fed. Cl. 399. United States ⟨=⟩ 73(9)

Claim certifications filed by contractor under the Contract Disputes Act (CDA) were technically deficient, where they failed to include the required representations that the claim was made in good faith and that the certifier was duly authorized to certify the claim. Trafalgar House Constr., Inc. v. U.S., Fed.Cl.2006, 73 Fed.Cl. 675, subsequent determination 77 Fed. Cl. 48, affirmed 274 Fed.Appx. 898, 2008 WL 1734471. United States ⟨=⟩ 73(9) /

30. Jurisdictional prerequisite of certification

Even if United States had actual knowledge of amount and basis of construction contractor's claim for time extension on window and roof replacement project for Navy, nothing in the CDA excused construction contractor's noncompliance with CDA's explicit claim requirements, and thus Court of Federal Claims lacked subject matter jurisdiction over contractor's breach of contract claim against the United States under the CDA. M. Maropakis Carpentry, Inc. v. U.S., C.A.Fed.2010, 609 F.3d 1323. United States ⟨=⟩ 73(9)

Contractor's allegations that government breached implied in fact contract to provide employee training programs for Department of Health and Human Services (HHS), by withdrawing contract award in violation of Contract Disputes Act (CDA), was not subject to jurisdiction of Court of Federal Claims, since contractor had not alleged fulfillment of jurisdictional prerequisite of submission of contract claim to contracting officer, denial of claim, or issuance of final decision relating to claim. Gonzalez-McCaulley Inv. Group, Inc. v. U.S., Fed.Cl.2010, 93 Fed.Cl. 710. United States ⟨=⟩ 73(9)

Jurisdiction is appropriate under the Contract Disputes Act when a government contractor submits in writing to the contracting officer a clear and unequivocal statement that gives the contracting officer adequate notice of the basis and amount of the claim. Retirement Commu-

nities LLC v. U.S., Fed.Cl.2010, 92 Fed.Cl. 587. United States ⟨=⟩ 73(9)

Contractor's claims for equitable adjustment of prices, for contract to maintain and repair facilities and to provide hazardous waste management services for Department of Navy, satisfied jurisdictional requirements, under CDA, where claims were in writing and denied by final decision of contracting officer. LB&B Associates Inc. v. U.S., Fed.Cl.2010, 91 Fed.Cl. 142. Federal Courts ⟨=⟩ 1076

Under the CDA, jurisdiction of the Court of Federal Claims is predicated upon a contractor meeting two fundamental requirements: (1) the submission of a written claim to the contracting officer, and (2) the agency's issuance of a final decision. OK's Cascade Co. v. U.S., Fed.Cl. 2009, 87 Fed.Cl. 739. United States ⟨=⟩ 73(9); United States ⟨=⟩ 73(15)

Court of Federal Claims lacked jurisdiction over federal government's breach of contract and Contract Disputes Act counterclaims, with respect to action initiated by contractor seeking payment for construction of government facilities, since such claims had not been first submitted to Contracting Officer. Morse Diesel Intern., Inc. v. U.S., Fed.Cl.2007, 74 Fed.Cl. 601, reconsideration granted in part 2007 WL 5177405. United States ⟨=⟩ 73(9)

32. Authority to issue final decision

If a claim is already pending in litigation, a contracting officer has no authority to issue a final decision on the claim, as exclusive governmental authority rests with the Department of Justice. Universal Shelters of America, Inc. v. U.S., Fed.Cl.2009, 87 Fed.Cl. 127. United States ⟨=⟩ 73(9)

33. Failure to issue decision deemed denial of claim

Contracting officer's failure to issue decision on contractor's written comments to Air Force in response to allegedly unfair and inaccurate evaluation of contractor's past contract performance, in contractor performance assessment report (CPAR) that was required to be fair and accurate, under federal acquisition regulation (FAR), did not constitute deemed denial of CDA claim, since contractor had not submitted valid CDA claim demanding relief arising under or relating to contract, but rather, only submitted comments that contracting officer would have had no reason to believe required further action once comments were referred to reviewing official. BLR Group of America, Inc. v. U.S., Fed. Cl.2010, 94 Fed.Cl. 354, reconsideration denied 96 Fed.Cl. 9. United States ⟨=⟩ 73(13)

Contractor's choice of Armed Services Board of Contract Appeals (ASBCA), as forum for appealing contractor's claim that was deemed denied as to Department of Navy's alleged breach of contract for removal of storage tanks and contaminated materials, was not binding, under election doctrine applicable to CDA claims, thereby allowing contractor to pursue appeal in alternate forum of Court of Federal Claims, since ASBCA dismissed contractor's ap-

See Revised Title 41, post

peal of deemed denied claim for lack of jurisdiction rather than on merits. Environmental Safety Consultants, Inc. v. U.S., Fed.Cl.2010, 95 Fed.Cl. 77, subsequent determination 2011 WL 488685. United States ☞ 73(15)

In absence of evidence that the contracting officer (CO) received notice of contractor's claim before certain date, it could not be concluded that 60–day period had expired to transform CO's inaction on claim into a deemed denial under Contract Disputes Act (CDA). Metrotop Plaza Associates v. U.S., Fed.Cl.2008, 82 Fed.Cl. 598. United States ☞ 73(13)

Where contracting officer (CO) failed to issue a final decision regarding contractor's claims in his decision or notify contractor as to when he would issue a final decision on the claims, the claims were deemed denied as a matter of law under the Contract Disputes Act (CDA). NCLN20, Inc. v. U.S., Fed.Cl.2008, 82 Fed.Cl. 103. United States ☞ 73(13)

34a. Inaction as final decision

Contracting officer's inaction on a contractor's certified claim against the United States, under the CDA, is a deemed denial of the claim and constitutes a "final decision." Kenney Orthopedic, LLC v. U.S., Fed.Cl.2009, 88 Fed.Cl. 688. United States ☞ 73(13)

35. —— Jurisdictional prerequisite, final decision

Contractor satisfied jurisdictional requirements, under CDA and federal acquisition regulations, for claims arising from Defense Acquisition University's (DAU) alleged appropriation of contractor's proprietary data in breach of confidentiality and non-disclosure agreement and breach of contracts purportedly implied-in-fact from proprietary data legends on contractor's learning tool products purchased by DAU via General Services Administration (GSA) schedule contracts; contractor timely submitted written claim to contracting officer (CO) seeking, as matter of right, payment of breach of contract damages, CO either provided to contractor written decision setting forth CO's reason for denying claim and apprising contractor of right to appeal, or alternatively CO failed to issue decision thus resulting in deemed denial, contractor filed appeal in Court of Federal Claims within one year of receiving CO's decision, contractor's appeal arose from same facts and sought same relief as original claim submitted to CO, and contractor did not first appeal claim to another forum. Paradigm Learning, Inc. v. U.S., Fed. Cl.2010, 93 Fed.Cl. 465. United States ☞ 73(15)

Under the CDA, jurisdiction of the Court of Federal Claims is predicated upon a contractor meeting two fundamental requirements: (1) the submission of a written claim to the contracting officer, and (2) the agency's issuance of a final decision. OK's Cascade Co. v. U.S., Fed.Cl. 2009, 87 Fed.Cl. 739. United States ☞ 73(9); United States ☞ 73(15)

The jurisdictional prerequisite of a final decision by a contracting officer to the litigation of claims under the Contract Disputes Act (CDA) applies to the claims of both contractors and the government. Universal Shelters of America, Inc. v. U.S., Fed.Cl.2009, 87 Fed.Cl. 127. United States ☞ 73(15)

Contracting officer issued final decision on written demand, as required for Court of Federal Claims to have jurisdiction over nonmonetary dispute under Contract Disputes Act (CDA), where government issued its proposed final evaluations of contractor's work, contractor submitted its comments protesting those evaluations, government issued final evaluations, and contractor submitted claim and supplemental claim to government, asserting regulatory violations in preparation of evaluations and lack of factual accuracy. Todd Const. L.P. v. U.S., Fed.Cl. 2008, 85 Fed.Cl. 34, subsequent determination 88 Fed.Cl. 235, subsequent determination 94 Fed.Cl. 100. United States ☞ 73(15)

Submission of a claim to the contracting officer and obtaining a decision on that claim is a jurisdictional prerequisite to an action in the Court of Federal Claims seeking review of the contracting officer's decision. Todd Const. L.P. v. U.S., Fed.Cl.2008, 85 Fed.Cl. 34, subsequent determination 88 Fed.Cl. 235, subsequent determination 94 Fed.Cl. 100. United States ☞ 73(9)

37. —— Miscellaneous decisions, final decision

Contracting officer's determination that United States was entitled to reduction in contract price for dam construction project as result of its decision permitting contractor to rewater site before testing gates and associated equipment was not product of her personal and independent judgment, and thus final decision was invalid, where contracting officer did not follow standard guidelines for issuing decisions on claims, final decision was entirely drafted by Army Corps of Engineers' counsel, and contracting officer did not attempt to verify accuracy of 564–day period that decision found was saved and did not review clauses and specifications of cited documents that were appended to final decision. Fireman's Fund Ins. Co. v. U.S., Fed. Cl.2010, 92 Fed.Cl. 598. United States ☞ 73(9)

Contracting officer's letters awarding damages to contractor based on National Interagency Fire Center's (NIFC) reassignment of contract to provide meals to firefighting crews did not constitute "final decision," as required under CDA, on grounds that contractor failed to comply with CDA requirement of certifying claims to contracting officer, and thus, NIFC was not bound by contracting officer's damages determinations that exceeded scope of his authority. OK's Cascade Co. v. U.S., Fed.Cl.2009, 87 Fed.Cl. 739. United States ☞ 73(15)

Army's refusal to allow military contractor admission to base in Iraq during deconstruction of contractor's temporary concrete factory for constructing concrete barriers, and Army's alleged failure to respond substantively to contractor's complaint filed in Court of Federal Claims asserting claim for $31 million in damages, did not constitute "final decision" by contracting officer constructively denying written certified claim, as required by CDA, thus barring claim for failure to exhaust administrative remedies. SITCO General Trading and Contracting Co. v. U.S., Fed.Cl.2009, 87 Fed.Cl. 506. United States ☞ 73(9)

Contracting officer's (CO) decision on government's defective pricing claim met the requirements of a valid final decision under the Contract Disputes Act; by referencing Defense Contract Audit Agency (DCAA) audit report as the grounds for the government's claim, the CO provided contractor with the reasons for her decision, and it was therefore not necessary for the CO to respond to contractor's later-refined version of its same arguments in her final decision. Saudi Logistics and Technical Support v. U.S., Fed.Cl.2009, 85 Fed.Cl. 747. United States ☞ 73(9)

38. Dismissal of claim

Contractor's claim under the Contract Disputes Act (CDA) was deemed denied, where contracting officer failed to issue a final decision after more than twenty-two months since contractor presented claim. BLR Group of America, Inc. v. U.S., Fed.Cl.2008, 84 Fed.Cl. 634. United States ☞ 73(13)

39a. Time for decision

The date of mailing of a contractor's claim to the contracting officer (CO) does not establish the starting date for the 60-day period required under the Contract Disputes Act (CDA) for a CO's deemed decision in the absence of facts confirming the contracting agency's receipt of the claim. Metrotop Plaza Associates v. U.S., Fed.Cl.2008, 82 Fed.Cl. 598. United States ☞ 73(13)

43a. Reconsideration

Contractor seeking declaratory judgment, under CDA, that government's change requests constituted breach of and cardinal change to lease for design, finance, and construction of project for National Oceanic and Atmospheric Administration failed to satisfy extraordinary circumstances required to justify reconsideration of order determining that Court of Federal Claims had jurisdiction to adjudicate contractor's claims but declining to grant declaratory relief at that juncture, since contractor had not challenged court's bases for declining declaratory relief due to fact questions that could not be resolved by declaratory judgment and due to court's substantial discretion to determine whether declaratory relief was appropriate, and contractor had not invoked special need for early resolution of legal issue. Maryland Enterprise, LLC v. U.S., Fed.Cl.2010, 93 Fed.Cl. 658.

44. Fraud exception

Contract claims against employees of tribal business involved fraud, and thus jurisdictional bar in Contract Disputes Act (CDA) did not apply to claims that employees filed false claims for brushing and road grading work performed under contract with Bureau of Indian Affairs (BIA); claims asserted that employees knowingly submitted invoices for work not performed and used false records to do so, and government alleged that motivation behind acts was fact that tribal business had used up substantial contract resources on unauthorized purchases, which resulted in need to submit false billings to government. U.S. v. Menominee Tribal Enterprises, E.D.Wis.2009, 601 F.Supp.2d 1061, reconsideration denied 2009 WL 1373952, entered 2009 WL 2877083. United States ☞ 73(9)

Under the Contract Disputes Act (CDA), contractor's claim certifications were substantively defective as to subcontractor's portion of claim, where contractor did not certify subcontractor's portion of claim in disregard of requirement that prime contractor must certify claim of subcontractor, where contractor was advised by outside consultant that subcontractor's claim might be fraudulent. Trafalgar House Constr., Inc. v. U.S., Fed.Cl.2006, 73 Fed.Cl. 675, subsequent determination 77 Fed.Cl. 48, affirmed 274 Fed. Appx. 898, 2008 WL 1734471. United States ☞ 73(9)

48. Weight and sufficiency of evidence

Sufficient evidence supported finding as to size of maintenance backlog of government vehicles inherited by contractor at start of vehicle maintenance contract, and as to costs of reducing backlog, in damages phase of contractor's Contract Disputes Act (CDA) claim seeking special compensation under contract for repair of inherited vehicle defects; in addition to evidence of defects already identified as of contract start date, contractor proffered evidence of inherited defects subsequently identified, based on parts found to be so far below standard that defects must have occurred before contract turnover. Tecom, Inc. v. U.S., Fed.Cl.2009, 86 Fed.Cl. 437, motion to amend denied 2009 WL 1470475. United States ☞ 74(11)

In government contractor's Contract Disputes Act (CDA) claim seeking special compensation under vehicle maintenance contract for repair of inherited vehicle defects, government expert's damages testimony was entitled to little weight, both because of expert's use of disfavored "total cost method" for analyzing contractor's increased costs, and because expert ignored contract's special compensation clause applicable to any excess maintenance backlog left over from incumbent contractor; expert incorrectly assumed that clause provided for compensation only to extent that costs exceeded bid amounts. Tecom, Inc. v. U.S., Fed.Cl.2009, 86 Fed.Cl. 437, motion to amend denied 2009 WL 1470475. United States ☞ 74(12.1)

See Revised Title 41, post

§ 606. Contractor's right of appeal to board of contract appeals

Notes of Decisions

2. Election of forum

Pursuant to election doctrine, contractor's election of forum by pursuing appeal with Armed Services Board of Contract Appeals (ASBCA), challenging contracting officer's final decision (COFD) on contract with Navy to remove and dispose of industrial waste sludge, under CDA, precluded contractor from pursuing appeal of same COFD in Court of Federal Claims. Nwogu v. U.S., Fed.Cl.2010, 94 Fed.Cl. 637. United States ⬤ 73(15).

4. Time of filing appeal

Contractor satisfied jurisdictional requirements, under CDA and federal acquisition regulations, for claims arising from Defense Acquisition University's (DAU) alleged appropriation of contractor's proprietary data in breach of confidentiality and non-disclosure agreement and breach of contracts purportedly implied-in-fact from proprietary data legends on contractor's learning tool products purchased by DAU via General Services Administration (GSA) schedule contracts; contractor timely submitted written claim to contracting officer (CO) seeking, as matter of right, payment of breach of contract damages, CO either provided to contractor written decision setting forth CO's reason for denying claim and apprising contractor of right to appeal, or alternatively CO failed to issue decision thus resulting in deemed denial, contractor filed appeal in Court of Federal Claims within one year of receiving CO's decision, contractor's appeal arose from same facts and sought same relief as original claim submitted to CO, and contractor did not first appeal claim to another forum. Paradigm Learning, Inc. v. U.S., Fed. Cl.2010, 93 Fed.Cl. 465. United States ⬤ 73(15).

§ 607. Agency boards of contract appeals

[See main volume for text of (a) to (c)]

(d) Jurisdiction

The Armed Services Board shall have jurisdiction to decide any appeal from a decision of a contracting officer of the Department of Defense, the Department of the Army, the Department of the Navy, the Department of the Air Force, or the National Aeronautics and Space Administration relative to a contract made by that department or agency. The Civilian Board shall have jurisdiction to decide any appeal from a decision of a contracting officer of any executive agency (other than the Department of Defense, the Department of the Army, the Department of the Navy, the Department of the Air Force, the National Aeronautics and Space Administration, the United States Postal Service, the Postal Regulatory Commission, or the Tennessee Valley Authority) relative to a contract made by that agency. Each other agency board shall have jurisdiction to decide any appeal from a decision of a contracting officer relative to a contract made by its agency. In exercising this jurisdiction, the agency board is authorized to grant any relief that would be available to a litigant asserting a contract claim in the United States Court of Federal Claims. Notwithstanding any other provision of this section and any other provision of law, an appeal from a decision of a contracting officer of the Central Intelligence Agency relative to a contract made by that Agency may be filed with whichever of the Armed Services Board of Contract Appeals or the Civilian Board of Contract Appeals is specified by such contracting officer as the Board to which such an appeal may be made and such Board shall have jurisdiction to decide that appeal.

[See main volume for text of (e) to (i)]

(Pub.L. 95–563, § 8, Nov. 1, 1978, 92 Stat. 2385; Pub.L. 97–164, Title I, §§ 156, 160(a)(15), Apr. 2, 1982, 96 Stat. 47, 48; Pub.L. 101–509, Title V, § 529 [Title I, § 104(d)(4)], Nov. 5, 1990, 104 Stat. 1447; Pub.L. 101–552, § 6(b), Nov. 15, 1990, 104 Stat. 2746; Pub.L. 102–572, Title IX, § 902(b)(1), Oct. 29, 1992, 106 Stat. 4516; Pub.L. 103–355, Title II, § 2351(c), Oct. 13, 1994, 108 Stat. 3322; Pub.L. 109–163, Div. A, Title VIII, § 847(d)(2) to (4), Jan. 6, 2006, 119 Stat. 3393, 3394; Pub.L. 109–435, Title VI, § 604(f), Dec. 20, 2006, 120 Stat. 3242; Pub.L. 111–259, Title IV, § 422, Oct. 7, 2010, 124 Stat. 2727.)

HISTORICAL AND STATUTORY NOTES

Amendments

2010 Amendments. Subsec. (d). Pub.L. 111–259, § 421, following the last sentence, inserted "Notwithstanding any other provision of this section and any other provision of law, an appeal from a decision of a contracting officer of the Central Intelligence Agency relative to a contract made by that Agency may be filed with whichever of the Armed Services Board of Contract Appeals or the Civilian Board of Contract

Text Repealed by Pub.L. 111–350, effective Jan. 4, 2011

Appeals is specified by such contracting officer as the Board to which such an appeal may be made and such Board shall have jurisdiction to decide that appeal."

Boards of Contract Appeals; Transfers; Termination; References

Pub.L. 109–163, Div. A, Title VIII, § 847(b), (c), (e), Jan. 6, 2006, 119 Stat. 3392, 3394, which provided for transfer of personnel employed in connection with, and the assets, liabilities, contracts, property, records, and unexpended balance of appropriations, authorizations, allocations, and other funds employed, held, used, arising from, available to, or to be made available in connection with the functions vested by

law in the agency boards of contract appeals, termination of certain agency boards of contract appeals, and provides that references to agency boards of contract appeals other than Armed Services Board of Contract Appeals, the board of contract appeals of the Tennessee Valley Authority, or the Postal Service Board of Contract Appeals in any provision of law or in any rule, regulation, or other paper of the United States shall be treated as referring to the Civilian Board of Contract Appeals, was editorially eliminated from the Code as a result of the enactment into positive law of Title 41, Public Contracts, by Pub.L. 111–350, Jan. 4, 2011, 124 Stat. 3677.

CODE OF FEDERAL REGULATIONS

Housing and Urban Development Department, see 24 CFR § 20.1 et seq.

LAW REVIEW AND JOURNAL COMMENTARIES

Arbitration: A permissible or desirable method for resolving disputes involving federal acquisition and assistance contracts? Kirby Behre, 16 Pub.Cont.L.J. 66 (1986)

Doing business with the government. Peter C. Mieres (February 1982) 4 L.A.Law. 34.

LIBRARY REFERENCES

American Digest System

United States ⊚33, 73(15).
Key Number System Topic No. 393.

Research References

ALR Library

185 ALR, Fed. 419, Construction and Application of Federal Crop Insurance Act, 7 U.S.C.A. §§ 1501 et seq.

96 ALR, Fed. 336, What Constitutes "Adversary Adjudication" by Administrative Agency Entitling Prevailing Party to Award of Attorneys' Fees Under Equal Access to Justice Act (5 U.S.C.A. § 504).

97 ALR, Fed. 694, Jurisdiction of United States Court of Appeals for Federal Circuit Under 28 U.S.C.A. §§ 1292 and 1295.

93 ALR, Fed. 886, Federal Government Liability for Loss Of, or Damage To, Vessels or Vehicles Seized in Course of Drug Enforcement Activity.

2 ALR, Fed. 691, Judicial Review Under Wunderlich Act (41 U.S.C.A. §§ 321, 322), of Federal Administrative Decisions Made Under Standard "Disputes" Clauses in Government Contracts.

Encyclopedias

14 Am. Jur. Trials 437, Representing the Government Contractor.

Am. Jur. 2d Federal Courts § 2011, Suits Under Contract Disputes Act.

Am. Jur. 2d Public Works and Contracts § 212, Appeal to an Agency Board of Contract Appeals.

Am. Jur. 2d Public Works and Contracts § 213, Appeal to an Agency Board of Contract Appeals--Appeals; Finality of Decisions of Agen-

cy Board of Contract Appeals; Questions of Law and Fact.

Forms

Federal Procedural Forms § 34:102, Introduction to Boards of Contract Appeals.

Federal Procedural Forms § 34:116, Relief Available.

Federal Procedural Forms § 34:220, Finality of Decision.

Federal Procedural Forms § 34:277, Motion in Limine to Establish Order of Proof and Limit Proof--Before Armed Services Board of Contract Appeals [48 C.F.R. Ch 2, Appx A, ASBCA Rule 5(B)].

Federal Procedural Forms § 34:302, Appeals by Contractors.

Federal Procedural Forms § 34:303, Appeals by the Government.

Federal Procedural Forms § 34:304, Appeals from Decisions of TVA BCA.

Federal Procedural Forms § 34:311, Petition in Court of Appeals--For Review of Decision of Board of Contract Appeals--Liquidated Damages Wrongfully Assessed Against Contractor [28 U.S.C.A. § 1295(A)(10); 41 U.S.C.A....

Federal Procedural Forms § 34:516, Introduction.

8 West's Federal Forms § 13011, Overview.

8 West's Federal Forms § 13023, Appeals from the Boards of Contract Appeals Under the Contract Disputes Act.

8 West's Federal Forms § 13102, Formal Brief of Appellant--Appeal from Board of Contract Appeals.

See Revised Title 41, post

8 West's Federal Forms § 13223, Government Contract Claims--Claims Under the Contract Disputes Act.

Am. Jur. Pl. & Pr. Forms Aviation § 98, Petition in Federal Court--Inverse Condemnation--Invasion of Airspace--Flights of Military Aircraft at Low Level Over Land Adjoining Military Airfield.

Am. Jur. Pl. & Pr. Forms Public Works & Contracts § 80, Notice of Appeal--To Board of Contract Appeals--Short Form.

Am. Jur. Pl. & Pr. Forms Space Law § 25, Notice of Appeal--To Board of Contract Appeals--Under Contract Disputes Act of 1978.

Treatises and Practice Aids

Federal Procedure, Lawyers Edition § 76:6, Department of Transportation Proceedings Covered by the Equal Access to Justice Act.

Federal Procedure, Lawyers Edition § 19:65, Suits Under Contract Disputes Act.

Federal Procedure, Lawyers Edition § 2:253, Adversary Adjudication Defined.

Federal Procedure, Lawyers Edition § 7:902, Introduction; Covered Proceedings and Applicants.

Federal Procedure, Lawyers Edition § 34:126, Types of Proceedings Covered.

Federal Procedure, Lawyers Edition § 34:134, Further Proceedings.

Federal Procedure, Lawyers Edition § 34:136, Administrative and Judicial Review.

Federal Procedure, Lawyers Edition § 39:824, Judicial Review of Arbitration Award.

Federal Procedure, Lawyers Edition § 39:849, Introduction.

Federal Procedure, Lawyers Edition § 39:850, Composition of Boards of Contract Appeals.

Federal Procedure, Lawyers Edition § 39:911, Form and Content of Notice.

Federal Procedure, Lawyers Edition § 44:126, Proceedings to Which EAJA and Implementing Rules Apply.

Federal Procedure, Lawyers Edition § 39:1081, Form of Decision.

Federal Procedure, Lawyers Edition § 39:1082, Transmission to Parties.

Federal Procedure, Lawyers Edition § 39:1083, Finality of Decision.

Federal Procedure, Lawyers Edition § 39:1121, Appeals by Contractors, Generally.

Federal Procedure, Lawyers Edition § 39:1122, Appeals by Government, Generally.

Federal Procedure, Lawyers Edition § 39:1123, Appeals from Decisions of Tennessee Valley Authority BCA.

Federal Procedure, Lawyers Edition § 39:1390, Applicability to Nasa Adjudications.

Immigration Law Service 2d PSD 1991 GEN COUNCEL OP, General Counsel's Opinions.

Patent Law Fundamentals App. 20(A), 28 U.S.C.A. § 1295--Jurisdiction of U.S. Court of Appeals for the Federal Circuit.

West's Federal Administrative Practice § 446, Department of Veterans Affairs--Board of Contract Appeals.

West's Federal Administrative Practice § 673, Contract Disputes Litigation--Boards of Contract Appeals.

West's Federal Administrative Practice § 675, Types of Proceedings.

West's Federal Administrative Practice § 676, Remedies and Appeals.

West's Federal Administrative Practice § 810, Time in Which to File; Statutes of Limitations; Laches; Equitable Estoppel.

West's Federal Administrative Practice § 819, Jurisdiction Concurrent With United States District Courts; Transfer of Jurisdiction.

West's Federal Administrative Practice § 8005, Courts of Special Jurisdiction--Federal Circuit.

Wright & Miller: Federal Prac. & Proc. App E.A.J.A., Equal Access to Justice Act.

Notes of Decisions

Court of Federal Claims review   11a
Small claims accelerated procedure   12

7. Court of appeals review—Generally

To extent that contractor appealed Interior Board of Contract Appeals' (IBCA) dismissal of contractor's appeal of National Park Service's (NPS) termination for default of contract to replace underground storage tanks, based on settlement agreement between contractor and NPS, and to extent that contractor appealed IBCA's dismissal of contractor's motion for reconsideration and subsequent duplicative appeal, such appeals were not reviewable in Court of Federal Claims, under CDA, authorizing exclusive review of IBCA's actions by Federal Circuit. Environmental Safety Consultants, Inc. v. U.S., Fed.Cl.2010, 95 Fed.Cl. 77, subsequent determination 2011 WL 488685. United States ☞ 73(15)

8. —— Issues reviewable, court of appeals review

Contractor's alleged settlement agreement with government was not valid, whereby contractor purportedly agreed to dismiss judicial appeals of breach of contract claims in exchange for government's agreement not to pursue setoff and to pay contractor $93,989.00, plus interest, awarded by Armed Services Board of Contract Appeals (ASBCA), since there was no evidence of meeting of minds as to critical elements of agreement or that any individual with requisite authority consented to agreement on behalf of government. Nwogu v. U.S., Fed.Cl.2010, 94 Fed.Cl. 637. United States ☞ 74(6)

11a. Court of Federal Claims review

Any claims by contractor that Armed Services Board of Contract Appeals (ASBCA) wrongfully dismissed contractor's breach of contract claims, arising from Department of Navy's termination for default on contract for removal of storage tanks and contaminated materials, and that ASBCA's dismissal was ultimate breach, were

Text Repealed by Pub.L. 111–350, effective Jan. 4, 2011

not reviewable in Court of Federal Claims, under election doctrine applicable to CDA claims, since ASBCA's actions were reviewable only by Federal Circuit after contractor elected to appeal contracting officer's final decision to ASBCA rather than to Court of Federal Claims. Environmental Safety Consultants, Inc. v. U.S., Fed.Cl.2010, 95 Fed.Cl. 77, subsequent determination 2011 WL 488685. United States ⌖ 73(15)

12. Small claims accelerated procedure

A contractor does not have an absolute right under the Contract Disputes Act (CDA) to the Small Claims Accelerated Procedure on appeal to the board of contract appeals to prevent the application of claim preclusion. Phillips/May Corp. v. U.S., C.A.Fed.2008, 524 F.3d 1264, rehearing denied. Administrative Law And Procedure ⌖ 501; United States ⌖ 73(15)

§ 609. Judicial review of board decisions

Notes of Decisions

Abuse of discretion standard of review, review of board decisions 22b
Attorney fees 52
Claims preclusion doctrine 26a
Damages 53
De novo standard of review, review of board decisions 22a
Mootness, time for filing 14a
Reconsideration of decision, time of filing 13a
Review of board decisions 22-26
    Abuse of discretion standard of review 22b
    De novo standard of review 22a
Time for filing 11-20
    Mootness 14a
    Reconsideration of decision 13a

3. Law governing

Use of general principles, due to lack of directly applicable Mexican statute, was not warranted to hold United States, as tenant of residence in Juárez, Chihuahua, Mexico, accountable for multiple ten percent increases of rent over four-year period, where landlord had legal recourse under CDA three years earlier and related statute did not contemplate multiple extensions and increases in rent. Fernandez de Iglesias v. U.S., Fed.Cl.2010, 2010 WL 5176664. United States ⌖ 70(16)

Transportation service providers' (TSPs) claims for reimbursement by Surface Deployment and Distribution Command (SDDC) of one-percent fees charged by bank as middle man for TSPs and SDDC on contracts to transport personal property were governed under Interstate Commerce Act (ICA), not CDA, even though TSPs argued that they sought reimbursement of fees rather than transportation charges, since claims for payment of money arose out of transportation service contracts with SDDC, and more specific provisions of ICA trumped provisions of CDA. Allstar Mayflower, LLC v. U.S., Fed.Cl.2010, 93 Fed.Cl. 169. United States ⌖ 73(9)

5. Election of forum

Pursuant to election doctrine, contractor's election of forum by pursuing appeal with Armed Services Board of Contract Appeals (ASBCA), challenging contracting officer's final decision (COFD) on contract with Navy to remove and dispose of industrial waste sludge,

under CDA, precluded contractor from pursuing appeal of same COFD in Court of Federal Claims. Nwogu v. U.S., Fed.Cl.2010, 94 Fed.Cl. 637. United States ⌖ 73(15)

Action in Court of Federal Claims by provider of information security solutions seeking damages for federal agency's alleged breach of license agreement was barred by pendency of provider's district court action alleging that agency's actions violated Lanham Act, even though provider included certain facts in one complaint and not in other, and suits were based on different legal theories, where both actions were based on agency's allegedly wrongful development of competing product, in contravention of its agreement to cooperate with provider in submission and promotion of its offering, and both suits sought $15 million in monetary damages. Trusted Integration, Inc. v. U.S., Fed.Cl. 2010, 93 Fed.Cl. 94. Federal Courts ⌖ 1145

Under Election Doctrine, lessor's prior appeal of contracting officer's final decision to agency board of contract appeals barred lessor's action against federal government in Court of Federal Claims which alleged that government breached lease by withholding rent on account of subcontractor's alleged failure to achieve final completion of construction project under lease-to-build arrangement; lessor's action challenged government's monthly cure proposal notices regarding amount of rent withheld to cover costs of curing subcontractor's default, but notices were supplemental to, not distinct from, contracting officer's final decision which determined that subcontractor was in default and which elected to withhold rent. BRC Lease Co. v. U.S., Fed.Cl.2010, 93 Fed.Cl. 67. United States ⌖ 73(15)

Under the election of forum doctrine of the Contract Disputes Act (CDA), Court of Federal Claims lacked jurisdiction to enforce awards of Value Engineering Change Proposal (VECP) royalty payments made to contractor by the Armed Services Board of Contract Appeals (ASBCA) but paid to bank as contractor's assignee; since contractor elected to pursue his VECP claims before the ASBCA instead of the Court of Federal Claims, any disagreement concerning payment of the royalties to bank should have been brought to the ASBCA or to the Court of Appeals for the Federal Circuit. Bianchi v. U.S., Fed.Cl.2005, 68 Fed.Cl. 442, affirmed in part, reversed in part and remanded 475 F.3d 1268, rehearing and rehearing en banc denied. United States ⌖ 73(15)

See Revised Title 41, post

6. Jurisdiction of Court of Federal Claims—Generally

Claims concerning termination of a contract between an executive agency and an independent contractor are contractual, and thus fall within the exclusive jurisdiction of the Court of Federal Claims. Vero Technical Support, Inc. v. U.S. Dept. of Defense, S.D.Fla.2010, 733 F.Supp.2d 1336. Federal Courts ☞ 1139

Court of Federal Claims had exclusive jurisdiction, under Administrative Dispute Resolution Act (ADRA) amendments to Tucker Act, over government contractor's challenge to Department of Defense's (DOD's) decision to insource weather-related services which were currently provided by contractor under procurement arrangement; despite contention that insourcing was not procurement-related, it was DOD's decision not to procure something, not the act of insourcing itself, that was at issue, moreover, statutory definition of procurement was broad enough to include decision not to procure, either as a matter of "determining a need" for procurement or deciding whether to continue procurement arrangement, and determination that insourcing dispute was within Court of Federal Claims's exclusive jurisdiction was consistent with policy behind ADRA to create a place of uniform jurisdiction over all manner of procurement-related disputes. Vero Technical Support, Inc. v. U.S. Dept. of Defense, S.D.Fla.2010, 733 F.Supp.2d 1336. Federal Courts ☞ 1141

Contractor's claim for enforcement of monetary judgment by Armed Services Board of Contract Appeals (ASBCA), in amount of $93,989.00, plus interest, arising from terminated contract with Navy to remove and dispose of industrial waste sludge, was not reviewable by Court of Federal Claims, since ASBCA final decisions could only be reviewed by Court of Appeals for Federal Circuit. Nwogu v. U.S., Fed.Cl.2010, 94 Fed.Cl. 637. United States ☞ 73(15)

Incumbent small business contractor's claims challenging Air Force's alleged statutory and regulatory violations by exiting small business program and instead procuring credit reports using General Services Administration (GSA) Federal Supply Schedule (FSS), after declining to exercise option to extend credit reports contract with incumbent contractor, involved "procurement," within meaning of Tucker Act provision governing bid protest jurisdiction, since claims did not concern administration of prior contract, but rather, concerned new FSS procurement of credit reports that allegedly should have been obtained through small business program. K-Lak Corp. v. U.S., Fed.Cl.2010, 93 Fed.Cl. 749. United States ☞ 64.60(1)

To extent that contractor appealed Interior Board of Contract Appeals' (IBCA) dismissal of contractor's appeal of National Park Service's (NPS) termination for default of contract to replace underground storage tanks, based on settlement agreement between contractor and NPS, and to extent that contractor appealed IBCA's dismissal of contractor's motion for reconsideration and subsequent duplicative appeal,

such appeals were not reviewable in Court of Federal Claims, under CDA, authorizing exclusive review of IBCA's actions by Federal Circuit. Environmental Safety Consultants, Inc. v. U.S., Fed.Cl.2010, 95 Fed.Cl. 77, subsequent determination 2011 WL 488685. United States ☞ 73(15)

Potential competitors' claims that Air Force's non-competitive exercise of options for four other holders of contracts to supply medical services violated Competition in Contracting Act (CICA) and federal acquisition regulation concerned "procurement or a proposed procurement," within meaning of Tucker Act's bid protest jurisdiction, not a matter of contract administration as would have required competitors to pursue remedy under CDA, since competitors were not protesting Air Force's refusal to exercise their own options, and no cardinal change in modification to existing contracts was required for bid protest alleging violation of statute or regulation in connection with procurement that should have been bid competitively. Magnum Opus Technologies, Inc. v. U.S., Fed.Cl.2010, 94 Fed.Cl. 512, motion to amend denied 94 Fed.Cl. 553. United States ☞ 64.60(1)

Court of Federal Claims has jurisdiction under the Contract Disputes Act (CDA) to hear claims of bad faith and abuse of discretion in the administration and termination of a contract. Digital Technologies, Inc. v. U.S., Fed.Cl.2009, 89 Fed.Cl. 711. United States ☞ 73(15)

Equitable considerations are not within the Court of Federal Claims' review, under the CDA. Public Service Co. Of Oklahoma v. U.S., Fed.Cl.2009, 88 Fed.Cl. 250. United States ☞ 73(15)

Plaintiff asserting a claim against the United States, under the CDA, must establish jurisdiction by a preponderance of the evidence. SIT-CO General Trading and Contracting Co. v. U.S., Fed.Cl.2009, 87 Fed.Cl. 506. United States ☞ 73(15)

8. —— Submission of claim, jurisdiction of Court of Federal Claims

Even if United States had actual knowledge of amount and basis of construction contractor's claim for time extension on window and roof replacement project for Navy, nothing in the CDA excused construction contractor's noncompliance with CDA's explicit claim requirements, and thus Court of Federal Claims lacked subject matter jurisdiction over contractor's breach of contract claim against the United States under the CDA. M. Maropakis Carpentry, Inc. v. U.S., C.A.Fed.2010, 609 F.3d 1323. United States ☞ 73(9)

Unsuccessful bidder's letter to Army and Air Force Exchange Service (AAFES) official did not satisfy Contract Disputes Act's (CDA) written demand requirement, and thus Court of Federal Claims lacked jurisdiction over bidder's challenge to award of concessionaire contract, where letter concerned different contract, official was not contracting officer overseeing her concessionaire contract, and letter did not address bidder's concessionaire contract. Terry v. U.S., Fed.Cl.2010, 2010 WL 5097766. United States ☞ 73(9)

Contractor's letter sent to counsel for United States Postal Service (USPS), seeking unspecified amount of reimbursement for costs of delays allegedly caused by USPS on contract to construct carrier annex, for additional work performed, and for associated interest, did not qualify as "claim," within meaning of CDA, precluding jurisdiction over contractor's breach of contract claim based on allegedly unpaid costs of continued work, since letter was neither addressed to nor offered to contracting officer (CO) for final decision, letter did not make specific claim for sum certain or establish any entitlement to relief, CO never issued final decision regarding letter, and claim could not have been deemed denied as CO never received letter. L.A. Ruiz Associates, Inc. v. U.S., Fed.Cl.2010, 94 Fed.Cl. 768. United States ☞ 73(9)

10. —— Decision of contracting officer, jurisdiction of Court of Federal Claims

Construction contractor's letter to contracting officer for United States Navy on window and roof replacement project, which reiterated contractor's earlier request for extension of time to complete project, was not valid "claim" within meaning of Contract Disputes Act (CDA), and thus Court of Federal Claims lacked subject matter jurisdiction over contractor's breach of contract claim under the CDA, where contractor's letter did not provide contracting officer adequate notice of total number of days actually requested in extension, did not state sum certain that contractor sought, and did not request officer issue final decision on contractor's request. M. Maropakis Carpentry, Inc. v. U.S., C.A.Fed. 2010, 609 F.3d 1323. United States ☞ 73(9)

Contractor satisfied jurisdictional requirements, under CDA and federal acquisition regulations, for claims arising from Defense Acquisition University's (DAU) alleged appropriation of contractor's proprietary data in breach of confidentiality and non-disclosure agreement and breach of contracts purportedly implied-in-fact from proprietary data legends on contractor's learning tool products purchased by DAU via General Services Administration (GSA) schedule contracts; contractor timely submitted written claim to contracting officer (CO) seeking, as matter of right, payment of breach of contract damages, CO either provided to contractor written decision setting forth CO's reason for denying claim and apprising contractor of right to appeal, or alternatively CO failed to issue decision thus resulting in deemed denial, contractor filed appeal in Court of Federal Claims within one year of receiving CO's decision, contractor's appeal arose from same facts and sought same relief as original claim submitted to CO, and contractor did not first appeal claim to another forum. Paradigm Learning, Inc. v. U.S., Fed. Cl.2010, 93 Fed.Cl. 465. United States ☞ 73(15)

Contractor's written response to the initial CPAR (Contractor Performance Assessment Reporting System) did not constitute a "claim"

so as to satisfy the Contract Disputes Act (CDA) jurisdictional prerequisites for asserting a claim for nonmonetary relief; although contractor requested that the initial CPAR be reevaluated, it did not request that the contracting officer exercise his discretion to reevaluate the initial CPAR and correct the ratings and narrative. Kemron Environmental Services, Inc. v. U.S., Fed.Cl. 2010, 93 Fed.Cl. 74. United States ☞ 73(9)

Court of Federal Claims had jurisdiction under Tucker Act over timber contractor's claim under Contract Disputes Act (CDA) that Forest Service wrongfully suspended timber sales contracts, where contracting officer issued final decisions granting contractor limited relief on, but otherwise denying, its claims on contracts. Scott Timber, Inc. v. U.S., Fed.Cl.2009, 86 Fed. Cl. 102. Federal Courts ☞ 1076; United States ☞ 73(9)

11. Time for filing—Generally

One year limitations period for government to bring suit to recover equitable adjustment allowed by contracting officer in contract modification began to run when Federal Circuit affirmed decision of Court of Federal Claims denying contractor leave to amend its complaint to challenge contracting officer's final decision to not award entire amount that contractor had requested. U.S. v. Renda Marine, Inc., E.D.Tex.2010, 2010 WL 3909237. Limitation Of Actions ☞ 46(6)

Contractor's breach of contract claim, based on Navy allegedly preventing contractor from performing contract to remove and dispose of industrial waste sludge, was timely filed with contracting officer, under CDA provision, requiring claims to be submitted to contracting officer for final decision within six years of accrual of claim, within six years of contractor and Navy executing bilateral modification terminating contract. Nwogu v. U.S., Fed.Cl.2010, 94 Fed.Cl. 637. United States ☞ 73(9)

The passage of time does not transform a claim brought pursuant to the deemed denial provision of the CDA into one covered by the Tucker Act's general six-year statute of limitations. System Planning Corp. v. U.S., Fed.Cl. 2010, 95 Fed.Cl. 1. United States ☞ 73(13)

Period under Contracts Dispute Act (CDA) to dispute decision of contracting officer in federal court had to be calculated as 12 calendar months, instead of 365 days. Quillen v. U.S., Fed.Cl.2009, 89 Fed.Cl. 148. United States ☞ 73(15)

Contractor's certified monetary claim for $329,457.75 against United States for alleged breach of contract, under which contractor provided prosthetic and orthotic devices and services to veterans on behalf of Department of Veterans Affairs (VA), accrued, commencing under CDA's 12-month limitations period, on date of contracting officer's (CO) final decision in letter denying contractor's certified monetary claim, not CO's prior final decision in letter terminating contract. Kenney Orthopedic, LLC v. U.S., Fed.Cl.2009, 88 Fed.Cl. 688. Federal Courts ☞ 1107

See Revised Title 41, post

13. —— Decision of contracting officer, time for filing

Contractor's breach of contract claim against United States, arising from Navy allegedly preventing contractor from performing contract to remove and dispose of industrial waste sludge, accrued, commencing under Contract Disputes Act's one-year statute of limitations, on date that contractor received contracting officer's final decision (COFD) denying majority of contractor's claim. Nwogu v. U.S., Fed.Cl.2010, 94 Fed.Cl. 637. Federal Courts ☞ 1107

Contractor's claim that Department of Navy breached contract for removal of storage tanks and contaminated materials, by allegedly withholding progress payments and failing to pay for work completed, would accrue, commencing under CDA's one-year limitations period, on date that contractor would receive contracting officer's final decision. Environmental Safety Consultants, Inc. v. U.S., Fed.Cl.2010, 95 Fed.Cl. 77, subsequent determination 2011 WL 488685. United States ☞ 73(15)

Contractor's appeal of decision of contracting officer denying its claims for indirect contract support costs for fiscal years 1993-1996 was barred as untimely under the Contract Disputes Act (CDA), where action was filed more that one year after CO's final decision. Ramah Navajo School Bd., Inc. v. U.S., Fed.Cl.2008, 83 Fed.Cl. 786, appeal filed. United States ☞ 73(15)

13a. —— Reconsideration of decision, time of filing

Finality of decision of contracting officer (CO) denying contractor's claim for real estates taxes on office space leased to the General Services Administration (GSA) was suspended for purposes of statute of limitations of the Contract Disputes Act (CDA), where efforts that contractor pursued to engage agency in discussions regarding the tax issue after receipt of CO's final decision could substantively be viewed as a request for reconsideration, and CO's letter proposing a compromise of the dispute reflected reconsideration of CO's prior decision. Metrotop Plaza Associates v. U.S., Fed.Cl.2008, 82 Fed.Cl. 598. Federal Courts ☞ 1107

14. —— Deemed denials, time for filing

Contracting officer's failure to issue decision on contractor's written comments to Air Force in response to allegedly unfair and inaccurate evaluation of contractor's past contract performance, in contractor performance assessment report (CPAR) that was required to be fair and accurate, under federal acquisition regulation (FAR), did not constitute deemed denial of CDA claim, since contractor had not submitted valid CDA claim demanding relief arising under or relating to contract, but rather, only submitted comments that contracting officer would have had no reason to believe required further action once comments were referred to reviewing official. BLR Group of America, Inc. v. U.S., Fed. Cl.2010, 94 Fed.Cl. 354, reconsideration denied 96 Fed.Cl. 9. United States ☞ 73(13)

CDA's one-year limitations period, accruing from date of contractor's receipt of decision of contracting officer, applied to contractor's deemed denied claim against United States for additional negotiated fee of $7,039,870 pursuant to amendment of contract to provide new security system to protect United States Air Force (USAF) facilities, rather than general six-year limitations period under Tucker Act, governing claims over which Court of Federal Claims had jurisdiction. System Planning Corp. v. U.S., Fed.Cl.2010, 95 Fed.Cl. 1. United States ☞ 73(15)

14a. —— Mootness, time for filing

Contractor's action seeking revision or rescission of Air Force's allegedly unfair and inaccurate performance evaluation, in contractor performance assessment report (CPAR) posted on past performance informational retrieval system (PPIRS), was not rendered moot by removal and archival of contractor's CPAR from PPIRS or by either former or amended version of federal acquisition regulation (FAR), requiring procuring agencies to use contractor's PPIRS information if related to contract performance completed within last three years, since contractor had legally cognizable interest in outcome due to CPAR's continued availability to agencies and potential to substantially damage contractor's business reputation, as agencies could request information from contractor concerning prior contract even though CPAR no longer appeared on PPIRS and performance was completed over three years ago. BLR Group of America, Inc. v. U.S., Fed.Cl.2010, 94 Fed.Cl. 354, reconsideration denied 96 Fed.Cl. 9. United States ☞ 73(15)

15. —— Receipt by contractor, time for filing

Contract Disputes Act (CDA) barred judicial review of final decision of contracting officer (CO) in favor of government on its counterclaims against contractor, where contractor failed to challenge decision in Court of Federal Claims within twelve months after receipt of decision. Renda Marine, Inc. v. U.S., C.A.Fed.2007, 509 F.3d 1372, rehearing and rehearing en banc denied. United States ☞ 73(15)

Contractor's claim that Department of Navy breached contract for removal of storage tanks and contaminated materials, by terminating contract and transferring contractor's contractual rights to local contractor, accrued, commencing under CDA's one-year limitations period, on date of contractor's receipt of final decision of contracting officer terminating contract for default. Environmental Safety Consultants, Inc. v. U.S., Fed.Cl.2010, 95 Fed.Cl. 77, subsequent determination 2011 WL 488685. United States ☞ 73(15)

A contracting officer must present objective indicia of receipt by the contractor in order to establish the date of receipt, to determine compliance with the dispute provision of the Contracts Dispute Act (CDA). Quillen v. U.S., Fed. Cl.2009, 89 Fed.Cl. 148. United States ☞ 73(9)

Text Repealed by Pub.L. 111–350, effective Jan. 4, 2011

21. Finality of decision

There was no just reason for delaying government's payment, pursuant to judgment fund statute, of partial final judgment in favor of contractor on CDA claims, with respect to unpaid balance of contract price for constructing laboratory building for National Institutes of Health (NIH), damages for unresolved changes not addressed in any contract modification, and pass through claims on behalf of subcontractors, since judgment on those damages claims was final, government's liability was established, claims would have no possible effect on remand proceedings, claims would never again be reviewed on appeal, and delayed payment would needlessly increase interest on damages. Bell BCI Co. v. U.S., Fed.Cl.2010, 91 Fed.Cl. 664. United States ☞ 73(15)

Contractor satisfied CDA requirements for commencing suit against United States, by submitting certified claim to contracting officer (CO) alleging that United States owed additional negotiated fee of $7,039,870 pursuant to amendment on contract to provide new security system to protect United States Air Force (USAF) facilities, even though CO had not issued final decision, since contractor's claim was deemed denied by CO after waiting nearly seven years for final decision that CO failed to issue within reasonable time. System Planning Corp. v. U.S., Fed. Cl.2010, 95 Fed.Cl. 1. United States ☞ 73(13)

Contracting officer's letter terminating contract, due to alleged default by contractor providing prosthetic and orthotic devices and services to veterans on behalf of Department of Veterans Affairs (VA), constituted appealable "final decision," under CDA, on government claim of termination for cause against contractor. Kenney Orthopedic, LLC v. U.S., Fed.Cl. 2009, 88 Fed.Cl. 688. United States ☞ 73(15)

Original decision by Department of Transportation Board of Contract Appeals, regarding corrections center service company's claim for interest on unpaid wages, fringe benefits, and associated taxes under Contract Dispute Act (CDA), was not final, since quantum issues were still outstanding, and thus board was free to reexamine claim in light of intervening case law. Schleicher Community Corrections Center, Inc. v. Gonzales, C.A.Fed.2007, 212 Fed.Appx. 972, 2007 WL 43260, Unreported, rehearing and rehearing en banc denied 219 Fed.Appx. 996, 2007 WL 930738. United States ☞ 73(15)

22. Review of board decisions—Generally

Contractor's alleged settlement agreement with government was not valid, whereby contractor purportedly agreed to dismiss judicial appeals of breach of contract claims in exchange for government's agreement not to pursue setoff and to pay contractor $93,989.00, plus interest, awarded by Armed Services Board of Contract Appeals (ASBCA), since there was no evidence of meeting of minds as to critical elements of agreement or that any individual with requisite authority consented to agreement on behalf of government. Nwogu v. U.S., Fed.Cl.2010, 94 Fed.Cl. 637. United States ☞ 74(6)

22a. —— De novo standard of review, review of board decisions,

Administrative Procedure Act (APA) standard of review applies to bid protests, while de novo review is mandated for CDA claims. Todd Const., L.P. v. U.S., Fed.Cl.2009, 88 Fed.Cl. 235, subsequent determination 94 Fed.Cl. 100. United States ☞ 64.60(3.1); United States ☞ 73(15)

22b. —— Abuse of discretion standard of review, review of board decisions

Government contractor's allegations regarding lack of responsibility for subcontractors working on roofing projects were legal conclusions, not fact, and were inconsistent with applicable law, holding contractor responsible for unexcused performance failures of subcontractors, and thus, allegations did not plausibly suggest entitlement to relief from contractor's negative performance evaluation by Corps of Engineers (COE), which did not abuse discretion in evaluating the contractor. Todd Construction, L.P. v. U.S., Fed.Cl.2010, 94 Fed.Cl. 100. United States ☞ 74(9)

Although Corps of Engineers' (COE) compliance with required procedures in preparing performance evaluation of roofing contractor was subject to de novo review, under CDA, COE's assignment of particular rating for contractor warranted deferential abuse of discretion review to determine whether evaluation was fair and accurate, since discretionary assignment of rating was subjective and within sole purview of COE. Todd Const., L.P. v. U.S., Fed.Cl.2009, 88 Fed.Cl. 235, subsequent determination 94 Fed.Cl. 100. United States ☞ 73(15)

23. —— Deference, review of board decisions

Construction of the language of a contract under the Contract Disputes Act to determine whether there is an ambiguity is a question of law which a court of appeals reviews without deference; whether ambiguities are latent or patent and whether the contractor's interpretation thereof is reasonable are also questions of law subject to de novo review. States Roofing Corp. v. Winter, C.A.Fed.2009, 587 F.3d 1364, on remand 2010 WL 1186021. United States ☞ 73(15)

In accordance with Contract Disputes Act, contract's interpretation is reviewed as matter of law with no deference owing to interpretation adopted by agency. Scott Timber, Inc. v. U.S., Fed.Cl.2009, 86 Fed.Cl. 102. United States ☞ 73(15)

24. —— Questions of law, review of board decisions

Contract interpretation under the Contract Disputes Act is a question of law, requiring plenary determination on appeal, with no deference owing to the interpretation adopted by either the agency or the Armed Services Board of Contract Appeals. States Roofing Corp. v. Winter, C.A.Fed.2009, 587 F.3d 1364, on remand 2010 WL 1186021. United States ☞ 73(15)

See Revised Title 41, post

The determination of jurisdiction under the Contract Disputes Act (CDA) is a question of law; it is therefore subject to de novo review. Winter v. FloorPro, Inc., C.A.Fed.2009, 570 F.3d 1367. United States ⟜ 73(15)

26. —— Substantial evidence standard, review of board decisions

Government contractor's interpretation of its contract to perform roofing work at a Naval facility as permitting use of waterproofing paint on the parapet walls of all roof cells, rather than requiring three-ply flashing material, was reasonable under the Contract Disputes Act, in view of all of the evidence and circumstances, including the prior use of waterproofing paint on parapet walls of the same roof, the Armed Services Board of Contract Appeals' agreement that waterproofing paint was required for some parapet walls, the consistent use of "ply" and other more precise terms wherever flashing material was specified, the Navy's admitted omission of the relevant specification, the conflicting expert testimony, and due attention to the rule of contra proferentem. States Roofing Corp. v. Winter, C.A.Fed.2009, 587 F.3d 1364, on remand 2010 WL 1186021. United States ⟜ 70(8)

26a. Claims preclusion doctrine

Contract Disputes Act (CDA) did not abrogate claim preclusion doctrine and thus did not permit splitting of claims based on same set of transactional facts. Phillips/May Corp. v. U.S., C.A.Fed.2008, 524 F.3d 1264, rehearing denied. Administrative Law And Procedure ⟜ 501; United States ⟜ 73(15)

27. Claims or issues reviewable—Generally

Contractor's written communication to Air Force in response to allegedly unfair and inaccurate evaluation of contractor's past contract performance, in contractor performance assessment report (CPAR) that was required to be fair and accurate, under federal acquisition regulation (FAR), was not valid "claim," within meaning of CDA, requiring written demand by contracting party seeking relief arising under or relating to contract, since communication constituted merely contractor comments in response to evaluation, contractor was only acting within confines of FAR's performance evaluation procedures, and contracting officer was not expected to treat as CDA claim contractor's communication that officer received in context wholly separate and distinct from CDA claim process. BLR Group of America, Inc. v. U.S., Fed.Cl.2010, 94 Fed.Cl. 354, reconsideration denied 96 Fed.Cl. 9.

28. —— Interpretation or construction of contracts, claims or issues reviewable

Contract interpretation under the Contract Disputes Act is a question of law, which Court of Appeals reviews de novo with no deference owing to the interpretation adopted by either the agency or the Board of Contract Appeals. McHugh v. DLT Solutions, Inc., C.A.Fed.2010, 618 F.3d 1375. United States ⟜ 73(15)

Contract interpretation is question of law over which Court of Appeals exercises complete and independent review on appeal from Armed Services Board of Contract Appeals. LAI Services, Inc. v. Gates, C.A.Fed.2009, 573 F.3d 1306, rehearing denied. United States ⟜ 73(15)

In putative bid protest action, incumbent contractor seeking temporary restraining order to prevent termination of its bridge contract to develop software for Army Corps of Engineers (COE) did not have substantial likelihood of prevailing on merits of bid protest, since Court of Federal Claims would likely lack Tucker Act bid protest jurisdiction to enjoin termination of contract, as COE's failure to exercise option to extend bridge contract was matter of contract administration, under Contract Disputes Act (CDA), rather than bid protest action, under Tucker Act. Jones Automation, Inc. v. U.S., Fed.Cl.2010, 92 Fed.Cl. 368. Injunction ⟜ 150

29. —— Liquidated damages, claims or issues reviewable

Contractor's amended claim against government for unpaid contract earnings was a new claim that had not been the subject of contractor's certified claim, and thus was outside Court of Federal Claims' subject matter jurisdiction under Contract Disputes Act (CDA), although contractor's original complaint sought liquidated damages; request for liquidated damages could not possibly foreshadow contractor's request for unpaid contract earnings. Renda Marine, Inc. v. U.S., Fed.Cl.2005, 65 Fed.Cl. 152, reconsideration denied 71 Fed.Cl. 782, appeal dismissed 208 Fed.Appx. 880, 2006 WL 3497269, order recalled and vacated 212 Fed.Appx. 969, 2006 WL 3922781, affirmed 509 F.3d 1372, rehearing and rehearing en banc denied. United States ⟜ 73(15)

30. —— Same operative facts, claims or issues reviewable

Contractor's duty under CDA to submit written claim to contracting officer (CO), demanding payment of money in sum certain for reimbursement for costs of delays allegedly caused by United States Postal Service (USPS) on contract to construct carrier annex, for additional work performed, and for associated interest, was not discharged by same claim principle, as would have allowed retention of jurisdiction over contractor's alleged counterclaim or request for set-off from CO's affirmative contract claim against contractor that resulted in $1,131,166 refund owed to USPS, even though contractor's setoff claim and USPS's affirmative contract claim arose out of performance of same contract, since claims did not arise out of same set of facts. L.A. Ruiz Associates, Inc. v. U.S., Fed.Cl.2010, 94 Fed.Cl. 768. Federal Courts ⟜ 1076

Under the Contract Disputes Act (CDA), a contractor may not present a claim to the Court of Federal Claims that was not first presented to the contracting officer for a final decision; however, a claim presented to the Court is not a new claim if it arises from the same operative facts and seeks the same categories of relief as the original claims. P.R. Contractors, Inc. v. U.S., Fed.Cl.2007, 76 Fed.Cl. 621, affirmed 274

Text Repealed by Pub.L. 111–350, effective Jan. 4, 2011

Fed.Appx. 897, 2008 WL 1734281. United States ☞ 73(9)

32. —— Miscellaneous claims or issues reviewable

Contractor's claim for revision or rescission of Air Force's allegedly unfair and inaccurate performance evaluation in contractor performance assessment report (CPAR) asserted entitlement to relief as matter of right, under federal acquisition regulation (FAR), requiring government to provide fair and accurate performance evaluation of contractors, in support of validity of contractor's CDA claim, since FAR was intended to benefit both private contractors and government, as contractors were not merely incidental beneficiaries of FAR. BLR Group of America, Inc. v. U.S., Fed.Cl.2010, 94 Fed.Cl. 354, reconsideration denied 96 Fed.Cl. 9. United States ☞ 73(9)

33. —— Miscellaneous claims or issues not reviewable

Plaintiff's submission of suggestion proposal to Social Security Administration (SSA) that Supplemental Security Income (SSI) benefits should be delivered to recipients by debit card transaction, rather than by paper check, did not create procurement contract subject to CDA, thus precluding exercise of jurisdiction over CDA claim that government breached contract. Grayton v. U.S., Fed.Cl.2010, 92 Fed.Cl. 327. United States ☞ 73(9)

35. Consolidation or transfer

Transfer of contract claim before the Court of Federal Claims to the Civilian Board of Contract Appeals (CBCA) where contractor also had a pending claim was appropriate, where contractor's claims stemmed from the same contract and implicated overlapping issues, both claims sought an equitable adjustment for contracting agency's alleged breach of duty to cooperate, same documents and witnesses would be central to proof of causation, contractor chose to initially file claim with the CBCA , and separate proceeding would result in inefficiency and inconsistent results. CH2M Hill Hanford Group, Inc. v. U.S., Fed.Cl.2008, 82 Fed.Cl. 139. Federal Courts ☞ 1101

39. Persons entitled to maintain action

Subcontractors are generally not in privity of contract with the government, so as to be able to avail themselves of the Contract Dispute Act's (CDA) appeal provisions; if the prime contractor is acting as the government's agent when it enters into the subcontractor agreement, however, the subcontractor may be permitted to sue the government directly. Winter v. FloorPro, Inc., C.A.Fed.2009, 570 F.3d 1367. United States ☞ 74.2

Incumbent small business contractor challenging Air Force's alleged statutory and regulatory violations, by exiting small business program and instead procuring credit reports using General Services Administration (GSA) Federal Supply Schedule (FSS), was "interested party," within meaning of Tucker Act's bid protest juris-

dictional provision, as required for contractor's standing as "actual or prospective bidder" for work being performed by larger contractor via FSS, although contractor had been successfully awarded prior contract that Air Force declined to exercise option to extend and although contractor was not FSS bidder, since contractor's claims were not related to prior contract, but prior contract provided link to FSS procurement that harmed contractor's economic interests. K-Lak Corp. v. U.S., Fed.Cl.2010, 93 Fed.Cl. 749.

Corps of Engineers' (COE) obligation to provide accurate and fair performance evaluation of contractor providing roofing services, pursuant to former version of federal acquisition regulation (FAR), mandating that performance report "shall be" prepared for each construction contract for $550,000 or more "in accordance with agency procedures," provided contractor with legally protected rights enforceable against government, under CDA, in accordance with *Christian* doctrine, although contractor could only succeed on challenge if COE had abused broad discretion, since regulation and implementing procedures reflected significant procurement policy intended to benefit both government and contractor being evaluated. Todd Construction, L.P. v. U.S., Fed.Cl.2010, 94 Fed.Cl. 100. United States ☞ 74(3)

Under ordinary government prime contracts, subcontractors do not have standing to sue the government under the Tucker Act to enforce a claim for equitable adjustment under the Contract Disputes Act; yet the law allows a prime contractor to sue the government on behalf of its subcontractor, by means of a pass-through suit, for costs incurred by the subcontractor for which the prime contractor is liable. Haddon Housing Associates, LLC v. U.S., Fed.Cl.2010, 92 Fed.Cl. 8. United States ☞ 74.2

Subcontractor lacked any basis to move in its own name for entry of partial final judgment in contractor's suit against government, under CDA, for breach of contract to construct laboratory building for National Institutes of Health (NIH), where subcontractor did not have privity of contract with government. Bell BCI Co. v. U.S., Fed.Cl.2010, 91 Fed.Cl. 664. United States ☞ 73(15)

40. Burden of proof

Contracting officer's decision letter, stating only that "amount of $259,840.85 represents the balance remaining in retainage," did not establish beyond peradventure that government withheld $259,840.85 from amount asserted in government's $11,860,016 counterclaim in prior lawsuit, as required to prove offset, since "retainage" was percentage of what landowner paid contractor, withheld until construction had been satisfactorily completed and all mechanic's liens were released or had expired. U.S. v. Renda Marine, Inc., E.D.Tex.2010, 2010 WL 3909237. United States ☞ 130(3)

43. Declaratory judgment

Contractor's claim seeking declaratory review of contracting officer's affirmative contract claim against contractor, that resulted in $1,131,166

See Revised Title 41, post

refund owed by contractor to United States Postal Service (USPS) on construction contract for carrier annex, was tied and subordinate to contractor's CDA money judgment claim challenging USPS's affirmative contract claim, as required for Tucker Act jurisdiction over equitable claim for declaratory relief. L.A. Ruiz Associates, Inc. v. U.S., Fed.Cl.2010, 94 Fed.Cl. 768. Federal Courts ⟐ 1078

44. Summary judgment

Genuine issue of material fact existed as to whether single ten percent increase in monthly rent was appropriate for unilateral extension of lease by United States, as tenant of residence in Juárez, Chihuahua, Mexico, precluding summary judgment on claim under Contract Disputes Act (CDA). Fernandez de Iglesias v. U.S., Fed.Cl. 2010, 2010 WL 5176664. Federal Courts ⟐ 1120

52. Attorney fees

Government's litigation position that Air Force lawfully terminated contract for default, even after contractor raised excusability defense for failing to complete contract to provide prefabricated modular buildings, was not "substantially justified," within meaning of Equal Access to Justice Act (EAJA), authorizing award of attorney fees and expenses to contractor as prevailing party in CDA action against government, since Air Force directly contravened pro-curement regulations governing termination for default and persisted in that error to prejudice of contractor, despite decisions by military board and reviewing court that Air Force lacked authority to terminate contract for default, and then Air Force refused to allow contractor opportunity to cure single valid defect in materials, and instead permitted contractor's allegedly defective materials to be used by reprocurement contractor in constructing replacement building. United Partition Systems, Inc. v. U.S., Fed.Cl. 2010, 95 Fed.Cl. 42. United States ⟐ 147(12)

53. Damages

Although government would be allowed continued deposition of certified small business contractor's expert witness, limited to alterations he made to his original expert report, and deposition of contractor's principal, limited to reasoning and particulars for reallocation of damages calculation to which expert opined, contractor was not precluded from any further honing of damages calculation, in CDA suit against United States to recover sums allegedly due for work performed at government's request that was beyond scope of fixed-price construction contract, since failure of contractor to support CDA claims could have serious ramifications. Hernandez, Kroone and Associates, Inc. v. U.S., Fed.Cl.2010, 95 Fed.Cl. 392. Federal Courts ⟐ 1112

§ 610. Subpena, discovery, and deposition

NOTES OF DECISIONS

1. Scope of discovery

Given broad scope of discovery, government was entitled to limited inquiry regarding identity of subcontractors and suppliers referenced in contractor's claims for subcontractor costs, on government's claims for fraud, violation of the anti-fraud provision of the Contract Disputes Act, and violation of the False Claims Act, mindful of the limits of attorney/client and work product privileges, and whether any results might be relevant or admissible were questions reserved for trial. Hernandez, Kroone and As-sociates, Inc. v. U.S., Fed.Cl.2010, 95 Fed.Cl. 395. Federal Courts ⟐ 1112

2. Interrogatories

Contractor was required to identify individual or individuals that calculated amounts it claimed based upon anticipated subcontractor and supplier expenses, in response to government's interrogatory seeking such identification, in connection with government's claims against contractor for fraud, violation of the anti-fraud provision of the Contract Disputes Act, and violation of the False Claims Act; contractor's response that it calculated those amounts was self evident and not responsive. Hernandez, Kroone and Associates, Inc. v. U.S., Fed.Cl. 2010, 95 Fed.Cl. 395. Federal Courts ⟐ 1112

§ 611. Interest

HISTORICAL AND STATUTORY NOTES

Accrual of Interest Where Certification is Defective

Pub.L. 102–572, Title IX, § 907(a)(3), Oct. 29, 1992, 106 Stat. 4518, which provided that If any interest is due under this section on a claim for which the certification under former section 605(c)(1) of this title is, on or after Oct. 29, 1992, found to be defective shall be paid from the later of the date on which the contracting officer initially received the claim or Oct. 29, 1992, was repealed in the enactment into positive law of Title 41, Public Contracts, by Pub.L. 111–350, § 7(b), Jan. 4, 2011, 124 Stat. 3855.

Text Repealed by Pub.L. 111–350, effective Jan. 4, 2011

Notes of Decisions

Construction with other laws ½

½. Construction with other laws

Prompt Payment Act (PPA) applies only in cases in which no disagreement exists over the contractor's claim for interest when the government is late in paying for goods or services under a written contract; that is, if there is a dispute over payment of a claim, the claim is subject to the CDA interest provision, rather than the PPA. Environmental Safety Consultants, Inc. v. U.S., Fed.Cl.2010, 95 Fed.Cl. 77, subsequent determination 2011 WL 488685. United States ⇔ 110

7. Rate of interest

Government was obligated to pay interest only at Contract Disputes Act (CDA) rate, on claim under CDA alleging that United States, as tenant of residence in Juárez, Chihuahua, Mexico, improperly held over; although lease generally specified that Mexican law governed construction of terms of the contract, lease specifically dealt with amount of judgment interest which was for CDA interest. Fernandez de Iglesias v. U.S., Fed.Cl.2010, 2010 WL 5176664. United States ⇔ 110

8. Settlements

Settlement agreement, outlining prospective arrangement with government to reconcile amounts allegedly owed under 23 underlying supply contracts, was not contract for procurement of goods or services, as required for payment of interest, under CDA, on alleged balance remaining on agreement, since agreement was merely tangentially connected to underlying government contracts for goods and services by provisionally determining amount due, but government did not obtain goods or services under agreement that was executed 14 years after obligations under supply contracts ceased to accrue. Marquardt Co. v. U.S., Fed.Cl.2010, 95 Fed.Cl. 14. United States ⇔ 110

10. Particular claims requiring payment of interest

Federal government's award of $3,032,051 for temporary physical taking of blanket easement over owners' private property adjacent to Mexican border, by placing seismic sensors on five parcels to allow Border Patrol to detect illegal aliens, entitled owners to award of compounded interest, under Contract Disputes Act (CDA), since compounded CDA interest was most accurate measure of owners' economic harm from government's decade-long delay in paying owners for use of their property by what should have been contractual arrangement, and award of simple interest would undervalue worth of property due to extended delay in compensating owners. Otay Mesa Property L.P. v. U.S., Fed. Cl.2010, 93 Fed.Cl. 476. Interest ⇔ 60

11. Particular claims not requiring payment of interest

Government contractor was not entitled under Contract Disputes Act (CDA) to recover interest on amounts paid by agency to discharge contractor's back wage liability following reformation of contract, even though contractor was obligated by contract to pay employees amount required by Service Contract Act, and to pay related tax amounts to appropriate tax authorities, where back wages and associated taxes were paid by government through escrow mechanism, and contractor did not itself advance any payments to employees or tax authorities. Richlin Sec. Service Co. v. Chertoff, C.A.Fed.2006, 437 F.3d 1296, rehearing and rehearing en banc denied, certiorari denied 127 S.Ct. 253, 549 U.S. 886, 166 L.Ed.2d 149. United States ⇔ 110

Corrections center service company was not entitled to interest on increased wages, fringe benefits, and taxes resulting from belated incorporation and subsequent revision of wage determination from Department of Labor (DOL); company was serving as mere conduit for back wages to be transferred to DOL for distribution to employees. Schleicher Community Corrections Center, Inc. v. Gonzales, C.A.Fed.2007, 212 Fed.Appx. 972, 2007 WL 43260, Unreported, rehearing and rehearing en banc denied 219 Fed.Appx. 996, 2007 WL 930738. United States ⇔ 70(33)

---

§ 612. Payment of claims

Notes of Decisions

Constructive changes 2
Time of payment 3

---

2. Constructive changes

Requirement that flashing material be used on all of the parapet walls instead of waterproofing paint was a constructive change in government contract for roofing work at a Naval facility, for which compensation was appropriate under the Contract Disputes Act. States Roofing Corp. v. Winter, C.A.Fed.2009, 587 F.3d 1364, on remand 2010 WL 1186021. United States ⇔ 70(26)

Federal Emergency Management Agency (FEMA), as lessee of residential property used for temporary housing facilities after Hurricane Ivan, was not required to pay water and sewer connection fees, under lease agreement with lessor requiring FEMA to pay utility bills that came due during term of lease and to install and leave installed only infrastructure that FEMA determined necessary for operation of temporary housing, since water authority did not require FEMA to pay utility fees during lease in order to receive utility services on property for which FEMA had installed and left installed water and sewer infrastructure, so lessor could not require FEMA to pay fees that were not

See Revised Title 41, post

necessary to operate temporary housing. Retirement Communities LLC v. U.S., Fed.Cl. 2010, 92 Fed.Cl. 587. Water Law ⟷ 2138

3. Time of payment

There was no just reason for delaying government's payment, pursuant to judgment fund statute, of partial final judgment in favor of contractor on CDA claims, with respect to unpaid balance of contract price for constructing laboratory building for National Institutes of Health (NIH), damages for unresolved changes not addressed in any contract modification, and pass through claims on behalf of subcontractors, since judgment on those damages claims was final, government's liability was established, claims would have no possible effect on remand proceedings, claims would never again be reviewed on appeal, and delayed payment would

needlessly increase interest on damages. Bell BCI Co. v. U.S., Fed.Cl.2010, 91 Fed.Cl. 664. United States ⟷ 73(15)

Any claims by contractor that federal government failed to pay contractor promptly for completed work on three contracts with Department of Navy, Army Corps of Engineers, and National Park Service (NPS) that were terminated for default were not actionable, under CDA, requiring prompt payment of judgments against United States and monetary awards to contractor by agency board of contract appeals, since government had not failed to pay judgment or award owed to contractor. Environmental Safety Consultants, Inc. v. U.S., Fed.Cl.2010, 95 Fed.Cl. 77, subsequent determination 2011 WL 488685. United States ⟷ 118

CHAPTER 10—DRUG–FREE WORKPLACE

§ 701. Drug-free workplace requirements for Federal contractors

HISTORICAL AND STATUTORY NOTES

Effective and Applicability Provisions

1988 Acts. Section 5160 of Pub.L. 100–690, which provided that this section and former section 702 of this title should be effective 120 days after Nov. 18, 1988, was repealed in the enactment into positive law of Title 41, Public Contracts, by Pub.L. 111–350, § 7(b), Jan. 4, 2011, 124 Stat. 3855.

Short Title

1988 Amendments. Section 5151 of Pub.L. 100–690, which provided a Short Title for the Drug-Free Workplace Act of 1988, was repealed in the enactment into positive law of Title 41, Public Contracts, by Pub.L. 111–350, § 7(b), Jan. 4, 2011, 124 Stat. 3855.

Text Repealed by Pub.L. 111–350, effective Jan. 4, 2011

TITLE 41

PUBLIC CONTRACTS

Table—Codification of Title 41 as Positive Law by Pub.L. 111–350

The table below shows the disposition of all sections of former Title 41, Public Contracts, affected by Pub.L. 111–350, Jan. 4, 2011, 124 Stat. 3677. The sections listed in the second column throughout this table are sections of new Title 41, Public Contracts, except as otherwise indicated.

Former Title 41	New Title 41 unless otherwise specified
1 to 4a	Previously repealed.
5, 5a	6101
5 note (Act Aug. 2, 1946, § 9(b))	Elim.
6	Previously repealed.
6a(a)	6102
6a(b) to (e)	Previously repealed.
6a(f)	6102
6a(g)	Previously repealed.
6a(h)	6102
6a(i)	Previously repealed.
6a(j)	6102
6a(k) to (n)	Previously repealed.
6a(o)	Superseded. Most recently based on Public Law 85–75, § 101 (last par. on p. 251), July, 1, 1957, 71 Stat. 251, provided that 41:5 would not apply to the Architect of the Capitol in the purchase of supplies and equipment or the procurement of services when the aggregate amount of supplies and equipment or services did not exceed $1,000. Superseded by 41:6a–1.
6a(p)	Previously repealed.
6a note (Act July 30, 1947, c. 359, Title I)	Elim.
6a–1	6102
6a–2	2:1816
6a–2	2:1816b
6a–3, 6a–4	6102

Former Title 41	New Title 41 unless otherwise specified
6b(a)	Obsolete. Provided that materials and equipment needed for control of emergency outbreaks of insects could be procured, without regard to 41:5, using amounts appropriated to carry out 7:148–148e. Provisions classified to 7:148–148e have previously been repealed.
6b(b)	Obsolete. Provided that 41:5 would not apply to certain expenditures related to the Civilian Conservation Corps. The Corps was liquidated June 30, 1944.
6b(c)	Limited interest. Provides that 41:5 does not apply to contracts for labor or supplies necessary to carry out operations on the Menominee Indian Reservation pursuant to "the Act of March 28, 1908 (35 Stat. 51)" (probably means the Act of March 28, 1908, ch. 111, 35 Stat. 51, which is not classified to the Code).
6b(c)	25:903g

Former Title 41	New Title 41 unless otherwise specified
6b(d)	6102
6b(e)	Obsolete. Provision, which related to the employment of experts or consultants in the Canal Zone, was from the General Government Matters Appropriation Act, 1962 (Public Law 87–125, title III, § 301, 75 Stat. 279). The provision was not repeated in subsequent appropriation acts and expired on June 30, 1962.
6b note [tbl] (Pub.L. 86–451, § 201)	Elim.
6b note [tbl] (Pub.L. 86–88, § 201)	Elim.
6b note [tbl] (Pub.L. 85–469, § 203)	Elim.
6b note [tbl] (Pub.L. 85–52, § 203)	Elim.
6b note [tbl] (Act June 20, 1956, c. 415, § 203)	Elim.
6b note [tbl] (Act June 30, 1955, c. 253, § 203)	Elim.
6b note [tbl] (Act June 30, 1954, c. 425, § 104)	Elim.
6b note [tbl] (Act July 27, 1953, c. 245, § 104)	Elim.
6b note [tbl] (Act July 11, 1952, c. 669, § 104)	Elim.
6b note [tbl] (Act Oct. 24, 1951, c. 556, § 104)	Elim.
6b note [tbl] (Act Sept. 6, 1950, c. 896, § 103)	Elim.
6b note [tbl] (Act Oct. 13, 1949, c. 688, § 4)	Elim.
6b note [tbl] (Act June 25, 1948, c. 655, § 4)	Elim.
6b note [tbl] (Act July 31, 1947, c. 411, § 4)	Elim.
6b note [tbl] (Act May 2, 1946, c. 247, § 4)	Elim.

Former Title 41	New Title 41 unless otherwise specified
6b note [tbl] (Act Mar. 31, 1945, c. 45, § 4)	Elim.
6b note [tbl] (Act June 26, 1944, c. 275, § 4)	Elim.
6b note [tbl] (Act June 2, 1943, c. 115, § 4)	Elim.
6b note [tbl] (Act Apr. 28, 1942, c. 246, § 5)	Elim.
6c to 6jj	Previously repealed.
6kk	Superseded. Provisions classified to this section were contained in annual appropriation Acts. The provisions created an exemption from 41:5 and 41:16 for certain purchases for the Botanic Garden when the amount involved did not exceed $50. With respect to an exemption from 41:5, the section appears to have been previously repealed by the Act of August 2, 1946, ch. 744, § 9(b), 60 Stat. 809. In any event, the section was superseded by 41:6a(b), which was subsequently repealed by the Act of October 31, 1951, ch. 654, § 1(107), 65 Stat. 705.
6ll	Previously repealed.
6mm	Previously transferred to 41:6b(d) prior to repeal.
7 to 7d	Previously repealed.
8	6103
9	Previously repealed.
10	Superseded. Provision related to preferential treatment of American material in contracts for public improvements. Superseded by 41:10a et seq.
10a	8302
10a note (Pub.L. 103–355, § 4301(c))	Elim.

PUBLIC CONTRACTS

Former Title 41	New Title 41 unless otherwise specified
10a note (Pub.L. 100–418, § 7001)	101 note
10a note (Pub.L. 100–418, § 7004)	19:2511 note
10a note (Pub.L. 100–418, § 7005(f))	19:2511 note
10a note (Pub.L. 100–371, § 508)	8301 note
10a note (Act Mar. 3, 1933, c. 212, § 7)	101 note
10b	8303
10b note (Pub.L. 101–516, § 340)	Elim.
10b note (Pub.L. 101–514, § 511)	Elim.
10b note (Pub.L. 100–202, § 109)	Elim.
10b–1	Obsolete. Provided that a Federal agency shall not award certain procurement contracts. This section ceased to be effective on April 30, 1996. See section 7004 of Public Law 100–418 (102 Stat. 1552).
10b–2	8304
10b–2 note (Pub.L. 111–118, § 8030)	8304 note
10b–2 note (Pub.L. 110–329, § 8030)	8304 note
10b–2 note (Pub.L. 110–116, § 8029)	8304 note
10b–2 note (Pub.L. 109–289, § 8027)	8304 note
10b–2 note (Pub.L. 109–148, § 8030)	8304 note
10b–2 note (Pub.L. 108–287, § 8032)	8304 note
10b–2 note (Pub.L. 108–87, § 8033)	8304 note
10b–2 note (Pub.L. 107–248, § 8033)	8304 note
10b–2 note (Pub.L. 107–117, § 8036)	8304 note
10b–2 note (Pub.L. 106–259, § 8036)	8304 note
10b–2 note (Pub.L. 106–79, § 8038)	8304 note
10b–2 note (Pub.L. 105–262, § 8038)	8304 note
10b–2 note (Pub.L. 105–56, § 8040)	8304 note
10b–2 note (Pub.L. 104–208, § 101(b) [Title VIII, § 8042])	8304 note
10b–2 note (Pub.L. 104–61, § 8051)	8304 note
10b–2 note (Pub.L. 103–335, § 8058)	8304 note
10b–2 note (Pub.L. 103–139, § 8069)	8304 note
10b–2 note (Pub.L. 102–396, § 9096)	8304 note
10b–2 note (Pub.L. 102–190, § 833)	8304 note
10b–2 note (Pub.L. 102–172, § 8123)	8304 note
10b–2 note (Pub.L. 101–189, § 823)	8304 note
10b–3	8305
10c	8301
10c note (Act Mar. 3, 1933, § 5)	Elim.
10d	8303
10d note (Ex Ord 10582)	8303 note
11	6301
11a	6302
12	6303
13	6304
13a	Previously repealed.
14	6301
15	6305
15 note (Memorandum, Oct. 3, 1995)	6305 note
16	Previously repealed.
16a	Obsolete. Section authorized purchases by the Department of the Interior without compliance with 41:16, which was repealed.
16b	Obsolete. Section authorized purchases by the Botanic Garden without compliance with 41:16, which was repealed.
16c	Obsolete. Section authorized purchases by the Architect of the Capitol without compliance with 41:16, which was repealed.
16d	Obsolete. Section authorized purchases by the Bureau of Reclamation without compliance with 41:16, which was repealed.
17 to 21	Previously repealed.
22	6306
23	6307
24	6308

See Main Volume and Repealed Title 41, ante, for annotations

Former Title 41	New Title 41 unless otherwise specified
24a	Obsolete. Provided for cancellation on or before March 31, 1936, of contracts for transportation entered into prior to June 16, 1933.
25 to 27	Previously repealed.
28 to 33	Obsolete. The Act of June 16, 1934, ch. 553, 48 Stat. 974, consisting of sections 1 through 6, which were classified to 41:28 through 41:33, respectively, provided for settlement of certain claims related to contracts with the Federal Government made prior to August 10, 1933.
34	Obsolete. Provision, consisting of the Act of August 29, 1935, ch. 815, 49 Stat. 990, provided that bids made subject to codes of fair competition prior to August 29, 1935 should not be rejected where bidder agreed to be subject to Acts requiring observance of minimum wages, maximum hours, or limitations as to age of employees in performance of contracts with Federal agencies. Table III of the Code indicates that provision is classified to 41:28 through 41:34. However, provision is classified only to 41:34. See text in 1940 edition of the Code and source credits.
35 (matter before subsec. (a) less words related to definition of "agency of the United States")	6502
35 (matter before subsec. (a) related to definition of "agency	

Former Title 41	New Title 41 unless otherwise specified
of the United States")	6501
35(a) to (d)	6502
35 note (Pub.L. 99–145, § 1241(c))	Elim.
35 note (Act June 30, 1936, c. 881, § 14)	101 note
35 note (Ex Ord 13126)	6501 note
36	6503
37	6504
38	6506
39	6507
40	6508
41	6501
42	6511
43	6505
43a(a)	6509
43a(b) (1st sentence)	6507
43a(b) (last sentence), (c)	6509
43b	6510
44	Unnecessary. Severability provisions of laws included in the codification are unnecessary.
45	6502
46	8502
46 note (Pub.L. 109–364, § 856(a), (d))	8501 note
46 note (Pub.L. 109–163, § 848(b), (c))	8501 note
46 note (Pub.L. 92–28, § 2)	Elim.
47	8503
48	8504
48a	8505
48b	8501
48c	8506
49, 50	6309
51	Unnecessary. Short titles of laws included in the codification are unnecessary.
51 note (Pub.L. 99–634, § 3)	Elim.
51 note (Pub.L. 99–634, § 1)	101 note
52	8701
53	8702
54	8707
55	8706
56	8705
57	8703
58	8704
101, 102(a)	Obsolete. Provided for the settlement of

Former Title 41	New Title 41 unless otherwise specified
	claims under terminated contracts for war production during World War II.
102(b)	Previously repealed.
103	Obsolete. Provided for the settlement of claims under terminated contracts for war production during World War II.
104(a)	Previously repealed.
104(b) to 113(c)	Obsolete. Provided for the settlement of claims under terminated contracts for war production during World War II.
106 note (Act Aug. 7, 1946, c. 864).....................	Elim.
113(d)	Obsolete. Provided for the appointment and duties of an Appeal Board. The Appeal Board was abolished no later than 9 months after July 14, 1952.
113(e) to 115	Obsolete. Provided for the settlement of claims under terminated contracts for war production during World War II.
114 note (Act July 28, 1953, § 4(b))	Elim.
114 note (Act June 25, 1948, c. 646, § 2(d))	Elim.
116	Previously repealed.
117, 118(a)	Obsolete. Provided for the settlement of claims under terminated contracts for war production during World War II.
117 note (Act June 28, 1954, § 2)....................	Elim.
118(b)	Previously repealed.
118(c) to 125	Obsolete. Provided for the settlement of claims under terminated contracts for war production during World War II.
151 to 162	Previously repealed.
201 to 205	Previously transferred to 40:471 to 475 prior to repeal.

Former Title 41	New Title 41 unless otherwise specified
211 to 213	Previously transferred to 40:751 to 753 prior to repeal.
214	Previously transferred to 44:391 prior to repeal.
215	Previously transferred to 5:630c prior to repeal.
216	Previously transferred to 5:630d and 40:754 prior to repeal.
217	Previously transferred to 5:630e and 40:755 prior to repeal.
218	Previously transferred to 5:630f prior to repeal.
219	Previously transferred to 5:630g and 40:756 prior to repeal.
231 to 237	Previously transferred to 40:481 to 488 prior to repeal.
238	Previously transferred to 5:630h and 40:758 prior to repeal.
239 to 240	Previously transferred to 40:489 to 492 prior to repeal.
251	Unnecessary. Sets out the purpose of the subchapter.
251 note (Pub.L. 110–417, § 861)...............	101 note
251 note (Pub. L. 110–417, § 867)	4711
251 note (Pub.L. 110–252, § 6101)...............	101 note
251 note (Pub. L. 110–252, § 6102, 6103)...........................	3509
251 note (Pub.L. 104–106, § 4001)...............	101 note
251 note (Pub.L. 104–106, § 4401)...........	10:2302 note
251 note (Pub.L. 104–106, § 4402).................	Elim.
251 note (Pub.L. 103–355, § 1)..................	101 note
251 note (Pub.L. 103–355, § 10001)..........	10:2302 note
251 note (Pub.L. 103–355, § 10002).................	Elim.
251 note (Pub.L. 103–355, § 10003).................	Elim.

See Main Volume and Repealed Title 41, ante, for annotations

Former Title 41	New Title 41 unless otherwise specified
251 note (Pub.L. 98–577, § 1)	101 note
251 note (Pub.L. 98–577, § 101)	3701 note
251 note (Pub.L. 98–369, § 2701)	101 note
251 note (Pub.L. 98–369, § 2751)	10:2302 note
251 note (Pub.L. 91–129)	Elim.
251 note (Act June 30, 1949, c. 288, § 1(a))	101 note
251 note (Act June 30, 1949, c. 288, § 604)	prec § 3901 note
251 note (Ex Ord 13005)	3101 note
251 note (Ex Ord 13502)	prec § 3901 note
251 note (Memorandum, Mar. 4, 2009)	3101 note
252(a)	3101
252(b)	3104
252(c)(1)	3106
252(c)(2)	3301
252 note (Pub.L. 94–190)	Elim.
252a, 252b	3101
252c	4709
253(a)	3301
253(b)	3303
253(c) to (f)	3304
253(g)	3305
253(h)	3301
253(i)	3105
253(j)	3304
253 note (Pub.L. 108–136, § 1442)	Elim.
253 note (Pub.L. 98–369, § 2711(c))	3301 note
253a	3306
253a note (Pub. L. 108–136, § 1428)	3306
253b(a), (b)	3701
253b(c)	3702
253b(d)	3703
253b(e)	3704
253b(f)	3705
253b(g) (related to 41:253b(e))	3704
253b(g) (related to 41:253b(f))	3705
253b(h)	3706
253b(i)	3707
253b(j)	3308
253b(k), (l)	3708
253b(m)	4702

Former Title 41	New Title 41 unless otherwise specified
253b note (Pub.L. 104–201, § 1074(b)(7))	Elim.
253b note (Pub.L. 98–577, § 201(b))	Elim.
253b note (Ex Ord 12979)	3701 note
253c	3311
253c note (Pub.L. 98–577, § 202(b))	Elim.
253d	4703
253d note (Pub.L. 98–577, § 203(b))	Elim.
253e	Previously repealed.
253f	3310
253f note (Pub.L. 98–577, § 205(b))	Elim.
253g	4704
253g note (Pub.L. 98–577, § 206(b))	Elim.
253h	4103
253h note (Pub. L. 110–417, § 863(a)-(e))	3302
253h note (Pub.L. 110–181, § 843(b)(3)(A))	Elim.
253h note (Pub. L. 106–65, § 804)	4104
253h note (Pub. L. 103–355, § 1054(b))	4102
253i	4105
253i note (Pub.L. 109–364, § 834)	10:2304b note
253i note (Pub. L. 109–364, § 834(b), (c) (related to (b))	4105
253j	4106
253j note (Pub.L. 110–181, § 843(b)(3)(B))	Elim.
253k	4101
253l	3902
253l–1 to 253l–8	3904
253m	3309
254(a)	3901
254(b)	3905
254 note (Pub. L. 110–417, § 864(a), (b), (d), (e), (f)(2), (g))	3906
254 note (Pub.L. 110–417, § 864(c))	Elim.
254 note (Pub.L. 110–417, § 864(f)(1))	Elim.
254 note (Ex Ord 13496)	prec § 3901 note
254a	4708
254b(a)	3502
254b(b)	3503
254b(c)	3504

Former Title 41	New Title 41 unless otherwise specified	Former Title 41	New Title 41 unless otherwise specified
254b(d)	3505	260	3101
254b(e)	3506	261	3102
254b(f)	3507	262	4701
254b(g)	3508	263	3103
254b(h)	3501	263 note (Pub.L.	
254b note (Pub. L.		103–355, § 5051(c))	1703 note
110–417, § 866)	4710	263 note (Pub.L.	
254b note (Pub. L.		103–355, § 5051(d))	Elim.
110–417, § 868)	3501	264	3307
254b note (Pub.L.		264 note (Pub. L.	
105–261, § 808(c))	Elim.	103–355, § 8002)	3307
254b note (Pub.L.		264 note (Pub.L.	
105–261, § 808(d))	Elim.	103–355, § 8304)	10:2375 note
254b note (Pub.L.		264a ("commercial	
103–355, § 1251(b))	Elim.	item")	103
254c	3903	264a ("nondevelop-	
254d	4706	mental item")	110
255(a)	4501	264a ("component")	105
255(b), (c)	4502	264a ("commercial	
255(d)	4503	component")	102
255(e)	4504	264b	3307
255(f)	4505	264b note (Pub.L.	
255(g)	4506	103–355, § 8305)	Elim.
255 note (Pub.L.		265	4705
103–355, § 2051(f))	4501 note	266	3105
256(a) to (d)	4303	266a	Temporary. Author-
256(e)	4304		izes the head of an
256(f)	4305		executive agency to
256(g)	4306		enter into a share-in-
256(h)	4307		savings contract for
256(i)	4308		information technolo-
256(j)	4309		gy. Those contracts
256(k)	4310		may not be entered
256(*l*)(1)	4301		into after September
256(*l*)(2)	4302		30, 2005.
256(m)	4301	266a	prec § 3901 note
256 note (Pub.L.		271 to 274	Previously trans-
103–355, § 2192)	4304 note		ferred to 40:511 to
256 note (Ex Ord			514 prior to repeal.
13494)	4304 note	281 to 291	Previously trans-
256a	4707		ferred to 44:392 to
257	4701		402 prior to repeal.
258	Previously repealed.	321 to 322	Superseded. Provi-
259(a)	151		sions superseded by
259(b)	152		section 10 of the
259(c)(1)	111		Contract Disputes
259(c)(2)	112		Act of 1978 (41
259(c)(3)	114		U.S.C. 609). Con-
259(c)(4)	107		gress intended to re-
259(c)(5)	113		peal provisions but,
259(c)(6)	116		due to apparent
259(c)(7)	109		oversight, repeal was
259(c)(8), (9)	108		not enacted. See
259(c)(10)	115		Senate Report No.
259(c)(11)	103		95–1118 (1978
259(c)(12)	110		U.S.C.C.A.N. p.
259(c)(13)	102		5235), especially
259(c)(14)	105		page 34 ("Section
259(d)	153		14(i) repeals 41
259(e)	106		U.S.C. 321–322") and

Former Title 41	New Title 41 unless otherwise specified
	pages 2, 3, 13 to 15, and 30. See also, Nash, Jr., Schooner, and O'Brien, Government Contracts Reference Book, 2d Ed., page 548.
351(a) (words before par. (1) related to applicability)	6702
351(a) (words before par. (1) related to required contract terms), (1) to (5).	6703
351(b)	6704
351 note (Ex Ord 13495)	6703 note
352	6705
353	6707
354(a)	6706
354(b)	6705
355	6707
356	6702
357	6701
357 note (Pub.L. 93–57, § 2)	Elim.
358	6707
401, 402	Previously repealed.
401 note (Pub.L. 108–136, § 1401)	101 note
401 note (Pub.L. 103–355, § 10005(b)(1))	Elim.
401 note (Pub.L. 102–394, § 502)	1101 note
401 note (Pub.L. 102–170, § 502)	1101 note
401 note (Pub.L. 101–517, § 502)	1101 note
401 note (Pub.L. 101–166, § 502)	1101 note
401 note (Pub.L. 100–679, § 1)	101 note
401 note (Pub.L. 100–202, § 101(h) [Title V, § 502])	1101 note
401 note (Pub.L. 99–591, § 101(i) [H.R. 5233, Title V, § 502])	1101 note
401 note (Pub.L. 99–500, § 101(i) [H.R. 5233, Title V, § 502])	1101 note
401 note (Pub.L. 99–178, § 502)	1101 note
401 note (Pub.L. 98–619, § 502)	1101 note
401 note (Pub.L. 98–191, § 1)	101 note

Former Title 41	New Title 41 unless otherwise specified
401 note (Pub.L. 98–139, § 502)	1101 note
401 note (Pub.L. 97–377, § 101(e)(1) [Title V, § 502])	1101 note
401 note (Pub.L. 96–83, § 1(a))	101 note
401 note (Pub.L. 96–83, § 12)	Elim.
401 note (Pub.L. 93–400, § 1(a))	101 note
401 note (Ex Ord 12073)	
401 note (Ex Ord 12931)	1701 note
401 note (Memorandum, Oct. 28, 1993)	2301 note
403(1)	133
403(2)	111
403(3)	112
403(4)	114
403(5)	132
403(6)	107
403(7)	113
403(8)	116
403(9)	109
403(10) ("item", "item of supply")	108
403(10) ("supplies")	115
403(11)	134
403(12)	103
403(13)	110
403(14)	105
403(15)	102
403(16)	131
403(17)	1301
403 note (Pub.L. 98–369, § 2752)	Elim.
404(a)	1101
404(b)	1102
405(a) to (c)	1121
405(d), (e)	1122
405(f)	1121
405(g)	1122
405(h)(1)	1130
405(h)(2)	2305
405(i)	1125
405(j)	1126
405(k)	1131
405 note (Pub. L. 110–417, § 874(a))	2311
405 note (Pub.L. 110–161, § 748)	1122 note
405 note (Pub.L. 108–136, § 803)	1121 note
405 note (Pub.L. 108–136, § 1423)	Elim.
405 note (Pub. L. 108–136, § 1431(b))	1129

Former Title 41	New Title 41 unless otherwise specified
405 note (Pub.L. 105–135, § 414)	1122 note
405 note (Pub.L. 103–355, § 1091(b)(1))	1126 note
405 note (Pub.L. 103–355, § 5052)	1122 note
405 note (Pub.L. 103–355, § 7107)	Elim.
405 note (Pub.L. 103–355, § 10004)	1122 note
405 note (Pub.L. 100–679, § 7)	1121 note
405a (1st sentence)	1121
405a (last sentence)	1123
405a note (Pub.L. 96–83, § 11)	1121 note
405b	2304
405c(a), (c)	2303
405c(b)	2303 note
406	1701
407	Previously repealed.
408	1121
409	Previously repealed.
410	1101
411	1122
412(a)	2307
412(b)	2306
413	1124
413 note (Pub.L. 103–355, § 5061)	Elim.
414	1702
414a	1706
414b(a) to (c)	1311
414b(d), (e)	1312
415	Previously repealed.
416	1708
416 note (Pub.L. 98–577, § 303(b))	Elim.
416 note (Pub.L. 98–577, § 303(c))	1708 note
417	1712
417a	1713
417b	2313
418	1705
418a	2302
418a note (Pub.L. 98–577, § 301(c))	Elim.
418b	1707
418b note (Pub.L. 98–577, § 302(b))	Elim.
419	1709
419 note (Pub.L. 103–355, § 6002(b))	1709 note
420	Previously repealed.
421(a), (b)	1302
421(c) to (f)	1303
421 note (Pub.L. 111–84, § 811)	Elim.
421 note (Pub.L. 102–190, § 809)	1302 note
422(a) to (e)	1501
422 note (Pub.L. 106–65, § 802(c)–(e), (g)–(i))	1502 note
422(f) to (h)(1)	1502
422(h)(2) to (4)	1503
422(i)	Expired. Required the Cost Accounting Standards Board to submit an annual report to Congress on the activities and operations of the Board. Section 3003 of the Federal Reports Elimination and Sunset Act of 1995 (31 U.S.C. 1113 note) provided that subject to certain provisions, each provision of law requiring the submittal to Congress or a committee of Congress of an annual, semiannual, or periodic report specified in the list prepared by the Clerk of the House of Representatives for the first session of the 103d Congress (House Document No. 103–7) ceased to be effective on May 15, 2000.
422(j)	1504
422(k)	1505
422(l)	1506
423(a), (b)	2102
423(c)	2103
423(d)	2104
423(e)	2105
423(f)	2101
423(g)	2106
423(h)	2107
423 note (Pub.L. 101–510, § 815(a)(1))	Elim.
423 note (Pub.L. 101–510, § 815(b))	Elim.
423 note (Pub.L. 101–194, § 507(1))	Elim.
423 note (Pub.L. 101–189, § 814(e))	Elim.
423 note (Pub.L. 100–679, § 6(b))	Elim.
424	Previously repealed.

See Main Volume and Repealed Title 41, ante, for annotations

Former Title 41	New Title 41 unless otherwise specified	Former Title 41	New Title 41 unless otherwise specified
425	1304	435 note (Pub.L. 105–85, § 808(f))	1127 note
425 note (Pub.L. 104–106, § 4301(b)(1))	1304 note	435 note (Pub.L. 105–85, § 808(g))	1127 note
426	2301	436	2309
426a	Previously repealed.	437	2310
427	1901	438	7105
427 note (Pub.L. 104–201, § 1074(b)(6))	Elim.	439	1710
428	1902	440	2312
428 note (Pub.L. 111–240, § 1332)	1902 note	501 to 509	Previously repealed.
428a	1903	601	7101
428a note (Pub. L. 108–136, § 1441)	1904	602, 603	7102
429	1905	604, 605	7103
430	1906	605 note (Pub.L. 102–572, § 907(a)(2))	Elim.
430 note (Pub.L. 103–355, § 8003(b))	Elim.	605 note (Pub.L. 102–572, § 907(a)(4))	Elim.
431(a), (b)	1907	605 note (Pub.L. 103–355, § 2351(a)(2))	Elim.
431(c)	104	606	7104
431a	1908	607(a) to (e)	7105
431a note (Pub. L. 108–375, § 807(c))	1908	607(f)	7106
432	1711	607(g)	7107
433	1703	607 note (Pub.L. 109–163, § 847(b), (c), (e))	Elim.
433 note (Pub.L. 111–240, § 1343(a))	1703 note	608	7106
433 note (Pub.L. 109–163, § 821(c))	Elim.	609(a)	7104
433 note (Pub.L. 109–163, § 821(d))	1703 note	609(b) to (f)	7107
433 notes (Pub. L. 108–136, §§ 1412(a), 1413)	1703	610	7105
433 note (Pub. L. 108–136, § 1414)	1128	611, 611 note (Pub. L. 102–572, § 907(a)(3))	7109
433a	1704	612	7108
433a note (Pub. L. 110–417, § 869)	1704	613	Unnecessary. Severability provisions of laws included in the codification are unnecessary.
434	2308	701	8102
435	1127	702	8103
435 note (Pub.L. 105–85, § 808(d))	10:2324 note	703	8104
435 note (Pub.L. 105–85, § 808(e))	Elim.	704	8105
		705	8106
		706, 707	8101

HISTORICAL AND STATUTORY NOTES

Enactment of Title 41

Pub.L. 111–350, § 3, Jan. 4, 2011, 124 Stat. 3677, provided in part that: "Certain general and permanent laws of the United States, related to public contracts, are revised, codified, and enacted as title 41, United States Code, 'Public Contracts'."

Purpose; Conformity with Original Intent

Pub.L. 111–350, § 2, Jan. 4, 2011, 124 Stat. 3677, provided that:

"(a) **Purpose.**—The purpose of this Act [Pub.L. 111–350, Jan. 4, 2011, 124 Stat. 3677] is to enact certain laws relating to public contracts as title 41, United States Code, 'Public Contracts'.

"(b) **Conformity with original intent.**—In the codification of laws by this Act [Pub.L. 111–350, Jan. 4, 2011, 124 Stat. 3677], the intent is to conform to the understood policy, intent, and purpose of Congress in the original enactments, with such amendments and corrections as will remove ambiguities, contradictions, and

Revised Title 41 effective Jan. 4, 2011

PUBLIC CONTRACTS

other imperfections, in accordance with section 205(c)(1) of House Resolution No. 988, 93d Congress, as enacted into law by Public Law 93–554 (2 U.S.C. 285b(1))."

Transitional and Savings Provisions

Pub.L. 111–350, § 6(a) to (e), Jan. 4, 2011, 124 Stat. 3854, provided that:

"(a) Cutoff date.—This Act [Pub.L. 111–350, Jan. 4, 2011, 124 Stat. 3677, which principally codified this title, Public Contracts, as positive law. See Tables for complete classification] replaces certain provisions of law enacted on or before December 31, 2008. If a law enacted after that date amends or repeals a provision replaced by this Act, that law is deemed to amend or repeal, as the case may be, the corresponding provision enacted by this Act. If a law enacted after that date is otherwise inconsistent with this Act, it supersedes this Act to the extent of the inconsistency.

"(b) Original date of enactment unchanged.—For purposes of determining whether one provision of law supersedes another based on enactment later in time, the date of enactment of a provision enacted by this Act [Pub.L. 111–350, Jan. 4, 2011, 124 Stat. 3677, which principally codified this title, Public Contracts, as positive law. See Tables for complete classification] is deemed to be the date of enactment of the provision it replaced.

"(c) References to provisions replaced.—A reference to a provision of law replaced by this Act [Pub.L. 111–350, Jan. 4, 2011, 124 Stat. 3677, which principally codified this title, Public Contracts, as positive law. See Tables for complete classification], including a reference in a regula-tion, order, or other law, is deemed to refer to the corresponding provision enacted by this Act.

"(d) Regulations, orders, and other administrative actions.—A regulation, order, or other administrative action in effect under a provision of law replaced by this Act [Pub.L. 111–350, Jan. 4, 2011, 124 Stat. 3677, which principally codified this title, Public Contracts, as positive law. See Tables for complete classification] continues in effect under the corresponding provision enacted by this Act.

"(e) Actions taken and offenses committed.—An action taken or an offense committed under a provision of law replaced by this Act [Pub.L. 111–350, Jan. 4, 2011, 124 Stat. 3677, which principally codified this title, Public Contracts, as positive law. See Tables for complete classification] is deemed to have been taken or committed under the corresponding provision enacted by this Act."

Inference of Repeal

Pub.L. 111–350, § 7(a), Jan. 4, 2011, 124 Stat. 3855, provided that: "The repeal of a law by this Act [Pub.L. 111–350, Jan. 4, 2011, 124 Stat. 3677, which principally codified this title, Public Contracts, as positive law. See Tables for complete classification] may not be construed as a legislative inference that the provision was or was not in effect before its repeal."

Repeals

Pub.L. 111–350, § 7(b), Jan. 4, 2011, 124 Stat. 3855, repealed specified laws, except with respect to rights and duties that matured, penalties that were incurred, or proceedings that were begun before Jan. 4, 2011.

SUBTITLE I—FEDERAL PROCUREMENT POLICY

DIVISION A—GENERAL

See Main Volume and Repealed Title 41, ante, for annotations

DIVISION A—GENERAL

CHAPTER 1—DEFINITIONS

SUBCHAPTER I—SUBTITLE DEFINITIONS

§ 101. Administrator

In this subtitle, the term "Administrator" means the Administrator for Federal Procurement Policy appointed under section 1102 of this title.

(Pub.L. 111–350, § 3, Jan. 4, 2011, 124 Stat. 3678.)

HISTORICAL AND STATUTORY NOTES

Short Title

2008 Amendments. Pub.L. 110–417, Div. A, Title VIII, § 861, Oct. 14, 2008, 122 Stat. 4546, provided that: "This subtitle [subtitle G of Title VIII of Pub.L. 110–417, Div. A, Title VIII, §§ 861 to 874, which enacted former 41 U.S.C.A. §§ 417b and 440, amended 10 U.S.C.A. §§ 2304 and 2313, and former 41 U.S.C.A. §§ 253, 254d, and 417, enacted provisions set out as notes under 31 U.S.C.A. §§ 1535 and 6101, and former 41 U.S.C.A. §§ 251, 253h, 254, 254b, 405, and 433a, and repealed provisions set out as a note under 10 U.S.C.A. § 2304] may be cited as the 'Clean Contracting Act of 2008'."

[Note was classified as a note under former 41 U.S.C.A. § 251 prior to the enactment into positive law of Title 41, Public Contracts, by Pub.L. 111–350, Jan. 4, 2011, 124 Stat. 3677.]

Pub.L. 110–252, Title VI, § 6101, June 30, 2008, 122 Stat. 2386, provided that: "This chapter [Pub.L. 110–252, Title VI, §§ 6101 to 6103, June 30, 2008, 122 Stat. 2386, which enacted provisions formerly set out as notes under former 41 U.S.C.A. § 251] may be cited as the 'Close the Contractor Fraud Loophole Act'."

[Note was classified as a note under former 41 U.S.C.A. § 251 prior to the enactment into positive law of Title 41, Public Contracts, by Pub.L. 111–350, Jan. 4, 2011, 124 Stat. 3677.]

2003 Amendments. Pub.L. 108–136, § 1401, provided that: "This title [enacting former 41 U.S.C.A. §§ 414b, 428a, and 437, amending 10 U.S.C.A. § 2855, 31 U.S.C.A. 1115, and former 41 U.S.C.A. §§ 403, 414, 433, and 436, enacting provisions set out as notes under 31 U.S.C.A. § 501, 40 U.S.C.A. § 1103, and former 41 U.S.C.A. §§ 253, 253a, 405, 428a, and 433, amending provisions set out as notes under 10 U.S.C.A. § 2304 and former 41 U.S.C.A. § 264, and repealing provisions set out as a note under 10 U.S.C.A. § 2302] may be cited as the "Services Acquisition Reform Act of 2003'."

[Note was classified as a note under former 41 U.S.C.A. § 401 prior to the enactment into positive law of Title 41, Public Contracts, by Pub.L. 111–350, Jan. 4, 2011, 124 Stat. 3677.]

1996 Amendments. Pub.L. 104–106, Div. D, § 4001, Feb. 10, 1996, 110 Stat. 642, as amended Pub.L. 104–208, Div. A, Title I, § 101(f) [Title VIII, § 808(a)], Sept. 30, 1996, 110 Stat. 3009–393, provided that: "This division [enacting section 2305a of Title 10, Armed Forces, and enacting former sections 253m, 432, 432, and 433 of this title, amending section 11 of Appendix 3 of Title 5, Government Organization & Employees, sections 2220, 2302, 2304, 2305, 2306a, 2323, 2324, 2350b, 2372, 2384, 2400, 2405, 2410b, 2410d, 2410g, 2424, 2431, 2461, 2533, 2539b, 2662, and 2701 of Title 10, sections 637 and 644 of Title 15, Commerce and Trade, section 799 of Title 16, Conservation, section 2761 of Title 22, Foreign Relations and Intercourse, section 721 of Title 29, Labor, sections 1352, 3551, 3553, and 3554 of Title 31, Money and Finance, and former sections 11, 15, 22, 43a, 57, 253, 253a, 253b, 254b, 254d, 257, 264a, 265, 403, 404, 405, 410, 416, 421, 422, 423, 425, 427, 428, 601, 605, 612, and 701 of this title, redesignating sections 2247 and 2304a as 2249 and 2304e of Title 10, respectively, repealing sections 2397, 2397a, 2397b, and 2397c of Title 10, section 789 of Title 15, section 281 of Title 18, Crimes and Criminal Procedure, former sections 20a, 20b, 401, 402, 407, and 409 of this title, and sections 5816a, 5918, 6392, 7211, 7212 and 7218 of Title 42, Public Health and Welfare, enacting provisions set out as notes under section 11 of Appendix 3 of Title 5, sections 1701, 2304, and 2306a of Title 10, section 2761 of Title 22, section 481 of Title 40, Public Buildings, Property, and Works, and former sections 251 and 425 of this title, amending provisions set out as notes under section 571 of Title 5, sections 2326, 2401, and 2431 of Title 10, section 270a of Title 40, and former sections 10a, 254b, and 413 of this title, and repealing provisions set out as a note under section 2432 of Title 10] and division E [enacting chapter 25 (section 1401 et seq.) of Title 40, Public Buildings, Property, and Works, and former section 434 of this title, amending section 5315 of Title 5, Government Organization and Employees, sections 2305, 2306b, and 2315 of Title 10, Armed Forces, section 278g–3 of Title 15, Commerce and Trade, section 612 of Title 28, Judiciary and Judicial Procedure, sections 1558, 3552, 3553, and 3554 of Title 31, Money and Finance, section 310 of Title 38, Veterans' Benefits, former sections 253b and 405 of this title, section 8287 of Title 42, The Public Health and Welfare, sections 3502, 3504, 3506, 3507, and 3518 of Title 44, Public Printing and Documents, section 40112 of Title 49, Transportation, and section 403c of Title 50, War and National Defense, repealing former section 759 of this title, and enacting provisions set out as notes under former section 251 of this title] may be cited as the 'Clinger-Cohen Act of 1996'."

[Note was classified as a note under former 41 U.S.C.A. § 251 prior to the enactment into positive law of Title 41, Public Contracts, by Pub.L. 111–350, Jan. 4, 2011, 124 Stat. 3677.]

1994 Amendments. Pub.L. 103–355, § 1, Oct. 13, 1994, 108 Stat. 3243, provided that: "This Act [see Tables for classification] may be cited as the 'Federal Acquisition Streamlining Act of 1994'."

[Note was classified as a note under former 41 U.S.C.A. § 251 prior to the enactment into positive law of Title 41, Public Contracts, by Pub.L. 111–350, Jan. 4, 2011, 124 Stat. 3677.]

1988 Amendments. Section 1 of Pub.L. 100–679 provided that: "This Act [enacting former sections 421 to 424 of this title, amending former sections 401, 402, 403, 405, 410, and 420 of this title, sections 5312 to 5315, 8331, 8401, 8701, and 8901 of Title 5, and section 541 of former Title 40, repealing section 2168 of Title 50, Appendix, and enacting provisions set out as

notes under former sections 405 and 423 of this title and section 5312 of Title 5] may be cited as the 'Office of Federal Procurement Policy Act Amendments of 1988'."

[Note was classified as a note under former 41 U.S.C.A. § 401 prior to the enactment into positive law of Title 41, Public Contracts, by Pub.L. 111–350, Jan. 4, 2011, 124 Stat. 3677.]

Section 7001 of Pub.L. 100–418 provided that: "This title [enacting former section 10b–1 of this title, amending 19 U.S.C.A. §§ 2511 and 2515, and former sections 10a, 10b, 10c, and 10d of this title, enacting provisions set out as notes under former section 10a of this title, and amending provisions set out as notes under former section 10c of this title] may be cited as the 'Buy American Act of 1988'."

[Note was classified as a note under former 41 U.S.C.A. § 10a prior to the enactment into positive law of Title 41, Public Contracts, by Pub.L. 111–350, Jan. 4, 2011, 124 Stat. 3677.]

1986 Amendments. Section 1 of Pub.L. 99–634 provided: "That this Act [enacting former sections 55 to 58 of this title, amending former sections 51 to 54 of this title, and enacting provisions set out as a note under former section 51 of this title] may be cited as the 'Anti-Kickback Enforcement Act of 1986'."

[Note was classified as a note under former 41 U.S.C.A. § 51 prior to the enactment into positive law of Title 41, Public Contracts, by Pub.L. 111–350, Jan. 4, 2011, 124 Stat. 3677.]

1984 Amendments. Pub.L. 98–577, § 1, Oct. 30, 1984, 98 Stat. 3066 provided, in part, that this Act [enacting former sections 253c to 253g, 414a, 418a and 418b of this title, repealing section 2303a of Title 10, Armed Forces, amending sections 2302, 2304, 2311 and 2320 of Title 10, Armed Forces, sections 637 and 644 of Title 15, Commerce and Trade, and former sections 253, 253b, 259, 403, and 416 of this title, and enacting provisions set out as notes under sections 637 and 644 of Title 15, Commerce and Trade and former sections 251 and 416 of this title] may be cited as the "Small Business and Federal Procurement Competition Enhancement Act of 1984".

[Note was classified as a note under former 41 U.S.C.A. § 251 prior to the enactment into positive law of Title 41, Public Contracts, by Pub.L. 111–350, Jan. 4, 2011, 124 Stat. 3677.]

Pub.L. 98–369, Title VII, § 2701, July 18, 1984, 98 Stat. 1175, provided that: "This title [enacting, sections 3551–3556 of Title 31, Money and Finance, and former sections 253a, 253b, 416–419 of this title, amending sections 2301–2306, 2310, 2311, 2313 and 2356 of Title 10, Armed Forces, section 759 of Title 40, Public Buildings, Property, and Works, and amending former sections 252, 253, 254, 257, 258, 259, 260, 403, 405, and 414 of this title, and enacting provisions set out as notes under section 2304 of Title 10, Armed Forces, and section 759 of Title 40, Public Buildings, Property, and Works, and former sections 251, 253, 403, and 407 of this title] may be cited as the 'Competition in Contracting Act of 1984'."

See Main Volume and Repealed Title 41, ante, for annotations

[Note was classified as a note under former 41 U.S.C.A. § 251 prior to the enactment into positive law of Title 41, Public Contracts, by Pub.L. 111–350, Jan. 4, 2011, 124 Stat. 3677.]

1983 Amendments. Section 1 of Pub.L. 98–191 provided: "That this Act [enacting former sections 413 to 415 of this title, amending former sections 5, 6a–1, 252, 401, 403, 405, 407, 409, 410, and 411 of this title, section 831h of Title 16, and sections 474, 481, and 487 of former Title 40,] may be cited as the 'Office of Federal Procurement Policy Act Amendments of 1983'."

[Note was classified as a note under former 41 U.S.C.A. § 401 prior to the enactment into positive law of Title 41, Public Contracts, by Pub.L. 111–350, Jan. 4, 2011, 124 Stat. 3677.]

1979 Amendments. Section 1(a) of Pub.L. 96–83 provided that: "This Act [amending former sections 401, 403, 405, 407, and 409 to 412 of this title, and sections 474, 481, and 487 of former Title 40, and enacting provisions set out as notes under former sections 401 and 405a of this title] may be cited as the 'Office of Federal Procurement Policy Act Amendments of 1979'."

[Note was classified as a note under former 41 U.S.C.A. § 401 prior to the enactment into positive law of Title 41, Public Contracts, by Pub.L. 111–350, Jan. 4, 2011, 124 Stat. 3677.]

1974 Amendments. Section 1(a) of Pub.L. 93–400, as amended by Pub.L. 103–355, Title X, § 10005(a)(1), Oct. 13, 1994, 108 Stat. 3406, provided that: "This Act [enacting former chapter 7 of this title, 41 U.S.C.A. § 401 et seq., and amending section 5315 of Title 5, and sections 474, 481, and 487 of former Title 40,] may be cited as the 'Office of Federal Procurement Policy Act'."

[Note was classified as a note under former 41 U.S.C.A. § 401 prior to the enactment into positive law of Title 41, Public Contracts, by Pub.L. 111–350, Jan. 4, 2011, 124 Stat. 3677.]

1949 Amendments. Act, June 30, 1949, c. 288, § 1(a), 63 Stat. 377, amended Oct. 13, 1994, Pub.L. 103–355, Title X, § 10005(a)(2), 108 Stat. 3406, provided that: "This Act may be cited as the 'Federal Property and Administrative Services Act of 1949'." Title III of the Act is classified to former subchapter IV of former chapter 4 of this title, 41 U.S.C.A. § 251 et seq.

while the remainder was formerly classified to chapter 10 of former Title 40, 40 U.S.C.A. § 471 et seq., prior to being repealed by Pub.L. 107–217, § 6(b), Aug. 21, 2002, 116 Stat. 1313; see now generally chapter 1 of Title 40, 40 U.S.C.A. § 101 et seq.

[Note was classified as a note under former 41 U.S.C.A. § 251 prior to the enactment into positive law of Title 41, Public Contracts, by Pub.L. 111–350, Jan. 4, 2011, 124 Stat. 3677.]

[The repeal of section 1(a) by Pub.L. 107–217, § 6(b), Aug. 21, 2002, 116 Stat. 1313, was repealed and "revived to read as if section 6(b) had not been enacted" by Pub.L. 108–178, § 2(b)(1), Dec. 19, 2003, 117 Stat. 2640.]

[Amendments by Pub.L. 108–178 effective August 21, 2002, see Pub.L. 108–178, § 5, set out as a note under 5 U.S.C.A. § 5334.]

1936 Amendments. Act June 30, 1936, c. 881, § 14, formerly § 12, of Act June 30, 1936, as added Pub.L. 103–355, Title X, § 10005(f)(5), Oct. 13, 1994, 108 Stat. 3409, and renumbered § 14 by Pub.L. 104–106, Div. D, Title XLIII, § 4321(f)(1)(B), Feb. 10, 1996, 110 Stat. 675, provided that: "This Act [enacting former sections 35, and 36 to 45 of this title] may be cited as the 'Walsh–Healey Act'."

[Note was classified as a note under former 41 U.S.C.A. § 35 prior to the enactment into positive law of Title 41, Public Contracts, by Pub.L. 111–350, Jan. 4, 2011, 124 Stat. 3677.]

1933 Amendments. Section 7, formerly § 5, of Act Mar. 3, 1933, c. 212, as added Pub.L. 103–355, Title X, § 10005(f)(4), Oct. 13, 1994, 108 Stat. 3409, renumbered § 7 and amended Pub.L. 104–106, Div. D, Title XLIII, § 4321(a)(11), Feb. 10, 1996, 110 Stat. 671, provided that: "This title [enacting former sections 10a, 10b, and 10c of this title] may be cited as the 'Buy American Act'."

[Note was classified as a note under former 41 U.S.C.A. § 10a prior to the enactment into positive law of Title 41, Public Contracts, by Pub.L. 111–350, Jan. 4, 2011, 124 Stat. 3677.]

[Amendment by Pub.L. 104–106 effective Oct. 13, 1994, see section 4321(a) of Pub.L. 104–106, set out as a note under section 2306a of Title 10, Armed Forces.]

§ 102. Commercial component

In this subtitle, the term "commercial component" means a component that is a commercial item.

(Pub.L. 111–350, § 3, Jan. 4, 2011, 124 Stat. 3678.)

§ 103. Commercial item

In this subtitle, the term "commercial item" means—

(1) an item, other than real property, that—

(A) is of a type customarily used by the general public or by nongovernmental entities for purposes other than governmental purposes; and

(B) has been sold, leased, or licensed, or offered for sale, lease, or license, to the general public;

Revised Title 41 effective Jan. 4, 2011

(2) an item that—

    (A) evolved from an item described in paragraph (1) through advances in technology or performance; and

    (B) is not yet available in the commercial marketplace but will be available in the commercial marketplace in time to satisfy the delivery requirements under a Federal Government solicitation;

(3) an item that would satisfy the criteria in paragraph (1) or (2) were it not for—

    (A) modifications of a type customarily available in the commercial marketplace; or

    (B) minor modifications made to meet Federal Government requirements;

(4) any combination of items meeting the requirements of paragraph (1), (2), (3), or (5) that are of a type customarily combined and sold in combination to the general public;

(5) installation services, maintenance services, repair services, training services, and other services if—

    (A) those services are procured for support of an item referred to in paragraph (1), (2), (3), or (4), regardless of whether the services are provided by the same source or at the same time as the item; and

    (B) the source of the services provides similar services contemporaneously to the general public under terms and conditions similar to those offered to the Federal Government;

(6) services offered and sold competitively, in substantial quantities, in the commercial marketplace based on established catalog or market prices for specific tasks performed or specific outcomes to be achieved and under standard commercial terms and conditions;

(7) any item, combination of items, or service referred to in paragraphs (1) to (6) even though the item, combination of items, or service is transferred between or among separate divisions, subsidiaries, or affiliates of a contractor; or

(8) a nondevelopmental item if the procuring agency determines, in accordance with conditions in the Federal Acquisition Regulation, that the item was developed exclusively at private expense and has been sold in substantial quantities, on a competitive basis, to multiple State and local governments.

(Pub.L. 111–350, § 3, Jan. 4, 2011, 124 Stat. 3679.)

§ 104. Commercially available off-the-shelf item

In this subtitle, the term "commercially available off-the-shelf item"—

    (1) means an item that—

        (A) is a commercial item (as described in section 103(1) of this title);

        (B) is sold in substantial quantities in the commercial marketplace; and

        (C) is offered to the Federal Government, without modification, in the same form in which it is sold in the commercial marketplace; but

    (2) does not include bulk cargo, as defined in section 40102(4) of title 46, such as agricultural products and petroleum products.

(Pub.L. 111–350, § 3, Jan. 4, 2011, 124 Stat. 3679.)

§ 105. Component

In this subtitle, the term "component" means an item supplied to the Federal Government as part of an end item or of another component.

(Pub.L. 111–350, § 3, Jan. 4, 2011, 124 Stat. 3680.)

§ 106. Federal Acquisition Regulation

In this subtitle, the term "Federal Acquisition Regulation" means the regulation issued under section 1303(a)(1) of this title.

(Pub.L. 111–350, § 3, Jan. 4, 2011, 124 Stat. 3680.)

See Main Volume and Repealed Title 41, ante, for annotations

§ 107. Full and open competition

In this subtitle, the term "full and open competition", when used with respect to a procurement, means that all responsible sources are permitted to submit sealed bids or competitive proposals on the procurement.

(Pub.L. 111–350, § 3, Jan. 4, 2011, 124 Stat. 3680.)

§ 108. Item and item of supply

In this subtitle, the terms "item" and "item of supply"—

(1) mean an individual part, component, subassembly, assembly, or subsystem integral to a major system, and other property which may be replaced during the service life of the system, including spare parts and replenishment spare parts; but

(2) do not include packaging or labeling associated with shipment or identification of an item.

(Pub.L. 111–350, § 3, Jan. 4, 2011, 124 Stat. 3680.)

§ 109. Major system

(a) **In general**—In this subtitle, the term "major system" means a combination of elements that will function together to produce the capabilities required to fulfill a mission need. These elements may include hardware, equipment, software, or a combination of hardware, equipment, and software, but do not include construction or other improvements to real property.

(b) **System deemed to be major system.**—A system is deemed to be a major system if—

(1) the Department of Defense is responsible for the system and the total expenditures for research, development, testing, and evaluation for the system are estimated to exceed $75,000,000 (based on fiscal year 1980 constant dollars) or the eventual total expenditure for procurement exceeds $ 300,000,000 (based on fiscal year 1980 constant dollars);

(2) a civilian agency is responsible for the system and total expenditures for the system are estimated to exceed the greater of $750,000 (based on fiscal year 1980 constant dollars) or the dollar threshold for a major system established by the agency pursuant to Office of Management and Budget (OMB) Circular A–109, entitled "Major Systems Acquisitions"; or

(3) the head of the agency responsible for the system designates the system a major system.

(Pub.L. 111–350, § 3, Jan. 4, 2011, 124 Stat. 3680.)

§ 110. Nondevelopmental item

In this subtitle, the term "nondevelopmental item" means—

(1) a commercial item;

(2) a previously developed item of supply that is in use by a department or agency of the Federal Government, a State or local government, or a foreign government with which the United States has a mutual defense cooperation agreement;

(3) an item of supply described in paragraph (1) or (2) that requires only minor modification or modification of the type customarily available in the commercial marketplace to meet the requirements of the procuring department or agency; or

(4) an item of supply currently being produced that does not meet the requirements of paragraph (1), (2), or (3) solely because the item is not yet in use.

(Pub.L. 111–350, § 3, Jan. 4, 2011, 124 Stat. 3680.)

Revised Title 41 effective Jan. 4, 2011

§ 111. Procurement

In this subtitle, the term "procurement" includes all stages of the process of acquiring property or services, beginning with the process for determining a need for property or services and ending with contract completion and closeout.

(Pub.L. 111–350, § 3, Jan. 4, 2011, 124 Stat. 3681.)

§ 112. Procurement system

In this subtitle, the term "procurement system" means the integration of the procurement process, the professional development of procurement personnel, and the management structure for carrying out the procurement function.

(Pub.L. 111–350, § 3, Jan. 4, 2011, 124 Stat. 3681.)

§ 113. Responsible source

In this subtitle, the term "responsible source" means a prospective contractor that—

(1) has adequate financial resources to perform the contract or the ability to obtain those resources;

(2) is able to comply with the required or proposed delivery or performance schedule, taking into consideration all existing commercial and Government business commitments;

(3) has a satisfactory performance record;

(4) has a satisfactory record of integrity and business ethics;

(5) has the necessary organization, experience, accounting and operational controls, and technical skills, or the ability to obtain the organization, experience, controls, and skills;

(6) has the necessary production, construction, and technical equipment and facilities, or the ability to obtain the equipment and facilities; and

(7) is otherwise qualified and eligible to receive an award under applicable laws and regulations.

(Pub.L. 111–350, § 3, Jan. 4, 2011, 124 Stat. 3681.)

§ 114. Standards

In this subtitle, the term "standards" means the criteria for determining the effectiveness of the procurement system by measuring the performance of the various elements of the system.

(Pub.L. 111–350, § 3, Jan. 4, 2011, 124 Stat. 3681.)

§ 115. Supplies

In this subtitle, the term "supplies" has the same meaning as the terms "item" and "item of supply".

(Pub.L. 111–350, § 3, Jan. 4, 2011, 124 Stat. 3681.)

§ 116. Technical data

In this subtitle, the term "technical data"—

(1) means recorded information (regardless of the form or method of the recording) of a scientific or technical nature (including computer software documentation) relating to supplies procured by an agency; but

(2) does not include computer software or financial, administrative, cost or pricing, or management data or other information incidental to contract administration.

(Pub.L. 111–350, § 3, Jan. 4, 2011, 124 Stat. 3681.)

See Main Volume and Repealed Title 41, ante, for annotations

SUBCHAPTER II—DIVISION B DEFINITIONS

§ 131. Acquisition

In division B, the term "acquisition"—

(1) means the process of acquiring, with appropriated amounts, by contract for purchase or lease, property or services (including construction) that support the missions and goals of an executive agency, from the point at which the requirements of the executive agency are established in consultation with the chief acquisition officer of the executive agency; and

(2) includes—

(A) the process of acquiring property or services that are already in existence, or that must be created, developed, demonstrated, and evaluated;

(B) the description of requirements to satisfy agency needs;

(C) solicitation and selection of sources;

(D) award of contracts;

(E) contract performance;

(F) contract financing;

(G) management and measurement of contract performance through final delivery and payment; and

(H) technical and management functions directly related to the process of fulfilling agency requirements by contract.

(Pub.L. 111–350, § 3, Jan. 4, 2011, 124 Stat. 3682.)

HISTORICAL AND STATUTORY NOTES

References in Text

Division B, referred to in text, is Division B of this subtitle, which is classified to 41 U.S.C.A. § 1101 et seq.

§ 132. Competitive procedures

In division B, the term "competitive procedures" means procedures under which an agency enters into a contract pursuant to full and open competition.

(Pub.L. 111–350, § 3, Jan. 4, 2011, 124 Stat. 3682.)

HISTORICAL AND STATUTORY NOTES

References in Text

Division B, referred to in text, is Division B of this subtitle, which is classified to 41 U.S.C.A. § 1101 et seq.

§ 133. Executive agency

In division B, the term "executive agency" means—

(1) an executive department specified in section 101 of title 5;

(2) a military department specified in section 102 of title 5;

(3) an independent establishment as defined in section 104(1) of title 5; and

(4) a wholly owned Government corporation fully subject to chapter 91 of title 31.

(Pub.L. 111–350, § 3, Jan. 4, 2011, 124 Stat. 3682.)

HISTORICAL AND STATUTORY NOTES

References in Text

Division B, referred to in text, is Division B of this subtitle, which is classified to 41 U.S.C.A. § 1101 et seq.

Chapter 91 of title 31, referred to in par. (4), is classified to 31 U.S.C.A. § 9101 et seq.

Revised Title 41 effective Jan. 4, 2011

§ 134. Simplified acquisition threshold

In division B, the term "simplified acquisition threshold" means $100,000.

(Pub.L. 111–350, § 3, Jan. 4, 2011, 124 Stat. 3682.)

HISTORICAL AND STATUTORY NOTES

References in Text

Division B, referred to in text, is Division B of this subtitle, which is classified to 41 U.S.C.A. § 1101 et seq.

SUBCHAPTER III—DIVISION C DEFINITIONS

§ 151. Agency head

In division C, the term "agency head" means the head or any assistant head of an executive agency, and may at the option of the Administrator of General Services include the chief official of any principal organizational unit of the General Services Administration.

(Pub.L. 111–350, § 3, Jan. 4, 2011, 124 Stat. 3682.)

HISTORICAL AND STATUTORY NOTES

References in Text

Division C, referred to in text, is Division C of this subtitle, which is classified to 41 U.S.C.A. § 3101 et seq.

§ 152. Competitive procedures

In division C, the term "competitive procedures" means procedures under which an executive agency enters into a contract pursuant to full and open competition. The term also includes—

    (1) procurement of architectural or engineering services conducted in accordance with chapter 11 of title 40;

    (2) the competitive selection of basic research proposals resulting from a general solicitation and the peer review or scientific review (as appropriate) of those proposals;

    (3) the procedures established by the Administrator of General Services for the multiple awards schedule program of the General Services Administration if—

        (A) participation in the program has been open to all responsible sources; and

        (B) orders and contracts under those procedures result in the lowest overall cost alternative to meet the needs of the Federal Government;

    (4) procurements conducted in furtherance of section 15 of the Small Business Act (15 U.S.C. 644) as long as all responsible business concerns that are entitled to submit offers for those procurements are permitted to compete; and

    (5) a competitive selection of research proposals resulting from a general solicitation and peer review or scientific review (as appropriate) solicited pursuant to section 9 of that Act (15 U.S.C. 638).

(Pub.L. 111–350, § 3, Jan. 4, 2011, 124 Stat. 3683.)

HISTORICAL AND STATUTORY NOTES

References in Text

Division C, referred to in text, is Division C of this subtitle, which is classified to 41 U.S.C.A. § 3101 et seq.

Chapter 11 of title 40, referred to in par. (1) is classified to 40 U.S.C.A. § 1101 et seq.

The Small Business Act, referred to in pars. (4) and (5), is Act July 18, 1958, Pub.L. 85–536, 72 Stat. 384, as amended, also known as the SBA, which is principally classified to chapter 14A of Title 15, 15 U.S.C.A. § 631 et seq. Section 15 of such Act, referred to in par. (4), is classified to 15 U.S.C.A. § 644. Section 9 of such Act, referred to in par. (5), is classified to

See Main Volume and Repealed Title 41, ante, for annotations

15 U.S.C.A. § 638. For complete classification, see Short Title note set out under 15 U.S.C.A. § 631 and Tables.

§ 153. Simplified acquisition threshold for contract in support of humanitarian or peacekeeping operation

(1) **In general**—In division C, the term "simplified acquisition threshold" has the meaning provided that term in section 134 of this title, except that, in the case of a contract to be awarded and performed, or purchase to be made, outside the United States in support of a humanitarian or peacekeeping operation, the term means an amount equal to two times the amount specified for that term in section 134 of this title.

(2) **Definition.**—In paragraph (1), the term "humanitarian or peacekeeping operation" means a military operation in support of the provision of humanitarian or foreign disaster assistance or in support of a peacekeeping operation under chapter VI or VII of the Charter of the United Nations. The term does not include routine training, force rotation, or stationing.

(Pub.L. 111–350, § 3, Jan. 4, 2011, 124 Stat. 3683.)

HISTORICAL AND STATUTORY NOTES

References in Text

Division C, referred to in text, is Division C of this subtitle, which is classified to 41 U.S.C.A. § 3101 et seq.

CROSS REFERENCES

Increased simplified acquisition threshold for procurements in support of humanitarian or peacekeeping operations or contingency operations, see 6 USCA § 423.

Limitation on amounts that may be obligated or accrued by the United States, see 10 USCA § 2347.

Noncombatant assistance to United Nations, see 22 USCA § 287d–1.

Peacekeeping operations, military assistance and sales, see 22 USCA § 2348.

DIVISION B—OFFICE OF FEDERAL PROCUREMENT POLICY

CHAPTER 11—ESTABLISHMENT OF OFFICE AND AUTHORITY AND FUNCTIONS OF ADMINISTRATOR

SUBCHAPTER I—GENERAL

§ 1101. Office of Federal Procurement Policy

(a) **Organization**—There is an Office of Federal Procurement Policy in the Office of Management and Budget.

(b) **Purposes.**—The purposes of the Office of Federal Procurement Policy are to—

(1) provide overall direction of Government-wide procurement policies, regulations, procedures, and forms for executive agencies; and

(2) promote economy, efficiency, and effectiveness in the procurement of property and services by the executive branch of the Federal Government.

(c) **Authorization of appropriations.**—Necessary amounts may be appropriated each fiscal year for the Office of Federal Procurement Policy to carry out the responsibilities of the Office for that fiscal year.

(Pub.L. 111–350, § 3, Jan. 4, 2011, 124 Stat. 3684.)

HISTORICAL AND STATUTORY NOTES

Services by Contract

Pub.L. 102–394, Title V, § 502, Oct. 6, 1992, 106 Stat. 1825, provided that:

"No part of any appropriation contained in this Act or subsequent Departments of Labor, Health and Human Services, and Education, and Related Agencies Appropriations Acts shall be expended by an executive agency, as referred to in the Office of Federal Procurement Policy Act (41 U.S.C. 401 et seq.) [former 41 U.S.C.A. § 401 et seq.], pursuant to any obligation for services by contract, unless such executive agency has awarded and entered into such contract in full compliance with such Act and regulations promulgated thereunder."

Similar provisions were contained in the following prior appropriation acts:

Pub.L. 102–170, Title V, § 502, Nov. 26, 1991, 105 Stat. 1140.

Pub.L. 101–517, Title V, § 502, Nov. 5, 1990, 104 Stat. 2221.

Pub.L. 101–166, Title V, § 502, Nov. 21, 1989, 103 Stat. 1189.

Pub.L. 100–202, § 101(h) [Title V, § 502], Dec. 22, 1987, 101 Stat. 1329–256, 1329–287.

Pub.L. 99–500, § 101(i) [H.R. 5233, Title V, § 502], Oct. 18, 1986, 100 Stat. 1783–287, and Pub.L. 99–591, § 101(i) [H.R. 5233, Title V, § 502], Oct. 30, 1986, 100 Stat. 3341–287.

Pub.L. 99–178, Title V, § 502, Dec. 12, 1985, 99 Stat. 1132.

Pub.L. 98–619, Title V, § 502, Nov. 8, 1984, 98 Stat. 3332.

Pub.L. 98–139, Title V, § 502, Oct. 31, 1983, 97 Stat. 899.

Pub.L. 97–377, Title I, § 101(e)(1) [Title V, § 502], Dec. 21, 1982, 96 Stat. 1878, 1904.

[Note was classified as a note under former 41 U.S.C.A. § 401 prior to the enactment into positive law of Title 41, Public Contracts, by Pub.L. 111–350, Jan. 4, 2011, 124 Stat. 3677.]

CROSS REFERENCES

Executive agency, defined for division B of subtitle I of this title, see 41 USCA § 133.

Office of Management and Budget, organization, Office of Federal Procurement Policy, see 31 USCA § 506.

§ 1102. Administrator

(a) **Head of Office**—The head of the Office of Federal Procurement Policy is the Administrator for Federal Procurement Policy.

(b) **Appointment.**—The Administrator is appointed by the President, by and with the advice and consent of the Senate.

(Pub.L. 111–350, § 3, Jan. 4, 2011, 124 Stat. 3684.)

CROSS REFERENCES

Administrator, defined for Subtitle I of this title, see 41 USCA § 101.

SUBCHAPTER II—AUTHORITY AND FUNCTIONS OF THE ADMINISTRATOR

CROSS REFERENCES

Administrator, defined for Subtitle I of this title, see 41 USCA § 101.

§ 1121. General authority

(a) **Overall direction and leadership**—The Administrator shall provide overall direction of procurement policy and leadership in the development of procurement systems of the executive agencies.

(b) **Federal Acquisition Regulation.**—To the extent that the Administrator considers appropriate in carrying out the policies and functions set forth in this division, and with due regard for applicable laws and the program activities of the executive agencies, the Administrator may prescribe Government–wide procurement policies. The policies shall be implemented in a single Government–wide procurement regulation called the Federal Acquisition Regulation.

(c) Policies to be followed by executive agencies.—

    (1) Areas of procurement for which policies are to be followed.—The policies implemented in the Federal Acquisition Regulation shall be followed by executive agencies in the procurement of—

        (A) property other than real property in being;

        (B) services, including research and development; and

        (C) construction, alteration, repair, or maintenance of real property.

    (2) Procedures to ensure compliance.—The Administrator shall establish procedures to ensure compliance with the Federal Acquisition Regulation by all executive agencies.

    (3) Application of other laws.—The authority of an executive agency under another law to prescribe policies, regulations, procedures, and forms for procurement is subject to the authority conferred in this section and sections 1122(a) to (c)(1), 1125, 1126, 1130, 1131, and 2305 of this title.

(d) When certain agencies are unable to agree or fail to act.—In any instance in which the Administrator determines that the Department of Defense, the National Aeronautics and Space Administration, and the General Services Administration are unable to agree on or fail to issue Government–wide regulations, procedures, and forms in a timely manner, including regulations, procedures, and forms necessary to implement prescribed policy the Administrator initiates under subsection (b), the Administrator, with due regard for applicable laws and the program activities of the executive agencies and consistent with the policies and functions set forth in this division, shall prescribe Government-wide regulations, procedures, and forms which executive agencies shall follow in procuring items listed in subsection (c)(1).

(e) Oversight of procurement regulations of other agencies.—The Administrator, with the concurrence of the Director of the Office of Management and Budget, and with consultation with the head of the agency concerned, may deny the promulgation of or rescind any Government-wide regulation or final rule or regulation of any executive agency relating to procurement if the Administrator determines that the rule or regulation is inconsistent with any policies, regulations, or procedures issued pursuant to subsection (b).

(f) Limitation on authority.—The authority of the Administrator under this division shall not be construed to—

    (1) impair or interfere with the determination by executive agencies of their need for, or their use of, specific property, services, or construction, including particular specifications for the property, services, or construction; or

    (2) interfere with the determination by executive agencies of specific actions in the award or administration of procurement contracts.

(Pub.L. 111–350, § 3, Jan. 4, 2011, 124 Stat. 3684.)

HISTORICAL AND STATUTORY NOTES

Federal Support for Enhancement of State and Local Anti-Terrorism Response Capabilities

Pub.L. 108–136, Div. A, Title VIII, § 803, Nov. 24, 2003, 117 Stat. 1541, provided that:

"**(a) Procurements of anti-terrorism technologies and services by State and local Governments.—**The Administrator for Federal Procurement Policy shall establish a program under which States and units of local government may procure through contracts entered into by the Department of Defense or the Department of Homeland Security anti-terrorism technologies or anti-terrorism services for the purpose of preventing, detecting, identifying, deterring, or recovering from acts of terrorism.

"**(b) Authorities.—**Under the program, the Secretary of Defense and the Secretary of Homeland Security may, but shall not be required to, award contracts using the procedures established by the Administrator of General Services for the multiple awards schedule program of the General Services Administration.

"**(c) Definition.—**In this section, the term 'State or local government' has the meaning provided in section 502(c)(3) of title 40, United States Code."

[Note was classified as a note under former 41 U.S.C.A. § 405 prior to the enactment into positive law of Title 41, Public Contracts, by Pub.L. 111–350, Jan. 4, 2011, 124 Stat. 3677.]

Profit Methodology Study

Pub.L. 100–679, § 7, Nov. 17, 1988, 102 Stat. 4068, provided that:

"(a) In general.—The Administrator shall conduct a study to develop a consistent methodology which executive agencies should use for measuring the profits earned by government contractors on procurements, other than procurements where the price is based on adequate price competition or on established catalog or market prices of commercial items sold in substantial quantities to the general public.

"(b) Contractors' financial data.—The methodology developed under subsection (a) shall include adequate procedures for verifying

and maintaining the confidentiality of contractors' financial data."

[Note was classified as a note under former 41 U.S.C.A. § 405 prior to the enactment into positive law of Title 41, Public Contracts, by Pub.L. 111–350, Jan. 4, 2011, 124 Stat. 3677.]

Supersedure of Inconsistent Statutory Provisions

Pub.L. 96–83, § 11, Oct. 10, 1979, 93 Stat. 652, provided that: "The provisions of the Act as amended by this Act [see Short Title and Short Title of 1979 Amendment notes set out under section 101 of this title] shall supersede the provisions of section 222 of the Act of October 24, 1978, entitled 'An Act to amend the Small Business Act and the Small Business Investment Act of 1958' (former 41 U.S.C. 405a) [this section] to the extent they are inconsistent therewith."

[Note was classified as a note under former 41 U.S.C.A. § 405a prior to the enactment into positive law of Title 41, Public Contracts, by Pub.L. 111–350, Jan. 4, 2011, 124 Stat. 3677.]

CROSS REFERENCES

Executive agency, defined for division B of subtitle I of this title, see 41 USCA § 133.
Federal Acquisition Regulation, defined for subtitle I of this title, functions and general authority, see 41 USCA §§ 106 and 1303.

Procurement, defined for subtitle I of this title, see 41 USCA § 111.
Procurement system, defined for subtitle I of this title, see 41 USCA § 112.

§ 1122. Functions

(a) In general.—The functions of the Administrator include—

(1) providing leadership and ensuring action by the executive agencies in establishing, developing, and maintaining the single system of simplified Government–wide procurement regulations and resolving differences among the executive agencies in developing simplified Government–wide procurement regulations, procedures, and forms;

(2) coordinating the development of Government–wide procurement system standards that executive agencies shall implement in their procurement systems;

(3) providing leadership and coordination in formulating the executive branch position on legislation relating to procurement;

(4)(A) providing for and directing the activities of the computer-based Federal Procurement Data System (including recommending to the Administrator of General Services a sufficient budget for those activities), which shall be located in the General Services Administration, in order to adequately collect, develop, and disseminate procurement data; and

(B) ensuring executive agency compliance with the record requirements of section 1712 of this title;

(5) providing for and directing the activities of the Federal Acquisition Institute (including recommending to the Administrator of General Services a sufficient budget for those activities), which shall be located in the General Services Administration, in order to—

(A) foster and promote the development of a professional acquisition workforce Government–wide;

(B) promote and coordinate Government–wide research and studies to improve the procurement process and the laws, policies, methods, regulations, procedures, and forms relating to acquisition by the executive agencies;

(C) collect data and analyze acquisition workforce data from the Office of Personnel Management, from the heads of executive agencies, and, through periodic surveys, from individual employees;

(D) periodically analyze acquisition career fields to identify critical competencies, duties, tasks, and related academic prerequisites, skills, and knowledge;

(E) coordinate and assist agencies in identifying and recruiting highly qualified candidates for acquisition fields;

(F) develop instructional materials for acquisition personnel in coordination with private and public acquisition colleges and training facilities;

(G) evaluate the effectiveness of training and career development programs for acquisition personnel;

(H) promote the establishment and utilization of academic programs by colleges and universities in acquisition fields;

(I) facilitate, to the extent requested by agencies, interagency intern and training programs; and

(J) perform other career management or research functions as directed by the Administrator;

(6) administering section 1703(a) to (i) of this title;

(7) establishing criteria and procedures to ensure the effective and timely solicitation of the viewpoints of interested parties in the development of procurement policies, regulations, procedures, and forms;

(8) developing standard contract forms and contract language in order to reduce the Federal Government's cost of procuring property and services and the private sector's cost of doing business with the Federal Government;

(9) providing for a Government–wide award to recognize and promote vendor excellence;

(10) providing for a Government–wide award to recognize and promote excellence in officers and employees of the Federal Government serving in procurement-related positions;

(11) developing policies, in consultation with the Administrator of the Small Business Administration, that ensure that small businesses, qualified HUBZone small business concerns (as defined in section 3(p) of the Small Business Act (15 U.S.C. 632(p))), small businesses owned and controlled by socially and economically disadvantaged individuals, and small businesses owned and controlled by women are provided with the maximum practicable opportunities to participate in procurements that are conducted for amounts below the simplified acquisition threshold;

(12) developing policies that will promote achievement of goals for participation by small businesses, small business concerns owned and controlled by service-disabled veterans, qualified HUBZone small business concerns (as defined in section 3(p) of the Small Business Act (15 U.S.C. 632(p))), small businesses owned and controlled by socially and economically disadvantaged individuals, and small businesses owned and controlled by women; and

(13) completing action, as appropriate, on the recommendations of the Commission on Government Procurement.

(b) Consultation and assistance.—In carrying out the functions in subsection (a), the Administrator—

(1) shall consult with the affected executive agencies, including the Small Business Administration;

(2) with the concurrence of the heads of affected executive agencies, may designate one or more executive agencies to assist in performing those functions; and

(3) may establish advisory committees or other interagency groups to assist in providing for the establishment, development, and maintenance of a single system of simplified Government–wide procurement regulations and to assist in performing any other function the Administrator considers appropriate.

(c) Assignment, delegation, or transfer.—

(1) To administrator.—Except as otherwise provided by law, only duties, functions, or responsibilities expressly assigned by this division shall be assigned, delegated, or transferred to the Administrator.

(2) By administrator.—

(A) **Within office.**—The Administrator may make and authorize delegations within the Office of Federal Procurement Policy that the Administrator determines to be necessary to carry out this division.

(B) **To another executive agency.**—The Administrator may delegate, and authorize successive redelegations of, an authority, function, or power of the Administrator under this division (other than the authority to provide overall direction of Federal procurement policy and to prescribe policies and regulations to carry out the policy) to another executive agency with the consent of the head of the executive agency or at the direction of the President.

(Pub.L. 111–350, § 3, Jan. 4, 2011, 124 Stat. 3685.)

HISTORICAL AND STATUTORY NOTES

References in Text

The Small Business Act, referred to in subsec. (a)(11), is Act July 18, 1958, Pub.L. 85–536, 72 Stat. 384, as amended, also known as the SBA, which is principally classified to chapter 14A of Title 15, 15 U.S.C.A. § 631 et seq. Section 3 of such Act, referred to in subsec. (a)(11) and (12), is classified to 15 U.S.C.A. § 632. For complete classification, see Short Title note set out under 15 U.S.C.A. § 631 and Tables.

Pilot Program for Development and Implementation of an Inventory to Track the Cost and Size of Service Contracts

Pub.L. 110–161, Div. D, Title VII, § 748, Dec. 26, 2007, 121 Stat. 2035, provided that: "No later than 180 days after enactment of this Act [Dec. 26, 2007], the Office of Management and Budget shall establish a pilot program to develop and implement an inventory to track the cost and size (in contractor manpower equivalents) of service contracts, particularly with respect to contracts that have been performed poorly by a contractor because of excessive costs or inferior quality, as determined by a contracting officer within the last five years, involve inherently governmental functions, or were undertaken without competition. The pilot program shall be established in at least three Cabinet-level departments, based on varying levels of annual contracting for services, as reported by the Federal Procurement Data System's Federal Procurement Report for fiscal year 2005, including at least one Cabinet-level department that contracts out annually for $10,000,000,000 or more in services, at least one Cabinet-level department that contracts out annually for between $5,000,000,000 and $9,000,000,000 in services, and at least one Cabinet-level department that contracts out annually for under $5,000,000,000 in services."

[Note was classified as a note under former 41 U.S.C.A. § 405 prior to the enactment into positive law of Title 41, Public Contracts, by Pub.L. 111–350, Jan. 4, 2011, 124 Stat. 3677.]

Reporting of Bundled Contract Opportunities

Pub.L. 105–135, § 414, Dec. 2, 1997, 111 Stat. 2619 provided that:

"(a) **Data collection required**

"The Federal Procurement Data System described in section 6(d)(4)(A) of the Office of Federal Procurement Policy Act (41 U.S.C. 405(d)(4)(A) [former 41 U.S.C.A. § 405(d)(5)(A)])

shall be modified to collect data regarding bundling of contract requirements when the contracting officer anticipates that the resulting contract price, including all options, is expected to exceed $5,000,000. The data shall reflect a determination made by the contracting officer regarding whether a particular solicitation constitutes a contract bundling.

"(b) **Definitions**

"In this section, the term 'bundling of contract requirements' has the meaning given that term in section 3(o) of the Small Business Act (15 U.S.C. 632(o)) (as added by section 412 of this subtitle [Pub.L. 105–135, Title IV, § 412, Dec. 2, 1997, 111 Stat. 2617])."

[Pub.L. 105–135 effective Oct. 1, 1997, see section 3 of Pub.L. 105–135, set out as a note under 15 U.S.C.A. § 631.]

[Note was classified as a note under former 41 U.S.C.A. § 405 prior to the enactment into positive law of Title 41, Public Contracts, by Pub.L. 111–350, Jan. 4, 2011, 124 Stat. 3677.]

Results-Oriented Acquisition Process

Pub.L. 103–355, § 5052, Oct. 13, 1994, 108 Stat. 3352, provided that:

"(a) **Development of process required.**— The Administrator for Federal Procurement Policy, in consultation with the heads of appropriate Federal agencies, shall develop results-oriented acquisition process guidelines for implementation by agencies in acquisitions of property and services by the Federal agencies. The process guidelines shall include the identification of quantitative measures and standards for determining the extent to which an acquisition of items other than commercial items by a Federal agency satisfies the needs for which the items are being acquired.

"(b) **Inapplicability of process to Department of Defense.**—The process guidelines developed pursuant to subsection (a) may not be applied to the Department of Defense."

[Note was classified as a note under former 41 U.S.C.A. § 405 prior to the enactment into positive law of Title 41, Public Contracts, by Pub.L. 111–350, Jan. 4, 2011, 124 Stat. 3677.]

Data Collection Through the Federal Procurement Data System

Pub.L. 103–355, § 10004, Oct. 13, 1994, 108 Stat. 3405, provided that:

"(a) **Data collection required.**—The Federal Procurement Data System described in section 6(d)(4)(A) of the Office of Federal Procurement Policy Act (former 41 U.S.C. 405(d)(4)(A)) [subsec.(d)(4)(A) of former 41 U.S.C.A. § 405] shall be modified to collect from contracts in excess of the simplified acquisition threshold data identifying the following matters:

"(1) Contract awards made pursuant to competitions conducted pursuant to section 2323 of title 10, United States Code [section 2323 of Title 10, Armed Forces], or section 7102 of the Federal Acquisition Streamlining Act of 1994 [section 7102 of Pub.L. 103–355, set out as a note under section 644 of Title 15, Commerce and Trade].

"(2) Awards to business concerns owned and controlled by women.

"(3) Number of offers received in response to a solicitation.

"(4) Task order contracts.

"(5) Contracts for the acquisition of commercial items.

"(b) **Definition.**—In this section, the term 'simplified acquisition threshold' has the meaning given such term in section 4(11) of the Office of Federal Procurement Policy Act (41 U.S.C. 403(11)) [former 41 U.S.C.A. § 403(11)]."

[Note was classified as a note under former 41 U.S.C.A. § 405 prior to the enactment into positive law of Title 41, Public Contracts, by Pub.L. 111–350, Jan. 4, 2011, 124 Stat. 3677.]

CROSS REFERENCES

Acquisition, defined for division B of subtitle I of this title, see 41 USCA § 131.

Executive agency, defined for division B of subtitle I of this title, see 41 USCA § 133.

Procurement, defined for subtitle I of this title, see 41 USCA § 111.

Simplified acquisition threshold, defined for division B of subtitle I of this title, see 41 USCA § 134.

§ 1123. Small business concerns

In formulating the Federal Acquisition Regulation and procedures to ensure compliance with the Regulation, the Administrator, in consultation with the Small Business Administration, shall—

(1) conduct analyses of the impact on small business concerns resulting from revised procurement regulations; and

(2) incorporate into revised procurement regulations simplified bidding, contract performance, and contract administration procedures for small business concerns.

(Pub.L. 111–350, § 3, Jan. 4, 2011, 124 Stat. 3687.)

CROSS REFERENCES

Federal Acquisition Regulation, defined for subtitle I of this title, functions and general authority, see 41 USCA §§ 106 and 1303.

Procurement, defined for subtitle I of this title, see 41 USCA § 111.

§ 1124. Tests of innovative procurement methods and procedures

(a) **In general.**—The Administrator may develop innovative procurement methods and procedures to be tested by selected executive agencies. In developing a program to test innovative procurement methods and procedures under this subsection, the Administrator shall consult with the heads of executive agencies to—

(1) ascertain the need for and specify the objectives of the program;

(2) develop the guidelines and procedures for carrying out the program and the criteria to be used in measuring the success of the program;

(3) evaluate the potential costs and benefits which may be derived from the innovative procurement methods and procedures tested under the program;

(4) select the appropriate executive agencies or components of executive agencies to carry out the program;

(5) specify the categories and types of products or services to be procured under the program; and

(6) develop the methods to be used to analyze the results of the program.

(b) **Approval of executive agencies required.**—A program to test innovative procurement methods and procedures may not be carried out unless approved by the heads of the executive agencies selected to carry out the program.

(c) **Request for waiver of law.**—If the Administrator determines that it is necessary to waive the application of a provision of law to carry out a proposed program to test innovative procurement methods and procedures under subsection (a), the Administrator shall transmit notice of the proposed program to the Committee on Oversight and Government Reform of the House of Representatives and the Committee on Homeland Security and Governmental Affairs of the Senate and request that the Committees take the necessary action to provide that the provision of law does not apply with respect to the proposed program. The notification to Congress shall include—

(1) a description of the proposed program (including the scope and purpose of the proposed program);

(2) the procedures to be followed in carrying out the proposed program;

(3) the provisions of law affected and the application of any provision of law that must be waived in order to carry out the proposed program; and

(4) the executive agencies involved in carrying out the proposed program.

(Pub.L. 111–350, § 3, Jan. 4, 2011, 124 Stat. 3688.)

CROSS REFERENCES

Executive agency, defined for division B of subtitle I of this title, see 41 USCA § 133.

Procurement, defined for subtitle I of this title, see 41 USCA § 111.

§ 1125. Recipients of Federal grants or assistance

(a) **Authority.**—With due regard to applicable laws and the program activities of the executive agencies administering Federal programs of grants or assistance, the Administrator may prescribe Government–wide policies, regulations, procedures, and forms that the Administrator considers appropriate and that executive agencies shall follow in providing for the procurement, to the extent required under those programs, of property or services referred to in section 1121(c)(1) of this title by recipients of Federal grants or assistance under the programs.

(b) **Limitation.**—Subsection (a) does not—

(1) permit the Administrator to authorize procurement or supply support, either directly or indirectly, to a recipient of a Federal grant or assistance; or

(2) authorize action by a recipient contrary to State and local law in the case of a program to provide a Federal grant or assistance to a State or political subdivision.

(Pub.L. 111–350, § 3, Jan. 4, 2011, 124 Stat. 3688.)

CROSS REFERENCES

Executive agency, defined for division B of subtitle I of this title, see 41 USCA § 133.

Procurement, defined for subtitle I of this title, see 41 USCA § 111.

§ 1126. Policy regarding consideration of contractor past performance

(a) **Guidance.**—The Administrator shall prescribe for executive agencies guidance regarding consideration of the past contract performance of offerors in awarding contracts. The guidance shall include—

(1) standards for evaluating past performance with respect to cost (when appropriate), schedule, compliance with technical or functional specifications, and other relevant performance factors that facilitate consistent and fair evaluation by all executive agencies;

(2) policies for the collection and maintenance of information on past contract performance that, to the maximum extent practicable, facilitate automated collection, maintenance, and dissemination of information and provide for ease of collection, maintenance, and dissemination of information by other methods, as necessary;

(3) policies for ensuring that—

(A) offerors are afforded an opportunity to submit relevant information on past contract performance, including performance under contracts entered into by the executive agency concerned, other departments and agencies of the Federal Government, agencies of State and local governments, and commercial customers; and

(B) the information submitted by offerors is considered; and

See Main Volume and Repealed Title 41, ante, for annotations

(4) the period for which information on past performance of offerors may be maintained and considered.

(b) Information not available.—If there is no information on past contract performance of an offeror or the information on past contract performance is not available, the offeror may not be evaluated favorably or unfavorably on the factor of past contract performance.

(Pub.L. 111–350, § 3, Jan. 4, 2011, 124 Stat. 3689.)

HISTORICAL AND STATUTORY NOTES

Congressional Findings and Policy Regarding Consideration of Contractor Past Performance

Pub.L. 103–355, 1091(b)(1), Oct. 13, 1994, 108 Stat. 3272, provided that:

"(1) Congress makes the following findings:

"(A) Past contract performance of an offeror is one of the relevant factors that a contracting official of an executive agency should consider in awarding a contract.

"(B) It is appropriate for a contracting official to consider past contract performance of an offeror as an indicator of the likelihood that the offeror will successfully perform a contract to be awarded by that official."

[Note was classified as a note under former 41 U.S.C.A. § 405 prior to the enactment into positive law of Title 41, Public Contracts, by Pub.L. 111–350, Jan. 4, 2011, 124 Stat. 3677.]

CROSS REFERENCES

Executive agency, defined for division B of subtitle I of this title, see 41 USCA § 133.

Standards, defined for subtitle I of this title, see 41 USCA § 114.

§ 1127. Determining benchmark compensation amount

(a) Definitions.—In this section:

(1) Benchmark compensation amount.—The term "benchmark compensation amount", for a fiscal year, is the median amount of the compensation provided for all senior executives of all benchmark corporations for the most recent year for which data is available at the time the determination under subsection (b) is made.

(2) Benchmark corporation.—The term "benchmark corporation", with respect to a fiscal year, means a publicly-owned United States corporation that has annual sales in excess of $50,000,000 for the fiscal year.

(3) Compensation.—The term "compensation", for a fiscal year, means the total amount of wages, salary, bonuses, and deferred compensation for the fiscal year, whether paid, earned, or otherwise accruing, as recorded in an employer's cost accounting records for the fiscal year.

(4) Fiscal year.—The term "fiscal year" means a fiscal year a contractor establishes for accounting purposes.

(5) Publicly-owned United States corporation.—The term "publicly-owned United States corporation" means a corporation—

(A) organized under the laws of a State of the United States, the District of Columbia, Puerto Rico, or a possession of the United States; and

(B) whose voting stock is publicly traded.

(6) Senior executives.—The term "senior executives", with respect to a contractor, means the 5 most highly compensated employees in management positions at each home office and each segment of the contractor.

(b) Determining benchmark compensation amount.—For purposes of section 4304(a)(16) of this title and section 2324(e)(1)(P) of title 10, the Administrator shall review commercially available surveys of executive compensation and, on the basis of the results of the review, determine a benchmark compensation amount to apply for each fiscal year. In making determinations under this subsection, the Administrator shall consult with the Director of the Defense Contract Audit Agency and other officials of executive agencies as the Administrator considers appropriate.

(Pub.L. 111–350, § 3, Jan. 4, 2011, 124 Stat. 3689.)

HISTORICAL AND STATUTORY NOTES

Exclusive Applicability of Provisions Limiting Allowability of Compensation for Certain Contractor Personnel

Pub.L. 105–85, § 808(f), Nov. 18, 1997, 111 Stat. 1838, provided that: "Notwithstanding any other provision of law, no other limitation in law on the allowability of costs of compensation of senior executives under covered contracts shall apply to such costs of compensation incurred after January 1, 1998."

[Note was classified as a note under former 41 U.S.C.A. § 435 prior to the enactment into positive law of Title 41, Public Contracts, by Pub.L. 111–350, Jan. 4, 2011, 124 Stat. 3677.]

Definition of Certain Terms for Purposes of Section 808 of Pub.L. 105–85

Pub.L. 105–85, § 808(g), Nov. 18, 1997, 111 Stat. 1838, as amended Pub.L. 105–261, Div. A,

Title VIII, § 804(c)(2), Oct. 17, 1998, 112 Stat. 2083, provided that: "In this section:

"(1) The term 'covered contract' has the meaning given such term in section 2324(*l*) of title 10, United States Code, and section 306(*l*) of the Federal Property and Administrative Services Act of 1949 (41 U.S.C. 256(*l*)) [former 41 U.S.C.A. § 256(*l*)].

"(2) The terms 'compensation' and 'senior executives' have the meanings given such terms in section 2324(*l*) of title 10, United States Code, and section 306(m) of the Federal Property and Administrative Services Act of 1949 [former 41 U.S.C.A. § 256]."

[Note was classified as a note under former 41 U.S.C.A. § 435 prior to the enactment into positive law of Title 41, Public Contracts, by Pub.L. 111–350, Jan. 4, 2011, 124 Stat. 3677.]

CROSS REFERENCES

Executive agency, defined for division B of subtitle I of this title, see 41 USCA § 133.

§ 1128. Maintaining necessary capability with respect to acquisition of architectural and engineering services

The Administrator, in consultation with the Secretary of Defense, the Administrator of General Services, and the Director of the Office of Personnel Management, shall develop and implement a plan to ensure that the Federal Government maintains the necessary capability with respect to the acquisition of architectural and engineering services to—

(1) ensure that Federal Government employees have the expertise to determine agency requirements for those services;

(2) establish priorities and programs, including acquisition plans;

(3) establish professional standards;

(4) develop scopes of work; and

(5) award and administer contracts for those services.

(Pub.L. 111–350, § 3, Jan. 4, 2011, 124 Stat. 3690.)

CROSS REFERENCES

Acquisition, defined for division B of subtitle I of this title, see 41 USCA § 131.

Standards, defined for subtitle I of this title, see 41 USCA § 114.

§ 1129. Center of excellence in contracting for services

The Administrator shall maintain a center of excellence in contracting for services. The center shall assist the acquisition community by identifying, and serving as a clearinghouse for, best practices in contracting for services in the public and private sectors.

(Pub.L. 111–350, § 3, Jan. 4, 2011, 124 Stat. 3690.)

CROSS REFERENCES

Acquisition, defined for division B of subtitle I of this title, see 41 USCA § 131.

§ 1130. Effect of division on other law

This division does not impair or affect the authorities or responsibilities relating to the procurement of real property conferred by division C of this subtitle and chapters 1 to 11 of title 40.

(Pub.L. 111–350, § 3, Jan. 4, 2011, 124 Stat. 3690.)

See Main Volume and Repealed Title 41, ante, for annotations

HISTORICAL AND STATUTORY NOTES

References in Text

Division C of this subtitle, referred to in text, is classified to 41 U.S.C.A. § 3101 et seq.

Chapters 1 to 11 of title 40, referred to in text, are classified to 40 U.S.C.A. §§ 101 et seq., 301

et seq., 501 et seq., 701 et seq., 901 et seq., and 1101 et seq., respectively.

CROSS REFERENCES

Procurement, defined for subtitle I of this title, see 41 USCA § 111.

§ 1131. Annual report

The Administrator annually shall submit to Congress an assessment of the progress made in executive agencies in implementing the policy regarding major acquisitions that is stated in section 3103(a) of this title. The Administrator shall use data from existing management systems in making the assessment.

(Pub.L. 111–350, § 3, Jan. 4, 2011, 124 Stat. 3690.)

CROSS REFERENCES

Acquisition, defined for division B of subtitle I of this title, see 41 USCA § 131.

Executive agency, defined for division B of subtitle I of this title, see 41 USCA § 133.

CHAPTER 13—ACQUISITION COUNCILS

SUBCHAPTER I—FEDERAL ACQUISITION REGULATORY COUNCIL

§ 1301. Definition

In this subchapter, the term "Council" means the Federal Acquisition Regulatory Council established under section 1302(a) of this title.

(Pub.L. 111–350, § 3, Jan. 4, 2011, 124 Stat. 3691.)

§ 1302. Establishment and membership

(a) Establishment.—There is a Federal Acquisition Regulatory Council to assist in the direction and coordination of Government–wide procurement policy and Government–wide procurement regulatory activities in the Federal Government.

(b) Membership.—

    (1) Makeup of Council.—The Council consists of—

        (A) the Administrator;

        (B) the Secretary of Defense;

        (C) the Administrator of National Aeronautics and Space; and

        (D) the Administrator of General Services.

    (2) Designation of other officials.—

        (A) Officials who may be designated.—Notwithstanding section 121(d)(1) and (2) of title 40, the officials specified in subparagraphs (B) to (D) of paragraph (1) may designate to serve on and attend meetings of the Council in place of that official—

            (i) the official assigned by statute with the responsibility for acquisition policy in each of their respective agencies or, in the case of the Secretary of Defense, an official at an organizational level not lower than an Assistant Secretary of Defense within the Office of the Under Secretary of Defense for Acquisition, Technology, and Logistics; or

(ii) if no official of that agency is assigned by statute with the responsibility for acquisition policy for that agency, the official designated pursuant to section 1702(c) of this title.

(B) **Limitation on designation.**—No other official or employee may be designated to serve on the Council.

(Pub.L. 111–350, § 3, Jan. 4, 2011, 124 Stat. 3691.)

HISTORICAL AND STATUTORY NOTES

Status of the Director of Defense Procurement

Pub.L. 102–190, Div. A, Title VIII, § 809, Dec. 5, 1991, 105 Stat. 1423, as amended Pub.L. 103–160, Div. A, Title IX, § 904(f), Nov. 30, 1993, 107 Stat. 1729; Pub.L. 106–65, Div. A, Title IX, § 911(a)(1), Oct. 5, 1999, 113 Stat. 717, provided that: "For the purposes of the amendment made by section 807 of the National Defense Authorization Act for Fiscal Year 1991 (Public Law 101–510; 104 Stat. 1593) to section 25(b)(2) of the Office of Federal Procurement

Policy Act (41 U.S.C. 421(b)(2) [former 41 U.S.C.A. § 421(b)(2)]), the Director of Defense Procurement of the Department of Defense shall be considered to be an official at an organizational level of an Assistant Secretary of Defense within the Office of the Under Secretary of Defense for Acquisition, Technology, and Logistics."

[Note was classified as a note under former 41 U.S.C.A. § 421 prior to the enactment into positive law of Title 41, Public Contracts, by Pub.L. 111–350, Jan. 4, 2011, 124 Stat. 3677.]

CROSS REFERENCES

Acquisition, defined for division B of subtitle I of this title, see 41 USCA § 131.

Procurement, defined for subtitle I of this title, see 41 USCA § 111.

§ 1303. Functions and authority

(a) **Functions.**—

(1) **Issue and maintain Federal Acquisition Regulation.**—Subject to sections 1121, 1122(a) to (c)(1), 1125, 1126, 1130, 1131, and 2305 of this title, the Administrator of General Services, the Secretary of Defense, and the Administrator of National Aeronautics and Space, pursuant to their respective authorities under division C of this subtitle, chapters 4 and 137 of title 10, and the National Aeronautics and Space Act of 1958 (42 U.S.C. 2451 et seq.), shall jointly issue and maintain in accordance with subsection (d) a single Government–wide procurement regulation, to be known as the Federal Acquisition Regulation.

(2) **Limitation on other regulations.**—Other regulations relating to procurement issued by an executive agency shall be limited to—

(A) regulations essential to implement Government–wide policies and procedures within the agency; and

(B) additional policies and procedures required to satisfy the specific and unique needs of the agency.

(3) **Ensure consistent regulations.**—The Administrator, in consultation with the Council, shall ensure that procurement regulations prescribed by executive agencies are consistent with the Federal Acquisition Regulation and in accordance with the policies prescribed pursuant to section 1121(b) of this title.

(4) **Request to review regulation.**—

(A) **Basis for request.**—Under procedures the Administrator establishes, a person may request the Administrator to review a regulation relating to procurement on the basis that the regulation is inconsistent with the Federal Acquisition Regulation.

(B) **Period of review.**—Unless the request is frivolous or does not, on its face, state a valid basis for the review, the Administrator shall complete the review not later than 60 days after receiving the request. The time for completion of the review may be extended if the Administrator determines that an additional period of review is required. The Administrator shall advise the

See Main Volume and Repealed Title 41, ante, for annotations

requester of the reasons for the extension and the date by which the review will be completed.

(5) When regulation is inconsistent or needs to be improved.—If the Administrator determines that a regulation relating to procurement is inconsistent with the Federal Acquisition Regulation or that the regulation otherwise should be revised to remove an inconsistency with the policies prescribed under section 1121(b) of this title, the Administrator shall rescind or deny the promulgation of the regulation or take other action authorized under sections 1121, 1122(a) to (c)(1), 1125, 1126, 1130, 1131, and 2305 of this title as may be necessary to remove the inconsistency. If the Administrator determines that the regulation, although not inconsistent with the Federal Acquisition Regulation or those policies, should be revised to improve compliance with the Regulation or policies, the Administrator shall take action authorized under sections 1121, 1122(a) to (c)(1), 1125, 1126, 1130, 1131, and 2305 as may be necessary and appropriate.

(6) Decisions to be in writing and publicly available.—The decisions of the Administrator shall be in writing and made publicly available.

(b) Additional responsibilities of membership.—

(1) In general.—Subject to the authority, direction, and control of the head of the agency concerned, each official who represents an agency on the Council pursuant to section 1302(b) of this title shall—

(A) approve or disapprove all regulations relating to procurement that are proposed for public comment, prescribed in final form, or otherwise made effective by that agency before the regulation may be prescribed in final form, or otherwise made effective, except that the official may grant an interim approval, without review, for not more than 60 days for a procurement regulation in urgent and compelling circumstances;

(B) carry out the responsibilities of that agency set forth in chapter 35 of title 44 for each information collection request that relates to procurement rules or regulations; and

(C) eliminate or reduce—

(i) any redundant or unnecessary levels of review and approval in the procurement system of that agency; and

(ii) redundant or unnecessary procurement regulations which are unique to that agency.

(2) Limitation on delegation.—The authority to review and approve or disapprove regulations under paragraph (1)(A) may not be delegated to an individual outside the office of the official who represents the agency on the Council pursuant to section 1302(b) of this title.

(c) Governing policies.—All actions of the Council and of members of the Council shall be in accordance with and furtherance of the policies prescribed under section 1121(b) of this title.

(d) General authority with respect to Federal Acquisition Regulation.—Subject to section 1121(d) of this title, the Council shall manage, coordinate, control, and monitor the maintenance of, issuance of, and changes in, the Federal Acquisition Regulation.

(Pub.L. 111–350, § 3, Jan. 4, 2011, 124 Stat. 3691.)

HISTORICAL AND STATUTORY NOTES

References in Text

Division C of this subtitle, referred to in subsec. (a)(1), is classified to 41 U.S.C.A. § 3101 et seq.

Chapters 4 and 137 of title 10, referred to in subsec. (a)(1), are classified to 10 U.S.C.A. §§ 131 et seq. and 2301 et seq., respectively.

The National Aeronautics and Space Act of 1958, referred to in subsec. (a)(1), also known as NASA, is Pub.L. 85–568, July 29, 1958, 72 Stat.

426, classified principally to chapter 26 of Title 42, 42 U.S.C.A. § 2451 et seq., and repealed by Pub.L. 111–314, § 6, Dec. 18, 2010, 124 Stat. 3444, as a result of the enactment into positive law of Title 51. For complete classification, see Short Title note set out under 42 U.S.C.A. § 2451 and Tables. See, also Disposition Table preceding 51 U.S.C. A. § 10101.

Chapter 35 of title 44, referred to in subsec. (b)(1)(B), is classified to 44 U.S.C.A. § 3501 et seq.

Administrator, defined for subtitle I of this title, see 41 USCA § 101.

Administrator of the National Aeronautics and Space Administration, appointment, see 51 USCA § 20111.

Executive agency, defined for division B of subtitle I of this title, see 41 USCA § 133.

Federal Acquisition Regulation, defined for subtitle I of this title, see 41 USCA § 106.

National Aeronautics and Space Administration and Department of Defense coordination, see 51 USCA § 20114.

Procurement, defined for subtitle I of this title, see 41 USCA § 111.

Procurement system, defined for subtitle I of this title, see 41 USCA § 112.

§ 1304. Contract clauses and certifications

(a) **Repetitive nonstandard contract clauses discouraged.**—The Council shall prescribe regulations to discourage the use of a nonstandard contract clause on a repetitive basis. The regulations shall include provisions that—

(1) clearly define what types of contract clauses are to be treated as nonstandard clauses; and

(2) require prior approval for the use of a nonstandard clause on a repetitive basis by an official at a level of responsibility above the contracting officer.

(b) **When certification required.**—

(1) **By law.**—A provision of law may not be construed as requiring a certification by a contractor or offeror in a procurement made or to be made by the Federal Government unless that provision of law specifically provides that such a certification shall be required.

(2) **In Federal Acquisition Regulation.**—A requirement for a certification by a contractor or offeror may not be included in the Federal Acquisition Regulation unless—

(A) the certification requirement is specifically imposed by statute; or

(B) written justification for the certification requirement is provided to the Administrator by the Council and the Administrator approves in writing the inclusion of the certification requirement.

(3) **Executive agency procurement regulation.**—

(A) **Definition.**—In subparagraph (B), the term "head of the executive agency" with respect to a military department means the Secretary of Defense.

(B) **When certification requirement may be included in regulation.**—A requirement for a certification by a contractor or offeror may not be included in a procurement regulation of an executive agency unless—

(i) the certification requirement is specifically imposed by statute; or

(ii) written justification for the certification requirement is provided to the head of the executive agency by the senior procurement executive of the agency and the head of the executive agency approves in writing the inclusion of the certification requirement.

(Pub.L. 111–350, § 3, Jan. 4, 2011, 124 Stat. 3693.)

Current Certification Requirements

Pub.L. 104–106, § 4301(b)(1), Feb. 10, 1996, 110 Stat. 656, provided that:

"(A) Not later than 210 days after the date of the enactment of this Act [Feb. 10, 1996], the Administrator for Federal Procurement Policy shall issue for public comment a proposal to amend the Federal Acquisition Regulation to remove from the Federal Acquisition Regulation certification requirements for contractors and offerors that are not specifically imposed by statute. The Administrator may omit such a certification requirement from the proposal only if—

"(i) the Federal Acquisition Regulatory Council provides the Administrator with a written justification for the requirement and a determination that there is no less burdensome means for administering and enforcing the particular regulation that contains the certification requirement; and

"(ii) the Administrator approves in writing the retention of the certification requirement.

"(B)(i) Not later than 210 days after the date of the enactment of this Act [Feb. 10, 1996], the head of each executive agency that has agency procurement regulations containing one or more certification requirements for contractors and offerors that are not specifically imposed by statute shall issue for public comment a proposal to amend the regulations to remove the certification requirements. The head of the executive agency may omit such a certification requirement from the proposal only if—

　　"(I) the senior procurement executive for the executive agency provides the head of the executive agency with a written justification for the requirement and a determination that there is no less burdensome means for administering and enforcing the particular regulation that contains the certification requirement; and

　　"(II) the head of the executive agency approves in writing the retention of such certification requirement.

　　"(ii) For purposes of clause (i), the term 'head of the executive agency' with respect to a military department means the Secretary of Defense."

[Note was classified as a note under former 41 U.S.C.A. § 425 prior to the enactment into positive law of Title 41, Public Contracts, by Pub.L. 111–350, Jan. 4, 2011, 124 Stat. 3677.]

MEMORANDA OF PRESIDENT
PRESIDENTIAL MEMORANDUM
January 20, 2010, 75 F.R. 3979

ADDRESSING TAX DELINQUENCY BY GOVERNMENT CONTRACTORS

Memorandum for the Heads of Executive Departments and Agencies

The Federal Government pays more than half a trillion dollars a year to contractors and has an important obligation to protect American taxpayer money and the integrity of the Federal acquisition process. Yet reports by the Government Accountability Office (GAO) state that Federal contracts are awarded to tens of thousands of companies with serious tax delinquencies. The total amount in unpaid taxes owed by these contracting companies is estimated to be more than $5 billion.

Too often, Federal contracting officials do not have the most basic information they need to make informed judgments about whether a company trying to win a Federal contract is delinquent in paying its taxes. We need to give our contracting officials the tools they need to protect taxpayer dollars.

Accordingly, I hereby direct the Commissioner of Internal Revenue (Commissioner) to direct a review of certifications of non-delinquency in taxes that companies bidding for Federal contracts are required to submit pursuant to a 2008 amendment to the Federal Acquisition Regulation. I further direct that the Commissioner report to me within 90 days on the overall accuracy of contractors' certifications.

I also direct the Director of the Office of Management and Budget, working with the Secretary of the Treasury and other agency heads, to evaluate practices of contracting officers and debarring officials in response to contractors' certifications of serious tax delinquencies and to provide me, within 90 days, recommendations on process improvements to ensure these contractors are not awarded new contracts, including a plan to make contractor certifications available in a Government-wide database, as is already being done with other information on contractors.

Executive departments and agencies shall carry out the provisions of this memorandum to the extent permitted by law. This memorandum is not intended to, and does not, create any right or benefit, substantive or procedural, enforceable at law or in equity by any party against the United States, its departments, agencies, or entities, its officers, employees, or agents, or any other person.

The Director of the Office of Management and Budget is hereby authorized and directed to publish this memorandum in the Federal Register.

BARACK OBAMA

CROSS REFERENCES

Administrator, defined for Subtitle I of this title, see 41 USCA § 101.

Executive agency, defined for division B of subtitle I of this title, see 41 USCA § 133.

Federal Acquisition Regulation, defined for subtitle I of this title, functions and general authority, see 41 USCA §§ 106 and 1303.

Procurement, defined for subtitle I of this title, see 41 USCA § 111.

SUBCHAPTER II—CHIEF ACQUISITION OFFICERS COUNCIL

§ 1311. Establishment and membership

　(a) **Establishment.**—There is in the executive branch a Chief Acquisition Officers Council.

　(b) **Membership.**—The members of the Council are—

　　(1) the Deputy Director for Management of the Office of Management and Budget;

(2) the Administrator;

(3) the Under Secretary of Defense for Acquisition, Technology, and Logistics;

(4) the chief acquisition officer of each executive agency that is required to have a chief acquisition officer under section 1702 of this title and the senior procurement executive of each military department; and

(5) any other senior agency officer of each executive agency, appointed by the head of the agency in consultation with the Chairman of the Council, who can effectively assist the Council in performing the functions set forth in section 1312(b) of this title and supporting the associated range of acquisition activities.

(c) **Leadership and support.**—

(1) **Chairman.**—The Deputy Director for Management of the Office of Management and Budget is the Chairman of the Council.

(2) **Vice Chairman.**—The Vice Chairman of the Council shall be selected by the Council from among its members. The Vice Chairman serves for one year and may serve multiple terms.

(3) **Leader of activities.**—The Administrator shall lead the activities of the Council on behalf of the Deputy Director for Management.

(4) **Support.**—The Administrator of General Services shall provide administrative and other support for the Council.

(Pub.L. 111–350, § 3, Jan. 4, 2011, 124 Stat. 3694.)

CROSS REFERENCES

Acquisition, defined for division B of subtitle I of this title, see 41 USCA § 131.

Administrator, defined for Subtitle I of this title, see 41 USCA § 101.

Executive agency, defined for division B of subtitle I of this title, see 41 USCA § 133.

Procurement, defined for subtitle I of this title, see 41 USCA § 111.

§ 1312. Functions

(a) **Principal forum.**—The Chief Acquisition Officers Council is the principal interagency forum for monitoring and improving the Federal acquisition system.

(b) **Functions.**—The Council shall perform functions that include the following:

(1) Develop recommendations for the Director of the Office of Management and Budget on Federal acquisition policies and requirements.

(2) Share experiences, ideas, best practices, and innovative approaches related to Federal acquisition.

(3) Assist the Administrator in the identification, development, and coordination of multiagency projects and other innovative initiatives to improve Federal acquisition.

(4) Promote effective business practices that ensure the timely delivery of best value products to the Federal Government and achieve appropriate public policy objectives.

(5) Further integrity, fairness, competition, openness, and efficiency in the Federal acquisition system.

(6) Work with the Office of Personnel Management to assess and address the hiring, training, and professional development needs of the Federal Government related to acquisition.

(7) Work with the Administrator and the Federal Acquisition Regulatory Council to promote the business practices referred to in paragraph (4) and other results of the functions carried out under this subsection.

(Pub.L. 111–350, § 3, Jan. 4, 2011, 124 Stat. 3694.)

CROSS REFERENCES

Acquisition, defined for division B of subtitle I of this title, see 41 USCA § 131.

Administrator, defined for Subtitle I of this title, see 41 USCA § 101.

See Main Volume and Repealed Title 41, ante, for annotations

CHAPTER 15—COST ACCOUNTING STANDARDS

§ 1501. Cost Accounting Standards Board

(a) **Organization.**—The Cost Accounting Standards Board is an independent board in the Office of Federal Procurement Policy.

(b) **Membership.**—

(1) **Number of members, Chairman, and appointment.**—The Board consists of 5 members. One member is the Administrator, who serves as Chairman. The other 4 members, all of whom shall have experience in Federal Government contract cost accounting, are as follows:

(A) 2 representatives of the Federal Government—

(i) one of whom is a representative of the Department of Defense appointed by the Secretary of Defense; and

(ii) one of whom is an officer or employee of the General Services Administration appointed by the Administrator of General Services.

(B) 2 individuals from the private sector, each of whom is appointed by the Administrator, and—

(i) one of whom is a representative of industry; and

(ii) one of whom is particularly knowledgeable about cost accounting problems and systems.

(2) **Term of office.**—

(A) **Length of term.**—The term of office of each member, other than the Administrator, is 4 years. The terms are staggered, with the terms of 2 members expiring in the same year, the term of another member expiring the next year, and the term of the last member expiring the year after that.

(B) **Individual required to remain with appointing agency.**—A member appointed under paragraph (1)(A) may not continue to serve after ceasing to be an officer or employee of the agency from which that member was appointed.

(3) **Vacancy.**—A vacancy on the Board shall be filled in the same manner in which the original appointment was made. A member appointed to fill a vacancy serves for the remainder of the term for which that member's predecessor was appointed.

(c) **Senior staff.**—The Administrator, after consultation with the Board, may—

(1) appoint an executive secretary and 2 additional staff members without regard to the provisions of title 5 governing appointments in the competitive service; and

(2) pay those employees without regard to the provisions of chapter 51 and subchapter III of chapter 53 of title 5 relating to classification and General Schedule pay rates, except that those employees may not receive pay in excess of the maximum rate of basic pay payable for level IV of the Executive Schedule.

(d) **Other staff.**—The Administrator may appoint, fix the compensation of, and remove additional employees of the Board under the applicable provisions of title 5.

(e) **Detailed and temporary personnel.**—For service on advisory committees and task forces to assist the Board in carrying out its functions and responsibilities—

(1) the Board, with the consent of the head of a Federal agency, may use, without reimbursement, personnel of that agency; and

(2) the Administrator, after consultation with the Board, may procure temporary and intermittent services of personnel under section 3109(b) of title 5.

(f) **Compensation.**—

(1) **Officers and employees of the Government.**—Members of the Board who are officers or employees of the Federal Government, and officers and employees of

other agencies of the Federal Government who are used under subsection (e)(1), shall not receive additional compensation for services but shall continue to be compensated by the employing department or agency of the officer or employee.

(2) **Appointees from private sector.**—Each member of the Board appointed from the private sector shall receive compensation at a rate not to exceed the daily equivalent of the rate for level IV of the Executive Schedule for each day (including travel time) in which the member is engaged in the actual performance of duties vested in the Board.

(3) **Temporary and intermittent personnel.**—An individual hired under subsection (e)(2) may receive compensation at a rate fixed by the Administrator, but not to exceed the daily equivalent of the rate for level V of the Executive Schedule for each day (including travel time) in which the individual is properly engaged in the actual performance of duties under this chapter.

(4) **Travel expenses.**—While serving away from home or regular place of business, Board members and other individuals serving on an intermittent basis under this chapter shall be allowed travel expenses in accordance with section 5703 of title 5.

(Pub.L. 111–350, § 3, Jan. 4, 2011, 124 Stat. 3695.)

HISTORICAL AND STATUTORY NOTES

References in Text

Chapter 51 of title 5, referred to in subsec. (c)(1), is classified to 5 U.S.C.A. § 5101 et seq.

Subchapter III of chapter 53 of title 5, referred to in subsec. (c)(1), is classified to 5 U.S.C.A. § 5331 et seq.

Level IV of the Executive Schedule, referred to in subsecs. (c)(2) and (f)(2), is set out in 5 U.S.C.A. § 5315.

Level V of the Executive Schedule, referred to in subsec. (f)(3), is set out in 5 U.S.C.A. § 5316.

CROSS REFERENCES

Administrator, defined for Subtitle I of this title, see 41 USCA § 101.

§ 1502. Cost accounting standards

(a) **Authority.**—

(1) **Cost Accounting Standards Board.**—The Cost Accounting Standards Board has exclusive authority to prescribe, amend, and rescind cost accounting standards, and interpretations of the standards, designed to achieve uniformity and consistency in the cost accounting standards governing measurement, assignment, and allocation of costs to contracts with the Federal Government.

(2) **Administrator for Federal Procurement Policy.**—The Administrator, after consultation with the Board, shall prescribe rules and procedures governing actions of the Board under this chapter. The rules and procedures shall require that any action to prescribe, amend, or rescind a standard or interpretation be approved by majority vote of the Board.

(b) **Mandatory use of standards.**—

(1) **Subcontract.**—

(A) **Definition.**—In this paragraph, the term "subcontract" includes a transfer of commercial items between divisions, subsidiaries, or affiliates of a contractor or subcontractor.

(B) **When standards are to be used.**—Cost accounting standards prescribed under this chapter are mandatory for use by all executive agencies and by contractors and subcontractors in estimating, accumulating, and reporting costs in connection with the pricing and administration of, and settlement of disputes concerning, all negotiated prime contract and subcontract procurements with the Federal Government in excess of the amount set forth in section 2306a(a)(1)(A)(i) of title 10 as the amount is adjusted in accordance with applicable requirements of law.

(C) **Nonapplication of standards.**—Subparagraph (B) does not apply to—

(i) a contract or subcontract for the acquisition of a commercial item;

See Main Volume and Repealed Title 41, ante, for annotations

(ii) a contract or subcontract where the price negotiated is based on a price set by law or regulation;

(iii) a firm, fixed-price contract or subcontract awarded on the basis of adequate price competition without submission of certified cost or pricing data; or

(iv) a contract or subcontract with a value of less than $7,500,000 if, when the contract or subcontract is entered into, the segment of the contractor or subcontractor that will perform the work has not been awarded at least one contract or subcontract with a value of more than $7,500,000 that is covered by the standards.

(2) **Exemptions and waivers by Board.**—The Board may—

(A) exempt classes of contractors and subcontractors from the requirements of this chapter; and

(B) establish procedures for the waiver of the requirements of this chapter for individual contracts and subcontracts.

(3) **Waiver by head of executive agency.**—

(A) **In general.**—The head of an executive agency may waive the applicability of the cost accounting standards for a contract or subcontract with a value of less than $15,000,000 if that official determines in writing that the segment of the contractor or subcontractor that will perform the work—

(i) is primarily engaged in the sale of commercial items; and

(ii) would not otherwise be subject to the cost accounting standards under this section.

(B) **In exceptional circumstances.**—The head of an executive agency may waive the applicability of the cost accounting standards for a contract or subcontract under exceptional circumstances when necessary to meet the needs of the agency. A determination to waive the applicability of the standards under this subparagraph shall be set forth in writing and shall include a statement of the circumstances justifying the waiver.

(C) **Restriction on delegation of authority.**—The head of an executive agency may not delegate the authority under subparagraph (A) or (B) to an official in the executive agency below the senior policymaking level in the executive agency.

(D) **Contents of Federal Acquisition Regulation.**—The Federal Acquisition Regulation shall include—

(i) criteria for selecting an official to be delegated authority to grant waivers under subparagraph (A) or (B); and

(ii) the specific circumstances under which the waiver may be granted.

(E) **Report.**—The head of each executive agency shall report the waivers granted under subparagraphs (A) and (B) for that agency to the Board on an annual basis.

(c) **Required Board action for prescribing standards and interpretations.**—Before prescribing cost accounting standards and interpretations, the Board shall—

(1) take into account, after consultation and discussions with the Comptroller General, professional accounting organizations, contractors, and other interested parties—

(A) the probable costs of implementation, including any inflationary effects, compared to the probable benefits;

(B) the advantages, disadvantages, and improvements anticipated in the pricing and administration of, and settlement of disputes concerning, contracts; and

(C) the scope of, and alternatives available to, the action proposed to be taken;

(2) prepare and publish a report in the Federal Register on the issues reviewed under paragraph (1);

(3)(A) publish an advanced notice of proposed rulemaking in the Federal Register to solicit comments on the report prepared under paragraph (2);

(B) provide all parties affected at least 60 days after publication to submit their views and comments; and

(C) during the 60–day period, consult with the Comptroller General and consider any recommendation the Comptroller General may make; and

(4) publish a notice of proposed rulemaking in the Federal Register and provide all parties affected at least 60 days after publication to submit their views and comments.

(d) Effective dates.—Rules, regulations, cost accounting standards, and modifications thereof prescribed or amended under this chapter shall have the full force and effect of law, and shall become effective within 120 days after publication in the Federal Register in final form, unless the Board determines that a longer period is necessary. The Board shall determine implementation dates for contractors and subcontractors. The dates may not be later than the beginning of the second fiscal year of the contractor or subcontractor after the standard becomes effective.

(e) Accompanying material.—Rules, regulations, cost accounting standards, and modifications thereof prescribed or amended under this chapter shall be accompanied by prefatory comments and by illustrations, if necessary.

(f) Implementing regulations.—The Board shall prescribe regulations for the implementation of cost accounting standards prescribed or interpreted under this section. The regulations shall be incorporated into the Federal Acquisition Regulation and shall require contractors and subcontractors as a condition of contracting with the Federal Government to—

(1) disclose in writing their cost accounting practices, including methods of distinguishing direct costs from indirect costs and the basis used for allocating indirect costs; and

(2) agree to a contract price adjustment, with interest, for any increased costs paid to the contractor or subcontractor by the Federal Government because of a change in the contractor's or subcontractor's cost accounting practices or a failure by the contractor or subcontractor to comply with applicable cost accounting standards.

(g) Nonapplicability of certain sections of title 5.—Functions exercised under this chapter are not subject to sections 551, 553 to 559, and 701 to 706 of title 5.

(Pub.L. 111–350, § 3, Jan. 4, 2011, 124 Stat. 3696.)

HISTORICAL AND STATUTORY NOTES

Effective and Applicability Provisions

1999 Acts. Pub.L. 106–65, Div. A, Title VIII, § 802(i), Oct. 5, 1999, 113 Stat. 702, provided that:

"The amendments made by subsections (a) and (b) [amending former 41 U.S.C.A. § 422] shall take effect 180 days after the date of enactment of this Act [Oct. 5, 1999], and shall apply with respect to—

"(1) contracts that are entered into on or after such effective date; and

"(2) determinations made on or after such effective date regarding whether a segment of a contractor or subcontractor is subject to the cost accounting standards under section 26(f) of the Office of Federal Procurement Policy Act (41 U.S.C. 422(f) [former 41 U.S.C.A. § 422(f)]), regardless of whether the contracts on which such determinations are made were entered into before, on, or after such date."

[Note was classified as a note under former 41 U.S.C.A. § 422 prior to the enactment into positive law of Title 41, Public Contracts, by Pub.L. 111–350, Jan. 4, 2011, 124 Stat. 3677.]

Regulations; Implementation

Pub.L. 106–65, Div. A, Title VIII, § 802(c) to (e), Oct. 5, 1999, 113 Stat. 701, provided that:

"**(c) Regulation on types of CAS coverage.**—(1) The Administrator for Federal Procurement Policy shall revise the rules and procedures prescribed pursuant to section 26(f) of the Office of Federal Procurement Policy Act (41 U.S.C. 422(f) [former 41 U.S.C.A. § 422(f)]) to the extent necessary to increase the thresholds established in section 9903.201–2 of title 48 of the Code of Federal Regulations from $25,000,000 to $50,000,000.

"(2) Paragraph (1) requires only a change of the statement of a threshold condition in the regulation referred to by section number in that paragraph, and shall not be construed as—

"(A) a ratification or expression of approval of—

"(i) any aspect of the regulation; or

"(ii) the manner in which section 26 of the Office of Federal Procurement Policy Act [former 41 U.S.C.A. § 422] is administered through the regulation; or

"(B) a requirement to apply the regulation.

See Main Volume and Repealed Title 41, ante, for annotations

"**(d) Implementation.**—The Administrator for Federal Procurement Policy shall ensure that this section and the amendments made by this section [amending 41 U.S.C.A. § 422] are implemented in a manner that ensures that the Federal Government can recover costs, as appropriate, in a case in which noncompliance with cost accounting standards, or a change in the cost accounting system of a contractor segment or subcontractor segment that is not determined to be desirable by the Federal Government, results in a shift of costs from contracts that are not covered by the cost accounting standards to contracts that are covered by the cost accounting standards.

"**(e) Implementation of requirements for revision of regulations.**—(1) Final regulations required by subsection (c) shall be issued not later than 180 days after the date of the enactment of this Act [Oct. 5, 1999].

"**(2)** Subsection (c) shall cease to be effective one year after the date on which final regulations issued in accordance with that subsection take effect."

[Note was classified as a note under former 41 U.S.C.A. § 422 prior to the enactment into positive law of Title 41, Public Contracts, by Pub.L. 111–350, Jan. 4, 124 Stat. 3677.]

Inapplicability of Standards to Certain Contracts; Construction Regarding Certain Not-for-Profit Entities

Pub.L. 106–65, Div. A, Title VIII, § 802(g), (h), Oct. 5, 1999, 113 Stat. 702, provided that:

"**(g) Inapplicability of standards to certain contracts.**—The cost accounting standards issued pursuant to section 26(f) of the Office of Federal Procurement Policy Act (41 U.S.C. 422(f)) [former 41 U.S.C.A. § 422(f)], as amended by this section, shall not apply during fiscal year 2000 with respect to a contract entered into under the authority provided in chapter 89 of title 5, United States Code [5 U.S.C.A. § 8901 et seq.] (relating to health benefits for Federal employees).

"**(h) Construction regarding certain not-for-profit entities.**—The amendments made by subsections (a) and (b) [amending former 41 U.S.C.A. § 422] shall not be construed as modifying or superseding, nor as intended to impair or restrict, the applicability of the cost accounting standards described in section 26(f) of the Office of Federal Procurement Policy Act (41 U.S.C. 422(f)) [former 41 U.S.C.A. § 422(f)] to—

"**(1)** any educational institution or federally funded research and development center that is associated with an educational institution in accordance with Office of Management and Budget Circular A–21, as in effect on January 1, 1999; or

"**(2)** any contract with a nonprofit entity that provides research and development and related products or services to the Department of Defense."

[Note was classified as a note under former 41 U.S.C.A. § 422 prior to the enactment into positive law of Title 41, Public Contracts, by Pub.L. 111–350, Jan. 4, 124 Stat. 3677.]

CROSS REFERENCES

Acquisition, defined for division B of subtitle I of this title, see 41 USCA § 131.

Administrator, defined for subtitle I of this title, see 41 USCA § 101.

Commercial item, defined for subtitle I of this title, see 41 USCA § 103.

Executive agency, defined for division B of subtitle I of this title, see 41 USCA § 133.

Federal Acquisition Regulation, defined for subtitle I of this title, functions and general authority, see 41 USCA §§ 106 and 1303.

Procurement, defined for subtitle I of this title, see 41 USCA § 111.

§ 1503. Contract price adjustment

(a) Disagreement constitutes a dispute.—If the Federal Government and a contractor or subcontractor fail to agree on a contract price adjustment, including whether the contractor or subcontractor has complied with the applicable cost accounting standards, the disagreement will constitute a dispute under chapter 71 of this title.

(b) Amount of adjustment.—A contract price adjustment undertaken under section 1502(f)(2) of this title shall be made, where applicable, on relevant contracts between the Federal Government and the contractor that are subject to the cost accounting standards so as to protect the Federal Government from payment, in the aggregate, of increased costs, as defined by the Cost Accounting Standards Board. The Federal Government may not recover costs greater than the aggregate increased cost to the Federal Government, as defined by the Board, on the relevant contracts subject to the price adjustment unless the contractor made a change in its cost accounting practices of which it was aware or should have been aware at the time of the price negotiation and which it failed to disclose to the Federal Government.

(c) Interest.—The interest rate applicable to a contract price adjustment is the annual rate of interest established under section 6621 of the Internal Revenue Code of 1986 (26 U.S.C. 6621) for the period. Interest accrues from the time payments of the increased costs were made to the contractor or subcontractor to the time the Federal Government receives full compensation for the price adjustment.

(Pub.L. 111–350, § 3, Jan. 4, 2011, 124 Stat. 3699.)

HISTORICAL AND STATUTORY NOTES

References in Text

Chapter 71 of this title, referred to in subsec. (a), is classified to 41 U.S.C.A. § 7101 et seq.

The Internal Revenue Code of 1986, referred to in subsec. (c), is classified generally to Title

26, 26 U.S.C.A. § 1 et seq. Section 6621 is classified to 26 U.S.C.A. § 6621.

§ 1504. Effect on other standards and regulations

(a) Previously existing standards—All cost accounting standards, waivers, exemptions, interpretations, modifications, rules, and regulations prescribed by the Cost Accounting Standards Board under section 719 of the Defense Production Act of 1950 (50 U.S.C. App. 2168)—

(1) remain in effect until amended, superseded, or rescinded by the Board under this chapter; and

(2) are subject to the provisions of this division in the same manner as if prescribed by the Board under this division.

(b) Inconsistent agency regulations.—To ensure that a regulation or proposed regulation of an executive agency is not inconsistent with a cost accounting standard prescribed or amended under this chapter, the Administrator, under the authority in sections 1121, 1122(a) to (c)(1), 1125, 1126, 1130, 1131, and 2305 of this title, shall rescind or deny the promulgation of the inconsistent regulation or proposed regulation and take other appropriate action authorized under sections 1121, 1122(a) to (c)(1), 1125, 1126, 1130, 1131, and 2305.

(c) Costs not subject to different standards.—Costs that are the subject of cost accounting standards prescribed under this chapter are not subject to regulations established by another executive agency that differ from those standards with respect to the measurement, assignment, and allocation of those costs.

(Pub.L. 111–350, § 3, Jan. 4, 2011, 124 Stat. 3699.)

HISTORICAL AND STATUTORY NOTES

References in Text

The Defense Production Act of 1950, referred to in subsec. (a), is Act Sept. 8, 1950, c. 932, 64 Stat. 798, as amended, which enacted section 2061 et seq. of the Appendix to Title 50. Section

719 of such Act was classified to 2168 of the Appendix to Title 50, which was repealed by Pub.L. 100–679, § 5(b), Nov. 17, 1988, 102 Stat. 4063. For complete classification, see section 2061 of the Appendix to Title 50, and Tables.

CROSS REFERENCES

Administrator, defined for Subtitle I of this title, see 41 USCA § 101.

Executive agency, defined for division B of subtitle I of this title, see 41 USCA § 133.

Standards, defined for subtitle I of this title, see 41 USCA § 114.

§ 1505. Examinations

To determine whether a contractor or subcontractor has complied with cost accounting standards prescribed under this chapter and has followed consistently the contractor's or subcontractor's disclosed cost accounting practices, an authorized representative of the head of the agency concerned, of the offices of inspector general established under the Inspector General Act of 1978 (5 U.S.C. App.), or of the Comptroller General shall have the right to examine and copy documents, papers, or records of the contractor or subcontractor relating to compliance with the standards.

(Pub.L. 111–350, § 3, Jan. 4, 2011, 124 Stat. 3700.)

See Main Volume and Repeated Title 41, ante, for annotations

HISTORICAL AND STATUTORY NOTES

References in Text

The Inspector General Act of 1978, referred to in text, is Pub.L. 95–452, Oct. 12, 1978, 92 Stat. 1101, as amended, which is set out as 5 App. 3 U.S.C.A. § 1 et seq.

§ 1506. Authorization of appropriations

Necessary amounts may be appropriated to carry out this chapter.

(Pub.L. 111–350, § 3, Jan. 4, 2011, 124 Stat. 3700.)

CHAPTER 17—AGENCY RESPONSIBILITIES AND PROCEDURES

Sec.		Sec.	
1701.	Cooperation with the Administrator.	1708.	Procurement notice.
1702.	Chief Acquisition Officers and senior procurement executives.	1709.	Contracting functions performed by Federal personnel.
1703.	Acquisition workforce.	1710.	Public-private competition required before conversion to contractor performance.
1704.	Planning and policy-making for acquisition workforce.		
1705.	Advocates for competition.	1711.	Value engineering.
1706.	Personnel evaluation.	1712.	Record requirements.
1707.	Publication of proposed regulations.	1713.	Procurement data.

§ 1701. Cooperation with the Administrator

On the request of the Administrator, each executive agency shall—

(1) make its services, personnel, and facilities available to the Office of Federal Procurement Policy to the greatest practicable extent for the performance of functions under this division; and

(2) except when prohibited by law, furnish to the Administrator, and give the Administrator access to, all information and records in its possession that the Administrator may determine to be necessary for the performance of the functions of the Office.

(Pub.L. 111–350, § 3, Jan. 4, 2011, 124 Stat. 3700.)

EXECUTIVE ORDERS
EXECUTIVE ORDER NO. 12073.
Aug. 16, 1978, 43 F.R. 36873

FEDERAL PROCUREMENT IN LABOR SURPLUS AREAS

By the authority vested in me as President by the Constitution of the United States of America, and in order to strengthen the economic base of our Nation, it is hereby ordered as follows:

1–1. PROCUREMENTS IN LABOR SURPLUS AREAS

1–101. Executive agencies shall emphasize procurement set-asides in labor surplus areas in order to strengthen our Nation's economy.

1–102. Labor surplus area procurements shall be consistent with this Order and, to the extent funds are available, the priorities of Section 15 of the Small Business Act, as amended by Public Law 95–89 (15 U.S.C. 644).

1–2. ADMINISTRATOR OF GENERAL SERVICES

1–201. The Administrator shall coordinate with and advise State and local officials with regard to Federal efforts to encourage procurements in labor surplus areas with the aim of fostering economic development in labor surplus areas.

1–202. The Administrator shall establish specific labor surplus area procurement targets for Executive agencies in consultation with the heads of those agencies.

1–203. In cooperation with the heads of Executive agencies, the Administrator shall encourage the use of set-asides or other appropriate methods for meeting procurement targets in labor surplus areas.

1–204. The Administrator shall report every six months to the President on the progress of the agencies in achieving the procurement targets.

1–3. AGENCY RESPONSIBILITIES

1–301. The Secretary of Labor shall classify and designate labor markets which are labor surplus areas. The Secretary shall provide labor market data to the heads of agencies and State and local officials in order to promote the development of business opportunities in labor surplus areas.

1–302. The heads of Executive agencies shall cooperate with the Administrator in carrying out his responsibilities for labor surplus area programs and shall provide the information necessary for setting procurement targets and recording achievement. They shall keep the Administrator informed of plans and programs which affect labor surplus procurements, with particular attention to opportunities for minority firms.

1–303. In accord with Section 6 of the Office of Federal Procurement Policy Act (41 U.S.C. 405), the Administrator for Federal Procurement Policy shall be responsible for the overall direction and oversight of the policies affecting procurement programs for labor surplus areas.

JIMMY CARTER

[Order was set out under former 41 U.S.C.A. § 401 prior to the enactment into positive law of Title 41, Public Contracts, by Pub.L. 111–350, Jan. 4, 2011, 124 Stat. 3677.]

EXECUTIVE ORDER NO. 12931.

Oct. 13, 1994, 59 F.R. 52387

FEDERAL PROCUREMENT REFORM

By the authority vested in me as President by the Constitution and the laws of the United States of America, and in order to ensure effective and efficient spending of public funds through fundamental reforms in Government procurement, it is hereby ordered as follows:

Section 1. To make procurement more effective in support of mission accomplishment and consistent with recommendations of the National Performance Review, heads of executive agencies engaged in the procurement of supplies and services shall:

(a) Review agency procurement rules, reporting requirements, contractual requirements, certification procedures, and other administrative procedures over and above those required by statute, and, where practicable, replace them with guiding principles that encourage and reward innovation;

(b) Review existing and planned agency programs to assure that such programs meet agency mission needs;

(c) Ensure that procurement organizations focus on measurable results and on increased attention to understanding and meeting customer needs;

(d) Increase the use of commercially available items where practicable, place more emphasis on past contractor performance, and promote best value rather than simply low cost in selecting sources for supplies and services;

(e) Ensure that simplified acquisition procedures are used, to the maximum extent practicable, for procurements under the simplified acquisition threshold in order to reduce administrative burdens and more effectively support the accomplishment of agency missions;

(f) Expand the use of the Government purchase card by the agency and take maximum advantage of the micro-purchase authority provided in the Federal Acquisition Streamlining Act of 1994 [Pub. L. 103–355, see Tables for classification] by delegating the authority, to the maximum extent practicable, to the offices that will be using the supplies or services to be purchased;

(g) Establish clear lines of contracting authority and accountability;

(h) Establish career education programs for procurement professionals, including requirements for successful completion of educational requirements or mandatory training for entry level positions and for promotion to higher level positions, in order to ensure a highly qualified procurement work force;

(i) Designate a Procurement Executive with agency-wide responsibility to oversee development of procurement goals, guidelines, and innovation, measure and evaluate procurement office performance against stated goals, enhance career development of the procurement work force, and advise the agency heads whether goals are being achieved; and

(j) Review existing and planned information technology acquisitions and contracts to ensure that the agency receives the best value with regard to price and technology, and consider alternatives in cases where best value is not being obtained.

Sec. 2. The Director of the Office of Personnel Management, in consultation with the heads of executive agencies, shall ensure that personnel policies and classification standards meet the needs of executive agencies for a professional procurement work force.

Sec. 3. The Administrator of the Office of Federal Procurement Policy, after consultation with the Director of the Office of Management and Budget, shall work jointly with the heads of executive agencies to provide broad policy guidance and overall leadership necessary to achieve procurement reform, including, but not limited to:

(a) Coordinating Government-wide efforts;

(b) Assisting executive agencies in streamlining guidance for procurement processes;

(c) Identifying desirable Government-wide procurement system criteria; and

(d) Identifying major inconsistencies in law and policies relating to procurement that impose unnecessary burdens on the private sector and Federal procurement officials, and, following coordination with executive agencies, submitting necessary legislative initiatives to the Office of Management and Budget for the resolution of such inconsistencies.

See Main Volume and Repealed Title 41, ante, for annotations

Sec. 4. Executive Order No. 12352 is revoked.

WILLIAM J. CLINTON

[Order was set out under former 41 U.S.C.A. § 401 prior to the enactment into positive law of Title 41, Public Contracts, by Pub.L. 111–350, Jan. 4, 2011, 124 Stat. 3677.]

CROSS REFERENCES

Administrator, defined for Subtitle I of this title, see 41 USCA § 101.

Executive agency, defined for division B of subtitle I of this title, see 41 USCA § 133.

§ 1702. Chief Acquisition Officers and senior procurement executives

(a) **Appointment or designation of Chief Acquisition Officer.**—The head of each executive agency described in section 901(b)(1) (other than the Department of Defense) or 901(b)(2)(C) of title 31 with a Chief Financial Officer appointed or designated under section 901(a) of title 31 shall appoint or designate a non-career employee as Chief Acquisition Officer for the agency.

(b) **Authority and functions of Chief Acquisition Officer.—**

(1) **Primary duty.**—The primary duty of a Chief Acquisition Officer is acquisition management.

(2) **Advice and assistance.**—A Chief Acquisition Officer shall advise and assist the head of the executive agency and other agency officials to ensure that the mission of the executive agency is achieved through the management of the agency's acquisition activities.

(3) **Other functions.**—The functions of each Chief Acquisition Officer include—

(A) monitoring the performance of acquisition activities and acquisition programs of the executive agency, evaluating the performance of those programs on the basis of applicable performance measurements, and advising the head of the executive agency regarding the appropriate business strategy to achieve the mission of the executive agency;

(B) increasing the use of full and open competition in the acquisition of property and services by the executive agency by establishing policies, procedures, and practices that ensure that the executive agency receives a sufficient number of sealed bids or competitive proposals from responsible sources to fulfill the Federal Government's requirements (including performance and delivery schedules) at the lowest cost or best value considering the nature of the property or service procured;

(C) increasing appropriate use of performance-based contracting and performance specifications;

(D) making acquisition decisions consistent with all applicable laws and establishing clear lines of authority, accountability, and responsibility for acquisition decisionmaking within the executive agency;

(E) managing the direction of acquisition policy for the executive agency, including implementation of the unique acquisition policies, regulations, and standards of the executive agency;

(F) developing and maintaining an acquisition career management program in the executive agency to ensure that there is an adequate professional workforce; and

(G) as part of the strategic planning and performance evaluation process required under section 306 of title 5 and sections 1105(a)(28), 1115, 1116, and 9703 (added by section 5(a) of Public Law 103–62 (107 Stat. 289)) of title 31—

(i) assessing the requirements established for agency personnel regarding knowledge and skill in acquisition resources management and the adequacy of those requirements for facilitating the achievement of the performance goals established for acquisition management;

(ii) developing strategies and specific plans for hiring, training, and professional development to rectify a deficiency in meeting those requirements; and

(iii) reporting to the head of the executive agency on the progress made in improving acquisition management capability.

(c) **Senior procurement executive.**—

(1) **Designation.**—The head of each executive agency shall designate a senior procurement executive.

(2) **Responsibility.**—The senior procurement executive is responsible for management direction of the procurement system of the executive agency, including implementation of the unique procurement policies, regulations, and standards of the executive agency.

(3) **When Chief Acquisition Officer appointed or designated.**—For an executive agency for which a Chief Acquisition Officer has been appointed or designated under subsection (a), the head of the executive agency shall—

(A) designate the Chief Acquisition Officer as the senior procurement executive for the executive agency; or

(B) ensure that the senior procurement executive designated under paragraph (1) reports directly to the Chief Acquisition Officer without intervening authority.

(Pub.L. 111–350, § 3, Jan. 4, 2011, 124 Stat. 3701.)

CROSS REFERENCES

Acquisition, defined for division B of subtitle I of this title, see 41 USCA § 131.

Executive agency, defined for division B of subtitle I of this title, see 41 USCA § 133.

Full and open competition, defined for subtitle I of this title, see 41 USCA § 107.

Procurement, defined for subtitle I of this title, see 41 USCA § 111.

Procurement system, defined for subtitle I of this title, see 41 USCA § 112.

Responsible source, defined for subtitle I of this title, see 41 USCA § 113.

Standards, defined for subtitle I of this title, see 41 USCA § 114.

§ 1703. Acquisition workforce

(a) **Description**—.For purposes of this section, the acquisition workforce of an agency consists of all employees serving in acquisition positions listed in subsection (g)(1)(A).

(b) **Applicability.**—

(1) **Nonapplicability to certain executive agencies.**—Except as provided in subsection (i), this section does not apply to an executive agency that is subject to chapter 87 of title 10.

(2) **Applicability of programs.**—The programs established by this section apply to the acquisition workforce of each executive agency.

(c) **Management policies.**—

(1) **Duties of head of executive agency.**—

(A) **Establish policies and procedures.**—After consultation with the Administrator, the head of each executive agency shall establish policies and procedures for the effective management (including accession, education, training, career development, and performance incentives) of the acquisition workforce of the agency. The development of acquisition workforce policies under this section shall be carried out consistent with the merit system principles set forth in section 2301(b) of title 5.

(B) **Ensure uniform implementation.**—The head of each executive agency shall ensure that, to the maximum extent practicable, acquisition workforce policies and procedures established are uniform in their implementation throughout the agency.

(2) **Duties of Administrator.**—The Administrator shall issue policies to promote uniform implementation of this section by executive agencies, with due regard for differences in program requirements among agencies that may be appropriate and warranted in view of the agency mission. The Administrator shall coordinate with the Deputy Director for Management of the Office of Management and Budget to ensure that the policies are consistent with the policies and procedures established, and enhanced system of incentives provided, pursuant to section 5051(c) of the Federal Acquisition Streamlining Act of 1994 (Public Law 103–355, 108 Stat. 3351).

See Main Volume and Repealed Title 41, ante, for annotations

The Administrator shall evaluate the implementation of this section by executive agencies.

(d) Authority and responsibility of senior procurement executive.—Subject to the authority, direction, and control of the head of an executive agency, the senior procurement executive of the agency shall carry out all powers, functions, and duties of the head of the agency with respect to implementing this section. The senior procurement executive shall ensure that the policies of the head of the executive agency established in accordance with this section are implemented throughout the agency.

(e) Collecting and maintaining information.—The Administrator shall ensure that the heads of executive agencies collect and maintain standardized information on the acquisition workforce related to implementing this section. To the maximum extent practicable, information requirements shall conform to standards the Director of the Office of Personnel Management establishes for the Central Personnel Data File.

(f) Career development.—

   (1) Career paths.—

      (A) Identification.—The head of each executive agency shall ensure that appropriate career paths for personnel who desire to pursue careers in acquisition are identified in terms of the education, training, experience, and assignments necessary for career progression to the most senior acquisition positions. The head of each executive agency shall make available information on those career paths.

      (B) Critical duties and tasks.—For each career path, the head of each executive agency shall identify the critical acquisition-related duties and tasks in which, at minimum, employees of the agency in the career path shall be competent to perform at full performance grade levels. For this purpose, the head of the executive agency shall provide appropriate coverage of the critical duties and tasks identified by the Director of the Federal Acquisition Institute.

      (C) Mandatory training and education.—For each career path, the head of each executive agency shall establish requirements for the completion of course work and related on-the-job training in the critical acquisition-related duties and tasks of the career path. The head of each executive agency also shall encourage employees to maintain the currency of their acquisition knowledge and generally enhance their knowledge of related acquisition management disciplines through academic programs and other self-developmental activities.

   (2) Performance incentives.—The head of each executive agency shall provide for an enhanced system of incentives to encourage excellence in the acquisition workforce that rewards performance of employees who contribute to achieving the agency's performance goals. The system of incentives shall include provisions that—

      (A) relate pay to performance (including the extent to which the performance of personnel in the workforce contributes to achieving the cost goals, schedule goals, and performance goals established for acquisition programs pursuant to section 3103(b) of this title); and

      (B) provide for consideration, in personnel evaluations and promotion decisions, of the extent to which the performance of personnel in the workforce contributes to achieving the cost goals, schedule goals, and performance goals.

(g) Qualification requirements.—

   (1) In general.—Subject to paragraph (2), the Administrator shall—

      (A) establish qualification requirements, including education requirements, for—

         (i) entry-level positions in the General Schedule Contracting series (GS–1102);

         (ii) senior positions in the General Schedule Contracting series (GS–1102);

         (iii) all positions in the General Schedule Purchasing series (GS–1105); and

(iv) positions in other General Schedule series in which significant acquisition-related functions are performed; and

(B) prescribe the manner and extent to which the qualification requirements shall apply to an individual serving in a position described in subparagraph (A) at the time the requirements are established.

(2) **Relationship to requirements applicable to defense acquisition workforce.**—The Administrator shall establish qualification requirements and make prescriptions under paragraph (1) that are comparable to those established for the same or equivalent positions pursuant to chapter 87 of title 10 with appropriate modifications.

(3) **Approval of requirements.**—The Administrator shall submit any requirement established or prescription made under paragraph (1) to the Director of the Office of Personnel Management for approval. The Director is deemed to have approved the requirement or prescription if the Director does not disapprove the requirement or prescription within 30 days after receiving it.

(h) Education and training.—

(1) **Funding levels.**—The head of an executive agency shall set forth separately the funding levels requested for educating and training the acquisition workforce in the budget justification documents submitted in support of the President's budget submitted to Congress under section 1105 of title 31.

(2) **Tuition assistance.**—The head of an executive agency may provide tuition reimbursement in education (including a full-time course of study leading to a degree) in accordance with section 4107 of title 5 for personnel serving in acquisition positions in the agency.

(3) **Restricted obligation.**—Amounts appropriated for education and training under this section may not be obligated for another purpose.

(i) Training fund.—

(1) **Purposes.**—The purposes of this subsection are to ensure that the Federal acquisition workforce—

(A) adapts to fundamental changes in the nature of Federal Government acquisition of property and services associated with the changing roles of the Federal Government; and

(B) acquires new skills and a new perspective to enable it to contribute effectively in the changing environment of the 21st century.

(2) **Establishment and management of fund.**—There is an acquisition workforce training fund. The Administrator of General Services shall manage the fund through the Federal Acquisition Institute to support the training of the acquisition workforce of the executive agencies, except as provided in paragraph (5). The Administrator of General Services shall consult with the Administrator in managing the fund.

(3) **Credits to fund.**—Five percent of the fees collected by executive agencies (other than the Department of Defense) under the following contracts shall be credited to the fund:

(A) Government–wide task and delivery-order contracts entered into under sections 4103 and 4105 of this title.

(B) Government–wide contracts for the acquisition of information technology as defined in section 11101 of title 40 and multiagency acquisition contracts for that technology authorized by section 11314 of title 40.

(C) multiple-award schedule contracts entered into by the Administrator of General Services.

(4) **Remittance by head of executive agency.**—The head of an executive agency that administers a contract described in paragraph (3) shall remit to the General Services Administration the amount required to be credited to the fund with respect to the contract at the end of each quarter of the fiscal year.

(5) **Transfer and use of fees collected from Department of Defense.**—The Administrator of General Services shall transfer to the Secretary of Defense fees

collected from the Department of Defense pursuant to paragraph (3). The Defense Acquisition University shall use the fees for acquisition workforce training.

(6) Amounts not to be used for other purposes.—The Administrator of General Services, through the Office of Federal Procurememt Policy, shall ensure that amounts collected for training under this subsection are not used for a purpose other than the purpose specified in paragraph (2).

(7) Amounts are in addition to other amounts for education and training.—Amounts credited to the fund are in addition to amounts requested and appropriated for education and training referred to in subsection (h)(1).

(8) Availability of amounts.—Amounts credited to the fund remain available to be expended only in the fiscal year for which they are credited and the 2 succeeding fiscal years.

(j) Recruitment program.—

(1) Shortage category positions.—For purposes of sections 3304, 5333, and 5753 of title 5, the head of a department or agency of the Federal Government (other than the Secretary of Defense) may determine, under regulations prescribed by the Office of Personnel Management, that certain Federal acquisition positions (as described in subsection (g)(1)(A)) are shortage category positions in order to use the authorities in those sections to recruit and appoint highly qualified individuals directly to those positions in the department or agency.

(2) Termination of authority.—The head of a department or agency may not appoint an individual to a position of employment under this subsection after September 30, 2012.

(k) Reemployment without loss of annuity.—

(1) Establishment of policies and procedures.—The head of each executive agency, after consultation with the Administrator and the Director of the Office of Personnel Management, shall establish policies and procedures under which the agency head may reemploy in an acquisition-related position (as described in subsection (g)(1)(A)) an individual receiving an annuity from the Civil Service Retirement and Disability Fund, on the basis of the individual's service, without discontinuing the annuity. The head of each executive agency shall keep the Administrator informed of the agency's use of this authority.

(2) Criteria for continuation of annuity.—Policies and procedures established under paragraph (1) shall authorize the head of the executive agency, on a case-by-case basis, to continue an annuity if any of the following makes the reemployment of an individual essential:

(A) The unusually high or unique qualifications of an individual receiving an annuity from the Civil Service Retirement and Disability Fund on the basis of the individual's service.

(B) The exceptional difficulty in recruiting or retaining a qualified employee.

(C) A temporary emergency hiring need.

(3) Service not subject to CSRS or FERS.—An individual reemployed under this subsection shall not be deemed an employee for purposes of chapter 83 or 84 of title 5.

(4) Reporting requirement.—The Administrator shall submit annually to the Committee on Oversight and Government Reform of the House of Representatives and the Committee on Homeland Security and Governmental Affairs of the Senate a report on the use of the authority under this subsection, including the number of employees reemployed under authority of this subsection.

(5) Sunset provision.—The authority under this subsection expires on December 31, 2011.

(Pub.L. 111–350, § 3, Jan. 4, 2011, 124 Stat. 3702.)

Revised Title 41 effective Jan. 4, 2011

HISTORICAL AND STATUTORY NOTES

References in Text

Chapter 87 of Title 10, referred to in subsecs. (b)(1) and (g)(2), is classified to 10 U.S.C.A. § 1701 et seq.

The Federal Acquisition Streamlining Act of 1994, referred to in subsec. (c)(2), is Pub.L. 103–355, Oct. 13, 1994, 108 Stat. 3243. Section 5051(c) of such Act, is set out as a note under section 1703 of this title. For complete classification, see Short Title note set out under 41 U.S.C.A. § 101 and Tables.

Chapter 83 or 84 of title 5, referred to in subsec. (k)(3), is classified to 5 U.S.C.A. §§ 8301 et seq. and 8401 et seq., respectively.

Training for Contracting and Enforcement Personnel

Pub.L. 111–240, Title I, § 1343(a), Sept. 27, 2010, 124 Stat. 2545, provided that: "Not later than 1 year after the date of enactment of this Act [Sept. 27, 2010], the Federal Acquisition Institute, in consultation with the Administrator for Federal Procurement Policy, the Defense Acquisition University, and the Administrator, shall develop courses for acquisition personnel concerning proper classification of business concerns and small business size and status for purposes of Federal contracts, subcontracts, grants, cooperative agreements, and cooperative research and development agreements."

[Note was classified as a note under former 41 U.S.C.A. § 433 prior to the enactment into positive law of Title 41, Public Contracts, by Pub.L. 111–350, Jan. 4, 2011, 124 Stat. 3677.]

Defense Acquisition University Funding

Pub.L. 109–163, Div. A, Title VIII, § 821(c), Jan. 6, 2006, 119 Stat. 3386, provided that: "Amounts transferred under section 37(h)(3)(D) of the Office of Federal Procurement Policy Act (as amended by subsection (a) [Pub.L. 109–163, Div. A, Title VIII, § 821(a), Jan. 6, 2006, 119 Stat. 3386, which amended former 41 U.S.C.A. § 433(h)(3)]) for use by the Defense Acquisition University shall be in addition to other amounts authorized for the University."

[Note was classified as a note under former 41 U.S.C.A. § 433 prior to the enactment into positive law of Title 41, Public Contracts, by Pub.L. 111–350, Jan. 4, 2011, 124 Stat. 3677.]

Enhanced System of Performance Incentives

Pub.L. 103–355, § 5051(c), Oct. 13, 1994, 108 Stat. 3551, provided that: "Within one year after the date of the enactment of this Act [Oct. 13, 1994], the Deputy Director for Management of the Office of Management and Budget, in consultation with appropriate officials in other departments and agencies of the Federal Government, shall, to the maximum extent consistent with applicable law—

"(1) establish policies and procedures for the heads of such departments and agencies to designate acquisition positions and manage employees (including the accession, education, training and career development of employees) in the designated acquisition positions; and

"(2) review the incentives and personnel actions available to the heads of departments and agencies of the Federal Government for encouraging excellence in the acquisition workforce of the Federal Government and provide an enhanced system of incentives for the encouragement of excellence in such workforce which—

"(A) relates pay to performance (including the extent to which the performance of personnel in such workforce contributes to achieving the cost goals, schedule goals, and performance goals established for acquisition programs pursuant to section 313(b) of the Federal Property and Administrative Services Act of 1949, as added by subsection (a) [subsec. (b) of this section]); and

"(B) provides for consideration, in personnel evaluations and promotion decisions, of the extent to which the performance of personnel in such workforce contributes to achieving such cost goals, schedule goals, and performance goals."

[Note was classified as a note under former 41 U.S.C.A. § 263 prior to the enactment into positive law of Title 41, Public Contracts, by Pub.L. 111–350, Jan. 4, 2011, 124 Stat. 3677.]

CROSS REFERENCES

Acquisition, defined for division B of subtitle I of this title, see 41 USCA § 131.

Administrator, defined for Subtitle I of this title, see 41 USCA § 101.

Executive agency, defined for division B of subtitle I of this title, see 41 USCA § 133.

Standards, defined for subtitle I of this title, see 41 USCA § 114.

§ 1704. Planning and policy-making for acquisition workforce

(a) **Definitions.**—In this section:

(1) **Associate Administrator.**—The term "Associate Administrator" means the Associate Administrator for Acquisition Workforce Programs as designated by the Administrator pursuant to subsection (b).

(2) **Chief Acquisition Officer.**—The term "Chief Acquisition Officer" means a Chief Acquisition Officer for an executive agency appointed pursuant to section 1702 of this title.

(b) **Associate Administrator for Acquisition Workforce Programs.**—The Administrator shall designate a member of the Senior Executive Service as the Associate

Administrator for Acquisition Workforce Programs. The Associate Administrator shall be located in the Federal Acquisition Institute (or its successor). The Associate Administrator shall be responsible for—

    (1) supervising the acquisition workforce training fund established under section 1703(i) of this title;

    (2) developing, in coordination with Chief Acquisition Officers and Chief Human Capital Officers, a strategic human capital plan for the acquisition workforce of the Federal Government;

    (3) reviewing and providing input to individual agency acquisition workforce succession plans;

    (4) recommending to the Administrator and other senior government officials appropriate programs, policies, and practices to increase the quantity and quality of the Federal acquisition workforce; and

    (5) carrying out other functions that the Administrator may assign.

(c) Acquisition and contracting training programs within executive agencies.—

    (1) **Chief Acquisition Officer authorities and responsibilities.**—Subject to the authority, direction, and control of the head of an executive agency, the Chief Acquisition Officer for that agency shall carry out all powers, functions, and duties of the head of the agency with respect to implementation of this subsection. The Chief Acquisition Officer shall ensure that the policies established by the head of the agency in accordance with this subsection are implemented throughout the agency.

    (2) **Requirement.**—The head of each executive agency, after consultation with the Associate Administrator, shall establish and operate acquisition and contracting training programs. The programs shall—

      (A) have curricula covering a broad range of acquisition and contracting disciplines corresponding to the specific acquisition and contracting needs of the agency involved;

      (B) be developed and applied according to rigorous standards; and

      (C) be designed to maximize efficiency, through the use of self-paced courses, online courses, on-the-job training, and the use of remote instructors, wherever those features can be applied without reducing the effectiveness of the training or negatively affecting academic standards.

(d) Government-wide policies and evaluation.—The Administrator shall issue policies to promote the development of performance standards for training and uniform implementation of this section by executive agencies, with due regard for differences in program requirements among agencies that may be appropriate and warranted in view of the agency mission. The Administrator shall evaluate the implementation of the provisions of subsection (c) by executive agencies.

(e) Information on acquisition and contracting training.—The Administrator shall ensure that the heads of executive agencies collect and maintain standardized information on the acquisition and contracting workforce related to the implementation of subsection (c).

(f) Acquisition Workforce Human Capital Succession Plan.—

    (1) **In general**—Each Chief Acquisition Officer for an executive agency shall develop, in consultation with the Chief Human Capital Officer for the agency and the Associate Administrator, a succession plan consistent with the agency's strategic human capital plan for the recruitment, development, and retention of the agency's acquisition workforce, with a particular focus on warranted contracting officers and program managers of the agency.

    (2) **Content of plan.**—The acquisition workforce succession plan shall address—

      (A) recruitment goals for personnel from procurement intern programs;

      (B) the agency's acquisition workforce training needs;

      (C) actions to retain high performing acquisition professionals who possess critical relevant skills;

(**D**) recruitment goals for personnel from the Federal Career Intern Program; and

(**E**) recruitment goals for personnel from the Presidential Management Fellows Program.

(g) Acquisition Workforce Development Strategic Plan.—

(1) **Purpose.**—The purpose of this subsection is to authorize the preparation and completion of the Acquisition Workforce Development Strategic Plan, which is a plan for Federal agencies other than the Department of Defense to—

(**A**) develop a specific and actionable 5–year plan to increase the size of the acquisition workforce; and

(**B**) operate a government-wide acquisition intern program for the Federal agencies.

(2) **Establishment of plan.**—The Associate Administrator shall be responsible for the management, oversight, and administration of the Acquisition Workforce Development Strategic Plan in cooperation and consultation with the Office of Federal Procurement Policy and with the assistance of the Federal Acquisition Institute.

(3) **Criteria.**—The Acquisition Workforce Development Strategic Plan shall include an examination of the following matters:

(**A**) The variety and complexity of acquisitions conducted by each Federal agency covered by the plan, and the workforce needed to effectively carry out the acquisitions.

(**B**) The development of a sustainable funding model to support efforts to hire, retain, and train an acquisition workforce of appropriate size and skill to effectively carry out the acquisition programs of the Federal agencies covered by the plan, including an examination of interagency funding methods and a discussion of how the model of the Defense Acquisition Workforce Development Fund could be applied to civilian agencies.

(**C**) Any strategic human capital planning necessary to hire, retain, and train an acquisition workforce of appropriate size and skill at each Federal agency covered by the plan.

(**D**) Methodologies that Federal agencies covered by the plan can use to project future acquisition workforce personnel hiring requirements, including an appropriate distribution of such personnel across each category of positions designated as acquisition workforce personnel under section 1703(g) of this title.

(**E**) Government-wide training standards and certification requirements necessary to enhance the mobility and career opportunities of the Federal acquisition workforce within the Federal agencies covered by the plan.

(**F**) If the Associate Administrator recommends as part of the plan a growth in the acquisition workforce of the Federal agencies covered by the plan below 25 percent over the next 5 years, an examination of each of the matters specified in subparagraphs (A) to (E) in the context of a 5–year plan that increases the size of such acquisition workforce by not less than 25 percent, or an explanation why such a level of growth would not be in the best interest of the Federal Government.

(4) **Deadline for completion.**—The Acquisition Workforce Development Strategic Plan shall be completed not later than one year after October 14, 2008, and in a fashion that allows for immediate implementation of its recommendations and guidelines.

(5) **Funds.**—The acquisition workforce development strategic plan shall be funded from the acquisition workforce training fund under section 1703(i) of this title.

(h) Training in the acquisition of architect and engineering services.—The Administrator shall ensure that a sufficient number of Federal employees are trained in the acquisition of architect and engineering services.

(i) Utilization of recruitment and retention authorities.—The Administrator, in coordination with the Director of the Office of Personnel Management, shall encourage

See Main Volume and Repealed Title 41, ante, for annotations

executive agencies to use existing authorities, including direct hire authority and tuition assistance programs, to recruit and retain acquisition personnel and consider recruiting acquisition personnel who may be retiring from the private sector, consistent with existing laws and regulations.

(Pub.L. 111–350, § 3, Jan. 4, 2011, 124 Stat. 3706; Pub.L. 111–383, Div. A, Title X, § 1075(e)(15), Jan. 7, 2011, 124 Stat. 4375.)

Amendment Subsequent to December 31, 2008

Pub.L. 111–350, Jan. 4, 2011, 124 Stat. 3677, which codified T. 41, Public Contracts, as positive law, directed that if a law enacted after Dec. 31, 2008, amends or repeals a provision replaced by Pub.L. 111–350, that law is deemed to amend or repeal, as the case may be, the corresponding provision enacted by Pub.L. 111–350, see Pub.L. 111–350, § 6(a), Jan. 4, 2011, 124 Stat. 3854, set out as a note provision preceding 41 U.S.C.A. § 101.

Pub.L. 111–383, Div. A, Title X, § 1075(e)(15), Jan. 7, 2011, 124 Stat. 4375, amended Pub.L. 110–417, § 869, which was set out as a note under former 41 U.S.C.A. § 433a, from which this section was derived, by substituting "433a(a)" for "433(a)" in subsec. (b) of the note, and by substituting "37(g)" for "37(j)" and substituting "433(g)" for "433(j)" in subsec. (c)(4) of the note.

CROSS REFERENCES

Acquisition, defined for division B of subtitle I of this title, see 41 USCA § 131.

Administrator, defined for Subtitle I of this title, see 41 USCA § 101.

Executive agency, defined for division B of subtitle I of this title, see 41 USCA § 133.

Standards, defined for subtitle I of this title, see 41 USCA § 114.

§ 1705. Advocates for competition

(a) Establishment and designation.—

   (1) Establishment.—Each executive agency has an advocate for competition.

   (2) Designation.—The head of each executive agency shall—

     (A) designate for the executive agency and for each procuring activity of the executive agency one officer or employee serving in a position authorized for the executive agency on July 18, 1984 (other than the senior procurement executive designated pursuant to section 1702(c) of this title) to serve as the advocate for competition;

     (B) not assign those officers or employees duties or responsibilities that are inconsistent with the duties and responsibilities of the advocates for competition; and

     (C) provide those officers or employees with the staff or assistance necessary to carry out the duties and responsibilities of the advocate for competition, such as individuals who are specialists in engineering, technical operations, contract administration, financial management, supply management, and utilization of small and disadvantaged business concerns.

(b) Duties and functions.—The advocate for competition of an executive agency shall—

   (1) be responsible for challenging barriers to, and promoting full and open competition in, the procurement of property and services by the executive agency;

   (2) review the procurement activities of the executive agency;

   (3) identify and report to the senior procurement executive of the executive agency—

     (A) opportunities and actions taken to achieve full and open competition in the procurement activities of the executive agency; and

     (B) any condition or action which has the effect of unnecessarily restricting competition in the procurement actions of the executive agency;

   (4) prepare and transmit to the senior procurement executive an annual report describing—

     (A) the advocate's activities under this section;

(B) new initiatives required to increase competition; and

(C) remaining barriers to full and open competition;

(5) recommend to the senior procurement executive—

   (A) goals and the plans for increasing competition on a fiscal year basis; and

   (B) a system of personal and organizational accountability for competition, which may include the use of recognition and awards to motivate program managers, contracting officers, and others in authority to promote competition in procurement programs; and

(6) describe other ways in which the executive agency has emphasized competition in programs for procurement training and research.

(c) Responsibilities.—The advocate for competition for each procuring activity is responsible for promoting full and open competition, promoting the acquisition of commercial items, and challenging barriers to acquisition, including unnecessarily restrictive statements of need, unnecessarily detailed specifications, and unnecessarily burdensome contract clauses.

(Pub.L. 111–350, § 3, Jan. 4, 2011, 124 Stat. 3709.)

§ 1706. Personnel evaluation

The head of each executive agency subject to division C shall ensure, with respect to the employees of that agency whose primary duties and responsibilities pertain to the award of contracts subject to the provisions of the Small Business and Federal Procurement Competition Enhancement Act of 1984 (Public Law 98–577, 98 Stat. 3066), that the performance appraisal system applicable to those employees affords appropriate recognition to, among other factors, efforts to—

(1) increase competition and achieve cost savings through the elimination of procedures that unnecessarily inhibit full and open competition;

(2) further the purposes of the Small Business and Federal Procurement Competition Enhancement Act of 1984 (Public Law 98–577, 98 Stat. 3066) and the Defense Procurement Reform Act of 1984 (Public Law 98–525, title XII, 98 Stat. 2588); and

(3) further other objectives and purposes of the Federal acquisition system authorized by law.

(Pub.L. 111–350, § 3, Jan. 4, 2011, 124 Stat. 3710.)

§ 1707. Publication of proposed regulations

(a) Covered policies, regulations, procedures, and forms.—

  (1) Required comment period.—Except as provided in subsection (d), a procurement policy, regulation, procedure, or form (including an amendment or modification thereto) may not take effect until 60 days after it is published for public comment in the Federal Register pursuant to subsection (b) if it—

    (A) relates to the expenditure of appropriated funds; and

    (B)(i) has a significant effect beyond the internal operating procedures of the agency issuing the policy, regulation, procedure, or form; or

    (ii) has a significant cost or administrative impact on contractors or offerors.

    (2) Exception.—A policy, regulation, procedure, or form may take effect earlier than 60 days after the publication date when there are compelling circumstances for the earlier effective date, but the effective date may not be less than 30 days after the publication date.

  (b) Publication in Federal Register and comment period.—Subject to subsection (c), the head of the agency shall have published in the Federal Register a notice of the proposed procurement policy, regulation, procedure, or form and provide for a public comment period for receiving and considering the views of all interested parties on the proposal. The length of the comment period may not be less than 30 days.

  (c) Contents of notice.—Notice of a proposed procurement policy, regulation, procedure, or form prepared for publication in the Federal Register shall include—

    (1) the text of the proposal or, if it is impracticable to publish the full text of the proposal, a summary of the proposal and a statement specifying the name, address, and telephone number of the officer or employee of the executive agency from whom the full text may be obtained; and

    (2) a request for interested parties to submit comments on the proposal and the name and address of the officer or employee of the Federal Government designated to receive the comments.

  (d) Waiver.—The requirements of subsections (a) and (b) may be waived by the officer authorized to issue a procurement policy, regulation, procedure, or form if urgent and compelling circumstances make compliance with the requirements impracticable.

  (e) Effectiveness of policy, regulation, procedure, or form.—

    (1) Temporary basis.—A procurement policy, regulation, procedure, or form for which the requirements of subsections (a) and (b) are waived under subsection (d) is effective on a temporary basis if—

      (A) a notice of the policy, regulation, procedure, or form is published in the Federal Register and includes a statement that the policy, regulation, procedure, or form is temporary; and

      (B) provision is made for a public comment period of 30 days beginning on the date on which the notice is published.

    (2) Final policy, regulation, procedure, or form.—After considering the comments received, the head of the agency waiving the requirements of subsections (a) and (b) under subsection (d) may issue the final procurement policy, regulation, procedure, or form.

(Pub.L. 111–350, § 3, Jan. 4, 2011, 124 Stat. 3710.)

CROSS REFERENCES

Executive agency, defined for division B of subtitle I of this title, see 41 USCA § 133.   Procurement, defined for subtitle I of this title, see 41 USCA § 111.

§ 1708. Procurement notice

  (a) Notice requirement.—Except as provided in subsection (b)—

    (1) an executive agency intending to solicit bids or proposals for a contract for property or services for a price expected to exceed $10,000, but not to exceed $25,000, shall post, for not less than 10 days, in a public place at the contracting office issuing the solicitation a notice of solicitation described in subsection (c);

    (2) an executive agency shall publish a notice of solicitation described in subsection (c) if the agency intends to—

      (A) solicit bids or proposals for a contract for property or services for a price expected to exceed $25,000; or

(B) place an order, expected to exceed $25,000, under a basic agreement, basic ordering agreement, or similar arrangement; and

(3) an executive agency awarding a contract for property or services for a price exceeding $25,000, or placing an order exceeding $25,000 under a basic agreement, basic ordering agreement, or similar arrangement, shall furnish for publication a notice announcing the award or order if there is likely to be a subcontract under the contract or order.

(b) **Exemptions.**—

(1) **In general.**—A notice is not required under subsection (a) if—

(A) the proposed procurement is for an amount not greater than the simplified acquisition threshold and is to be conducted by—

(i) using widespread electronic public notice of the solicitation in a form that allows convenient and universal user access through a single, Government–wide point of entry; and

(ii) permitting the public to respond to the solicitation electronically;

(B) the notice would disclose the executive agency's needs and disclosure would compromise national security;

(C) the proposed procurement would result from acceptance of—

(i) an unsolicited proposal that demonstrates a unique and innovative research concept and publication of a notice of the unsolicited research proposal would disclose the originality of thought or innovativeness of the proposal or would disclose proprietary information associated with the proposal; or

(ii) a proposal submitted under section 9 of the Small Business Act (15 U.S.C. 638);

(D) the procurement is made against an order placed under a requirements contract, a task order contract, or a delivery order contract;

(E) the procurement is made for perishable subsistence supplies;

(F) the procurement is for utility services, other than telecommunication services, and only one source is available; or

(G) the procurement is for the services of an expert for use in any litigation or dispute (including any reasonably foreseeable litigation or dispute) involving the Federal Government in a trial, hearing, or proceeding before a court, administrative tribunal, or agency, or in any part of an alternative dispute resolution process, whether or not the expert is expected to testify.

(2) **Certain procurements.**—The requirements of subsection (a)(2) do not apply to a procurement—

(A) under conditions described in paragraph (2), (3), (4), (5), or (7) of section 3304(a) of this title or paragraph (2), (3), (4), (5), or (7) of section 2304(c) of title 10; or

(B) for which the head of the executive agency makes a determination in writing, after consultation with the Administrator and the Administrator of the Small Business Administration, that it is not appropriate or reasonable to publish a notice before issuing a solicitation.

(3) **Implementation consistent with international agreements.**—Paragraph (1)(A) shall be implemented in a manner consistent with applicable international agreements.

(c) **Contents of notice.**—Each notice of solicitation required by paragraph (1) or (2) of subsection (a) shall include—

(1) an accurate description of the property or services to be contracted for, which description—

(A) shall not be unnecessarily restrictive of competition; and

(B) shall include, as appropriate, the agency nomenclature, National Stock Number or other part number, and a brief description of the item's form, fit, or function, physical dimensions, predominant material of manufacture, or similar information that will assist a prospective contractor to make an informed business judgment as to whether a copy of the solicitation should be requested;

(2) provisions that—

(A)(i) state whether the technical data required to respond to the solicitation will not be furnished as part of the solicitation; and

(ii) identify the source in the Federal Government, if any, from which the technical data may be obtained; and

(B)(i) state whether an offeror or its product or service must meet a qualification requirement in order to be eligible for award; and

(ii) if so, identify the office from which the qualification requirement may be obtained;

(3) the name, business address, and telephone number of the contracting officer;

(4) a statement that all responsible sources may submit a bid, proposal, or quotation (as appropriate) that the agency shall consider;

(5) in the case of a procurement using procedures other than competitive procedures, a statement of the reason justifying the use of those procedures and the identity of the intended source; and

(6) in the case of a contract in an amount estimated to be greater than $25,000 but not greater than the simplified acquisition threshold, or a contract for the procurement of commercial items using special simplified procedures—

(A) a description of the procedures to be used in awarding the contract; and

(B) a statement specifying the periods for prospective offerors and the contracting officer to take the necessary preaward and award actions.

(d) **Electronic publication of notice of solicitation, award, or order.**—A notice of solicitation, award, or order required to be published under subsection (a) shall be published by electronic means. The notice must be electronically accessible in a form that allows convenient and universal user access through the single Government–wide point of entry designated in the Federal Acquisition Regulation.

(e) **Time limitations.—**

(1) **Issuing notice of solicitation and establishing deadline for submitting bids and proposals.**—An executive agency required by subsection (a) (2) to publish a notice of solicitation may not—

(A) issue the solicitation earlier than 15 days after the date on which the notice is published; or

(B) in the case of a contract or order expected to be greater than the simplified acquisition threshold, establish a deadline for the submission of all bids or proposals in response to the notice required by subsection (a)(2) that—

(i) in the case of a solicitation for research and development, is earlier than 45 days after the date the notice required for a bid or proposal for a contract described in subsection (a)(2)(A) is published;

(ii) in the case of an order under a basic agreement, basic ordering agreement, or similar arrangement, is earlier than 30 days after the date the notice required for an order described in subsection (a)(2)(B) is published; or

(iii) in any other case, is earlier than 30 days after the date the solicitation is issued.

(2) **Establishing deadline when none provided by statute.**—An executive agency shall establish a deadline for the submission of all bids or proposals in response to a solicitation for which a deadline is not provided by statute. Each deadline for the submission of offers shall afford potential offerors a reasonable opportunity to respond.

(3) **Flexible deadlines.**—The Administrator shall prescribe regulations defining limited circumstances in which flexible deadlines can be used under paragraph (1) for the issuance of solicitations and the submission of bids or proposals for the procurement of commercial items.

(f) **Consideration of certain timely received offers.**—An executive agency intending to solicit offers for a contract for which a notice of solicitation is required to be posted under subsection (a)(1) shall ensure that contracting officers consider each responsive offer timely received from an offeror.

(g) **Availability of complete solicitation package and payment of fee.**—An executive agency shall make available to a business concern, or the authorized representative of a concern, the complete solicitation package for any on-going procurement announced pursuant to a notice of solicitation under subsection (a). An executive agency may require the payment of a fee, not exceeding the actual cost of duplication, for a copy of the package.

(Pub.L. 111–350, § 3, Jan. 4, 2011, 124 Stat. 3711.)

HISTORICAL AND STATUTORY NOTES

References in Text

The Small Business Act, referred to in subsec. (b)(1)(C)(ii), is Act July 18, 1958, Pub.L. 85–536, 72 Stat. 384, as amended, also known as the SBA, which is principally classified to chapter 14A of Title 15, 15 U.S.C.A. § 631 et seq. Section 9 of such Act is classified to 15 U.S.C.A. § 638. For complete classification, see Short Title note set out under 15 U.S.C.A. § 631 and Tables.

Applicability to Tennessee Valley Authority

Pub. L. 98–577, § 303(c), Oct. 30, 1994, 98 Stat. 3079, provided that: "The provisions of the amendments made by subsection (a) of this section [amending former 41 U.S.C.A. § 416] shall apply to the Tennessee Valley Authority only with respect to procurements to be paid from appropriated funds."

[Note was classified as a note under former 41 U.S.C.A. § 416 prior to the enactment into positive law of Title 41, Public Contracts, by Pub.L. 111–350, Jan. 4, 2011, 124 Stat. 3677.]

CROSS REFERENCES

Administrator, defined for subtitle I of this title, see 41 USCA § 101.

Commercial item, defined for subtitle I of this title, see 41 USCA § 103.

Competitive procedures, defined for division B of subtitle I of this title, see 41 USCA § 132.

Executive agency, defined for division B of subtitle I of this title, see 41 USCA § 133.

Federal Acquisition Regulation, defined for subtitle I of this title, functions and general authority, see 41 USCA §§ 106 and 1303.

Item and item of supply, defined for subtitle I of this title, see 41 USCA § 108.

Procurement, defined for subtitle I of this title, see 41 USCA § 111.

Responsible source, defined for subtitle I of this title, see 41 USCA § 113.

Simplified acquisition threshold, defined for division B of subtitle I of this title, see 41 USCA § 134.

Supplies, defined for subtitle I of this title, see 41 USCA § 115.

Technical data, defined for subtitle I of this title, see 41 USCA § 116.

§ 1709. Contracting functions performed by Federal personnel

(a) **Covered personnel.**—Personnel referred to in subsection (b) are—

(1) an employee, as defined in section 2105 of title 5;

(2) a member of the armed forces; and

(3) an individual assigned to a Federal agency pursuant to subchapter VI of chapter 33 of title 5.

(b) **Limitation on payment for advisory and assistance services.**—No individual who is not an individual described in subsection (a) may be paid by an executive agency for services to conduct evaluations or analyses of any aspect of a proposal submitted for an acquisition unless personnel described in subsection (a) with adequate training and capabilities to perform the evaluations and analyses are not readily available in the agency or another Federal agency. When administering this subsection, the head of each executive agency shall determine in accordance with standards and procedures prescribed in the Federal Acquisition Regulation whether—

(1) a sufficient number of personnel described in subsection (a) in the agency or another Federal agency are readily available to perform a particular evaluation or analysis for the head of the executive agency making the determination; and

(2) the readily available personnel have the training and capabilities necessary to perform the evaluation or analysis.

See Main Volume and Repealed Title 41, ante, for annotations

(c) Certain relationship not affected.—This section does not affect the relationship between the Federal Government and a Federally funded research and development center.

(Pub.L. 111–350, § 3, Jan. 4, 2011, 124 Stat. 3714.)

HISTORICAL AND STATUTORY NOTES

References in Text

Subchapter VI of chapter 33 of title 5, referred to in subsec. (a)(3), is classified to 5 U.S.C.A. § 3371 et seq.

Requirement for Guidance and Regulations

Pub.L. 103–355, § 6002(b), Oct. 13, 1994, 108 Stat. 3363, provided that:

"The Federal Acquisition Regulatory Council established by section 25(a) of the Office of Federal Procurement Policy Act (41 U.S.C. 421(a) [former 41 U.S.C.A. § 421(a)]) shall—

"(1) review part 37 of title 48 of the Code of Federal Regulations as it relates to the use of advisory and assistance services; and

"(2) provide guidance and promulgate regulations regarding—

"(A) what actions Federal agencies are required to take to determine whether expertise is readily available within the Federal Government before contracting for advisory and technical services to conduct acquisitions; and

"(B) the manner in which personnel with expertise may be shared with agencies needing expertise for such acquisitions."

[Note was classified as a note under former 41 U.S.C.A. § 419 prior to the enactment into positive law of Title 41, Public Contracts, by Pub.L. 111–350, Jan. 4, 2011, 124 Stat. 3677.]

CROSS REFERENCES

Acquisition, defined for division B of subtitle I of this title, see 41 USCA § 131.

Executive agency, defined for division B of subtitle I of this title, see 41 USCA § 133.

Federal Acquisition Regulation, defined for subtitle I of this title, functions and general authority, see 41 USCA §§ 106 and 1303.

Standards, defined for subtitle I of this title, see 41 USCA § 114.

§ 1710. Public-private competition required before conversion to contractor performance

(a) Public-private competition.—

(1) When conversion to contractor performance is allowed.—A function of an executive agency performed by 10 or more agency civilian employees may not be converted, in whole or in part, to performance by a contractor unless the conversion is based on the results of a public-private competition that—

(A) formally compares the cost of performance of the function by agency civilian employees with the cost of performance by a contractor;

(B) creates an agency tender, including a most efficient organization plan, in accordance with Office of Management and Budget Circular A76, as implemented on May 29, 2003, or any successor circular;

(C) includes the issuance of a solicitation;

(D) determines whether the submitted offers meet the needs of the executive agency with respect to factors other than cost, including quality, reliability, and timeliness;

(E) examines the cost of performance of the function by agency civilian employees and the cost of performance of the function by one or more contractors to demonstrate whether converting to performance by a contractor will result in savings to the Federal Government over the life of the contract, including—

(i) the estimated cost to the Federal Government (based on offers received) for performance of the function by a contractor;

(ii) the estimated cost to the Federal Government for performance of the function by agency civilian employees; and

(iii) an estimate of all other costs and expenditures that the Federal Government would incur because of the award of the contract;

(F) requires continued performance of the function by agency civilian employees unless the difference in the cost of performance of the function by a

Revised Title 41 effective Jan. 4, 2011

contractor compared to the cost of performance of the function by agency civilian employees would, over all performance periods required by the solicitation, be equal to or exceed the lesser of—

    (i) 10 percent of the personnel-related costs for performance of that function in the agency tender; or

    (ii) $10,000,000; and

  (G) examines the effect of performance of the function by a contractor on the agency mission associated with the performance of the function.

(2) **Not a new requirement.**—A function that is performed by the executive agency and is reengineered, reorganized, modernized, upgraded, expanded, or changed to become more efficient, but still essentially provides the same service, shall not be considered a new requirement.

(3) **Prohibitions.**—In no case may a function being performed by executive agency personnel be—

  (A) modified, reorganized, divided, or in any way changed for the purpose of exempting the conversion of the function from the requirements of this section; or

  (B) converted to performance by a contractor to circumvent a civilian personnel ceiling.

(b) **Consulting with affected employees or their representatives.**—

(1) **Consulting with affected employees.**—Each civilian employee of an executive agency responsible for determining under Office of Management and Budget Circular A76 whether to convert to contractor performance any function of the executive agency—

  (A) shall, at least monthly during the development and preparation of the performance work statement and the management efficiency study used in making that determination, consult with civilian employees who will be affected by that determination and consider the views of the employees on the development and preparation of that statement and that study; and

  (B) may consult with the employees on other matters relating to that determination.

(2) **Consulting with representatives.**—

  (A) **Employees represented by a labor organization.**—In the case of employees represented by a labor organization accorded exclusive recognition under section 7111 of title 5, consultation with representatives of that labor organization shall satisfy the consultation requirement in paragraph (1).

  (B) **Employees not represented by a labor organization.**—In the case of employees other than employees referred to in subparagraph (A), consultation with appropriate representatives of those employees shall satisfy the consultation requirement in paragraph (1).

(3) **Regulations.**—The head of each executive agency shall prescribe regulations to carry out this subsection. The regulations shall include provisions for the selection or designation of appropriate representatives of employees referred to in paragraph (2)(B) for purposes of consultation required by paragraph (1).

(c) **Congressional notification.**—

(1) **Report.**—Before commencing a public-private competition under subsection (a), the head of an executive agency shall submit to Congress a report containing the following:

  (A) The function for which the public-private competition is to be conducted.

  (B) The location at which the function is performed by agency civilian employees.

  (C) The number of agency civilian employee positions potentially affected.

  (D) The anticipated length and cost of the public-private competition, and a specific identification of the budgetary line item from which funds will be used to cover the cost of the public-private competition.

See Main Volume and Repealed Title 41, ante, for annotations

(E) A certification that a proposed performance of the function by a contractor is not a result of a decision by an official of an executive agency to impose predetermined constraints or limitations on agency civilian employees in terms of man years, end strengths, full-time equivalent positions, or maximum number of employees.

(2) Examination of potential economic effect.—The report required under paragraph (1) shall include an examination of the potential economic effect of performance of the function by a contractor on—

(A) agency civilian employees who would be affected by such a conversion in performance; and

(B) the local community and the Federal Government, if more than 50 agency civilian employees perform the function.

(3) Objections to public-private competition.—

(A) Grounds.—A representative individual or entity at a facility where a public-private competition is conducted may submit to the head of the executive agency an objection to the public-private competition on the grounds that—

(i) the report required by paragraph (1) has not been submitted; or

(ii) the certification required by paragraph (1)(E) was not included in the report required by paragraph (1).

(B) Deadlines.—The objection shall be in writing and shall be submitted within 90 days after the following date:

(i) In the case of a failure to submit the report when required, the date on which the representative individual or an official of the representative entity authorized to pose the objection first knew or should have known of that failure.

(ii) In the case of a failure to include the certification in a submitted report, the date on which the report was submitted to Congress.

(C) Report and certification required before solicitation or award of contract.—If the head of the executive agency determines that the report required by paragraph (1) was not submitted or that the required certification was not included in the submitted report, the function for which the public-private competition was conducted for which the objection was submitted may not be the subject of a solicitation of offers for, or award of, a contract until, respectively, the report is submitted or a report containing the certification in full compliance with the certification requirement is submitted.

(d) Exemption for the purchase of products and services of the blind and other severely disabled people.—This section shall not apply to a commercial or industrial type function of an executive agency that is—

(1) included on the procurement list established pursuant to section 8503 of this title; or

(2) planned to be changed to performance by a qualified nonprofit agency for the blind or by a qualified nonprofit agency for other severely disabled people in accordance with chapter 85 of this title.

(e) Inapplicability during war or emergency.—The provisions of this section shall not apply during war or during a period of national emergency declared by the President or Congress.

(Pub.L. 111–350, § 3, Jan. 4, 2011, 124 Stat. 3715.)

HISTORICAL AND STATUTORY NOTES

References in Text

Chapter 85 of this title, referred to in subsec. (d)(2), is classified to 41 U.S.C.A. § 8501 et seq.

CROSS REFERENCES

Executive agency, defined for division B of subtitle I of this title, see 41 USCA § 133.

Procurement, defined for subtitle I of this title, see 41 USCA § 111.

Revised Title 41 effective Jan. 4, 2011

§ 1711. Value engineering

Each executive agency shall establish and maintain cost-effective procedures and processes for analyzing the functions of a program, project, system, product, item of equipment, building, facility, service, or supply of the agency. The analysis shall be—

   (1) performed by qualified agency or contractor personnel; and

   (2) directed at improving performance, reliability, quality, safety, and life cycle costs.

(Pub.L. 111–350, § 3, Jan. 4, 2011, 124 Stat. 3718.)

CROSS REFERENCES

Executive agency, defined for division B of subtitle I of this title, see 41 USCA § 133.

§ 1712. Record requirements

   (a) **Maintaining records on computer.**—Each executive agency shall establish and maintain for 5 years a computer file, by fiscal year, containing unclassified records of all procurements greater than the simplified acquisition threshold in that fiscal year.

   (b) **Contents.**—The record established under subsection (a) shall include, with respect to each procurement carried out using—

   (1) competitive procedures—

      (A) the date of contract award;

      (B) information identifying the source to whom the contract was awarded;

      (C) the property or services the Federal Government obtains under the procurement; and

      (D) the total cost of the procurement; or

   (2) procedures other than competitive procedures—

      (A) the information described in paragraph (1);

      (B) the reason under section 3304(a) of this title or section 2304(c) of title 10 for using the procedures; and

      (C) the identity of the organization or activity that conducted the procurement.

   (c) **Separate record category for procurements resulting in one bid or proposal.**—Information included in a record pursuant to subsection (b)(1) that relates to procurements resulting in the submission of a bid or proposal by only one responsible source shall be separately categorized from the information relating to other procurements included in the record. The record of that information shall be designated "noncompetitive procurements using competitive procedures".

   (d) **Transmission and data entry of information.**—The head of each executive agency shall—

   (1) ensure the accuracy of the information included in the record established and maintained by the agency under subsection (a); and

   (2) transmit in a timely manner such information to the General Services Administration for entry into the Federal Procurement Data System referred to in section 1122(a)(4) of this title, or any successor system.

(Pub.L. 111–350, § 3, Jan. 4, 2011, 124 Stat. 3718.)

CROSS REFERENCES

Competitive procedures, defined for division B of subtitle I of this title, see 41 USCA § 132.

Executive agency, defined for division B of subtitle I of this title, see 41 USCA § 133.

Procurement, defined for subtitle I of this title, see 41 USCA § 111.

Responsible source, defined for subtitle I of this title, see 41 USCA § 113.

Simplified acquisition threshold, defined for division B of subtitle I of this title, see 41 USCA § 134.

§ 1713. Procurement data

   (a) **Definitions.**—In this section:

See Main Volume and Repealed Title 41, ante, for annotations

(1) **Qualified HUBZone small business concern.**—The term "qualified HUBZone small business concern" has the meaning given that term in section 3(p) of the Small Business Act (15 U.S.C. 632(p)).

(2) **Small business concern owned and controlled by socially and economically disadvantaged individuals.**—The term "small business concern owned and controlled by socially and economically disadvantaged individuals" has the meaning given that term in section 8(d) of the Small Business Act (15 U.S.C. 637(d)).

(3) **Small business concern owned and controlled by women.**—The term "small business concern owned and controlled by women" has the meaning given that term in section 8(d) of the Small Business Act (15 U.S.C. 637(d)) and section 204 of the Women's Business Ownership Act of 1988 (Public Law 100–533, 102 Stat. 2692).

(b) **Reporting.**—Each Federal agency shall report to the Office of Federal Procurement Policy the number of qualified HUBZone small business concerns, the number of small businesses owned and controlled by women, and the number of small business concerns owned and controlled by socially and economically disadvantaged individuals, by gender, that are first time recipients of contracts from the agency. The Office shall take appropriate action to ascertain, for each fiscal year, the number of those small businesses that have newly entered the Federal market.

(Pub.L. 111–350, § 3, Jan. 4, 2011, 124 Stat. 3719.)

HISTORICAL AND STATUTORY NOTES

References in Text

The Small Business Act, referred to in subsec. (a), is Act July 18, 1958, Pub.L. 85–536, 72 Stat. 384, as amended, also known as the SBA, which is principally classified to chapter 14A of Title 15, 15 U.S.C.A. § 631 et seq. Section 3 of such Act is classified to 15 U.S.C.A. § 632. Section 8 of such Act is classified to 15 U.S.C.A. § 637.

For complete classification, see Short Title note set out under 15 U.S.C.A. § 631 and Tables.

The Women's Business Ownership Act of 1988, referred to in subsec. (a)(3), is Pub.L. 100–533, Oct. 25, 1988, 102 Stat. 2689, as amended. Section 204 of such Act is set out as a note under 15 U.S.C.A. § 637. For complete classification, see Short Title note set out under 15 U.S.C.A. § 631 and Tables.

CROSS REFERENCES

Procurement, defined for subtitle I of this title, see 41 USCA § 111.

CHAPTER 19—SIMPLIFIED ACQUISITION PROCEDURES

§ 1901. Simplified acquisition procedures

(a) **When procedures are to be used.**—To promote efficiency and economy in contracting and to avoid unnecessary burdens for agencies and contractors, the Federal Acquisition Regulation shall provide for special simplified procedures for purchases of property and services for amounts—

(1) not greater than the simplified acquisition threshold; and

(2) greater than the simplified acquisition threshold but not greater than $5,000,000 for which the contracting officer reasonably expects, based on the nature of the property or services sought and on market research, that offers will include only commercial items.

(b) **Prohibition on dividing purchases.**—A proposed purchase or contract for an amount above the simplified acquisition threshold may not be divided into several purchases or contracts for lesser amounts to use the simplified acquisition procedures required by subsection (a).

(c) **Promotion of competition required.**—When using simplified acquisition procedures, the head of an executive agency shall promote competition to the maximum extent practicable.

(d) **Consideration of offers timely received.**—The simplified acquisition procedures contained in the Federal Acquisition Regulation shall include a requirement that a contracting officer consider each responsive offer timely received from an eligible offeror.

(e) **Special rules for commercial items.**—The Federal Acquisition Regulation shall provide that an executive agency using special simplified procedures to purchase commercial items—

(1) shall publish a notice in accordance with section 1708 of this title and, as provided in section 1708(c)(4) of this title, permit all responsible sources to submit a bid, proposal, or quotation (as appropriate) that the agency shall consider;

(2) may not conduct the purchase on a sole source basis unless the need to do so is justified in writing and approved in accordance with section 2304(f) of title 10 or section 3304(e) of this title, as applicable; and

(3) shall include in the contract file a written description of the procedures used in awarding the contract and the number of offers received.

(Pub.L. 111–350, § 3, Jan. 4, 2011, 124 Stat. 3719.)

CROSS REFERENCES

Commercial item, defined for subtitle I of this title, see 41 USCA § 103.

Executive agency, defined for division B of subtitle I of this title, see 41 USCA § 133.

Federal Acquisition Regulation, defined for subtitle I of this title, functions and general authority, see 41 USCA §§ 106 and 1303.

Responsible source, defined for subtitle I of this title, see 41 USCA § 113.

Simplified acquisition threshold, defined for division B of subtitle I of this title, see 41 USCA § 134.

§ 1902. Procedures applicable to purchases below micro-purchase threshold

(a) **Definition.**—For purposes of this section, the micro-purchase threshold is $3,000.

(b) **Compliance with certain requirements and nonapplicability of certain authority.**—

(1) **Compliance with certain requirements.**—The head of each executive agency shall ensure that procuring activities of that agency, when awarding a contract with a price exceeding the micro-purchase threshold, comply with the requirements of section 8(a) of the Small Business Act (15 U.S.C. 637(a)), section 2323 of title 10, and section 7102 of the Federal Acquisition Streamlining Act of 1994 (Public Law 103–355, 15 U.S.C. 644 note).

(2) **Nonapplicability of certain authority.**—The authority under part 13.106(a)(1) of the Federal Acquisition Regulation (48 C.F.R. 13.106(a)(1)), as in effect on November 18, 1993, to make purchases without securing competitive quotations does not apply to a purchase with a price exceeding the micro-purchase threshold.

(c) **Nonapplicability of certain provisions.**—An executive agency purchase with an anticipated value of the micro-purchase threshold or less is not subject to section 15(j) of the Small Business Act (15 U.S.C. 644(j)) and chapter 83 of this title.

(d) **Purchases without competitive quotations.**—A purchase not greater than $3,000 may be made without obtaining competitive quotations if an employee of an executive agency or a member of the armed forces, authorized to do so, determines that the price for the purchase is reasonable.

(e) **Equitable distribution.**—Purchases not greater than $3,000 shall be distributed equitably among qualified suppliers.

See Main Volume and Repealed Title 41, ante, for annotations

(f) Implementation through Federal Acquisition Regulation.—This section shall be implemented through the Federal Acquisition Regulation.

(Pub.L. 111–350, § 3, Jan. 4, 2011, 124 Stat. 3720.)

HISTORICAL AND STATUTORY NOTES

References in Text

The Small Business Act, referred to in subsecs. (b)(1) and (c), is Act July 18, 1958, Pub.L. 85–536, 72 Stat. 384, as amended, also known as the SBA, which is principally classified to chapter 14A of Title 15, 15 U.S.C.A. § 631 et seq. Section 8 of such Act is classified to 15 U.S.C.A. § 637. Section 15 of such Act is classified to 15 U.S.C.A. § 644. For complete classification, see Short Title note set out under 15 U.S.C.A. § 631 and Tables.

The Federal Acquisition Streamlining Act of 1994, referred to in subsec. (b)(1), is Pub.L. 103–355, Oct. 13, 1994, 108 Stat. 3243. Section 7102 of such Act is set out as a note under 15 U.S.C.A. § 644. For complete classification, see Short Title note set out under 41 U.S.C.A. § 101 and Tables.

Chapter 83 of this title, referred to in subsec. (c), is classified to 41 U.S.C.A. § 8301 et seq.

Micro-purchase Guidelines

Pub.L. 111–240, Title I, § 1332, Sept. 27, 2010, 124 Stat. 2541, provided that: "Not later than 1 year after the date of enactment of this Act [Sept. 27, 2010], the Director of the Office of Management and Budget, in coordination with the Administrator of General Services, shall issue guidelines regarding the analysis of purchase card expenditures to identify opportunities for achieving and accurately measuring fair participation of small business concerns in purchases in an amount not in excess of the micro-purchase threshold, as defined in section 32 of the Office of Federal Procurement Policy Act (41 U.S.C. 428 [former 41 U.S.C.A. § 428]) (in this section referred to as 'micro-purchases'), consistent with the national policy on small business participation in Federal procurements set forth in sections 2(a) and 15(g) of the Small Business Act (15 U.S.C. 631(a) and 644(g)), and dissemination of best practices for participation of small business concerns in micro-purchases."

[Note was classified as a note under former 41 U.S.C.A. § 428 prior to the enactment into positive law of Title 41, Public Contracts, by Pub.L. 111–350, Jan. 4, 2011, 124 Stat. 3677.]

CROSS REFERENCES

Executive agency, defined for division B of subtitle I of this title, see 41 USCA § 133.

Federal Acquisition Regulation, defined for subtitle I of this title, functions and general authority, see 41 USCA §§ 106 and 1303.

§ 1903. Special emergency procurement authority

(a) Applicability.—The authorities provided in subsections (b) and (c) apply with respect to a procurement of property or services by or for an executive agency that the head of the executive agency determines are to be used—

(1) in support of a contingency operation (as defined in section 101(a) of title 10); or

(2) to facilitate the defense against or recovery from nuclear, biological, chemical, or radiological attack against the United States.

(b) Increased thresholds and limitation.—For a procurement to which this section applies under subsection (a)—

(1) the amount specified in section 1902(a), (d), and (e) of this title shall be deemed to be—

(A) $15,000 in the case of a contract to be awarded and performed, or purchase to be made, in the United States; and

(B) $25,000 in the case of a contract to be awarded and performed, or purchase to be made, outside the United States;

(2) the term "simplified acquisition threshold" means—

(A) $250,000 in the case of a contract to be awarded and performed, or purchase to be made, in the United States; and

(B) $1,000,000 in the case of a contract to be awarded and performed, or purchase to be made, outside the United States; and

(3) the $5,000,000 limitation in sections 1901(a)(2) and 3305(a)(2) of this title and section 2304(g)(1)(B) of title 10 is deemed to be $10,000,000.

(c) Authority to treat property or service as commercial item.—

Revised Title 41 effective Jan. 4, 2011

(1) **In general.**—The head of an executive agency carrying out a procurement of property or a service to which this section applies under subsection (a)(2) may treat the property or service as a commercial item for the purpose of carrying out the procurement.

(2) **Certain contracts not exempt from standards or requirements.**—A contract in an amount of more than $15,000,000 that is awarded on a sole source basis for an item or service treated as a commercial item under paragraph (1) is not exempt from—

(A) cost accounting standards prescribed under section 1502 of this title; or

(B) cost or pricing data requirements (commonly referred to as truth in negotiating) under chapter 35 of this title and section 2306a of title 10.

(Pub.L. 111–350, § 3, Jan. 4, 2011, 124 Stat. 3721.)

HISTORICAL AND STATUTORY NOTES

References in Text

Chapter 35 of this title, referred to in subsec. (c)(2)(B), is classified to 41 U.S.C.A. § 3501 et seq.

CROSS REFERENCES

Commercial item, defined for subtitle I of this title, see 41 USCA § 103.

Executive agency, defined for division B of subtitle I of this title, see 41 USCA § 133.

Item and item of supply, defined for subtitle I of this title, see 41 USCA § 108.

Procurement, defined for subtitle I of this title, see 41 USCA § 111.

Simplified acquisition threshold, defined for division B of subtitle I of this title, see 41 USCA § 134.

Standards, defined for subtitle I of this title, see 41 USCA § 114.

§ 1904. Certain transactions for defense against attack

(a) **Authority.**—

(1) **In general.**—The head of an executive agency that engages in basic research, applied research, advanced research, and development projects that are necessary to the responsibilities of the executive agency in the field of research and development and have the potential to facilitate defense against or recovery from terrorism or nuclear, biological, chemical, or radiological attack may exercise the same authority (subject to the same restrictions and conditions) with respect to the research and projects as the Secretary of Defense may exercise under section 2371 of title 10, except for subsections (b) and (f) of section 2371.

(2) **Prototype projects.**—The head of an executive agency, under the authority of paragraph (1), may carry out prototype projects that meet the requirements of paragraph (1) in accordance with the requirements and conditions provided for carrying out prototype projects under section 845 of the National Defense Authorization Act for Fiscal Year 1994 (Public Law 103–160, 10 U.S.C. 2371 note), including that, to the maximum extent practicable, competitive procedures shall be used when entering into agreements to carry out projects under section 845(a) of that Act and that the period of authority to carry out projects under section 845(a) of that Act terminates as provided in section 845(i) of that Act.

(3) **Application of requirements and conditions.**—In applying the requirements and conditions of section 845 of that Act under this subsection—

(A) section 845(c) of that Act shall apply with respect to prototype projects carried out under paragraph (2); and

(B) the Director of the Office of Management and Budget shall perform the functions of the Secretary of Defense under section 845(d) of that Act.

(4) **Applicability to selected executive agencies.**—

(A) **Office of Management and Budget.**—The head of an executive agency may exercise authority under this subsection for a project only if authorized by the Director of the Office of Management and Budget.

See Main Volume and Repealed Title 41, ante, for annotations

(B) **Department of Homeland Security.**—Authority under this subsection does not apply to the Secretary of Homeland Security while section 831 of the Homeland Security Act of 2002 (6 U.S.C. 391) is in effect.

(b) **Regulations.**—The Director of the Office of Management and Budget shall prescribe regulations to carry out this section. No transaction may be conducted under the authority of this section before the regulations take effect.

(c) **Annual report.**—The annual report of the head of an executive agency that is required under section 2371(h) of title 10, as applied to the head of the executive agency by subsection (a), shall be submitted to the Committee on Homeland Security and Governmental Affairs of the Senate and the Committee on Oversight and Government Reform of the House of Representatives.

(d) **Termination of authority.**—The authority to carry out transactions under subsection (a) terminates on September 30, 2008.

(Pub.L. 111–350, § 3, Jan. 4, 2011, 124 Stat. 3721.)

HISTORICAL AND STATUTORY NOTES

References in Text

The National Defense Authorization Act for Fiscal Year 1994, referred to in subsec. (a)(2), (3), is Pub.L. 103–160, Nov. 30, 1993, 107 Stat. 1547. Section 845 of such Act is classified as a note under 10 U.S.C.A. § 2371. For complete classification, see Tables.

The Homeland Security Act of 2002, referred to in subsec. (a)(4)(B), is Pub.L. 107–296, Nov. 25, 2002, 116 stat. 2135, as amended, which is classified principally to chapter 1 of Title 6, 6 U.S.C.A. § 101 et seq. Section 831 of such Act is classified to 6 U.S.C.A. § 391. For complete classification, see Short Title note set out under 6 U.S.C.A. § 101 and Tables.

CROSS REFERENCES

Competitive procedures, defined for division B of subtitle I of this title, see 41 USCA § 132.

Executive agency, defined for division B of subtitle I of this title, see 41 USCA § 133.

§ 1905. List of laws inapplicable to contracts or subcontracts not greater than simplified acquisition threshold

(a) **Definition.**—In this section, the term "Council" has the meaning given that term in section 1301 of this title.

(b) **Inclusion in Federal Acquisition Regulation.—**

(1) **In general.**—The Federal Acquisition Regulation shall include a list of provisions of law that are inapplicable to contracts or subcontracts in amounts not greater than the simplified acquisition threshold. A provision of law properly included on the list pursuant to paragraph (2) does not apply to contracts or subcontracts in amounts not greater than the simplified acquisition threshold that are made by an executive agency. This section does not render a provision of law not included on the list inapplicable to contracts and subcontracts in amounts not greater than the simplified acquisition threshold.

(2) **Laws enacted after October 13, 1994.**—A provision of law described in subsection (c) that is enacted after October 13, 1994, shall be included on the list of inapplicable provisions of laws required by paragraph (1) unless the Council makes a written determination that it would not be in the best interest of the Federal Government to exempt contracts or subcontracts in amounts not greater than the simplified acquisition threshold from the applicability of the provision.

(c) **Covered law.**—A provision of law referred to in subsection (b)(2) is a provision of law that the Council determines sets forth policies, procedures, requirements, or restrictions for the procurement of property or services by the Federal Government, except for a provision of law that—

(1) provides for criminal or civil penalties; or

(2) specifically refers to this section and provides that, notwithstanding this section, it shall be applicable to contracts or subcontracts in amounts not greater than the simplified acquisition threshold.

(d) **Petition.**—A person may petition the Administrator to take appropriate action when a provision of law described in subsection (c) is not included on the list of inapplicable provisions of law as required by subsection (b) and the Council has not made a written determination pursuant to subsection (b)(2). The Administrator shall revise the Federal Acquisition Regulation to include the provision on the list of inapplicable provisions of law unless the Council makes a determination pursuant to subsection (b)(2) within 60 days after the petition is received.

(Pub.L. 111–350, § 3, Jan. 4, 2011, 124 Stat. 3722.)

CROSS REFERENCES

Administrator, defined for Subtitle I of this title, see 41 USCA § 101.
Executive agency, defined for division B of subtitle I of this title, see 41 USCA § 133.
Federal Acquisition Regulation, defined for subtitle I of this title, functions and general authority, see 41 USCA §§ 106 and 1303.

Procurement, defined for subtitle I of this title, see 41 USCA § 111.
Simplified acquisition threshold, defined for division B of subtitle I of this title, see 41 USCA § 134.

§ 1906. List of laws inapplicable to procurements of commercial items

(a) **Definition**—In this section, the term "Council" has the meaning given that term in section 1301 of this title.

(b) **Contracts.**—

(1) **Inclusion in Federal Acquisition Regulation.**—The Federal Acquisition Regulation shall include a list of provisions of law that are inapplicable to contracts for the procurement of commercial items. A provision of law properly included on the list pursuant to paragraph (2) does not apply to purchases of commercial items by an executive agency. This section does not render a provision of law not included on the list inapplicable to contracts for the procurement of commercial items.

(2) **Laws enacted after October 13, 1994.**—A provision of law described in subsection (d) that is enacted after October 13, 1994, shall be included on the list of inapplicable provisions of law required by paragraph (1) unless the Council makes a written determination that it would not be in the best interest of the Federal Government to exempt contracts for the procurement of commercial items from the applicability of the provision.

(c) **Subcontracts.**—

(1) **Definition.**—In this subsection, the term " subcontract" includes a transfer of commercial items between divisions, subsidiaries, or affiliates of a contractor or subcontractor.

(2) **Inclusion in Federal Acquisition Regulation.**—The Federal Acquisition Regulation shall include a list of provisions of law that are inapplicable to subcontracts under a contract or subcontract for the procurement of commercial items. A provision of law properly included on the list pursuant to paragraph (3) does not apply to those subcontracts. This section does not render a provision of law not included on the list inapplicable to subcontracts under a contract for the procurement of commercial items.

(3) **Provisions to be excluded from list.**—A provision of law described in subsection (d) shall be included on the list of inapplicable provisions of law required by paragraph (2) unless the Council makes a written determination that it would not be in the best interest of the Federal Government to exempt subcontracts under a contract for the procurement of commercial items from the applicability of the provision.

(4) **Waiver not authorized.**—This subsection does not authorize the waiver of the applicability of any provision of law with respect to any subcontract under a contract with a prime contractor reselling or distributing commercial items of another contractor without adding value.

(d) **Covered law.**—A provision of law referred to in subsections (b)(2) and (c) is a provision of law that the Council determines sets forth policies, procedures, requirements, or restrictions for the procurement of property or services by the Federal Government, except for a provision of law that—

(1) provides for criminal or civil penalties; or

(2) specifically refers to this section and provides that, notwithstanding this section, it shall be applicable to contracts for the procurement of commercial items.

(e) Petition.—A person may petition the Administrator to take appropriate action when a provision of law described in subsection (d) is not included on the list of inapplicable provisions of law as required by subsection (b) or (c) and the Council has not made a written determination pursuant to subsection (b)(2) or (c)(3). The Administrator shall revise the Federal Acquisition Regulation to include the provision on the list of inapplicable provisions of law unless the Council makes a determination pursuant to subsection (b)(2) or (c)(3) within 60 days after the petition is received.

(Pub.L. 111–350, § 3, Jan. 4, 2011, 124 Stat. 3723.)

CROSS REFERENCES

Administrator, defined for subtitle I of this title, see 41 USCA § 101.

Commercial item, defined for subtitle I of this title, see 41 USCA § 103.

Executive agency, defined for division B of subtitle I of this title, see 41 USCA § 133.

Federal Acquisition Regulation, defined for subtitle I of this title, functions and general authority, see 41 USCA §§ 106 and 1303.

Procurement, defined for subtitle I of this title, see 41 USCA § 111.

§ 1907. List of laws inapplicable to procurements of commercially available off-the-shelf items

(a) Inclusion in Federal Acquisition Regulation.—

(1) In general.—The Federal Acquisition Regulation shall include a list of provisions of law that are inapplicable to contracts for the procurement of commercially available off-the-shelf items. A provision of law properly included on the list pursuant to paragraph (2) does not apply to contracts for the procurement of commercially available off-the-shelf items. This section does not render a provision of law not included on the list inapplicable to contracts for the procurement of commercially available off-the-shelf items.

(2) Laws to be included.—A provision of law described in subsection (b) shall be included on the list of inapplicable provisions of law required by paragraph (1) unless the Administrator makes a written determination that it would not be in the best interest of the Federal Government to exempt contracts for the procurement of commercially available off-the-shelf items from the applicability of the provision.

(3) Other authorities or responsibilities not affected.—This section does not modify, supersede, impair, or restrict authorities or responsibilities under—

(A) section 15 of the Small Business Act (15 U.S.C. 644); or

(B) bid protest procedures developed under the authority of—

(i) subchapter V of chapter 35 of title 31;

(ii) section 2305(e) and (f) of title 10; or

(iii) sections 3706 and 3707 of this title.

(b) Covered law.—Except as provided in subsection (a)(3), a provision of law referred to in subsection (a)(1) is a provision of law that the Administrator determines imposes Federal Government-unique policies, procedures, requirements, or restrictions for the procurement of property or services on persons whom the Federal Government has awarded contracts for the procurement of commercially available off-the-shelf items, except for a provision of law that—

(1) provides for criminal or civil penalties; or

(2) specifically refers to this section and provides that, notwithstanding this section, it shall be applicable to contracts for the procurement of commercially available off-the-shelf items.

(Pub.L. 111–350, § 3, Jan. 4, 2011, 124 Stat. 3724.)

HISTORICAL AND STATUTORY NOTES

References in Text

The Small Business Act, referred to in subsec. (a)(3)(A), is Act July 18, 1958, Pub.L. 85–536, 72 Stat. 384, as amended, also known as the SBA, which is principally classified to chapter 14A of Title 15, 15 U.S.C.A. § 631 et seq. Section 15 of such Act is classified to 15 U.S.C.A. § 644. For complete classification, see Short Title note set out under 15 U.S.C.A. § 631 and Tables.

Subchapter V of chapter 35 of title 31, referred to in subsec. (a)(3)(B)(i), is classified to 31 U.S.C.A. 3551 et seq.

CROSS REFERENCES

Administrator, defined for subtitle I of this title, see 41 USCA § 101.

Commercially available off-the-shelf item, defined for subtitle I of this title, see 41 USCA § 104.

Federal Acquisition Regulation, defined for subtitle I of this title, functions and general authority, see 41 USCA §§ 106 and 1303.

Procurement, defined for subtitle I of this title, see 41 USCA § 111.

§ 1908. Inflation adjustment of acquisition-related dollar thresholds

(a) **Definition.**—In this section, the term "Council" has the meaning given that term in section 1301 of this title.

(b) **Application.**—

(1) **In general.**—Except as provided in paragraph (2), the requirement for adjustment under subsection (c) applies to a dollar threshold that is specified in law as a factor in defining the scope of the applicability of a policy, procedure, requirement, or restriction provided in that law to the procurement of property or services by an executive agency, as the Council determines.

(2) **Exceptions.**—Subsection (c) does not apply to dollar thresholds—

(A) in chapter 67 of this title;

(B) in sections 3141 to 3144, 3146, and 3147 of title 40; or

(C) the United States Trade Representative establishes pursuant to title III of the Trade Agreements Act of 1979 (19 U.S.C. 2511 et seq.).

(3) **Relationship to other inflation adjustment authorities.**—This section supersedes the applicability of other provisions of law that provide for the adjustment of a dollar threshold that is adjustable under this section.

(c) **Requirement for periodic adjustment.**—

(1) **Baseline constant dollar value.**—For purposes of paragraph (2), the baseline constant dollar value for a dollar threshold—

(A) in effect on October 1, 2000, that was first specified in a law that took effect on or before October 1, 2000, is the October 1, 2000, constant dollar value of that dollar threshold; and

(B) specified in a law that takes effect after October 1, 2000, is the constant dollar value of that threshold as of the effective date of that dollar threshold pursuant to that law.

(2) **Adjustment.**—On October 1 of each year evenly divisible by 5, the Council shall adjust each acquisition-related dollar threshold provided by law, as described in subsection (b)(1), to the baseline constant dollar value of that threshold.

(3) **Exclusive means of adjustment.**—A dollar threshold adjustable under this section shall be adjusted only as provided in this section.

(d) **Publication.**—The Council shall publish a notice of the adjusted dollar thresholds under this section in the Federal Register. The thresholds take effect on the date of publication.

(e) **Calculation.**—An adjustment under this section shall be—

(1) calculated on the basis of changes in the Consumer Price Index for all-urban consumers published monthly by the Secretary of Labor; and

(2) rounded, in the case of a dollar threshold that on the day before the adjustment is—

(A) less than $10,000, to the nearest $500;

(B) not less than $10,000, but less than $100,000, to the nearest $5, 000;

(C) not less than $100,000, but less than $1,000,000, to the nearest $ 50,000; and

(D) $1,000,000 or more, to the nearest $500,000.

(f) **Petition for inclusion of omitted threshold.**—

See Main Volume and Repealed Title 41, ante, for annotations

(1) **Petition submitted to Administrator.**—A person may request adjustment of a dollar threshold adjustable under this section that is not included in a notice of adjustment published under subsection (d) by submitting a petition for adjustment to the Administrator.

(2) **Actions of Administrator.**—On receipt of a petition for adjustment of a dollar threshold under paragraph (1), the Administrator—

(A) shall determine, in writing, whether the dollar threshold is required to be adjusted under this section; and

(B) on determining that it should be adjusted, shall publish in the Federal Register a revised notice of the adjustment dollar thresholds under this section that includes the adjustment of the dollar threshold covered by the petition.

(3) **Effective date of adjustment by petition.**—The adjustment of a dollar threshold pursuant to a petition under this subsection takes effect on the date the revised notice adding the adjustment under paragraph (2)(B) is published.

(Pub.L. 111–350, § 3, Jan. 4, 2011, 124 Stat. 3725.)

HISTORICAL AND STATUTORY NOTES

References in Text

Chapter 67 of this title, referred to in subsec. (b)(2)(A), is classified to 41 U.S.C.A. § 6701 et seq.

The Trade Agreements Act of 1979, referred to in subsec. (b)(2)(C), is Pub.L. 96–39, July 26, 1979, 93 Stat. 144, as amended, which principally enacted chapter 13 of Title 19, 19 U.S.C.A. § 2501 et seq. Title III of such Act is classified to subchapter I of chapter 13 of Title 19, 19 U.S.C.A. § 2511 et seq. For complete classification, see 19 U.S.C.A. § 2501 and Tables.

CROSS REFERENCES

Acquisition, defined for division B of subtitle I of this title, see 41 USCA § 131.

Administrator, defined for Subtitle I of this title, see 41 USCA § 101.

Executive agency, defined for division B of subtitle I of this title, see 41 USCA § 133.

Procurement, defined for subtitle I of this title, see 41 USCA § 111.

Publication of proposed regulations, covered policies, regulations, procedures, and form, contents of notice, see 41 USCA § 1707.

CHAPTER 21—RESTRICTIONS ON OBTAINING AND DISCLOSING CERTAIN INFORMATION

§ 2101. Definitions

In this chapter:

(1) **Contracting officer.**—The term "contracting officer" means an individual who, by appointment in accordance with applicable regulations, has the authority to enter into a Federal agency procurement contract on behalf of the Government and to make determinations and findings with respect to the contract.

(2) **Contractor bid or proposal information.**—The term "contractor bid or proposal information" means any of the following information submitted to a Federal agency as part of, or in connection with, a bid or proposal to enter into a Federal agency procurement contract, if that information previously has not been made available to the public or disclosed publicly:

(A) Cost or pricing data (as defined in section 2306a(h) of title 10 with respect to procurements subject to that section and section 3501(a) of this title with respect to procurements subject to that section).

(B) Indirect costs and direct labor rates.

(C) Proprietary information about manufacturing processes, operations, or techniques marked by the contractor in accordance with applicable law or regulation.

(D) Information marked by the contractor as "contractor bid or proposal information", in accordance with applicable law or regulation.

(3) **Federal agency.**—The term "Federal agency" has the meaning given that term in section 102 of title 40.

(4) **Federal agency procurement.**—The term "Federal agency procurement" means the acquisition (by using competitive procedures and awarding a contract) of goods or services (including construction) from non-Federal sources by a Federal agency using appropriated funds.

(5) **Official.**—The term "official" means—

(A) an officer, as defined in section 2104 of title 5;

(B) an employee, as defined in section 2105 of title 5; and

(C) a member of the uniformed services, as defined in section 2101(3) of title 5.

(6) **Protest.**—The term "protest" means a written objection by an interested party to the award or proposed award of a Federal agency procurement contract, pursuant to subchapter V of chapter 35 of title 31.

(7) **Source selection information.**—The term "source selection information" means any of the following information prepared for use by a Federal agency to evaluate a bid or proposal to enter into a Federal agency procurement contract, if that information previously has not been made available to the public or disclosed publicly:

(A) Bid prices submitted in response to a Federal agency solicitation for sealed bids, or lists of those bid prices before public bid opening.

(B) Proposed costs or prices submitted in response to a Federal agency solicitation, or lists of those proposed costs or prices.

(C) Source selection plans.

(D) Technical evaluation plans.

(E) Technical evaluations of proposals.

(F) Cost or price evaluations of proposals.

(G) Competitive range determinations that identify proposals that have a reasonable chance of being selected for award of a contract.

(H) Rankings of bids, proposals, or competitors.

(I) Reports and evaluations of source selection panels, boards, or advisory councils.

(J) Other information marked as "source selection information" based on a case-by-case determination by the head of the agency, the head's designee, or the contracting officer that its disclosure would jeopardize the integrity or successful completion of the Federal agency procurement to which the information relates.

(Pub.L. 111–350, § 3, Jan. 4, 2011, 124 Stat. 3727.)

HISTORICAL AND STATUTORY NOTES

References in Text

Subchapter V of chapter 35 of title 31, referred to in par. (6), is classified to 31 U.S.C.A. 3551 et seq.

CROSS REFERENCES

Acquisition, defined for division B of subtitle I of this title, see 41 USCA § 131.

Competitive procedures, defined for division B of subtitle I of this title, see 41 USCA § 132.

Procurement, defined for subtitle I of this title, see 41 USCA § 111.

See Main Volume and Repealed Title 41, ante, for annotations

§ 2102. Prohibitions on disclosing and obtaining procurement information

(a) Prohibition on disclosing procurement information.—

(1) **In general.**—Except as provided by law, a person described in paragraph (3) shall not knowingly disclose contractor bid or proposal information or source selection information before the award of a Federal agency procurement contract to which the information relates.

(2) **Employee of private sector organization.**—In addition to the restriction in paragraph (1), an employee of a private sector organization assigned to an agency under chapter 37 of title 5 shall not knowingly disclose contractor bid or proposal information or source selection information during the 3–year period after the employee's assignment ends, except as provided by law.

(3) **Application.**—Paragraph (1) applies to a person that—

(A)(i) is a present or former official of the Federal Government; or

(ii) is acting or has acted for or on behalf of, or who is advising or has advised the Federal Government with respect to, a Federal agency procurement; and

(B) by virtue of that office, employment, or relationship has or had access to contractor bid or proposal information or source selection information.

(b) Prohibition on obtaining procurement information.—

Except as provided by law, a person shall not knowingly obtain contractor bid or proposal information or source selection information before the award of a Federal agency procurement contract to which the information relates.

(Pub.L. 111–350, § 3, Jan. 4, 2011, 124 Stat. 3728.)

§ 2103. Actions required of procurement officers when contacted regarding non-Federal employment

(a) Actions required.—

An agency official participating personally and substantially in a Federal agency procurement for a contract in excess of the simplified acquisition threshold who contacts or is contacted by a person that is a bidder or offeror in that Federal agency procurement regarding possible non–Federal employment for that official shall—

(1) promptly report the contact in writing to the official's supervisor and to the designated agency ethics official (or designee) of the agency in which the official is employed; and

(2)(A) reject the possibility of non–Federal employment; or

(B) disqualify himself or herself from further personal and substantial participation in that Federal agency procurement until the agency authorizes the official to resume participation in the procurement, in accordance with the requirements of section 208 of title 18 and applicable agency regulations on the grounds that—

(i) the person is no longer a bidder or offeror in that Federal agency procurement; or

(ii) all discussions with the bidder or offeror regarding possible non–Federal employment have terminated without an agreement or arrangement for employment.

(b) Retention of reports.—

The agency shall retain each report required by this section for not less than 2 years following the submission of the report. The reports shall be made available to the public on request, except that any part of a report that is exempt from the disclosure requirements of section 552 of title 5 under subsection (b)(1) of that section may be withheld from disclosure to the public.

(c) Persons subject to penalties.—The following are subject to the penalties and administrative actions set forth in section 2105 of this title:

(1) An official who knowingly fails to comply with the requirements of this section.

(2) A bidder or offeror that engages in employment discussions with an official who is subject to the restrictions of this section, knowing that the official has not complied with paragraph (1) or (2) of subsection (a).

(Pub.L. 111–350, § 3, Jan. 4, 2011, 124 Stat. 3728.)

CROSS REFERENCES

Procurement, defined for subtitle I of this title, see 41 USCA § 111.

Simplified acquisition threshold, defined for division B of subtitle I of this title, see 41 USCA § 134.

§ 2104. Prohibition on former official's acceptance of compensation from contractor

(a) Prohibition.—A former official of a Federal agency may not accept compensation from a contractor as an employee, officer, director, or consultant of the contractor within one year after the official—

(1) served, when the contractor was selected or awarded a contract, as the procuring contracting officer, the source selection authority, a member of the source selection evaluation board, or the chief of a financial or technical evaluation team in a procurement in which that contractor was selected for award of a contract in excess of $10,000,000;

(2) served as the program manager, deputy program manager, or administrative contracting officer for a contract in excess of $10,000,000 awarded to that contractor; or

(3) personally made for the Federal agency a decision to—

(A) award a contract, subcontract, modification of a contract or subcontract, or a task order or delivery order in excess of $10,000,000 to that contractor;

(B) establish overhead or other rates applicable to one or more contracts for that contractor that are valued in excess of $10,000,000;

(C) approve issuance of one or more contract payments in excess of $10,000,000 to that contractor; or

(D) pay or settle a claim in excess of $10,000,000 with that contractor.

(b) When compensation may be accepted.—Subsection (a) does not prohibit a former official of a Federal agency from accepting compensation from a division or affiliate of a contractor that does not produce the same or similar products or services as the entity of the contractor that is responsible for the contract referred to in paragraph (1), (2), or (3) of subsection (a).

(c) Implementing regulations.—Regulations implementing this section shall include procedures for an official or former official of a Federal agency to request advice from the appropriate designated agency ethics official regarding whether the official or former official is or would be precluded by this section from accepting compensation from a particular contractor.

(d) Persons subject to penalties.—The following are subject to the penalties and administrative actions set forth in section 2105 of this title:

(1) A former official who knowingly accepts compensation in violation of this section.

(2) A contractor that provides compensation to a former official knowing that the official accepts the compensation in violation of this section.

(Pub.L. 111–350, § 3, Jan. 4, 2011, 124 Stat. 3729.)

See Main Volume and Repealed Title 41, ante, for annotations

CROSS REFERENCES

Procurement, defined for subtitle I of this title, see 41 USCA § 111.

§ 2105.   Penalties and administrative actions

(a) **Criminal penalties.**—A person that violates section 2102 of this title to exchange information covered by section 2102 of this title for anything of value or to obtain or give a person a competitive advantage in the award of a Federal agency procurement contract shall be fined under title 18, imprisoned for not more than 5 years, or both.

(b) **Civil penalties.**—The Attorney General may bring a civil action in an appropriate district court of the United States against a person that engages in conduct that violates section 2102, 2103, or 2104 of this title. On proof of that conduct by a preponderance of the evidence—

(1) an individual is liable to the Federal Government for a civil penalty of not more than $50,000 for each violation plus twice the amount of compensation that the individual received or offered for the prohibited conduct; and

(2) an organization is liable to the Federal Government for a civil penalty of not more than $500,000 for each violation plus twice the amount of compensation that the organization received or offered for the prohibited conduct.

(c) **Administrative actions.**—

(1) **Types of action that Federal agency may take.**—A Federal agency that receives information that a contractor or a person has violated section 2102, 2103, or 2104 of this title shall consider taking one or more of the following actions, as appropriate:

(A) Canceling the Federal agency procurement, if a contract has not yet been awarded.

(B) Rescinding a contract with respect to which—

(i) the contractor or someone acting for the contractor has been convicted for an offense punishable under subsection (a); or

(ii) the head of the agency that awarded the contract has determined, based on a preponderance of the evidence, that the contractor or a person acting for the contractor has engaged in conduct constituting the offense.

(C) Initiating a suspension or debarment proceeding for the protection of the Federal Government in accordance with procedures in the Federal Acquisition Regulation.

(D) Initiating an adverse personnel action, pursuant to the procedures in chapter 75 of title 5 or other applicable law or regulation.

(2) **Amount Government entitled to recover.**—When a Federal agency rescinds a contract pursuant to paragraph (1)(B), the Federal Government is entitled to recover, in addition to any penalty prescribed by law, the amount expended under the contract.

(3) **Present responsibility affected by conduct.**—For purposes of a suspension or debarment proceeding initiated pursuant to paragraph (1)(C), engaging in conduct constituting an offense under section 2102, 2103, or 2104 of this title affects the present responsibility of a Federal Government contractor or subcontractor.

(Pub.L. 111–350, § 3, Jan. 4, 2011, 124 Stat. 3730.)

HISTORICAL AND STATUTORY NOTES

References in Text

Chapter 75 of title 5, referred to in subsec. (c)(1)(D), is classified to 5 U.S.C.A. § 7501 et seq.

CROSS REFERENCES

Federal Acquisition Regulation, defined for subtitle I of this title, functions and general authority, see 41 USCA §§ 106 and 1303.

Procurement, defined for subtitle I of this title, see 41 USCA § 111.

Revised Title 41 effective Jan. 4, 2011

§ 2106. Reporting information believed to constitute evidence of offense

A person may not file a protest against the award or proposed award of a Federal agency procurement contract alleging a violation of section 2102, 2103, or 2104 of this title, and the Comptroller General may not consider that allegation in deciding a protest, unless the person, no later than 14 days after the person first discovered the possible violation, reported to the Federal agency responsible for the procurement the information that the person believed constitutes evidence of the offense.

(Pub.L. 111–350, § 3, Jan. 4, 2011, 124 Stat. 3731.)

CROSS REFERENCES

Procurement, defined for subtitle I of this title, see 41 USCA § 111.

§ 2107. Savings provisions

This chapter does not—

(1) restrict the disclosure of information to, or its receipt by, a person or class of persons authorized, in accordance with applicable agency regulations or procedures, to receive that information;

(2) restrict a contractor from disclosing its own bid or proposal information or the recipient from receiving that information;

(3) restrict the disclosure or receipt of information relating to a Federal agency procurement after it has been canceled by the Federal agency before contract award unless the Federal agency plans to resume the procurement;

(4) prohibit individual meetings between a Federal agency official and an offeror or potential offeror for, or a recipient of, a contract or subcontract under a Federal agency procurement, provided that unauthorized disclosure or receipt of contractor bid or proposal information or source selection information does not occur;

(5) authorize the withholding of information from, nor restrict its receipt by, Congress, a committee or subcommittee of Congress, the Comptroller General, a Federal agency, or an inspector general of a Federal agency;

(6) authorize the withholding of information from, nor restrict its receipt by, the Comptroller General in the course of a protest against the award or proposed award of a Federal agency procurement contract; or

(7) limit the applicability of a requirement, sanction, contract penalty, or remedy established under another law or regulation.

(Pub.L. 111–350, § 3, Jan. 4, 2011, 124 Stat. 3731.)

CROSS REFERENCES

Procurement, defined for subtitle I of this title, see 41 USCA § 111.

CHAPTER 23—MISCELLANEOUS

See Main Volume and Repealed Title 41, ante, for annotations

§ 2301. Use of electronic commerce in Federal procurement

(a) Definition.—For the purposes of this section, the term "electronic commerce" means electronic techniques for accomplishing business transactions, including electronic mail or messaging, World Wide Web technology, electronic bulletin boards, purchase cards, electronic funds transfers, and electronic data interchange.

(b) Establishment, maintenance, and use of electronic commerce procedures and processes.—The head of each executive agency, after consulting with the Administrator, shall establish, maintain, and use, to the maximum extent that is practicable and cost-effective, procedures and processes that employ electronic commerce in the conduct and administration of the procurement system of the agency.

(c) Applicable standards.—In conducting electronic commerce, the head of an executive agency shall apply nationally and internationally recognized standards that broaden interoperability and ease the electronic interchange of information.

(d) Requirements of systems, technologies, procedures, and processes.—The head of each executive agency shall ensure that systems, technologies, procedures, and processes established pursuant to this section—

(1) are implemented with uniformity throughout the agency, to the extent practicable;

(2) are implemented only after granting due consideration to the use or partial use, as appropriate, of existing electronic commerce and electronic data interchange systems and infrastructures such as the Federal acquisition computer network architecture known as FACNET;

(3) facilitate access to Federal Government procurement opportunities, including opportunities for small business concerns, socially and economically disadvantaged small business concerns, and business concerns owned predominantly by women; and

(4) ensure that any notice of agency requirements or agency solicitation for contract opportunities is provided in a form that allows convenient and universal user access through a single, Government-wide point of entry.

(e) Implementation.—In carrying out the requirements of this section, the Administrator shall—

(1) issue policies to promote, to the maximum extent practicable, uniform implementation of this section by executive agencies, with due regard for differences in program requirements among agencies that may require departures from uniform procedures and processes in appropriate cases, when warranted because of the agency mission;

(2) ensure that the head of each executive agency complies with the requirements of subsection (d); and

(3) consult with the heads of appropriate Federal agencies with applicable technical and functional expertise, including the Office of Information and Regulatory Affairs, the National Institute of Standards and Technology, the General Services Administration, and the Department of Defense.

(Pub.L. 111–350, § 3, Jan. 4, 2011, 124 Stat. 3732.)

MEMORANDA OF PRESIDENT
PRESIDENTIAL MEMORANDUM
Oct. 28, 1993, 58 F.R. 58095

STREAMLINING PROCUREMENT THROUGH ELECTRONIC COMMERCE

Memorandum for the Heads of Executive Departments and Agencies [and] the President's Management Council

The Federal Government spends $200 billion annually buying goods and services. Unfortunately, the red tape and burdensome paperwork of the current procurement system increases costs, produces unnecessary delays, and reduces Federal work force productivity.

Moving to an electronic commerce system to simplify and streamline the purchasing process will promote customer service and cost-effectiveness. The electronic exchange of acquisition information between the private sector and the Federal Government also will increase competition by improving access to Federal contracting opportunities for the more than 300,000 vendors currently doing business with the Government, particularly small businesses, as well as many other vendors who find access to bidding opportunities difficult under the current system. For these reasons, I am committed to fundamentally altering and improving the way the Federal Government buys goods and services by ensuring that electronic commerce is implemented for appropriate Federal purchases as quickly as possible.

1. OBJECTIVES.

The objectives of this electronic commerce initiative are to:

(a) exchange procurement information – such as solicitations, offers, contracts, purchase orders, invoices, payments, and other contractual documents – electronically between the private sector and the Federal Government to the maximum extent practical;

(b) provide businesses, including small, small disadvantaged, and women-owned businesses, with greater access to Federal procurement opportunities;

(c) ensure that potential suppliers are provided simplified access to the Federal Government's electronic commerce system;

(d) employ nationally and internationally recognized data formats that serve to broaden and ease the electronic interchange of data; and

(e) use agency and industry systems and networks to enable the Government and potential suppliers to exchange information and access Federal procurement data.

2. IMPLEMENTATION.

The President's Management Council, in coordination with the Office of Federal Procurement Policy of the Office of Management and Budget, and in consultation with appropriate Federal agencies with applicable technical and functional expertise, as necessary, shall provide overall leadership, management oversight, and policy direction to implement electronic commerce in the executive branch through the following actions:

(a) by March 1994, define the architecture for the Government-wide electronic commerce acquisition system and identify executive departments or agencies responsible for developing, implementing, operating, and maintaining the Federal electronic system;

(b) by September 1994, establish an initial electronic commerce capability to enable the Federal Government and private vendors to electronically exchange standardized requests for quotations, quotes, purchase orders, and notice of awards and begin Government-wide implementation;

(c) by July 1995, implement a full scale Federal electronic commerce system that expands initial capabilities to include electronic payments, document interchange, and supporting databases; and

(d) by January 1997, complete Government-wide implementation of electronic commerce for appropriate Federal purchases, to the maximum extent possible.

This implementation schedule should be accelerated where practicable.

The head of each executive department or agency shall:

(a) ensure that budgetary resources are available, within approved budget levels, for electronic commerce implementation in each respective department or agency;

(b) assist the President's Management Council in implementing the electronic commerce system as quickly as possible in accordance with the schedules established herein; and

(c) designate one or more senior level employees to assist the President's Management Council and serve as a point of contact for the development and implementation of the Federal electronic commerce system within each respective department or agency.

3. NO PRIVATE RIGHTS CREATED.

This directive is for the internal management of the executive branch and does not create any right or benefit, substantive or procedural, enforceable by a party against the United States, its agencies or instrumentalities, its officers or employees, or any other person.

The Director of the Office of Management and Budget is authorized and directed to publish this memorandum in the Federal Register.

WILLIAM J. CLINTON

[Memorandum was set out under former 41 U.S.C.A. § 401 prior to the enactment into positive law of Title 41, Public Contracts, by Pub.L. 111–350, Jan. 4, 2011, 124 Stat. 3677.]

CROSS REFERENCES

Administrator, defined for Subtitle I of this title, see 41 USCA § 101.

Electronic records and signatures in commerce, see 15 USCA § 7001 et seq.

Executive agency, defined for division B of subtitle I of this title, see 41 USCA § 133.

Procurement, defined for subtitle I of this title, see 41 USCA § 111.

Procurement system, defined for subtitle I of this title, see 41 USCA § 112.

Standards, defined for subtitle I of this title, see 41 USCA § 114.

§ 2302. Rights in technical data

(a) **Where defined.**—The legitimate proprietary interest of the Federal Government and of a contractor in technical or other data shall be defined in regulations prescribed as part of the Federal Acquisition Regulation.

See Main Volume and Repealed Title 41, ante, for annotations

(b) General extent of regulations.—

(1) **Other rights not impaired.**—Regulations prescribed under subsection (a) may not impair a right of the Federal Government or of a contractor with respect to a patent or copyright or another right in technical data otherwise established by law.

(2) **Limitation on requiring data be provided to the Government.**—With respect to executive agencies subject to division C, regulations prescribed under subsection (a) shall provide that the Federal Government may not require a person that has developed a product (or process offered or to be offered for sale to the public) to provide to the Federal Government technical data relating to the design (or development or manufacture of the product or process) as a condition of procurement by the Federal Government of the product or process. This paragraph does not apply to data that may be necessary for the Federal Government to operate and maintain the product or use the process if the Federal Government obtains it as an element of performance under the contract.

(c) Technical data developed with Federal funds.—

(1) **Use by Government and agencies.**—Except as otherwise expressly provided by Federal statute, with respect to executive agencies subject to division C, regulations prescribed under subsection (a) shall provide that—

(A) the Federal Government has unlimited rights in technical data developed exclusively with Federal funds if delivery of the data—

(i) was required as an element of performance under a contract; and

(ii) is needed to ensure the competitive acquisition of supplies or services that will be required in substantial quantities in the future; and

(B) the Federal Government and each agency of the Federal Government has an unrestricted, royalty-free right to use, or to have its contractors use, for governmental purposes (excluding publication outside the Federal Government) technical data developed exclusively with Federal funds.

(2) **Requirements in addition to other rights of the Government.**—The requirements of paragraph (1) are in addition to and not in lieu of any other rights the Federal Government may have pursuant to law.

(d) Factors to be considered in prescribing regulations.—The following factors shall be considered in prescribing regulations under subsection (a):

(1) Whether the item or process to which the technical data pertains was developed—

(A) exclusively with Federal funds;

(B) exclusively at private expense; or

(C) in part with Federal funds and in part at private expense.

(2) The statement of congressional policy and objectives in section 200 of title 35, the statement of purposes in section 2(b) of the Small Business Innovation Development Act of 1982 (Public Law 97–219, 15 U.S.C. 638 note), and the declaration of policy in section 2 of the Small Business Act (15 U.S. C. 631).

(3) The interest of the Federal Government in increasing competition and lowering costs by developing and locating alternative sources of supply and manufacture.

(e) Provisions required in contracts.—Regulations prescribed under subsection (a) shall require that a contract for property or services entered into by an executive agency contain appropriate provisions relating to technical data, including provisions—

(1) defining the respective rights of the Federal Government and the contractor or subcontractor (at any tier) regarding technical data to be delivered under the contract;

(2) specifying technical data to be delivered under the contract and schedules for delivery;

(3) establishing or referencing procedures for determining the acceptability of technical data to be delivered under the contract;

(4) establishing separate contract line items for technical data to be delivered under the contract;

(5) to the maximum practicable extent, identifying, in advance of delivery, technical data which is to be delivered with restrictions on the right of the Federal Government to use the data;

(6) requiring the contractor to revise any technical data delivered under the contract to reflect engineering design changes made during the performance of the contract and affecting the form, fit, and function of the items specified in the contract and to deliver the revised technical data to an agency within a time specified in the contract;

(7) requiring the contractor to furnish written assurance, when technical data is delivered or is made available, that the technical data is complete and accurate and satisfies the requirements of the contract concerning technical data;

(8) establishing remedies to be available to the Federal Government when technical data required to be delivered or made available under the contract is found to be incomplete or inadequate or to not satisfy the requirements of the contract concerning technical data; and

(9) authorizing the head of the agency to withhold payments under the contract (or exercise another remedy the head of the agency considers appropriate) during any period if the contractor does not meet the requirements of the contract pertaining to the delivery of technical data.

(Pub.L. 111–350, § 3, Jan. 4, 2011, 124 Stat. 3733.)

HISTORICAL AND STATUTORY NOTES

References in Text

Division C, referred to in text, is division C of this subtitle, which is classified to 41 U.S.C.A. § 3101 et seq.

The Small Business Innovation Development Act of 1982, referred to in subsec. (d)(2), is Pub.L. 97–219, July 22, 1982, 96 Stat. 217, as amended, which amended 15 U.S.C.A. § 638, and enacted provisions set out as notes under 15 U.S.C.A. § 638. Section 2(b) of such Act, is set out as a note under 15 U.S.C.A. § 638. For

complete classification, see Short Title note set out under 15 U.S.C.A. § 631 and Tables.

The Small Business Act, referred to in subsec. (d)(2), is Act July 18, 1958, Pub.L. 85–536, 72 Stat. 384, as amended, also known as the SBA, which is principally classified to chapter 14A of Title 15, 15 U.S.C.A. § 631 et seq. Section 2 of such Act is classified to 15 U.S.C.A. § 631. For complete classification, see Short Title note set out under 15 U.S.C.A. § 631 and Tables.

CROSS REFERENCES

Acquisition, defined for division B of subtitle I of this title, see 41 USCA § 131.

Executive agency, defined for division B of subtitle I of this title, see 41 USCA § 133.

Federal Acquisition Regulation, defined for subtitle I of this title, functions and general authority, see 41 USCA §§ 106 and 1303.

Item and item of supply, defined for subtitle I of this title, see 41 USCA § 108.

Procurement, defined for subtitle I of this title, see 41 USCA § 111.

Supplies, defined for subtitle I of this title, see 41 USCA § 115.

Technical data, defined for subtitle I of this title, see 41 USCA § 116.

§ 2303. Ethics safeguards related to contractor conflicts of interest

(a) **Definition.**—In this section, the term "relevant acquisition function" means an acquisition function closely associated with inherently governmental functions.

(b) **Policy on personal conflicts of interest by contractor employees.**—

(1) **Development and issuance of policy.**—The Administrator shall develop and issue a standard policy to prevent personal conflicts of interest by contractor employees performing relevant acquisition functions (including the development, award, and administration of Federal Government contracts) for or on behalf of a Federal agency or department.

(2) **Elements of policy.**—The policy shall—

(A) define "personal conflict of interest" as it relates to contractor employees performing relevant acquisition functions; and

(B) require each contractor whose employees perform relevant acquisition functions to—

(i) identify and prevent personal conflicts of interest for the employees;

(ii) prohibit contractor employees who have access to non-public government information obtained while performing relevant acquisition functions from using the information for personal gain;

(iii) report any personal conflict-of-interest violation by an employee to the applicable contracting officer or contracting officer's representative as soon as it is identified;

(iv) maintain effective oversight to verify compliance with personal conflict-of-interest safeguards;

(v) have procedures in place to screen for potential conflicts of interest for all employees performing relevant acquisition functions; and

(vi) take appropriate disciplinary action in the case of employees who fail to comply with policies established pursuant to this section.

(3) **Contract clause.**—

(A) **Contents.**—The Administrator shall develop a personal conflicts-of-interest clause or a set of clauses for inclusion in solicitations and contracts (and task or delivery orders) for the performance of relevant acquisition functions that sets forth—

(i) the personal conflicts-of-interest policy developed under this subsection; and

(ii) the contractor's responsibilities under the policy.

(B) **Effective date.**—Subparagraph (A) shall take effect 300 days after October 14, 2008, and shall apply to—

(i) contracts entered into on or after that effective date; and

(ii) task or delivery orders awarded on or after that effective date, regardless of whether the contracts pursuant to which the task or delivery orders are awarded are entered before, on, or after October 14, 2008.

(4) **Applicability.**—

(A) **Contracts in excess of the simplified acquisition threshold.**—This subsection shall apply to any contract for an amount in excess of the simplified acquisition threshold (as defined in section 134 of this title) if the contract is for the performance of relevant acquisition functions.

(B) **Partial applicability.**—If only a portion of a contract described in subparagraph (A) is for the performance of relevant acquisition functions, then this subsection applies only to that portion of the contract.

(c) **Best practices.**—The Administrator shall, in consultation with the Director of the Office of Government Ethics, develop and maintain a repository of best practices relating to the prevention and mitigation of organizational and personal conflicts of interest in Federal contracting.

(Pub.L. 111–350, § 3, Jan. 4, 2011, 124 Stat. 3735.)

HISTORICAL AND STATUTORY NOTES

Effective Date for Issuance of Policy on Personal Conflicts of Interest by Contractor Employees

Pub.L. 111–350, § 6(f)(1), Jan. 4, 2011, 124 Stat. 3854, provided that: "The requirement in section 2303(b)(1) of title 41, United States Code, to issue a policy shall be done not later than 270 days after October 14, 2008."

Review of Federal Acquisition Regulation Relating to Conflicts of Interest

Pub.L. 110–417, Div. A, Title VIII, § 841(b), Oct. 14, 2008, 122 Stat. 4538, provided that:

"(1) **Review**

"Not later than 12 months after the date of enactment of this Act [October 14, 2008], the Administrator for Federal Procurement Policy, in consultation with the Director of the Office of Government Ethics, shall review the Federal Acquisition Regulation to—

"(A) identify contracting methods, types and services that raise heightened concerns for potential personal and organizational conflicts of interest; and

"(B) determine whether revisions to the Federal Acquisition Regulation are necessary to—

"(i) address personal conflicts of interest by contractor employees with respect to functions other than those described in subsection (a); or

"(ii) achieve sufficiently rigorous, comprehensive, and uniform government-wide policies to prevent and mitigate organizational conflicts of interest in Federal contracting.

"(2) Regulatory revisions

"If the Administrator determines pursuant to the review under paragraph (1)(B) that revisions to the Federal Acquisition Regulation are necessary, the Administrator shall work with the Federal Acquisition Regulatory Council to prescribe appropriate revisions to the regulations, including the development of appropriate contract clauses.

"(3) Report

"Not later than March 1, 2010, the Administrator shall submit to the Committees on Armed Services of the Senate and House of Representatives, the Committee on Homeland Security and Governmental Affairs in the Senate, and the Committee on Oversight and Government Reform of the House of Representatives a report setting forth such findings and determinations under subparagraphs (A) and (B) of paragraph (1), together with an assessment of any revisions to the Federal Acquisition Regulation that may be necessary."

[Note was classified to former 41 U.S.C.A. § 405c(b) prior to the enactment into positive law of Title 41, Public Contracts, by Pub.L. 111–350, Jan. 4, 2011, 124 Stat. 3677.]

CROSS REFERENCES

Acquisition, defined for division B of subtitle I of this title, see 41 USCA § 131.

Administrator, defined for Subtitle I of this title, see 41 USCA § 101.

§ 2304. Conflict of interest standards for consultants

(a) **Content of regulations.**—The Administrator shall prescribe under this division Government–wide regulations that set forth—

(1) conflict of interest standards for persons who provide consulting services described in subsection (b); and

(2) procedures, including registration, certification, and enforcement requirements as may be appropriate, to promote compliance with the standards.

(b) **Services subject to regulations.**—Regulations required by subsection (a) apply to—

(1) advisory and assistance services provided to the Federal Government to the extent necessary to identify and evaluate the potential for conflicts of interest that could be prejudicial to the interests of the United States;

(2) services related to support of the preparation or submission of bids and proposals for Federal contracts to the extent that inclusion of the services in the regulations is necessary to identify and evaluate the potential for conflicts of interest that could be prejudicial to the interests of the United States; and

(3) other services related to Federal contracts as specified in the regulations prescribed under subsection (a) to the extent necessary to identify and evaluate the potential for conflicts of interest that could be prejudicial to the interests of the United States.

(c) **Intelligence activities exemption.**—

(1) **Activities that may be exempt.**—Intelligence activities as defined in section 3.4(e) of Executive Order No. 12333 or a comparable definitional section in any successor order may be exempt from the regulations required by subsection (a).

(2) **Report.**—The Director of National Intelligence shall report to the Intelligence and Appropriations Committees of Congress each January 1, delineating the activities and organizations that have been exempted under paragraph (1).

(d) **Presidential determination.**—Before the regulations required by subsection (a) are prescribed, the President shall determine if prescribing the regulations will have a significantly adverse effect on the accomplishment of the mission of the Defense Department or another Federal agency. If the President determines that the regulations will have such an adverse effect, the President shall so report to the appropriate committees of the Senate and the House of Representatives, stating in full the reasons for the determination. If such a report is submitted, the requirement for the regulations shall be null and void.

(Pub.L. 111–350, § 3, Jan. 4, 2011, 124 Stat. 3736.)

See Main Volume and Repealed Title 41, ante, for annotations

References in Text

Executive Ord. No. 12333, Dec. 4, 1981, 46 F.R. 59941, as amended, relating to United States Intelligence Activities, is set out as a note under 50 U.S.C.A. § 401.

CROSS REFERENCES

Administrator, defined for Subtitle I of this title, see 41 USCA § 101.

§ 2305. Authority of Director of Office of Management and Budget not affected

This division does not limit the authorities and responsibilities of the Director of the Office of Management and Budget in effect on December 1, 1983.

(Pub.L. 111–350, § 3, Jan. 4, 2011, 124 Stat. 3737.)

§ 2306. Openness of meetings

The Administrator by regulation shall require that—

(1) formal meetings of the Office of Federal Procurement Policy, as designated by the Administrator, for developing procurement policies and regulations be open to the public; and

(2) public notice of each meeting be given not less than 10 days prior to the meeting.

(Pub.L. 111–350, § 3, Jan. 4, 2011, 124 Stat. 3737.)

CROSS REFERENCES

Administrator, defined for Subtitle I of this title, see 41 USCA § 101.

Open meetings, administrative procedures, generally, see 5 U.S.C.A. § 552b.

Procurement, defined for subtitle I of this title, see 41 USCA § 111.

§ 2307. Comptroller General's access to information

The Administrator and personnel in the Office of Federal Procurement Policy shall furnish information the Comptroller General may require to discharge the responsibilities of the Comptroller General. For this purpose, the Comptroller General or representatives of the Comptroller General shall have access to all books, documents, papers, and records of the Office of Federal Procurement Policy.

(Pub.L. 111–350, § 3, Jan. 4, 2011, 124 Stat. 3737.)

CROSS REFERENCES

Administrator, defined for Subtitle I of this title, see 41 USCA § 101.

§ 2308. Modular contracting for information technology

(a) Use.—To the maximum extent practicable, the head of an executive agency should use modular contracting for an acquisition of a major system of information technology.

(b) Modular contracting described.—Under modular contracting, an executive agency's need for a system is satisfied in successive acquisitions of interoperable increments. Each increment complies with common or commercially accepted standards applicable to information technology so that the increments are compatible with other increments of information technology comprising the system.

(c) Provisions in Federal Acquisition Regulation.—The Federal Acquisition Regulation shall provide that—

(1) under the modular contracting process, an acquisition of a major system of information technology may be divided into several smaller acquisition increments that—

(A) are easier to manage individually than would be one comprehensive acquisition;

(B) address complex information technology objectives incrementally in order to enhance the likelihood of achieving workable solutions for attaining those objectives;

(C) provide for delivery, implementation, and testing of workable systems or solutions in discrete increments, each of which comprises a system or solution that is not dependent on a subsequent increment in order to perform its principal functions; and

(D) provide an opportunity for subsequent increments of the acquisition to take advantage of any evolution in technology or needs that occurs during conduct of the earlier increments;

(2) to the maximum extent practicable, a contract for an increment of an information technology acquisition should be awarded within 180 days after the solicitation is issued and, if the contract for that increment cannot be awarded within that period, the increment should be considered for cancellation; and

(3) the information technology provided for in a contract for acquisition of information technology should be delivered within 18 months after the solicitation resulting in award of the contract was issued.

(Pub.L. 111–350, § 3, Jan. 4, 2011, 124 Stat. 3737.)

CROSS REFERENCES

Acquisition, defined for division B of subtitle I of this title, see 41 USCA § 131.

Executive agency, defined for division B of subtitle I of this title, see 41 USCA § 133.

Federal Acquisition Regulation, defined for subtitle I of this title, functions and general authority, see 41 USCA §§ 106 and 1303.

Major system, defined for subtitle I of this title, see 41 USCA § 109.

Standards, defined for subtitle I of this title, see 41 USCA § 114.

§ 2309. Protection of constitutional rights of contractors

(a) **Prohibition on requiring waiver of rights.**—A contractor may not be required, as a condition for entering into a contract with the Federal Government, to waive a right under the Constitution for a purpose relating to the Chemical Weapons Convention Implementation Act of 1998 (22 U.S.C. 6701 et seq.) or the Chemical Weapons Convention (as defined in section 3 of that Act (22 U.S.C. 6701)).

(b) **Permissible contract clauses.**—Subsection (a) does not prohibit an executive agency from including in a contract a clause that requires the contractor to permit inspections to ensure that the contractor is performing the contract in accordance with the provisions of the contract.

(Pub.L. 111–350, § 3, Jan. 4, 2011, 124 Stat. 3738.)

HISTORICAL AND STATUTORY NOTES

References in Text

The Chemical Weapons Convention Implementation Act of 1998, referred to in subsec. (a), is Division I of Pub.L. 105–277, Oct. 21, 1998, 112 Stat. 2681–860, which enacted chapter 75 of Title 22, 22 U.S.C.A. § 6701 et seq., and chapter 11B of Title 18, 18 U.S.C.A. § 229 et seq. Section 3 of such Act is classified to 22 U.S.C.A. § 6701. For complete classification, see Short Title note set out under 22 U.S.C.A. § 6701 and Tables.

CROSS REFERENCES

Executive agency, defined for division B of subtitle I of this title, see 41 USCA § 133.

§ 2310. Performance-based contracts or task orders for services to be treated as contracts for the procurement of commercial items

(a) **Criteria.**—A performance-based contract for the procurement of services entered into by an executive agency or a performance-based task order for services issued by an executive agency may be treated as a contract for the procurement of commercial items if—

(1) the value of the contract or task order is estimated not to exceed $ 25,000,000;

See Main Volume and Repealed Title 41, ante, for annotations

(2) the contract or task order sets forth specifically each task to be performed and, for each task—

    (A) defines the task in measurable, mission-related terms;

    (B) identifies the specific end products or output to be achieved; and

    (C) contains firm, fixed prices for specific tasks to be performed or outcomes to be achieved; and

(3) the source of the services provides similar services to the general public under terms and conditions similar to those offered to the Federal Government.

(b) Regulations.—Regulations implementing this section shall require agencies to collect and maintain reliable data sufficient to identify the contracts or task orders treated as contracts for commercial items using the authority of this section. The data may be collected using the Federal Procurement Data System or other reporting mechanism.

(c) Report.—Not later than 2 years after November 24, 2003, the Director of the Office of Management and Budget shall prepare and submit to the Committees on Homeland Security and Governmental Affairs and on Armed Services of the Senate and the Committees on Oversight and Government Reform and on Armed Services of the House of Representatives a report on the contracts or task orders treated as contracts for commercial items using the authority of this section. The report shall include data on the use of the authority, both government-wide and for each department and agency.

(d) Expiration.—The authority under this section expires 10 years after November 24, 2003.

(Pub.L. 111–350, § 3, Jan. 4, 2011, 124 Stat. 3738.)

CROSS REFERENCES

Commercial item, defined for subtitle I of this title, see 41 USCA § 103.

Executive agency, defined for division B of subtitle I of this title, see 41 USCA § 133.

Procurement, defined for subtitle I of this title, see 41 USCA § 111.

§ 2311. Enhanced transparency on interagency contracting and other transactions

The Director of the Office of Management and Budget shall direct appropriate revisions to the Federal Procurement Data System or any successor system to facilitate the collection of complete, timely, and reliable data on interagency contracting actions and on transactions other than contracts, grants, and cooperative agreements issued pursuant to section 2371 of title 10 or similar authorities. The Director of the Office of Management and Budget shall ensure that data, consistent with what is collected for contract actions, is obtained on—

    (1) interagency contracting actions, including data at the task or delivery-order level; and

    (2) other transactions, including the initial award and any subsequent modifications awarded or orders issued (other than transactions that are reported through the Federal Assistance Awards Data System).

(Pub.L. 111–350, § 3, Jan. 4, 2011, 124 Stat. 3739.)

HISTORICAL AND STATUTORY NOTES

Effective Date for Revisions in Federal Procurement Data System or Successor System

Pub.L. 111–350, § 6(f)(2), Jan. 4, 2011, 124 Stat. 3855, provided that: "The requirement in section 2311 of title 41, United States Code, to direct appropriate revisions in the Federal Procurement Data System or any successor system shall be done not later than one year after October 14, 2008."

§ 2312. Contingency Contracting Corps

(a) Definition.—In this section, the term "Corps" means the Contingency Contracting Corps established in subsection (b).

(b) Establishment.—The Administrator of General Services, pursuant to policies established by the Office of Management and Budget, and in consultation with the

Secretary of Defense and the Secretary of Homeland Security, shall establish a Government-wide Contingency Contracting Corps.

(c) Function.—The members of the Corps shall be available for deployment in responding to an emergency or major disaster, or a contingency operation, both within or outside the continental United States.

(d) Applicability.—The authorities provided in this section apply with respect to any procurement of property or services by or for an executive agency that, as determined by the head of the executive agency, are to be used—

(1) in support of a contingency operation as defined in section 101(a) (13) of title 10; or

(2) to respond to an emergency or major disaster as defined in section 102 of the Robert T. Stafford Disaster Relief and Emergency Assistance Act (42 U.S.C. 5122).

(e) Membership.—Membership in the Corps shall be voluntary and open to all Federal employees and members of the Armed Forces who are members of the Federal acquisition workforce.

(f) Education and training.—The Administrator of General Services may, in consultation with the Director of the Federal Acquisition Institute and the Chief Acquisition Officers Council, establish educational and training requirements for members of the Corps. Education and training carried out pursuant to the requirements shall be paid for from funds available in the acquisition workforce training fund established pursuant to section 1703(i) of this title.

(g) Salary.—The salary for a member of the Corps shall be paid—

(1) in the case of a member of the Armed Forces, out of funds available to the Armed Force concerned; and

(2) in the case of a Federal employee, out of funds available to the employing agency.

(h) Authority to deploy the Corps.—

(1) Director of the Office of Management and Budget.—The Director of the Office of Management and Budget shall have the authority, upon request by an executive agency, to determine when members of the Corps shall be deployed, with the concurrence of the head of the agency or agencies employing the members to be deployed.

(2) Secretary of Defense.—Nothing in this section shall preclude the Secretary of Defense or the Secretary's designee from deploying members of the Armed Forces or civilian personnel of the Department of Defense in support of a contingency operation as defined in section 101(a)(13) of title 10.

(i) Annual report.—

(1) In general.—The Administrator of General Services shall provide to the Committee on Homeland Security and Governmental Affairs and the Committee on Armed Services of the Senate and the Committee on Oversight and Government Reform and the Committee on Armed Services of the House of Representatives an annual report on the status of the Corps as of September 30 of each fiscal year.

(2) Content.—Each report under paragraph (1) shall include the number of members of the Corps, the total cost of operating the program, the number of deployments of members of the program, and the performance of members of the program in deployment.

(Pub.L. 111–350, § 3, Jan. 4, 2011, 124 Stat. 3739.)

HISTORICAL AND STATUTORY NOTES

References in Text

The Robert T. Stafford Disaster Relief and Emergency Assistance Act, referred to in subsec. (d)(2), is Pub.L. 93–288, May 22, 1974, 88 Stat. 143, as amended, also known as the Disaster Relief Act of 1974, which is classified principally to chapter 68 of Title 42, 42 U.S.C.A. § 5121 et seq. Section 102 of such Act is classified to 42 U.S.C.A. § 5122. For complete classification, see Short Title note set out under 42 U.S.C.A. § 5121 and Tables.

See Main Volume and Repealed Title 41, ante, for annotations

Acquisition, defined for division B of subtitle I of this title, see 41 USCA § 131.

Disaster relief, generally, see 42 USCA § 5121 et seq.

Executive agency, defined for division B of subtitle I of this title, see 41 USCA § 133.

Federal coordinating offices, major disaster and emergency assistance administration, see 42 USCA § 5143.

National emergency management, personnel and comprehensive preparedness system, see 6 USCA § 701 et seq.

Procurement, defined for subtitle I of this title, see 41 USCA § 111.

Registry of disaster response contractors, prevention of fraud, waste, and abuse under comprehensive, preparedness system, see 6 USCA § 796.

§ 2313. Database for Federal agency contract and grant officers and suspension and debarment officials

(a) **In general.**—Subject to the authority, direction, and control of the Director of the Office of Management and Budget, the Administrator of General Services shall establish and maintain a database of information regarding the integrity and performance of certain persons awarded Federal agency contracts and grants for use by Federal agency officials having authority over contracts and grants.

(b) **Persons covered.**—The database shall cover the following:

(1) Any person awarded a Federal agency contract or grant in excess of $500,000, if any information described in subsection (c) exists with respect to the person.

(2) Any person awarded such other category or categories of Federal agency contract as the Federal Acquisition Regulation may provide, if any information described in subsection (c) exists with respect to the person.

(c) **Information included.**—With respect to a covered person, the database shall include information (in the form of a brief description) for the most recent 5–year period regarding the following:

(1) Each civil or criminal proceeding, or any administrative proceeding, in connection with the award or performance of a contract or grant with the Federal Government with respect to the person during the period to the extent that the proceeding results in the following dispositions:

(A) In a criminal proceeding, a conviction.

(B) In a civil proceeding, a finding of fault and liability that results in the payment of a monetary fine, penalty, reimbursement, restitution, or damages of $5,000 or more.

(C) In an administrative proceeding, a finding of fault and liability that results in—

(i) the payment of a monetary fine or penalty of $5,000 or more; or

(ii) the payment of a reimbursement, restitution, or damages in excess of $100,000.

(D) To the maximum extent practicable and consistent with applicable laws and regulations, in a criminal, civil, or administrative proceeding, a disposition of the matter by consent or compromise with an acknowledgment of fault by the person if the proceeding could have led to any of the outcomes specified in subparagraph (A), (B), or (C).

(2) Each Federal contract and grant awarded to the person that was terminated in the period due to default.

(3) Each Federal suspension and debarment of the person.

(4) Each Federal administrative agreement entered into by the person and the Federal Government in the period to resolve a suspension or debarment proceeding.

(5) Each final finding by a Federal official in the period that the person has been determined not to be a responsible source under paragraph (3) or (4) of section 113 of this title.

(6) Other information that shall be provided for purposes of this section in the Federal Acquisition Regulation.

Revised Title 41 effective Jan. 4, 2011

(7) To the maximum extent practicable, information similar to the information covered by paragraphs (1) to (4) in connection with the award or performance of a contract or grant with a State government.

(d) Requirements relating to database information.—

(1) **Direct input and update.**—The Administrator of General Services shall design and maintain the database in a manner that allows the appropriate Federal agency officials to directly input and update information in the database relating to actions that the officials have taken with regard to contractors or grant recipients.

(2) **Timeliness and accuracy.**—The Administrator of General Services shall develop policies to require—

(A) the timely and accurate input of information into the database;

(B) the timely notification of any covered person when information relevant to the person is entered into the database; and

(C) opportunities for any covered person to submit comments pertaining to information about the person for inclusion in the database.

(e) Use of database.—

(1) **Availability to Government officials.**—The Administrator of General Services shall ensure that the information in the database is available to appropriate acquisition officials of Federal agencies, other government officials as the Administrator of General Services determines appropriate, and, on request, the Chairman and Ranking Member of the committees of Congress having jurisdiction.

(2) **Review and assessment of data.—**

(A) **In general.**—Before awarding a contract or grant in excess of the simplified acquisition threshold under section 134 of this title, the Federal agency official responsible for awarding the contract or grant shall review the database and consider all information in the database with regard to any offer or proposal, and in the case of a contract, shall consider other past performance information available with respect to the offeror in making any responsibility determination or past performance evaluation for the offeror.

(B) **Documentation in contract file.**—The contract file for each contract of a Federal agency in excess of the simplified acquisition threshold shall document the manner in which the material in the database was considered in any responsibility determination or past performance evaluation.

(f) Disclosure in applications.—The Federal Acquisition Regulation shall require that persons with Federal agency contracts and grants valued in total greater than $10,000,000 shall—

(1) submit to the Administrator of General Services, in a manner determined appropriate by the Administrator of General Services, the information subject to inclusion in the database as listed in subsection (c) current as of the date of submittal of the information under this subsection; and

(2) update the information submitted under paragraph (1) on a semiannual basis.

(g) Rulemaking.—The Administrator of General Services shall prescribe regulations that may be necessary to carry out this section.

(Pub.L. 111–350, § 3, Jan. 4, 2011, 124 Stat. 3740; Pub.L. 111–212, Title III, § 3010, July 29, 2010, 124 Stat. 2340; Pub.L. 111–383, Div. A, Title VIII, § 834(d), Jan. 4, 2011, 124 Stat. 4279.)

Amendment Subsequent to December 31, 2008

Pub.L. 111–350, Jan. 4, 2011, 124 Stat. 3677, which codified T. 41, Public Contracts, as positive law, directed that if a law enacted after Dec. 31, 2008, amends or repeals a provision replaced by Pub.L. 111–350, that law is deemed to amend or repeal, as the case may be, the corresponding provision enacted by Pub.L. 111–350, see Pub.L. 111–350, § 6(a), Jan. 4, 2011, 124 Stat. 3854, set out as a note provision preceding 41 U.S.C.A. § 101.

Pub.L. 111–383, Div. A, Title VIII, § 834(d), Jan. 7, 2011, 124 Stat. 4279, amended Pub.L. 110–417, § 872(c)(1), which was set out as former 41 U.S.C.A. § 417b, from which this section was derived, by adding subpar. (E) to subsec. (c)(1) which read:

See Main Volume and Repealed Title 41, ante, for annotations

"(E) In an administrative proceeding, a final determination of contractor fault by the Secretary of Defense pursuant to section 823(d) of the National Defense Authorization Act for Fiscal Year 2010 (10 U.S.C. 2302 note)."

Pub.L. 111–212, Title III, § 3010, July 29, 2010, 124 Stat. 2340, amended Pub.L. 110–417, § 872(e)(1), which was set out as former 41 U.S.C.A. § 417b, from which this section was derived, by adding at the end of subsec. (e)(1) the following: "In addition, the Administrator shall post all such information, excluding past performance reviews, on a publicly available Internet website."

HISTORICAL AND STATUTORY NOTES

References in Text

The National Defense Authorization Act for Fiscal Year 2010, referred to in subsec. (c)(1)(E), is Pub.L. 111–84, Oct. 28, 2009, 123 Stat. 2190. Section 823(d) of such Act is set out as a note under 10 U.S.C.A. § 2302. For complete classification, see Tables.

Amendments

2011 Amendments. Subsec. (c)(1)(E). Pub.L. 111–383, § 834, added subpar. (E).

2010 Amendments. Subsec. (e)(1). Pub.L. 111–212, § 3010, inserted "In addition, the Administrator shall post all such information, excluding past performance reviews, on a publicly available Internet website." following "committees of Congress having jurisdiction.".

Effective Date for Establishment of Database

Pub.L. 111–350, § 6(f)(3), Jan. 4, 2011, 124 Stat. 3855, provided that: "The requirement in section 2313(a) of title 41, United States Code, to establish a database shall be done not later than one year after October 14, 2008."

Effective Date for Amendment of Federal Acquisition Regulation

Pub.L. 111–350, § 6(f)(4), Jan. 4, 2011, 124 Stat. 3855, provided that: "The Federal Acquisition Regulation shall be amended to meet the requirements of sections 2313(f), 3302(b) and (d), 4710(b), and 4711(b) of title 41, United States Code, not later than one year after October 14, 2008."

CROSS REFERENCES

Addressing tax delinquency by government contractors, see Memorandum of the President of the United States, January 20, 2010, 75 F.R. 3979, set out as a note under 41 USCA § 1304.

Federal Acquisition Regulation, defined for subtitle I of this title, functions and general authority, see 41 USCA §§ 106 and 1303.

Records maintained on individuals, administrative procedures, see 5 USCA 552a.

Simplified acquisition threshold, defined for division B of subtitle I of this title, see 41 USCA § 134.

DIVISION C—PROCUREMENT

CHAPTER 31—GENERAL

§ 3101. Applicability

(a) In general.—An executive agency shall make purchases and contracts for property and services in accordance with this division and implementing regulations of the Administrator of General Services.

(b) Simplified acquisition threshold and procedures.—

(1) Simplified acquisition threshold.—

(A) Definition.—For purposes of an acquisition by an executive agency, the simplified acquisition threshold is as specified in section 134 of this title.

(B) Inapplicable laws.—A law properly listed in the Federal Acquisition Regulation pursuant to section 1905 of this title does not apply to or with respect to a contract or subcontract that is not greater than the simplified acquisition threshold.

Revised Title 41 effective Jan. 4, 2011

(2) **Simplified acquisition procedures.**—Simplified acquisition procedures contained in the Federal Acquisition Regulation pursuant to section 1901 of this title apply in executive agencies as provided in section 1901.

(c) **Exceptions.**—

(1) **In general.**—This division does not apply—

(A) to the Department of Defense, the Coast Guard, and the National Aeronautics and Space Administration; or

(B) except as provided in paragraph (2), when this division is made inapplicable pursuant to law.

(2) **Applicability of certain laws related to advertising, opening of bids, and length of contract.**—Sections 6101, 6103, and 6304 of this title do not apply to the procurement of property or services made by an executive agency pursuant to this division. However, when this division is made inapplicable by any law, sections 6101 and 6103 of this title apply in the absence of authority conferred by statute to procure without advertising or without regard to section 6101 of this title. A law that authorizes an executive agency (other than an executive agency exempted from this division by this subsection) to procure property or services without advertising or without regard to section 6101 of this title is deemed to authorize the procurement pursuant to the provisions of this division relating to procedures other than sealed-bid procedures.

(Pub.L. 111–350, § 3, Jan. 4, 2011, 124 Stat. 3742.)

EXECUTIVE ORDERS
EXECUTIVE ORDER NO. 13005
May 21, 1996, 61 F.R. 26069

EMPOWERMENT CONTRACTING

In order to promote economy and efficiency in Federal procurement, it is necessary to secure broad-based competition for Federal contracts. This broad competition is best achieved where there is an expansive pool of potential contractors capable of producing quality goods and services at competitive prices. A great and largely untapped opportunity for expanding the pool of such contractors can be found in this Nation's economically distressed communities.

Fostering growth of Federal contractors in economically distressed communities and ensuring that those contractors become viable businesses for the long term will promote economy and efficiency in Federal procurement and help to empower those communities. Fostering growth of long-term viable contractors will be promoted by offering appropriate incentives to qualified businesses.

Accordingly, by the authority vested in me as President by the Constitution and the laws of the United States, including section 486(a) of title 40, United States Code [see now 40 U.S.C.A. § 121(a)], and section 301 of title 3, United States Code [3 U.S.C.A. § 301], it is hereby ordered as follows:

Section 1. Policy. The purpose of this order is to strengthen the economy and to improve the efficiency of the Federal procurement system by encouraging business development that expands the industrial base and increases competition.

Sec. 2. Empowerment Contracting Program. In consultation with the Secretaries of the Departments of Housing and Urban Development, Labor, and Defense; the Administrator of General Services; the Administrator of the National Aeronautics and Space Administration; the Administrator of the Small Business Administration; and the Administrator for Federal Procurement Policy, the Secretary of the Department of Commerce shall develop policies and procedures to ensure that agencies, to the extent permitted by law, grant qualified large businesses and qualified small businesses appropriate incentives to encourage business activity in areas of general economic distress, including a price or an evaluation credit, when assessing offers for government contracts in unrestricted competitions, where the incentives would promote the policy set forth in this order. In developing such policies and procedures, the Secretary shall consider the size of the qualified businesses.

Sec. 3. Monitoring and Evaluation. The Secretary shall:

(a) monitor the implementation and operation of the policies and procedures developed in accordance with this order;

(b) develop a process to ensure the proper administration of the program and to reduce the potential for fraud by the intended beneficiaries of the program;

(c) develop principles and a process to evaluate the effectiveness of the policies and procedures developed in accordance with this order; and

(d) by December 1 of each year, issue a report to the President on the status and effectiveness of the program.

See Main Volume and Repealed Title 41, ante, for annotations

Sec. 4. Implementation Guidelines. In implementing this order, the Secretary shall:

(a) issue rules, regulations, and guidelines necessary to implement this order, including a requirement for the periodic review of the eligibility of qualified businesses and distressed areas;

(b) draft all rules, regulations, and guidelines necessary to implement this order within 90 days of the date of this order; and

(c) ensure that all policies and procedures and all rules, regulations, and guidelines adopted and implemented in accordance with this order minimize the administrative burden on affected agencies and the procurement process.

Sec. 5. Definitions. For purposes of this Executive order:

(a) "Agency" means any authority of the United States that is an "agency" under 44 U.S.C. 3502(1), other than those considered to be independent regulatory agencies, as defined in 44 U.S.C. 3502(10).

(b) "Area of general economic distress" shall be defined, for all urban and rural communities, as any census tract that has a poverty rate of at least 20 percent or any designated Federal Empowerment Zone, Supplemental Empowerment Zone, Enhanced Enterprise Community, or Enterprise Community. In addition, the Secretary may designate as an area of general economic distress any additional rural or Indian reservation area after considering the following factors:

(1) Unemployment rate;

(2) Degree of poverty;

(3) Extent of outmigration; and

(4) Rate of business formation and rate of business growth.

(c) "Qualified large business" means a large for-profit or not-for-profit trade or business that (1) employs a significant number of residents from the area of general economic distress; and (2) either has a significant physical presence in the area of general economic distress or has a direct impact on generating significant economic activity in the area of general economic distress.

(d) "Qualified small business" means a small for-profit or not-for-profit trade or business that (1) employs a significant number of residents from the area of general economic distress; (2) has a significant physical presence in the area of general economic distress; or (3) has a direct impact on generating significant economic activity in the area of general economic distress.

(e) "Secretary" means the Secretary of Commerce.

Sec. 6. Agency Authority. Nothing in this Executive order shall be construed as displacing the agencies' authority or responsibilities, as authorized by law, including specifically other programs designed to promote the development of small or disadvantaged businesses.

Sec. 7. Judicial Review. This Executive order does not create any right or benefit, substantive or procedural, enforceable at law or equity by a party against the United States, its agencies or instrumentalities, its officers or employees, or any other person.

WILLIAM J. CLINTON

[Executive Order was set out under former 41 U.S.C.A. § 251 prior to the enactment into positive law of Title 41, Public Contracts, by Pub.L. 111–350, Jan. 4, 2011, 124 Stat. 3677.]

MEMORANDA OF PRESIDENT

PRESIDENTIAL MEMORANDUM

GOVERNMENT CONTRACTING

Mar. 4, 2009, 74 F.R. 9755

Memorandum for the Heads of Executive Departments and Agencies

The Federal Government has an overriding obligation to American taxpayers. It should perform its functions efficiently and effectively while ensuring that its actions result in the best value for the taxpayers.

Since 2001, spending on Government contracts has more than doubled, reaching over $500 billion in 2008. During this same period, there has been a significant increase in the dollars awarded without full and open competition and an increase in the dollars obligated through cost-reimbursement contracts. Between fiscal years 2000 and 2008, for example, dollars obligated under cost-reimbursement contracts nearly doubled, from $71 billion in 2000 to $135 billion in 2008. Reversing these trends away from full and open competition and toward cost-reimbursement contracts could result in savings of billions of dollars each year for the American taxpayer.

Excessive reliance by executive agencies on sole-source contracts (or contracts with a limited number of sources) and cost-reimbursement contracts creates a risk that taxpayer funds will be spent on contracts that are wasteful, inefficient, subject to misuse, or otherwise not well designed to serve the needs of the Federal Government or the interests of the American taxpayer. Reports by agency Inspectors General, the Government Accountability Office (GAO), and other independent reviewing bodies have shown that noncompetitive and cost-reimbursement contracts have been misused, resulting in wasted taxpayer resources, poor contractor performance, and inadequate accountability for results.

When awarding Government contracts, the Federal Government must strive for an open and competitive process. However, executive agencies must have the flexibility to tailor contracts to carry out their missions and achieve the policy goals of the Government. In certain exigent circumstances, agencies may need to consider whether a competitive process will not accomplish the agency's mission. In such cases, the agency must ensure that the risks associated with noncompetitive contracts are minimized.

Moreover, it is essential that the Federal Government have the capacity to carry out robust and thorough management and oversight of its contracts in order to achieve programmatic goals, avoid significant overcharges, and curb wasteful spending. A GAO study last year of 95 major defense acquisitions projects found cost overruns of 26 percent, totaling $295 billion over the life of the projects. Improved contract oversight could reduce such sums significantly.

Government outsourcing for services also raises special concerns. For decades, the Federal Government has relied on the private sector for necessary commercial services used by the Government, such as transportation, food, and maintenance. Office of Management and Budget Circular A-76, first issued in 1966, was based on the reasonable premise that while inherently governmental activities should be performed by Government employees, taxpayers may receive more value for their dollars if non-inherently governmental activities that can be provided commercially are subject to the forces of competition.

However, the line between inherently governmental activities that should not be outsourced and commercial activities that may be subject to private sector competition has been blurred and inadequately defined. As a result, contractors may be performing inherently governmental functions. Agencies and departments must operate under clear rules prescribing when outsourcing is and is not appropriate.

It is the policy of the Federal Government that executive agencies shall not engage in noncompetitive contracts except in those circumstances where their use can be fully justified and where appropriate safeguards have been put in place to protect the taxpayer. In addition, there shall be a preference for fixed-price type contracts. Cost-reimbursement contracts shall be used only when circumstances do not allow the agency to define its requirements sufficiently to allow for a fixed-price type contract. Moreover, the Federal Government shall ensure that taxpayer dollars are not spent on contracts that are wasteful, inefficient, subject to misuse, or otherwise not well designed to serve the Federal Government's needs and to manage the risk associated with the goods and services being procured. The Federal Government must have sufficient capacity to manage and oversee the contracting process from start to finish, so as to ensure that taxpayer funds are spent wisely and are not subject to excessive risk. Finally, the Federal Government must ensure that those functions that are inherently governmental in nature are performed by executive agencies and are not outsourced.

I hereby direct the Director of the Office of Management and Budget (OMB), in collaboration with the Secretary of Defense, the Administrator of the National Aeronautics and Space Administration, the Administrator of General Services, the Director of the Office of Personnel Management, and the heads of such other agencies as the Director of OMB determines to be appropriate, and with the participation of appropriate management councils and program management officials, to develop and issue by July 1, 2009, Government-wide guidance to assist agencies in reviewing, and creating processes for ongoing review of, existing contracts in order to identify contracts that are wasteful, inefficient, or not otherwise likely to meet the agency's needs, and to formulate appropriate corrective action in a timely manner. Such corrective action may include modifying or canceling such contracts in a manner and to the extent consistent with applicable laws, regulations, and policy.

I further direct the Director of OMB, in collaboration with the aforementioned officials and councils, and with input from the public, to develop and issue by September 30, 2009, Government-wide guidance to:

(1) govern the appropriate use and oversight of sole-source and other types of noncompetitive contracts and to maximize the use of full and open competition and other competitive procurement processes;

(2) govern the appropriate use and oversight of all contract types, in full consideration of the agency's needs, and to minimize risk and maximize the value of Government contracts generally, consistent with the regulations to be promulgated pursuant to section 864 of Public Law 110–417;

(3) assist agencies in assessing the capacity and ability of the Federal acquisition workforce to develop, manage, and oversee acquisitions appropriately; and

(4) clarify when governmental outsourcing for services is and is not appropriate, consistent with section 321 of Public Law 110–417 (31 U.S.C. 501 note).

Executive departments and agencies shall carry out the provisions of this memorandum to the extent permitted by law. This memorandum is not intended to, and does not, create any right or benefit, substantive or procedural, enforceable at law or in equity by any party against the United States, its departments, agencies, or entities, its officers, employees, or agents, or any other person.

The Director of OMB is hereby authorized and directed to publish this memorandum in the **Federal Register**.

BARACK OBAMA

[Memorandum was set out under former 42 U.S.C.A. § 251 prior to the enactment into positive law of Title 41, Public Contracts, by Pub.L. 111–350, Jan. 4, 2011, 124 Stat. 3677.]

See Main Volume and Repealed Title 41, ante, for annotations

CROSS REFERENCES

Federal Acquisition Regulation, defined for subtitle I of this title, functions and general authority, see 41 USCA §§ 106 and 1303.

Procurement, defined for subtitle I of this title, see 41 USCA § 111.

§ 3102. Delegation and assignment of powers, functions, and responsibilities

(a) In general.—Except to the extent expressly prohibited by another law, the head of an executive agency may delegate to another officer or official of that agency any power under this division.

(b) Procurements for or with another agency.—Subject to subsection (a), to facilitate the procurement of property and services covered by this division by an executive agency for another executive agency, and to facilitate joint procurement by executive agencies—

(1) the head of an executive agency may delegate functions and assign responsibilities relating to procurement to any officer or employee within the agency;

(2) the heads of 2 or more executive agencies, consistent with section 1535 of title 31 and regulations prescribed under section 1074 of the Federal Acquisition Streamlining Act of 1994 (Public Law 103–355, 31 U.S.C. 1535 note), may by agreement delegate procurement functions and assign procurement responsibilities from one executive agency to another of those executive agencies or to an officer or civilian employee of another of those executive agencies; and

(3) the heads of 2 or more executive agencies may establish joint or combined offices to exercise procurement functions and responsibilities.

(Pub.L. 111–350, § 3, Jan. 4, 2011, 124 Stat. 3743.)

HISTORICAL AND STATUTORY NOTES

References in Text

The Federal Acquisition Streamlining Act of 1994, referred to in subsec. (b)(2), is Pub.L. 103–355, Oct. 13, 1994, 108 Stat. 3243. Section 1074 of such Act is set out as a note under 31 U.S.C.A. § 1535. For complete classification, see Short Title note set out under 41 U.S.C.A. § 101 and Tables.

CROSS REFERENCES

Procurement, defined for subtitle I of this title, see 41 USCA § 111.

§ 3103. Acquisition programs

(a) Congressional policy.—It is the policy of Congress that the head of each executive agency should achieve, on average, 90 percent of the cost, performance, and schedule goals established for major acquisition programs of the agency.

(b) Establishment of goals.—

(1) By head of executive agency.—The head of each executive agency shall approve or define the cost, performance, and schedule goals for major acquisition programs of the agency.

(2) By chief financial officer.—The chief financial officer of an executive agency shall evaluate the cost goals proposed for each major acquisition program of the agency.

(c) Identification of noncompliant programs.—When it is necessary to implement the policy set out in subsection (a), the head of an executive agency shall—

(1) determine whether there is a continuing need for programs that are significantly behind schedule, over budget, or not in compliance with performance or capability requirements; and

(2) identify suitable actions to be taken, including termination, with respect to those programs.

(Pub.L. 111–350, § 3, Jan. 4, 2011, 124 Stat. 3743.)

§ 3104. Small business concerns

It is the policy of Congress that a fair proportion of the total purchases and contracts for property and services for the Federal Government shall be placed with small business concerns.

(Pub.L. 111–350, § 3, Jan. 4, 2011, 124 Stat. 3744.)

§ 3105. New contracts and grants and merit-based selection procedures

(a) **Congressional policy.**—It is the policy of Congress that—

(1) an executive agency should not be required by legislation to award—

(A) a new contract to a specific non-Federal Government entity; or

(B) a new grant for research, development, test, or evaluation to a non–Federal Government entity; and

(2) a program, project, or technology identified in legislation be procured or awarded through merit-based selection procedures.

(b) **New contract and new grant described.**—For purposes of this section—

(1) a contract is a new contract unless the work provided for in the contract is a continuation of the work performed by the specified entity under a prior contract; and

(2) a grant is a new grant unless the work provided for in the grant is a continuation of the work performed by the specified entity under a prior grant.

(c) **Requirements for awarding new contract or new grant.**—A provision of law may not be construed as requiring a new contract or a new grant to be awarded to a specified non–Federal Government entity unless the provision of law specifically—

(1) refers to this section;

(2) identifies the particular non–Federal Government entity involved; and

(3) states that the award to that entity is required by the provision of law in contravention of the policy set forth in subsection (a).

(d) **Exception.**—This section does not apply to a contract or grant that calls on the National Academy of Sciences to investigate, examine, or experiment on a subject of science or art of significance to an executive agency and to report on those matters to Congress or an agency of the Federal Government.

(Pub.L. 111–350, § 3, Jan. 4, 2011, 124 Stat. 3744.)

§ 3106. Erection, repair, or furnishing of public buildings and improvements not authorized, and certain contracts not permitted, by this division

This division does not—

(1) authorize the erection, repair, or furnishing of a public building or public improvement; or

(2) permit a contract for the construction or repair of a building, road, sidewalk, sewer, main, or similar item using procedures other than sealed-bid procedures under section 3301(b)(1)(A) of this title if the conditions set forth in section 3301(b)(1)(A) of this title apply or the contract is to be performed outside the United States.

(Pub.L. 111–350, § 3, Jan. 4, 2011, 124 Stat. 3745.)

CHAPTER 33—PLANNING AND SOLICITATION

§ 3301. Full and open competition

(a) **In general.**—Except as provided in sections 3303, 3304(a), and 3305 of this title and except in the case of procurement procedures otherwise expressly authorized by statute, an executive agency in conducting a procurement for property or services shall—

(1) obtain full and open competition through the use of competitive procedures in accordance with the requirements of this division and the Federal Acquisition Regulation; and

(2) use the competitive procedure or combination of competitive procedures that is best suited under the circumstances of the procurement.

(b) **Appropriate competitive procedures.**—

(1) **Use of sealed bids.**—In determining the competitive procedures appropriate under the circumstance, an executive agency shall—

(A) solicit sealed bids if—

(i) time permits the solicitation, submission, and evaluation of sealed bids;

(ii) the award will be made on the basis of price and other price- related factors;

(iii) it is not necessary to conduct discussions with the responding sources about their bids; and

(iv) there is a reasonable expectation of receiving more than one sealed bid; or

(B) request competitive proposals if sealed bids are not appropriate under subparagraph (A).

(2) **Sealed bid not required.**—Paragraph (1)(A) does not require the use of sealed-bid procedures in cases in which section 204(e) of title 23 applies.

(c) **Efficient fulfillment of Government requirements.**—The Federal Acquisition Regulation shall ensure that the requirement to obtain full and open competition is implemented in a manner that is consistent with the need to efficiently fulfill the Federal Government's requirements.

(Pub.L. 111–350, § 3, Jan. 4, 2011, 124 Stat. 3745.)

HISTORICAL AND STATUTORY NOTES

Small Business Act

Pub.L. 98–369, § 2711(c), July 18, 1984, 98 Stat. 1181, provided that: "The amendments made by this section [enacting former sections 253a and 253b of this title, and amending former sections 253 and 259 of this title] do not super-sede or affect the provisions of section 8(a) of the Small Business Act (15 U.S.C. 637(a))."

[Note was classified as a note under former 41 U.S.C.A. § 253 prior to the enactment into positive law of Title 41, Public Contracts, by Pub.L. 111–350, Jan. 4, 2011, 124 Stat. 3677.]

CROSS REFERENCES

Competitive procedures, defined for division C of subtitle I of this title, see 41 USCA § 152.

Federal Acquisition Regulation, defined for subtitle I of this title, functions and general authority, see 41 USCA §§ 106 and 1303.

Full and open competition, defined for subtitle I of this title, see 41 USCA § 107.

Procurement, defined for subtitle I of this title, see 41 USCA § 111.

§ 3302. **Requirements for purchase of property and services pursuant to multiple award contracts**

(a) **Definitions**—In this section:

(1) **Executive agency.**— The term "executive agency" has the same meaning given in section 133 of this title.

(2) **Individual purchase.**—The term "individual purchase" means a task order, delivery order, or other purchase.

(3) **Multiple award contract.**—The term "multiple award contract" means—

(A) a contract that is entered into by the Administrator of General Services under the multiple award schedule program referred to in section 2302(2)(C) of title 10;

(B) a multiple award task order contract that is entered into under the authority of sections 2304a to 2304d of title 10, or chapter 41 of this title; and

(C) any other indefinite delivery, indefinite quantity contract that is entered into by the head of an executive agency with 2 or more sources pursuant to the same solicitation.

(4) **Sole source task or delivery order.**—The term "sole source task or delivery order" means any order that does not follow the competitive procedures in paragraph (2) or (3) of subsection (c).

(b) **Regulations required.**—The Federal Acquisition Regulation shall require enhanced competition in the purchase of property and services by all executive agencies pursuant to multiple award contracts.

(c) **Content of regulations.**—

(1) **In general.**—The regulations required by subsection (b) shall provide that each individual purchase of property or services in excess of the simplified acquisition threshold that is made under a multiple award contract shall be made on a competitive basis unless a contracting officer—

(A) waives the requirement on the basis of a determination that—

(i) one of the circumstances described in paragraphs (1) to (4) of section 4106(c) of this title or section 2304c(b) of title 10 applies to the individual purchase; or

(ii) a law expressly authorizes or requires that the purchase be made from a specified source; and

(B) justifies the determination in writing.

(2) **Competitive basis procedures.**—For purposes of this subsection, an individual purchase of property or services is made on a competitive basis only if it is made pursuant to procedures that—

(A) require fair notice of the intent to make that purchase (including a description of the work to be performed and the basis on which the selection will be made) to be provided to all contractors offering the property or services under the multiple award contract; and

(B) afford all contractors responding to the notice a fair opportunity to make an offer and have that offer fairly considered by the official making the purchase.

(3) **Exception to notice requirement.**—

(A) **In general.**—Notwithstanding paragraph (2), and subject to subparagraph (B), notice may be provided to fewer than all contractors offering the property or services under a multiple award contract as described in subsection (a)(3) (A) if notice is provided to as many contractors as practicable.

(B) **Limitation on exception.**—A purchase may not be made pursuant to a notice that is provided to fewer than all contractors under subparagraph (A) unless—

(i) offers were received from at least 3 qualified contractors; or

    (ii) a contracting officer of the executive agency determines in writing that no additional qualified contractors were able to be identified despite reasonable efforts to do so.

(d) Public notice requirements related to sole source task or delivery orders.—

    (1) Public notice required.—The Federal Acquisition Regulation shall require the head of each executive agency to—

    (A) publish on FedBizOpps notice of all sole source task or delivery orders in excess of the simplified acquisition threshold that are placed against multiple award contracts not later than 14 days after the orders are placed, except in the event of extraordinary circumstances or classified orders; and

    (B) disclose the determination required by subsection (c)(1) related to sole source task or delivery orders in excess of the simplified acquisition threshold placed against multiple award contracts through the same mechanism and to the same extent as the disclosure of documents containing a justification and approval required by section 2304(f)(1) of title 10 and section 3304(e)(1) of this title, except in the event of extraordinary circumstances or classified orders.

    (2) Exemption.—This subsection does not require the public availability of information that is exempt from public disclosure under section 552(b) of title 5.

(e) Applicability.—The regulations required by subsection (b) shall apply to all individual purchases of property or services that are made under multiple award contracts on or after the effective date of the regulations, without regard to whether the multiple award contracts were entered into before, on, or after the effective date.

(Pub.L. 111–350, § 3, Jan. 4, 2011, 124 Stat. 3746; Pub.L. 111–383, Div. A, Title X, § 1075(e)(14), Jan. 7, 2011, 124 Stat. 4375.)

Amendment Subsequent to December 31, 2008

    Pub.L. 111–350, Jan. 4, 2011, 124 Stat. 3677, which codified T. 41, Public Contracts, as positive law, directed that if a law enacted after Dec. 31, 2008, amends or repeals a provision replaced by Pub.L. 111–350, that law is deemed to amend or repeal, as the case may be, the corresponding provision enacted by Pub.L. 111–350, see Pub.L. 111–350, § 6(a), Jan. 4, 2011, 124 Stat. 3854, set out as a note provision preceding 41 U.S.C.A. § 101.

    Pub.L. 111–383, Div. A, Title X, § 1075(e)(14), Jan. 7, 2011, 124 Stat. 4375, amended Pub.L. 110–417, § 863, which was set out as a note under former 41 U.S.C.A. § 253h, from which this section was derived, by substituting "subsection (d)(3)(A)" for "subsection (d)(2)(A)" in subsec. (b)(3)(A) of the note.

HISTORICAL AND STATUTORY NOTES

References in Text

    Chapter 41 referred to in subsec. (a)(3)(B), is classified to 41 U.S.C.A. § 4101 et seq.

Effective Date for Amendment of Federal Acquisition Regulation

    Pub.L. 1111–350, § 6(f)(4), provided that the Federal Acquisition Regulation shall be amended to meet the requirements of subsecs. (b) and (d) of this section not later than one year after Oct. 14, 2008, see Pub.L. 111–350, § 6(f)(4), set out as a note under 41 U.S.C.A. § 2313.

CROSS REFERENCES

    Competitive procedures, defined for division C of subtitle I of this title, see 41 USCA § 152.

    Consolidation of contract requirements, policy and restriction, military procurement provisions, see 10 USCA § 2382.

    Federal Acquisition Regulation, defined for subtitle I of this title, functions and general authority, see 41 USCA §§ 106 and 1303.

    Simplified acquisition threshold, defined for division C of subtitle I of this title, see 41 USCA § 153.

§ 3303. Exclusion of particular source or restriction of solicitation to small business concerns

(a) Exclusion of particular source.—

(1) Criteria for exclusion.—An executive agency may provide for the procurement of property or services covered by section 3301 of this title using competitive procedures but excluding a particular source to establish or maintain an alternative source of supply for that property or service if the agency head determines that to do so would—

(A) increase or maintain competition and likely result in reduced overall cost for the procurement, or for an anticipated procurement, of the property or services;

(B) be in the interest of national defense in having a facility (or a producer, manufacturer, or other supplier) available for furnishing the property or service in case of a national emergency or industrial mobilization;

(C) be in the interest of national defense in establishing or maintaining an essential engineering, research, or development capability to be provided by an educational or other nonprofit institution or a Federally funded research and development center

(D) ensure the continuous availability of a reliable source of supply of the property or service;

(E) satisfy projected needs for the property or service determined on the basis of a history of high demand for the property or service; or

(F) satisfy a critical need for medical, safety, or emergency supplies.

(2) Determination for class disallowed.—A determination under paragraph (1) may not be made for a class of purchases or contracts.

(b) Exclusion of other than small business concerns.—An executive agency may provide for the procurement of property or services covered by section 3301 of this title using competitive procedures, but excluding other than small business concerns in furtherance of sections 9 and 15 of the Small Business Act (15 U.S.C. 638, 644).

(c) Nonapplication of justification and approval requirements.—A contract awarded pursuant to the competitive procedures referred to in subsections (a) and (b) is not subject to the justification and approval required by section 3304(e)(1) of this title.

(Pub.L. 111–350, § 3, Jan. 4, 2011, 124 Stat. 3747.)

HISTORICAL AND STATUTORY NOTES

References in Text

The Small Business Act, referred to in subsec. (b), is Act July 18, 1958, Pub.L. 85–536, 72 Stat. 384, as amended, also known as the SBA, which is principally classified to chapter 14A of Title 15, 15 U.S.C.A. § 631 et seq. Section 9 of such Act is classified to 15 U.S.C.A. § 638. Section 15 of such Act is classified to 15 U.S.C.A. § 644. For complete classification, see Short Title note set out under 15 U.S.C.A. § 631 and Tables.

CROSS REFERENCES

Agency head, defined for division C of subtitle I of this title, see 41 USCA § 151.
Competitive procedures, defined for division C of subtitle I of this title, see 41 USCA § 152.
Federal Acquisition Regulation, defined for subtitle I of this title, functions and general authority, see 41 USCA §§ 106 and 1303.

Procurement, defined for subtitle I of this title, see 41 USCA § 111.
Small—business concerns, criteria, aid to small business, see 15 USCA § 632.
Supplies, defined for subtitle I of this title, see 41 USCA § 115.

§ 3304. Use of noncompetitive procedures

(a) When noncompetitive procedures may be used.—An executive agency may use procedures other than competitive procedures only when—

(1) the property or services needed by the executive agency are available from only one responsible source and no other type of property or services will satisfy the needs of the executive agency;

(2) the executive agency's need for the property or services is of such an unusual and compelling urgency that the Federal Government would be seriously injured unless the executive agency is permitted to limit the number of sources from which it solicits bids or proposals;

(3) it is necessary to award the contract to a particular source—

(A) to maintain a facility, producer, manufacturer, or other supplier available for furnishing property or services in case of a national emergency or to achieve industrial mobilization;

(B) to establish or maintain an essential engineering, research, or development capability to be provided by an educational or other nonprofit institution or a Federally funded research and development center;

(C) to procure the services of an expert for use, in any litigation or dispute (including any reasonably foreseeable litigation or dispute) involving the Federal Government, in any trial, hearing, or proceeding before a court, administrative tribunal, or agency, whether or not the expert is expected to testify; or

(D) to procure the services of an expert or neutral for use in any part of an alternative dispute resolution or negotiated rulemaking process, whether or not the expert is expected to testify;

(4) the terms of an international agreement or treaty between the Federal Government and a foreign government or an international organization, or the written directions of a foreign government reimbursing the executive agency for the cost of the procurement of the property or services for that government, have the effect of requiring the use of procedures other than competitive procedures;

(5) subject to section 3105 of this title, a statute expressly authorizes or requires that the procurement be made through another executive agency or from a specified source, or the agency's need is for a brand-name commercial item for authorized resale;

(6) the disclosure of the executive agency's needs would compromise the national security unless the agency is permitted to limit the number of sources from which it solicits bids or proposals; or

(7) the head of the executive agency (who may not delegate the authority under this paragraph)—

(A) determines that it is necessary in the public interest to use procedures other than competitive procedures in the particular procurement concerned; and

(B) notifies Congress in writing of that determination not less than 30 days before the award of the contract.

(b) **Property or services deemed available from only one source.**—For the purposes of subsection (a)(1), in the case of—

(1) a contract for property or services to be awarded on the basis of acceptance of an unsolicited research proposal, the property or services are deemed to be available from only one source if the source has submitted an unsolicited research proposal that demonstrates a unique and innovative concept, the substance of which is not otherwise available to the Federal Government and does not resemble the substance of a pending competitive procurement; or

(2) a follow-on contract for the continued development or production of a major system or highly specialized equipment, the property may be deemed to be available only from the original source and may be procured through procedures other than competitive procedures when it is likely that award to a source other than the original source would result in—

(A) substantial duplication of cost to the Federal Government that is not expected to be recovered through competition; or

(B) unacceptable delay in fulfilling the executive agency's needs.

(c) **Property or services needed with unusual and compelling urgency.**—

(1) **Allowable contract period.**—The contract period of a contract described in paragraph (2) that is entered into by an executive agency pursuant to the authority provided under subsection (a)(2)—

(A) may not exceed the time necessary—

(i) to meet the unusual and compelling requirements of the work to be performed under the contract; and

(ii) for the executive agency to enter into another contract for the required goods or services through the use of competitive procedures; and

(**B**) may not exceed one year unless the head of the executive agency entering into the contract determines that exceptional circumstances apply.

(2) **Applicability of allowable contract period.**—This subsection applies to any contract in an amount greater than the simplified acquisition threshold.

(**d**) **Offer requests to potential sources.**—An executive agency using procedures other than competitive procedures to procure property or services by reason of the application of paragraph (2) or (6) of subsection (a) shall request offers from as many potential sources as is practicable under the circumstances.

(**e**) **Justification for use of noncompetitive procedures.**—

(1) **Prerequisites for awarding contract.**—Except as provided in paragraphs (3) and (4), an executive agency may not award a contract using procedures other than competitive procedures unless—

(**A**) the contracting officer for the contract justifies the use of those procedures in writing and certifies the accuracy and completeness of the justification;

(**B**) the justification is approved, in the case of a contract for an amount—

(**i**) exceeding $500,000 but equal to or less than $10,000,000, by the advocate for competition for the procuring activity (without further delegation) or by an official referred to in clause (ii) or (iii);

(**ii**) exceeding $10,000,000 but equal to or less than $50,000,000, by the head of the procuring activity or by a delegate who, if a member of the armed forces, is a general or flag officer or, if a civilian, is serving in a position in which the individual is entitled to receive the daily equivalent of the maximum annual rate of basic pay payable for level IV of the Executive Schedule (or in a comparable or higher position under another schedule); or

(**iii**) exceeding $50,000,000, by the senior procurement executive of the agency designated pursuant to section 1702(c) of this title (without further delegation); and

(**C**) any required notice has been published with respect to the contract pursuant to section 1708 of this title and the executive agency has considered all bids or proposals received in response to that notice.

(2) **Elements of justification.**—The justification required by paragraph (1)(A) shall include—

(**A**) a description of the agency's needs;

(**B**) an identification of the statutory exception from the requirement to use competitive procedures and a demonstration, based on the proposed contractor's qualifications or the nature of the procurement, of the reasons for using that exception;

(**C**) a determination that the anticipated cost will be fair and reasonable;

(**D**) a description of the market survey conducted or a statement of the reasons a market survey was not conducted;

(**E**) a listing of any sources that expressed in writing an interest in the procurement; and

(**F**) a statement of any actions the agency may take to remove or overcome a barrier to competition before a subsequent procurement for those needs.

(3) **Justification allowed after contract awarded.**—In the case of a procurement permitted by subsection (a)(2), the justification and approval required by paragraph (1) may be made after the contract is awarded.

(4) **Justification not required.**—The justification and approval required by paragraph (1) are not required if—

(**A**) a statute expressly requires that the procurement be made from a specified source;

(**B**) the agency's need is for a brand-name commercial item for authorized resale;

(**C**) the procurement is permitted by subsection (a)(7); or

(D) the procurement is conducted under chapter 85 of this title or section 8(a) of the Small Business Act (15 U.S.C. 637(a)).

(5) Restrictions on executive agencies.—

(A) Contracts and procurement of property or services.—In no case may an executive agency—

(i) enter into a contract for property or services using procedures other than competitive procedures on the basis of the lack of advance planning or concerns related to the amount available to the agency for procurement functions; or

(ii) procure property or services from another executive agency unless the other executive agency complies fully with the requirements of this division in its procurement of the property or services.

(B) Additional restriction.—The restriction set out in subparagraph (A)(ii) is in addition to any other restriction provided by law.

(f) Public availability of justification and approval required for using noncompetitive procedures.—

(1) Time requirement.—

(A) Within 14 days after contract award.—Except as provided in subparagraph (B), in the case of a procurement permitted by subsection (a), the head of an executive agency shall make publicly available, within 14 days after the award of the contract, the documents containing the justification and approval required by subsection (e)(1) with respect to the procurement.

(B) Within 30 days after contract award.—In the case of a procurement permitted by subsection (a)(2), subparagraph (A) shall be applied by substituting "30 days" for "14 days".

(2) Availability on websites.—The documents referred to in subparagraph (A) of paragraph (1) shall be made available on the website of the agency and through a Government–wide website selected by the Administrator.

(3) Exception to availability and approval requirement.—This subsection does not require the public availability of information that is exempt from public disclosure under section 552(b) of title 5.

(Pub.L. 111–350, § 3, Jan. 4, 2011, 124 Stat. 3748.)

HISTORICAL AND STATUTORY NOTES

References in Text

Level IV of the Executive Schedule, referred to in subsec. (e)(1)(B)(ii), is set out in 5 U.S.C.A. § 5315.

Chapter 85 of this title, referred to in subsec. (e)(4)(D), is classified to 41 U.S.C.A. § 8501 et seq.

The Small Business Act, referred to in subsec. (e)(4)(D), is Act July 18, 1958, Pub.L. 85–536, 72 Stat. 384, as amended, also known as the SBA, which is principally classified to chapter 14A of Title 15, 15 U.S.C.A. § 631 et seq. Section 8 of such Act is classified to 15 U.S.C.A. § 637. For complete classification, see Short Title note set out under 15 U.S.C.A. § 631 and Tables.

CROSS REFERENCES

Administrator, defined for subtitle I of this title, see 41 USCA § 101.

Commercial item, defined for subtitle I of this title, see 41 USCA § 103.

Competitive procedures, defined for division C of subtitle I of this title, see 41 USCA § 152.

Major system, defined for subtitle I of this title, see 41 USCA § 109.

Procurement, defined for subtitle I of this title, see 41 USCA § 111.

Responsible source, defined for subtitle I of this title, see 41 USCA § 113.

Simplified acquisition threshold, defined for division C of subtitle I of this title, see 41 USCA § 153.

§ 3305. Simplified procedures for small purchases

(a) Authorization.—To promote efficiency and economy in contracting and to avoid unnecessary burdens for agencies and contractors, the Federal Acquisition Regulation shall provide for special simplified procedures for purchases of property and services for amounts—

(1) not greater than the simplified acquisition threshold; and

(2) greater than the simplified acquisition threshold but not greater than $5,000,000 for which the contracting officer reasonably expects, based on the nature of the property or services sought and on market research, that offers will include only commercial items.

(b) Leasehold interests in real property.—The Administrator of General Services shall prescribe regulations that provide special simplified procedures for acquisitions of leasehold interests in real property at rental rates that do not exceed the simplified acquisition threshold. The rental rate under a multiyear lease does not exceed the simplified acquisition threshold if the average annual amount of the rent payable for the period of the lease does not exceed the simplified acquisition threshold.

(c) Prohibition on dividing contracts.—A proposed purchase or contract for an amount above the simplified acquisition threshold may not be divided into several purchases or contracts for lesser amounts to use the simplified procedures required by subsection (a).

(d) Promotion of competition.—In using the simplified procedures, an executive agency shall promote competition to the maximum extent practicable.

(e) Compliance with special requirements of Federal Acquisition Regulation.— An executive agency shall comply with the Federal Acquisition Regulation provisions referred to in section 1901(e) of this title.

(Pub.L. 111–350, § 3, Jan. 4, 2011, 124 Stat. 3752.)

CROSS REFERENCES

Commercial item, defined for subtitle I of this title, see 41 USCA § 103.

Federal Acquisition Regulation, defined for subtitle I of this title, functions and general authority, see 41 USCA §§ 106 and 1303.

Simplified acquisition threshold, defined for division B provisions, see 41 USCA § 134.

Simplified acquisition threshold, defined for division C of subtitle I of this title, see 41 USCA § 153.

§ 3306. Planning and solicitation requirements

(a) Planning and specifications.—

(1) **Preparing for procurement.**—In preparing for the procurement of property or services, an executive agency shall—

(A) specify its needs and solicit bids or proposals in a manner designed to achieve full and open competition for the procurement;

(B) use advance procurement planning and market research; and

(C) develop specifications in the manner necessary to obtain full and open competition with due regard to the nature of the property or services to be acquired.

(2) **Requirements of specifications.**—Each solicitation under this division shall include specifications that—

(A) consistent with this division, permit full and open competition; and

(B) include restrictive provisions or conditions only to the extent necessary to satisfy the needs of the executive agency or as authorized by law.

(3) **Types of specifications.**—For the purposes of paragraphs (1) and (2), the type of specification included in a solicitation shall depend on the nature of the needs of the executive agency and the market available to satisfy those needs. Subject to those needs, specifications may be stated in terms of—

(A) function, so that a variety of products or services may qualify;

(B) performance, including specifications of the range of acceptable characteristics or of the minimum acceptable standards; or

(C) design requirements.

(b) Contents of solicitation.—In addition to the specifications described in subsection (a), each solicitation for sealed bids or competitive proposals (other than for a procurement for commercial items using special simplified procedures or a purchase for an amount not greater than the simplified acquisition threshold) shall at a minimum include—

See Main Volume and Repealed Title 41, ante, for annotations

(1) a statement of—

    (A) all significant factors and significant subfactors that the executive agency reasonably expects to consider in evaluating sealed bids (including price) or competitive proposals (including cost or price, cost- related or price-related factors and subfactors, and noncost-related or nonprice-related factors and subfactors); and

    (B) the relative importance assigned to each of those factors and subfactors; and

(2)(A) in the case of sealed bids—

    (i) a statement that sealed bids will be evaluated without discussions with the bidders; and

    (ii) the time and place for the opening of the sealed bids; or

(B) in the case of competitive proposals—

    (i) either a statement that the proposals are intended to be evaluated with, and the award made after, discussions with the offerors, or a statement that the proposals are intended to be evaluated, and the award made, without discussions with the offerors (other than discussions conducted for the purpose of minor clarification) unless discussions are determined to be necessary; and

    (ii) the time and place for submission of proposals.

(c) Evaluation factors.—

    (1) In general.—In prescribing the evaluation factors to be included in each solicitation for competitive proposals, an executive agency shall—

        (A) establish clearly the relative importance assigned to the evaluation factors and subfactors, including the quality of the product or services to be provided (including technical capability, management capability, prior experience, and past performance of the offeror);

        (B) include cost or price to the Federal Government as an evaluation factor that must be considered in the evaluation of proposals; and

        (C) disclose to offerors whether all evaluation factors other than cost or price, when combined, are—

            (i) significantly more important than cost or price;

            (ii) approximately equal in importance to cost or price; or

            (iii) significantly less important than cost or price.

    (2) Restriction on implementing regulations.—Regulations implementing paragraph (1)(C) may not define the terms "significantly more important" and "significantly less important" as specific numeric weights that would be applied uniformly to all solicitations or a class of solicitations.

(d) Additional information in solicitation.—This section does not prohibit an executive agency from—

    (1) providing additional information in a solicitation, including numeric weights for all evaluation factors and subfactors on a case-by-case basis; or

    (2) stating in a solicitation that award will be made to the offeror that meets the solicitation's mandatory requirements at the lowest cost or price.

(e) Limitation on evaluation of purchase options.—An executive agency, in issuing a solicitation for a contract to be awarded using sealed bid procedures, may not include in the solicitation a clause providing for the evaluation of prices for options to purchase additional property or services under the contract unless the executive agency has determined that there is a reasonable likelihood that the options will be exercised.

(f) Authorization of telecommuting for Federal contractors.—

    (1) Definition.—In this subsection, the term "executive agency" has the meaning given that term in section 133 of this title.

    (2) Federal acquisition regulation to allow telecommuting.—The Federal Acquisition Regulation issued in accordance with sections 1121(b) and 1303(a)(1) of this title shall permit telecommuting by employees of Federal Government contractors in the performance of contracts entered into with executive agencies.

(3) **Scope of allowance.**—The Federal Acquisition Regulation at a minimum shall provide that a solicitation for the acquisition of property or services may not set forth any requirement or evaluation criteria that would—

(A) render an offeror ineligible to enter into a contract on the basis of the inclusion of a plan of the offeror to allow the offeror's employees to telecommute, unless the contracting officer concerned first determines that the requirements of the agency, including security requirements, cannot be met if telecommuting is allowed and documents in writing the basis for the determination; or

(B) reduce the scoring of an offer on the basis of the inclusion in the offer of a plan of the offeror to allow the offeror's employees to telecommute, unless the contracting officer concerned first determines that the requirements of the agency, including security requirements, would be adversely impacted if telecommuting is allowed and documents in writing the basis for the determination.

(Pub.L. 111–350, § 3, Jan. 4, 2011, 124 Stat. 3752.)

CROSS REFERENCES

Commercial item, defined for subtitle I of this title, see 41 USCA § 103.

Federal Acquisition Regulation, defined for subtitle I of this title, functions and general authority, see 41 USCA §§ 106 and 1303.

Full and open competition, defined for subtitle I of this title, see 41 USCA § 107.

Procurement, defined for subtitle I of this title, see 41 USCA § 111.

Simplified acquisition threshold, defined for division C of subtitle I of this title, see 41 USCA § 153.

Standards, defined for subtitle I of this title, see 41 USCA § 114.

Telecommuting and other alternative workplace arrangements, operations requirements relating to Federal property and administrative services, see 41 USCA § 587.

Telework, attendance and leave requirements for Federal employees, see 5 USCA § 6501 et seq.

§ 3307. Preference for commercial items

(a) **Relationship of provisions of law to procurement of commercial items.**—

(1) **This division.**—Unless otherwise specifically provided, all other provisions in this division also apply to the procurement of commercial items.

(2) **Laws listed in Federal Acquisition Regulation.**—A contract for the procurement of a commercial item entered into by the head of an executive agency is not subject to a law properly listed in the Federal Acquisition Regulation pursuant to section 1906 of this title.

(b) **Preference.**—The head of each executive agency shall ensure that, to the maximum extent practicable—

(1) requirements of the executive agency with respect to a procurement of supplies or services are stated in terms of—

(A) functions to be performed;

(B) performance required; or

(C) essential physical characteristics;

(2) those requirements are defined so that commercial items or, to the extent that commercial items suitable to meet the executive agency's needs are not available, nondevelopmental items other than commercial items may be procured to fulfill those requirements; and

(3) offerors of commercial items and nondevelopmental items other than commercial items are provided an opportunity to compete in any procurement to fill those requirements.

(c) **Implementation.**—The head of each executive agency shall ensure that procurement officials in that executive agency, to the maximum extent practicable—

(1) acquire commercial items or nondevelopmental items other than commercial items to meet the needs of the executive agency;

(2) require that prime contractors and subcontractors at all levels under contracts of the executive agency incorporate commercial items or nondevelopmental

items other than commercial items as components of items supplied to the executive agency;

(3) modify requirements in appropriate cases to ensure that the requirements can be met by commercial items or, to the extent that commercial items suitable to meet the executive agency's needs are not available, nondevelopmental items other than commercial items;

(4) state specifications in terms that enable and encourage bidders and offerors to supply commercial items or, to the extent that commercial items suitable to meet the executive agency's needs are not available, nondevelopmental items other than commercial items in response to the executive agency solicitations;

(5) revise the executive agency's procurement policies, practices, and procedures not required by law to reduce any impediments in those policies, practices, and procedures to the acquisition of commercial items; and

(6) require training of appropriate personnel in the acquisition of commercial items.

(d) Market research.—

(1) **When to be used.**—The head of an executive agency shall conduct market research appropriate to the circumstances—

(A) before developing new specifications for a procurement by that executive agency; and

(B) before soliciting bids or proposals for a contract in excess of the simplified acquisition threshold.

(2) **Use of results.**—The head of an executive agency shall use the results of market research to determine whether commercial items or, to the extent that commercial items suitable to meet the executive agency's needs are not available, nondevelopmental items other than commercial items are available that—

(A) meet the executive agency's requirements;

(B) could be modified to meet the executive agency's requirements; or

(C) could meet the executive agency's requirements if those requirements were modified to a reasonable extent.

(3) **Only minimum information required to be submitted.**—In conducting market research, the head of an executive agency should not require potential sources to submit more than the minimum information that is necessary to make the determinations required in paragraph (2).

(e) Regulations.—

(1) **In general.**—The Federal Acquisition Regulation shall provide regulations to implement this section, sections 102, 103, 105, and 110 of this title, and chapter 140 of title 10.

(2) **Contract clauses.—**

(A) **Definition.**—In this paragraph, the term "subcontract" includes a transfer of commercial items between divisions, subsidiaries, or affiliates of a contractor or subcontractor.

(B) **List of clauses to be included.**—The regulations prescribed under paragraph (1) shall contain a list of contract clauses to be included in contracts for the acquisition of commercial end items. To the maximum extent practicable, the list shall include only those contract clauses that are—

(i) required to implement provisions of law or executive orders applicable to acquisitions of commercial items or commercial components; or

(ii) determined to be consistent with standard commercial practice.

(C) **Requirements of prime contractor.**—The regulations shall provide that the Federal Government shall not require a prime contractor to apply to any of its divisions, subsidiaries, affiliates, subcontractors, or suppliers that are furnishing commercial items any contract clause except those that are—

(i) required to implement provisions of law or executive orders applicable to subcontractors furnishing commercial items or commercial components; or

(ii) determined to be consistent with standard commercial practice.

(D) Clauses that may be used in a contract.—To the maximum extent practicable, only the contract clauses listed pursuant to subparagraph (B) may be used in a contract, and only the contract clauses referred to in subparagraph (C) may be required to be used in a subcontract, for the acquisition of commercial items or commercial components by or for an executive agency.

(E) Waiver of contract clauses.—The Federal Acquisition Regulation shall provide standards and procedures for waiving the use of contract clauses required pursuant to subparagraph (B), other than those required by law, including standards for determining the cases in which a waiver is appropriate.

(3) Market acceptance.—

(A) Requirement of offerors.—The Federal Acquisition Regulation shall provide that under appropriate conditions the head of an executive agency may require offerors to demonstrate that the items offered—

(i) have achieved commercial market acceptance or been satisfactorily supplied to an executive agency under current or recent contracts for the same or similar requirements; and

(ii) otherwise meet the item description, specifications, or other criteria prescribed in the public notice and solicitation relating to the contract.

(B) Regulation to provide guidance on criteria.—The Federal Acquisition Regulation shall provide guidance to ensure that the criteria for determining commercial market acceptance include the consideration of—

(i) the minimum needs of the executive agency concerned; and

(ii) the entire relevant commercial market, including small businesses.

(4) Provisions relating to types of contracts.—

(A) Types of contracts that may be used.—The Federal Acquisition Regulation shall include, for acquisitions of commercial items—

(i) a requirement that firm, fixed price contracts or fixed price with economic price adjustment contracts be used to the maximum extent practicable;

(ii) a prohibition on use of cost type contracts; and

(iii) subject to subparagraph (B), authority for use of a time-and-materials or labor-hour contract for the procurement of commercial services that are commonly sold to the general public through those contracts and are purchased by the procuring agency on a competitive basis.

(B) When time-and-materials or labor-hour contract may be used.—A time-and-materials or labor-hour contract may be used pursuant to the authority referred to in subparagraph (A)(iii)—

(i) only for a procurement of commercial services in a category of commercial services described in subparagraph (C); and

(ii) only if the contracting officer for the procurement—

(I) executes a determination and findings that no other contract type is suitable;

(II) includes in the contract a ceiling price that the contractor exceeds at its own risk; and

(III) authorizes a subsequent change in the ceiling price only on a determination, documented in the contract file, that it is in the best interest of the procuring agency to change the ceiling price.

(C) Categories of commercial services.—The categories of commercial services referred to in subparagraph (B) are as follows:

(i) Commercial services procured for support of a commercial item, as described in section 103(5) of this title.

(ii) Any other category of commercial services that the Administrator for Federal Procurement Policy designates in the Federal Acquisition Regulation for the purposes of this subparagraph on the basis that—

(I) the commercial services in the category are of a type of commercial services that are commonly sold to the general public through use of time-and- materials or labor-hour contracts; and

(II) it would be in the best interests of the Federal Government to authorize use of time-and-materials or labor-hour contracts for purchases of the commercial services in the category.

(5) **Contract quality requirements.**—Regulations prescribed under paragraph (1) shall include provisions that—

(A) allow, to the maximum extent practicable, a contractor under a commercial items acquisition to use the existing quality assurance system of the contractor as a substitute for compliance with an otherwise applicable requirement for the Federal Government to inspect or test the commercial items before the contractor's tender of those items for acceptance by the Federal Government;

(B) require that, to the maximum extent practicable, the executive agency take advantage of warranties (including extended warranties) offered by offerors of commercial items and use those warranties for the repair and replacement of commercial items; and

(C) set forth guidance regarding the use of past performance of commercial items and sources as a factor in contract award decisions.

(Pub.L. 111–350, § 3, Jan. 4, 2011, 124 Stat. 3754.)

HISTORICAL AND STATUTORY NOTES

References in Text

Chapter 140 of title 10, referred to in subsec. (e)(1), is classified to 10 U.S.C.A. § 2375 et seq.

CROSS REFERENCES

Commercial component, defined for subtitle I of this title, see 41 USCA § 102.

Commercial item, defined for subtitle I of this title, see 41 USCA § 103.

Federal Acquisition Regulation, defined for subtitle I of this title, functions and general authority, see 41 USCA §§ 106 and 1303.

Item and item of supply, defined for subtitle I of this title, see 41 USCA § 108.

Nondevelopmental item, defined for subtitle I of this title, see 41 USCA § 110.

Procurement, defined for subtitle I of this title, see 41 USCA § 111.

Simplified acquisition threshold, defined for division C of subtitle I of this title, see 41 USCA § 153.

Standards, defined for subtitle I of this title, see 41 USCA § 114.

Supplies, defined for subtitle I of this title, see 41 USCA § 115.

§ 3308. Planning for future competition in contracts for major systems

(a) Development contract.—

(1) **Determining whether proposals are necessary.**—In preparing a solicitation for the award of a development contract for a major system, the head of an agency shall consider requiring in the solicitation that an offeror include in its offer proposals described in paragraph (2). In determining whether to require the proposals, the head of the agency shall consider the purposes for which the system is being procured and the technology necessary to meet the system's required capabilities. If the proposals are required, the head of the agency shall consider them in evaluating the offeror's price.

(2) **Contents of proposals.**—The proposals that the head of an agency is to consider requiring in a solicitation for the award of a development contract are the following:

(A) Proposals to incorporate in the design of the major system items that are currently available within the supply system of the Federal agency responsible for the major system, available elsewhere in the national supply system, or commercially available from more than one source.

(B) With respect to items that are likely to be required in substantial quantities during the system's service life, proposals to incorporate in the design of the major system items that the Federal Government will be able to acquire competitively in the future.

(b) Production contract.—

(1) **Determining whether proposals are necessary.**—In preparing a solicitation for the award of a production contract for a major system, the head of an agency shall consider requiring in the solicitation that an offeror include in its offer proposals described in paragraph (2). In determining whether to require the proposals, the head of the agency shall consider the purposes for which the system is being procured and the technology necessary to meet the system's required capabilities. If the proposals are required, the head of the agency shall consider them in evaluating the offeror's price.

(2) **Content of proposals.**—The proposals that the head of an agency is to consider requiring in a solicitation for the award of a production contract are proposals identifying opportunities to ensure that the Federal Government will be able to obtain on a competitive basis items procured in connection with the system that are likely to be reprocured in substantial quantities during the service life of the system. Proposals submitted in response to this requirement may include the following:

(A) Proposals to provide to the Federal Government the right to use technical data to be provided under the contract for competitive reprocurement of the item, together with the cost to the Federal Government of acquiring the data and the right to use the data.

(B) Proposals for the qualification or development of multiple sources of supply for the item.

(c) Consideration of factors as objectives in negotiations.—If the head of an agency is making a noncompetitive award of a development contract or a production contract for a major system, the factors specified in subsections (a) and (b) to be considered in evaluating an offer for a contract may be considered as objectives in negotiating the contract to be awarded.

(Pub.L. 111–350, § 3, Jan. 4, 2011, 124 Stat. 3758.)

CROSS REFERENCES

Intelligence community, cost of acquisition of major systems, accountability for intelligence activities, see 50 USCA § 415a–1.

Item and item of supply, defined for subtitle I of this title, see 41 USCA § 108.

Major system, defined for subtitle I of this title, see 41 USCA § 109.

Major systems, definitional threshold amounts, military procurement provisions, generally, see 10 USCA § 2302d.

Technical data, defined for subtitle I of this title, see 41 USCA § 116.

§ 3309. Design-build selection procedures

(a) Authorization.—Unless the traditional acquisition approach of design-bid-build established under sections 1101 to 1104 of title 40 or another acquisition procedure authorized by law is used, the head of an executive agency shall use the two-phase selection procedures authorized in this section for entering into a contract for the design and construction of a public building, facility, or work when a determination is made under subsection (b) that the procedures are appropriate for use.

(b) Criteria for use.—A contracting officer shall make a determination whether two-phase selection procedures are appropriate for use for entering into a contract for the design and construction of a public building, facility, or work when—

(1) the contracting officer anticipates that 3 or more offers will be received for the contract;

(2) design work must be performed before an offeror can develop a price or cost proposal for the contract;

(3) the offeror will incur a substantial amount of expense in preparing the offer; and

(4) the contracting officer has considered information such as the following:

    (A) The extent to which the project requirements have been adequately defined.

    (B) The time constraints for delivery of the project.

    (C) The capability and experience of potential contractors.

    (D) The suitability of the project for use of the two-phase selection procedures.

    (E) The capability of the agency to manage the two-phase selection process.

    (F) Other criteria established by the agency.

 (c) Procedures described.—Two-phase selection procedures consist of the following:

    (1) Development of scope of work statement.—The agency develops, either in-house or by contract, a scope of work statement for inclusion in the solicitation that defines the project and provides prospective offerors with sufficient information regarding the Federal Government's requirements (which may include criteria and preliminary design, budget parameters, and schedule or delivery requirements) to enable the offerors to submit proposals that meet the Federal Government's needs. If the agency contracts for development of the scope of work statement, the agency shall contract for architectural and engineering services as defined by and in accordance with sections 1101 to 1104 of title 40.

    (2) Solicitation of phase-one proposals.—The contracting officer solicits phase-one proposals that—

    (A) include information on the offeror's—

        (i) technical approach; and

        (ii) technical qualifications; and

    (B) do not include—

        (i) detailed design information; or

        (ii) cost or price information.

    (3) Evaluation factors.—The evaluation factors to be used in evaluating phase-one proposals are stated in the solicitation and include specialized experience and technical competence, capability to perform, past performance of the offeror's team (including the architect-engineer and construction members of the team), and other appropriate factors, except that cost-related or price-related evaluation factors are not permitted. Each solicitation establishes the relative importance assigned to the evaluation factors and subfactors that must be considered in the evaluation of phase-one proposals. The agency evaluates phase-one proposals on the basis of the phase-one evaluation factors set forth in the solicitation.

    (4) Selection by contracting officer.—

    (A) Number of offerors selected and what is to be evaluated.—The contracting officer selects as the most highly qualified the number of offerors specified in the solicitation to provide the property or services under the contract and requests the selected offerors to submit phase-two competitive proposals that include technical proposals and cost or price information. Each solicitation establishes with respect to phase two—

        (i) the technical submission for the proposal, including design concepts or proposed solutions to requirements addressed within the scope of work, or both; and

        (ii) the evaluation factors and subfactors, including cost or price, that must be considered in the evaluations of proposals in accordance with subsections (b) to (d) of section 3306 of this title.

    (B) Separate evaluations.—The contracting officer separately evaluates the submissions described in clauses (i) and (ii) of subparagraph (A).

    (5) Awarding of contract.—The agency awards the contract in accordance with chapter 37 of this title.

 (d) Solicitation to State number of offerors to be selected for phase-two requests for competitive proposals.—A solicitation issued pursuant to the procedures described in subsection (c) shall state the maximum number of offerors that are to be selected to submit competitive proposals pursuant to subsection (c)(4). The maximum number specified in the solicitation shall not exceed 5 unless the agency determines with respect to an individual solicitation that a specified number greater than 5 is in the Federal Government's interest and is consistent with the purposes and objectives of the two-phase selection process.

(e) Requirement for guidance and regulations.—The Federal Acquisition Regulation shall include guidance—

    (1) regarding the factors that may be considered in determining whether the two-phase contracting procedures authorized by subsection (a) are appropriate for use in individual contracting situations;

    (2) regarding the factors that may be used in selecting contractors; and

    (3) providing for a uniform approach to be used Government-wide.

(Pub.L. 111–350, § 3, Jan. 4, 2011, 124 Stat. 3759.)

HISTORICAL AND STATUTORY NOTES

References in Text

Chapter 37 of this title, referred to in subsec. (c)(5), is classified to 41 U.S.C.A. § 3701 et seq.

CROSS REFERENCES

Armed Forces, design–build selection procedures, see 10 USCA § 2305a.

Airport development and improvement, design–build contracting, approvals by Administrator of Federal Aviation Administration, see 49 USCA § 47142.

Architect of the Capitol, design–build contracts, general powers and duties, see 2 USCA § 1816a.

Federal Acquisition Regulation, defined for subtitle I of this title, functions and general authority, see 41 USCA §§ 106 and 1303.

§ 3310. Quantities to order

(a) Factors affecting quantity to order.—Each executive agency shall procure supplies in a quantity that—

    (1) will result in the total cost and unit cost most advantageous to the Federal Government, where practicable; and

    (2) does not exceed the quantity reasonably expected to be required by the agency.

(b) Offeror's opinion of quantity.—Each solicitation for a contract for supplies shall, if practicable, include a provision inviting each offeror responding to the solicitation to state an opinion on whether the quantity of supplies proposed to be procured is economically advantageous to the Federal Government and, if applicable, to recommend a quantity that would be more economically advantageous to the Federal Government. Each recommendation shall include a quotation of the total price and the unit price for supplies procured in each recommended quantity.

(Pub.L. 111–350, § 3, Jan. 4, 2011, 124 Stat. 3761.)

CROSS REFERENCES

Armed Forces procurement of supplies, economic order quantities, see 10 USCA § 2384a.

Supplies, defined for subtitle I of this title, see 41 USCA § 115.

§ 3311. Qualification requirement

(a) Definition.—In this section, the term "qualification requirement" means a requirement for testing or other quality assurance demonstration that must be completed by an offeror before award of a contract.

(b) Actions before enforcing qualification requirement.—Except as provided in subsection (c), the head of an agency, before enforcing any qualification requirement, shall—

    (1) prepare a written justification stating the necessity for establishing the qualification requirement and specify why the qualification requirement must be demonstrated before contract award;

See Main Volume and Repealed Title 41, ante, for annotations

(2) specify in writing and make available to a potential offeror on request all requirements that a prospective offeror, or its product, must satisfy to become qualified, with those requirements to be limited to those least restrictive to meet the purposes necessitating the establishment of the qualification requirement;

(3) specify an estimate of the cost of testing and evaluation likely to be incurred by a potential offeror to become qualified;

(4) ensure that a potential offeror is provided, on request, a prompt opportunity to demonstrate at its own expense (except as provided in subsection (d)) its ability to meet the standards specified for qualification using—

    (A) qualified personnel and facilities—

        (i) of the agency concerned;

        (ii) of another agency obtained through interagency agreement; or

        (iii) under contract; or

    (B) other methods approved by the agency (including use of approved testing and evaluation services not provided under contract to the agency);

(5) if testing and evaluation services are provided under contract to the agency for the purposes of paragraph (4), provide to the extent possible that those services be provided by a contractor that—

    (A) is not expected to benefit from an absence of additional qualified sources; and

    (B) is required in the contract to adhere to any restriction on technical data asserted by the potential offeror seeking qualification; and

(6) ensure that a potential offeror seeking qualification is promptly informed whether qualification is attained and, if not attained, is promptly furnished specific information about why qualification was not attained.

(c) Applicability, waiver authority, and referral of offers.—

(1) **Applicability.**—Subsection (b) does not apply to a qualification requirement established by statute prior to October 30, 1984.

(2) **Waiver authority.—**

    (A) **Submission of determination of unreasonableness.**—Except as provided in subparagraph (C), if it is unreasonable to specify the standards for qualification that a prospective offeror or its product must satisfy, a determination to that effect shall be submitted to the advocate for competition of the procuring activity responsible for the purchase of the item subject to the qualification requirement.

    (B) **Authority to grant waiver.**—After considering any comments of the advocate for competition reviewing the determination, the head of the procuring activity may waive the requirements of paragraphs (2) to (5) of subsection (b) for up to 2 years with respect to the item subject to the qualification requirement.

    (C) **Nonapplicability to qualified products list.**—Waiver authority under this paragraph does not apply with respect to a qualified products list.

(3) **Submission and consideration of offer not to be denied.**—A potential offeror may not be denied the opportunity to submit and have considered an offer for a contract solely because the potential offeror has not been identified as meeting a qualification requirement if the potential offeror can demonstrate to the satisfaction of the contracting officer that the potential offeror or its product meets the standards established for qualification or can meet those standards before the date specified for award of the contract.

(4) **Referral to Small Business Administration not required.**—This subsection does not require the referral of an offer to the Small Business Administration pursuant to section 8(b)(7) of the Small Business Act (15 U.S.C. 637(b)(7)) if the basis for the referral is a challenge by the offeror to either the validity of the qualification requirement or the offeror's compliance with that requirement.

(5) **Delay of procurement not required.**—The head of an agency need not delay a proposed procurement to comply with subsection (b) or to provide a potential

offeror with an opportunity to demonstrate its ability to meet the standards specified for qualification.

(d) Fewer than 2 actual manufacturers.—

(1) **Solicitation and testing of additional sources or products.**—If the number of qualified sources or qualified products available to compete actively for an anticipated future requirement is fewer than 2 actual manufacturers or the products of 2 actual manufacturers, respectively, the head of the agency concerned shall—

(A) publish notice periodically soliciting additional sources or products to seek qualification, unless the contracting officer determines that doing so would compromise national security; and

(B) subject to paragraph (2), bear the cost of conducting the specified testing and evaluation (excluding the cost associated with producing the item or establishing the production, quality control, or other system to be tested and evaluated) for a small business concern or a product manufactured by a small business concern that has met the standards specified for qualification and that could reasonably be expected to compete for a contract for that requirement.

(2) **When agency may bear cost.**—The head of the agency concerned may bear the cost under paragraph (1)(B) only if the head of the agency determines that the additional qualified sources or products are likely to result in cost savings from increased competition for future requirements sufficient to offset (within a reasonable period of time considering the duration and dollar value of anticipated future requirements) the cost incurred by the agency.

(3) **Certification required.**—The head of the agency shall require a prospective contractor requesting the Federal Government to bear testing and evaluation costs under paragraph (1)(B) to certify its status as a small business concern under section 3 of the Small Business Act (15 U.S.C. 632).

(e) Examination and revalidation of qualification requirement.—Within 7 years after the establishment of a qualification requirement, the need for the requirement shall be examined and the standards of the requirement revalidated in accordance with the requirements of subsection (b). This subsection does not apply in the case of a qualification requirement for which a waiver is in effect under subsection (c)(2).

(f) When enforcement of qualification requirement not allowed.—Except in an emergency as determined by the head of the agency, after the head of the agency determines not to enforce a qualification requirement for a solicitation, the agency may not enforce the requirement unless the agency complies with the requirements of subsection (b).

(Pub.L. 111–350, § 3, Jan. 4, 2011, 124 Stat. 3761.)

HISTORICAL AND STATUTORY NOTES

References in Text

The Small Business Act, referred to in subsec. (c)(4) and (d)(3), is Act July 18, 1958, Pub.L. 85–536, 72 Stat. 384, as amended, also known as the SBA, which is principally classified to chapter 14A of Title 15, 15 U.S.C.A. § 631 et seq. Section 8 of such Act is classified to 15 U.S.C.A. § 637. Section 3 of such Act is classified to 15 U.S.C.A. § 632. For complete classification, see Short Title note set out under 15 U.S.C.A. § 631 and Tables.

CROSS REFERENCES

Item and item of supply, defined for subtitle I of this title, see 41 USCA § 108.

Procurement, defined for subtitle I of this title, see 41 USCA § 111.

Standards, defined for subtitle I of this title, see 41 USCA § 114.

Technical data, defined for subtitle I of this title, see 41 USCA § 116.

CHAPTER 35—TRUTHFUL COST OR PRICING DATA

See Main Volume and Repealed Title 41, ante, for annotations

§ 3501.   General

(a) **Definitions.**—In this chapter:

(1) **Commercial item.**—The term "commercial item" has the meaning provided the term by section 103 of this title.

(2) **Cost or pricing data.**—The term "cost or pricing data" means all facts that, as of the date of agreement on the price of a contract (or the price of a contract modification) or, if applicable consistent with section 3506(a)(2) of this title, another date agreed upon between the parties, a prudent buyer or seller would reasonably expect to affect price negotiations significantly. The term does not include information that is judgmental, but does include factual information from which a judgment was derived.

(3) **Subcontract.**—The term "subcontract" includes a transfer of commercial items between divisions, subsidiaries, or affiliates of a contractor or a subcontractor.

(b) **Regulations.**—

(1) **Minimizing abuse of commercial services item authority.**—The Federal Acquisition Regulation shall ensure that services that are not offered and sold competitively in substantial quantities in the commercial marketplace, but are of a type offered and sold competitively in substantial quantities in the commercial marketplace, may be treated as commercial items for purposes of this chapter only if the contracting officer determines in writing that the offeror has submitted sufficient information to evaluate, through price analysis, the reasonableness of the price for the services.

(2) **Information to submit.**—To the extent necessary to make a determination under paragraph (1), the contracting officer may request the offeror to submit—

(A) prices paid for the same or similar commercial items under comparable terms and conditions by both government and commercial customers; and

(B) if the contracting officer determines that the information described in subparagraph (A) is not sufficient to determine the reasonableness of price, other relevant information regarding the basis for price or cost, including information on labor costs, material costs, and overhead rates.

(Pub.L. 111–350, § 3, Jan. 4, 2011, 124 Stat. 3764.)

CROSS REFERENCES

Commercial item, defined for subtitle I of this title, see 41 USCA § 103.

Federal Acquisition Regulation, defined for subtitle I of this title, functions and general authority, see 41 USCA §§ 106 and 1303.

§ 3502.   Required cost or pricing data and certification

(a) **When required.**—The head of an executive agency shall require offerors, contractors, and subcontractors to make cost or pricing data available as follows:

(1) **Offeror for prime contract.**—An offeror for a prime contract under this division to be entered into using procedures other than sealed-bid procedures shall be required to submit cost or pricing data before the award of a contract if—

(A) in the case of a prime contract entered into after October 13, 1994, the price of the contract to the Federal Government is expected to exceed $500,000; and

(B) in the case of a prime contract entered into on or before October 13, 1994, the price of the contract to the Federal Government is expected to exceed $100,000.

(2) **Contractor.**—The contractor for a prime contract under this division shall be required to submit cost or pricing data before the pricing of a change or modification to the contract if—

(A) in the case of a change or modification made to a prime contract referred to in paragraph (1)(A), the price adjustment is expected to exceed $ 500,000;

(B) in the case of a change or modification made to a prime contract that was entered into on or before October 13, 1994, and that has been modified pursuant to subsection (f), the price adjustment is expected to exceed $500,000; and

(C) in the case of a change or modification not covered by subparagraph (A) or (B), the price adjustment is expected to exceed $100,000.

(3) Offeror for subcontract.—An offeror for a subcontract (at any tier) of a contract under this division shall be required to submit cost or pricing data before the award of the subcontract if the prime contractor and each higher-tier subcontractor have been required to make available cost or pricing data under this chapter and—

(A) in the case of a subcontract under a prime contract referred to in paragraph (1)(A), the price of the subcontract is expected to exceed $500, 000;

(B) in the case of a subcontract entered into under a prime contract that was entered into on or before October 13, 1994, and that has been modified pursuant to subsection (f), the price of the subcontract is expected to exceed $500,000; and

(C) in the case of a subcontract not covered by subparagraph (A) or (B), the price of the subcontract is expected to exceed $100,000.

(4) Subcontractor.—The subcontractor for a subcontract covered by paragraph (3) shall be required to submit cost or pricing data before the pricing of a change or modification to the subcontract if—

(A) in the ease of a change or modification to a subcontract referred to in paragraph (3)(A) or (B), the price adjustment is expected to exceed $ 500,000; and

(B) in the case of a change or modification to a subcontract referred to in paragraph (3)(C), the price adjustment is expected to exceed $100,000.

(b) Certification.—A person required, as an offeror, contractor, or subcontractor, to submit cost or pricing data under subsection (a) (or required by the head of the procuring activity concerned to submit the data under section 3504 of this title) shall be required to certify that, to. the best of the person's knowledge and belief, the cost or pricing data submitted are accurate, complete, and current.

(c) To whom submitted.—Cost or pricing data required to be submitted under subsection (a) (or under section 3504 of this title), and a certification required to be submitted under subsection (b), shall be submitted—

(1) in the case of a submission by a prime contractor (or an offeror for a prime contract), to the contracting officer for the contract (or a designated representative of the contracting officer); or

(2) in the case of a submission by a subcontractor (or an offeror for a subcontract), to the prime contractor.

(d) Application of chapter.—Except as provided under section 3503 of this title, this chapter applies to contracts entered into by the head of an executive agency on behalf of a foreign government.

(e) Subcontracts not affected by waiver.—A waiver of requirements for submission of certified cost or pricing data that is granted under section 3503(a)(3) of this title in the case of a contract or subcontract does not waive the requirement under subsection (a)(3) of this section for submission of cost or pricing data in the case of subcontracts under that contract or subcontract unless the head of the procuring activity granting the waiver determines that the requirement under subsection (a)(3) of this section should be waived in the case of those subcontracts and justifies in writing the reason for the determination.

(f) Modifications to prior contracts.—On the request of a contractor that was required to submit cost or pricing data under subsection (a) in connection with a prime contract entered into on or before October 13, 1994, the head of the executive agency that entered into the contract shall modify the contract to reflect paragraphs (2)(B) and (3)(B) of subsection (a). All those modifications shall be made without requiring consideration.

(g) Adjustment of amounts.—Effective on October 1 of each year that is divisible by 5, each amount set forth in subsection (a) shall be adjusted to the amount that is equal to the fiscal year 1994 constant dollar value of the amount set forth. Any amount, as so adjusted, that is not evenly divisible by $50,000 shall be rounded to the nearest multiple of $50,000. In the case of an amount that is evenly divisible by $25,000 but not evenly divisible by $50,000, the amount shall be rounded to the next higher multiple of $50,000.

(Pub.L. 111–350, § 3, Jan. 4, 2011, 124 Stat. 3765.)

§ 3503. Exceptions

(a) In general.—Submission of certified cost or pricing data shall not be required under section 3502 of this title in the case of a contract, a subcontract, or a modification of a contract or subcontract—

    (1) for which the price agreed on is based on—

        (A) adequate price competition; or

        (B) prices set by law or regulation;

    (2) for the acquisition of a commercial item; or

    (3) in an exceptional case when the head of the procuring activity, without delegation, determines that the requirements of this chapter may be waived and justifies in writing the reasons for the determination.

(b) Modifications of contracts and subcontracts for commercial items.—In the case of a modification of a contract or subcontract for a commercial item that is not covered by the exception to the submission of certified cost or pricing data in paragraph (1) or (2) of subsection (a), submission of certified cost or pricing data shall not be required under section 3502 of this title if—

    (1) the contract or subcontract being modified is a contract or subcontract for which submission of certified cost or pricing data may not be required by reason of paragraph (1) or (2) of subsection (a); and

    (2) the modification would not change the contract or subcontract from a contract or subcontract for the acquisition of a commercial item to a contract or subcontract for the acquisition of an item other than a commercial item.

(Pub.L. 111–350, § 3, Jan. 4, 2011, 124 Stat. 3766.)

CROSS REFERENCES

Commercial item, defined for subtitle I of this title, see 41 USCA § 103.

Item and item of supply, defined for subtitle I of this title, see 41 USCA § 108.

Item and item of supply, defined for subtitle I of this title, see 41 USCA § 108.

§ 3504. Cost or pricing data on below-threshold contracts

(a) Authority to require submission.—Subject to subsection (b), when certified cost or pricing data are not required to be submitted by section 3502 of this title for a contract, subcontract, or modification of a contract or subcontract, the data may nevertheless be required to be submitted by the head of the procuring activity, but only if the head of the procuring activity determines that the data are necessary for the evaluation by the agency of the reasonableness of the price of the contract, subcontract, or modification of a contract or subcontract. In any case in which the head of the procuring activity requires the data to be submitted under this section, the head of the procuring activity shall justify in writing the reason for the requirement.

(b) Exception.—The head of the procuring activity may not require certified cost or pricing data to be submitted under this section for any contract or subcontract, or modification of a contract or subcontract, covered by the exceptions in section 3503(a)(1) or (2) of this title.

(c) Delegation of authority prohibited.—The head of a procuring activity may not delegate the functions under this section.

(Pub.L. 111–350, § 3, Jan. 4, 2011, 124 Stat. 3767.)

Revised Title 41 effective Jan. 4, 2011

§ 3505. Submission of other information

(a) **Authority to require submission.**—When certified cost or pricing data are not required to be submitted under this chapter for a contract, subcontract, or modification of a contract or subcontract, the contracting officer shall require submission of data other than certified cost or pricing data to the extent necessary to determine the reasonableness of the price of the contract, subcontract, or modification of the contract or subcontract.   Except in the case of a contract or subcontract covered by the exceptions in section 3503(a)(1) of this title, the contracting officer shall require that the data submitted include, at a minimum, appropriate information on the prices at which the same item or similar items have previously been sold that is adequate for evaluating the reasonableness of the price for the procurement.

(b) **Limitations on authority.**—The Federal Acquisition Regulation shall include the following provisions regarding the types of information that contracting officers may require under subsection (a):

    (1) **Reasonable limitations.**—Reasonable limitations on requests for sales data relating to commercial items.

    (2) **Limitation on scope of request.**—A requirement that a contracting officer limit, to the maximum extent practicable, the scope of any request for information relating to commercial items from an offeror to only that information that is in the form regularly maintained by the offeror in commercial operations.

    (3) **Information not to be disclosed.**—A statement that any information received relating to commercial items that is exempt from disclosure under section 552(b) of title 5 shall not be disclosed by the Federal Government.

(Pub.L. 111–350, § 3, Jan. 4, 2011, 124 Stat. 3767.)

CROSS REFERENCES

Commercial item, defined for subtitle I of this title, see 41 USCA § 103.

Federal Acquisition Regulation, defined for subtitle I of this title, functions and general authority, see 41 USCA §§ 106 and 1303.

Item and item of supply, defined for subtitle I of this title, see 41 USCA § 108.

Procurement, defined for subtitle I of this title, see 41 USCA § 111.

§ 3506. Price reductions for defective cost or pricing data

(a) **Provision requiring adjustment.**—

    (1) **In general.**—A prime contract (or change or modification to a prime contract) under which a certificate under section 3502(b) of this title is required shall contain a provision that the price of the contract to the Federal Government, including profit or fee, shall be adjusted to exclude any significant amount by which it may be determined by the head of the executive agency that the price was increased because the contractor (or any subcontractor required to make the certificate available) submitted defective cost or pricing data.

    (2) **What constitutes defective cost or pricing data.**—For the purposes of this chapter, defective cost or pricing data are cost or pricing data that, as of the date of agreement on the price of the contract (or another date agreed on between the parties), were inaccurate, incomplete, or noncurrent.   If for purposes of the preceding sentence the parties agree on a date other than the date of agreement on the price of the contract, the date agreed on by the parties shall be as close to the date of agreement on the price of the contract as is practicable.

(b) **Valid defense.**—In determining for purposes of a contract price adjustment under a contract provision required by subsection (a) whether, and to what extent, a contract price was increased because the contractor (or a subcontractor) submitted defective cost or pricing data, it is a defense that the Federal Government did not rely on the defective data submitted by the contractor or subcontractor.

(c) **Invalid defenses.**—It is not a defense to an adjustment of the price of a contract under a contract provision required by subsection (a) that—

    (1) the price of the contract would not have been modified even if accurate, complete, and current cost or pricing data had been submitted by the contractor or subcontractor because the contractor or subcontractor—

See Main Volume and Repealed Title 41, ante, for annotations

(A) was the sole source of the property or services procured; or

(B) otherwise was in a superior bargaining position with respect to the property or services procured;

(2) the contracting officer should have known that the cost or pricing data in issue were defective even though the contractor or subcontractor took no affirmative action to bring the character of the data to the attention of the contracting officer;

(3) the contract was based on an agreement between the contractor and the Federal Government about the total cost of the contract and there was no agreement about the cost of each item procured under the contract; or

(4) the prime contractor or subcontractor did not submit a certification of cost or pricing data relating to the contract as required by section 3502(b) of this title.

(d) Offsets.—

(1) **When allowed.—**A contractor shall be allowed to offset an amount against the amount of a contract price adjustment under a contract provision required by subsection (a) if—

(A) the contractor certifies to the contracting officer (or to a designated representative of the contracting officer) that, to the best of the contractor's knowledge and belief, the contractor is entitled to the offset; and

(B) the contractor proves that the cost or pricing data were available before the date of agreement on the price of the contract (or price of the modification), or, if applicable, consistent with subsection (a)(2), another date agreed on by the parties, and that the data were not submitted as specified in section 3502(c) of this title before that date.

(2) **When not allowed.—**A contractor shall not be allowed to offset an amount otherwise authorized to be offset under paragraph (1) if—

(A) the certification under section 3502(b) of this title with respect to the cost or pricing data involved was known to be false when signed; or

(B) the Federal Government proves that, had the cost or pricing data referred to in paragraph (1)(B) been submitted to the Federal Government before date of agreement on the price of the contract (or price of the modification), or, if applicable, under subsection (a)(2), another date agreed on by the parties, the submission of the cost or pricing data would not have resulted in an increase in that price in the amount to be offset.

(Pub.L. 111–350, § 3, Jan. 4, 2011, 124 Stat. 3768.)

CROSS REFERENCES

Item and item of supply, defined for subtitle I of this title, see 41 USCA § 108.

§ 3507. Interest and penalties for certain overpayments

(a) In general.—If the Federal Government makes an overpayment to a contractor under a contract with an executive agency subject to this chapter and the overpayment was due to the submission by the contractor of defective cost or pricing data, the contractor shall be liable to the Federal Government—

(1) for interest on the amount of the overpayment, to be computed—

(A) for the period beginning on the date the overpayment was made to the contractor and ending on the date the contractor repays the amount of the overpayment to the Federal Government; and

(B) at the current rate prescribed by the Secretary of the Treasury under section 6621 of the Internal Revenue Code of 1986 (26 U.S.C. 6621); and

(2) if the submission of the defective data was a knowing submission, for an additional amount equal to the amount of the overpayment.

(b) Liability not affected by refusal to submit certification.—Any liability under this section of a contractor that submits cost or pricing data but refuses to submit the certification required by section 3502(b) of this title with respect to the cost or pricing data is not affected by the refusal to submit the certification.

(Pub.L. 111–350, § 3, Jan. 4, 2011, 124 Stat. 3769.)

HISTORICAL AND STATUTORY NOTES

References in Text

The Internal Revenue Code of 1986, referred to in subsec. (a)(1)(B), is classified generally to

Title 26, 26 U.S.C.A. § 1 et seq. Section 6621 of the Code is classified to 26 U.S.C.A. § 6621.

§ 3508. Right to examine contractor records

For the purpose of evaluating the accuracy, completeness, and currency of cost or pricing data required to be submitted by this chapter, an executive agency shall have the authority provided by section 4706(b)(2) of this title.

(Pub.L. 111–350, § 3, Jan. 4, 2011, 124 Stat. 3770.)

§ 3509. Notification of violations of Federal criminal law or overpayments

(a) **Definition.**—In this section, the term "covered contract" means any contract in an amount greater than $5,000,000 and more than 120 days in duration.

(b) **Federal Acquisition Regulation.**—The Federal Acquisition Regulation shall include, pursuant to FAR Case 2007–006 (as published at 72 Fed. Reg. 64019, November 14, 2007) or any follow-on FAR case, provisions that require timely notification by Federal contractors of violations of Federal criminal law or overpayments in connection with the award or performance of covered contracts or subcontracts, including those performed outside the United States and those for commercial items.

(Pub.L. 111–350, § 3, Jan. 4, 2011, 124 Stat. 3770.)

CROSS REFERENCES

Commercial item, defined for subtitle I of this title, see 41 USCA § 103.

Enhancing payment accuracy through a "Do Not Pay List," see Memorandum of the President of the United States, June 18, 2010, 75 F.R. 35953, set out under 31 USCA § 3321.

Federal Acquisition Regulation, defined for subtitle I of this title, functions and general authority, see 41 USCA §§ 106 and 1303.

Finding and recapturing improper payments, see Memorandum of the President of the United States, March 10, 2010, 75 F.R. 12119, set out under 31 USCA § 3321.

Reducing improper payments, see Executive Order No. 13520, Nov. 20, 2009, 74 F.R. 62201, set out under 31 USCA § 3321.

CHAPTER 37—AWARDING OF CONTRACTS

§ 3701. Basis of award and rejection

(a) **Award.**—An executive agency shall evaluate sealed bids and competitive proposals, and award a contract, based solely on the factors specified in the solicitation.

(b) **Rejection.**—All sealed bids or competitive proposals received in response to a solicitation may be rejected if the agency head determines that rejection is in the public interest.

(Pub.L. 111–350, § 3, Jan. 4, 2011, 124 Stat. 3770.)

HISTORICAL AND STATUTORY NOTES

Congressional Statement of Purpose

Pub.L. 98–577, Title I, § 101, Oct. 30, 1984, 98 Stat. 3066, provided that: "The purposes of this

Act [see Short Title note, Pub.L. 98–577, § 1, Oct. 30, 1984, 98 Stat. 3066, set out under 41 U.S.C.A. § 101] are to—

See Main Volume and Repealed Title 41, ante, for annotations

"(1) eliminate procurement procedures and practices that unnecessarily inhibit full and open competition for contracts;

"(2) promote the use of contracting opportunities as a means to expand the industrial base of the United States in order to ensure adequate responsive capability of the economy to the increased demands of the Government in times of national emergency; and

"(3) foster opportunities for the increased participation in the competitive procurement process of small business concerns and small business concerns owned and controlled by socially and economically disadvantaged individuals."

[Note was classified as a note under former 41 U.S.C.A. § 251 prior to the enactment into positive law of Title 41, Public Contracts, by Pub.L. 111–350, Jan. 4, 2011, 124 Stat. 3677.]

EXECUTIVE ORDERS
EXECUTIVE ORDER NO 12979
Oct. 25, 1995, 60 F.R. 55171

AGENCY PROCUREMENT PROTESTS

By the authority vested in me as President by the Constitution and the laws of the United States of America, and in order to ensure effective and efficient expenditure of public funds and fair and expeditious resolution of protests to the award of Federal procurement contracts, it is hereby ordered as follows:

Section 1. Heads of executive departments and agencies ("agencies") engaged in the procurement of supplies and services shall prescribe administrative procedures for the resolution of protests to the award of their procurement contracts as an alternative to protests in fora outside the procuring agencies. Procedures prescribed pursuant to this order shall:

(a) emphasize that whenever conduct of a procurement is contested, all parties should use their best efforts to resolve the matter with agency contracting officers;

(b) to the maximum extent practicable, provide for inexpensive, informal, procedurally simple, and expeditious resolution of protests, including, where appropriate and as permitted by law, the use of alternative dispute resolution techniques, third party neutrals, and another agency's personnel;

(c) allow actual or prospective bidders or offerors whose direct economic interests would be affected by the award or failure to award the contract to request a review, at a level above the contracting officer, of any decision by a contracting officer that is alleged to have violated a statute or regulation and, thereby, caused prejudice to the protester; and

(d) except where immediate contract award or performance is justified for urgent and compelling reasons or is determined to be in the best interest of the United States, prohibit award or performance of the contract while a timely filed protest is pending before the agency. To allow for the withholding of a contract award or performance, the agency must have received notice of the protest within either 10 calendar days after the contract award or 5 calendar days after the bidder or offeror who is protesting the contract award was given the opportunity to be debriefed by the agency, whichever date is later.

Sec. 2. The Administrator for Federal Procurement Policy shall: **(a)** work with the heads of executive agencies to provide policy guidance and leadership necessary to implement provisions of this order; and

(b) review and evaluate agency experience and performance under this order, and report on any findings to the President within 2 years from the date of this order.

Sec. 3. The Administrator of General Services, the Secretary of Defense, and the Administrator of the National Aeronautics and Space Administration, in coordination with the Office of Federal Procurement Policy, shall amend the Federal Acquisition Regulation, 48 C.F.R. 1, within 180 days of the date of this order to further the purposes of this order.

WILLIAM J. CLINTON

[Executive Order was set out under former 41 U.S.C.A. § 253b prior to the enactment into positive law of Title 41, Public Contracts, by Pub.L. 111–350, Jan. 4, 2011, 124 Stat. 3677.]

CROSS REFERENCES

Agency head, defined for division C of subtitle I of this title, see 41 USCA § 151.

§ 3702.   Sealed bids

(a) Opening of bids.—Sealed bids shall be opened publicly at the time and place stated in the solicitation.

(b) Criteria for awarding contract.—The executive agency shall evaluate the bids in accordance with section 3701(a) of this title without discussions with the bidders and, except as provided in section 3701(b) of this title, shall award a contract with reasonable promptness to the responsible source whose bid conforms to the solicitation and is most advantageous to the Federal Government, considering only price and the other price-related factors included in the solicitation.

(c) **Notice of award.**—The award of a contract shall be made by transmitting, in writing or by electronic means, notice of the award to the successful bidder. Within 3 days after the date of contract award, the executive agency shall notify, in writing or by electronic means, each bidder not awarded the contract that the contract has been awarded.

(Pub.L. 111–350, § 3, Jan. 4, 2011, 124 Stat. 3770.)

§ 3703. Competitive proposals

(a) **Evaluation and award.**—An executive agency shall evaluate competitive proposals in accordance with section 3701(a) of this title and may award a contract—

(1) after discussions with the offerors, provided that written or oral discussions have been conducted with all responsible offerors who submit proposals within the competitive range; or

(2) based on the proposals received and without discussions with the offerors (other than discussions conducted for the purpose of minor clarification), if, as required by section 3306(b)(2)(B)(i) of this title, the solicitation included a statement that proposals are intended to be evaluated, and award made, without discussions unless discussions are determined to be necessary.

(b) **Limit on number of proposals.**—If the contracting officer determines that the number of offerors that would otherwise be included in the competitive range under subsection (a)(1) exceeds the number at which an efficient competition can be conducted, the contracting officer may limit the number of proposals in the competitive range, in accordance with the criteria specified in the solicitation, to the greatest number that will permit an efficient competition among the offerors rated most highly in accordance with those criteria.

(c) **Criteria for awarding contract.**—Except as otherwise provided in section 3701(b) of this title, the executive agency shall award a contract with reasonable promptness to the responsible source whose proposal is most advantageous to the Federal Government, considering only cost or price and the other factors included in the solicitation.

(d) **Notice of award.**—The executive agency shall award the contract by transmitting, in writing or by electronic means, notice of the award to that source and, within 3 days after the date of contract award, shall notify, in writing or by electronic means, all other offerors of the rejection of their proposals.

(Pub.L. 111–350, § 3, Jan. 4, 2011, 124 Stat. 3771.)

CROSS REFERENCES
Responsible source, defined for subtitle I of this title, see 41 USCA § 113.

§ 3704. Post-award debriefings

(a) **Request for debriefing.**—When a contract is awarded by the head of an executive agency on the basis of competitive proposals, an unsuccessful offeror, on written request received by the agency within 3 days after the date on which the unsuccessful offeror receives the notification of the contract award, shall be debriefed and furnished the basis for the selection decision and contract award.

(b) **When debriefing to be conducted.**—The executive agency shall debrief the offeror within, to the maximum extent practicable, 5 days after receipt of the request by the executive agency.

(c) **Information to be provided.**—The debriefing shall include, at a minimum—

(1) the executive agency's evaluation of the significant weak or deficient factors in the offeror's offer;

(2) the overall evaluated cost and technical rating of the offer of the contractor awarded the contract and the overall evaluated cost and technical rating of the offer of the debriefed offeror;

(3) the overall ranking of all offers;

(4) a summary of the rationale for the award;

(5) in the case of a proposal that includes a commercial item that is an end item under the contract, the make and model of the item being provided in accordance with the offer of the contractor awarded the contract; and

(6) reasonable responses to relevant questions posed by the debriefed offeror as to whether source selection procedures set forth in the solicitation, applicable regulations, and other applicable authorities were followed by the executive agency.

(d) Information not to be included.—The debriefing may not include point-by-point comparisons of the debriefed offeror's offer with other offers and may not disclose any information that is exempt from disclosure under section 552(b) of title 5.

(e) Inclusion of statement in solicitation.—Each solicitation for competitive proposals shall include a statement that information described in subsection (c) may be disclosed in post-award debriefings.

(f) After successful protest.—If, within one year after the date of the contract award and as a result of a successful procurement protest, the executive agency seeks to fulfill the requirement under the protested contract either on the basis of a new solicitation of offers or on the basis of new best and final offers requested for that contract, the head of the executive agency shall make available to all offerors—

(1) the information provided in debriefings under this section regarding the offer of the contractor awarded the contract; and

(2) the same information that would have been provided to the original offerors.

(g) Summary to be included in file.—The contracting officer shall include a summary of the debriefing in the contract file.

(Pub.L. 111–350, § 3, Jan. 4, 2011, 124 Stat. 3771.)

CROSS REFERENCES

Commercial item, defined for subtitle I of this title, see 41 USCA § 103.

Procurement, defined for subtitle I of this title, see 41 USCA § 111.

§ 3705.　Pre-award debriefings

(a) Request for debriefing.—When the contracting officer excludes an offeror submitting a competitive proposal from the competitive range (or otherwise excludes that offeror from further consideration prior to the final source selection decision), the excluded offeror may request in writing, within 3 days after the date on which the excluded offeror receives notice of its exclusion, a debriefing prior to award.

(b) When debriefing to be conducted.—The contracting officer shall make every effort to debrief the unsuccessful offeror as soon as practicable but may refuse the request for a debriefing if it is not in the best interests of the Federal Government to conduct a debriefing at that time.

(c) Precondition for post-award debriefing.—The contracting officer is required to debrief an excluded offeror in accordance with section 3704 of this title only if that offeror requested and was refused a pre-award debriefing under subsections (a) and (b).

(d) Information to be provided.—The debriefing conducted under this section shall include—

(1) the executive agency's evaluation of the significant elements in the offeror's offer;

(2) a summary of the rationale for the offeror's exclusion; and

(3) reasonable responses to relevant questions posed by the debriefed offeror as to whether source selection procedures set forth in the solicitation, applicable regulations, and other applicable authorities were followed by the executive agency.

(e) Information not to be disclosed.—The debriefing conducted pursuant to this section may not disclose the number or identity of other offerors and shall not disclose information about the content, ranking, or evaluation of other offerors' proposals.

(f) Summary to be included in file.—The contracting officer shall include a summary of the debriefing in the contract file.

(Pub.L. 111–350, § 3, Jan. 4, 2011, 124 Stat. 3772.)

§ 3706. Encouragement of alternative dispute resolution

The Federal Acquisition Regulation shall include a provision encouraging the use of alternative dispute resolution techniques to provide informal, expeditious, and inexpensive procedures for an offeror to consider using before filing a protest, prior to the award of a contract, of the exclusion of the offeror from the competitive range (or otherwise from further consideration) for that contract.

(Pub.L. 111–350, § 3, Jan. 4, 2011, 124 Stat. 3773.)

CROSS REFERENCES

Alternative Dispute Resolution, judicial procedures, see 28 USCA § 651 et seq.

Alternative means of dispute resolution in the administrative process, see 5 USCA § 571 et seq.

Federal Acquisition Regulation, defined for subtitle I of this title, functions and general authority, see 41 USCA §§ 106 and 1303.

§ 3707. Antitrust violations

If the agency head considers that a bid or proposal evidences a violation of the antitrust laws, the agency head shall refer the bid or proposal to the Attorney General for appropriate action.

(Pub.L. 111–350, § 3, Jan. 4, 2011, 124 Stat. 3773.)

CROSS REFERENCES

Agency head, defined for division C of subtitle I of this title, see 41 USCA § 151.

Antitrust laws,
  Actions under, see 15 USCA §§ 15 and 22.

Monopolies and combinations in restraint of trade, see 15 USCA § 1 et seq.

§ 3708. Protests

(a) Protest file.—

(1) Establishment and access.—If, in the case of a solicitation for a contract issued by, or an award or proposed award of a contract by, the head of an executive agency, a protest is filed pursuant to the procedures in subchapter V of chapter 35 of title 31, and an actual or prospective offeror requests, a file of the protest shall be established by the procuring activity and reasonable access shall be provided to actual or prospective offerors.

(2) Redacted information.—Information exempt from disclosure under section 552 of title 5 may be redacted in a file established pursuant to paragraph (1) unless an applicable protective order provides otherwise.

(b) Agency actions on protests.—If, in connection with a protest, the head of an executive agency determines that a solicitation, proposed award, or award does not comply with the requirements of law or regulation, the head of the executive agency may—

(1) take any action set out in subparagraphs (A) to (F) of subsection (b) (1) of section 3554 of title 31; and

(2) pay costs described in paragraph (1) of section 3554(c) of title 31 within the limits referred to in paragraph (2) of section 3554(c).

(Pub.L. 111–350, § 3, Jan. 4, 2011, 124 Stat. 3773.)

HISTORICAL AND STATUTORY NOTES

References in Text

Subchapter V of chapter 35 of title 31, referred to in subsec. (a)(1), is classified to 31 U.S.C.A. § 3551 et seq.

See Main Volume and Repealed Title 41, ante, for annotations

CHAPTER 39—SPECIFIC TYPES OF CONTRACTS

HISTORICAL AND STATUTORY NOTES

Severability of Provisions

Act June 30, 1949, c. 288, 63 Stat. 403, § 604, formerly § 504, renumbered by Act Sept. 5, 1950, c. 849, 6(a), (b), 64 Stat. 583, provided that: "If any provision of this Act [Act June 30, 1949, c. 288, 63 Stat. 377; see Tables]or the application thereof to any person or circumstances, is held invalid, the remainder of this Act, and the application of such provision to other persons or circumstances, shall not be affected thereby."

[Note was classified as a note under former 41 U.S.C.A. § 251 prior to the enactment into positive law of Title 41, Public Contracts, by Pub.L. 111–350, Jan. 4, 2011, 124 Stat. 3677.]

Share-in-Savings Contracts

Act June 30, 1949, c. 288, Title III, § 317, as added Dec. 17, 2002, Pub.L. 107–347, Title II, § 210(b), 116 Stat. 2934, provided that:

"(a) **Authority to enter into share-in-savings contracts**

"(1) The head of an executive agency may enter into a share-in-savings contract for information technology (as defined in section 11101(6) of Title 40) in which the Government awards a contract to improve mission-related or administrative processes or to accelerate the achievement of its mission and share with the contractor in savings achieved through contract performance.

"(2)(A) Except as provided in subparagraph (B), a share-in-savings contract shall be awarded for a period of not more than five years.

"(B) A share-in-savings contract may be awarded for a period greater than five years, but not more than 10 years, if the head of the agency determines in writing prior to award of the contract that—

"(i) the level of risk to be assumed and the investment to be undertaken by the contractor is likely to inhibit the government from obtaining the needed information technology competitively at a fair and reasonable price if the contract is limited in duration to a period of five years or less; and

"(ii) usage of the information technology to be acquired is likely to continue for a period of time sufficient to generate reasonable benefit for the government.

"(3) Contracts awarded pursuant to the authority of this section shall, to the maximum extent practicable, be performance-based contracts that identify objective outcomes and contain performance standards that will be used to measure achievement and milestones that must be met before payment is made.

"(4) Contracts awarded pursuant to the authority of this section shall include a provision containing a quantifiable baseline that is to be the basis upon which a savings share ratio is established that governs the amount of payment a contractor is to receive under the contract. Before commencement of performance of such a contract, the senior procurement executive of the agency shall determine in writing that the terms of the provision are quantifiable and will likely yield value to the Government.

"(5)(A) The head of the agency may retain savings realized through the use of a share-in-savings contract under this section that are in excess of the total amount of savings paid to the contractor under the contract, but may not retain any portion of such savings that is attributable to a decrease in the number of civilian employees of the Federal Government performing the function. Except as provided in subparagraph (B), savings shall be credited to the appropriation or fund against which charges were made to carry out the contract and shall be used for information technology.

"(B) Amounts retained by the agency under this subsection shall—

"(i) without further appropriation, remain available until expended; and

"(ii) be applied first to fund any contingent liabilities associated with share-in-savings procurements that are not fully funded.

"(b) **Cancellation and termination**

"(1) If funds are not made available for the continuation of a share-in-savings contract entered into under this section in a subsequent fiscal year, the contract shall be canceled or terminated. The costs of cancellation or termination may be paid out of—

"(A) appropriations available for the performance of the contract;

"(B) appropriations available for acquisition of the information technology procured under the contract, and not otherwise obligated; or

"(C) funds subsequently appropriated for payments of costs of cancellation or termination, subject to the limitations in paragraph (3).

"(2) The amount payable in the event of cancellation or termination of a share-in-savings contract shall be negotiated with the contractor at the time the contract is entered into.

"(3)(A) Subject to subparagraph (B), the head of an executive agency may enter into share-in-savings contracts under this section in any given fiscal year even if funds are not made specifically available for the full costs of cancellation or termination of the contract if funds are available and sufficient to make payments with respect to the first fiscal year of the contract and the following conditions are met regarding the funding of cancellation and termination liability:

"(i) The amount of unfunded contingent liability for the contract does not exceed the lesser of—

"(I) 25 percent of the estimated costs of a cancellation or termination; or

"(II) $5,000,000.

"(ii) Unfunded contingent liability in excess of $1,000,000 has been approved by the Director of the Office of Management and Budget or the Director's designee.

"(B) The aggregate number of share-in-savings contracts that may be entered into under subparagraph (A) by all executive agencies to which this chapter [Title III of Act June 30, 1949, c. 288] applies in a fiscal year may not exceed 5 in each of fiscal years 2003, 2004, and 2005.

"(c) Definitions

"In this section:

"(1) The term 'contractor' means a private entity that enters into a contract with an agency.

"(2) The term 'savings' means—

"(A) monetary savings to an agency; or

"(B) savings in time or other benefits realized by the agency, including enhanced revenues (other than enhanced revenues from the collection of fees, taxes, debts, claims, or other amounts owed the Federal Government).

"(3) The term 'share-in-savings contract' means a contract under which—

"(A) a contractor provides solutions for—

"(i) improving the agency's mission-related or administrative processes; or

"(ii) accelerating the achievement of agency missions; and

"(B) the head of the agency pays the contractor an amount equal to a portion of the savings derived by the agency from—

"(i) any improvements in mission-related or administrative processes that result from implementation of the solution; or

"(ii) acceleration of achievement of agency missions."

[Note was classified to former 41 U.S.C.A. § 266a prior to the enactment into positive law of Title 41, Public Contracts, by Pub.L. 111–350, Jan. 4, 2011, 124 Stat. 3677.]

EXECUTIVE ORDERS
EXECUTIVE ORDER NO. 13496
Jan. 30, 2009, 74 F.R. 6107

NOTIFICATION OF EMPLOYEE RIGHTS UNDER FEDERAL LABOR LAWS

By the authority vested in me as President by the Constitution and the laws of the United States of America, including the Federal Property and Administrative Services Act, 40 U.S.C. 101 et seq., and in order to ensure the economical and efficient administration and completion of Government contracts, it is hereby ordered that:

Section 1. Policy. This order is designed to promote economy and efficiency in Government procurement. When the Federal Government contracts for goods or services, it has a proprietary interest in ensuring that those contracts will be performed by contractors whose work will not be interrupted by labor unrest. The attainment of industrial peace is most easily achieved and workers' productivity is enhanced when workers are well informed of their rights under Federal labor laws, including the National Labor Relations Act (Act), 29 U.S.C. 151 et seq. As the Act recognizes, "encouraging the practice and procedure of collective bargaining and . . . protecting the exercise by workers of full freedom of association, self-organization, and designation of representatives of their own choosing, for the purpose of negotiating the terms and conditions of their employment or other mutual aid or protection" will "eliminate the causes of certain substantial obstructions to the free flow of commerce" and "mitigate and eliminate these obstructions when they have occurred." 29

U.S.C. 151. Relying on contractors whose employees are informed of such rights under Federal labor laws facilitates the efficient and economical completion of the Federal Government's contracts.

Sec. 2. Contract Clause. Except in contracts exempted in accordance with section 3 of this order, all Government contracting departments and agencies shall, to the extent consistent with law, include the following provisions in every Government contract, other than collective bargaining agreements as defined in 5 U.S.C. 7103(a)(8) and purchases under the simplified acquisition threshold as defined in the Office of Federal Procurement Policy Act, 41 U.S.C. 403.

"1. During the term of this contract, the contractor agrees to post a notice, of such size and in such form, and containing such content as the Secretary of Labor shall prescribe, in conspicuous places in and about its plants and offices where employees covered by the National Labor Relations Act engage in activities relating to the performance of the contract, including all places where notices to employees are customarily posted both physically and electronically. The notice shall include the information contained in the notice published by the Secretary of Labor in the **Federal Register** (Secretary's Notice).

"2. The contractor will comply with all provisions of the Secretary's Notice, and related rules, regulations, and orders of the Secretary of Labor.

"3. In the event that the contractor does not comply with any of the requirements set forth in paragraphs (1) or (2) above, this contract may be cancelled, terminated, or suspended in whole or in part, and the contractor may be declared ineligible for further Government contracts in accordance with procedures authorized in or adopted pursuant to Executive Order [number as provided by the Federal Register] of [insert new date]. Such other sanctions or remedies may be imposed as are provided in Executive Order [number as provided by the Federal Register] of [insert new date], or by rule, regulation, or order of the Secretary of Labor, or as are otherwise provided by law.

"4. The contractor will include the provisions of paragraphs (1) through (3) above in every subcontract entered into in connection with this contract (unless exempted by rules, regulations, or orders of the Secretary of Labor issued pursuant to section 3 of Executive Order [number as provided by the Federal Register] of [insert new date]) so that such provisions will be binding upon each subcontractor. The contractor will take such action with respect to any such subcontract as may be directed by the Secretary of Labor as a means of enforcing such provisions, including the imposition of sanctions for non-compliance: Provided, however, that if the contractor becomes involved in litigation with a subcontractor, or is threatened with such involvement, as a result of such direction, the contractor may request the United States to enter into such litigation to protect the interests of the United States."

Sec. 3. Administration.

(a) The Secretary of Labor (Secretary) shall be responsible for the administration and enforcement of this order. The Secretary shall adopt such rules and regulations and issue such orders as are necessary and appropriate to achieve the purposes of this order.

(b) Within 120 days of the effective date of this order, the Secretary shall initiate a rulemaking to prescribe the size, form, and content of the notice to be posted by a contractor under paragraph 1 of the contract clause described in section 2 of this order. Such notice shall describe the rights of employees under Federal labor laws, consistent with the policy set forth in section 1 of this order.

(c) Whenever the Secretary finds that an act of Congress, clarification of existing law by the courts or the National Labor Relations Board, or other circumstances make modification of the contractual provisions set out in subsection (a) of this section necessary to achieve the purposes of this order, the Secretary promptly shall issue such rules, regulations, or orders as are needed to cause the substitution or addition of appropriate contractual provisions in Government contracts thereafter entered into.

Sec. 4. Exemptions.

(a) If the Secretary finds that the application of any of the requirements of this order would not serve the purposes of this order or would impair the ability of the Government to procure goods or services on an economical and efficient basis, the Secretary may exempt a contracting department or agency or group of departments or agencies from the requirements of any or all of the provisions of this order with respect to a particular contract or subcontract or any class of contracts or subcontracts.

(b) The Secretary may, if the Secretary finds that special circumstances require an exemption in order to serve the national interest, exempt a contracting department or agency from the requirements of any or all of the provisions of section 2 of this order with respect to a particular contract or subcontract or class of contracts or subcontracts.

Sec. 5. Investigation.

(a) The Secretary may investigate any Government contractor, subcontractor, or vendor to determine whether the contractual provisions required by section 2 of this order have been violated.

Such investigations shall be conducted in accordance with procedures established by the Secretary.

(b) The Secretary shall receive and investigate complaints by employees of a Government contractor or subcontractor, where such complaints allege a failure to perform or a violation of the contractual provisions required by section 2 of this order.

Sec. 6. Compliance.

(a) The Secretary, or any agency or officer in the executive branch lawfully designated by rule, regulation, or order of the Secretary, may hold such hearings, public or private, regarding compliance with this order as the Secretary may deem advisable.

(b) The Secretary may hold hearings, or cause hearings to be held, in accordance with subsection (a) of this section, prior to imposing, ordering, or recommending the imposition of sanctions under this order. Neither an order for cancellation, termination, or suspension of any contract or debarment of any contractor from further Government contracts under section 7(b) of this order nor the inclusion of a contractor on a published list of noncomplying contractors under section 7(c) of this order shall be carried out without affording the contractor an opportunity for a hearing.

Sec. 7. Remedies.

In accordance with such rules, regulations, or orders as the Secretary may issue or adopt, the Secretary may:

(a) after consulting with the contracting department or agency, direct that department or agency to cancel, terminate, suspend, or cause to be cancelled, terminated, or suspended, any contract, or any portion or portions thereof, for failure of the contractor to comply with the contractual provisions required by section 2 of this order; contracts may be cancelled, terminated, or suspended absolutely, or continuance of contracts may be conditioned upon future compliance: Provided, that before issuing a directive under this subsection, the Secretary shall provide the head of the contracting department or agency an opportunity to offer written objections to the issuance of such a directive, which objections shall include a complete statement of reasons for the objections, among which reasons shall be a finding that completion of the contract is essential to the agency's mission: And provided further, that no directive shall be issued by the Secretary under this subsection so long as the head of the contracting department or agency, or his or her designee, continues to object to the issuance of such directive;

(b) after consulting with each affected contracting department or agency, provide that one or more contracting departments or agencies shall refrain from entering into further contracts, or extensions or other modifications of existing contracts, with any noncomplying contractor, until such contractor has satisfied the Secretary that such contractor has complied with and will carry out the provisions of this order: Provided, that before issuing a directive under this subsection, the Secretary shall provide the head of each contracting department or agency an opportunity to offer written objections to the issuance of such a directive, which objections shall include a complete statement of reasons for the objections, among which reasons shall be a finding that further contracts or extensions or other modifications of existing contracts with the noncomplying contractor are essential to the agency's mission: And provided further, that no directive shall be issued by the Secretary under this subsection so long as the head of a contracting department or agency, or his or her designee, continues to object to the issuance of such directive; and

(c) publish, or cause to be published, the names of contractors that have, in the judgment of the Secretary, failed to comply with the provisions of this order or of related rules, regulations, and orders of the Secretary.

Sec. 8. Reports. Whenever the Secretary invokes section 7(a) or 7(b) of this order, the contracting department or agency shall report to the Secretary the results of the action it has taken within such time as the Secretary shall specify.

Sec. 9. Cooperation. Each contracting department and agency shall cooperate with the Secretary and provide such information and assistance as the Secretary may require in the performance of the Secretary's functions under this order.

Sec. 10. Sufficiency of Remedies. If the Secretary finds that the authority vested in the Secretary by sections 5 through 9 of this order is not sufficient to effectuate the purposes of this order, the Secretary shall develop recommendations on how better to effectuate those purposes.

Sec. 11. Delegation. The Secretary may, in accordance with law, delegate any function or duty of the Secretary under this order to any officer in the Department of Labor or to any other officer in the executive branch of the Government, with the consent of the head of the department or agency in which that officer serves.

Sec. 12. Implementation. To the extent permitted by law, the Federal Acquisition Regulatory Council (FAR Council) shall take whatever action is required to implement in the Federal Acquisition Regulation (FAR) the provisions of this order and any related rules, regulations, or orders issued by the Secretary under this order and shall amend the FAR to require each solicitation of offers for a contract to include a provision that implements section 2 of this order.

Sec. 13. Revocation of Prior Order and Actions. Executive Order 13201 of February 17, 2001, is revoked. The heads of executive departments and agencies shall, to the extent permitted by law, revoke expeditiously any orders, rules, regulations, guidelines, or policies implementing or enforcing Executive Order 13201.

Sec. 14. Severability. If any provision of this order, or the application of such provision to any person or circumstance, is held to be invalid, the remainder of this order and the application of the provisions of such to any person or circumstances shall not be affected thereby.

Sec. 15. General Provisions.

(a) Nothing in this order shall be construed to impair or otherwise affect:

(i) authority granted by law to a department, agency, or the head thereof; or

(ii) functions of the Director of the Office of Management and Budget relating to budgetary, administrative, or legislative proposals.

(b) This order shall be implemented consistent with applicable law and subject to the availability of appropriations.

(c) This order is not intended to, and does not, create any right or benefit, substantive or procedural, enforceable at law or in equity by any party against the United States, its departments, agencies, or entities, its officers, employees, or agents, or any other person.

Sec. 16. Effective Date. This order shall become effective immediately, and shall apply to contracts resulting from solicitations issued on or after the effective date of the rule promulgated by the Secretary pursuant to section 3(b) of this order.

BARACK OBAMA

[Order was set out under former 41 U.S.C.A. § 254 prior to the enactment into positive law of Title 41, Public Contracts, by Pub.L. 111–350, Jan. 4, 2011, 124 Stat. 3677.]

EXECUTIVE ORDER NO. 13502
Feb.6, 2009, 74 F.R. 6985

USE OF PROJECT LABOR AGREEMENTS FOR FEDERAL CONSTRUCTION PROJECTS

By the authority vested in me as President by the Constitution and the laws of the United States of America, including the Federal Property and Administrative Services Act, 40 U.S.C. 101et seq., and in order to promote the efficient administration and completion of Federal construction projects, it is hereby ordered that:

Section 1. Policy. (a) Large-scale construction projects pose special challenges to efficient and timely procurement by the Federal Government. Construction employers typically do not have a permanent workforce, which makes it difficult for them to predict labor costs when bidding on contracts and to ensure a steady supply of labor on contracts being performed. Challenges also arise due to the fact that construction projects typically involve multiple employers at a single location. A labor dispute involving one employer can delay the entire project. A lack of coordination among various employers, or uncertainty about the terms and conditions of employment of various groups of workers, can create frictions and disputes in the absence of an agreed-upon resolution mechanism. These problems threaten the efficient and timely completion of construction projects undertaken by Federal contractors. On larger projects, which are generally more complex and of longer duration, these problems tend to be more pronounced.

(b) The use of a project labor agreement may prevent these problems from developing by providing structure and stability to large-scale construction projects, thereby promoting the efficient and expeditious completion of Federal construction contracts. Accordingly, it is the policy of the Federal Government to encourage executive agencies to consider requiring the use of project labor agreements in connection with large-scale construction projects in order to promote economy and efficiency in Federal procurement.

Sec. 2. Definitions.

(a) The term "labor organization" as used in this order means a labor organization as defined in 29 U.S.C. 152(5).

(b) The term "construction" as used in this order means construction, rehabilitation, alteration, conversion, extension, repair, or improvement of buildings, highways, or other real property.

(c) The term "large-scale construction project" as used in this order means a construction project where the total cost to the Federal Government is $25 million or more.

(d) The term "executive agency" as used in this order has the same meaning as in 5 U.S.C. 105, but excludes the Government Accountability Office.

(e) The term "project labor agreement" as used in this order means a pre-hire collective bargaining agreement with one or more labor organizations that establishes the terms and conditions of employment for a specific construction project and is an agreement described in 29 U.S.C. 158(f).

Sec. 3. (a) In awarding any contract in connection with a large-scale construction project, or obligating funds pursuant to such a contract, executive agencies may, on a project-by-project basis, require the use of a project labor agreement by a contractor where use of such an agreement will (i) advance the Federal Government's interest in achieving economy and efficiency in Federal procurement, producing labor-management stability, and ensuring compliance with laws and regulations governing safety and health, equal employment opportunity, labor and employment standards, and other matters, and (ii) be consistent with law.

(b) If an executive agency determines under subsection (a) that the use of a project labor agreement will satisfy the criteria in clauses (i) and (ii) of that subsection, the agency may, if appropriate, require that every contractor or subcontractor on the project agree, for that project, to negotiate or become a party to a project labor agreement with one or more appropriate labor organizations.

Sec. 4. Any project labor agreement reached pursuant to this order shall:

(a) bind all contractors and subcontractors on the Construction project through the inclusion of appropriate specifications in all relevant solicitation provisions and contract documents;

(b) allow all contractors and subcontractors to compete for contracts and subcontracts without regard to whether they are otherwise parties to collective bargaining agreements;

(c) contain guarantees against strikes, lockouts, and similar job disruptions;

(d) set forth effective, prompt, and mutually binding procedures for resolving labor disputes arising during the project labor agreement;

(e) Provide other mechanisms for labor-management cooperation on matters of mutual interest and concern, including productivity, quality of work, safety, and health; and

(f) fully conform to all statutes, regulations, and Executive Orders.

Sec. 5. This order does not require an executive agency to use a project labor agreement on any construction project, nor does it preclude the use of a project labor agreement in circumstances not covered by this order, including leasehold arrangements and projects receiving Federal financial assistance. This order also does not require contractors or subcontractors to enter into a project labor agreement with any particular labor organization.

Sec. 6. Within 120 days of the date of this order, the Federal Acquisition Regulatory Council (FAR Council), to the extent permitted by law, shall take whatever action is required to amend the Federal Acquisition Regulation to implement the provisions of this order.

Sec. 7. The Director of OMB, in consultation with the Secretary of Labor and with other officials as appropriate, shall provide the President within 180 days of this order, recommendations about whether broader use of project labor agreements, with respect to both construction projects undertaken under Federal contracts and construction projects receiving Federal financial assistance, would help to promote the economical, efficient, and timely completion of such projects.

Sec. 8. Revocation of Prior Orders, Rules, and Regulations. Executive Order 13202 of February 17, 2001, and Executive Order 13208 of April 6, 2001, are revoked. The heads of executive agencies shall, to the extent permitted by law, revoke expeditiously any orders, rules, or regulations implementing Executive Orders 13202 and 13208.

Sec. 9. Severability. If any provision of this order, or the application of such provision to any person or circumstance, is held to be invalid, the remainder of this order and the application of the provisions of such to any person or circumstance shall not be affected thereby.

Sec. 10. General. (a) Nothing in this order shall be construed to impair or otherwise affect:

(i) authority granted by law to an executive department, agency, or the head thereof; or

(ii) functions of the Director of the Office of Management and Budget relating to budgetary, administrative, or legislative proposals.

(b) This order shall be implemented consistent with applicable law and subject to the availability of appropriations.

(c) This order is not intended to, and does not, create any right or benefit, substantive or procedural, enforceable at law or in equity by any party against the United States, its departments, agencies, or entities, its officers, employees, or agents, or any other person.

Sec. 11. Effective Date. This order shall be effective immediately and shall apply to all solicitations for contracts issued on or after the effective date of the action taken by the FAR Council under section 6 of this order.

BARACK OBAMA

[Executive Order was set out under former 41 U.S.C.A. § 251 prior to the enactment into positive law of Title 41, Public Contracts, by Pub.L. 111–350, Jan. 4, 2011, 124 Stat. 3677.]

§ 3901. Contracts awarded using procedures other than sealed-bid procedures

(a) Authorized types.—Except as provided in section 3905 of this title, contracts awarded after using procedures other than sealed-bid procedures may be of any type which in the opinion of the agency head will promote the best interests of the Federal Government.

(b) Required warranty.—

(1) Content.—Every contract awarded after using procedures other than sealed-bid procedures shall contain a suitable warranty, as determined by the agency head, by the contractor that no person or selling agency has been employed or retained to solicit or secure the contract on an agreement or understanding for a commission, percentage, brokerage, or contingent fee, except for bona fide employees or bona fide established commercial or selling agencies the contractor maintains to secure business.

(2) Remedy for breach or violation.—For the breach or violation of the warranty, the Federal Government may annul the contract without liability or deduct from the contract price or consideration the full amount of the commission, percentage, brokerage, or contingent fee.

(3) Nonapplication.—Paragraph (1) does not apply to a contract for an amount that is not greater than the simplified acquisition threshold or to a contract for the acquisition of commercial items.

(Pub.L. 111–350, § 3, Jan. 4, 2011, 124 Stat. 3774.)

CROSS REFERENCES

Agency head, defined for division C of subtitle I of this title, see 41 USCA § 151.

Commercial item, defined for subtitle I of this title, see 41 USCA § 103.

Simplified acquisition threshold, defined for division C of subtitle I of this title, see 41 USCA § 153.

§ 3902. Severable services contracts for periods crossing fiscal years

(a) Authority to enter into contract.—The head of an executive agency may enter into a contract for the procurement of severable services for a period that begins in one fiscal year and ends in the next fiscal year if (without regard to any option to extend the period of the contract) the contract period does not exceed one year.

See Main Volume and Repealed Title 41, ante, for annotations

(b) Obligation of funds.—Funds made available for a fiscal year may be obligated for the total amount of a contract entered into under the authority of this section.

(Pub.L. 111–350, § 3, Jan. 4, 2011, 124 Stat. 3774.)

CROSS REFERENCES

Procurement, defined for subtitle I of this title, see 41 USCA § 111.

§ 3903. Multiyear contracts

(a) Definition.—In this section, a multiyear contract is a contract for the purchase of property or services for more than one, but not more than 5, program years.

(b) Authority to enter into contract.—An executive agency may enter into a multiyear contract for the acquisition of property or services if—

    (1) funds are available and obligated for the contract, for the full period of the contract or for the first fiscal year in which the contract is in effect, and for the estimated costs associated with a necessary termination of the contract; and

    (2) the executive agency determines that—

        (A) the need for the property or services is reasonably firm and continuing over the period of the contract; and

        (B) a multiyear contract will serve the best interests of the Federal Government by encouraging full and open competition or promoting economy in administration, performance, and operation of the agency's programs.

(c) Termination clause.—A multiyear contract entered into under the authority of this section shall include a clause that provides that the contract shall be terminated if funds are not made available for the continuation of the contract in a fiscal year covered by the contract. Funds available for paying termination costs shall remain available for that purpose until the costs associated with termination of the contract are paid.

(d) Cancellation ceiling notice.—Before a contract described in subsection (b) that contains a clause setting forth a cancellation ceiling in excess of $10,000,000 may be awarded, the executive agency shall give written notification of the proposed contract and of the proposed cancellation ceiling for that contract to Congress. The contract may not be awarded until the end of the 30–day period beginning on the date of the notification.

(e) Contingency clause for appropriation of funds.—A multiyear contract may provide that performance under the contract after the first year of the contract is contingent on the appropriation of funds and (if the contract does so provide) that a cancellation payment shall be made to the contractor if the funds are not appropriated.

(f) Other law not affected.—This section does not modify or affect any other provision of law that authorizes multiyear contracts.

(Pub.L. 111–350, § 3, Jan. 4, 2011, 124 Stat. 3774.)

CROSS REFERENCES

Full and open competition, defined for subtitle I of this title, see 41 USCA § 107.

§ 3904. Contract authority for severable services contracts and multiyear contracts

(a) Comptroller General.—The Comptroller General may use available funds to enter into contracts for the procurement of severable services for a period that begins in one fiscal year and ends in the next fiscal year and to enter into multiyear contracts for the acquisition of property and nonaudit-related services to the same extent as executive agencies under sections 3902 and 3903 of this title.

(b) Library of Congress.—The Library of Congress may use available funds to enter into contracts for the lease or procurement of severable services for a period that begins in one fiscal year and ends in the next fiscal year and to enter into multiyear contracts for the acquisition of property and services pursuant to sections 3902 and 3903 of this title.

(c) **Chief Administrative Officer of the House of Representatives.**—The Chief Administrative Officer of the House of Representatives may enter into—

(1) contracts for the procurement of severable services for a period that begins in one fiscal year and ends in the next fiscal year to the same extent as the head of an executive agency under the authority of section 3902 of this title; and

(2) multiyear contracts for the acquisitions of property and nonaudit- related services to the same extent as executive agencies under the authority of section 3903 of this title.

(d) **Congressional Budget Office.**—The Congressional Budget Office may use available funds to enter into contracts for the procurement of severable services for a period that begins in one fiscal year and ends in the next fiscal year and may enter into multiyear contracts for the acquisition of property and services to the same extent as executive agencies under the authority of sections 3902 and 3903 of this title.

(e) **Secretary and Sergeant at Arms and Doorkeeper of the Senate.**—Subject to regulations prescribed by the Committee on Rules and Administration of the Senate, the Secretary and the Sergeant at Arms and Doorkeeper of the Senate may enter into—

(1) contracts for the procurement of severable services for a period that begins in one fiscal year and ends in the next fiscal year to the same extent and under the same conditions as the head of an executive agency under the authority of section 3902 of this title; and

(2) multiyear contracts for the acquisition of property and services to the same extent and under the same conditions as executive agencies under the authority of section 3903 of this title.

(f) **Capitol Police.**—The United States Capitol Police may enter into—

(1) contracts for the procurement of severable services for a period that begins in one fiscal year and ends in the next fiscal year to the same extent as the head of an executive agency under the authority of section 3902 of this title; and

(2) multiyear contracts for the acquisitions of property and nonaudit- related services to the same extent as executive agencies under the authority of section 3903 of this title.

(g) **Architect of the Capitol.**—The Architect of the Capitol may enter into—

(1) contracts for the procurement of severable services for a period that begins in one fiscal year and ends in the next fiscal year to the same extent as the head of an executive agency under the authority of section 3902 of this title; and

(2) multiyear contracts for the acquisitions of property and nonaudit- related services to the same extent as executive agencies under the authority of section 3903 of this title.

(h) **Secretary of the Smithsonian Institution.**—The Secretary of the Smithsonian Institution may enter into—

(1) contracts for the procurement of severable services for a period that begins in one fiscal year and ends in the next fiscal year under the authority of section 3902 of this title; and

(2) multiyear contracts for the acquisition of property and services under the authority of section 3903 of this title.

(Pub.L. 111–350, § 3, Jan. 4, 2011, 124 Stat. 3775.)

CROSS REFERENCES

Procurement, defined for subtitle I of this title, see 41 USCA § 111.

§ 3905. Cost contracts

(a) **Cost-plus-a-percentage-of-cost contracts disallowed.**—The cost-plus-a- percentage-of-cost system of contracting shall not be used.

See Main Volume and Repealed Title 41, ante, for annotations

(b) Cost-plus-a-fixed-fee contracts.—

　(1) In general.—Except as provided in paragraphs (2) and (3), the fee in a cost-plus-a-fixed-fee contract shall not exceed 10 percent of the estimated cost of the contract, not including the fee, as determined by the agency head at the time of entering into the contract.

　(2) Experimental, developmental, or research work.—The fee in a cost-plus-a-fixed-fee contract for experimental, developmental, or research work shall not exceed 15 percent of the estimated cost of the contract, not including the fee.

　(3) Architectural or engineering services.—The fee in a cost-plus-a-fixed-fee contract for architectural or engineering services relating to any public works or utility project may include the contractor's costs and shall not exceed 6 percent of the estimated cost, not including the fee, as determined by the agency head at the time of entering into the contract, of the project to which the fee applies.

(c) Notification.—All cost and cost-plus-a-fixed-fee contracts shall provide for advance notification by the contractor to the procuring agency of any subcontract on a cost-plus-a-fixed-fee basis and of any fixed-price subcontract or purchase order which exceeds in dollar amount either the simplified acquisition threshold or 5 percent of the total estimated cost of the prime contract.

(d) Right to audit.—A procuring agency, through any authorized representative thereof, has the right to inspect the plans and to audit the books and records of a prime contractor or subcontractor engaged in the performance of a cost or cost-plus-a-fixed-fee contract.

(Pub.L. 111–350, § 3, Jan. 4, 2011, 124 Stat. 3776.)

CROSS REFERENCES

Agency head, defined for division C of subtitle I of this title, see 41 USCA § 151.

Simplified acquisition threshold, defined for division C of subtitle I of this title, see 41 USCA § 153.

§ 3906.　Cost-reimbursement contracts

(a) Definition.—In this section, the term "executive agency" has the same meaning given in section 133 of this title.

(b) Regulations on the use of cost-reimbursement contracts.—The Federal Acquisition Regulation shall address the use of cost-reimbursement contracts.

(c) Content.—The regulations promulgated under subsection (b) shall include guidance regarding—

　(1) when and under what circumstances cost-reimbursement contracts are appropriate;

　(2) the acquisition plan findings necessary to support a decision to use cost-reimbursement contracts; and

　(3) the acquisition workforce resources necessary to award and manage cost-reimbursement contracts.

(d) Annual report.—

　(1) In general.—The Director of the Office of Management and Budget shall submit an annual report to Congressional committees identified in subsection (e) on the use of cost-reimbursement contracts and task or delivery orders by all executive agencies.

　(2) Contents.—The report shall include—

　　(A) the total number and value of contracts awarded and orders issued during the covered fiscal year;

　　(B) the total number and value of cost-reimbursement contracts awarded and orders issued during the covered fiscal year; and

　　(C) an assessment of the effectiveness of the regulations promulgated pursuant to subsection (b) in ensuring the appropriate use of cost- reimbursement contracts.

　(3) Time requirements.—

(A) **Deadline.**—The report shall be submitted no later than March 1 and shall cover the fiscal year ending September 30 of the prior year.

(B) **Limitation.**—The report shall be submitted from March 1, 2009, until March 1, 2014.

(e) **Congressional committees.**—The report required by subsection (d) shall be submitted to—

(1) the Committee on Oversight and Government Reform of the House of Representatives;

(2) the Committee on Homeland Security and Governmental Affairs of the Senate;

(3) the Committees on Appropriations of the House of Representatives and the Senate; and

(4) in the case of the Department of Defense and the Department of Energy, the Committees on Armed Services of the Senate and the House of Representatives.

(Pub.L. 111–350, § 3, Jan. 4, 2011, 124 Stat. 3777.)

HISTORICAL AND STATUTORY NOTES

Effective Date for Amendment of Federal Acquisition Regulation

Pub.L. 111–350, § 6(f)(5), Jan. 4, 2011, 124 Stat. 3855. provided that: "The Federal Acquisi-

tion Regulation shall be amended to meet the requirements of section 3906(b) of title 41, United States Code, not later than 270 days after October 14, 2008."

CROSS REFERENCES

Federal Acquisition Regulation, defined for subtitle I of this title, functions and general authority, see 41 USCA §§ 106 and 1303.

CHAPTER 41—TASK AND DELIVERY ORDER CONTRACTS

§ 4101. Definitions in this chapter:

(1) **Delivery order contract.**—The term "delivery order .contract" means a contract for property that—

(A) does not procure or specify a firm quantity of property (other than a minimum or maximum quantity); and

(B) provides for the issuance of orders for the delivery of property during the period of the contract.

(2) **Task order contract.**—The term "task order contract" means a contract for services that—

(A) does not procure or specify a firm quantity of services (other than a minimum or maximum quantity); and

(B) provides for the issuance of orders for the performance of tasks during the period of the contract.

(Pub.L. 111–350, § 3, Jan. 4, 2011, 124 Stat. 3778.)

§ 4102. Authorities or responsibilities not affected

This chapter does not modify or supersede, and is not intended to impair or restrict, authorities or responsibilities under sections 1101 to 1104 of title 40.

(Pub.L. 111–350, § 3, Jan. 4, 2011, 124 Stat. 3778.)

See Main Volume and Repealed Title 41, ante, for annotations

§ 4103. General authority

(a) **Authority to award.**—Subject to the requirements of this section, section 4106 of this title, and other applicable law, the head of an executive agency may enter into a task or delivery order contract for procurement of services or property.

(b) **Solicitation.**—The solicitation for a task or delivery order contract shall include—

(1) the period of the contract, including the number of options to extend the contract and the period for which the contract may be extended under each option;

(2) the maximum quantity or dollar value of the services or property to be procured under the contract; and

(3) a statement of work, specifications, or other description that reasonably describes the general scope, nature, complexity, and purposes of the services or property to be procured under the contract.

(c) **Applicability of restriction on use of noncompetitive procedures.**—The head of an executive agency may use procedures other than competitive procedures to enter into a task or delivery order contract under this section only if an exception in section 3304(a) of this title applies to the contract and the use of those procedures is approved in accordance with section 3304(e) of this title.

(d) **Single and multiple contract awards.**—

(1) **Exercise of authority.**—The head of an executive agency may exercise the authority provided in this section—

(A) to award a single task or delivery order contract; or

(B) if the solicitation states that the head of the executive agency has the option to do so, to award separate task or delivery order contracts for the same or similar services or property to 2 or more sources.

(2) **Determination not required.**—No determination under section 3303 of this title is required for an award of multiple task or delivery order contracts under paragraph (1)(B).

(3) **Single source award for task or delivery order contracts exceeding $100,000,000.**—

(A) **When single awards are allowed.**—No task or delivery order contract in an amount estimated to exceed $100,000,000 (including all options) may be awarded to a single source unless the head of the executive agency determines in writing that—

(i) the task or delivery orders expected under the contract are so integrally related that only a single source can reasonably perform the work;

(ii) the contract provides only for firm, fixed price task orders or delivery orders for—

(I) products for which unit prices are established in the contract; or

(II) services for which prices are established in the contract for the specific tasks to be performed;

(iii) only one source is qualified and capable of performing the work at a reasonable price to the Federal Government; or

(iv) because of exceptional circumstances, it is necessary in the public interest to award the contract to a single source.

(B) **Notification of Congress.**—The head of the executive agency shall notify Congress within 30 days after any determination under subparagraph (A)(iv).

(4) **Regulations.**—Regulations implementing this subsection shall establish—

(A) a preference for awarding, to the maximum extent practicable, multiple task or delivery order contracts for the same or similar services or property under paragraph (1)(B); and

(B) criteria for determining when award of multiple task or delivery order contracts would not be in the best interest of the Federal Government.

(e) **Contract modifications.**—A task or delivery order may not increase the scope, period, or maximum value of the task or delivery order contract under which the order is issued. The scope, period, or maximum value of the contract may be increased only by modification of the contract.

(f) **Inapplicability to contracts for advisory and assistance services.**—Except as otherwise specifically provided in section 4105 of this title, this section does not apply to a task or delivery order contract for the acquisition of advisory and assistance services (as defined in section 1105(g) of title 31).

(g) **Relationship to other contracting authority.**—Nothing in this section may be construed to limit or expand any authority of the head of an executive agency or the Administrator of General Services to enter into schedule, multiple award, or task or delivery order contracts under any other provision of law.

(Pub.L. 111–350, § 3, Jan. 4, 2011, 124 Stat. 3778.)

CROSS REFERENCES

Competitive procedures, defined for division C of subtitle I of this title, see 41 USCA § 152.

Procurement, defined for subtitle I of this title, see 41 USCA § 111.

§ 4104. Guidance on use of task and delivery order contracts

(a) **Guidance in Federal Acquisition Regulation.**—The Federal Acquisition Regulation issued in accordance with sections 1121(b) and 1303(a)(1) of this title shall provide guidance to agencies on the appropriate use of task and delivery order contracts in accordance with this chapter and sections 2304a to 2304d of title 10.

(b) **Content of regulations.**—The regulations issued pursuant to subsection (a) at a minimum shall provide specific guidance on—

   (1) the appropriate use of Government–wide and other multiagency contracts entered into in accordance with this chapter and sections 2304a to 2304d of title 10; and

   (2) steps that agencies should take in entering into and administering multiple award task and delivery order contracts to ensure compliance with the requirement in—

      (A) section 11312 of title 40 for capital planning and investment control in purchases of information technology products and services;

      (B) section 4106(c) of this title and section 2304c(b) of title 10 to ensure that all contractors are afforded a fair opportunity to be considered for the award of task and delivery orders; and

      (C) section 4106(e) of this title and section 2304c(c) of title 10 for a statement of work in each task or delivery order issued that clearly specifies all tasks to be performed or property to be delivered under the order.

(c) **Federal supply schedules program.**—The Administrator for Federal Procurement Policy shall consult with the Administrator of General Services to assess the effectiveness of the multiple awards schedule program of the General Services Administration referred to in section 152(3) of this title that is administered as the Federal Supply Schedules program. The assessment shall include examination of—

   (1) the administration of the program by the Administrator of General Services; and

   (2) the ordering and program practices followed by Federal customer agencies in using schedules established under the program.

(Pub.L. 111–350, § 3, Jan. 4, 2011, 124 Stat. 3780.)

CROSS REFERENCES

Federal Acquisition Regulation, defined for subtitle I of this title, functions and general authority, see 41 USCA §§ 106 and 1303.

See Main Volume and Repealed Title 41, ante, for annotations

§ 4105. Advisory and assistance services

(a) **Definition.**—In this section, the term "advisory and assistance services" has the same meaning given that term in section 1105(g) of title 31.

(b) **Authority to award.**—

(1) **In general.**—Subject to the requirements of this section, section 4106 of this title, and other applicable law, the head of an executive agency may enter into a task order contract for procurement of advisory and assistance services.

(2) **Only under this section.**—The head of an executive agency may enter into a task order contract for advisory and assistance services only under this section.

(c) **Contract period.**—The period of a task order contract entered into under this section, including all periods of extensions of the contract under options, modifications, or otherwise, may not exceed 5 years unless a longer period is specifically authorized in a law that is applicable to the contract.

(d) **Content of notice.**—The notice required by section 1708 of this title and section 8(e) of the Small Business Act (15 U.S.C. 637(e)) shall reasonably and fairly describe the general scope, magnitude, and duration of the proposed task order contract in a manner that would reasonably enable a potential offeror to decide whether to request the solicitation and consider submitting an offer.

(e) **Required content of solicitation and contract.**—

(1) **Solicitation.**—The solicitation shall include the information (regarding services) described in section 4103(b) of this title.

(2) **Contract.**—A task order contract entered into under this section shall contain the same information that is required by paragraph (1) to be included in the solicitation of offers for that contract.

(f) **Multiple awards.**—

(1) **Authority to make multiple awards.**—On the basis of one solicitation, the head of an executive agency may award separate task order contracts under this section for the same or similar services to 2 or more sources if the solicitation states that the head of the executive agency has the option to do so.

(2) **Content of solicitation.**—In the case of a task order contract for advisory and assistance services to be entered into under this section, if the contract period is to exceed 3 years and the contract amount is estimated to exceed $10,000,000 (including all options), the solicitation shall—

(A) provide for a multiple award authorized under paragraph (1); and

(B) include a statement that the head of the executive agency may also elect to award only one task order contract if the head of the executive agency determines in writing that only one of the offerors is capable of providing the services required at the level of quality required.

(3) **Nonapplication.**—Paragraph (2) does not apply in the case of a solicitation for which the head of the executive agency concerned determines in writing that, because the services required under the contract are unique or highly specialized, it is not practicable to award more than one contract.

(g) **Contract modifications.**—

(1) **Increase in scope, period, or maximum value of contract only by modification of contract.**—A task order may not increase the scope, period, or maximum value of the task order contract under which the order is issued. The scope, period, or maximum value of the contract may be increased only by modification of the contract.

(2) **Use of competitive procedures.**—Unless use of procedures other than competitive procedures is authorized by an exception in section 3304(a) of this title and approved in accordance with section 3304(e) of this title, competitive procedures shall be used for making such a modification.

(3) **Notice.**—Notice regarding the modification shall be provided in accordance with section 1708 of this title and section 8(e) of the Small Business Act (15 U.S.C. 637(e)).

(h) Contract extensions.—

(1) **When contract may be extended.**—Notwithstanding the limitation on the contract period set forth in subsection (c) or in a solicitation or contract pursuant to subsection (f), a contract entered into by the head of an executive agency under this section may be extended on a sole-source basis for a period not exceeding 6 months if the head of the executive agency determines that—

(A) the award of a follow-on contract has been delayed by circumstances that were not reasonably foreseeable at the time the initial contract was entered into; and

(B) the extension is necessary to ensure continuity of the receipt of services pending the award of, and commencement of performance under, the follow-on contract.

(2) **Limit of one extension.**—A task order contract may be extended under paragraph (1) only once and only in accordance with the limitations and requirements of this subsection.

(i) Inapplicability to certain contracts.—This section does not apply to a contract for the acquisition of property or services that includes acquisition of advisory and assistance services if the head of the executive agency entering into the contract determines that, under the contract, advisory and assistance services are necessarily incident to, and not a significant component of, the contract.

(Pub.L. 111–350, § 3, Jan. 4, 2011, 124 Stat. 3780.)

HISTORICAL AND STATUTORY NOTES

References in Text

The Small Business Act, referred to in subsecs. (d), (g)(3), is Act July 18, 1958, Pub.L. 85–536, 72 Stat. 384, as amended, also known as the SBA, which is principally classified to chapter 14A of Title 15, 15 U.S.C.A. § 631 et seq. Section 8 of the Act is classified to 15 U.S.C.A. § 637. For complete classification, see Short Title note set out under 15 U.S.C.A. § 631 and Tables.

CROSS REFERENCES

Competitive procedures, defined for division C of subtitle I of this title, see 41 USCA § 152.

Procurement, defined for subtitle I of this title, see 41 USCA § 111.

§ 4106. Orders

(a) **Application.**—This section applies to task and delivery order contracts entered into under sections 4103 and 4105 of this title.

(b) **Actions not required for issuance of orders.**—The following actions are not required for issuance of a task or delivery order under a task or delivery order contract:

(1) A separate notice for the order under section 1708 of this title or section 8(e) of the Small Business Act (15 U.S.C. 637(e)).

(2) Except as provided in subsection (c), a competition (or a waiver of competition approved in accordance with section 3304(e) of this title) that is separate from that used for entering into the contract.

(c) **Multiple award contracts.**—When multiple contracts are awarded under section 4103(d)(1)(B) or 4105(f) of this title, all contractors awarded the contracts shall be provided a fair opportunity to be considered, pursuant to procedures set forth in the contracts, for each task or delivery order in excess of $2,500 that is to be issued under any of the contracts, unless—

(1) the executive agency's need for the services or property ordered is of such unusual urgency that providing the opportunity to all of those contractors would result in unacceptable delays in fulfilling that need;

(2) only one of those contractors is capable of providing the services or property required at the level of quality required because the services or property ordered are unique or highly specialized;

(3) the task or delivery order should be issued on a sole-source basis in the interest of economy and efficiency because it is a logical follow-on to a task or delivery order already issued on a competitive basis; or

(4) it is necessary to place the order with a particular contractor to satisfy a minimum guarantee.

(d) **Enhanced competition for orders in excess of $5,000,000.**—In the case of a task or delivery order in excess of $5,000,000, the requirement to provide all contractors a fair opportunity to be considered under subsection (c) is not met unless all such contractors are provided, at a minimum—

(1) a notice of the task or delivery order that includes a clear statement of the executive agency's requirements;

(2) a reasonable period of time to provide a proposal in response to the notice;

(3) disclosure of the significant factors and subfactors, including cost or price, that the executive agency expects to consider in evaluating such proposals, and their relative importance;

(4) in the case of an award that is to be made on a best value basis, a written statement documenting—

(A) the basis for the award; and

(B) the relative importance of quality and price or cost factors; and

(5) an opportunity for a post-award debriefing consistent with the requirements of section 3704 of this title.

(e) **Statement of work.**—A task or delivery order shall include a statement of work that clearly specifies all tasks to be performed or property to be delivered under the order.

(f) **Protests.**—

(1) **Protest not authorized.**—A protest is not authorized in connection with the issuance or proposed issuance of a task or delivery order except for—

(A) a protest on the ground that the order increases the scope, period, or maximum value of the contract under which the order is issued; or

(B) a protest of an order valued in excess of $10,000,000.

(2) **Jurisdiction over protests.**—Notwithstanding section 3556 of title 31, the Comptroller General shall have exclusive jurisdiction of a protest authorized under paragraph (1)(B).

(3) **Effective period.**—This subsection shall be in effect for three years, beginning on the date that is 120 days after January 28, 2008.

(g) **Task and delivery order ombudsman.**—

(1) **Appointment or designation and responsibilities.**—The head of each executive agency who awards multiple task or delivery order contracts under section 4103(d)(1)(B) or 4105(f) of this title shall appoint or designate a task and delivery order ombudsman who shall be responsible for reviewing complaints from the contractors on those contracts and ensuring that all of the contractors are afforded a fair opportunity to be considered for task or delivery orders when required under subsection (c).

(2) **Who is eligible.**—The task and delivery order ombudsman shall be a senior agency official who is independent of the contracting officer for the contracts and may be the executive agency's advocate for competition.

(Pub.L. 111–350, § 3, Jan. 4, 2011, 124 Stat. 3782; Pub.L. 111–383, Div. A, Title X, § 1075(f)(5)(B), Jan. 7, 2011, 124 Stat. 4376.)

Amendment Subsequent to December 31, 2008

Pub.L. 111–350, Jan. 4, 2011, 124 Stat. 3677, which codified T. 41, Public Contracts, as positive law, directed that if a law enacted after Dec. 31, 2008, amends or repeals a provision replaced by Pub.L. 111–350, that law is deemed to amend or repeal, as the case may be, the corresponding provision enacted by Pub.L. 111–350, see Pub.L. 111–350, § 6(a), Jan. 4, 2011, 124 Stat. 3854, set out as a note provision preceding 41 U.S.C.A. § 101.

Pub.L. 111–383, Div. A, Title X, § 1075(f)(5)(B), Jan. 7, 2011, 124 Stat. 4376, amended directory language of Pub.L. 110–181, § 843(b)(2)(C), which amended former 41 U.S.C.A. § 253j, from which this section was derived, resulting in no change in text.

HISTORICAL AND STATUTORY NOTES

References in Text

The Small Business Act, referred to in subsec. (b)(1), is Act July 18, 1958, Pub.L. 85–536, 72 Stat. 384, as amended, also known as the SBA, which is principally classified to chapter 14A of Title 15, 15 U.S.C.A. § 631 et seq. Section 8 of the Act is classified to 15 U.S.C.A. § 637. For complete classification, see Short Title note set out under 15 U.S.C.A. § 631 and Tables.

CHAPTER 43—ALLOWABLE COSTS

§ 4301. Definitions

In this chapter:

(1) Compensation.—The term "compensation", for a fiscal year, means the total amount of wages, salary, bonuses, and deferred compensation for the fiscal year, whether paid, earned, or otherwise accruing, as recorded in an employer's cost accounting records for the fiscal year.

(2) Covered contract.—The term "covered contract" means a contract for an amount in excess of $500,000 that is entered into by an executive agency, except that the term does not include a fixed-price contract without cost incentives or any firm fixed-price contract for the purchase of commercial items.

(3) Fiscal year.—The term "fiscal year" means a fiscal year established by a contractor for accounting purposes.

(4) Senior executive.—The term "senior executive", with respect to a contractor, means the 5 most highly compensated employees in management positions at each home office and each segment of the contractor.

(Pub.L. 111–350, § 3, Jan. 4, 2011, 124 Stat. 3784.)

CROSS REFERENCES

Commercial item, defined for subtitle I of this title, see 41 USCA § 103.

§ 4302. Adjustment of threshold amount of covered contract

Effective on October 1 of each year that is divisible by 5, the amount set forth in section 4301(2) of this title shall be adjusted to the equivalent amount in constant fiscal year 1994 dollars. An adjusted amount that is not evenly divisible by $50,000 shall be rounded to the nearest multiple of $50, 000. If an amount is evenly divisible by $25,000 but is not evenly divisible by $50,000, the amount shall be rounded to the next higher multiple of $50,000.

(Pub.L. 111–350, § 3, Jan. 4, 2011, 124 Stat. 3784.)

§ 4303. Effect of submission of unallowable costs

(a) Indirect cost that violates Federal acquisition regulation cost principle.—An executive agency shall require that a covered contract provide that if the contractor submits to the executive agency a proposal for settlement of indirect costs incurred by the contractor for any period after those costs have been accrued and if that proposal includes the submission of a cost that is unallowable because the cost violates a cost principle in the Federal Acquisition Regulation or an executive agency supplement to the Federal Acquisition Regulation, the cost shall be disallowed.

(b) Penalty for violation of cost principle.—

(1) Unallowable cost in proposal.—If the executive agency determines that a cost submitted by a contractor in its proposal for settlement is expressly unallowable under a cost principle referred to in subsection (a) that defines the allowability of specific selected costs, the executive agency shall assess a penalty against the contractor in an amount equal to—

    (A) the amount of the disallowed cost allocated to covered contracts for which a proposal for settlement of indirect costs has been submitted; plus

    (B) interest (to be computed based on provisions in the Federal Acquisition Regulation) to compensate the Federal Government for the use of the amount which a contractor has been paid in excess of the amount to which the contractor was entitled.

(2) Cost determined to be unallowable before proposal submitted.—If the executive agency determines that a proposal for settlement of indirect costs submitted by a contractor includes a cost determined to be unallowable in the case of that contractor before the submission of that proposal, the executive agency shall assess a penalty against the contractor in an amount equal to 2 times the amount of the disallowed cost allocated to covered contracts for which a proposal for settlement of indirect costs has been submitted.

(c) Waiver of penalty.—The Federal Acquisition Regulation shall provide for a penalty under subsection (b) to be waived in the case of a contractor's proposal for settlement of indirect costs when—

    (1) the contractor withdraws the proposal before the formal initiation of an audit of the proposal by the Federal Government and resubmits a revised proposal;

    (2) the amount of unallowable costs subject to the penalty is insignificant; or

    (3) the contractor demonstrates, to the contracting officer's satisfaction, that—

        (A) it has established appropriate policies and personnel training and an internal control and review system that provide assurances that unallowable costs subject to penalties are precluded from being included in the contractor's proposal for settlement of indirect costs; and

        (B) the unallowable costs subject to the penalty were inadvertently incorporated into the proposal.

(d) Applicability of contract disputes procedure.—An action of an executive agency under subsection (a) or (b)—

    (1) shall be considered a final decision for the purposes of section 7103 of this title; and

    (2) is appealable in the manner provided in section 7104(a) of this title.

(Pub.L. 111–350, § 3, Jan. 4, 2011, 124 Stat. 3784.)

CROSS REFERENCES

Federal Acquisition Regulation, defined for subtitle I of this title, functions and general authority, see 41 USCA §§ 106 and 1303.

§ 4304. Specific costs not allowable

(a) Specific costs.—The following costs are not allowable under a covered contract:

    (1) Costs of entertainment, including amusement, diversion, and social activities, and any costs directly associated with those costs (such as tickets to shows or sports events, meals, lodging, rentals, transportation, and gratuities).

    (2) Costs incurred to influence (directly or indirectly) legislative action on any matter pending before Congress, a State legislature, or a legislative body of a political subdivision of a State.

    (3) Costs incurred in defense of any civil or criminal fraud proceeding or similar proceeding (including filing of any false certification) brought by the Federal Government where the contractor is found liable or had pleaded nolo contendere to a charge of fraud or similar proceeding (including filing of a false certification).

(4) Payments of fines and penalties resulting from violations of, or failure to comply with, Federal, State, local, or foreign laws and regulations, except when incurred as a result of compliance with specific terms and conditions of the contract or specific written instructions from the contracting officer authorizing in advance those payments in accordance with applicable provisions of the Federal Acquisition Regulation.

(5) Costs of membership in any social, dining, or country club or organization.

(6) Costs of alcoholic beverages.

(7) Contributions or donations, regardless of the recipient.

(8) Costs of advertising designed to promote the contractor or its products.

(9) Costs of promotional items and memorabilia, including models, gifts, and souvenirs.

(10) Costs for travel by commercial aircraft that exceed the amount of the standard commercial fare.

(11) Costs incurred in making any payment (commonly known as a "golden parachute payment") that is—

    (A) in an amount in excess of the normal severance pay paid by the contractor to an employee on termination of employment; and

    (B) paid to the employee contingent on, and following, a change in management control over, or ownership of, the contractor or a substantial portion of the contractor's assets.

(12) Costs of commercial insurance that protects against the costs of the contractor for correction of the contractor's own defects in materials or workmanship.

(13) Costs of severance pay paid by the contractor to foreign nationals employed by the contractor under a service contract performed outside the United States, to the extent that the amount of severance pay paid in any case exceeds the amount paid in the industry involved under the customary or prevailing practice for firms in that industry providing similar services in the United States, as determined under the Federal Acquisition Regulation.

(14) Costs of severance pay paid by the contractor to a foreign national employed by the contractor under a service contract performed in a foreign country if the termination of the employment of the foreign national is the result of the closing of, or the curtailment of activities at, a Federal Government facility in that country at the request of the government of that country.

(15) Costs incurred by a contractor in connection with any criminal, civil, or administrative proceeding commenced by the Federal Government or a State, to the extent provided in section 4310 of this title.

(16) Costs of compensation of senior executives of contractors for a fiscal year, regardless of the contract funding source, to the extent that the compensation exceeds the benchmark compensation amount determined applicable for the fiscal year by the Administrator under section 1127 of this title.

(b) Waiver of severance pay restrictions for foreign nationals.—

(1) **Executive agency determination.—**Pursuant to the Federal Acquisition Regulation and subject to the availability of appropriations, an executive agency, in awarding a covered contract, may waive the application of paragraphs (13) and (14) of subsection (a) to that contract if the executive agency determines that—

    (A) the application of those provisions to that contract would adversely affect the continuation of a program, project, or activity that provides significant support services for employees of the executive agency posted outside the United States;

    (B) the contractor has taken (or has established plans to take) appropriate actions within the contractor's control to minimize the amount and number of incidents of the payment of severance pay by the contractor to employees under the contract who are foreign nationals; and

    (C) the payment of severance pay is necessary to comply with a law that is generally applicable to a significant number of businesses in the country in which the foreign national receiving the payment performed services under the contract or is necessary to comply with a collective bargaining agreement.

(2) Solicitation to include statement about waiver.—An executive agency shall include in the solicitation for a covered contract a statement indicating—

(A) that a waiver has been granted under paragraph (1) for the contract; or

(B) whether the executive agency will consider granting a waiver and, if the executive agency will consider granting a waiver, the criteria to be used in granting the waiver.

(3) Determination to be made before contract awarded.—An executive agency shall make the final determination whether to grant a waiver under paragraph (1) with respect to a covered contract before award of the contract.

(c) Establishment of definitions, exclusions, limitations, and qualifications.— The provisions of the Federal Acquisition Regulation implementing this chapter may establish appropriate definitions, exclusions, limitations, and qualifications. A submission by a contractor of costs that are incurred by the contractor and that are claimed to be allowable under Department of Energy management and operating contracts shall be considered a proposal for settlement of indirect costs incurred by the contractor for any period after those costs have been accrued.

(Pub.L. 111–350, § 3, Jan. 4, 2011, 124 Stat. 3785.)

HISTORICAL AND STATUTORY NOTES

Revision of Cost Principle Relating to Entertainment, Gift, and Recreation Costs for Contractor Employees

Pub.L. 103–355, § 2192, Oct. 13, 1994, 108 Stat. 3315, provided that:

"**(a) Costs not allowable.**—(1) The costs of gifts or recreation for employees of a contractor or members of their families that are provided by the contractor to improve employee morale or performance or for any other purpose are not allowable under a covered contract unless, within 120 days after the date of the enactment of this Act [Oct. 13, 1994], the Federal Acquisition Regulatory Council prescribes amendments to the Federal Acquisition Regulation specifying circumstances under which such costs are allowable under a covered contract.

"(2) Not later than 90 days after the date of the enactment of this Act [Oct. 13, 1994], the Federal Acquisition Regulatory Council shall amend the cost principle in the Federal Acquisition Regulation that is set out in section 31.205–14 of title 48, Code of Federal Regulations, relating to unallowability of entertainment costs—

"(A) by inserting in the cost principle a statement that costs made specifically unallowable under that cost principle are not allowable under any other cost principle; and

"(B) by striking out '(but see 31.205–1 and 31.205–13)'.

"**(b) Definitions.**—In this section:

"(1) The term 'employee' includes officers and directors of a contractor.

"(2) The term 'covered contract' has the meaning given such term in section 2324(l) of title 10, United States Code (as amended by section 2101(c) ([section 2324(l) of Title 10, Armed Forces], and section 306(1) of the Federal Property and Administrative Services Act of 1949 (as added by section 2151) [subsec. (l) of former 41 U.S.C.A. § 256].

"**(c) Effective date.**—Any amendments to the Federal Acquisition Regulation made pursuant to subsection (a) shall apply with respect to costs incurred after the date on which the amendments made by section 2101 apply (as provided in section 10001 [Oct. 1, 1995, or earlier, see section 10001 of Pub.L. 103–355, set out as a note under section 251 of this title]) or the date on which the amendments made by section 2151 apply (as provided in section 10001 [Oct. 1, 1995, or earlier, see section 10001 of Pub.L. 103–355]), whichever is later."

[Note was classified as a note under former 41 U.S.C.A. § 256 prior to the enactment into positive law of Title 41, Public Contracts, by Pub.L. 111–350, Jan. 4, 2011, 124 Stat. 3677.]

EXECUTIVE ORDERS
EXECUTIVE ORDER NO. 13494

Jan. 30, 2009, 74 F.R. 6101, as amended Ex. Ord. No. 13517, Sec. 2, Oct. 30, 2009, 74 F.R. 57239

ECONOMY IN GOVERNMENT CONTRACTING

By the authority vested in me as President by the Constitution and the laws of the United States of America, including the Federal Prop-erty and Administrative Services Act, 40 U.S.C. 101et seq., it is hereby ordered that:

Section 1. To promote economy and efficiency in Government contracting, certain costs that are not directly related to the contractors' provision of goods and services to the Government shall be unallowable for payment, thereby directly reducing Government expenditures. This order is also consistent with the policy of the United States to remain impartial concerning any labor-management dispute involving Government contractors. This order does not restrict the manner in which recipients of Federal funds may expend those funds.

Sec. 2. It is the policy of the executive branch in procuring goods and services that, to ensure the economical and efficient administration of Government contracts, contracting departments and agencies, when they enter into, receive proposals for, or make disbursements pursuant to a contract as to which certain costs are treated as unallowable, shall treat as unallowable the costs of any activities undertaken to persuade employees—whether employees of the recipient of the Federal disbursements or of any other entity—to exercise or not to exercise, or concerning the manner of exercising, the right to organize and bargain collectively through representatives of the employees' own choosing. Such unallowable costs shall be excluded from any billing, claim, proposal, or disbursement applicable to any such Federal Government contract.

Sec. 3. Contracting departments and agencies shall treat as allowable costs incurred in maintaining satisfactory relations between the contractor and its employees (other than the costs of any activities undertaken to persuade employees to exercise or not to exercise, or concerning the manner of exercising, the right to organize and bargain collectively), including costs of labor management committees, employee publications, and other related activities. See 48 C.F.R. 31.205–21.

Sec. 4. Examples of costs unallowable under section 2 of this order include the costs of the following activities, when they are undertaken to persuade employees to exercise or not to exercise, or concern the manner of exercising, rights to organize and bargain collectively:

(a) preparing and distributing materials;

(b) hiring or consulting legal counsel or consultants;

(c) holding meetings (including paying the salaries of the attendees at meetings held for this purpose); and

(d) planning or conducting activities by managers, supervisors, or union representatives during work hours.

Sec. 5. Within 150 days of the effective date of this order, the Federal Acquisition Regulatory Council (FAR Council) shall adopt such rules and regulations and issue such orders as are deemed necessary and appropriate to carry out this order. Such rules, regulations, and orders shall minimize the costs of compliance for contractors and shall not interfere with the ability of contractors to engage in advocacy through activities for which they do not claim reimbursement.

Sec. 6. Each contracting department or agency shall cooperate with the FAR Council and provide such information and assistance as the FAR Council may require in the performance of its functions under this order.

Sec. 7. (a) This order shall be implemented consistent with applicable law and subject to the availability of appropriations.

(b) This order is not intended to, and does not, create any right or benefit, substantive or procedural, enforceable at law or in equity by any party against the United States, its departments, agencies, or entities, its officers, employees, or agents, or any other person.

Sec. 8. This order shall become effective immediately, and shall apply to contracts resulting from solicitations issued on or after the effective date of the action taken by the FAR Council under section 5 of this order.

BARACK OBAMA

[Order was set out under former 41 U.S.C.A. § 256 prior to the enactment into positive law of Title 41, Public Contracts, by Pub.L. 111–350, Jan. 4, 2011, 124 Stat. 3677.]

CROSS REFERENCES

Federal Acquisition Regulation, defined for subtitle I of this title, functions and general authority, see 41 USCA §§ 106 and 1303.

§ 4305. Required regulations

(a) In general.—The Federal Acquisition Regulation shall contain provisions on the allowability of contractor costs. Those provisions shall define in detail and in specific terms the costs that are unallowable, in whole or in part, under covered contracts.

(b) Specific items.—The regulations shall, at a minimum, clarify the cost principles applicable to contractor costs of the following:

(1) Air shows.

(2) Membership in civic, community, and professional organizations.

(3) Recruitment.

(4) Employee morale and welfare.

See Main Volume and Repealed Title 41, ante, for annotations

(5) Actions to influence (directly or indirectly) executive branch action on regulatory and contract matters (other than costs incurred in regard to contract proposals pursuant to solicited or unsolicited bids).

(6) Community relations.

(7) Dining facilities.

(8) Professional and consulting services, including legal services.

(9) Compensation.

(10) Selling and marketing.

(11) Travel.

(12) Public relations.

(13) Hotel and meal expenses.

(14) Expense of corporate aircraft.

(15) Company–furnished automobiles.

(16) Advertising.

(17) Conventions.

(c) **Additional requirements.—**

(1) **When questioned costs may be resolved.**—The Federal Acquisition Regulation shall require that a contracting officer not resolve any questioned costs until the contracting officer has obtained—

(A) adequate documentation of those costs; and

(B) the opinion of the contract auditor on the allowability of those costs.

(2) **Presence of contract auditor.**—The Federal Acquisition Regulation shall provide that, to the maximum extent practicable, a contract auditor be present at any negotiation or meeting with the contractor regarding a determination of the allowability of indirect costs of the contractor.

(3) **Settlement to reflect amount of individual questioned costs.**—The Federal Acquisition Regulation shall require that all categories of costs designated in the report of a contract auditor as questioned with respect to a proposal for settlement be resolved in a manner so that the amount of the individual questioned costs that are paid will be reflected in the settlement.

(Pub.L. 111–350, § 3, Jan. 4, 2011, 124 Stat. 3787.)

CROSS REFERENCES

Federal Acquisition Regulation, defined for subtitle I of this title, functions and general authority, see 41 USCA §§ 106 and 1303.

§ 4306. Applicability of regulations to subcontractors

The regulations referred to in sections 4304 and 4305(a) and (b) of this title shall require prime contractors of a covered contract, to the maximum extent practicable, to apply the provisions of those regulations to all subcontractors of the covered contract.

(Pub.L. 111–350, § 3, Jan. 4, 2011, 124 Stat. 3788.)

§ 4307. Contractor certification

(a) **Content and form.**—A proposal for settlement of indirect costs applicable to a covered contract shall include a certification by an official of the contractor that, to the best of the certifying official's knowledge and belief, all indirect costs included in the proposal are allowable. The certification shall be in a form prescribed in the Federal Acquisition Regulation.

(b) **Waiver.**—An executive agency may, in an exceptional case, waive the requirement for certification under subsection (a) in the case of a contract if the agency—

(1) determines that it would be in the interest of the Federal Government to waive the certification; and

(2) states in writing the reasons for the determination and makes the determination available to the public.

(Pub.L. 111–350, § 3, Jan. 4, 2011, 124 Stat. 3788.)

§ 4308. Penalties for submission of cost known to be unallowable

The submission to an executive agency of a proposal for settlement of costs for any period after those costs have been accrued that includes a cost that is expressly specified by statute or regulation as being unallowable, with the knowledge that the cost is unallowable, is subject to section 287 of title 18 and section 3729 of title 31.

(Pub.L. 111–350, § 3, Jan. 4, 2011, 124 Stat. 3788.)

§ 4309. Burden of proof on contractor

In a proceeding before a board of contract appeals, the United States Court of Federal Claims, or any other Federal court in which the reasonableness of indirect costs for which a contractor seeks reimbursement from the Federal Government is in issue, the burden of proof is on the contractor to establish that those costs are reasonable.

(Pub.L. 111–350, § 3, Jan. 4, 2011, 124 Stat. 3788.)

§ 4310. Proceeding costs not allowable

(a) **Definitions**—In this section:

(1) **Costs.**—The term "costs", with respect to a proceeding, means all costs incurred by a contractor, whether before or after the commencement of the proceeding, including—

(A) administrative and clerical expenses;

(B) the cost of legal services, including legal services performed by an employee of the contractor;

(C) the cost of the services of accountants and consultants retained by the contractor; and

(D) the pay of directors, officers, and employees of the contractor for time devoted by those directors, officers, and employees to the proceeding.

(2) **Penalty.**—The term "penalty" does not include restitution, reimbursement, or compensatory damages.

(3) **Proceeding.**—The term "proceeding" includes an investigation.

(b) **In general.**—Except as otherwise provided in this section, costs incurred by a contractor in connection with a criminal, civil, or administrative proceeding commenced by the Federal Government or a State are not allowable as reimbursable costs under a covered contract if the proceeding—

(1) relates to a violation of, or failure to comply with, a Federal or State statute or regulation; and

(2) results in a disposition described in subsection (c).

(c) **Covered dispositions.**—A disposition referred to in subsection (b)(2) is any of the following:

(1) In a criminal proceeding, a conviction (including a conviction pursuant to a plea of nolo contendere) by reason of the violation or failure referred to in subsection (b).

See Main Volume and Repealed Title 41, ante, for annotations

(2) In a civil or administrative proceeding involving an allegation of fraud or similar misconduct, a determination of contractor liability on the basis of the violation or failure referred to in subsection (b).

(3) In any civil or administrative proceeding, the imposition of a monetary penalty by reason of the violation or failure referred to in subsection (b).

(4) A final decision to do any of the following, by reason of the violation or failure referred to in subsection (b):

    (A) Debar or suspend the contractor.

    (B) Rescind or void the contract.

    (C) Terminate the contract for default.

(5) A disposition of the proceeding by consent or compromise if the disposition could have resulted in a disposition described in paragraph (1), (2), (3), or (4).

(d) Costs allowed by settlement agreement in proceeding commenced by Federal Government.—In the case of a proceeding referred to in subsection (b) that is commenced by the Federal Government and is resolved by consent or compromise pursuant to an agreement entered into by a contractor and the Federal Government, the costs incurred by the contractor in connection with the proceeding that are otherwise not allowable as reimbursable costs under subsection (b) may be allowed to the extent specifically provided in that agreement.

(e) Costs specifically authorized by executive agency in proceeding commenced by state.—In the case of a proceeding referred to in subsection (b) that is commenced by a State, the executive agency that awarded the covered contract involved in the proceeding may allow the costs incurred by the contractor in connection with the proceeding as reimbursable costs if the executive agency determines, in accordance with the Federal Acquisition Regulation, that the costs were incurred as a result of—

(1) a specific term or condition of the contract; or

(2) specific written instructions of the executive agency.

(f) Other allowable costs.—

(1) **In general.**—Except as provided in paragraph (3), costs incurred by a contractor in connection with a criminal, civil, or administrative proceeding commenced by the Federal Government or a State in connection with a covered contract may be allowed as reimbursable costs under the contract if the costs are not disallowable under subsection (b), but only to the extent provided in paragraph (2).

(2) **Amount of allowable costs.**—

    (A) **Maximum amount allowed.**—The amount of the costs allowable under paragraph (1) in any case may not exceed the amount equal to 80 percent of the amount of the costs incurred, to the extent that the costs are determined to be otherwise allowable and allocable under the Federal Acquisition Regulation.

    (B) **Content of regulations.**—Regulations issued for the purpose of subparagraph (A) shall provide for appropriate consideration of the complexity of procurement litigation, generally accepted principles governing the award of legal fees in civil actions involving the Federal Government as a party, and other factors as may be appropriate.

(3) **When otherwise allowable costs are not allowable.**—In the case of a proceeding referred to in paragraph (1), contractor costs otherwise allowable as reimbursable costs under this subsection are not allowable if—

    (A) the proceeding involves the same contractor misconduct alleged as the basis of another criminal, civil, or administrative proceeding; and

    (B) the costs of the other proceeding are not allowable under subsection (b).

(Pub.L. 111–350, § 3, Jan. 4, 2011, 124 Stat. 3789.)

CROSS REFERENCES

Procurement, defined for subtitle I of this title, see 41 USCA § 111.

Revised Title 41 effective Jan. 4, 2011

CHAPTER 45—CONTRACT FINANCING

§ 4501. Authority of executive agency

An executive agency may—

(1) make advance, partial, progress or other payments under contracts for property or services made by the agency; and

(2) insert in solicitations for procurement of property or services a provision limiting to small business concerns advance or progress payments.

(Pub.L. 111–350, § 3, Jan. 4, 2011, 124 Stat. 3790.)

HISTORICAL AND STATUTORY NOTES

Relationship Between 1994 Amendments and Prompt Payment Requirements

Section 2051(f) of Pub.L. 103–355 provided that: "The amendments made by this section [amending former 41 U.S.C.A. § 255] are not intended to impair or modify procedures required by the provisions of chapter 39 of title 31, United States Code [section 3901 et seq. of Title 31, Money and Finance], and the regulations issued pursuant to such provisions of law (as

such procedures are in effect on the date of the enactment of this Act [Oct. 13, 1994]), except that the Government may accept payment terms offered by a contractor offering a commercial item."

[Note was classified as a note under former 41 U.S.C.A. § 255 prior to the enactment into positive law of Title 41, Public Contracts, by Pub.L. 111–350, Jan. 4, 2011, 124 Stat. 3677.]

CROSS REFERENCES

Procurement, defined for subtitle I of this title, see 41 USCA § 111.

§ 4502. Payment

(a) **Basis for payment.**—When practicable, payments under section 4501 of this title shall be made on any of the following bases:

(1) Performance measured by objective, quantifiable methods such as delivery of acceptable items, work measurement, or statistical process controls.

(2) Accomplishment of events defined in the program management plan.

(3) Other quantifiable measures of results.

(b) **Payment amount.**—Payments made under section 4501 of this title may not exceed the unpaid contract price.

(Pub.L. 111–350, § 3, Jan. 4, 2011, 124 Stat. 3791.)

CROSS REFERENCES

Item and item of supply, defined for subtitle I of this title, see 41 USCA § 108.

Item and item of supply, defined for subtitle I of this title, see 41 USCA § 108.

§ 4503. Security for advance payments

Advance payments under section 4501 of this title may be made only on adequate security and a determination by the agency head that to do so would be in the public interest. The security may be in the form of a lien in favor of the Federal Government on the property contracted for, on the balance in an account in which the payments are deposited, and on such of the property acquired for performance of the contract as the parties may agree. This lien shall be paramount to all other liens and is effective immediately upon the first advancement of funds without filing, notice, or any other action by the Federal Government.

(Pub.L. 111–350, § 3, Jan. 4, 2011, 124 Stat. 3791.)

See Main Volume and Repealed Title 41, ante, for annotations

CROSS REFERENCES

Agency head, defined for division C of subtitle
I of this title, see 41 USCA § 151.

§ 4504. Conditions for progress payments

(a) Payment commensurate with work.—The executive agency shall ensure that a payment for work in progress (including materials, labor, and other items) under a contract of an executive agency that provides for those payments is commensurate with the work accomplished that meets standards established under the contract. The contractor shall provide information and evidence the executive agency determines is necessary to permit the executive agency to carry out this subsection.

(b) Limitation.—The executive agency shall ensure that progress payments referred to in subsection (a) are not made for more than 80 percent of the work accomplished under the contract as long as the executive agency has not made the contractual terms, specifications, and price definite.

(c) Application.—This section applies to a contract in an amount greater than $25,000.

(Pub.L. 111–350, § 3, Jan. 4, 2011, 124 Stat. 3791.)

CROSS REFERENCES

Item and item of supply, defined for subtitle I of this title, see 41 USCA § 108.

Standards, defined for subtitle I of this title, see 41 USCA § 114.

§ 4505. Payments for commercial items

(a) Terms and conditions for payments.—Payments under section 4501 of this title for commercial items may be made under terms and conditions that the head of the executive agency determines are appropriate or customary in the commercial marketplace and are in the best interests of the Federal Government.

(b) Security for payments.—The head of the executive agency shall obtain adequate security for the payments. If the security is in the form of a lien in favor of the Federal Government, the lien is paramount to all other liens and is effective immediately on the first payment, without filing, notice, or other action by the Federal Government.

(c) Limitation on advance payments.—Advance payments made under section 4501 of this title for commercial items may include payments, in a total amount not more than 15 percent of the contract price, in advance of any performance of work under the contract.

(d) Nonapplication of certain conditions.—The conditions of sections 4503 and 4504 of this title need not be applied if they would be inconsistent, as determined by the head of the executive agency, with commercial terms and conditions pursuant to this section.

(Pub.L. 111–350, § 3, Jan. 4, 2011, 124 Stat. 3791.)

CROSS REFERENCES

Commercial item, defined for subtitle I of this title, see 41 USCA § 103.

§ 4506. Action in case of fraud

(a) Definition.—In this section, the term "remedy coordination official", with respect to an executive agency, means the individual or entity in that executive agency who coordinates within that executive agency the administration of criminal, civil, administrative, and contractual remedies resulting from investigations of fraud or corruption related to procurement activities.

(b) Recommendation to reduce or suspend payments.—In any case in which the remedy coordination official of an executive agency finds that there is substantial evidence that the request of a contractor for advance, partial, or progress payment under a contract awarded by that executive agency is based on fraud, the remedy coordination official shall recommend that the executive agency reduce or suspend further payments to that contractor.

(c) Reduction or suspension of payments.—The head of an executive agency receiving a recommendation under subsection (b) in the case of a contractor's request for payment under a contract shall determine whether there is substantial evidence that the request is based on fraud. On making an affirmative determination, the head of the executive agency may reduce or suspend further payments to the contractor under the contract.

(d) Extent of reduction or suspension.—The extent of any reduction or suspension of payments by an executive agency under subsection (c) on the basis of fraud shall be reasonably commensurate with the anticipated loss to the Federal Government resulting from the fraud.

(e) Written justification.—A written justification for each decision of the head of an executive agency whether to reduce or suspend payments under subsection (c), and for each recommendation received by the executive agency in connection with the decision, shall be prepared and be retained in the files of the executive agency.

(f) Notice.—The head of each executive agency shall prescribe procedures to ensure that, before the head of the executive agency decides to reduce or suspend payments in the case of a contractor under subsection (c), the contractor is afforded notice of the proposed reduction or suspension and an opportunity to submit matters to the executive agency in response to the proposed reduction or suspension.

(g) Review.—Not later than 180 days after the date on which the head of an executive agency reduces or suspends payments to a contractor under subsection (c), the remedy coordination official of the executive agency shall—

(1) review the determination of fraud on which the reduction or suspension is based; and

(2) transmit a recommendation to the head of the executive agency whether the suspension or reduction should continue.

(h) Report.—The head of each executive agency who receives recommendations made by the remedy coordination official of the executive agency to reduce or suspend payments under subsection (c) during a fiscal year shall prepare for that year a report that contains the recommendations, the actions taken on the recommendations and the reasons for those actions, and an assessment of the effects of those actions on the Federal Government. The report shall be available to any Member of Congress on request.

(i) Restriction on delegation.—The head of an executive agency may not delegate responsibilities under this section to an individual in a position below level IV of the Executive Schedule.

(Pub.L. 111–350, § 3, Jan. 4, 2011, 124 Stat. 3792.)

CROSS REFERENCES

Procurement, defined for subtitle I of this title, see 41 USCA § 111.

CHAPTER 47—MISCELLANEOUS

See Main Volume and Repealed Title 41, ante, for annotations

Sec.
4711.   Linking of award and incentive fees to
             acquisition outcomes.

§ 4701.   Determinations and decisions

(a) Individual or class determinations and decisions authorized.—

(1) In general.—Determinations and decisions required to be made under this division by the head of an executive agency or provided in this division or chapters 1 to 11 of title 40 to be made by the Administrator of General Services or other agency head may be made for an individual purchase or contract or, except for determinations or decisions made under sections 3105, 3301, 3303 to 3305, 3306(a)–(e), and 3308, chapter 37, and section 4702 of this title or to the extent expressly prohibited by another law, for a class of purchases or contracts.

(2) Delegation.—Except as provided in section 3304(a)(7) of this title, and except as provided in section 121(d)(1) and (2) of title 40 with respect to the Administrator of General Services, the agency head, in the discretion and subject to the direction of the agency head, may delegate powers provided by this division or chapters 1 to 11 of title 40, including the making of determinations and decisions described in paragraph (1), to other officers or officials of the agency.

(3) Finality.—The determinations and decisions are final.

(b) Written findings.—

(1) Basis for certain determinations.—Each determination or decision under section 3901, 3905, 4503, or 4706(d)(2)(B) of this title shall be based on a written finding by the individual making the determination or decision. A finding under section 4503 or 4706(d)(2)(B) shall set out facts and circumstances that support the determination or decision.

(2) Finality.—Each finding referred to in paragraph (1) is final.

(3) Maintaining copies of findings.—The head of an executive agency shall maintain for a period of not less than 6 years a copy of each finding referred to in paragraph (1) that is made by an individual in that executive agency. The period begins on the date of the determination or decision to which the finding relates.

(Pub.L. 111–350, § 3, Jan. 4, 2011, 124 Stat. 3793.)

HISTORICAL AND STATUTORY NOTES

References in Text

Chapters 1 to 11 of title 40, referred to in subsec. (a)(1), (2), are classified to 40 U.S.C.A. § 101 et seq. to 40 U.S.C.A. § 1101 et seq.

Chapter 37 of this title, referred to in subsec. (a)(1), is classified to 41 U.S.C.A. § 3701 et seq.

CROSS REFERENCES

Agency head, defined for division C of subtitle I of this title, see 41 USCA § 151.

§ 4702.   Prohibition on release of contractor proposals

(a) Definition.—In this section, the term "proposal" means a proposal, including a technical, management, or cost proposal, submitted by a contractor in response to the requirements of a solicitation for a competitive proposal.

(b) Prohibition.—A proposal in the possession or control of an executive agency may not be made available to any person under section 552 of title 5.

(c) Nonapplication.—Subsection (b) does not apply to a proposal that is set forth or incorporated by reference in a contract entered into between the agency and the contractor that submitted the proposal.

(Pub.L. 111–350, § 3, Jan. 4, 2011, 124 Stat. 3794.)

§ 4703.   Validation of proprietary data restrictions

(a) Contract that provides for delivery of technical data.—A contract for property or services entered into by an executive agency that provides for the delivery of technical data shall provide that—

(1) a contractor or subcontractor at any tier shall be prepared to furnish to the contracting officer a written justification for any restriction the contractor or subcontractor asserts on the right of the Federal Government to use the data; and

(2) the contracting officer may review the validity of a restriction the contractor or subcontractor asserts under the contract on the right of the Federal Government to use technical data furnished to the Federal Government under the contract if the contracting officer determines that reasonable grounds exist to question the current validity of the asserted restriction and that the continued adherence to the asserted restriction by the Federal Government would make it impracticable to procure the item competitively at a later time.

(b) Challenge of restriction.—If after a review the contracting officer determines that a challenge to the asserted restriction is warranted, the contracting officer shall provide written notice to the contractor or subcontractor asserting the restriction. The notice shall state—

(1) the grounds for challenging the asserted restriction; and

(2) the requirement for a response within 60 days justifying the current validity of the asserted restriction.

(c) Additional time for responses.—If a contractor or subcontractor asserting a restriction subject to this section submits to the contracting officer a written request showing the need for additional time to comply with the requirement to justify the current validity of the asserted restriction, the contracting officer shall provide appropriate additional time to adequately permit the justification to be submitted.

(d) Multiple challenges.—If a party asserting a restriction receives notices of challenges to restrictions on technical data from more than one contracting officer, and notifies each contracting officer of the existence of more than one challenge, the contracting officer initiating the earliest challenge, after consultation with the party asserting the restriction and the other contracting officers, shall formulate a schedule of responses to each of the challenges that will afford the party asserting the restriction with an equitable opportunity to respond to each challenge.

(e) Decision on validity of asserted restriction.—

(1) **No response submitted.**—The contracting officer shall issue a decision pertaining to the validity of the asserted restriction if the contractor or subcontractor does not submit a response under subsection (b).

(2) **Response submitted.**—Within 60 days of receipt of a justification submitted in response to the notice provided pursuant to subsection (b), a contracting officer shall issue a decision or notify the party asserting the restriction of the time within which a decision will be issued.

(f) Claim deemed claim within chapter 71.—A claim pertaining to the validity of the asserted restriction that is submitted in writing to a contracting officer by a contractor or subcontractor at any tier is deemed to be a claim within the meaning of chapter 71 of this title.

(g) Final disposition of challenge.—

(1) **Challenge is sustained.**—If the contracting officer's challenge to the restriction on the right of the Federal Government to use technical data is sustained on final disposition—

(A) the restriction is cancelled; and

(B) if the asserted restriction is found not to be substantially justified, the contractor or subcontractor, as appropriate, is liable to the Federal Government for payment of the cost to the Federal Government of reviewing the asserted restriction and the fees and other expenses (as defined in section 2412(d)(2)(A) of title 28) incurred by the Federal Government in challenging the asserted restriction, unless special circumstances would make the payment unjust.

(2) **Challenge not sustained.**—If the contracting officer's challenge to the restriction on the right of the Federal Government to use technical data is not sustained on final disposition, the Federal Government—

(A) continues to be bound by the restriction; and

(B) is liable for payment to the party asserting the restriction for fees and other expenses (as defined in section 2412(d)(2)(A) of title 28) incurred by the party asserting the restriction in defending the asserted restriction if the challenge by the Federal Government is found not to be made in good faith.

(Pub.L. 111–350, § 3, Jan. 4, 2011, 124 Stat. 3794.)

HISTORICAL AND STATUTORY NOTES

References in Text

Chapter 71 of this title, referred to in subsec. (f), is classified to 41 U.S.C.A. § 7101 et seq.

CROSS REFERENCES

Item and item of supply, defined for subtitle I of this title, see 41 USCA § 108.

Technical data, defined for subtitle I of this title, see 41 USCA § 116.

§ 4704. Prohibition of contractors limiting subcontractor sales directly to Federal Government

(a) Contract restrictions.—Each contract for the purchase of property or services made by an executive agency shall provide that the contractor will not—

(1) enter into an agreement with a subcontractor under the contract that has the effect of unreasonably restricting sales by the subcontractor directly to the Federal Government of any item or process (including computer software) made or furnished by the subcontractor under the contract (or any follow-on production contract); or

(2) otherwise act to restrict unreasonably the ability of a subcontractor to make sales described in paragraph (1) to the Federal Government.

(b) Rights under law preserved.—This section does not prohibit a contractor from asserting rights it otherwise has under law.

(c) Inapplicability to certain contracts.—This section does not apply to a contract for an amount that is not greater than the simplified acquisition threshold.

(d) Inapplicability when Government treated similarly to other purchasers. —An agreement between the contractor in a contract for the acquisition of commercial items and a subcontractor under the contract that restricts sales by the subcontractor directly to persons other than the contractor may not be considered to unreasonably restrict sales by that subcontractor to the Federal Government in violation of the provision included in the contract pursuant to subsection (a) if the agreement does not result in the Federal Government being treated differently with regard to the restriction than any other prospective purchaser of the commercial items from that subcontractor.

(Pub.L. 111–350, § 3, Jan. 4, 2011, 124 Stat. 3795.)

CROSS REFERENCES

Commercial item, defined for subtitle I of this title, see 41 USCA § 103.

Item and item of supply, defined for subtitle I of this title, see 41 USCA § 108.

Simplified acquisition threshold, defined for division C of subtitle I of this title, see 41 USCA § 153.

§ 4705. Protection of contractor employees from reprisal for disclosure of certain information

(a) Definitions.—In this section:

(1) Contract.—The term "contract" means a contract awarded by the head of an executive agency.

(2) Contractor.—The term "contractor" means a person awarded a contract with an executive agency.

(3) Inspector General.—The term "Inspector General" means an Inspector General appointed under the Inspector General Act of 1978 (5 U.S.C. App.).

(b) Prohibition of reprisals.—An employee of a contractor may not be discharged, demoted, or otherwise discriminated against as a reprisal for disclosing to a Member of

Congress or an authorized official of an executive agency or the Department of Justice information relating to a substantial violation of law related to a contract (including the competition for, or negotiation of, a contract).

(c) **Investigation of complaints.**—An individual who believes that the individual has been subjected to a reprisal prohibited by subsection (b) may submit a complaint to the Inspector General of the executive agency. Unless the Inspector General determines that the complaint is frivolous, the Inspector General shall investigate the complaint and, on completion of the investigation, submit a report of the findings of the investigation to the individual, the contractor concerned, and the head of the agency. If the executive agency does not have an Inspector General, the duties of the Inspector General under this section shall be performed by an official designated by the head of the executive agency.

(d) **Remedy and enforcement authority.**—

(1) **Actions contractor may be ordered to take.**—If the head of an executive agency determines that a contractor has subjected an individual to a reprisal prohibited by subsection (b), the head of the executive agency may take one or more of the following actions:

(A) **Abatement.**—Order the contractor to take affirmative action to abate the reprisal.

(B) **Reinstatement.**—Order the contractor to reinstate the individual to the position that the individual held before the reprisal, together with the compensation (including back pay), employment benefits, and other terms and conditions of employment that would apply to the individual in that position if the reprisal had not been taken.

(C) **Payment.**—Order the contractor to pay the complainant an amount equal to the aggregate amount of all costs and expenses (including attorneys' fees and expert witnesses' fees) that the complainant reasonably incurred for, or in connection with, bringing the complaint regarding the reprisal, as determined by the head of the executive agency.

(2) **Enforcement order.**—When a contractor fails to comply with an order issued under paragraph (1), the head of the executive agency shall file an action for enforcement of the order in the United States district court for a district in which the reprisal was found to have occurred. In an action brought under this paragraph, the court may grant appropriate relief, including injunctive relief and compensatory and exemplary damages.

(3) **Review of enforcement order.**—A person adversely affected or aggrieved by an order issued under paragraph (1) may obtain review of the order's conformance with this subsection, and regulations issued to carry out this section, in the United States court of appeals for a circuit in which the reprisal is alleged in the order to have occurred. A petition seeking review must be filed no more than 60 days after the head of the agency issues the order. Review shall conform to chapter 7 of title 5.

(e) **Scope of section.**—This section does not—

(1) authorize the discharge of, demotion of, or discrimination against an employee for a disclosure other than a disclosure protected by subsection (b); or

(2) modify or derogate from a right or remedy otherwise available to the employee.

(Pub.L. 111–350, § 3, Jan. 4, 2011, 124 Stat. 3796.)

HISTORICAL AND STATUTORY NOTES

References in Text

The Inspector General Act of 1978, referred to in subsec. (a)(3), is Pub.L. 95–452, Oct. 12, 1978, 92 Stat. 1101, as amended, which is set out as 5 App. 3 U.S.C.A. § 1 et seq.

Chapter 7 of title 5, referred to in subsec. (d)(3), is classified to 5 U.S.C.A. § 701 et seq.

§ 4706. Examination of facilities and records of contractor

(a) **Definition.**—In this section, the term "records" includes books, documents, accounting procedures and practices, and other data, regardless of type and regardless of whether the items are in written form, in the form of computer data, or in any other form.

(b) Agency authority.—

(1) Inspection of plant and audit of records.—The head of an executive agency, acting through an authorized representative, may inspect the plant and audit the records of—

(A) a contractor performing a cost-reimbursement, incentive, time-and- materials, labor-hour, or price-redeterminable contract, or any combination of those contracts, the executive agency makes under this division; and

(B) a subcontractor performing a cost-reimbursement, incentive, time-and-materials, labor-hour, or price-redeterminable subcontract, or any combination of those subcontracts, under a contract referred to in subparagraph (A).

(2) Examination of records.—The head of an executive agency, acting through an authorized representative, may, for the purpose of evaluating the accuracy, completeness, and currency of certified cost or pricing data required to be submitted pursuant to chapter 35 of this title with respect to a contract or subcontract, examine all records of the contractor or subcontractor related to—

(A) the proposal for the contract or subcontract;

(B) the discussions conducted on the proposal;

(C) pricing of the contract or subcontract; or

(D) performance of the contract or subcontract.

(c) Subpoena power.—

(1) Authority to require the production of records.—The Inspector General of an executive agency appointed under section 3 or 8G of the Inspector General Act of 1978 (5 U.S.C. App.) or, on request of the head of an executive agency, the Director of the Defense Contract Audit Agency (or any successor agency) of the Department of Defense or the Inspector General of the General Services Administration may require by subpoena the production of records of a contractor, access to which is provided for that executive agency by subsection (b).

(2) Enforcement of subpoena.—A subpoena under paragraph (1), in the case of contumacy or refusal to obey, is enforceable by order of an appropriate United States district court.

(3) Authority not delegable.—The authority provided by paragraph (1) may not be delegated.

(4) Report.—In the year following a year in which authority provided in paragraph (1) is exercised for an executive agency, the head of the executive agency shall submit to the Committee on Homeland Security and Governmental Affairs of the Senate and the Committee on Oversight and Government Reform of the House of Representatives a report on the exercise of the authority during the preceding year and the reasons why the authority was exercised in any instance.

(d) Authority of Comptroller General.—

(1) In general.—Except as provided in paragraph (2), each contract awarded after using procedures other than sealed bid procedures shall provide that the Comptroller General and representatives of the Comptroller General may examine records of the contractor, or any of its subcontractors, that directly pertain to, and involve transactions relating to, the contract or subcontract and to interview any current employee regarding the transactions.

(2) Exception for foreign contractor or subcontractor.—Paragraph (1) does not apply to a contract or subcontract with a foreign contractor or foreign subcontractor if the executive agency concerned determines, with the concurrence of the Comptroller General or the designee of the Comptroller General, that applying paragraph (1) to the contract or subcontract would not be in the public interest. The concurrence of the Comptroller General or the designee is not required when—

(A) the contractor or subcontractor is—

(i) the government of a foreign country or an agency of that government; or

    (ii) precluded by the laws of the country involved from making its records available for examination; and

    (B) the executive agency determines, after taking into account the price and availability of the property and services from United States sources, that the public interest would be best served by not applying paragraph (1).

    (3) Additional records not required.—Paragraph (1) does not require a contractor or subcontractor to create or maintain a record that the contractor or subcontractor does not maintain in the ordinary course of business or pursuant to another law.

  (e) Limitation on audits relating to indirect costs.—An executive agency may not perform an audit of indirect costs under a contract, subcontract, or modification before or after entering into the contract, subcontract, or modification when the contracting officer determines that the objectives of the audit can reasonably be met by accepting the results of an audit that was conducted by another department or agency of the Federal Government within one year preceding the date of the contracting officer's determination.

  (f) Expiration of authority.—The authority of an executive agency under subsection (b) and the authority of the Comptroller General under subsection (d) shall expire 3 years after final payment under the contract or subcontract.

  (g) Inapplicability to certain contracts.—This section does not apply to the following contracts:

    (1) Contracts for utility services at rates not exceeding those established to apply uniformly to the public, plus any applicable reasonable connection charge.

    (2) A contract or subcontract that is not greater than the simplified acquisition threshold.

  (h) Electronic form allowed.—This section does not preclude a contractor from duplicating or storing original records in electronic form.

  (i) Original records not required.—An executive agency shall not require a contractor or subcontractor to provide original records in an audit carried out pursuant to this section if the contractor or subcontractor provides photographic or electronic images of the original records and meets the following requirements:

    (1) Preservation procedures established.—The contractor or subcontractor has established procedures to ensure that the imaging process preserves the integrity, reliability, and security of the original records.

    (2) Indexing system maintained.—The contractor or subcontractor maintains an effective indexing system to permit timely and convenient access to the imaged records.

    (3) Original records retained.—The contractor or subcontractor retains the original records for a minimum of one year after imaging to permit periodic validation of the imaging systems.

(Pub.L. 111–350, § 3, Jan. 4, 2011, 124 Stat. 3797.)

HISTORICAL AND STATUTORY NOTES

References in Text

  Chapter 35 of this title, referred to in subsec. (b)(2), is classified to 41 U.S.C.A. § 3501 et seq.

  The Inspector General Act of 1978, referred to in subsec. (c)(1), is Pub.L. 95–452, Oct. 12, 1978, 92 Stat. 1101, as amended, which is set out as 5 App. 3 U.S.C.A. § 1 et seq. Sections 3 and 8G of the Act are classified to 5 App. 3 U.S.C.A. §§ 3 and 8G, respectively.

CROSS REFERENCES

Armed Forces procurement, examination of records of contractor, see 10 USCA § 2313.

  Item and item of supply, defined for subtitle I of this title, see 41 USCA § 108.

Simplified acquisition threshold, defined for division C of subtitle I of this title, see 41 USCA § 153.

§ 4707. Remission of liquidated damages

  When a contract made on behalf of the Federal Government by the head of a Federal agency, or by an authorized officer of the agency, includes a provision for liquidated damages for delay, the Secretary of the Treasury on recommendation of the head of the agency may remit any part of the damages as the Secretary of the Treasury believes is just and equitable.

(Pub.L. 111–350, § 3, Jan. 4, 2011, 124 Stat. 3799.)

CROSS REFERENCES

Armed Forces procurement, remission of liquidated damages, see 10 USCA § 2312.

§ 4708. Payment of reimbursable indirect costs in cost-type research and development contracts with educational institutions

A cost-type research and development contract (including a grant) with a university, college, or other educational institution may provide for payment of reimbursable indirect costs on the basis of predetermined fixed-percentage rates applied to the total of the reimbursable direct costs incurred or to an element of the total of the reimbursable direct costs incurred.

(Pub.L. 111–350, § 3, Jan. 4, 2011, 124 Stat. 3799.)

§ 4709. Implementation of electronic commerce capability

(a) Role of head of executive agency.—The head of each executive agency shall implement the electronic commerce capability required by section 2301 of this title. In implementing the capability, the head of an executive agency shall consult with the Administrator.

(b) Program manager.—The head of each executive agency shall designate a program manager to implement the electronic commerce capability for the agency. The program manager reports directly to an official at a level not lower than the senior procurement executive designated for the agency under section 1702(c) of this title.

(Pub.L. 111–350, § 3, Jan. 4, 2011, 124 Stat. 3800.)

CROSS REFERENCES

Administrator, defined for subtitle I of this title, see 41 USCA § 101.

§ 4710. Limitations on tiering of subcontractors

(a) Definition.—In this section, the term "executive agency" has the same meaning given in section 133 of this title.

(b) Regulations.—For executive agencies other than the Department of Defense, the Federal Acquisition Regulation shall—

    (1) require contractors to minimize the excessive use of subcontractors, or of tiers of subcontractors, that add no or negligible value; and

    (2) ensure that neither a contractor nor a subcontractor receives indirect costs or profit on work performed by a lower-tier subcontractor to which the higher-tier contractor or subcontractor adds no or negligible value (but not to limit charges for indirect costs and profit based on the direct costs of managing lower-tier subcontracts).

(c) Covered contracts.—This section applies to any cost-reimbursement type contract or task or delivery order in an amount greater than the simplified acquisition threshold (as defined by section 134 of this title).

(d) Rule of construction.—Nothing in this section shall be construed as limiting the ability of the Department of Defense to implement more restrictive limitations on the tiering of subcontractors.

(e) Applicability.—The Department of Defense shall continue to be subject to guidance on limitations on tiering of subcontractors issued by the Department of

Defense pursuant to section 852 of the John Warner National Defense Authorization Act for Fiscal Year 2007 (Public Law 109–364, 10 U.S.C. 2324 note).

(Pub.L. 111–350, § 3, Jan. 4, 2011, 124 Stat. 3800.)

HISTORICAL AND STATUTORY NOTES

References in Text

The John Warner National Defense Authorization Act for Fiscal Year 2007, referred to in subsec. (e), is Pub.L. 109–364, Oct. 17, 2006, 120 Stat. 2083, also known as the National Defense Authorization Act for Fiscal Year 2007. Section 852 of the Act is set out as a note under 10 U.S.C.A. § 2324. For complete classification, see Tables.

Effective Date for Amendment of Federal Acquisition Regulation

Pub.L. 111–350, § 6(f)(4), provided that the Federal Acquisition Regulation shall be amended to meet the requirements of subsec. (b) of this section not later than one year after Oct. 14, 2008, see Pub.L. 111–350, § 6(f)(4), set out as a note under 41 U.S.C.A. § 2313.

CROSS REFERENCES

Federal Acquisition Regulation, defined for subtitle I of this title, functions and general authority, see 41 USCA §§ 106 and 1303.

Simplified acquisition threshold, defined for division C of subtitle I of this title, see 41 USCA § 153.

§ 4711. Linking of award and incentive fees to acquisition outcomes

(a) Definition.—In this section, the term "executive agency" has the same meaning given in section 133 of this title.

(b) Guidance for executive agencies on linking of award and incentive fees to acquisition outcomes.—The Federal Acquisition Regulation shall provide executive agencies other than the Department of Defense with instructions, including definitions, on the appropriate use of award and incentive fees in Federal acquisition programs.

(c) Elements.—The regulations under subsection (b) shall—

(1) ensure that all new contracts using award fees link the fees to acquisition outcomes (which shall be defined in terms of program cost, schedule, and performance);

(2) establish standards for identifying the appropriate level of officials authorized to approve the use of award and incentive fees in new contracts;

(3) provide guidance on the circumstances in which contractor performance may be judged to be "excellent" or "superior" and the percentage of the available award fee which contractors should be paid for the performance;

(4) establish standards for determining the percentage of the available award fee, if any, which contractors should be paid for performance that is judged to be "acceptable", "average", "expected", "good", or "satisfactory";

(5) ensure that no award fee may be paid for contractor performance that is judged to be below satisfactory performance or performance that does not meet the basic requirements of the contract;

(6) provide specific direction on the circumstances, if any, in which it may be appropriate to roll over award fees that are not earned in one award fee period to a subsequent award fee period or periods;

(7) ensure consistent use of guidelines and definitions relating to award and incentive fees across the Federal Government;

(8) ensure that each executive agency—

(A) collects relevant data on award and incentive fees paid to contractors; and

(B) has mechanisms in place to evaluate the data on a regular basis;

(9) include performance measures to evaluate the effectiveness of award and incentive fees as a tool for improving contractor performance and achieving desired program outcomes; and

(10) provide mechanisms for sharing proven incentive strategies for the acquisition of different types of products and services among contracting and program management officials.

See Main Volume and Repealed Title 41, ante, for annotations

(d) Guidance for Department of Defense.—The Department of Defense shall continue to be subject to guidance on award and incentive fees issued by the Secretary of Defense pursuant to section 814 of the John Warner National Defense Authorization Act for Fiscal Year 2007 (Public Law 109–364, 10 U.S.C. 2302 note).

(Pub.L. 111–350, § 3, Jan. 4, 2011, 124 Stat. 3800.)

HISTORICAL AND STATUTORY NOTES

References in Text

The John Warner National Defense Authorization Act for Fiscal Year 2007, referred to in subsec. (d), is Pub.L. 109–364, Oct. 17, 2006, 120 Stat. 2083, also known as the National Defense Authorization Act for Fiscal Year 2007. Section 814 of the Act is set out as a note under 10 U.S.C.A. § 2302. For complete classification, see Tables.

Effective Date for Amendment of Federal Acquisition Regulation

Pub.L. 111–350, § 6(f)(4), provided that the Federal Acquisition Regulation shall be amended to meet the requirements of subsec. (b) of this section not later than one year after Oct. 14, 2008, see Pub.L. 111–350, § 6(f)(4), set out as a note under 41 U.S.C.A. § 2313.

CROSS REFERENCES

Federal Acquisition Regulation, defined for subtitle I of this title, functions and general authority, see 41 USCA §§ 106 and 1303.

Standards, defined for subtitle I of this title, see 41 USCA § 114.

SUBTITLE II—OTHER ADVERTISING AND CONTRACT PROVISIONS

CHAPTER 61—ADVERTISING

§ 6101. Advertising requirement for Federal Government purchases and sales

(a) Definitions.—In this section—

(1) Appropriation.—The term "appropriation" includes amounts made available by legislation under section 9104 of title 31.

(2) Federal Government.—The term "Federal Government" includes the government of the District of Columbia.

(b) Purchases.—

(1) In general.—Unless otherwise provided in the appropriation concerned or other law, purchases and contracts for supplies or services for the Federal Government may be made or entered into only after advertising for proposals for a sufficient time.

(2) Limitations on applicability.—Paragraph (1) does not apply when—

(A) the amount involved in any one case does not exceed $25,000;

(B) public exigencies require the immediate delivery of articles or performance of services;

(C) only one source of supply is available and the Federal Government purchasing or contracting officer so certifies; or

(D) services are required to be performed by a contractor in person and are—

 (i) of a technical and professional nature; or

 (ii) under Federal Government supervision and paid for on a time basis.

(c) **Sales.**—Except when otherwise authorized by law or when the reasonable value involved in any one case does not exceed $500, sales and contracts of sale by the Federal Government are governed by the requirements of this section for advertising.

(d) **Application to wholly owned Government corporations.**—For wholly owned Government corporations, this section applies only to administrative transactions.

(Pub.L. 111–350, § 3, Jan. 4, 2011, 124 Stat. 3801.)

§ 6102. Exceptions from advertising requirement

(a) **American Battle Monuments Commission.**—Section 6101 of this title does not apply to the American Battle Monuments Commission with respect to leases in foreign countries for office or garage space.

(b) **Bureau of Interparliamentary Union for Promotion of International Arbitration.**—Section 6101 of this title does not apply to the Bureau of Interparliamentary Union for Promotion of International Arbitration with respect to necessary stenographic reporting services by contract.

(c) **Department of State.**—Section 6101 of this title does not apply to the Department of State when the purchase or service relates to the packing of personal and household effects of Diplomatic, Consular, and Foreign Service officers and clerks for foreign shipment.

(d) **International Committee of Aerial Legal Experts.**—Section 6101 of this title does not apply to the International Committee of Aerial Legal Experts with respect to necessary stenographic and other services by contract.

(e) **Architect of the Capitol.**—The purchase of supplies and equipment and the procurement of services for all branches under the Architect of the Capitol may be made in the open market according to common business practice, without compliance with section 6101 of this title, when the aggregate amount of the purchase or the service does not exceed $25,000 in any instance.

(f) **Forest products from Indian reservations.**—Lumber and other forest products produced by Indian enterprises from forests on Indian reservations may be sold under regulations the Secretary of the Interior prescribes, without compliance with section 6101 of this title.

(g) **House of Representatives.**—Section 6101 of this title does not apply to purchases and contracts for supplies or services for any office of the House of Representatives.

(h) **Congressional Budget Office.**—The Director of the Congressional Budget Office may enter into agreements or contracts without regard to section 6101 of this title.

(Pub.L. 111–350, § 3, Jan. 4, 2011, 124 Stat. 3802.)

§ 6103. Opening of bids

Whenever proposals for supplies have been solicited, the parties responding to the solicitation shall be notified of the time and place of the opening of the bids, and be permitted to be present either in person or by attorney. A record of each bid shall be made at the time and place of the opening of the bids.

(Pub.L. 111–350, § 3, Jan. 4, 2011, 124 Stat. 3803.)

CHAPTER 63—GENERAL CONTRACT PROVISIONS

See Main Volume and Repealed Title 41, ante, for annotations

§ 6301. Authorization requirement

(a) **In general.**—A contract or purchase on behalf of the Federal Government shall not be made unless the contract or purchase is authorized by law or is under an appropriation adequate to its fulfillment.

(b) **Exception.**—

    (1) **Definition.**—In this subsection, the term "defined Secretary" means—

        (A) the Secretary of Defense; or

        (B) the Secretary of Homeland Security with respect to the Coast Guard when the Coast Guard is not operating as a service in the Navy.

    (2) **In general.**—Subsection (a) does not apply to a contract or purchase made by a defined Secretary for clothing, subsistence, forage, fuel, quarters, transportation, or medical and hospital supplies.

    (3) **Current year limitation.**—A contract or purchase made by a defined Secretary under this subsection may not exceed the necessities of the current year.

    (4) **Reports.**—The defined Secretary shall immediately advise Congress when authority is exercised under this subsection. The defined Secretary shall report quarterly on the estimated obligations incurred pursuant to the authority granted in this subsection.

(c) **Special rule for purchase of land.**—Land may not be purchased by the Federal Government unless the purchase is authorized by law.

(Pub.L. 111–350, § 3, Jan. 4, 2011, 124 Stat. 3803; Pub.L. 111–281, Title IX, § 903(a)(4), Oct. 15, 2010, 124 Stat. 3010.)

Amendment Subsequent to December 31, 2008

Pub.L. 111–350, Jan. 4, 2011, 124 Stat. 3677, which codified T. 41, Public Contracts, as positive law, directed that if a law enacted after Dec. 31, 2008 amends or repeals a provision replaced by Pub.L. 111–350, that law is deemed to amend or repeal, as the case may be, the corresponding provision enacted by Pub.L. 111–350, see Pub.L. 111–350, § 6(a), Jan. 4, 2011, 124 Stat. 3854, set out as a note provision preceding 41 U.S.C.A. § 101.

Pub.L. 111–281, Title IX, § 903(a)(4), Oct. 15, 2010, 124 Stat. 3010, amended Pub.L. 109–241, § 902(c), which amended former 41 U.S.C.A. § 11, from which this section was derived, by amending directory language of Pub.L. 109–241, § 902(c), which resulted in no change in text.

Amendments

  2010 Amendments. Subsec. (c). Pub.L. 111–281, § 903(a)(4), amended directory language of Pub.L. 109–241, § 902(c), which resulted in no change in text.

Effective and Applicability Provisions

  2010 Acts. Amendments by Pub.L. 111–281, § 903(a) to Pub.L. 109–241 are effective with enactment of Pub.L. 109–241, July 11, 2006, see Pub.L. 111–281, § 903(a), set out in part as a note under 16 U.S.C.A. § 460kkk.

§ 6302. Contracts for fuel made by Secretary of the Army

The Secretary of the Army, when the Secretary believes it is in the interest of the United States, may enter into contracts and incur obligations for fuel in sufficient quantities to meet the requirements for one year without regard to the current fiscal year. Amounts appropriated for the fiscal year in which the contract is made or amounts appropriated or which may be appropriated for the following fiscal year may be used to pay for supplies delivered under a contract made pursuant to this section.

(Pub.L. 111–350, § 3, Jan. 4, 2011, 124 Stat. 3804.)

§ 6303. Certain contracts limited to appropriated amounts

A contract to erect, repair, or furnish a public building, or to make any public improvement, shall not be made on terms requiring the Federal Government to pay more than the amount specifically appropriated for the activity covered by the contract.

(Pub.L. 111–350, § 3, Jan. 4, 2011, 124 Stat. 3804.)

§ 6304. Certain contracts limited to one-year term

Except as otherwise provided, an executive department shall not make a contract for stationery or other supplies for a term longer than one year from the time the contract is made.

(Pub.L. 111–350, § 3, Jan. 4, 2011, 124 Stat. 3804.)

§ 6305. Prohibition on transfer of contract and certain allowable assignments

(a) **General prohibition on transfer of contracts.**—The party to whom the Federal Government gives a contract or order may not transfer the contract or order, or any interest in the contract or order, to another party. A purported transfer in violation of this subsection annuls the contract or order so far as the Federal Government is concerned, except that all rights of action for breach of contract are reserved to the Federal Government.

(b) **Assignment.**—

(1) **In general.**—Notwithstanding subsection (a) and in accordance with the requirements of this subsection, amounts due from the Federal Government under a contract may be assigned to a bank, trust company, Federal lending agency, or other financing institution.

(2) **Minimum amount.**—This subsection applies only to a contract under which the aggregate amounts due from the Federal Government total at least $1,000.

(3) **Accord with contract terms.**—Assignment may not be made under this subsection if the contract forbids the assignment.

(4) **Full balance due.**—Unless otherwise expressly permitted by the contract, an assignment under this subsection must cover the balance of all amounts due from the Federal Government under the contract.

(5) **Single assignment.**—Unless otherwise expressly permitted by the contract, an assignment under this subsection may not be made to more than one party or be subject to further assignment, except that assignment may be made to one party as agent or trustee for 2 or more parties participating in the financing.

(6) **Written notice.**—The assignee of an assignment under this subsection shall file written notice of the assignment and a true copy of the instrument of assignment with—

(A) the contracting officer or head of the officer's department or agency;

(B) the surety on any bond connected with the contract; and

(C) the disbursing officer, if any, designated in the contract to make payment.

(7) **Validity.**—Notwithstanding any law to the contrary governing the validity of assignments, an assignment under this subsection is a valid assignment for all purposes.

(8) **No refund to cover assignor's liability.**—The assignee of an assignment under this subsection is not liable to make any refund to the Federal Government because of an assignor's liability to the Federal Government, whether that liability arises from the contract or independently.

(9) **Avoiding reduction or setoff with certain contracts.**—

See Main Volume and Repealed Title 41, ante, for annotations

(A) **Contract provision.**—A contract of the Department of Defense, the General Services Administration, the Department of Energy, or another department or agency of the Federal Government designated by the President may, on a determination of need by the President, provide or be amended without consideration to provide that payments made to an assignee under the contract are not subject to reduction or setoff. Each determination of need by the President under this subparagraph shall be published in the Federal Register.

(B) **Carrying out contract provision.**—When a "no reduction or setoff" provision as described in subparagraph (A) is included in a contract, payments to the assignee are not subject to reduction or setoff for an assignor's liability arising—

(i) independently of the contract;

(ii) on account of renegotiation under a renegotiation statute or under a statutory renegotiation article in the contract;

(iii) on account of fines;

(iv) on account of penalties; or

(v) on account of taxes, social security contributions, or the withholding or non-withholding of taxes or social security contributions, whether arising from or independently of the contract.

(C) **Limitation.**—Subparagraph (B)(iv) does not apply to amounts which may be collected or withheld from the assignor in accordance with or for failure to comply with the terms of the contract.

(Pub.L. 111–350, § 3, Jan. 4, 2011, 124 Stat. 3804.)

MEMORANDA OF PRESIDENT
PRESIDENTIAL MEMORANDUM
Oct. 3, 1995, 60 F.R. 52289

DELEGATION OF AUTHORITY UNDER THE ASSIGNMENT OF CLAIMS ACT

Memorandum for the Heads of Executive Departments and Agencies

Section 2451 of the Federal Acquisition Streamlining Act of 1994, Public Law 103–355 (41 U.S.C. 15) ("Act"), provides, in part, that "[a]ny contract of the Department of Defense, the General Services Administration, the Department of Energy or any other department or agency of the United States designated by the President, except [contracts where] . . . full payment has been made, may, upon a determination of need by the President, provide or be amended without consideration to provide that payments to be made to the assignee of any moneys due or to become due under [the] contract shall not be subject to reduction or set-off."

By the authority vested in me as President by the Constitution and the laws of the United States of America, including section 301 of title 3, United States Code [section 301 of Title 3, The President], I hereby designate all other departments and agencies of the United States as subject to this provision. Furthermore, I hereby delegate to the Secretaries of Defense and Energy, the Administrator of General Services, and the heads of all other departments and agencies, the authority under section 2451 of the Act [this section] to make determinations of need for their respective agency's contracts, subject to such further guidance as issued by the Office of Federal Procurement Policy.

The authority delegated by this memorandum may be further delegated within the departments and agencies.

This memorandum shall be published in the **Federal Register.**

WILLIAM J. CLINTON

[Memorandum was set out under former 42 U.S.C.A. § 15 prior to the enactment into positive law of Title 41, Public Contracts, by Pub.L. 111–350, Jan. 4, 2011, 124 Stat. 3677.]

§ 6306. Prohibition on Members of Congress making contracts with Federal Government

(a) **In general.**—A Member of Congress may not enter into or benefit from a contract or agreement or any part of a contract or agreement with the Federal Government.

(b) **Exemptions.**—

(1) **In general.**—Subsection (a) does not apply to contracts that the Secretary of Agriculture may enter into with farmers.

(2) Certain acts.—Subsection (a) does not apply to a contract entered into under—

(A) the Agricultural Adjustment Act (7 U.S.C. 601 et seq.);

(B) the Farm Credit Act of 1971 (12 U.S.C. 2001 et seq.); or

(C) the Home Owners' Loan Act (12 U.S.C. 1461 et seq.).

(3) Public record.—An exemption under this subsection shall be made a matter of public record.

(Pub.L. 111–350, § 3, Jan. 4, 2011, 124 Stat. 3805.)

HISTORICAL AND STATUTORY NOTES

References in Text

The Agricultural Adjustment Act, referred to in subsec. (b)(2)(A), is Act May 12, 1933, c. 25, Title I, 48 Stat. 31, as amended, which is classified principally to chapter 26 of Title 7, 7 U.S.C.A. § 601 et seq. For complete classification, see Short Title note set out under 7 U.S.C.A. § 601 and Tables.

The Farm Credit Act of 1971, referred to in subsec. (b)(2)(B), is Pub.L. 92–181, Dec. 10, 1971, 85 Stat. 583, which is classified principally to chapter 23 of Title 12, 12 U.S.C.A. § 2001 et seq. For complete classification, see Short Title note set out under 12 USCA § 2001 and Tables.

The Home Owners' Loan Act, referred to in subsec. (b)(2)(C), is Act June 13, 1933, c. 64, 48 Stat. 128, as amended, which is classified principally to chapter 12 of Title 12, 12 U.S.C.A. § 1461 et seq. For complete classification, see 12 U.S.C.A. § 1461 and Tables.

§ 6307. Contracts with Federal Government-owned establishments and availability of appropriations

An order or contract placed with a Federal Government-owned establishment for work, material, or the manufacture of material pertaining to an approved project is deemed to be an obligation in the same manner that a similar order or contract placed with a commercial manufacturer or private contractor is an obligation. Appropriations remain available to pay an obligation to a Federal Government–owned establishment just as appropriations remain available to pay an obligation to a commercial manufacturer or private contractor.

(Pub.L. 111–350, § 3, Jan. 4, 2011, 124 Stat. 3806.)

§ 6308. Contracts for transportation of Federal Government securities

When practicable, a contract for transporting bullion, cash, or securities of the Federal Government shall be awarded to the lowest responsible bidder after notice to all parties with means of transportation.

(Pub.L. 111–350, § 3, Jan. 4, 2011, 124 Stat. 3806.)

§ 6309. Honorable discharge certificate in lieu of birth certificate

(a) In general.—An employer described in subsection (b) may not deny employment, on account of failure to produce a birth certificate, to an individual who submits, in lieu of the birth certificate, an honorable discharge certificate (or certificate issued in lieu of an honorable discharge certificate) from the Army, Air Force, Navy, Marine Corps, or Coast Guard of the United States, unless the honorable discharge certificate shows on its face that the individual may have been an alien at the time of its issuance.

(b) Employers to which section applies.—An employer referred to in subsection (a) is an employer—

(1) engaged in—

(A) the production, maintenance, or storage of arms, armament, ammunition, implements of war, munitions, machinery, tools, clothing, food, fuel, or any articles or supplies, or parts or ingredients of any articles or supplies; or

(B) the construction, reconstruction, repair, or installation of a building, plant, structure, or facility; and

(2) engaged in the activity described in paragraph (1) under—

(A) a contract with the Federal Government; or

See Main Volume and Repealed Title 41, ante, for annotations

(B) any contract that the President, the Secretary of the Army, the Secretary of the Air Force, the Secretary of the Navy, or the Secretary of the Department in which the Coast Guard is operating certifies to the employer to be necessary to the national defense.

(Pub.L. 111–350, § 3, Jan. 4, 2011, 124 Stat. 3806.)

CHAPTER 65—CONTRACTS FOR MATERIALS, SUPPLIES, ARTICLES, AND EQUIPMENT EXCEEDING $10,000

§ 6501. Definitions

In this chapter—

(1) **Agency of the United States**—The term "agency of the United States" means an executive department, independent establishment, or other agency or instrumentality of the United States, the District of Columbia, or a corporation in which all stock is beneficially owned by the Federal Government.

(2) **Person.**—The term "person" includes one or more individuals, partnerships, associations, corporations, legal representatives, trustees, trustees in cases under title 11, or receivers.

(3) **Secretary.**—The term "Secretary" means the Secretary of Labor.

(Pub.L. 111–350, § 3, Jan. 4, 2011, 124 Stat. 3807.)

HISTORICAL AND STATUTORY NOTES

References in Text

Title 11, referred to in par. (2), is classified to 11 U.S.C.A. § 101 et seq.

EXECUTIVE ORDERS
EXECUTIVE ORDER NO. 13126
June 12, 1999, 64 F.R. 32383

PROHIBITION OF ACQUISITION OF PRODUCTS PRODUCED BY FORCED OR INDENTURED CHILD LABOR

By the authority vested in me as President by the Constitution and the laws of the United States of America, and in order to continue the executive branch's commitment to fighting abusive child labor practices, it is hereby ordered as follows:

Section 1.   Policy. It shall be the policy of the United States Government, consistent with the Tariff Act of 1930, 19 U.S.C. 1307, the Fair Labor Standards Act, 29 U.S.C. 201 et. seq., and the Walsh–Healey Public Contracts Act, 41 U.S.C. 35 et seq., that executive agencies shall take appropriate actions to enforce the laws prohibiting the manufacture or importation of goods, wares, articles, and merchandise mined, produced, or manufactured wholly or in part by forced or indentured child labor.

Sec. 2.   Publication of List. Within 120 days after the date of this order, the Department of Labor, in consultation and cooperation with the Department of the Treasury and the Department of State, shall publish in the **Federal Register** a list of products, identified by their country of origin, that those Departments have a reasonable basis to believe might have been mined, produced, or manufactured by forced or indentured child labor. The Department of Labor may conduct hearings to assist in the identification of those products.

Sec. 3.   Procurement Regulations. Within 120 days after the date of this order, the Federal Acquisition Regulatory Council shall issue proposed rules to implement the following:

(a) Required Solicitation Provisions. Each solicitation of offers for a contract for the procurement of a product included on the list published under section 2 of this order shall include the following provisions:

(1) A provision that requires the contractor to certify to the contracting officer that the con-

tractor or, in the case of an incorporated contractor, a responsible official of the contractor has made a good faith effort to determine whether forced or indentured child labor was used to mine, produce, or manufacture any product furnished under the contract and that, on the basis of those efforts, the contractor is unaware of any such use of child labor; and

(2) A provision that obligates the contractor to cooperate fully in providing reasonable access to the contractor's records, documents, persons, or premises if reasonably requested by authorized officials of the contracting agency, the Department of the Treasury, or the Department of Justice, for the purpose of determining whether forced or indentured child labor was used to mine, produce, or manufacture any product furnished under the contract.

(b) Investigations. Whenever a contracting officer of an executive agency has reason to believe that forced or indentured child labor was used to mine, produce, or manufacture a product furnished pursuant to a contract subject to the requirements of subsection 3(a) of this order, the head of the executive agency shall refer the matter for investigation to the Inspector General of the executive agency and, as the head of the executive agency or the Inspector General determines appropriate, to the Attorney General and the Secretary of the Treasury.

(c) Remedies.

(1) The head of an executive agency may impose remedies as provided in this subsection in the case of a contractor under a contract of the executive agency if the head of the executive agency finds that the contractor:

(i) Has furnished under the contract products that have been mined, produced, or manufactured by forced or indentured child labor or uses forced or indentured child labor in the mining, production, or manufacturing operations of the contractor;

(ii) Has submitted a false certification under subsection 3(a)(1) of this order; or

(iii) Has failed to cooperate in accordance with the obligation imposed pursuant to subsection 3(a)(2) of this order.

(2) The head of an executive agency, in his or her sole discretion, may terminate a contract on the basis of any finding described in subsection 3(c)(1) of this order for any contract entered into after the date the regulation called for in section 3 of this order is published in final.

(3) The head of an executive agency may debar or suspend a contractor from eligibility for Federal contracts on the basis of a finding that the contractor has engaged in an act described in subsection 3(c)(1) of this order. The provision for debarment may not exceed 3 years.

(4) The Administrator of General Services shall include on the List of Parties Excluded from Federal Procurement and Nonprocurement Programs (maintained by the Administrator as described in the Federal Acquisition Regulation) each party that is debarred, suspended, proposed for debarment or suspension, or de

clared ineligible by the head of an agency on the basis that the person has engaged in an act described in subsection 3(c)(1) of this order.

(5) This section shall not be construed to limit the use of other remedies available to the head of an executive agency or any other official of the Federal Government on the basis of a finding described in subsection 3(c)(1) of this order.

Sec. 4. Report. Within 2 years after implementation of any final rule under this order, the Administrator of General Services, with the assistance of other executive agencies, shall submit to the Office of Management and Budget a report on the actions taken pursuant to this order.

Sec. 5. Scope. (a) Any proposed rules issued pursuant to section 3 of this order shall apply only to acquisitions for a total amount in excess of the micro-purchase threshold as defined in section 32(f) of the Office of Federal Procurement Policy Act (41 U.S.C. 428(f)).

(b) This order does not apply to a contract that is for the procurement of any product, or any article, material, or supply contained in a product that is mined, produced, or manufactured in any foreign country if:

(1) the foreign country is a party to the Agreement on Government Procurement annexed to the WTO Agreement or a party to the North American Free Trade Agreement ("NAFTA"); and

(2) the contract is of a value that is equal to or greater than the United States threshold specified in the Agreement on Government Procurement annexed to the WTO Agreement or NAFTA, whichever is applicable.

Sec. 6. Definitions. (a) "Executive agency" and "agency" have the meaning given to "executive agency" in section 4(1) of the Office of Federal Procurement Policy Act (41 U.S.C. 403(1)).

(b) "WTO Agreement" means the Agreement Establishing the World Trade Organization, entered into on April 15, 1994.

(c) "Forced or indentured child labor" means all work or service (1) exacted from any person under the age of 18 under the menace of any penalty for its nonperformance and for which the worker does not offer himself voluntarily; or (2) performed by any person under the age of 18 pursuant to a contract the enforcement of which can be accomplished by process or penalties.

Sec. 7. Judicial Review. This order is intended only to improve the internal management of the executive branch and does not create any rights or benefits, substantive or procedural, enforceable by law by a party against the United States, its agencies, its officers, or any other person.

WILLIAM J. CLINTON

[Executive Order was set out under former 41 U.S.C.A. § 35 prior to the enactment into positive law of Title 41, Public Contracts, by Pub.L. 111–350, Jan. 4, 2011, 124 Stat. 3677.]

See Main Volume and Repealed Title 41, ante, for annotations

§ 6502. Required contract terms

A contract made by an agency of the United States for the manufacture or furnishing of materials, supplies, articles, or equipment, in an amount exceeding $10,000, shall include the following representations and stipulations:

    (1) **Minimum wages to be paid.**—All individuals employed by the contractor in the manufacture or furnishing of materials, supplies, articles, or equipment under the contract will be paid, without subsequent deduction or rebate on any account, not less than the prevailing minimum wages, as determined by the Secretary, for individuals employed in similar work or in the particular or similar industries or groups of industries currently operating in the locality in which the materials, supplies, articles, or equipment are to be manufactured or furnished under the contract, except that this paragraph applies only to purchases or contracts relating to industries that have been the subject matter of a determination by the Secretary.

    (2) **Maximum number of hours to be worked in a week.**—No individual employed by the contractor in the manufacture or furnishing of materials, supplies, articles, or equipment under the contract shall be permitted to work in excess of 40 hours in any one week, except that this paragraph does not apply to an employer who has entered into an agreement with employees pursuant to paragraph (1) or (2) of section 7(b) of the Fair Labor Standards Act of 1938 (29 U.S.C. 207(b)(1) or (2)).

    (3) **Ineligible employees.**—No individual under 16 years of age and no incarcerated individual will be employed by the contractor in the manufacture or furnishing of materials, supplies, articles, or equipment under the contract, except that this section, or other law or executive order containing similar prohibitions against the purchase of goods by the Federal Government, does not apply to convict labor that satisfies the conditions of section 1761(c) of title 18.

    (4) **Standards of places and working conditions where contract performed.**—No part of the contract will be performed, and no materials, supplies, articles, or equipment will be manufactured or fabricated under the contract, in plants, factories, buildings, or surroundings, or under working conditions, that are unsanitary, hazardous, or dangerous to the health and safety of employees engaged in the performance of the contract. Compliance with the safety, sanitary, and factory inspection laws of the State in which the work or part of the work is to be performed is prima facie evidence of compliance with this paragraph.

(Pub.L. 111–350, § 3, Jan. 4, 2011, 124 Stat. 3807.)

HISTORICAL AND STATUTORY NOTES

References in Text

The Fair Labor Standards Act of 1938, referred to in par. (2), is Act June 25, 1938, c. 676, 52 Stat. 1060, as amended, which is principally classified to chapter 8 of Title 29, 29 U.S.C.A. § 201 et seq. Section 7 of the Act is classified to 29 U.S.C.A. § 207. For complete classification, see 29 U.S.C.A. § 201 and Tables.

§ 6503. Breach or violation of required contract terms

    (a) **Applicable breach or violation.**—This section applies in case of breach or violation of a representation or stipulation included in a contract under section 6502 of this title.

    (b) **Liquidated damages.**—In addition to damages for any other breach of the contract, the party responsible for a breach or violation described in subsection (a) is liable to the Federal Government for the following liquidated damages:

    (1) An amount equal to the sum of $10 per day for each individual under 16 years of age and each incarcerated individual knowingly employed in the performance of the contract.

    (2) An amount equal to the sum of each underpayment of wages due an employee engaged in the performance of the contract, including any underpayments arising from deductions, rebates, or refunds.

    (c) **Cancellation and alternative completion.**—In addition to the Federal Government being entitled to damages described in subsection (b), the agency of the United States that made the contract may cancel the contract and make open-market purchases or make other contracts for the completion of the original contract, charging any additional cost to the original contractor.

(d) Recovery of amounts due.—An amount due the Federal Government because of a breach or violation described in subsection (a) may be withheld from any amounts owed the contractor under any contract under section 6502 of this title or may be recovered in a suit brought by the Attorney General.

(e) Employee reimbursement for underpayment of wages.—An amount withheld or recovered under subsection (d) that is based on an underpayment of wages as described in subsection (b)(2) shall be held in a special deposit account. On order of the Secretary, the amount shall be paid directly to the underpaid employee on whose account the amount was withheld or recovered. However, an employee's claim for payment under this subsection may be entertained only if made within one year from the date of actual notice to the contractor of the withholding or recovery.

(Pub.L. 111–350, § 3, Jan. 4, 2011, 124 Stat. 3808.)

§ 6504. Three-year prohibition on new contracts in case of breach or violation

(a) Distribution of list.—The Comptroller General shall distribute to each agency of the United States a list containing the names of persons found by the Secretary to have breached or violated a representation or stipulation included in a contract under section 6502 of this title.

(b) Three-year prohibition.—Unless the Secretary recommends otherwise, a contract described in section 6502 of this title may not be awarded to a person named on the list under subsection (a), or to a firm, corporation, partnership, or association in which the person has a controlling interest, until 3 years have elapsed from the date of the determination by the Secretary that a breach or violation occurred.

(Pub.L. 111–350, § 3, Jan. 4, 2011, 124 Stat. 3808.)

§ 6505. Exclusions

(a) Items available in the open market.—This chapter does not apply to the purchase of materials, supplies, articles, or equipment that may usually be bought in the open market.

(b) Perishables and agricultural products.—This chapter does not apply to any of the following:

(1) Perishables, including dairy, livestock and nursery products.

(2) Agricultural or farm products processed for first sale by the original producers.

(3) Contracts made by the Secretary of Agriculture for the purchase of agricultural commodities or products of agricultural commodities.

(c) Carriage of freight or personnel.—This chapter may not be construed to apply to—

(1) the carriage of freight or personnel by vessel, airplane, bus, truck, express, or railway line where published tariff rates are in effect; or

(2) common carriers subject to the Communications Act of 1934 (47 U.S.C. 151 et seq.).

(Pub.L. 111–350, § 3, Jan. 4, 2011, 124 Stat. 3809.)

HISTORICAL AND STATUTORY NOTES

References in Text

The Communications Act of 1934, referred to in subsec. (c)(2), is Act June 19, 1934, c. 652, 48 Stat. 1064, also known as the Dill–Rayburn Communications Act, Petrillo Bill, Telegraph Company Merger Act, and Telecommunications Act of 1934, which is classified principally to chapter 5 of Title 47, 47 U.S.C.A. § 151 et seq. For complete classification, see 47 U.S.C.A. § 609 and Tables.

§ 6506. Administrative provisions

(a) In general.—The Secretary shall administer this chapter.

See Main Volume and Repealed Title 41, ante, for annotations

(b) Regulations.—The Secretary may make, amend, and rescind regulations as necessary to carry out this chapter.

(c) Use of Government officers and employees.—The Secretary shall use Federal officers and employees and, with a State's consent, State and local officers and employees as the Secretary finds necessary to assist in the administration of this chapter.

(d) Appointments.—The Secretary shall appoint an administrative officer and attorneys, experts, and other employees from time to time as the Secretary finds necessary for the administration of this chapter. The appointments are subject to chapter 51 and subchapter III of chapter 53 of title 5 and other law applicable to the employment and compensation of officers and employees of the Federal Government.

(e) Investigations.—The Secretary, or an authorized representative of the Secretary, may make investigations and findings as provided in this chapter and may, in any part of the United States, prosecute an inquiry necessary to carry out this chapter.

(Pub.L. 111–350, § 3, Jan. 4, 2011, 124 Stat. 3809.)

HISTORICAL AND STATUTORY NOTES

References in Text

Chapter 51 of title 5, referred to in subsec. (d), is classified to 5 U.S.C.A. § 5101 et seq.

Subchapter III of chapter 53 of title 5, referred to in subsec. (d), is classified to 5 U.S.C.A. § 5331 et seq.

§ 6507. Hearing authority and procedures

(a) Record and hearing requirements for wage determinations.—A wage determination under section 6502(1) of this title shall be made on the record after opportunity for a hearing.

(b) Authority to hold hearings.—The Secretary or an impartial representative designated by the Secretary may hold hearings when there is a complaint of breach or violation of a representation or stipulation included in a contract under section 6502 of this title. The Secretary may initiate hearings on the Secretary's own motion or on the application of a person affected by the ruling of an agency of the United States relating to a proposal or contract under this chapter.

(c) Orders to compel testimony.—The Secretary or an impartial representative designated by the Secretary may issue orders requiring witnesses to attend hearings held under this section and to produce evidence and testify under oath. Witnesses shall be paid fees and mileage at the same rates as witnesses in courts of the United States.

(d) Enforcement of orders.—If a person refuses or fails to obey an order issued under subsection (c), the Secretary or an impartial representative designated by the Secretary may bring an action to enforce the order in a district court of the United States or in the district court of a territory or possession of the United States. A court has jurisdiction to enforce the order if the inquiry is being carried out within the court's judicial district or if the person is found or resides or transacts business within the court's judicial district. The court may issue an order requiring the person to obey the order issued under subsection (c), and the court may punish any further refusal or failure as contempt of court.

(e) Findings of fact.—After notice and a hearing, the Secretary or an impartial representative designated by the Secretary shall make findings of fact. The findings are conclusive for agencies of the United States. If supported by a preponderance of the evidence, the findings are conclusive in any court of the United States.

(f) Decisions.—The Secretary or an impartial representative designated by the Secretary may make decisions, based on findings of fact, that are considered necessary to enforce this chapter.

(Pub.L. 111–350, § 3, Jan. 4, 2011, 124 Stat. 3809.)

§ 6508. Authority to make exceptions

(a) Duty of the Secretary to make exceptions.—When the head of an agency of the United States makes a written finding that the inclusion of representations or stipulations under section 6502 of this title in a proposal or contract will seriously impair the conduct of Federal Government business, the Secretary shall make exceptions, in specific cases or otherwise, when justice or the public interest will be served.

(b) Authority of the Secretary to modify existing contracts.—When an agency of the United States and a contractor jointly recommend, the Secretary may modify the terms of an existing contract with respect to minimum wages and maximum hours of labor as the Secretary finds necessary and proper in the public interest or to prevent injustice and undue hardship.

(c) Authority of the Secretary to allow limitations, variations, tolerances, and exemptions.—The Secretary may provide reasonable limitations and may prescribe regulations to allow reasonable variations, tolerances, and exemptions in the application of this chapter to contractors, including with respect to minimum wages and maximum hours of labor.

(d) Rate of pay for overtime.—When the Secretary permits an increase in the maximum hours of labor stipulated in a contract, the Secretary shall set a rate of pay for overtime. The overtime rate must be at least one and one-half times the basic hourly rate.

(e) Authority of the President to suspend.—The President may suspend any of the representations and stipulations contained in section 6502 of this title whenever, in the President's judgment, suspension is in the public interest.

(Pub.L. 111–350, § 3, Jan. 4, 2011, 124 Stat. 3810.)

§ 6509. Other procedures

(a) Applicability of certain administrative provisions.—Notwithstanding section 553 of title 5, subchapter II of chapter 5 and chapter 7 of title 5 are applicable in the administration of sections 6501 to 6507 and 6511 of this title.

(b) Judicial review in general.—Notwithstanding the inclusion of representations and stipulations in a contract under section 6502 of this title, an interested person has the right of judicial review of any legal question which might otherwise be raised, including wage determinations and the interpretation of the terms "locality" and "open market".

(c) Judicial review of wage determinations.—A person adversely affected or aggrieved by a wage determination under section 6502(1) of this title has the right of judicial review of the determination, or of the applicability of the determination, within 90 days after the determination is made, in the manner provided by chapter 7 of title 5. A person adversely affected or aggrieved by a wage determination is deemed to include a person in an industry to which the determination applies that is a supplier of materials, supplies, articles, or equipment that are purchased or intended to be purchased by the Federal Government from any source.

(Pub.L. 111–350, § 3, Jan. 4, 2011, 124 Stat. 3810.)

HISTORICAL AND STATUTORY NOTES

References in Text

Subchapter II of chapter 5 of title 5, referred to in subsec. (a), is classified to 5 U.S.C.A. § 551 et seq.

Chapter 7 of title 5, referred to in subsecs. (a), (c), is classified to 5 U.S.C.A. § 701 et seq.

§ 6510. Manufacturers and regular dealers

(a) Prescribing standards.—The Secretary may prescribe, in regulations, standards for determining whether a contractor is a manufacturer or regular dealer with respect to materials, supplies, articles, or equipment to be manufactured or furnished under, or used in the performance of, a contract entered into by an agency of the United States.

(b) Judicial review.—An interested person has the right of judicial review of any legal question relating to interpretation of the terms "regular dealer" and "manufacturer" as defined pursuant to subsection (a).

(Pub.L. 111–350, § 3, Jan. 4, 2011, 124 Stat. 3811.)

See Main Volume and Repealed Title 41, ante, for annotations

CROSS REFERENCES

Judicial review, government organizations and employees, see 5 USCA § 701 et seq.

§ 6511. Effect on other law

This chapter may not be construed to modify or amend the following provisions:

    (1) Chapter 83 of this title.

    (2) Sections 3141 to 3144, 3146, and 3147 of title 40.

    (3) Chapter 307 of title 18.

(Pub.L. 111–350, § 3, Jan. 4, 2011, 124 Stat. 3811.)

HISTORICAL AND STATUTORY NOTES

References in Text

Chapter 83 of this title, referred to in par. (1), is classified to 41 U.S.C.A. § 8301 et seq.

Chapter 307 of title 18, referred to in par. (3), is classified to 18 U.S.C.A. § 4121 et seq.

CHAPTER 67—SERVICE CONTRACT LABOR STANDARDS

Sec.		Sec.	
6701.	Definitions.	6705.	Violations.
6702.	Contracts to which this chapter applies.	6706.	Three-year prohibition on new contracts in case of violation.
6703.	Required contract terms.	6707.	Enforcement and administration of chapter.
6704.	Limitation on minimum wage.		

§ 6701. Definitions

In this chapter:

    (1) **Compensation.**—The term "compensation" means any of the payments or fringe benefits described in section 6703 of this title.

    (2) **Secretary.**—The term "Secretary" means the Secretary of Labor.

    (3) **Service employee.**—The term "service employee"—

        (A) means an individual engaged in the performance of a contract made by the Federal Government and not exempted under section 6702(b) of this title, whether negotiated or advertised, the principal purpose of which is to furnish services in the United States;

        (B) includes an individual without regard to any contractual relationship alleged to exist between the individual and a contractor or subcontractor; but

        (C) does not include an individual employed in a bona fide executive, administrative, or professional capacity, as those terms are defined in part 541 of title 29, Code of Federal Regulations.

    (4) **United States.**—The term "United States"—

        (A) includes any State of the United States, the District of Columbia, Puerto Rico, the Virgin Islands, the outer Continental Shelf as defined in the Outer Continental Shelf Lands Act (43 U.S.C. Sec. 1331 et seq.), American Samoa, Guam, Wake Island, and Johnston Island; but

        (B) does not include any other territory under the jurisdiction of the United States or any United States base or possession within a foreign country.

(Pub.L. 111–350, § 3, Jan. 4, 2011, 124 Stat. 3811.)

HISTORICAL AND STATUTORY NOTES

References in Text

The Outer Continental Shelf Lands Act, referred to in par. (4)(A), is Act Aug. 7, 1953, c. 345, 67 Stat. 462, also known as OCSLA, which is classified principally to subchapter III of chapter 29 of Title 43, 43 U.S.C.A. § 1331 et seq. For complete classification, see Tables.

§ 6702. Contracts to which this chapter applies

    (a) **In general.**—Except as provided in subsection (b), this chapter applies to any contract or bid specification for a contract, whether negotiated or advertised, that—

(1) is made by the Federal Government or the District of Columbia;

(2) involves an amount exceeding $2,500; and

(3) has as its principal purpose the furnishing of services in the United States through the use of service employees.

(b) **Exemptions.**—This chapter does not apply to—

(1) a contract of the Federal Government or the District of Columbia for the construction, alteration, or repair, including painting and decorating, of public buildings or public works;

(2) any work required to be done in accordance with chapter 65 of this title;

(3) a contract for the carriage of freight or personnel by vessel, airplane, bus, truck, express, railway line or oil or gas pipeline where published tariff rates are in effect;

(4) a contract for the furnishing of services by radio, telephone, telegraph, or cable companies, subject to the Communications Act of 1934 (47 U.S.C. 151 et seq.);

(5) a contract for public utility services, including electric light and power, water, steam, and gas;

(6) an employment contract providing for direct services to a Federal agency by an individual; and

(7) a contract with the United States Postal Service, the principal purpose of which is the operation of postal contract stations.

(Pub.L. 111–350, § 3, Jan. 4, 2011, 124 Stat. 3812.)

HISTORICAL AND STATUTORY NOTES

References in Text

Chapter 65 of this title, referred to in subsec. (b)(2), is classified to 41 U.S.C.A. § 6501 et seq.

The Communications Act of 1934, referred to in subsec. (b)(4), is Act June 19, 1934, c. 652, 48 Stat. 1064, also known as the Dill–Rayburn Communications Act, Petrillo Bill, Telegraph Company Merger Act, and Telecommunications Act of 1934, which is classified principally to chapter 5 of Title 47, 47 U.S.C.A. § 151 et seq. For complete classification, see section 47 U.S.C.A. § 609 and Tables.

§ 6703. Required contract terms

A contract, and bid specification for a contract, to which this chapter applies under section 6702 of this title shall contain the following terms:

(1) **Minimum wage.**—The contract and bid specification shall contain a provision specifying the minimum wage to be paid to each class of service employee engaged in the performance of the contract or any subcontract, as determined by the Secretary or the Secretary's authorized representative, in accordance with prevailing rates in the locality, or, where a collective-bargaining agreement covers the service employees, in accordance with the rates provided for in the agreement, including prospective wage increases provided for in the agreement as a result of arm's length negotiations. In any case the minimum wage may not be less than the minimum wage specified in section 6704 of this title.

(2) **Fringe benefits.**—The contract and bid specification shall contain a provision specifying the fringe benefits to be provided to each class of service employee engaged in the performance of the contract or any subcontract, as determined by the Secretary or the Secretary's authorized representative to be prevailing in the locality, or, where a collective-bargaining agreement covers the service employees, to be provided for under the agreement, including prospective fringe benefit increases provided for in the agreement as a result of arm's-length negotiations. The fringe benefits shall include medical or hospital care, pensions on retirement or death, compensation for injuries or illness resulting from occupational activity, or insurance to provide any of the foregoing, unemployment benefits, life insurance, disability and sickness insurance, accident insurance, vacation and holiday pay, costs of apprenticeship or other similar programs and other bona fide fringe benefits not otherwise required by Federal, State, or local law to be provided by the contractor or subcontractor. The obligation under this paragraph may be discharged by furnishing any equivalent combinations of fringe benefits or by making equivalent or differential payments in cash under regulations established by the Secretary.

(3) Working conditions.—The contract and bid specification shall contain a provision specifying that no part of the services covered by this chapter may be performed in buildings or surroundings or under working conditions, provided by or under the control or supervision of the contractor or any subcontractor, which are unsanitary or hazardous or dangerous to the health or safety of service employees engaged to provide the services.

(4) Notice.—The contract and bid specification shall contain a provision specifying that on the date a service employee begins work on a contract to which this chapter applies, the contractor or subcontractor will deliver to the employee a notice of the compensation required under paragraphs (1) and (2), on a form prepared by the Federal agency, or will post a notice of the required compensation in a prominent place at the worksite.

(5) General schedule pay rates and prevailing rate systems.—The contract and bid specification shall contain a statement of the rates that would be paid by the Federal agency to each class of service employee if section 5332 or 5341 of title 5 were applicable to them. The Secretary shall give due consideration to these rates in making the wage and fringe benefit determinations specified in this section.

(Pub.L. 111–350, § 3, Jan. 4, 2011, 124 Stat. 3812.)

EXECUTIVE ORDERS
EXECUTIVE ORDER NO. 13495
Jan. 30, 2009, 74 F.R. 6103

NONDISPLACEMENT OF QUALIFIED WORKERS UNDER SERVICE CONTRACTS

When a service contract expires, and a follow-on contract is awarded for the same service, at the same location, the successor contractor or its subcontractors often hires the majority of the predecessor's employees. On some occasions, however, a successor contractor or its subcontractors hires a new work force, thus displacing the predecessor's employees.

The Federal Government's procurement interests in economy and efficiency are served when the successor contractor hires the predecessor's employees. A carryover work force reduces disruption to the delivery of services during the period of transition between contractors and provides the Federal Government the benefits of an experienced and trained work force that is familiar with the Federal Government's personnel, facilities, and requirements.

Therefore, by the authority vested in me as President by the Constitution and the laws of the United States of America, including the Federal Property and Administrative Services Act, 40 U.S.C. 101 et seq., and in order to promote economy and efficiency in Federal Government procurement, it is hereby ordered as follows:

Section 1. Policy. It is the policy of the Federal Government that service contracts and solicitations for such contracts shall include a clause that requires the contractor, and its subcontractors, under a contract that succeeds a contract for performance of the same or similar services at the same location, to offer those employees (other than managerial and supervisory employees) employed under the predecessor contract whose employment will be terminated as a result of the award of the successor contract, a right of first refusal of employment under the contract in positions for which they are qualified. There shall be no employment

openings under the contract until such right of first refusal has been provided. Nothing in this order shall be construed to permit a contractor or subcontractor to fail to comply with any provision of any other Executive Order or law of the United States.

Sec. 2. Definitions.

(a) "Service contract" or "contract" means any contract or subcontract for services entered into by the Federal Government or its contractors that is covered by the Service Contract Act of 1965, as amended, 41 U.S.C. 351 et seq., and its implementing regulations.

(b) "Employee" means a service employee as defined in the Service Contract Act of 1965, 41 U.S.C. 357(b).

Sec. 3. Exclusions. This order shall not apply to:

(a) contracts or subcontracts under the simplified acquisition threshold as defined in 41 U.S.C. 403;

(b) contracts or subcontracts awarded pursuant to the Javits-Wagner-O'Day Act, 41 U.S.C. 46—48c;

(c) guard, elevator operator, messenger, or custodial services provided to the Federal Government under contracts or subcontracts with sheltered workshops employing the severely handicapped as described in section 505 of the Treasury, Postal Services and General Government Appropriations Act, 1995, Public Law 103–329;

(d) agreements for vending facilities entered into pursuant to the preference regulations issued under the Randolph-Sheppard Act, 20 U.S.C. 107; or

(e) employees who were hired to work under a Federal service contract and one or more nonfederal service contracts as part of a single job, provided that the employees were not deployed in a manner that was designed to avoid the purposes of this order.

Sec. 4. Authority to Exempt Contracts. If the head of a contracting department or agency finds that the application of any of the requirements of this order would not serve the purposes of this order or would impair the ability of the Federal Government to procure services on an economical and efficient basis, the head of such department or agency may exempt its department or agency from the requirements of any or all of the provisions of this order with respect to a particular contract, subcontract, or purchase order or any class of contracts, subcontracts, or purchase orders.

Sec. 5. Contract Clause. The following contract clause shall be included in solicitations for and service contracts that succeed contracts for performance of the same or similar work at the same location:

"NONDISPLACEMENT OF QUALIFIED WORKERS

"**(a)** Consistent with the efficient performance of this contract, the contractor and its subcontractors shall, except as otherwise provided herein, in good faith offer those employees (other than managerial and supervisory employees) employed under the predecessor contract whose employment will be terminated as a result of award of this contract or the expiration of the contract under which the employees were hired, a right of first refusal of employment under this contract in positions for which employees are qualified. The contractor and its subcontractors shall determine the number of employees necessary for efficient performance of this contract and may elect to employ fewer employees than the predecessor contractor employed in connection with performance of the work. Except as provided in paragraph (b) there shall be no employment opening under this contract, and the contractor and any subcontractors shall not offer employment under this contract, to any person prior to having complied fully with this obligation. The contractor and its subcontractors shall make an express offer of employment to each employee as provided herein and shall state the time within which the employee must accept such offer, but in no case shall the period within which the employee must accept the offer of employment be less than 10 days.

"**(b)** Notwithstanding the obligation under paragraph (a) above, the contractor and any subcontractors (1) may employ under this contract any employee who has worked for the contractor or subcontractor for at least 3 months immediately preceding the commencement of this contract and who would otherwise face layoff or discharge, (2) are not required to offer a right of first refusal to any employee(s) of the predecessor contractor who are not service employees within the meaning of the Service Contract Act of 1965, as amended, 41 U.S.C. 357(b), and (3) are not required to offer a right of first refusal to any employee(s) of the predecessor contractor whom the contractor or any of its subcontractors reasonably believes, based on the

particular employee's past performance, has failed to perform suitably on the job.

"**(c)** In accordance with Federal Acquisition Regulation 52.222–41(n), the contractor shall, not less than 10 days before completion of this contract, furnish the Contracting Officer a certified list of the names of all service employees working under this contract and its subcontracts during the last month of contract performance. The list shall also contain anniversary dates of employment of each service employee under this contract and its predecessor contracts either with the current or predecessor contractors or their subcontractors. The Contracting Officer will provide the list to the successor contractor, and the list shall be provided on request to employees or their representatives.

"**(d)** If it is determined, pursuant to regulations issued by the Secretary of Labor (Secretary), that the contractor or its subcontractors are not in compliance with the requirements of this clause or any regulation or order of the Secretary, appropriate sanctions may be imposed and remedies invoked against the contractor or its subcontractors, as provided in Executive Order (No.) _____, the regulations, and relevant orders of the Secretary, or as otherwise provided by law.

"**(e)** In every subcontract entered into in order to perform services under this contract, the contractor will include provisions that ensure that each subcontractor will honor the requirements of paragraphs (a) through (b) with respect to the employees of a predecessor subcontractor or subcontractors working under this contract, as well as of a predecessor contractor and its subcontractors. The subcontract shall also include provisions to ensure that the subcontractor will provide the contractor with the information about the employees of the subcontractor needed by the contractor to comply with paragraph 5(c), above. The contractor will take such action with respect to any such subcontract as may be directed by the Secretary as a means of enforcing such provisions, including the imposition of sanctions for non-compliance: provided, however, that if the contractor, as a result of such direction, becomes involved in litigation with a subcontractor, or is threatened with such involvement, the contractor may request that the United States enter into such litigation to protect the interests of the United States."

Sec. 6. Enforcement. (a) The Secretary of Labor (Secretary) is responsible for investigating and obtaining compliance with this order. In such proceedings, the Secretary shall have the authority to issue final orders prescribing appropriate sanctions and remedies, including, but not limited to, orders requiring employment and payment of wages lost. The Secretary also may provide that where a contractor or subcontractor has failed to comply with any order of the Secretary or has committed willful violations of this order or the regulations issued pursuant thereto, the contractor or subcontractor, and its responsible officers, and any firm in which the contractor or subcontractor has a substantial interest, shall be ineligible to be awarded any contract of the United States for a period of up to 3 years. Neither an order for debarment of any contractor or subcontractor from further Government contracts under this section nor the inclusion of a contractor or subcontractor on a published list of noncomplying contractors shall be carried out without affording the contractor or subcontractor an opportunity for a hearing.

(b) This order creates no rights under the Contract Disputes Act, and disputes regarding the requirement of the contract clause prescribed by section 5 of this order, to the extent permitted by law, shall be disposed of only as provided by the Secretary in regulations issued under this order. To the extent practicable, such regulations shall favor the resolution of disputes by efficient and informal alternative dispute resolution methods. The Secretary shall, in consultation with the Federal Acquisition Regulatory Council, issue regulations, within 180 days of the date of this order, to the extent permitted by law, to implement the requirements of this order. The Federal Acquisition Regulatory Council shall issue, within 180 days of the date of this order, to the extent permitted by law, regulations in the Federal Acquisition Regulation to provide for inclusion of the contract clause in Federal solicitations and contracts subject to this order.

Sec. 7. Revocation. Executive Order 13204 of February 17, 2001, is revoked.

Sec. 8. Severability. If any provision of this order, or the application of such provision or amendment to any person or circumstance, is held to be invalid, the remainder of this order and the application of the provisions of such to any person or circumstances shall not be affected thereby.

Sec. 9. General Provisions. (a) Nothing in this order shall be construed to impair or otherwise affect:

(i) authority granted by law to an executive department, agency, or the head thereof; or

(ii) functions of the Director of the Office of Management and Budget relating to budgetary, administrative, or legislative proposals.

(b) This order shall be implemented consistent with applicable law and subject to the availability of appropriations.

(c) This order is not intended to, and does not, create any right or benefit, substantive or procedural, enforceable at law or in equity by any party against the United States, its departments, agencies, or entities, its officers, employees, or agents, or any other person. This order is not intended, however, to preclude judicial review of final decisions by the Secretary in accordance with the Administrative Procedure Act, 5 U.S.C. 701 et seq.

Sec. 10. Effective Date. This order shall become effective immediately and shall apply to solicitations issued on or after the effective date for the action taken by the Federal Acquisition Regulatory Council under section 6(b) of this order.

BARACK OBAMA

[Order was set out under former 41 U.S.C.A. § 351 prior to the enactment into positive law of Title 41, Public Contracts, by Pub.L. 111–350, Jan. 4, 2011, 124 Stat. 3677.]

§ 6704. Limitation on minimum wage

(a) **In general.**—A contractor that makes a contract with the Federal Government, the principal purpose of which is to furnish services through the use of service employees, and any subcontractor, may not pay less than the minimum wage specified under section 6(a)(1) of the Fair Labor Standards Act of 1938 (29 U.S.C. 206(a)(1)) to an employee engaged in performing work on the contract.

(b) **Violations.**—Sections 6705 to 6707(d) of this title are applicable to a violation of this section.

(Pub.L. 111–350, § 3, Jan. 4, 2011, 124 Stat. 3813.)

HISTORICAL AND STATUTORY NOTES

References in Text

The Fair Labor Standards Act of 1938, referred to in subsec. (a), is Act June 25, 1938, c. 676, 52 Stat. 1060, as amended, which is principally classified to chapter 8 of Title 29, 29 U.S.C.A. § 201 et seq. Section 6 of the Act is classified to 29 U.S.C.A. § 206. For complete classification, see 29 U.S.C.A. § 201 and Tables.

§ 6705. Violations

(a) **Liability of responsible party.**—A party responsible for a violation of a contract provision required under section 6703(1) or (2) of this title or a violation of section 6704 of this title is liable for an amount equal to the sum of any deduction, rebate, refund, or underpayment of compensation due any employee engaged in the performance of the contract.

(b) **Recovery of amounts underpaid to employees.**—

(1) **Withholding accrued payments due on contracts.**—The total amount determined under subsection (a) to be due any employee engaged in the performance of a

contract may be withheld from accrued payments due on the contract or on any other contract between the same contractor and the Federal Government. The amount withheld shall be held in a deposit fund. On order of the Secretary, the compensation found by the Secretary or the head of a Federal agency to be due an underpaid employee pursuant to this chapter shall be paid from the deposit fund directly to the underpaid employee.

(2) **Bringing actions against contractors.**—If the accrued payments withheld under the terms of the contract are insufficient to reimburse a service employee with respect to whom there has been a failure to pay the compensation required pursuant to this chapter, the Federal Government may bring action against the contractor, subcontractor, or any sureties in any court of competent jurisdiction to recover the remaining amount of underpayment. Any amount recovered shall be held in the deposit fund and shall be paid, on order of the Secretary, directly to the underpaid employee. Any amount not paid to an employee because of inability to do so within 3 years shall be covered into the Treasury as miscellaneous receipts.

(c) **Cancellation and alternative completion.**—In addition to other actions in accordance with this section, when a violation of any contract stipulation is found, the Federal agency that made the contract may cancel the contract on written notice to the original contractor. The Federal Government may then make other contracts or arrangements for the completion of the original contract, charging any additional cost to the original contractor.

(d) **Enforcement of section.**—In accordance with regulations prescribed pursuant to section 6707(a)–(d) of this title, the Secretary or the head of a Federal agency may carry out this section.

(Pub.L. 111–350, § 3, Jan. 4, 2011, 124 Stat. 3814.)

§ 6706. Three-year prohibition on new contracts in case of violation

(a) **Distribution of list.**—The Comptroller General shall distribute to each agency of the Federal Government a list containing the names of persons or firms that a Federal agency or the Secretary has found to have violated this chapter.

(b) **Three-year prohibition.**—Unless the Secretary recommends otherwise because of unusual circumstances, a Federal Government contract may not be awarded to a person or firm named on the list under subsection (a) , or to an entity in which the person or firm has a substantial interest, until 3 years have elapsed from the date of publication of the list. If the Secretary does not recommend otherwise because of unusual circumstances, the Secretary shall, not later than 90 days after a hearing examiner has made a finding of a violation of this chapter, forward to the Comptroller General the name of the person or firm found to have violated this chapter.

(Pub.L. 111–350, § 3, Jan. 4, 2011, 124 Stat. 3814.)

§ 6707. Enforcement and administration of chapter

(a) **Enforcement of chapter.**—Sections 6506 and 6507 of this title govern the Secretary's authority to enforce this chapter, including the Secretary's authority to prescribe regulations, issue orders, hold hearings, make decisions based on findings of fact, and take other appropriate action under this chapter.

(b) **Limitations and regulations for variations, tolerances, and exemptions.**—The Secretary may provide reasonable limitations and may prescribe regulations allowing reasonable variation, tolerances, and exemptions with respect to this chapter (other than subsection (f)), but only in special circumstances where the Secretary determines that the limitation, variation, tolerance, or exemption is necessary and proper in the public interest or to avoid the serious impairment of Federal Government business, and is in accord with the remedial purpose of this chapter to protect prevailing labor standards.

(c) **Preservation of wages and benefits due under predecessor contracts.**—

(1) **In general.**—Under a contract which succeeds a contract subject to this chapter, and under which substantially the same services are furnished, a contractor or subcontractor may not pay a service employee less than the wages and fringe benefits the service employee would have received under the predecessor contract,

including accrued wages and fringe benefits and any prospective increases in wages and fringe benefits provided for in a collective-bargaining agreement as a result of arm's-length negotiations.

(2) **Exception.**—This subsection does not apply if the Secretary finds after a hearing in accordance with regulations adopted by the Secretary that wages and fringe benefits under the predecessor contract are substantially at variance with wages and fringe benefits prevailing in the same locality for services of a similar character.

(d) **Duration of contracts.**—Subject to limitations in annual appropriation acts but notwithstanding any other law, a contract to which this chapter applies may, if authorized by the Secretary, be for any term of years not exceeding 5, if the contract provides for periodic adjustment of wages and fringe benefits pursuant to future determinations, issued in the manner prescribed in section 6703 of this title at least once every 2 years during the term of the contract, covering each class of service employee.

(e) **Exclusion of fringe benefit payments in determining overtime pay.**—In determining any overtime pay to which a service employee is entitled under Federal law, the regular or basic hourly rate of pay of the service employee does not include any fringe benefit payments computed under this chapter which are excluded from the definition of "regular rate" under section 7(e) of the Fair Labor Standards Act of 1938 (29 U.S.C. 207(e)).

(f) **Timeliness of wage and fringe benefit determinations.**—It is the intent of Congress that determinations of minimum wages and fringe benefits under section 6703(1) and (2) of this title should be made as soon as administratively feasible for all contracts subject to this chapter. In any event, the Secretary shall at least make the determinations for contracts under which more than 5 service employees are to be employed.

(Pub.L. 111–350, § 3, Jan. 4, 2011, 124 Stat. 3815.)

HISTORICAL AND STATUTORY NOTES

References in Text

The Fair Labor Standards Act of 1938, referred to in subsec. (e), is Act June 25, 1938, c. 676, 52 Stat. 1060, as amended, which is principally classified to chapter 8 of Title 29, 29 U.S.C.A. § 201 et seq. Section 7 of the Act is classified to 29 U.S.C.A. § 207. For complete classification, see 29 U.S.C.A. § 207 and Tables.

SUBTITLE III—CONTRACT DISPUTES

CHAPTER 71—CONTRACT DISPUTES

§ 7101. Definitions

In this chapter:

(1) **Administrator.**—The term "Administrator" means the Administrator for Federal Procurement Policy appointed pursuant to section 1102 of this title.

(2) **Agency board or agency board of contract appeals.**—The term "agency board" or "agency board of contract appeals" means—

(A) the Armed Services Board;

    (B) the Civilian Board;

    (C) the board of contract appeals of the Tennessee Valley Authority; or

    (D) the Postal Service Board established under section 7105(d)(1) of this title.

  (3) Agency head.—The term "agency head" means the head and any assistant head of an executive agency. The term may include the chief official of a principal division of an executive agency if the head of the executive agency so designates that chief official.

  (4) Armed Services Board.—The term "Armed Services Board" means the Armed Services Board of Contract Appeals established under section 7105(a)(1) of this title.

  (5) Civilian Board.—The term "Civilian Board" means the Civilian Board of Contract Appeals established under section 7105(b)(1) of this title.

  (6) Contracting officer.—The term "contracting officer"—

    (A) means an individual who, by appointment in accordance with applicable regulations, has the authority to make and administer contracts and to make determinations and findings with respect to contracts; and

    (B) includes an authorized representative of the contracting officer, acting within the limits of the representative's authority.

  (7) Contractor.—The term "contractor" means a party to a Federal Government contract other than the Federal Government.

  (8) Executive agency.—The term "executive agency" means—

    (A) an executive department as defined in section 101 of title 5;

    (B) a military department as defined in section 102 of title 5;

    (C) an independent establishment as defined in section 104 of title 5, except that the term does not include the Government Accountability Office; and

    (D) a wholly owned Government corporation as defined in section 9101(3) of title 31.

  (9) Misrepresentation of fact.—The term "misrepresentation of fact" means a false statement of substantive fact, or conduct that leads to a belief of a substantive fact material to proper understanding of the matter in hand, made with intent to deceive or mislead.

(Pub.L. 111–350, § 3, Jan. 4, 2011, 124 Stat. 3816.)

§ 7102. Applicability of chapter

  (a) Executive agency contracts.—Unless otherwise specifically provided in this chapter, this chapter applies to any express or implied contract (including those of the nonappropriated fund activities described in sections 1346 and 1491 of title 28) made by an executive agency for—

  (1) the procurement of property, other than real property in being;

  (2) the procurement of services;

  (3) the procurement of construction, alteration, repair, or maintenance of real property; or

  (4) the disposal of personal property.

  (b) Tennessee Valley Authority contracts.—

  (1) In general.—With respect to contracts of the Tennessee Valley Authority, this chapter applies only to contracts containing a clause that requires contract disputes to be resolved through an agency administrative process.

  (2) Exclusion.—Notwithstanding any other provision of this chapter, this chapter does not apply to a contract of the Tennessee Valley Authority for the sale of fertilizer or electric power or related to the conduct or operation of the electric power system.

  (c) Foreign government or international organization contracts.—If an agency head determines that applying this chapter would not be in the public interest, this chapter does not apply to a contract with a foreign government, an agency of a foreign government, an international organization, or a subsidiary body of an international organization.

(d) Maritime contracts.—Appeals under section 7107(a) of this title and actions brought under sections 7104(b) and 7107(b) to (f) of this title, arising out of maritime contracts, are governed by chapter 309 or 311 of title 46, as applicable, to the extent that those chapters are not inconsistent with this chapter.

(Pub.L. 111–350, § 3, Jan. 4, 2011, 124 Stat. 3817.)

HISTORICAL AND STATUTORY NOTES

References in Text

Chapter 309 of title 46, referred to in subsec. (d), is classified to 46 U.S.C.A. § 30901 et seq.

Chapter 311 of title 46, referred to in subsec. (d), is classified to 46 U.S.C.A. § 31101 et seq.

CROSS REFERENCES

Tennessee Valley Authority, Generally, see 16 USCA § 831 et seq.

Actions involving Tennessee Valley Authority, jurisdiction of United States Claims Court, see 28 USCA § 1491.

§ 7103. Decision by contracting officer

(a) Claims generally.—

(1) **Submission of contractor's claims to contracting officer.**—Each claim by a contractor against the Federal Government relating to a contract shall be submitted to the contracting officer for a decision.

(2) **Contractor's claims in writing.**—Each claim by a contractor against the Federal Government relating to a contract shall be in writing.

(3) **Contracting officer to decide Federal Government's claims.**—Each claim by the Federal Government against a contractor relating to a contract shall be the subject of a written decision by the contracting officer.

(4) **Time for submitting claims.**—

(A) **In general.**—Each claim by a contractor against the Federal Government relating to a contract and each claim by the Federal Government against a contractor relating to a contract shall be submitted within 6 years after the accrual of the claim.

(B) **Exception.**—Subparagraph (A) of this paragraph does not apply to a claim by the Federal Government against a contractor that is based on a claim by the contractor involving fraud.

(5) **Applicability.**—The authority of this subsection and subsections (c)(1), (d), and (e) does not extend to a claim or dispute for penalties or forfeitures prescribed by statute or regulation that another Federal agency is specifically authorized to administer, settle, or determine.

(b) Certification of claims.—

(1) **Requirement generally.**—For claims of more than $100,000 made by a contractor, the contractor shall certify that—

(A) the claim is made in good faith;

(B) the supporting data are accurate and complete to the best of the contractor's knowledge and belief;

(C) the amount requested accurately reflects the contract adjustment for which the contractor believes the Federal Government is liable; and

(D) the certifier is authorized to certify the claim on behalf of the contractor.

(2) **Who may execute certification.**—The certification required by paragraph (1) may be executed by an individual authorized to bind the contractor with respect to the claim.

(3) **Failure to certify or defective certification.**—A contracting officer is not obligated to render a final decision on a claim of more than $100,000 that is not certified in accordance with paragraph (1) if, within 60 days after receipt of the claim, the contracting officer notifies the contractor in writing of the reasons why any attempted certification was found to be defective. A defect in the certification

of a claim does not deprive a court or an agency board of jurisdiction over the claim. Prior to the entry of a final judgment by a court or a decision by an agency board, the court or agency board shall require a defective certification to be corrected.

(c) Fraudulent claims.—

(1) **No authority to settle.**—This section does not authorize an agency head to settle, compromise, pay, or otherwise adjust any claim involving fraud.

(2) **Liability of contractor.**—If a contractor is unable to support any part of the contractor's claim and it is determined that the inability is attributable to a misrepresentation of fact or fraud by the contractor, then the contractor is liable to the Federal Government for an amount equal to the unsupported part of the claim plus all of the Federal Government' s costs attributable to reviewing the unsupported part of the claim. Liability under this paragraph shall be determined within 6 years of the commission of the misrepresentation of fact or fraud.

(d) Issuance of decision.—The contracting officer shall issue a decision in writing and shall mail or otherwise furnish a copy of the decision to the contractor.

(e) Contents of decision.—The contracting officer's decision shall state the reasons for the decision reached and shall inform the contractor of the contractor's rights as provided in this chapter. Specific findings of fact are not required. If made, specific findings of fact are not binding in any subsequent proceeding.

(f) Time for issuance of decision.—

(1) **Claim of $100,000 or less.**—A contracting officer shall issue a decision on any submitted claim of $100,000 or less within 60 days from the contracting officer's receipt of a written request from the contractor that a decision be rendered within that period.

(2) **Claim of more than $100,000.**—A contracting officer shall, within 60 days of receipt of a submitted certified claim over $100,000—

(A) issue a decision; or

(B) notify the contractor of the time within which a decision will be issued.

(3) **General requirement of reasonableness.**—The decision of a contracting officer on submitted claims shall be issued within a reasonable time, in accordance with regulations prescribed by the agency, taking into account such factors as the size and complexity of the claim and the adequacy of information in support of the claim provided by the contractor.

(4) **Requesting tribunal to direct issuance within specified time period.**—A contractor may request the tribunal concerned to direct a contracting officer to issue a decision in a specified period of time, as determined by the tribunal concerned, in the event of undue delay on the part of the contracting officer.

(5) **Failure to issue decision within required time period.**—Failure by a contracting officer to issue a decision on a claim within the required time period is deemed to be a decision by the contracting officer denying the claim and authorizes an appeal or action on the claim as otherwise provided in this chapter. However, the tribunal concerned may, at its option, stay the proceedings of the appeal or action to obtain a decision by the contracting officer.

(g) Finality of decision unless appealed.—The contracting officer's decision on a claim is final and conclusive and is not subject to review by any forum, tribunal, or Federal Government agency, unless an appeal or action is timely commenced as authorized by this chapter. This chapter does not prohibit an executive agency from including a clause in a Federal Government contract requiring that, pending final decision of an appeal, action, or final settlement, a contractor shall proceed diligently with performance of the contract in accordance with the contracting officer's decision.

(h) Alternative means of dispute resolution.—

(1) **In general.**—Notwithstanding any other provision of this chapter, a contractor and a contracting officer may use any alternative means of dispute resolution under subchapter IV of chapter 5 of title 5, or other mutually agreeable procedures, for resolving claims. All provisions of subchapter IV of chapter 5 of title 5 apply to alternative means of dispute resolution under this subsection.

See Main Volume and Repealed Title 41, ante, for annotations

(2) Certification of claim.—The contractor shall certify the claim when required to do so under subsection (b)(1) or other law.

(3) Rejecting request for alternative dispute resolution.—

    (A) Contracting officer.—A contracting officer who rejects a contractor's request for alternative dispute resolution proceedings shall provide the contractor with a written explanation, citing one or more of the conditions in section 572(b) of title 5 or other specific reasons that alternative dispute resolution procedures are inappropriate.

    (B) Contractor.—A contractor that rejects an agency's request for alternative dispute resolution proceedings shall inform the agency in writing of the contractor's specific reasons for rejecting the request.

(Pub.L. 111–350, § 3, Jan. 4, 2011, 124 Stat. 3817.)

HISTORICAL AND STATUTORY NOTES

References in Text

Subchapter IV of chapter 5 of title 5, referred to in subsec. (h)(1), is classified to 5 U.S.C.A. § 571 et seq.

CROSS REFERENCES

Tennessee Valley Authority, Generally, see 16 USCA § 831 et seq.

Actions involving Tennessee Valley Authority, jurisdiction of United States Claims Court, see 28 USCA § 1491.

§ 7104. Contractor's right of appeal from decision by contracting officer

(a) Appeal to agency board.—A contractor, within 90 days from the date of receipt of a contracting officer's decision under section 7103 of this title, may appeal the decision to an agency board as provided in section 7105 of this title.

(b) Bringing an action de novo in Federal Court.—

    (1) In general.—Except as provided in paragraph (2), and in lieu of appealing the decision of a contracting officer under section 7103 of this title to an agency board, a contractor may bring an action directly on the claim in the United States Court of Federal Claims, notwithstanding any contract provision, regulation, or rule of law to the contrary.

    (2) Tennessee Valley Authority.—In the case of an action against the Tennessee Valley Authority, the contractor may only bring an action directly on the claim in a district court of the United States pursuant to section 1337 of title 28, notwithstanding any contract provision, regulation, or rule of law to the contrary.

    (3) Time for filing.—A contractor shall file any action under paragraph (1) or (2) within 12 months from the date of receipt of a contracting officer's decision under section 7103 of this title.

    (4) De novo.—An action under paragraph (1) or (2) shall proceed de novo in accordance with the rules of the appropriate court.

(Pub.L. 111–350, § 3, Jan. 4, 2011, 124 Stat. 3820.)

CROSS REFERENCES

Tennessee Valley Authority, Generally, see 16 USCA § 831 et seq. Actions involving Tennessee Valley Authority, jurisdiction of United States Claims Court, see 28 USCA § 1491.

United States Court of Federal Claims, organization, and jurisdiction and venue, see 28 USCA § 171 et seq., and 28 USCA § 1491 et seq.

§ 7105. Agency boards

(a) Armed Services Board.—

    (1) Establishment.—An Armed Services Board of Contract Appeals may be established within the Department of Defense when the Secretary of Defense, after consultation with the Administrator, determines from a workload study that the volume of contract claims justifies the establishment of a full-time agency board of at least 3 members who shall have no other inconsistent duties. Workload studies will be updated at least once every 3 years and submitted to the Administrator.

(2) **Appointment of members and compensation.**—Members of the Armed Services Board shall be selected and appointed in the same manner as administrative law judges appointed pursuant to section 3105 of title 5, with an additional requirement that members must have had at least 5 years of experience in public contract law. The Secretary of Defense shall designate the chairman and vice chairman of the Armed Services Board from among the appointed members. Compensation for the chairman, vice chairman, and other members shall be determined under section 5372a of title 5.

(b) **Civilian Board.—**

(1) **Establishment.**—There is established in the General Services Administration the Civilian Board of Contract Appeals.

(2) **Membership.—**

(A) **Eligibility.**—The Civilian Board consists of members appointed by the Administrator of General Services (in consultation with the Administrator for Federal Procurement Policy) from a register of applicants maintained by the Administrator of General Services, in accordance with rules issued by the Administrator of General Services (in consultation with the Administrator for Federal Procurement Policy) for establishing and maintaining a register of eligible applicants and selecting Civilian Board members. The Administrator of General Services shall appoint a member without regard to political affiliation and solely on the basis of the professional qualifications required to perform the duties and responsibilities of a Civilian Board member.

(B) **Appointment of members and compensation.**—Members of the Civilian Board shall be selected and appointed to serve in the same manner as administrative law judges appointed pursuant to section 3105 of title 5, with an additional requirement that members must have had at least 5 years experience in public contract law. Compensation for the members shall be determined under section 5372a of title 5.

(3) **Removal.**—Members of the Civilian Board are subject to removal in the same manner as administrative law judges, as provided in section 7521 of title 5.

(4) **Functions.—**

(A) **In general.**—The Civilian Board has jurisdiction as provided by subsection (e)(1)(B).

(B) **Additional jurisdiction.**—With the concurrence of the Federal agencies affected, the Civilian Board may assume—

(i) jurisdiction over any additional category of laws or disputes over which an agency board of contract appeals established pursuant to section 8 of the Contract Disputes Act exercised jurisdiction before January 6, 2007; and

(ii) any other function the agency board performed before January 6, 2007, on behalf of those agencies.

(c) **Tennessee Valley Authority Board.—**

(1) **Establishment.**—The Board of Directors of the Tennessee Valley Authority may establish a board of contract appeals of the Tennessee Valley Authority of an indeterminate number of members.

(2) **Appointment of members and compensation.**—The Board of Directors of the Tennessee Valley Authority shall establish criteria for the appointment of members to the agency board established under paragraph (1), and shall designate a chairman of the agency board. The chairman and other members of the agency board shall receive compensation, at the daily equivalent of the rates determined under section 5372a of title 5, for each day they are engaged in the actual performance of their duties as members of the agency board.

(d) **Postal Service Board.—**

(1) **Establishment.**—There is established an agency board of contract appeals known as the Postal Service Board of Contract Appeals.

See Main Volume and Repealed Title 41, ante, for annotations

(2) **Appointment and service of members.**—The Postal Service Board of Contract Appeals consists of judges appointed by the Postmaster General. The judges shall meet the qualifications of and serve in the same manner as members of the Civilian Board.

(3) **Application.**—This chapter applies to contract disputes before the Postal Service Board of Contract Appeals in the same manner as it applies to contract disputes before the Civilian Board.

(e) **Jurisdiction.**—

(1) **In general.**—

(A) **Armed Services Board.**—The Armed Services Board has jurisdiction to decide any appeal from a decision of a contracting officer of the Department of Defense, the Department of the Army, the Department of the Navy, the Department of the Air Force, or the National Aeronautics and Space Administration relative to a contract made by that department or agency.

(B) **Civilian Board.**—The Civilian Board has jurisdiction to decide any appeal from a decision of a contracting officer of any executive agency (other than the Department of Defense, the Department of the Army, the Department of the Navy, the Department of the Air Force, the National Aeronautics and Space Administration, the United States Postal Service, the Postal Regulatory Commission, or the Tennessee Valley Authority) relative to a contract made by that agency.

(C) **Postal Service Board.**—The Postal Service Board of Contract Appeals has jurisdiction to decide any appeal from a decision of a contracting officer of the United States Postal Service or the Postal Regulatory Commission relative to a contract made by either agency.

(D) **Other agency boards.**—Each other agency board has jurisdiction to decide any appeal from a decision of a contracting officer relative to a contract made by its agency.

(2) **Relief.**—In exercising this jurisdiction, an agency board may grant any relief that would be available to a litigant asserting a contract claim in the United States Court of Federal Claims.

(f) **Subpoena, discovery, and deposition.**—A member of an agency board of contract appeals may administer oaths to witnesses, authorize depositions and discovery proceedings, and require by subpoena the attendance of witnesses, and production of books and papers, for the taking of testimony or evidence by deposition or in the hearing of an appeal by the agency board. In case of contumacy or refusal to obey a subpoena by a person who resides, is found, or transacts business within the jurisdiction of a United States district court, the court, upon application of the agency board through the Attorney General, or upon application by the board of contract appeals of the Tennessee Valley Authority, shall have jurisdiction to issue the person an order requiring the person to appear before the agency board or a member of the agency board, to produce evidence or to give testimony, or both. Any failure of the person to obey the order of the court may be punished by the court as contempt of court.

(g) **Decisions.**—An agency board shall—

(1) to the fullest extent practicable provide informal, expeditious, and inexpensive resolution of disputes;

(2) issue a decision in writing or take other appropriate action on each appeal submitted; and

(3) mail or otherwise furnish a copy of the decision to the contractor and the contracting officer.

(Pub.L. 111–350, § 3, Jan. 4, 2011, 124 Stat. 3820; Pub.L. 111–383, Div. A, Title X, § 1075(*o*), Jan. 7, 2011, 124 Stat. 4378.)

Amendment Subsequent to December 31, 2008

Pub.L. 111–350, Jan. 4, 2011, 124 Stat. 3677, which codified T. 41, Public Contracts, as positive law, directed that if a law enacted after Dec. 31, 2008, amends or repeals a provision replaced by Pub.L. 111–350, that law is deemed to amend or repeal, as the case may be, the corresponding provision enacted by Pub.L. 111–350, see Pub.L. 111–350, § 6(a), Jan. 4, 2011, 124 Stat. 3854, set out as a note provision preceding 41 U.S.C.A. § 101.

Pub.L. 111–383, Div. A, Title X, § 1075(o), Jan. 7, 2011, 124 Stat. 4378, amended former 41 U.S.C.A. § 438, from which this section was derived, resulting in no change in text.

HISTORICAL AND STATUTORY NOTES

References in Text

The Contract Disputes Act of 1978, referred to in subsec. (b)(4)(B)(i), is Pub.L. 95–563, Nov. 1, 1978, 92 Stat. 2383, which was classified principally to chapter 9 of former Title 41, 41 U.S.C.A. § 601 et seq., and was substantially repealed and restated as chapter 71 of Title 41, 41 U.S.C.A. § 7101 et seq., by Pub.L. 111–350, §§ 3, 7(b), Jan. 4, 2011, 124 Stat. 3677, 3855. For complete classification, see Tables. For disposition of sections of former Title 41, see Disposition Table preceding 41 U.S.C.A. § 101.

CROSS REFERENCES

Tennessee Valley Authority,
  Generally, see 16 USCA § 831 et seq.
  Actions involving Tennessee Valley Authority, jurisdiction of United States Claims Court, see 28 USCA § 1491.

Board of Directors, creation and duties, see 16 USCA §§ 831 and 831a.

§ 7106. Agency board procedures for accelerated and small claims

(a) Accelerated procedure where $100,000 or less in dispute.—The rules of each agency board shall include a procedure for the accelerated disposition of any appeal from a decision of a contracting officer where the amount in dispute is $100,000 or less. The accelerated procedure is applicable at the sole election of the contractor. An appeal under the accelerated procedure shall be resolved, whenever possible, within 180 days from the date the contractor elects to use the procedure.

(b) Small claims procedure.—

(1) In general.—The rules of each agency board shall include a procedure for the expedited disposition of any appeal from a decision of a contracting officer where the amount in dispute is $50,000 or less, or in the case of a small business concern (as defined in the Small Business Act (15 U.S.C. 631 et seq.) and regulations under that Act), $150,000 or less. The small claims procedure is applicable at the sole election of the contractor.

(2) Simplified rules of procedure.—The small claims procedure shall provide for simplified rules of procedure to facilitate the decision of any appeal. An appeal under the small claims procedure may be decided by a single member of the agency board with such concurrences as may be provided by rule or regulation.

(3) Time of decision.—An appeal under the small claims procedure shall be resolved, whenever possible, within 120 days from the date the contractor elects to use the procedure.

(4) Finality of decision.—A decision against the Federal Government or against the contractor reached under the small claims procedure is final and conclusive and may not be set aside except in cases of fraud.

(5) No precedent.—Administrative determinations and final decisions under this subsection have no value as precedent for future cases under this chapter.

(6) Review of requisite amounts in controversy.—The Administrator, from time to time, may review the dollar amounts specified in paragraph (1) and adjust the amounts in accordance with economic indexes selected by the Administrator.

(Pub.L. 111–350, § 3, Jan. 4, 2011, 124 Stat. 3823.)

HISTORICAL AND STATUTORY NOTES

References in Text

The Small Business Act, referred to in subsec. (b)(1), is Act July 18, 1958, Pub.L. 85–536, 72 Stat. 384, as amended, also known as the SBA, which is principally classified to chapter 14A of Title 15, 15 U.S.C.A. § 631 et seq. For complete classification, see Short Title note set out under 15 U.S.C.A. § 631 and Tables.

See Main Volume and Repealed Title 41, ante, for annotations

§ 7107.　Judicial review of agency board decisions

(a) Review.—

(1) In general.—The decision of an agency board is final, except that—

(A) a contractor may appeal the decision to the United States Court of Appeals for the Federal Circuit within 120 days from the date the contractor receives a copy of the decision; or

(B) if an agency head determines that an appeal should be taken, the agency head, with the prior approval of the Attorney General, may transmit the decision to the United States Court of Appeals for the Federal Circuit for judicial review under section 1295 of title 28, within 120 days from the date the agency receives a copy of the decision.

(2) Tennessee Valley Authority.—Notwithstanding paragraph (1), a decision of the board of contract appeals of the Tennessee Valley Authority is final, except that—

(A) a contractor may appeal the decision to a United States district court pursuant to section 1337 of title 28, within 120 days from the date the contractor receives a copy of the decision; or

(B) the Tennessee Valley Authority may appeal the decision to a United States district court pursuant to section 1337 of title 28, within 120 days from the date of the decision.

(3) Review of arbitration.—An award by an arbitrator under this chapter shall be reviewed pursuant to sections 9 to 13 of title 9, except that the court may set aside or limit any award that is found to violate limitations imposed by Federal statute.

(b) Finality of agency board decisions on questions of law and fact.—Notwithstanding any contract provision, regulation, or rule of law to the contrary, in an appeal by a contractor or the Federal Government from the decision of an agency board pursuant to subsection (a)—

(1) the decision of the agency board on a question of law is not final or conclusive; but

(2) the decision of the agency board on a question of fact is final and conclusive and may not be set aside unless the decision is—

(A) fraudulent, arbitrary, or capricious;

(B) so grossly erroneous as to necessarily imply bad faith; or

(C) not supported by substantial evidence.

(c) Remand.—In an appeal by a contractor or the Federal Government from the decision of an agency board pursuant to subsection (a), the court may render an opinion and judgment and remand the case for further action by the agency board or by the executive agency as appropriate, with direction the court considers just and proper.

(d) Consolidation.—If 2 or more actions arising from one contract are filed in the United States Court of Federal Claims and one or more agency boards, for the convenience of parties or witnesses or in the interest of justice, the United States Court of Federal Claims may order the consolidation of the actions in that court or transfer any actions to or among the agency boards involved.

(e) Judgments as to fewer than all claims or parties.—In an action filed pursuant to this chapter involving 2 or more claims, counterclaims, cross-claims, or third-party claims, and where a portion of one of the claims can be divided for purposes of decision or judgment, and in any action where multiple parties are involved, the court, whenever appropriate, may enter a judgment as to one or more but fewer than all of the claims or portions of claims or parties.

(f) Advisory opinions.—

(1) In general.—Whenever an action involving an issue described in paragraph (2) is pending in a district court of the United States, the district court may request an agency board to provide the court with an advisory opinion on the matters of contract interpretation under consideration.

(2) **Applicable issue.**—An issue referred to in paragraph (1) is any issue that could be the proper subject of a final decision of a contracting officer appealable under this chapter.

(3) **Referral to agency board with jurisdiction.**—A district court shall direct a request under paragraph (1) to the agency board having jurisdiction under this chapter to adjudicate appeals of contract claims under the contract being interpreted by the court.

(4) **Timely response.**—After receiving a request for an advisory opinion under paragraph (1), an agency board shall provide the advisory opinion in a timely manner to the district court making the request.

(Pub.L. 111–350, § 3, Jan. 4, 2011, 124 Stat. 3824.)

CROSS REFERENCES

Tennessee Valley Authority,
    Generally, see 16 USCA § 831 et seq.

Actions involving Tennessee Valley Authority, jurisdiction of United States Claims Court, see 28 USCA § 1491.

§ 7108. Payment of claims

(a) **Judgments.**—Any judgment against the Federal Government on a claim under this chapter shall be paid promptly in accordance with the procedures provided by section 1304 of title 31.

(b) **Monetary awards.**—Any monetary award to a contractor by an agency board shall be paid promptly in accordance with the procedures contained in subsection (a).

(c) **Reimbursement.**—Payments made pursuant to subsections (a) and (b) shall be reimbursed to the fund provided by section 1304 of title 31 by the agency whose appropriations were used for the contract out of available amounts or by obtaining additional appropriations for purposes of reimbursement.

(d) **Tennessee Valley Authority.**—

(1) **Judgments.**—Notwithstanding subsections (a) to (c), any judgment against the Tennessee Valley Authority on a claim under this chapter shall be paid promptly in accordance with section 9(b) of the Tennessee Valley Authority Act of 1933 (16 U.S.C. 831h(b)).

(2) **Monetary awards.**—Notwithstanding subsections (a) to (c), any monetary award to a contractor by the board of contract appeals of the Tennessee Valley Authority shall be paid in accordance with section 9(b) of the Tennessee Valley Authority Act of 1933 (16 U.S.C. 831h(b)).

(Pub.L. 111–350, § 3, Jan. 4, 2011, 124 Stat. 3825.)

HISTORICAL AND STATUTORY NOTES

References in Text

The Tennessee Valley Authority Act of 1933, referred to in subsec. (d), is Act May 18, 1933, c. 32, 48 Stat. 58, also known as the TVA Act, which is classified principally to chapter 12A of Title 16, 16 U.S.C.A. § 831 et seq. Section 9 of the Act is classified to 16 U.S.C.A. § 831h. For complete classification, see Short Title note set out under 16 U.S.C.A. § 831 and Tables.

CROSS REFERENCES

Tennessee Valley Authority,
    Generally, see 16 USCA § 831 et seq.

Actions involving Tennessee Valley Authority, jurisdiction of United States Claims Court, see 28 USCA § 1491.

§ 7109. Interest

(a) **Period.**—

(1) **In general.**—Interest on an amount found due a contractor on a claim shall be paid to the contractor for the period beginning with the date the contracting officer receives the contractor's claim, pursuant to section 7103(a) of this title, until the date of payment of the claim.

(2) **Defective certification.**—On a claim for which the certification under section 7103(b)(1) of this title is found to be defective, any interest due under this section

shall be paid for the period beginning with the date the contracting officer initially receives the contractor's claim until the date of payment of the claim.

(b) **Rate.**—Interest shall accrue and be paid at a rate which the Secretary of the Treasury shall specify as applicable for each successive 6–month period. The rate shall be determined by the Secretary of the Treasury taking into consideration current private commercial rates of interest for new loans maturing in approximately 5 years.

(Pub.L. 111–350, § 3, Jan. 4, 2011, 124 Stat. 3825.)

SUBTITLE IV—MISCELLANEOUS

CHAPTER 81—DRUG–FREE WORKPLACE

§ 8101. Definitions and construction

(a) **Definitions.**—In this chapter:

(1) **Contractor.**—The term "contractor" means the department, division, or other unit of a person responsible for the performance under the contract.

(2) **Controlled substance.**—The term "controlled substance" means a controlled substance in schedules I through V of section 202 of the Comprehensive Drug Abuse Prevention and Control Act of 1970 (21 U.S.C. 812).

(3) **Conviction.**—The term "conviction" means a finding of guilt (including a plea of nolo contendere), an imposition of sentence, or both, by a judicial body charged with the responsibility to determine violations of Federal or State criminal drug statutes.

(4) **Criminal drug statute.**—The term "criminal drug statute" means a criminal statute involving manufacture, distribution, dispensation, use, or possession of a controlled substance.

(5) **Drug-free workplace.**—The term "drug-free workplace" means a site of an entity—

(A) for the performance of work done in connection with a specific contract or grant described in section 8102 or 8103 of this title; and

(B) at which employees of the entity are prohibited from engaging in the unlawful manufacture, distribution, dispensation, possession, or use of a controlled substance in accordance with the requirements of the Anti–Drug Abuse Act of 1988 (Public Law 100–690, 102 Stat. 4181).

(6) **Employee.**—The term "employee" means the employee of a contractor or grantee directly engaged in the performance of work pursuant to the contract or grant described in section 8102 or 8103 of this title.

(7) **Federal agency.**—The term "Federal agency" means an agency as defined in section 552(f) of title 5.

(8) **Grantee.**—The term "grantee" means the department, division, or other unit of a person responsible for the performance under the grant.

(b) **Construction.**—This chapter does not require law enforcement agencies to comply with this chapter if the head of the agency determines it would be inappropriate in connection with the agency's undercover operations.

(Pub.L. 111–350, § 3, Jan. 4, 2011, 124 Stat. 3826.)

HISTORICAL AND STATUTORY NOTES

References in Text

The Comprehensive Drug Abuse Prevention and Control Act of 1970, referred to in subsec. (a)(2), is Pub.L. 91–513, Oct. 27, 1970, 84 Stat. 1236, as amended, which is classified principally to chapter 13 of Title 21, 21 U.S.C.A. § 801 et seq. Section 202 of the Act is classified to 21 U.S.C.A. § 812. For complete classification, see

Short Title note set out under 21 U.S.C.A. § 801 and Tables.

The Anti–Drug Abuse Act of 1988, referred to in subsec. (a)(5), is Pub.L. 100–690, Nov. 18, 1988, 102 Stat. 4181, also known as the Drug Kingpin Act. For classification, see Short Title note set out under 21 U.S.C.A. § 1501 and Tables.

§ 8102. Drug-free workplace requirements for Federal contractors

(a) **In general.**—

(1) **Persons other than individuals.**—A person other than an individual shall not be considered a responsible source (as defined in section 113 of this title) for the purposes of being awarded a contract for the procurement of any property or services of a value greater than the simplified acquisition threshold (as defined in section 134 of this title) by a Federal agency, other than a contract for the procurement of commercial items (as defined in section 103 of this title), unless the person agrees to provide a drug-free workplace by—

(A) publishing a statement notifying employees that the unlawful manufacture, distribution, dispensation, possession, or use of a controlled substance is prohibited in the person's workplace and specifying the actions that will be taken against employees for violations of the prohibition;

(B) establishing a drug–free awareness program to inform employees about—

(i) the dangers of drug abuse in the workplace;

(ii) the person's policy of maintaining a drug-free workplace;

(iii) available drug counseling, rehabilitation, and employee assistance programs; and

(iv) the penalties that may be imposed on employees for drug abuse violations;

(C) making it a requirement that each employee to be engaged in the performance of the contract be given a copy of the statement required by subparagraph (A);

(D) notifying the employee in the statement required by subparagraph (A) that as a condition of employment on the contract the employee will—

(i) abide by the terms of the statement; and

(ii) notify the employer of any criminal drug statute conviction for a violation occurring in the workplace no later than 5 days after the conviction;

(E) notifying the contracting agency within 10 days after receiving notice under subparagraph (D)(ii) from an employee or otherwise receiving actual notice of a conviction;

(F) imposing a sanction on, or requiring the satisfactory participation in a drug abuse assistance or rehabilitation program by, any employee who is convicted, as required by section 8104 of this title; and

(G) making a good faith effort to continue to maintain a drug-free workplace through implementation of subparagraphs (A) to (F).

(2) **Individuals.**—A Federal agency shall not make a contract with an individual unless the individual agrees not to engage in the unlawful manufacture, distribution, dispensation, possession, or use of a controlled substance in the performance of the contract.

See Main Volume and Repealed Title 41, ante, for annotations

(b) Suspension, termination, or debarment of contractor.—

 (1) Grounds for suspension, termination, or debarment.—Payment under a contract awarded by a Federal agency may be suspended and the contract may be terminated, and the contractor or individual who made the contract with the agency may be suspended or debarred in accordance with the requirements of this section, if the head of the agency determines that—

  (A) the contractor is violating, or has violated, the requirements of subparagraph (A), (B), (C), (D), (E), or (F) of subsection (a)(1); or

  (B) the number of employees of the contractor who have been convicted of violations of criminal drug statutes for violations occurring in the workplace indicates that the contractor has failed to make a good faith effort to provide a drug-free workplace as required by subsection (a).

 (2) Conduct of suspension, termination, and debarment proceedings.—A contracting officer who determines in writing that cause for suspension of payments, termination, or suspension or debarment exists shall initiate an appropriate action, to be conducted by the agency concerned in accordance with the Federal Acquisition Regulation and applicable agency procedures. The Federal Acquisition Regulation shall be revised to include rules for conducting suspension and debarment proceedings under this subsection, including rules providing notice, opportunity to respond in writing or in person, and other procedures as may be necessary to provide a full and fair proceeding to a contractor or individual.

 (3) Effect of debarment.—A contractor or individual debarred by a final decision under this subsection is ineligible for award of a contract by a Federal agency, and for participation in a future procurement by a Federal agency, for a period specified in the decision, not to exceed 5 years.

(Pub.L. 111–350, § 3, Jan. 4, 2011, 124 Stat. 3827.)

§ 8103. Drug-free workplace requirements for Federal grant recipients

(a) In general.—

 (1) Persons other than individuals.—A person other than an individual shall not receive a grant from a Federal agency unless the person agrees to provide a drug-free workplace by—

  (A) publishing a statement notifying employees that the unlawful manufacture, distribution, dispensation, possession, or use of a controlled substance is prohibited in the grantee's workplace and specifying the actions that will be taken against employees for violations of the prohibition;

  (B) establishing a drug–free awareness program to inform employees about—

   (i) the dangers of drug abuse in the workplace;

   (ii) the grantee's policy of maintaining a drug-free workplace;

   (iii) available drug counseling, rehabilitation, and employee assistance programs; and

   (iv) the penalties that may be imposed on employees for drug abuse violations;

  (C) making it a requirement that each employee to be engaged in the performance of the grant be given a copy of the statement required by subparagraph (A);

  (D) notifying the employee in the statement required by subparagraph (A) that as a condition of employment in the grant the employee will—

   (i) abide by the terms of the statement; and

   (ii) notify the employer of any criminal drug statute conviction for a violation occurring in the workplace no later than 5 days after the conviction;

  (E) notifying the granting agency within 10 days after receiving notice under subparagraph (D)(ii) from an employee or otherwise receiving actual notice of a conviction;

   (F) imposing a sanction on, or requiring the satisfactory participation in a drug abuse assistance or rehabilitation program by, any employee who is convicted, as required by section 8104 of this title; and

   (G) making a good faith effort to continue to maintain a drug-free workplace through implementation of subparagraphs (A) to (F).

  (2) Individuals.—A Federal agency shall not make a grant to an individual unless the individual agrees not to engage in the unlawful manufacture, distribution, dispensation, possession, or use of a controlled substance in conducting an activity with the grant.

(b) Suspension, termination, or debarment of grantee.—

  (1) Grounds for suspension, termination, or debarment.—Payment under a grant awarded by a Federal agency may be suspended and the grant may be terminated, and the grantee may be suspended or debarred, in accordance with the requirements of this section, if the head of the agency or the official designee of the head of the agency determines in writing that—

   (A) the grantee is violating, or has violated, the requirements of subparagraph (A), (B), (C), (D), (E), (F), or (G) of subsection (a)(1); or

   (B) the number of employees of the grantee who have been convicted of violations of criminal drug statutes for violations occurring in the workplace indicates that the grantee has failed to make a good faith effort to provide a drug-free workplace as required by subsection (a)(1).

  (2) Conduct of suspension, termination, and debarment proceedings.—A suspension of payments, termination, or suspension or debarment proceeding subject to this subsection shall be conducted in accordance with applicable law, including Executive Order 12549 or any superseding executive order and any regulations prescribed to implement the law or executive order.

  (3) Effect of debarment.—A grantee debarred by a final decision under this subsection is ineligible for award of a grant by a Federal agency, and for participation in a future grant by a Federal agency, for a period specified in the decision, not to exceed 5 years.

(Pub.L. 111–350, § 3, Jan. 4, 2011, 124 Stat. 3828.)

§ 8104. Employee sanctions and remedies

Within 30 days after receiving notice from an employee of a conviction pursuant to section 8102(a)(1)(D)(ii) or 8103(a)(1)(D)(ii) of this title, a contractor or grantee shall—

  (1) take appropriate personnel action against the employee, up to and including termination; or

  (2) require the employee to satisfactorily participate in a drug abuse assistance or rehabilitation program approved for those purposes by a Federal, State, or local health, law enforcement, or other appropriate agency.

(Pub.L. 111–350, § 3, Jan. 4, 2011, 124 Stat. 3830.)

§ 8105. Waiver

  (a) In general.—The head of an agency may waive a suspension of payments, termination of the contract or grant, or suspension or debarment of a contractor or grantee under this chapter with respect to a particular contract or grant if—

  (1) in the case of a contract, the head of the agency determines under section 8102(b)(1) of this title, after a final determination is issued under section 8102(b)(1), that suspension of payments, termination of the contract, suspension or debarment of the contractor, or refusal to permit a person to be treated as a responsible source for a contract would severely disrupt the operation of the agency to the detriment of the Federal Government or the general public; or

  (2) in the case of a grant, the head of the agency determines that suspension of payments, termination of the grant, or suspension or debarment of the grantee would not be in the public interest.

See Main Volume and Repealed Title 41, ante, for annotations

(b) Waiver authority may not be delegated.—The authority of the head of an agency under this section to waive a suspension, termination, or debarment shall not be delegated.

(Pub.L. 111–350, § 3, Jan. 4, 2011, 124 Stat. 3830.)

§ 8106. Regulations

Government–wide regulations governing actions under this chapter shall be issued pursuant to division B of subtitle I of this title.

(Pub.L. 111–350, § 3, Jan. 4, 2011, 124 Stat. 3830.)

CHAPTER 83—BUY AMERICAN

§ 8301. Definitions

In this chapter:

    (1) Public building, public use, and public work.—The terms "public building", "public use", and "public work" mean a public building of, use by, and a public work of, the Federal Government, the District of Columbia, Puerto Rico, American Samoa, and the Virgin Islands.

    (2) United States.—The term "United States" includes any place subject to the jurisdiction of the United States.

(Pub.L. 111–350, § 3, Jan. 4, 2011, 124 Stat. 3830.)

HISTORICAL AND STATUTORY NOTES

Water Resource Projects; Cofferdam

Pub.L. 100–371, Title V, § 508, July 19, 1988, 102 Stat. 875, provided that:

"**(a) General Rule.**—For purposes of title III of the Act of March 3, 1933 (47 Stat. 1520; 41 U.S.C. 10a–10c) [former sections 10a to 10c of this title], commonly known as the Buy American Act, a cofferdam or any other temporary structure to be constructed by the Secretary of the Army, acting through the Chief of Engi-

neers, shall be treated in the same manner as a permanent dam constructed by the Secretary of the Army.

"**(b) Applicability.**—Subsection (a) shall only apply to contracts entered into after the date of the enactment of this Act [July 19, 1988]."

[Note was classified as a note under former 41 U.S.C.A. § 10a prior to the enactment into positive law of Title 41, Public Contracts, by Pub.L. 111–350, Jan. 4, 2011, 124 Stat. 3677.]

§ 8302. American materials required for public use

(a) In general.—

    (1) Allowable materials.—Only unmanufactured articles, materials, and supplies that have been mined or produced in the United States, and only manufactured articles, materials, and supplies that have been manufactured in the United States substantially all from articles, materials, or supplies mined, produced, or manufactured in the United States, shall be acquired for public use unless the head of the department or independent establishment concerned determines their acquisition to be inconsistent with the public interest or their cost to be unreasonable.

    (2) Exceptions.—This section does not apply—

        (A) to articles, materials, or supplies for use outside the United States;

        (B) if articles, materials, or supplies of the class or kind to be used, or the articles, materials, or supplies from which they are manufactured, are not mined, produced, or manufactured in the United States in sufficient and reasonably available commercial quantities and are not of a satisfactory quality; and

(C) to manufactured articles, materials, or supplies procured under any contract with an award value that is not more than the micro-purchase threshold under section 1902 of this title.

(b) Reports.—

(1) In general.—Not later than 180 days after the end of each of fiscal years 2009 through 2011, the head of each Federal agency shall submit to the Committee on Homeland Security and Governmental Affairs of the Senate and the Committee on Oversight and Government Reform of the House of Representatives a report on the amount of the acquisitions made by the agency in that fiscal year of articles, materials, or supplies purchased from entities that manufacture the articles, materials, or supplies outside the United States.

(2) Contents of report.—The report required by paragraph (1) shall separately include, for the fiscal year covered by the report—

(A) the dollar value of any articles, materials, or supplies that were manufactured outside the United States;

(B) an itemized list of all waivers granted with respect to the articles, materials, or supplies under this chapter, and a citation to the treaty, international agreement, or other law under which each waiver was granted;

(C) if any articles, materials, or supplies were acquired from entities that manufacture articles, materials, or supplies outside the United States, the specific exception under this section that was used to purchase the articles, materials, or supplies; and

(D) a summary of—

(i) the total procurement funds expended on articles, materials, and supplies manufactured inside the United States; and

(ii) the total procurement funds expended on articles, materials, and supplies manufactured outside the United States.

(3) Public availability.—The head of each Federal agency submitting a report under paragraph (1) shall make the report publicly available to the maximum extent practicable.

(4) Exception for intelligence community.—This subsection shall not apply to acquisitions made by an agency, or component of an agency, that is an element of the intelligence community as specified in, or designated under, section 3 of the National Security Act of 1947 (50 U.S.C. 401a).

(Pub.L. 111–350, § 3, Jan. 4, 2011, 124 Stat. 3831.)

HISTORICAL AND STATUTORY NOTES

References in Text

The National Security Act of 1947, referred to in subsec. (b)(4), is Act July 26, 1947, c. 343, 61 Stat. 495, as amended. Section 3 of the Act is classified to 50 U.S.C.A. § 401a. For complete classification, see Short Title note set out under 50 U.S.C.A. § 401 and Tables.

CROSS REFERENCES

Aviation programs, buying goods produced in the United States, see 49 USCA § 50101.

§ 8303. Contracts for public works

(a) In general.—Every contract for the construction, alteration, or repair of any public building or public work in the United States shall contain a provision that in the performance of the work the contractor, subcontractors, material men, or suppliers shall use only—

(1) unmanufactured articles, materials, and supplies that have been mined or produced in the United States; and

(2) manufactured articles, materials, and supplies that have been manufactured in the United States substantially all from articles, materials, or supplies mined, produced, or manufactured in the United States.

(b) Exceptions.—

See Main Volume and Repealed Title 41, ante, for annotations

(1) **In general.**—This section does not apply—

(A) to articles, materials, or supplies for use outside the United States;

(B) if articles, materials, or supplies of the class or kind to be used, or the articles, materials, or supplies from which they are manufactured, are not mined, produced, or manufactured in the United States in sufficient and reasonably available commercial quantities and are not of a satisfactory quality; and

(C) to manufactured articles, materials, or supplies procured under any contract with an award value that is not more than the micro-purchase threshold under section 1902 of this title.

(2) **Particular article, material, or supply.**—If the head of the department or independent establishment making the contract finds that it is impracticable to comply with subsection (a) for a particular article, material, or supply or that it would unreasonably increase the cost, an exception shall be noted in the specifications for that article, material, or supply and a public record of the findings that justified the exception shall be made.

(3) **Inconsistent with public interest.**—Subsection (a) shall be regarded as requiring the purchase, for public use within the United States, of articles, materials, or supplies manufactured in the United States in sufficient and reasonably available commercial quantities and of a satisfactory quality, unless the head of the department or independent establishment concerned determines their purchase to be inconsistent with the public interest or their cost to be unreasonable.

(c) **Results of failure to comply.**—If the head of a department, bureau, agency, or independent establishment that has made a contract containing the provision required by subsection (a) finds that there has been a failure to comply with the provision in the performance of the contract, the head of the department, bureau, agency, or independent establishment shall make the findings public. The findings shall include the name of the contractor obligated under the contract. The contractor, and any subcontractor, material man, or supplier associated or affiliated with the contractor, shall not be awarded another contract for the construction, alteration, or repair of any public building or public work for 3 years after the findings are made public.

(Pub.L. 111–350, § 3, Jan. 4, 2011, 124 Stat. 3832.)

EXECUTIVE ORDERS
EXECUTIVE ORDER NO. 10582

Dec. 17, 1954, 19 F.R. 8723, as amended by Ex.Ord. No. 11051, Sept. 27, 1962, 27 F.R. 9683; Ex.Ord. No. 12148, July 20, 1979, 44 F.R. 43239; Ex.Ord. No. 12608, Sept. 9, 1987, 52 F.R. 34617

UNIFORM PROCEDURES FOR DETERMINATIONS

Section 1. As used in this order, (a) the term "materials" includes articles and supplies, (b) the term "executive agency" includes executive department, independent establishment, and other instrumentality of the executive branch of the Government, and (c) the term "bid or offered price of materials of foreign origin" means the bid or offered price of such materials delivered at the place specified in the invitation to bid including applicable duty and all costs incurred after arrival in the United States.

Sec. 2. (a) For the purposes of this order materials shall be considered to be of foreign origin if the cost of the foreign products used in such materials constitutes fifty per centum or more of the cost of all the products used in such materials.

(b) For the purposes of the said act of March 3, 1933 [enacting sections 10a to 10c of this title], and the other laws referred to in the first paragraph of the preamble of this order, the bid or offered price of materials of domestic origin shall be deemed to be unreasonable, or the purchase of such materials shall be deemed to be inconsistent with the public interest, if the bid or offered price thereof exceeds the sum of the bid or offered price of like materials of foreign origin and a differential computed as provided in subsection (c) of this section.

(c) The executive agency concerned shall in each instance determine the amount of the differential referred to in subsection (b) of this section on the basis of one of the following-described formulas, subject to the terms thereof:

(1) The sum determined by computing six per centum of the bid or offered price of materials of foreign origin.

(2) The sum determined by computing ten per centum of the bid or offered price of materials of foreign origin exclusive of applicable duty and all costs incurred after arrival in the United States: provided that when the

bid or offered price of materials of foreign origin amounts to less than $25,000, the sum shall be determined by computing ten per centum of such price exclusive only of applicable duty.

Sec. 3. Nothing in this order shall affect the authority or responsibility of an executive agency:

(a) To reject any bid or offer for reasons of the national interest not described or referred to in this order; or

(b) To place a fair proportion of the total purchases with small business concerns in accordance with section 302(b) of the Federal Property and Administrative Services Act of 1949, as amended [section 252(b) of this title], section 2(b) of the Armed Services Procurement Act of 1947, as amended [former section 151(b) of this title; now covered by sections 2301, 2303–2305 of Title 10, Armed Forces], and section 202 of the Small Business Act of 1953 [section 631 of Title 15, Commerce and Trade]; or

(c) To reject a bid or offer to furnish materials of foreign origin in any situation in which the domestic supplier offering the lowest price for furnishing the desired materials undertakes to produce substantially all of such materials in areas of substantial unemployment, as determined by the Secretary of Labor in accordance with such appropriate regulations as he may establish and during such period as the President may determine that it is in the national interest to provide to such areas preference in the award of Government contracts: *Provided*, that nothing in this section shall prevent the rejection of a bid or offered price which is excessive; or

(d) To reject any bid or offer for materials of foreign origin if such rejection is necessary to protect essential national-security interests after receiving advice with respect thereto from the President or from the Director of the Federal Emergency Management Agency. In providing this advice the Director shall be governed by the principle that exceptions under this section shall be made only upon a clear showing that the payment of a greater differential than the procedures of this section generally prescribe is justified by consideration of national security.

Sec. 4. The head of each executive agency shall issue such regulations as may be necessary to insure that procurement practices under his jurisdiction conform to the provisions of this order.

Sec. 5. This order shall apply only to contracts entered into after the date hereof. In any case in which the head of an executive agency proposing to purchase domestic materials determines that a greater differential than that provided in this order between the cost of such materials of domestic origin and materials of foreign origin is not unreasonable or that the purchase of materials of domestic origin is not inconsistent with the public interest, this order shall not apply. A written report of the facts of each case in which such a determination is made shall be submitted to the President through the Director of the Office of Management and Budget by the official making the determination within 30 days thereafter.

[Executive Order was set out under former 42 U.S.C.A. § 10d prior to the enactment into positive law of Title 41, Public Contracts, by Pub.L. 111–350, Jan. 4, 2011, 124 Stat. 3677.]

[For transfer of functions of the Federal Emergency Management Agency, including existing responsibilities for emergency alert systems and continuity of operations and continuity of government plans and programs as constituted on June 1, 2006, including all of its personnel, assets, components, authorities, grant programs, and liabilities, and including the functions of the Under Secretary for Federal Emergency Management relating thereto, see 6 U.S.C.A. § 315.]

§ 8304. Waiver rescission

(a) **Type of agreement.**—An agreement referred to in subsection (b) is a reciprocal defense procurement memorandum of understanding between the United States and a foreign country pursuant to which the Secretary of Defense has prospectively waived this chapter for certain products in that country.

(b) **Determination by Secretary of Defense.**—If the Secretary of Defense, after consultation with the United States Trade Representative, determines that a foreign country that is party to an agreement described in subsection (a) has violated the agreement by discriminating against certain types of products produced in the United States that are covered by the agreement, the Secretary of Defense shall rescind the Secretary's blanket waiver of this chapter with respect to those types of products produced in that country.

(Pub.L. 111–350, § 3, Jan. 4, 2011, 124 Stat. 3833.)

HISTORICAL AND STATUTORY NOTES

Similar Provisions

Provisions similar to those in this section and former 41 U.S.C.A. § 10b–3 were contained in the following Acts:

Pub.L. 112–10, Div. A, Title VIII, § 8028, Apr. 15, 2011, 125 Stat. 63.

Pub.L. 111–118, Div. A, Title VIII, § 8030, Dec. 19, 2009, 123 Stat. 3435.

See Main Volume and Repealed Title 41, ante, for annotations

Pub.L. 110–329, Div. C, Title VIII, § 8030, Sept. 30, 2008, 122 Stat. 3627.

Pub.L. 110–116, Div. A, Title VIII, § 8029, Nov. 13, 2007, 121 Stat. 1321.

Pub.L. 109–289, Div. A, Title VIII, § 8027, Sept. 29, 2006, 120 Stat. 1279.

Pub.L. 109–148, Div. A, Title VIII, § 8030, Dec. 30, 2005, 119 Stat. 2705.

Pub.L. 108–287, Title VIII, § 8032, Aug. 5, 2004, 118 Stat. 977.

Pub.L. 108–87, Title VIII, § 8033, Sept. 30, 2003, 117 Stat. 1079.

Pub.L. 107–248, Title VIII, § 8033, Oct. 23, 2002, 116 Stat. 1544.

Pub.L. 107–117, Div. A, Title VIII, § 8036, Jan. 10, 2002, 115 Stat. 2255.

Pub.L. 106–259, Title VIII, § 8036, Aug. 9, 2000, 114 Stat. 682.

Pub.L. 106–79, Title VIII, § 8038, Oct. 25, 1999, 113 Stat. 1239.

Pub.L. 105–262, Title VIII, § 8038, Oct. 17, 1998, 112 Stat. 2305.

Pub.L. 105–56, Title VIII, § 8040, Oct. 8, 1997, 111 Stat. 1229.

Pub.L. 104–208, Div. A, Title I, § 101(b) [Title VIII, § 8042], Sept. 30, 1996, 110 Stat. 3009–97.

Pub.L. 104–61, Title VIII, § 8051, Dec. 1, 1995, 109 Stat. 662.

Pub.L. 103–335, Title VIII, § 8058, Sept. 30, 1994, 108 Stat. 2631.

Pub.L. 103–139, Title VIII, § 8069, Nov. 11, 1993, 107 Stat. 1455.

Pub.L. 102–396, Title IX, § 9096, Oct. 6, 1992, 106 Stat. 1924.

Pub.L. 102–190, Div. A, Title VIII, § 833, Dec. 5, 1991, 105 Stat. 1447.

Pub.L. 102–172, Title VIII, § 8123, Nov. 26, 1991, 105 Stat. 1205.

Pub.L. 101–189, Div. A, Title VIII, § 823, Nov. 29, 1989, 103 Stat. 1504.

[Notes were classified as notes under former 41 U.S.C.A. § 10b–2 prior to the enactment into positive law of Title 41, Public Contracts, by Pub.L. 111–350, Jan. 4, 2011, 124 Stat. 3677.]

[Section 9096(b) of Pub.L. 102–396 was repealed by Pub.L. 103–355, Title VII, § 7206(b), Title X, § 10001, Oct. 13, 1994, 108 Stat. 3382, 3404, effective Oct. 13, 1994, and applicable on and after such date.]

§ 8305. Annual report

Not later than 60 days after the end of each fiscal year, the Secretary of Defense shall submit to Congress a report on the amount of purchases by the Department of Defense from foreign entities in that fiscal year. The report shall separately indicate the dollar value of items for which this chapter was waived pursuant to—

    (1) a reciprocal defense procurement memorandum of understanding described in section 8304(a) of this title;

    (2) the Trade Agreements Act of 1979 (19 U.S.C. 2501 et seq.); or

    (3) an international agreement to which the United States is a party.

(Pub.L. 111–350, § 3, Jan. 4, 2011, 124 Stat. 3833.)

HISTORICAL AND STATUTORY NOTES

References in Text

The Trade Agreements Act of 1979, referred to in par. (2), is Pub.L. 96–39, July 26, 1979, 93 Stat. 144. For complete classification, see References in Text note set out under 19 U.S.C.A. § 2501 and Tables.

CHAPTER 85—COMMITTEE FOR PURCHASE FROM PEOPLE WHO ARE BLIND OR SEVERELY DISABLED

§ 8501. Definitions

In this chapter:

    (1) Blind.—The term "blind" refers to an individual or class of individuals whose central visual acuity does not exceed 20/200 in the better eye with correcting lenses or whose visual acuity, if better than 20/200, is accompanied by a limit to the field of vision in the better eye to such a degree that its widest diameter subtends an angle of no greater than 20 degrees.

(2) **Committee.**—The term "Committee" means the Committee for Purchase From People Who Are Blind or Severely Disabled established under section 8502 of this title.

(3) **Direct labor.**—The term "direct labor"—

(A) includes all work required for preparation, processing, and packing of a product, or work directly relating to the performance of a service; but

(B) does not include supervision, administration, inspection, or shipping.

(4) **Entity of the Federal Government and Federal Government.**—The terms "entity of the Federal Government" and "Federal Government" include an entity of the legislative or judicial branch, a military department or executive agency (as defined in sections 102 and 105 of title 5, respectively), the United States Postal Service, and a nonappropriated fund instrumentality under the jurisdiction of the Armed Forces.

(5) **Other severely disabled.**—The term "other severely disabled" means an individual or class of individuals under a physical or mental disability, other than blindness, which (according to criteria established by the Committee after consultation with appropriate entities of the Federal Government and taking into account the views of non–Federal Government entities representing the disabled) constitutes a substantial handicap to employment and is of a nature that prevents the individual from currently engaging in normal competitive employment.

(6) **Qualified nonprofit agency for other severely disabled.**—The term "qualified nonprofit agency for other severely disabled" means an agency—

(A)(i) organized under the laws of the United States or a State;

(ii) operated in the interest of severely disabled individuals who are not blind; and

(iii) of which no part of the net income of the agency inures to the benefit of a shareholder or other individual;

(B) that complies with any applicable occupational health and safety standard prescribed by the Secretary of Labor; and

(C) that in the production of products and in the provision of services (whether or not the products or services are procured under this chapter) during the fiscal year employs blind or other severely disabled individuals for at least 75 percent of the hours of direct labor required for the production or provision of the products or services.

(7) **Qualified nonprofit agency for the blind.**—The term "qualified nonprofit agency for the blind" means an agency—

(A)(i) organized under the laws of the United States or a State;

(ii) operated in the interest of blind individuals; and

(iii) of which no part of the net income of the agency inures to the benefit of a shareholder or other individual;

(B) that complies with any applicable occupational health and safety standard prescribed by the Secretary of Labor; and

(C) that in the production of products and in the provision of services (whether or not the products or services are procured under this chapter) during the fiscal year employs blind individuals for at least 75 percent of the hours of direct labor required for the production or provision of the products or services.

(8) **Severely disabled individual.**—The term "severely disabled individual" means an individual or class of individuals under a physical or mental disability, other than blindness, which (according to criteria established by the Committee after consultation with appropriate entities of the Federal Government and taking into account the views of non-Federal Government entities representing the disabled) constitutes a substantial handicap to employment and is of a nature that prevents the individual from currently engaging in normal competitive employment.

(9) **State.**—The term "State" includes the District of Columbia, Puerto Rico, the Virgin Islands, Guam, American Samoa, and the Northern Mariana Islands.

(Pub.L. 111–350, § 3, Jan. 4, 2011, 124 Stat. 3833.)

HISTORICAL AND STATUTORY NOTES

Contracting with Employers of Persons with Disabilities

Pub.L. 109–364, Div. A, Title VIII, § 856(a), (d), Oct. 17, 2006, 120 Stat. 2347, 2349, provided that:

"(a) **Inapplicability of certain laws.**—

"(1) **Inapplicability of the Randolph-Sheppard Act to contracts and subcontracts for military dining facility support services covered by Javits-Wagner-O'Day Act.**—The Randolph-Sheppard Act (20 U.S.C. 107 et seq.) does not apply to full food services, mess attendant services, or services supporting the operation of a military dining facility that, as of the date of the enactment of this Act [Oct. 17, 2006], were services on the procurement list established under section 2 of the Javits-Wagner-O'Day Act (41 U.S.C. 47).

"(2) **Inapplicability of the Javits-Wagner-O'Day Act to contracts for the operation of a military dining facility.**—(A) The Javits-Wagner-O'Day Act (41 U.S.C. 46 et seq.) [Act June 25, 1938, c. 697, 52 Stat. 1196, which enacted former 41 U.S.C.A. § 46 et seq.; see Tables] does not apply at the prime contract level to any contract entered into by the Department of Defense as of the date of the enactment of this Act with a State licensing agency under the Randolph-Sheppard Act (20 U.S.C. 107 et seq.) for the operation of a military dining facility.

"(B) The Javits-Wagner-O'Day Act shall apply to any subcontract entered into by a Department of Defense contractor for full food services, mess attendant services, and other services supporting the operation of a military dining facility.

"(3) [Omitted. Repealed section 853(a), (b), of Pub.L. 108–375, 118 Stat. 2021.]

"(d) **Definitions.**—In this section [this note]:

"(1) The term 'State licensing agency' means any agency designated by the Secretary of Education under section 2(a)(5) of the Randolph-Sheppard Act (20 U.S.C. 107a(a)(5)).

"(2) The term 'military dining facility' means a facility owned, operated, leased, or wholly controlled by the Department of Defense and used to provide dining services to members of the Armed Forces, including a cafeteria, military mess hall, military troop dining facility, or any similar dining facility operated for the purpose of providing meals to members of the Armed Forces."

[Note was classified as a note under former 41 U.S.C.A. § 46 prior to the enactment into positive law of Title 41, Public Contracts, by Pub.L. 111–350, Jan. 4, 2011, 124 Stat. 3677.]

Statement of Policy; Report

Pub.L. 109–163, Div. A, Title VIII, § 848(b), (c), Jan. 6, 2006, 119 Stat. 3395, provided that:

"(b) **Statement of policy.**—The Secretary of Defense, the Secretary of Education, and the Chairman of the Committee for Purchase From People Who Are Blind or Severely Disabled shall jointly issue a statement of policy related to the implementation of the Randolph-Sheppard Act (20 U.S.C. 107 et seq.) and the Javits-Wagner-O'Day Act (41 U.S.C. 48) [Act June 25, 1938, c. 697, 52 Stat. 1196, which enacted former 41 U.S.C.A. § 46 et seq.; see Tables for complete classification] within the Department of Defense and the Department of Education. The joint statement of policy shall specifically address the application of those Acts to both operation and management of all or any part of a military mess hall, military troop dining facility, or any similar dining facility operated for the purpose of providing meals to members of the Armed Forces, and shall take into account and address, to the extent practicable, the positions acceptable to persons representing programs implemented under each Act.

"(c) **Report.**—Not later than April 1, 2006, the Secretary of Defense, the Secretary of Education, and the Chairman of the Committee for Purchase From People Who Are Blind or Severely Disabled shall submit to the Committees on Armed Services of the Senate and the House of Representatives, the Committee on Health, Education, Labor and Pensions of the Senate, and the Committee on Education and the Workforce of the House of Representatives a report describing the joint statement of policy issued under subsection (b) [of this note], with such findings and recommendations as the Secretaries consider appropriate."

[Note was classified as a note under former 41 U.S.C.A. § 46 prior to the enactment into positive law of Title 41, Public Contracts, by Pub.L. 111–350, Jan. 4, 2011, 124 Stat. 3677.]

§ 8502. Committee for purchase from people who are blind or severely disabled

(a) **Establishment.**—There is a Committee for Purchase From People Who Are Blind or Severely Disabled.

(b) **Composition.**—The Committee consists of 15 members appointed by the President as follows:

(1) One officer or employee from each of the following, nominated by the head of the department or agency:

(A) The Department of Agriculture.

(B) The Department of Defense.

(C) The Department of the Army.

(D) The Department of the Navy.

(E) The Department of the Air Force.

(F) The Department of Education.

(G) The Department of Commerce.

(H) The Department of Veterans Affairs.

(I) The Department of Justice.

(J) The Department of Labor.

(K) The General Services Administration.

(2) One member from individuals who are not officers or employees of the Federal Government and who are conversant with the problems incident to the employment of the blind.

(3) One member from individuals who are not officers or employees of the Federal Government and who are conversant with the problems incident to the employment of other severely disabled individuals.

(4) One member from individuals who are not officers or employees of the Federal Government and who represent blind individuals employed in qualified nonprofit agencies for the blind.

(5) One member from individuals who are not officers or employees of the Federal Government and who represent severely disabled individuals (other than blind individuals) employed in qualified nonprofit agencies for other severely disabled individuals.

(c) **Terms of office.**—Members appointed under paragraph (2), (3), (4), or (5) of subsection (b) shall be appointed for terms of 5 years and may be reappointed if the member meets the qualifications prescribed by those paragraphs.

(d) **Chairman.**—The members of the Committee shall elect one of the members to be Chairman.

(e) **Vacancy.**—

(1) **Manner in which filled.**—A vacancy in the membership of the Committee shall be filled in the manner in which the original appointment was made.

(2) **Unfulfilled term.**—A member appointed under paragraph (2), (3), (4), or (5) of subsection (b) to fill a vacancy occurring prior to the expiration of the term for which the predecessor was appointed shall be appointed only for the remainder of the term. The member may serve after the expiration of a term until a successor takes office.

(f) **Pay and travel expenses.**—

(1) **Amount to which members are entitled.**—Except as provided in paragraph (2), members of the Committee are entitled to receive the daily equivalent of the maximum annual rate of basic pay payable for level IV of the Executive Schedule for each day (including travel–time) during which they perform services for the Committee. A member is entitled to travel expenses, including a per diem allowance instead of subsistence, as provided under section 5703 of title 5.

(2) **Officers or employees of the Federal Government.**—Members who are officers or employees of the Federal Government may not receive additional pay because of their service on the Committee.

(g) **Staff.**—

(1) **Appointment and compensation.**—Subject to rules the Committee may adopt and to chapters 33 and 51 and subchapter III of chapter 53 of title 5, the Chairman may appoint and fix the pay of personnel the Committee determines are necessary to assist it in carrying out this chapter.

(2) **Personnel from other entities.**—On request of the Committee, the head of an entity of the Federal Government may detail, on a reimbursable basis, any personnel of the entity to the Committee to assist it in carrying out this chapter.

(h) **Obtaining official information.**—The Committee may secure directly from an entity of the Federal Government information necessary to enable it to carry out this chapter. On request of the Chairman, the head of the entity shall furnish the information to the Committee.

(i) Administrative support services.—The Administrator of General Services shall provide to the Committee, on a reimbursable basis, administrative support services the Committee requests.

(j) Annual report.—Not later than December 31 of each year, the Committee shall transmit to the President a report that includes the names of the Committee members serving in the prior fiscal year, the dates of Committee meetings in that year, a description of the activities of the Committee under this chapter in that year, and any recommendations for changes in this chapter which the Committee determines are necessary.

(Pub.L. 111–350, § 3, Jan. 4, 2011, 124 Stat. 3835.)

HISTORICAL AND STATUTORY NOTES

References in Text

Chapter 33 of title 5, referred to in subsec. (g)(1), is classified to 5 U.S.C.A. § 3301 et seq.

Chapter 51 of title 5, referred to in subsec. (g)(1), is classified to 5 U.S.C.A. § 5101 et seq.

Subchapter III of chapter 53 of title 5, referred to in subsec. (g)(1), is classified to 5 U.S.C.A. § 5331 et seq.

§ 8503. Duties and powers of the Committee

(a) Procurement list.—

(1) Maintenance of list.—The Committee shall maintain and publish in the Federal Register a procurement list. The list shall include the following products and services determined by the Committee to be suitable for the Federal Government to procure pursuant to this chapter:

(A) Products produced by a qualified nonprofit agency for the blind or by a qualified nonprofit agency for other severely disabled.

(B) The services those agencies provide.

(2) Changes to list.—The Committee may, by rule made in accordance with the requirements of section 553(b) to (e) of title 5, add to and remove from the procurement list products so produced and services so provided.

(b) Fair market price.—The Committee shall determine the fair market price of products and services contained on the procurement list that are offered for sale to the Federal Government by a qualified nonprofit agency for the blind or a qualified nonprofit agency for other severely disabled. The Committee from time to time shall revise its price determinations with respect to those products and services in accordance with changing market conditions.

(c) Central nonprofit agency or agencies.—The Committee shall designate a central nonprofit agency or agencies to facilitate the distribution, by direct allocation, subcontract, or any other means, of orders of the Federal Government for products and services on the procurement list among qualified nonprofit agencies for the blind or qualified nonprofit agencies for other severely disabled.

(d) Regulations.—The Committee—

(1) may prescribe regulations regarding specifications for products and services on the procurement list, the time of their delivery, and other matters as necessary to carry out this chapter; and

(2) shall prescribe regulations providing that when the Federal Government purchases products produced and offered for sale by qualified nonprofit agencies for the blind or qualified nonprofit agencies for other severely disabled, priority shall be given to products produced and offered for sale by qualified nonprofit agencies for the blind.

(e) Study and evaluation of activities.—The Committee shall make a continuing study and evaluation of its activities under this chapter to ensure effective and efficient administration of this chapter. The Committee on its own or in cooperation with other public or nonprofit private agencies may study—

(1) problems related to the employment of the blind and other severely disabled individuals; and

(2) the development and adaptation of production methods that would enable a greater utilization of the blind and other severely disabled individuals.

(Pub.L. 111–350, § 3, Jan. 4, 2011, 124 Stat. 3836.)

§ 8504. Procurement requirements for the Federal Government

(a) In general.—An entity of the Federal Government intending to procure a product or service on the procurement list referred to in section 8503 of this title shall procure the product or service from a qualified nonprofit agency for the blind or a qualified nonprofit agency for other severely disabled in accordance with regulations of the Committee and at the price the Committee establishes if the product or service is available within the period required by the entity.

(b) Exception.—This section does not apply to the procurement of a product that is available from an industry established under chapter 307 of title 18 and that is required under section 4124 of title 18 to be procured from that industry.

(Pub.L. 111–350, § 3, Jan. 4, 2011, 124 Stat. 3837.)

HISTORICAL AND STATUTORY NOTES
References in Text

Chapter 307 of title 18, referred to in subsec. (b), is classified to 18 U.S.C.A. § 4121 et seq.

§ 8505. Audit

For the purpose of audit and examination, the Comptroller General shall have access to the books, documents, papers, and other records of—

(1) the Committee and of each central nonprofit agency the Committee designates under section 8503(c) of this title; and

(2) qualified nonprofit agencies for the blind and qualified nonprofit agencies for other severely disabled that have sold products or services under this chapter to the extent those books, documents, papers, and other records relate to the activities of the agency in a fiscal year in which a sale was made under this chapter.

(Pub.L. 111–350, § 3, Jan. 4, 2011, 124 Stat. 3838.)

HISTORICAL AND STATUTORY NOTES
References in Text

Chapter 71, referred to in subsecs. (a), (d), is classified to 41 U.S.C.A. § 7101 et seq.

§ 8506. Authorization of appropriations

Necessary amounts may be appropriated to the Committee to carry out this chapter.

(Pub.L. 111–350, § 3, Jan. 4, 2011, 124 Stat. 3838.)

CHAPTER 87—KICKBACKS

§ 8701. Definitions

In this chapter:

(1) Contracting agency.—The term "contracting agency", when used with respect to a prime contractor, means a department, agency, or establishment of the Federal Government that enters into a prime contract with a prime contractor.

See Main Volume and Repealed Title 41, ante, for annotations

(2) **Kickback.**—The term "kickback" means any money, fee, commission, credit, gift, gratuity, thing of value, or compensation of any kind that is provided to a prime contractor, prime contractor employee, subcontractor, or subcontractor employee to improperly obtain or reward favorable treatment in connection with a prime contract or a subcontract relating to a prime contract.

(3) **Person.**—The term "person" means a corporation, partnership, business association of any kind, trust, joint-stock company, or individual.

(4) **Prime contract.**—The term "prime contract" means a contract or contractual action entered into by the Federal Government to obtain supplies, materials, equipment, or services of any kind.

(5) **Prime contractor.**—The term "prime contractor" means a person that has entered into a prime contract with the Federal Government.

(6) **Prime contractor employee.**—The term "prime contractor employee" means an officer, partner, employee, or agent of a prime contractor.

(7) **Subcontract.**—The term "subcontract" means a contract or contractual action entered into by a prime contractor or subcontractor to obtain supplies, materials, equipment, or services of any kind under a prime contract.

(8) **Subcontractor.**—The term "subcontractor"—

(A) means a person, other than the prime contractor, that offers to furnish or furnishes supplies, materials, equipment, or services of any kind under a prime contract or a subcontract entered into in connection with the prime contract; and

(B) includes a person that offers to furnish or furnishes general supplies to the prime contractor or a higher tier subcontractor.

(9) **Subcontractor employee.**—The term "subcontractor employee" means an officer, partner, employee, or agent of a subcontractor.

(Pub.L. 111–350, § 3, Jan. 4, 2011, 124 Stat. 3838.)

§ 8702. Prohibited conduct

A person may not—

(1) provide, attempt to provide, or offer to provide a kickback;

(2) solicit, accept, or attempt to accept a kickback; or

(3) include the amount of a kickback prohibited by paragraph (1) or (2) in the contract price—

(A) a subcontractor charges a prime contractor or a higher tier subcontractor; or

(B) a prime contractor charges the Federal Government.

(Pub.L. 111–350, § 3, Jan. 4, 2011, 124 Stat. 3839.)

§ 8703. Contractor responsibilities

(a) **Requirements included in contracts.**—Each contracting agency shall include in each prime contract awarded by the agency a requirement that the prime contractor shall—

(1) have in place and follow reasonable procedures designed to prevent and detect violations of section 8702 of this title in its own operations and direct business relationships; and

(2) cooperate fully with a Federal Government agency investigating a violation of section 8702 of this title.

(b) **Full cooperation required.**—Notwithstanding subsection (d), a prime contractor shall cooperate fully with a Federal Government agency investigating a violation of section 8702 of this title.

(c) **Reporting requirement.**—

(1) **In general.**—A prime contractor or subcontractor that has reasonable grounds to believe that a violation of section 8702 of this title may have occurred shall promptly report the possible violation in writing to the inspector general of the

contracting agency, the head of the contracting agency if the agency does not have an inspector general, or the Attorney General.

(2) Supplying information as favorable evidence.—In an administrative or contractual action to suspend or debar a person who is eligible to enter into contracts with the Federal Government, evidence that the person has supplied information to the Federal Government pursuant to paragraph (1) is favorable evidence of the person's responsibility for the purposes of Federal procurement laws and regulations.

(d) Inapplicability to certain prime contracts.—Subsection (a) does not apply to a prime contract—

    (1) that is not greater than $100,000; or

    (2) for the acquisition of commercial items (as defined in section 103 of this title).

(Pub.L. 111–350, § 3, Jan. 4, 2011, 124 Stat. 3839.)

§ 8704. Inspection authority

(a) In general.—To ascertain whether there has been a violation of section 8702 of this title with respect to a prime contract, the Comptroller General and the inspector general of the contracting agency, or a representative of the contracting agency designated by the head of the agency if the agency does not have an inspector general, shall have access to and may inspect the facilities and audit the books and records, including electronic data or records, of a prime contractor or subcontractor under a prime contract awarded by the agency.

(b) Exception.—This section does not apply to a prime contract for the acquisition of commercial items (as defined in section 103 of this title).

(Pub.L. 111–350, § 3, Jan. 4, 2011, 124 Stat. 3839.)

§ 8705. Administrative offsets

(a) Definition.—In this section, the term "contracting officer" has the meaning given that term in chapter 71 of this title.

(b) Offset authority.—A contracting officer of a contracting agency may offset the amount of a kickback provided, accepted, or charged in violation of section 8702 of this title against amounts the Federal Government owes the prime contractor under the prime contract to which the kickback relates.

(c) Duties of prime contractor.—

    (1) Withholding and paying over or retaining amounts.—On direction of a contracting officer of a contracting agency with respect to a prime contract, the prime contractor shall withhold from amounts owed to a subcontractor under a subcontract of the prime contract the amount of a kickback which was or may be offset against the prime contractor under subsection (b). The contracting officer may order that amounts withheld—

        (A) be paid over to the contracting agency; or

        (B) be retained by the prime contractor if the Federal Government has already offset the amount against the prime contractor.

    (2) Notice.—The prime contractor shall notify the contracting officer when an amount is withheld and retained under paragraph (1)(B).

(d) Offset, direction, or order is claim of Federal Government.—An offset under subsection (b) or a direction or order of a contracting officer under subsection (c) is a claim by the Federal Government for the purposes of chapter 71 of this title.

(Pub.L. 111–350, § 3, Jan. 4, 2011, 124 Stat. 3840.)

§ 8706. Civil actions

(a) Amount.—The Federal Government in a civil action may recover from a person—

    (1) that knowingly engages in conduct prohibited by section 8702 of this title a civil penalty equal to—

See Main Volume and Repealed Title 41, ante, for annotations

    (A) twice the amount of each kickback involved in the violation; and

    (B) not more than $10,000 for each occurrence of prohibited conduct; and

  (2) whose employee, subcontractor, or subcontractor employee violates section 8702 of this title by providing, accepting, or charging a kickback a civil penalty equal to the amount of that kickback.

  (b) Statute of limitations.—A civil action under this section must be brought within 6 years after the later of the date on which—

    (1) the prohibited conduct establishing the cause of action occurred; or

    (2) the Federal Government first knew or should reasonably have known that the prohibited conduct had occurred.

(Pub.L. 111–350, § 3, Jan. 4, 2011, 124 Stat. 3840.)

§ 8707. Criminal penalties

  A person that knowingly and willfully engages in conduct prohibited by section 8702 of this title shall be fined under title 18, imprisoned for not more than 10 years, or both.

(Pub.L. 111–350, § 3, Jan. 4, 2011, 124 Stat. 3841.)

INDEX

CONSULT GENERAL INDEX

†